Safire's Washington

Also by William Safire

NONFICTION

On Language (1980)

Before the Fall (1974)

The New Language of Politics: Safire's Political Dictionary
(1968, 1979)

Plunging Into Politics (1964)

The Relations Explosion (1963)

FICTION

Full Disclosure (1977)

★

SAFIRE'S
WASHINGTON

WILLIAM
SAFIRE

★

Times
BOOKS

Published by TIMES BOOKS, a division
of Quadrangle/The New York Times Book Co., Inc.
Three Park Avenue, New York, N.Y. 10016

Published simultaneously in Canada by
Fitzhenry & Whiteside, Ltd., Toronto.

Library of Congress Cataloging in Publication Data

Safire, William L.
   Safire's Washington.

   Includes index.
   1. United States—Politics and government—1977-
—Addresses, essays, lectures. 2. United States—Foreign relations—1977-   —Addresses, essays, lectures.
3. United States—Politics and government—1974–1977—
Addresses, essays, lectures. 4. United States—Foreign
relations—1974–1977—Addresses, essays, lectures.
5. Nixon, Richard Milhous, 1913-   —Addresses, essays,
lectures. I. Title.
E872.S23 1980   320.973   79-9649
ISBN 0-8129-0919-4

Manufactured in the United States of America.

For brother Len

CONTENTS

"William Safire must be a mind-reader. He always
writes exactly what I'm thinking."

Drawing by Joseph Farris; © 1979
The New Yorker Magazine, Inc.

Safire's Washington

Openers

WASHINGTON—When word spread like cooling lava through the Nixon Administration that I was to become a columnist for *The New York Times*, speechwriters who stayed behind wanted to know: "Will you continue to stand up for the President, the work ethic, and the Nixon doctrine, or will you sell out to the élitist establishment and become a darling of the Georgetown cocktail-party set?"

Sipping a bourbon in one of those dreaded drawing rooms—more dens of inequity than iniquity—I was asked substantially the same question by a new colleague in the press: "Will you speak out impartially without fear or favor, or will you continue to be a slavish, craven parroter of the Nixon line, a flack planted in our midst?"

I have never ducked the tough questions; my answer, in both cases, was "yes and no," which when delivered with crisp authority inspires confidence. Truth to tell, the only way the reader or the writer of this column will find the answer is to watch this space for further developments.

But not on opening day; before pulling a long face to deal with public affairs as befits a serious columnist, let me trot around the bases to get the feel of this place.

On flackery: A young, nervous aide of Henry Kissinger called me one day a couple of years ago to ask a strange question: "What does the word 'flack' mean?"

I was gratified to be consulted on a matter of meaning and etymology, a lifelong field of interest, but I had learned the first rule of bureaucratic survival: Never give out information without first finding out why it is being sought. So I misinterpreted the question and replied: "The word 'flak' is an acronym coined in World War II to describe anti-aircraft fire, from the German words *Fleiger Abwehr, Kanonen.*"

Moments later, the aide called back to say: "Dr. Kissinger says he doesn't need you to teach him German, but a columnist just called him 'an Administration flack' and he wants to know whether he should take offense."

With that background tucked away for use, I passed along the current usage of "flack": an apologist, or paid proponent, with a usually pejorative but occasionally madcap connotation. To cheer Henry up, I added that the role, if not the word, could be an honorable one—a skilled advocate was needed to explicate policy—but when I saw him next, he gloomily informed me: "I decided to take offense." Perhaps I will, too, someday— but not for a while.

On vogue words: Readers of these essays will not be bombarded with any of the "dirty dozen": relevant, meaningful, knowledgeable, hopefully, viable, input, exacerbate, dichotomy, the use as verbs of program, implement, and structure, and ambivalent, though I am of two minds about ambivalent.

On choosing a title: Columnists for *The Times* tend toward using generic titles, thereby laying claim to great chunks of subject matter. "Washington" is spoken for by James Reston, leaving another Washington columnist only the word "column" to head his piece, which is apt but a little pretentious for a newcomer. Arthur Krock's "In The Nation" is carried on by Tom Wicker, "Foreign Affairs" belongs to C. L. Sulzberger, and amused detachment is the province of Russell Baker's "Observer."

Anthony Lewis, with whom I will appear on this page every Monday and Thursday (we are paired like a couple of Senators whose votes are fated to cancel each other out), calls his column "At Home Abroad" when he is overseas and "Abroad at Home" when he writes from the United States. This leaves available only "At Home at Home," which is self-satisfied, and "Abroad Abroad," which must be angrily rejected as sexist.

I have chosen "Essay," which sounds innocuous enough but flies in under everybody's radar. The word might not have the verve, sparkle, and rallying power of, say, "The New Federalism," but it offers room to ruminate and holds out no false promise of total topicality, since I may want to fiddle around with some way-out subjects.

I'm pleased to meet you. To essay means to make a beginning, to try, to put to a test, which I undertake with zest and determination, along with appropriate false humility. I hope you have the need for another point of view, for I hope to have something to say.

PART I

★

1973–1976

The Fall of Nixon

ART BUCHWALD put it charitably: I was "the right man at the wrong time." As a former Nixon speechwriter beginning a *New York Times* column just as the Watergate scandal began to break, my time was hopelessly out of joint.

Here, for honesty's grim sake, is the early piece that most makes me look like a sap—welcoming a Nixon speech on the cover-up that I thought put him on the "right side of the Watergate investigation" and heralding a new comeback. That was hardly an auspicious beginning for a political pundit.

Subsequent columns were more realistic, but "hung tough" and went against the grain of most public opinion on the disintegrating Presidency. "A different point of view" was what *The Times* promised in its announcement of my employment, but I was not sure they expected it to be all this different. When I walked through the city room of the Washington bureau, silence fell. My new colleagues were unfailingly civil, a few even friendly, but my written opinions were ill-received; some *Times* reporters took pride in the paper's willingness to publish the unpopular views of "a Nixon apologist," but most felt the publisher had been suckered.

David Halberstam, a former *Times* man who won the Pulitzer Prize for reporting from Vietnam, wrote a letter to Arthur O. "Punch" Sulzberger, my boss, which typified that feeling: "Safire is not a conservative in any true sense, never has been one, and he has not come up in any way through the editorial processes. Rather he is a paid manipulator. He is not a man of ideas or politics but rather a man of tricks, which is the last thing *The Times* needed."

Halberstam judged my first three months of columnizing severely: "It is a very dishonest column—and a shabby one. A few years ago when you had just taken over the paper you were handed a tough decision on the

West Coast edition. You said—'it's a lousy paper. Close it.' So Punch, this time the play is to you. It's a lousy column and it's a dishonest one. So close it. Or you end up just as shabby as Safire." He added, "I do expect to hear from you on this."

The irony did not escape me: Halberstam had gained fame when an American President tried to get the publisher of *The New York Times* to fire him for his out-of-step Vietnam dispatches, and here was that same reporter trying to get *The Times*'s publisher to "close up" a point of view that, however shabby, was mine own. Since Halberstam had noted on the original of his letter that a copy was going to me, a copy of the Sulzberger reply was sent to me as well:

"I always answer my mail," wrote "Punch" Sulzberger, "so, of course, I shall reply to your letter of July 27 relating to Bill Safire." That was a nice way of handling Halberstam's peremptory demand for an answer. "I appreciate that you feel I am prepared to make a 'tough decision,' but right now, as far as I am concerned, one is not necessary in this case. While I have not always agreed with Bill, I think he is developing a style of his own and that he is reflecting a philosophy. I remain confident that over the years he will be an important contributor to *The New York Times.*"

That was heartening: Evidently *The Times* was willing to stand the gaff from infuriated readers inside and outside the profession. Despite the mail, I began to feel better about putting the feet of anti-Nixon civil libertarians to the fire of civil liberty. I thought a McCarthyite bloodlust was in the air, denying due process to those who were accused of denying it to others. Sophistry? I thought not, and am proudest of some of the essays that drove many readers up the wall at that time.

Life improved for me at the Washington bureau after the summer picnic of the office staff in 1974. A two-year-old child of one of the reporters fell in the pool and started to drown; my wife pushed me in with my clothes on to fish him out, and it was hard to hate me after that. Besides, after Nixon resigned, I was able to get off the defensive.

COMEBACK TIME

April 19, 1973

WASHINGTON—The President did it his way.

He did not stand in front of the cameras, bruised and embittered, apologizing about Watergate, saying he was misled by his subordinates or otherwise pushing an alibi. He neither submitted to cross-examination nor requested television time for a long explanation.

Instead, he wrote out his announcement, read it in a cold, stern voice, and left no doubt that he had stepped up to the situation and engaged it frontally.

The reaction is one of relief. Supporters of the President are happy to see him take charge and take action; critics of the President feel profoundly satisfied about their vigorous pursuit of the Watergate affair, but not many of them want to see the Presidency itself splattered with mud. A few will gloat "I told you so," and by their misreading of the public mind will help rally opinion behind the President.

Mr. Nixon has credentials as an investigator, long unused but still valid; like Thomas E. Dewey, that is how he first came on the scene. When this generation's version of the Pumpkin Papers was laid before him, the President switched from loyalist to pursuer.

His statement—"I condemn any attempts to cover up"—was forceful and positive, the appropriate tone for the first concession statement he has had to make since 1962. Mr. Nixon showed he has learned a lot in a decade. Contrary to Churchill's admonition, he is neither magnanimous in victory nor defiant in defeat, but he has often shown himself to be a tower of strength in a crisis. Watergate is not a significant defeat, but it was developing into one, and the President moved in the nick of time.

Plenty of juicy headlines and personal tragedies lie ahead. Once a case begins to break, it breaks wide open, and when the President joins the press, the courts, and the Senate in getting to the bottom of something, we can expect to hit new bottoms every day. A few points to keep in mind as the cloud named Watergate finally begins to burst:

1.   *We Wuz Wrong.* Our political enemies and media critics, from Larry O'Brien and Frank Mankiewicz to *The Washington Post*'s Ben Bradlee and Philip Geyelin, were right to keep the heat on the Watergate; we who worked at the White House, who were certain that nobody at a responsible level could be so stupid, now appear likely to be proven mistaken. Hats off to you fellows for hanging in there, which is more than any of you ever said to any of us when the President's bombing of Hanoi brought the North Vietnamese back to the negotiating table. (Why can I never admit a mistake graciously?)

2.   *No* Dolchstosslegende *can be made out of the Watergate.* There

was no "stab in the back" that changed the course of history in any of this. Mr. Nixon would have swamped Mr. McGovern with no help from zealots; indeed, the Watergate incident provided Democrats with their only useful 1972 campaign issue.

3. *Not every hardball is a beanball.* Let's wait and see if a connection is proven between the Watergate crime and other political activity that may be shady but is not criminal. Let's also watch out for *ex post facto* morality, condemning tactics in the most recent campaign that were tacitly condoned in other campaigns. We would be better off without such "hardball" but we should not pretend it never existed.

4. *Beware of linkage.* The word in this unfolding story that should concern civil libertarians is "linked"—"So and so linked to Watergate." Linked by what, linked according to whose sworn, firsthand testimony?

In the long run, the experience of swinging wide the Watergate should prove to be uplifting. In future campaigns, some idiot may be found stuffing a suitcase full of laundered credit cards, but such behavior would be treated as aberrant and—worse—impractical.

As we flip over this flat rock we call politics, Americans of different parties and ideologies now do so together, thanks to the President's action this week; we need not don a mantle of national guilt if we see something scurrying around. Political standards are getting higher, which is something to be proud of, not ashamed of, and as we make dirty politics too costly a game to play, cleaning the Augean stables becomes a snap.

This is not a tragic moment for Mr. Nixon, nor a sad day for democracy; on the contrary, for people who want all Presidents to succeed, this is a moment to take heart. For all players in the game of politics, as well as for Richard Nixon, this is comeback time—and when it comes to comebacks, the world's leading expert has just made his appearance on the right side of the Watergate investigation.

THE PENDULUM

May 17, 1973

WASHINGTON—Piercing through a couple of floors of the Smithsonian Institution's Museum of History and Technology in Washington is a great pendulum. To tourists and scientists, its long, slow swings demonstrate the motion of the earth, but to politicians it symbolizes the inexorability of change in public opinion.

Five years ago, Senator Edward Kennedy was widely regarded to be the Democrat most likely to be President. Four years ago, he was considered washed up. Today he is back in the lists, vigorously denouncing Watergate.

Nine years ago, Barry Goldwater was seen by many Americans as the embodiment of evil; "in your guts you know he's nuts," they said, and he received the worst trouncing since Alf Landon; today, because of his personal probity, his good humor in defeat, the discreditation of his opponents, and the fact that he is no threat, Goldwater has become the liberals' favorite conservative.

A decade ago, Richard Nixon was groping around the floor for the pieces of his career like a man who had lost both contact lenses; three months ago, he bestrode the earth like a Colossus, treating longtime detractors with a delighted vindictiveness; today, he's down there again picking up the pieces.

Most of us have had our ups and downs in life, but few of us have really ridden the giant pendulum back and forth. We think of our times as this week, not this year, and certainly not in four-year terms.

We are bedazzled by the hall of mirrors that is the media: Newspapers compete to extract the widest headline from an unfolding story; newsmagazines reflect the hysteria and put out excited press releases on Sunday about what will appear in their own pages the next week, and television reports on the reports of the reports. The fad in magazine covers is a photograph of a statue of a person or a collage of a subject, as if communications itself wanted to back off from reality when events move rapidly.

To a man who has ridden the pendulum as long as Richard Nixon, the hysteria, depression, secret delight, and genuine concern that form the amalgam of public opinion today can be viewed with a certain resigned perspective. The orders from the command post are to retreat in good order, taking care not to let the necessary withdrawal turn into a rout.

That is why we do not see new faces taking the place of men who had to be dropped or who left in a hurry. Critics complain this is only a reshuffle; but the President wants to show the nation he appointed a lot of trustworthy people in his first term who were untouched by Watergate. The President's inclination to deal with trusted old hands is a part of the reason why new people are not being brought in now: The major part, however, is to avert the appearance of rout, with new faces seeming to "save" the President. That is also primarily why the President's critics are demanding fresh troops and denouncing the game of musical chairs—it is a good way of getting the President to admit not only a lapse of attention but a fundamental misjudgment of people.

Besides his experience as an old pendulum-rider, the President has another reason for his "peace at the center": He knows what he did not know. He knows he was not guilty of a crime, and the worst that can be proved is misplaced trust, which is why he can confidently take the attitude that "this, too, shall pass."

And it will. The price of gold will come down, the stock market will go up, some Democrat with a suitcase full of cash will be exposed, the Mets will win the Series, a new Cliff Irving will seize the headlines, and public boredom will help stabilize the ship of state by proving once again that it is always darkest before the yawn. Nixon, the man who practically invented modern political survival, will survive, and finish in a bicentennial glow.

The President could speed this process by getting some perspective on his perspective: As Kipling did not say, "If you can keep your head while all others about you are losing theirs, perhaps you don't understand the seriousness of the situation." The usual Nixon tactic when the pendulum is far out on its latest arc is to lean back in hard, exuding confidence, dismissing scandal as an unfortunate incident, counterpunching at excessive charges that offend a spirit of fairness.

But more powerful forces are gathering to dispel what is semiannually described as "the crisis of confidence" by commentators who never know quite how to describe the times when confidence is not in crisis. When nobody can prove the President culpable; when the anti-Nixon brigade gets too strident and stimulates a reaction; when world leaders meet and peace and security are factored into the Nixon equation, then we will see these days as a strange, dark interlude in the midst of prosperous, peace-making times.

Someday the pendulum at the Smithsonian might smash through the wall and keep on going in one direction, but it is a safer bet that the pendulum will keep swinging back, and that the people who lightly bandy about words like "impeachment" will be ashamed of themselves, and the doomsayers, as always, will have to recalculate their dire predictions and move back the date of the end of the world.

GUNGA DEAN

June 18, 1973

WASHINGTON—

You may talk o' Hunt and Liddy
When you're feelin' gay and giddy
And you think you have th' White House in your sights,

But when your side is achin'
To prove Nixon said "Go break in"
You need an aide who sat there at the heights.
Now in D.C.'s sunny clime
Where I used to spend my time
A-servin' of the public, sight unseen,
Of all the crewcut crew
The straightest lace I knew
Was the man in charge of ethics, Gunga Dean.
     He was "Dean! Dean! Dean!
  "You smoothie of a lawyer, keep us clean!
    "With your ardor never dampened
    "We'll see rectitude is rampant
   "For no scandal can deflect us, Gunga Dean."
Nixon entered the campaign
And considered it insane
To concern himself with breakin' any rules,
For a-watchin' the committee
And its forty-million kitty
Was his counselor from all the finest schools.
But while leading lambs to slaughter
Came the shockin' gate o' water
And all the district fuzz began to fly.
To give him true reports
Of any White House torts
Nixon wrongly chose an implicated guy.
     It was "Dean! Dean! Dean!
  "I want the deepest probe you've ever seen!
    "Don't blow anybody's cover
    "But try and soon discover
  "If CREEP did anything illegal, Gunga Dean."
For six long months Dean battled
(Nobody caught had tattled)
And kept sendin' word he had the problem solved.
When the Oval Office queried
Dean would smile, and with eyes bleari(ed,
Say: "No one in the White House was involved."
Then McCord untied his knot
And the story went to pot
And the hunter was the hunted sudden-ly;
Dean ran out hell-for-leather,
Said: "We were in it altogether,
"—And nobody makes a scapegoat out of me."
     Then it was "Dean! Dean! Dean!

"For your testimony we are very keen!
  "Point the finger, show who's sleazy,
  "And we'll see the judge goes easy.
"Here's your chance to cop a plea, Gunga Dean."
"Thanks, but I'll not need ya.
"I've got contacts in the media
"Who'll print my leaks until the price has risen.
"I'll use them for my ends.
" 'According to Dean's friends,'
"For the likes of me does not belong in prison."
He would sing out any tune
To hear Sirica say "immune"
("No less than forty times I've made the scene!")
Justice balked, but Senate crumbled,
To Ervin's saving arms he tumbled.
And now they cannot jail you, Gunga Dean.
   · So it's Dean! Dean! Dean!
  Smear your leader, save your skin and vent your
    spleen!
    Though the Fifth Amendment aids you,
     By the TV that parades you—
You will never drag down Nixon, Gunga Dean.
    Yes, it's Dean! Dean! Dean!
    Star of everybody's television screen
    You will claim that you obeyed,
    But the truth is you betrayed
A far better man than you are, Gunga Dean!

NO DECENCY LEFT

July 16, 1973

WASHINGTON—A vicious attack by a 33-year-old Democratic law-yer, bedazzled by his moment in the limelight, upon the only witness to come before the Watergate committee with clean hands—an upright, re-spected, gentle human being of 59 named Richard Moore—is proof that the purpose of the Ervin committee is not to bring out the truth but to bring down the President.

    Richard Moore, of all the men on the White House staff, comes closest to being a hero on the Watergate matter: When in March he had evidence that a crime was being covered up, he urged the man who knew most about it—John Dean—to go to the President and tell him all he knew. One reason Dean then did so, after nine months of duplicity, was the knowledge that if he did not immediately spill all he knew to the President, Richard Moore would go in with whatever he had.

So there was Moore, a man not "involved"; not seeking immunity; not the target of an investigation; a man of substance and lifelong good repute, and a witness to some crucial meetings between Mr. Dean and the President, coming before the Senate committee.

Moore had been told on Monday evening that he would be called to testify on the coming Thursday. He began preparing his testimony, but was interrupted the next day by Special Prosecutor Archibald Cox, who wanted his information first and took most of the next day. That left Moore all day Wednesday to get ready for the Ervin committee, and he concentrated on the period central to the whole investigation—"what the President knew and when he knew it."

After a few hours' sleep Moore went to the committee; briefly, at lunchtime, committee lawyers went over the area of testimony to be covered that day, centering on the crucial March meetings with the President and Dean.

Then Moore's turn came. His prepared statement refuted John Dean's central conclusion that the President was aware of the cover-up. Moore said no; the first the President had known was on March 21, 1973, when Mr. Dean came clean.

Then young Terry Lenzner tore into him—not into the blockbuster testimony Mr. Moore had just given, nor on the matters about which Moore had properly been concentrating, but on some meetings that had taken place on another subject over a year ago. The line of questioning was a non sequitur; it had nothing to do with the matter at hand; in the language of football he "blindsided" the witness.

Moore was taken aback; Lenzner bored in with demands for dates and facts on an extraneous matter, effectively confusing and thereby discrediting the witness—after all, had not John Dean come equipped with every fact and date at his fingertips?

Next day, under questioning by others who wanted to find out what evidence he could contribute, Mr. Moore answered with some wit and the kind of occasionally precise recall that has an honest ring, and contrasts sharply with the carefully rehearsed stories of con men out to save their skins.

Because Moore did not lash into anybody, because his subsequent testimony showed he is a person not motivated by hatred, the unfairness of the attempted humiliation by Lenzner was underscored.

The thought must have occurred to many viewers: Of the two men in confrontation, who would be a better adviser to any President of the United States?

Terry Lenzner, born to wealth, captain of the Harvard football team, protégé of Ramsey Clark, and lawyer to the Reverend Philip Berrigan, is the essence of radical chic. He is a man on the make who strikes the pose of a stern guardian of civil liberties, but who has shown he has not the most rudimentary understanding of fairness and civility in human relationships.

Richard Moore, whom he sought to discredit, emerges from the hearings with dignity, good humor, and integrity intact. Viewers who do not automatically assume anybody connected with Mr. Nixon to be evil see Mr. Moore as the kind of man Presidents need to protect them from the gung-ho, ends-justify-the-means "team players" who flutter around the center of power.

The fury of the attack on a good man who did the right thing recalls the pivotal question asked by Joseph Welch, a man like Mr. Moore, at the Army-McCarthy hearings a generation ago: "Have you no decency left, sir?"

The Lenzner attack—which Senator Ervin made no effort to stop—is sure to be mentioned when the President confronts the Senator, and, with personal civility and all constitutional respect, tells him where to get off.

July 17, 1973

The New York Times

To The Editor:

The Times' Mr. Safire in his Monday column, gurgling with coldly slick rage over the plight of the White House's Richard Moore in the witness chair in the Watergate hearings, invoked the name of Joseph Welch to underline his protest over "the fury of the attack on a good man (Richard Moore, of course) who did the right thing."

In the process of his wringing-wet brief for the defense, Mr. Safire quoted what he thought Mr. Welch had said in another time, so much more innocent, to the late Sen. Joseph R. McCarthy: "Have you no decency left, sir?" Why did Mr. Welch bring up the matter of decency? Let's look back.

In that memorable moment in the real history of good men, Joe Welch was rising in the Army-McCarthy hearings (the date was June 9, 1954) to denounce an attempt by the Republican from Wisconsin to lay the red brush on a young Harvard lawyer in the Welch firm. Now what was Mr. Safire doing on your newsprint in his Monday essay?

Before he dragged in the ghost of Joe Welch, just two paragraphs before, he had turned the fury of his own attack on another young Harvard lawyer, the one who conducted the questioning of the suddenly forgetful Richard Moore for the majority on the Ervin committee. And here is how Mr. Safire identified that young lawyer: "Terry Lenzner, born to wealth, captain of the Harvard football team, protégé of Ramsey Clark, and lawyer to the Rev. Philip Berrigan, is the essence of radical chic."

Hell, all Joe McCarthy said about the kid in the Welch firm was that he was a member (and he wasn't then) of the National Lawyers Guild—"the legal bulwark of the Communist Party" in the Senator's reading of the record. A rather soft impeachment, it seems to me, alongside Mr. Safire's savage indictment of Terry Lenzner. At the least, your new columnist could have left out the football bit. Harvard was only 4–3 in the Ivy League in Mr. Lenzner's 1960 turn as captain.

The real question then, the way Mr. Welch really said it, is for Mr. Safire himself: "Have you no sense of decency, sir, at long last?"

Mr. Safire could look it up. It's on tape, like so many things today in the White House, *his* White House, in the time of Watergate and our national shame.

Paul Sann, Executive Editor
New York Post
New York, New York

THE SUSPICIOUS 17

August 9, 1973

WASHINGTON—From mid-1969 to February of 1971, at the direction of the President, the F.B.I. tapped the home telephones of 17 men—four newsmen and 13 Government officials—to find out why classified information had appeared in the press and to prevent future leaks.

"I authorized this entire program," the President asserted on May 22 of this year. "The persons who were subject to these wiretaps were determined through coordination among the Director of the F.B.I., my assistant for national security affairs, and the Attorney General." (J. Edgar Hoover, Henry Kissinger, John Mitchell.)

How were the suspicious 17 chosen? "Those wiretapped," said the President, "were selected on the basis of access to the information leaked, material in security files, and evidence that developed as the inquiry proceeded." That last category refers to people overheard talking to those being tapped and who subsequently were honored with a wiretap all their own.

Who were the suspicious 17? The Government will not publicly say, but tacitly admits that four were journalists: Marvin Kalb of CBS; Henry Brandon of the London *Sunday Times;* Hedrick Smith of *The New York Times,* now its Moscow correspondent; and William Beecher of *The New York Times,* now Deputy Assistant Secretary of Defense for Public Affairs. (Columnist Joseph Kraft was also bugged, but not by an official F.B.I. wiretapper, and so cannot claim membership in the 17.)

Of the 13 Government officials, it had been assumed until recently that all were members of the National Security Council staff. Those named up to now were Winston Lord, Helmut Sonnenfeldt, Daniel Davidson, Anthony Lake, Roger Morris, and Morton Halperin. This morning, let me add two more names of former N.S.C. men to the list of those whose home telephones were tapped: Richard Moose, now a consultant to the Senate Foreign Relations Committee, and Laurence Lynn Jr., now an Assistant Secretary of the Interior.

A few days ago, *New York Times* reporter John Crewdson dug up another name from his own Federal law enforcement sources: one William Safire, former special assistant to the President, now a columnist for *The New York Times* who is writing today's exercise in restrained fury.

And then there were four, as Agatha Christie might put it—out of the 17 taps, the names of four men still remain to be disclosed. Who are they? Obviously they include names of men, perhaps still working as loyal lieutenants to the President, who would be surprised, chagrined, and profoundly offended if they knew their longtime loyalty had been returned with mistrust, suspicion, and an unconscionable invasion of their privacy.

Of course, the men on the N.S.C. staff who were tapped usually pretend that it does not bother them at all; when prodded, they will recite some litany about men who deal in secret matters having to expect constant surveillance. Frankly, men who expect constant surveillance handling our national security betray a certain lack of understanding about our national traditions. Only one of the tappees, Morton Halperin, has expressed publicly his sense of outrage; his lawsuit might force more disclosure.

The reporters tapped and their news organizations have been curiously supine: Perhaps they are holding their fire until they build a factual case. Let's hope so—unless they resist, they cannot claim to have been raped. Acquiescence is approval.

For myself, I cannot go along with this fraternal silence of the suspicious 17. I did not knock myself loose for Mr. Nixon in 1959 and 1960, and then cast my lot with him through the long, arid comeback years of 1965 through 1968, to have him—or some lizard-lidded paranoid acting in his name without his approval—eavesdropping on my conversations.

"National security," my eye—during the 37 days in July and August of 1969 that some agent in earphones was illegally (as the Supreme Court later found) listening in to my every word, I was writing the (sh!) President's message and speech on welfare reform.

I still believe in the work ethic, the New Federalism, the Nixon doctrine, and the absence of Presidential involvement in Watergate—but I have been consistent, before, during, and after my White House days, about the right to privacy.

There are questions that must be answered: Who had the right to decide which White House aides would be tapped? Were other speechwriters tapped as well? Did the President know when he was talking to an aide who was being tapped?

If, as I have reason to suspect, the answer to that last question is no, a further question presents itself: Does the President realize that there are tapes and transcripts of his own conversations with aides now in the files of the F.B.I. out of his control, taken years before he began taping himself?

THE GREAT HOWCUM

August 2, 1973

WASHINGTON—President Eisenhower used to have a benign "enemies list" of his own. Whenever somebody irritated him, he would write that person's name on a scrap of paper, crumple it up, and throw it in a bottom drawer, thereby ridding himself of what later came to be called hangups.

When Senator Sam Ervin observed on "Face the Nation" last weekend, "Down in North Carolina, we say—'howcum?'" his remark sent me to my bottom drawer where I keep my crumpled-up howcums. Flattened out and presented here today, these collected howcums represent a cathartic checklist for diehards, some specifics to fling about in justifying that lingering feeling of helpless resentment.

Howcum the lack of investigation of massive vote frauds in the 1960 Kennedy-Nixon campaign has never been called a "cover-up"?

Howcum John Dean's flat assertion under oath that "I planted no stories" received no refutation from the dozens of people with whom Dean and his lawyers planted stories?

Howcum there has been no clamor to investigate the investigations inflicted on the 1968 Nixon-Agnew campaign?

Howcum people usually sensitive to ethnic or religious slurs feel free to disparage "the Germans" in the White House, and like to identify Haldeman and Ehrlichman as Christian Scientists when they identify no other witness' religious affiliation?

Howcum it is laudable to raise funds to ransom Cubans recruited to land at the Bay of Pigs, but terrible to raise funds for "support and lawyers' fees" to Cuban-Americans who broke into the Watergate? (This howcum collapses under examination of motive, but it has a certain symmetry.)

Howcum those rightly indignant at unfair prying into the private lives of public figures have shown no interest in the anti-Republican snooping activities of Carmine Bellino, as brought out into the open by George Bush?

Howcum it was right for the Internal Revenue Service to hand over tax returns to a Kennedy investigator, without so much as a written request, when it is wrong for Nixon investigators to even breathe the initials "I.R.S."?

Howcum the wrath of civil libertarians so properly aimed at the misuse of Government power to "get" individuals never managed to get cranked up (with the lonely exception of Wayne Morse) at the misuse of Government power by Robert Kennedy to "get" Jimmy Hoffa?

Howcum nobody is asking now what "foreign intelligence reasons" were given for the unconscionable tapping of Martin Luther King's telephone, or about the propriety of F.B.I. agents seeking to leak contents of those tapes to newspaper editors?

Howcum nobody ever objected before to the "dirty tricks" and "negative advance" perfected by Lyndon Johnson's campaign staff and described on page 349 of Theodore White's *The Making of the President 1964?*

Howcum Daniel Schorr of CBS, who was the subject of F.B.I. harassment and has more reason than any other reporter to be angry at this Administration, has been reporting the Ervin hearings with restraint and insight, while Carl Stern of NBC has felt free to indulge his biases?

Howcum Bob Haldeman, who was supposed to be so efficient, never arranged for the taping of Presidential conversations aboard the yacht *Sequoia?* (Maybe this howcum came out of the wrong drawer.)

Howcum the incredible similarity of the devotion of Gordon Liddy and Daniel Ellsberg to a "higher law" has led to one's lionization and the other's incarceration?

Howcum the people who are so irate about our secret bombing of North Vietnamese sanctuaries near the Cambodian border never so much as waggle a finger at North Vietnamese troops for assembling on Cambodian soil in the first place?

Howcum the scoffers who were so certain that the Vietnam cease-fire would not last longer than a few weeks are not admitting they may have been wrong after six months?

Howcum the report that President Johnson surreptitiously taped conversations with George Wallace has raised not a single eyebrow?

That cleans out my howcum drawer. An even longer list could be tellingly directed at the Nixon Administration, but these accumulated resentments are presented to suggest that much of what appalls us today has its roots in the callousness or apathy of too many of us in the past.

The great howcum, as they call it down in North Carolina, is this: Howcum we cannot agree to apply a single standard to political morality, and as we try to raise that standard together, to admit that nobody has the perfect right to cast the first stone?

HAIG'S ORATION

October 25, 1973

Haig: Friends, liberals, civilians, lend me your ears;
I come to bury Nixon, not to praise him.
The good that Presidents do lives after them;
The evil can be interred with their tapes;
So let it be with Nixon. The noble Elliot
Hath told you Nixon was ambitious:
If it were so, it was a grievous fault,
And grievously hath Nixon answer'd it.
He hath brought prosperity without war,
Whose revenues did the general coffers fill:
Did this in Nixon seem ambitious?
When the aggressed-against have cried, Nixon hath wept:
Ambition should be made of sterner stuff:
Yet critics say he was ambitious;
And critics are all honorable men.
I speak not to disprove what Elliot spoke
But here I am to speak what I do know.
Sixty-eight percent did love him once, not without cause:
What cause withholds you then to stick with him?

O judgment! Thou are fled to editorial writers
And men have lost their reason. Bear with me;
My heart is in the West Wing there with Nixon
And I must pause ere it come back to me.

First Citizen: Poor soul! His eyes are red as fire with weeping.

Second Citizen: There's not a nobler man in Washington than Al Haig.
Mark him, he begins again—

Haig: But yesterday the word of Nixon might
Have stood against the world: Now lies he there,
And none so poor to do him reverence.
If you have tears, prepare to shed them now.
You all do know this overcoat: I remember
the first time ever Nixon put it on;
'Twas on the trip to Peking, visiting the Great Wall,
Ten days that changed the world:
Look, in this place ran Ed Brooke's dagger through:
See what a rent the envious Muskie made:
Through this the well-beloved Elliot stabb'd;
For Elliot, as you know, was Nixon's angel:
Judge, O you gods, how often Nixon appointed him!
That was the most unkindest cut of all;
For when the noble Nixon saw Elliot's stab
On television, watched his friend refuse to say impeachment nay,
That vanquished him; then burst his mighty resolve,
And, gathering up his innocent tapes,
He made poor Wright accept Sirica's wrong,
And our Commander in Chief, Great Nixon, folded.
O, what a folding was there, my countrymen!
Then I, and you, and all of us caved in
Whilst the glee of élitist media flourished o'er us.

First Citizen: O piteous spectacle!

Second Citizen: Peace there, hear the noble Haig.

Haig: Moreover, he plans to leave you all his walks,
His private arbors and new-planted orchards
At San Clemente and Biscayne; he will leave them to you
And to your heirs forever, common pleasures,
To walk abroad and recreate yourselves.

Here was a Nixon! When comes such another?
O, the Cox-men who have done this deed are honorable:
What private griefs they have, alas, I know not.
I am no orator, as Elliot is,
But all my life a plain military man
That follows my leader; but were I Elliot,
And Elliot Haig, there were a Haig
Would ruffle up your spirits and put a tongue
In every wound of Nixon that should move
The silent majority to split the heavens with a roar!

First Citizen: O noble Nixon! We'll revenge his abasement!

Second Citizen: Impeach the would-be impeachers.
Exeunt.

Haig: Now let it work. Resentment, thou are afoot.
Take thou what course thou wilt!

    A reply to "Haig's Oration" was posted on the bulletin board of the Washington bureau of *The Times*, written by reporter Anthony Ripley, a devotee of poet Robert Frost:

A Bull in the woods on a snowy evening

Whose tapes these are I think I know
He's busy in the White House, though.
He will not mind my stopping here
To throw his tapes into the snow.

Charles Alan Wright must think it queer
To act without Sirica near
And hide them by a frozen lake
The darkest thieving of this year.

Dick's given Archibald the shake
Nor yet confessed to some mistake.
The only other sound's the weep
Of queasy friend and Senate flake.

The tapes were loaded, stark and steep.
But I've a cover-up to keep,
And cash to spend that came from Creep,
And cash to spend that came from Creep.

ON BEING WRONG

December 13, 1973

WASHINGTON—Avid readers of this space may recall an essay this summer that used the great pendulum at the Smithsonian Institution as a symbol.

My point was that the pendulum always swung back. The likelihood of the hue and cry about Watergate continuing without letup seemed to me as remote as that of the great pendulum swinging past its ordained outer limit to crash through the wall of the museum.

"Ol' Buddy," a former White House colleague of mine pointed out today, "that pendulum of yours not only crashed through the wall but it swung up high and came crashing through the opposite wall. That's not a pendulum anymore, it's a propeller."

As the year of retribution draws to a close, it might be good to claim to have experienced the secret thrill of being wrong in times like these; a hair shirt can be a fun fur.

The week this column began to appear was the week President Nixon announced he had been told of a massive cover-up in connection with Watergate. I opined that it was a good thing that Mr. Nixon had taken firm command and nipped the Watergate scandal in the bud.

That is what is called "being really wrong." Not mistaken, not slightly off base, not relatively inaccurate—but grandly, gloriously, egregiously wrong. (April 1973 might have been the wrong time to start writing a column but it was the right time to leave the White House.)

Rivaling this underestimation of the vulnerability of the first Administration equipped for instant replay was my decision, several months later, to defend Vice President Agnew against a campaign of leaks.

In that instance, I was more careful; no knee-jerk responses for this once-burnt warrior. I waited until the Vice President personally assured me that the charges were false and pledged to fight if indicted before I went up over the top.

However, while Mr. Agnew was telling me this on the telephone, he was negotiating his resignation. That left a few of us plodding ahead in no-man's-land, bullets whizzing 'round, while, back in the trenches, the platoon leader was waving his white flag. Wrong again.

To be wrong on the grand scale like that, twice in less than a year, tempts one to boast, with Fiorello La Guardia, "When I make a mistake, it's a beaut," and to inflate other, lesser errors into apparent whoppers.

For example, I recently breathed life into the late couturier Balenciaga, who died nearly two years ago; the report of his current success is exaggerated. Also, the word "Moxie" was erroneously etymologized here as the name of a Southern soft drink, but—as dozens of irate Moxie-drinkers puckeringly pointed out—Moxie is a Boston product only recently inflicted on Southerners. Worst of all, I have twice used "lies" for "lays."

These are inaccuracies and errors, but lack the thrill of profound wrongitude. People find it pretentious and lacking in suavity to confess unimportant mistakes; that is why nobody comes forward today to say, "I was wrong about wanting to cut down the oil depletion allowance a few years ago" or "I was wrong to oppose the President on the Alaska pipeline back when it was chic to be an environmentalist."

Presidents and other punching bags experience the thrill of being really wrong, from time to time, but with a difference: If you are at the center of action, *being* wrong is perceived as *doing* wrong. To be wrong is the privilege of free men; to do wrong is the activity of criminals. But with chiefs of state, that separating semicolon blurs, and wrongbeing is universally equated with wrongdoing.

At this sentimental time of year we can sympathize with those consistently on-target doomsayers who have not felt the guiltily pleasurable twinge of being really wrong. When to be in fashion is to be in error, those who plaintively cry "I told you so" must be counted among the Neediest Cases.

Years ago, when Brooklyn Dodger slugger Dolph Camilli would come to bat late in the game, after having struck out three times in succession, an ominous murmur would race through the bleachers: "He's due."

A year from now, the crazily whirling propeller may turn back into a stately pendulum, and optimists like me may then be writing smug and arid essays "on being right." Sooner or later, somebody up there is going to enforce the law of averages—God knows we're "due."

12/17/73

Dear Mr. Safire:

I read your column regularly in *The New York Times*—and do indeed enjoy your articles immensely. Your clear style and thought-provoking ideas are especially delightful. The depth of research manifested is refreshing.

But oh! you are also so wrong!! about almost everything!... and on

Thursday, December 13th, in your article "On Being Wrong," you revealed how wrong you *also* are concerning "the law of averages."

If you will check with any professional trained in statistical mathematics, you will find there is *no* such thing as "the law of averages" ... that when Dolph Camilli had struck out 3 times in succession he was *not* due. In fact, because he did not have a hit in his last 3 times at bat made his batting average even *lower* and his chances even *less* for getting a hit his fourth time at bat that day.

When a man has a .333 batting average, for example, his chances for hitting safely are 1 in 3 *each time* he comes to bat. The fact that he does not hit safely 2 times in a row does *not* mean he is *due* when he next comes to bat. It is still 1 chance in 3. And if, like yourself, he continues to be *unable* to hit safely, his chances become even worse the next time he comes to bat.

Mr. Safire, I'm afraid there is no "law of averages" to bale you out. What you need are some *genuine* safe hits to increase your batting average and your true chances the next time you come to bat.

Maybe President Nixon *too* believes in the "law of averages" to bale *him* out. Like you, he better not count on it because there's no such thing.

N. L. Seltzer
Lexington, Massachusetts

THE NEW TORTURE

December 20, 1973

WASHINGTON—With Judge "Maximum John" Sirica being talked about as the likely "Man of the Year" for 1973, with "law and order" no longer denounced as code words for repression or racism, and with widespread approval of the way society finally moved to protect itself against crime of all sorts, only a spoilsport would complain that the rights of the accused are being stolen away.

After all, we have finally reached a kind of national consensus on criminal justice: Conservatives have long held that criminals were being mollycoddled by lenient judges, and are happy that the trend is now in the direction of toughmindedness; liberals, meanwhile, watching the wrath of a Sirica turned against the Nixon men, have to admit they like the taste of no-nonsense prosecution.

Thus we have attained a kind of poetic injustice: The Nixon hard-liners who denounced the hamstringing of stern justice with petty civil liberties technicalities only five years ago now find themselves standing naked before their enemies.

One old device of the prosecution that has been sharpened anew, and now glints in every courtroom, is the inclination of judges to sentence a convicted man most horrendously—and then to dangle the bribe of a reduced sentence, perhaps even freedom, if the man under sentence is willing to "cooperate."

Of course a penitent offender who helps the law should be treated with more consideration than the criminal who chooses to hang tough, but consider how this sing-or-else device can be used to help justice miscarry:

You have just been sentenced to 35 years for breaking and entering. You know they will throw the key away, and you will never see your loved ones again, or be able to care for children dependent on you. But then the judge offers a way out—a short sentence, with a possibility of quick parole—if only you say what the prosecution wants you to say.

Let us say, just for the sake of argument, that what the prosecution wants you to say is something you know is not the truth. The prosecution suspects someone "higher up" but it just happens in your case that their target, Mr. Big, was not involved. What would you do—lie and get off, or stick to the truth and go to jail?

I do not suggest that this new torture resulted in a miscarriage of justice in Judge Sirica's courtroom: He used sing-or-else to crack the Watergate case, and it appears that justice prevailed. The technique worked; the new torture served a good end; but perhaps we should pause before we enshrine this method of breaking the resistance of individuals.

Another new weapon of the prosecution is now in rampant vogue: a way of getting around that part of the Bill of Rights that says no man shall be forced to bear witness against himself.

Five years ago, the only way a prosecutor could force a person to testify was to grant him immunity from prosecution. But good prosecutors were loath to give "immunity baths" to possibly guilty people, and so we law-and-order types came up with a "limited immunity" idea.

Without the immunity weapon, the prosecution would never have been able to build a case against Vice President Agnew; nor would we have been treated to John Dean's Senate testimony; and there must be instances in which Mafia leaders, for whom the statute was intended, have received their just deserts.

Of course, this "use" immunity idea has led to the roughening of justice: Prosecutors are making deals as never before, and suspects who feel themselves trapped can barter for their freedom by pointing their fingers in the desired directions. We'll jail more biggies that way—and what does it matter if some innocent men named as "higher-ups" get railroaded, or if some guilty men down the line get off scot-free?

Of course it matters. Presidential aide Dwight Chapin, for example, has been indicted for perjury because a couple of other men want reduced sentences and immunity; that psychological and financial squeeze was put on Mr. Chapin to get him to finger H. R. Haldeman or the President. By protesting his innocence, Mr. Chapin is breaking the chain. (I just sent a check to the Chapin Justice Fund at The American Security and Trust Company in Washington and don't care whose list that puts me on.)

By applying the devices of the new torture—in both its sing-or-else and limited immunity forms—we have undoubtedly purified our political system. Judge Sirica broke the Watergate case single-handedly and surely deserves all the applause he gets, having proven that the new torture—cruel but no longer unusual—is a means of obtaining evidence that can be used for the best of ends.

The applause has a special poignance to those who draw from Watergate the lesson that the noblest ends can never be used to justify immoral means.

TO "NIXON PEOPLE"

August 12, 1974

WASHINGTON—Not so long ago, about four out of ten adults in this country referred to themselves politically as "Nixon people." How should they react to the forced resignation of the man who for so long embodied their beliefs and their prejudices?

As a card-carrying member of that group, let me suggest a few reactions both to those who made it to the lifeboats and those who went down with the ship:

First, toward Richard Nixon. Despite the frequent hypocrisy of some of his pursuers he was not unfairly ejected.

He is now America's only living former President, for good reasons. When he first learned that some men acting in his name committed a crime, he put the bonds of friendship ahead of his oath of office. When he had the chance to destroy all the tapes just after their existence had become known, he made the wrong tactical decision, and nobody is patting him on the back now for his rectitude in not destroying the evidence that proved him guilty.

In retrospect, all the maneuvers his supporters considered so ill-advised in establishing his innocence gain an intelligent pattern when viewed as a means toward preventing revelation of his guilt. He "knew"; he knew that there was proof that he "knew"; and all his actions for the last year, from the firing of Archibald Cox to the rejection of subpoenas to the falsely based appeal to the Supreme Court, were absolutely consistent.

No wonder, then, he would allow no lawyer to listen to the tapes; he was stalling for time and playing for breaks, and on such a course there was nobody he could trust without making him a co-conspirator. Mr. Nixon was never indecisive, never floundering, as so many of us had anguished: His plan was to protect the tapes at all costs, and their cost was all.

Therefore, no torment of unfairness is due him from the "Nixon people." Black Sox slugger "Shoeless" Joe Jackson was approached by a fan crying, "Say it ain't so, Joe." The corrupted ballplayer said nothing; Mr. Nixon said it was not so.

As we spare him our tears, we can afford him more than a little respect. He was never the would-be dictator his severest critics have claimed, and his motives were either noble (to make a peace that would last) or at least not ignoble (to gain the adulation that would flow from being the man who made the peace).

The people who supported him, and most of those who worked for him, can look around now that the shelling has ceased and point out much of substance that was done domestically in reflecting the will of the people—which, lest we forget, earned such a ringing affirmation of support just a year and a half ago.

Toward President Ford, the reaction of the "Nixon people" should be far different from the reaction, say, of the Kennedy people to the ascension of President Johnson. Here is no cultural or stylistic usurper; Mr. Ford was not Mr. Nixon's necessary compromise, but his chosen heir, deserving of a transfer of old loyalties. (Mr. Nixon wound up with a lifetime batting average of .500 in picking Vice Presidents, better than F.D.R.'s .333.)

As President, Mr. Ford has chosen two of the best of the early Nixon supporters to be on his transition committee: Interior Secretary Rogers Morton and NATO Ambassador Donald Rumsfeld, both of whom bear the scars of battle with the Nixon Palace Guard. Mr. Rumsfeld, a former Congressman in his early forties, is especially valuable.

Finally, how should the former "Nixon people" view the ecstatic political opposition, so wrong about the country in 1972 and so right about Mr. Nixon in 1973? For the country's sake and our own, let us let them have their time of vindication without resentment. The triumph of justice is nobody's political defeat. Churchill's "in defeat, defiance" does not apply, because Mr. Nixon's defeat is not the defeat of the "Nixon people" nor of the causes the former President espoused, only the defeat of that misguided toughness which is a form of weakness.

Of course, "in victory, magnanimity" does apply; if in months to come, those who justly brought Mr. Nixon down want to make a martyr out of him, dragging him down Pennsylvania Avenue behind a chariot, here we go again on another round of vindictiveness.

For Mr. Nixon, who might not have shown enough contrition to satisfy everyone, in delivering his own epitaph as President showed that the underlying lesson of Watergate had finally sunk in ". . . those who hate you don't win unless you hate them—and then you destroy yourself."

WATERGATE'S THIRD CRIME

October 28, 1974

WASHINGTON—The man who appointed himself to be judge of the Watergate trial announced from the bench last week that he was "not trying to try this case on strict rules of evidence."

According to John Sirica, the reason why the normal rules of the criminal courtroom will not apply is that he wants to expose the "full story" of Watergate. For those simpletons who could not grasp his purpose, he spelled it out: "T-R-U-T-H."

The purpose of this celebrated trial, according to the judge, is only incidentally to determine the guilt or innocence of the five defendants: The basic purpose is to bring to light the truth. Most people will applaud that goal; most people do not understand the purpose of the criminal courts.

The one and only purpose of bringing a defendant to trial is to determine whether the evidence proves that specific individual committed the specific crime with which he has been charged.

That is why we have strict rules of evidence. Those rules must be strict to protect the individual against the power of government. To use the criminal court system for any other purpose than the trial of defendants for the particular charge is to pervert that system.

John Sirica, like Senator Sam Ervin before him, evidently believes that it is more important to find out the truth than to send a few men to jail. Accordingly, he is conducting his Nuremberg-on-the-Potomac trial in a way designed (a) to expose villainy in the highest places, (b) to convict the defendants, and (c) to guarantee that the appeals courts will overturn the convictions.

Thus, the "error bag" of the defense counsel is not the primary concern of this misguidedly patriotic man on the bench, because he envisions a trade-off: The nation will benefit from the full truth exposed in the trial court, and the defendants will get their protection and their freedom in the appeals courts. Everyone will find out what really happened and nobody will go to jail, as justice steps aside for truth.

On this theory, the ends justify the means. By means of a temporary abuse of the criminal justice system, the ends of the national interest in truth are served. And since the abuse will soon be set right in the expected reversals on appeal, what is the harm in loosening up the rules of evidence?

The harm is incalculable. The first crime of Watergate was the corruption of political power in the campaign process; the second crime was the corruption of government power in the cover-up; the third crime of Watergate is the corruption of the criminal justice system in the prosecution of the first two crimes.

All three crimes, all three corruptions of power, have been and are being committed in the names of high-sounding goals—at first, political victory; then, personal loyalty; now, the public's right to know. But they are all forms of the same corruption.

Judge Sirica's admissions, his Greek-chorus commentary, and his hints that he will call former President Nixon to the stand as a "court witness" which both defense and prosecution can treat as hostile, make plain that this is not intended to be the fair trial of five accused men. This is the trial of Richard Nixon, who is the target of the prosecution, the dumping ground of the defense, and the ultimate fount of the "full truth" that the judge seeks.

In years to come, as our children study the aberrations of these times, the classic horror story will be the way Watergate tainted nearly everyone connected with it, finally including the man who originally cracked the case.

The taint of the third Watergate crime is, once again, the unlawful use of the law: in the present instance, the unlawful use of the criminal courts to publicize crimes rather than to try defendants. Break-in, cover-up, vendetta—all illegal, all participated in by the self-righteous abusing their trust in the name of a higher cause—and in the end, with the great majority of public and press joining in.

At least the break-in and cover-up were intimate conspiracies. In the perversion of the criminal courts that is the third Watergate crime, we are all conspirators, even the civil libertarians who have registered a mild peep for the record about needing disinterested judges but who reserve their outrage for the denial of rights of more respectably disreputable defendants.

Those are not the rights of a handful of villains that are being ripped away in a good cause and to the delight of the public; those are your rights and mine, and there is no getting them back when we set the precedent for giving them away.

The criminal courts should never be used to vent our spleen, to get our enemies, to right political wrongs, nor even to lay the awful truth before the curious public eye—but used only for justice, the specific justice

demanded in the Constitution, or as somebody should spell out to
the adulated man who has cast himself in a role higher than judge:
"J-U-S-T-I-C-E."

ORCHESTRATING OUTRAGE

December 8, 1975

*He misused the Federal Bureau of Investigation ... to conduct or con-
tinue electronic surveillance or other investigations for purposes unrelated to national security, the enforcement of laws, or any other lawful
function of his office....
    From Article II, Section 2, of the Impeachment of Richard Nixon.*

WASHINGTON—We are all now permitted to recognize as truth one
central point that Richard Nixon's defenders have been making for two
years: that the use of the F.B.I. for political purposes in the Nixon Administration was mild compared to the misuse of that agency in the Johnson and Kennedy years.

M.I.T. Professor Noam Chomsky, that giant of linguistics who joined
or led just about every radical anti-war protest during the 60's, has this to
say in his introduction to *Cointelpro—The F.B.I.'s Secret War on Political Freedom*, published last week by Pathfinder Press:

"Illegal F.B.I. operations [under Kennedy and Johnson] ... while in-
comparably more serious than anything charged in the Congressional Articles of Impeachment or other denunciations of Nixon, aroused scant interest and little concern, specifically, in the organs of American liberalism
that were so agitated over the latest tax trickery or tape erasure.

"Ergo," concludes Professor Chomsky, "Nixon's defenders do have a
case."

Nicholas Von Hoffman, a modern Peter Porcupine whose Nixon-hat-
ing credentials have always been in good order, writes: "In the months
since his departure, his defense looks better and better. Half a dozen Congressional committees have brought forth volumes of information all ad-
ducing that the break-ins, the tapping, snooping and harassment have
been routine government activities for a generation at least."

But what of the frequently repeated charge that Mr. Nixon's abuses of
power far exceeded the occasional transgressions of his two predecessors?
My colleague, Tom Wicker, who is not often accused of being a Nixon
apologist, disposed of that the other day: "There is no great difference in

wiretapping the Democratic National Committee and the Mississippi Freedom Democratic Party."

And so it appears that revisionism is already doing its work. History will show the Nixon Administration not as the one that invented abuse of power, but the one that gloriously if unwittingly served the cause of individual liberty by the clumsy way it tried to continue the abuses of Kennedy and Johnson.

The real question we should be asking today is this: Why didn't the public know about the dirty tricks of the F.B.I. and the C.I.A. long before this?

The secrets being "revealed" now, accompanied by synthetic gasps of horror and an effort to make J. Edgar Hoover the sole scapegoat, were not secrets at all: They were known to Democratic Senators and their staffs, and to some timorous Republicans as well, for two long years.

Why was this vital information not vouchsafed to the public? Why was it not leaked to, or dug out by, investigative reporters who are otherwise busy being immortalized by our most glamorous movie stars?

Because the public, if possessed of the whole truth, might not have acted as the public opinion manipulators wanted them to. If the whole truth were let out, Mr. Nixon might have escaped. That explains the two-year delay in testimony tucked away by the Senate Watergate committee, much of which is still to come.

In his book, *At That Point in Time,* Fred Thompson, the inexperienced minority counsel of the Senate Watergate committee, blurts out why Republicans on the committee did not call F.B.I. Deputy Directors William Sullivan or Cartha DeLoach to the stand to recount the Kennedy-Johnson F.B.I. abuses we officially learned about only last week. "[Senator Lowell] Weicker was adamantly opposed. He said it would look like an attempt to justify some of the actions of the Nixon Administration."

And so the greatest cover-up of all took place: the suppression of the truth about Democratic precedents to Watergate, on the grounds that it might ameliorate the hatred being focused on Richard Nixon—on the assumption that the public was too stupid to take action if it were permitted to know the whole story.

The reason for the deliberate suppression of evidence in 1974, for the lackadaisical reportage then of what we see now, was the fear that a false claim that "everybody did it" might make it impossible to hound Mr. Nixon out of office.

Everybody did not do it; the Justice Department under President Eisenhower, for example, shows up far better than under Roosevelt, Kennedy, Johnson, or Nixon. But even assuming the fear of anti-Nixon partisans to be valid, did that give the orchestrators of outrage the right to suppress evidence? To manage the news and fan the hysteria? To prevent perspective?

As each new abuse of power finally dribbles out, we can ask ourselves: "Why now? Why not two years ago?"

THREE ATTORNEYS GENERAL

May 10, 1976

WASHINGTON—"Everybody did it" is no excuse for wrongdoing, but the Church committee reports demonstrate conclusively that the seeds of Watergate were planted and nourished in two Democratic administrations.

Using the Senate committee's findings, let us observe a trio of Attorneys General at their individual moments of truth.

1. *Nicholas Katzenbach and the bugging of hotel rooms of Martin Luther King.* Ben Bradlee, then head of *Newsweek*'s Washington bureau, alerted Mr. Katzenbach to the way F.B.I. officials were peddling salacious King tapes to newsmen in 1964. In his moment of truth, the Attorney General's response was "clearly inadequate," concludes the committee. In fact, he permitted the official wiretapping of Dr. King to go on for four months after receiving the warning of a smear campaign using unofficial "bugs."

When Mr. Katzenbach's complicity in the bugging of Dr. King was first suggested in this space a year ago, he exploded with a letter using all the libel code words.

But Church committee counsel confronted him with documentary evidence that he had been informed of the placement of microphones in Dr. King's suites. Three F.B.I. memos saying so bore Mr. Katzenbach's handwritten initials, and there was a separate handwritten note from him— dated and filed in sequence with a bugging notification—telling Director Hoover, "Obviously these are particularly delicate surveillances and we should be very cautious. . . ."

Mr. Katzenbach's reaction to this evidence was to insist he couldn't remember what his note was referring to—maybe it was some other surveillance that day. Nor could he remember initialing any of the bugging notifications, but—under oath—he added artfully: "If they are my initials and if I put them on, then I am clearly mistaken. . . ."

The Church staff report on Dr. King (written with admirable evenhandedness by Old Kennedy Hand Michael Epstein) permits the clear conclusion that (a) the wiretapping of Dr. King was originally Robert

Kennedy's idea, not J. Edgar Hoover's, and (b) the systematic program of snoop-and-smear could probably not have taken place without the sometimes tacit, sometimes explicit, toleration of Nicholas Katzenbach.

2. *Ramsey Clark and the Doar plan to spy on dissidents.* Under heat from the Johnson White House to crack down on black power groups and new left peaceniks, Attorney General Clark told his henchman, John Doar, to come up with a plan to bring the full power of government to bear on gathering intelligence about dissenters.

The Doar plan—forming the "Interdivision Information Unit," described last year in this column—was submitted, urging that agencies as disparate as the Narcotics Bureau, the Poverty Program, the I.R.S., and the Post Office Department be tapped to "funnel information" into a computer that a later Clark study said would create a "master index on individuals, or organizations."

Mr. Clark, in that moment of truth in 1967, approved the Doar plan, spawning the infamous I.D.I.U., which—in the Church committee's words—"was the focal point of a massive domestic intelligence apparatus . . . resulting in excessive collection of information about law-abiding citizens."

3. *John Mitchell and the Huston plan.* Thanks to the fine work of impeachment counsel John Doar, we have been treated to many lengthy denunciations of this proposal of a young man in the Nixon White House to combat dissidents with illegal "black bag jobs," mail openings, and eavesdroppings. It turns out that in making his scandalous suggestions, Tom Huston was not aware that most of them were already standard operating procedure for intelligence agencies under Presidents Kennedy and Johnson.

In his moment of truth, in the face of White House pressure urging him to approve the Huston plan, what did Attorney General John Mitchell do? Writes the Church committee: "C.I.A. Director Helms shortly thereafter indicated his support for the plan to the Attorney General, telling him 'We had put our backs into this exercise.' Nonetheless, Mitchell advised the President to withdraw his approval. Huston was told to rescind his memorandum. . . ."

These three moments are not cited to suggest Attorneys General Katzenbach and Clark were devils and Mitchell was a saint. But they might be remembered in reviewing what each of the trio is doing today:

Mr. Katzenbach, making no apology for his role in the King case, is taking down $300,000 per year in pay and benefits as I.B.M.'s general counsel. Mr. Clark, posing as a civil libertarian, is a candidate for the Democratic nomination for Senator from the state of New York. Mr. Mitchell, acquitted at one political show trial and convicted at another, has seen his career ruined and now faces jail.

Equal justice under law?

J. N. MITCHELL 24171-157
Fed Pr. Camp
Maxwell AFB - ALA 36112

Saturday

Dear Bill

Thanks for your note of the 18th and enclosures. I definitely appreciate the Safire essays and am glad you have "directed" they be sent.

Dick Moore is right about the library status. It takes more than a crack-down on the overdue list as many of my fellow vacationers have larceny in their souls.

Please keep after the establishment and make them account. You should continue to have a field day with Koreagate. Sooner or latter they will have to quit stonewalling and get on with the fireworks.

Please be assured that I am doing just fine & nothing else, which there will be, I'm determined to outlive the bastards.

Many thanks and warmest regards

John

P.S. Hope your book is a WOW!

Nothing Recedes
Like Recession

IN THE NIXON YEARS, some of the guys placed illegal wiretaps; some of the guys broke into the Watergate; some of the guys participated in a cover-up. My sin in those days was to write the President's August 15, 1971, speech imposing wage and price controls, and some economists think it may have been the most far-reaching sin of all.

But it taught me a lesson. The essays that follow reflect a passion for a free-market economy that is akin to the writings about alcoholism by a reformed drunk. In the soliloquy ascribed herein to Margaret Thatcher—written long before she came to power—there is some inkling of what her government would be like, and in many ways Britain's conservative experiment has been an example to us.

This group of essays begins with my first visit to the C.I.A., where my target was the soybean-and-anchovy man.

EL NIÑO

August 30, 1973

WASHINGTON—There is a warm and unwelcome current of water that flows down from the Equator past the coast of Peru every year around Christmastime that the fishermen call "El Niño De Navidad"— the Christmas Child. The warm current is unwelcome because it is bad for the fish.

Six years out of seven, the warm El Niño current is pushed out to sea and made harmless by the Humboldt current, an icy-cold stream from the South Pacific that flows northward up the coast of Peru and makes the huge anchovy catch proliferate happily.

But on the seventh year, El Niño cannot be denied; for as long as any of the old fishermen can remember, on the seventh year El Niño defeats the Humboldt current, making the waters warm and the fish sluggish. The anchovies huddle together, do not breed well, and the fishing is bad.

Last year was one of those seventh years. But the young, modern fishermen saw themselves not as mere men of the sea who pay respect to the cycle of nature, but as industrialists providing the world two million tons annually of protein-rich fish meal. So they equipped their boats with electronic fish-finders, located the unhappy schools of anchovies, and fished them heavily, and laughed at El Niño.

Suddenly there were no more fish off the coast of Peru. In the old days, on the seventh year, the anchovies that survived El Niño could hide from the fisherman and spawn for the next year, but thanks to the electronic fish-finders, the schools were decimated. The fishermen are now in a depression, and it serves them right, because they lost their sense of pride and courage and respect (and it's tempting to slip into Ernest Hemingway-style writing about the old men and the sea).

Perhaps by coincidence, two other great sources of protein in the world were hard hit: Drought harmed the peanut crops of West Africa and India, and in the United States, 75 million bushels of soybeans rotted.

What happens when you have a bad year for fish meal and soybeans and peanuts? As night follows day, you have higher prices for cattle feed and chicken feed and hogwash, and you have housewives in supermarkets infuriated by higher prices and blaming it all on Herb Stein and George Shultz which is unfair because neither ever insulted El Niño De Navidad.

To find out what might happen next in current events, this essayist ventured to the headquarters of the Central Intelligence Agency in McLean, Virginia. The protein experts of their bureau of economic research brilliantly foresaw the worldwide consequences of the fishermen's refusal to submit to El Niño memorandum ER-IM 72-149, "Peru's Fish Problem," which has come into my possession.

The soybean-and-anchovy man at the C.I.A. insists on anonymity because his friends and neighbors think he is a proper spy and not just a soybean-and-anchovy expert. He sees some hope in the situation: Although there are not the usual fourteen million tons of live fish off Peru right now, there are about four million tons splashing about in the Humboldt current and reproducing with great glee under the protection of a lock-the-barn-door Peruvian fishing ban.

How the C.I.A. has found out there are four million tons of fish out there they will not say—the picture of an intrepid agent in a rowboat with a can of worms and a sodden transmitter comes to mind—but their soybean-and-anchovy man was correct before and the agency has earned a certain credibility in this matter.

So chances are that next year there will be plenty of fish meal; if the law of averages holds up, there will be a normal peanut crop in Africa, a decent grain harvest in Russia, and an improved corn crop in the U.S. with our soybeans sprouting determinedly. When feed prices come down, food prices will stop going up so fast.

An increase in supply to meet the increase in worldwide demand will come about not because Peruvian fishermen have discovered better fish-finding gimmicks, or because the phase makers of American economic policy have hit the lucky number.

A secure, growing supply of anchovies for fish meal will be achieved because the fishermen have been taught humility by El Niño. When the warm current comes back strongly in 1979, it will be respected; there will be a downturn, sometimes called a recession, in the fishing industry that year, but the self-correcting process will provide stability in the years ahead.

In the same way, we will be able to moderate price rises and raise the average man's real income if we show respect for our own El Niño. A periodic slowdown is not a happy time, and its effect on unemployment might be lessened by better manpower training programs, but we must not let the economic slowdown likely to come next year panic us into using tax and monetary stimulants that would do the symbolic job of electronic fish-finders.

Let the economic currents turn awry in their cyclical way. We should help lessen their effects on people's lives, but before we start confidently tampering with fundamental forces, let us remember what El Niño taught the fishermen.

September 13, 1973

Dear Mr. Safire:

Your column entitled "El Niño" in *The New York Times* of August 30, 1973, was, as usual, well-written and very entertaining. Alas, as a discussion of the philosophy of history, it was all wrong. It confuses biologic law with the norms of civilization. There is no basis for assuming that economic factors that can cause periodic slowdowns are at all comparable to the laws of biologic behavior which have been selected by the evolutionary processes. Commentators are forever making the mistake of using biologic metaphors to explain complicated processes that occur in Civilization.

I am enclosing a copy of Paul Schrecker's *magnum opus, Work and History*, to show you the error of your ways.

Best wishes.

Cordially yours,
Richard J. Wurtman, M.D.
Cambridge, Massachusetts

"DO SOMETHING!"

February 14, 1974

WASHINGTON—Confronting the demon of economic downturn, President Nixon extended his arms, flashed the ancient thumbs-up sign, and pronounced the mystic incantation: "There will be no recession."

Doing their bits to shoo out the dybbuk, advisers like Treasury Secretary George Shultz allowed as how the bedeviled President's prophecy would self-fulfill, provided one accepts the Nixon definition of a recession, and economist Herbert Stein sturdily agreed, adding under his breath, "But we're sure gonna have the littlest boom you ever saw."

What must disturb these two believers in economic freedom is the President's willingness to make economic decisions for political reasons—that is, to listen to the populist demand to "do something!"

Last summer, popularity economics called for a wrongheaded price freeze; by satisfying the demagogic lust to "do something," the President—overruling Messrs. Shultz and Stein—succeeded only in creating shortages and confusion.

This year, popularity economics calls for an evasion of recession at any cost, in a perversion of Keynesianism that says "inflation irritates, but recession infuriates." Some recession is surely necessary to restrain inflation and improve productivity, but the natural downturn would not help the President's plan for political survival.

When his back is to the wall, Mr. Nixon tends to adopt the economic suggestions of his Democratic opponents, and with a vengeance: taking "bold action" to freeze prices, or crack down on profits, or throw Federal money at a possible recession. This frenetic activity gives the illusion of leadership and temporarily answers the demands that he "do something."

But when Senator William Proxmire ladled out the usual pap about "lack of vigorous, forceful economic leadership" to George Shultz last week at a Congressional hearing, the mild-mannered witness did not grin and bear it. To everyone's surprise, Mr. Shultz banged the table and exploded: "I do not see why you just keep saying, saying, saying something that is not true. . . . In the stampede for 'action, action, do something' . . . you find yourself doing the wrong thing."

Mr. Shultz, a free-markets man who fought against the kind of "vigorous, forceful leadership" that caved in years ago to the clamor for controls—and who turned out to be right—denounced the Senator's do-something fulminations as "a gross misrepresentation and I'm frankly tired of it." Senator Proxmire, ashamed at being caught in a demagogic posture by an economist he admires, said, "So am I" and backed off.

What brings about this lust for Government intervention, this dosomethingism, on the part of those who simultaneously decry excessive Presidential power? Why can't "forceful leadership" ever be equated with unpopular self-restraint? Think of the economic mischief that could be avoided if voters were to say to elected officials: "Don't just do something—stand there."

For example, part of Proxmire's Complaint was with the way the independent truckers' strike was handled by the President. Presumably, the Senator would have preferred the Lyndon Johnson method, with all-night bargaining sessions in the White House showing the President's personal concern.

That sort of stunting would have undermined the professional mediation which brought about a sensible settlement. It has taken five years to wean disputants away from Oval Office maternal care—and, of course, had the President injected himself into the settlement, the do-something set would promptly have berated him for grandstanding.

At a time when the President is especially tempted to take "the popular course," a special responsibility falls on those who airily call on him to "do something" about avoiding a recession and—in the same breath—demand he "do something" about rising prices and "do something" about shortages induced by price controls.

Such demagogic demands can no longer be made with impunity: The President is now all too likely to respond to them. (I had a small dog which, secure in the belief that my leash would restrain him, loved to lunge and snarl at a huge St. Bernard; one day I dropped his leash and the little dog looked at me as if I had lost my mind.)

Controls have failed; let's admit it. Heavy Federal spending and a tax cut could avert a recession, let's admit that, too—but at a cost in inflated prices and reduced real earnings that make it something that is wrong to do.

Instead, let's consider a capitalist's manifesto: Laissez-faires of the world, unite! You have nothing to lose but your Keynes.

THE 5¢ CUP OF COFFEE

March 14, 1974

WASHINGTON—In *The American Condition*, published today, Richard N. Goodwin, the former speechwriter for Presidents Kennedy and Johnson, provocatively explores the baneful effects of bureaucracy on individual freedom.

Although the author is eminently serious about the dangers of "submission to a process," and fairly describes the lava-like encroachment of bureaucracies that take on a life of their own, he offers a brief, self-mocking digression that enlivens his work and enlightens his readers.

Cooking, he says, tongue in chic, was the beginning of the descent of man into bureaucracy.

The desire to cook led to the need for fire; absent matches, a fire required somebody to tend it, hence the need for a home; this was followed by a man-woman division of labor between hunting and cooking, in turn necessitating grouping into communities. Thus society began the business of grabbing previously independent cavemen by their fur lapels.

Mr. Goodwin's point, as I get it, is that we should carefully measure the personal freedom that we pay out for every advantage we demand from society; experience has taught him that not every alliance is an alliance for progress.

People organize for a purpose—cooking, for example—but after a while that purpose is subsumed by the organization itself, which then gains a new purpose: to continue to exist.

Along these lines, for the past year, I have been silently observing an unwitting experiment in bureaucratic purpose and efficiency here at the Washington bureau of *The New York Times*.

There are two coffee pools, or "messes" as they say in the Navy. One is operated by the reporters and columnists, providing the needed beverage to some 40 coffee-lovers in the newsroom; the other is operated by and for the seven men in the wireroom who transmit the reporters' copy.

The reporters' coffee mess provides a self-service brew of uneven consistency; the charge is 15 cents per cup, and the loss from operations, breakage, and wastage is made up by periodic assessments of the members of the mess.

The wireroom coffee, on the other hand, is hearty and strong: It costs a nickel a cup; and the year's operations turned a profit that enabled the members to buy a small refrigerator.

There are those in the reporters' mess who, looking at the product and the balance sheet of the wireroom mess, are convinced that corruption must be afoot. But the fair-minded observer would say that there is something fundamental about management that the wireroom mess has to teach the reporters' mess.

First, the wireroom mess is a comparatively small-scale unit. In bureaucracies, mass production efficiencies are a myth; a small operation can have less overhead per cup.

Second, the men in the wireroom remember the name of the game—to produce a good cup of coffee cheaply—and not "to have a coffee mess" like the rest of society or to suit the convenience of visitors. (Visitors, who may be exemplars of probity in their journalistic or government endeavors, are invariably coffee thieves.)

Third, the wireroom exercises control: The coffee machine is in sight of the membership, not off in a hidden kitchen, and nobody is going to put an empty coffeepot down on a hot coil and walk off dreamily. Nor will a member or visitor "forget" to plunk down his nickel. Credit is not permitted.

Finally, there is a sense of community spirit in the wireroom coffee mess that can never exist in the larger newsroom.

Reporters and columnists, proud of their individuality, proclaim a distaste for the processes of organizations, and tend mutteringly to accept bureaucracy's dictates; in that paradoxical way, we foolishly abdicate some of our freedom.

Contrariwise, the wireroom men are proud of their teamwork and—by consciously participating in their organization—are able to hold their loss of personal freedom to a minimum.

The man who runs the wireroom, Earl Smith, likes to call his 5-cent coffee mess "the conservative mess" and the 15-cent product "the liberal mess" on the theory that conservatives are more efficient at managing programs developed by liberals, which is the story of modern Republicanism.

But there is more to the dynamics of the lopsided coffee situation here than can be explained in conventional ideological terms.

Perhaps Mr. Goodwin, in *The American Condition*, is making a variation of a point made long ago: Those who do not try to manage the management of necessary bureaucracies are condemned to be defeated by them.

Think about that. (Black, two sugars, please.)

BLESSINGS OF RECESSION

March 17, 1975

In a Cleveland tavern, the man on the barstool to my right looked bleak; he had been out of a job for two months, had no prospects, and was feeling the pinch. But the man on the barstool beyond him, who was buying the beer, had a different story:

"I work for a replacement-parts outfit," he explained guiltily, "and when new-car sales fall out of bed, our business is great."

Heartless though it seems to admit, here is how the ill wind of recession is blowing some good:

1. *Recession Brings Down Inflation.* For every worker thrown out of work by recession, ten workers—and retirees on fixed incomes—are slammed up against the wall by inflation. Last year, inflation surged by 13 percent, more than 1 percent a month.

Thanks to the recession, the consumer price index in December rose only 0.7 percent; in January, 0.6 percent; and figures to be released later this week will be in that ball park. On the basis of a full quarter, then, we will see that this measurement of inflation has been cut in half—down from an annual rate of 13 percent to an annual rate of less than 7 percent.

That slowdown in the rise in the cost of living is no fluke. Wholesale prices, which presage retail price trends, rose some 30 percent in 1974. But in the past three months, wholesale prices have not only slowed their rise, but have actually declined at an annual rate of more than 6 percent. And an even more significant indicator: Wholesale industrial prices have moderated to a pace not seen in two years.

If you look at inflation as a wasteful tax, cutting that tax in half is much the same as reducing personal income taxes by more than $50 billion this year—a whopping stimulus.

In real-life terms, the average family's earnings last year went up only 7 percent, not nearly enough to keep up with 13 percent inflation; this year, those who continue to have jobs will be ahead of inflation, with real income going up.

2. *Recession Gives Us an Opportunity to Break the Oil Cartel.*

The world's oil exporting countries had been producing about 30 million barrels every day, but last month, this production was cut back to an estimated 25 million barrels, with further reductions scheduled for this month. This has produced what headline writers like to call "an oil glut."

Oil gluttons of the consuming nations have been stockpiling the stuff, and are stickily awash with nearly a month's supply, as much as storage facilities can hold. Did this situation come about as a result of the new high prices, or because our gas conservation efforts are beginning to pay off, or because new sources of energy supply are being found?

Of course not; recession—"good old recession"—is the prime cause of the oil surplus. When industrial production drops, the use of oil declines, and industrial production in the United States has dropped 11 percent from its prerecession peaks.

As a result, the once-intransigent oil producers are talking about quiet deals: financing purchases at no interest, absorbing shipping costs, even secretly cutting prices.

The discomfort inflicted upon some oil producers by the cartel's need to curtail production—and to keep all the members of OPEC in line—offers us a black-golden opportunity to crack the cartel once and for all.

Suspicion, greed, disunity of purpose—all this is now going for us, if we will but use our financial muscle to exploit the recession-induced oil surplus. With preferential tariffs, slippery quotas, secret middlemen, negative-interest deposits, and the unleashing of entrepreneurs with a talent for legal larceny, consuming nations can divide and conquer the cartel.

In the face of this opportunity—which will last only as long as the recession, about six more months—Secretary Kissinger's scheme to provide the oil exporters with the security of a guaranteed minimum-price floor sticks out as a form of policy lunacy. "Protectionism" is no longer a dirty word, but it is ourselves whom we should try to protect, not our combined competitors.

In cracking a cartel, as well as in combating inflation, we will not always have a recession to rely upon. After the recession of 1975, we will have to come up with new ways to encourage energy competition, and to spur productivity on the job that reduces inflation in a more difficult but less unfair way. For as we walk through the valley of the shadow of the business cycle, the unfairness of sacrifice is what hurts most.

The man staring at the glass of beer during what had been working hours, feeling the indignity of forced idleness, is making today's most painful contribution to tomorrow's stability. Such random sacrifice is unfair—as life, love, and war is so often unfair—but perhaps it is worthwhile to point out that even recession has its blessings, and that such sacrifice is not in vain.

MRS. THATCHER'S SOLILOQUY

July 24, 1975

LONDON—Envision the farsightedness and courage of the government of New York City applied to a whole nation: That's the Government of Great Britain.

Too timorous to cut social services, too poor to pay for them, both governments face the same dilemma: Nobody believes they have the gumption to defy unions and other pressure groups long enough to set their houses in order.

In England, however, doctrinaire Socialists have never been so pleased. They have found an ally—inflation of 26 percent per year—in their effort to demolish the middle class and bring about the "classless society."

The situation is this: Union demands have kept the working classes ahead of inflation, while people on fixed incomes—and people with property and savings—have been falling far behind. Result: a redistribution of income by inflation's Robin Hood that would not have been possible even in Socialist England through the political process.

What hope is there for Great Britain to clamber back from the precipice of unwitting Marxism? Those of us who respect and admire the British— from whom we inherited the ideals of political freedom and capitalism— look now to Mrs. Margaret Thatcher, head of the Conservative Party, for a serious challenge to the dictatorship of the parliamentary proletariat.

Perhaps Mrs. Thatcher thinks of Britain's infidelity to the principles of economic freedom, just as Hamlet mused on the unfaithfulness of his mother:

O, that this frozen Welfare State would melt,
Thaw, and resolve itself to act anew!
Or that the me-too Tories had not joined
In trendy economics. John Maynard Keynes!
How weary, stale, flat and unprofitable
It's been to put a nation on the dole.
Fie on't! For shame! To let unseeded players
Grab center court; things sank when "share-the-wealth"
Obsessed us nearly. That it should come to this!
In three decades—nay, not so much, not three—
Free enterprise replaced; that was, to this,
High tragedy to a satire. So useful to free people
That we inspired great nations overseas
To copy our example. O, Adam Smith!
Can't we remember? Now, inflation rages,
Begun by those who advertised this pitch:
"Something for nothing." Hark, two percent a month
The cost of living soars—Frailty, thy name is Wilson!—
He huffs and "draws the line"; false posturing
Since union bosses formed his source of strength
And nourished him, for years. Now he talks restraint—
Too late; the far-left clique controls his party
And likes inflation's aid: married to class struggle,

Devaluation's way is no more like our own
Than I to Edward Heath. Observe the plan:
To mollify the middle class with pap
While workers' wages push inflation up;
Bankruptcy—O, most wicked way to strike
With such asperity pure Socialism's hour.
It is not, nor it cannot come to good.
But break, my heart—for Labor's still in power!

THE WELFARE WORLD

September 1, 1975

WASHINGTON—One day in 1963, Jawaharlal Nehru asked an American economist for some ideas on how to make India's poverty-laden economy more productive.

The economist, Dr. Arthur Burns, inquired if it were true that the average worker's day was much less than eight hours, and that managers had to go through long court hearings to get permission to fire workers who were lazy or uncaring.

Mr. Nehru said yes, that was true, but could not be changed: "For years, Mahatma Gandhi and I promised that after independence, the lot of the worker would be vastly improved."

Dr. Burns then turned to the need for investment capital, to build plants and create jobs. Why could not a foreign investor own majority control of the plant he builds for the first ten years?

Mr. Nehru shook his head; such a plan would attract capital, but would postpone for too long the pride of Indian ownership. Economic realities had to stand aside for political realities.

Today, Indian workers still have their jobs protected, and Indians own most of their production facilities, but India is more desperately poor than ever. Pride and poverty walk hand in hand.

The Indian example is worth recalling this week because India and other proud, poor nations are assembling at the United Nations in New York to demand that industrial nations share their wealth in (using Hitler's phrase) a "New Order" of world economics.

When the poor nations look at the way the Western world acquiesced in a holdup by the oil producers, they wonder: What about trying the same? Why don't we form cartels on our raw materials and hold up the industrial nations?

In the U.S. the self-flagellation set—at loose whip-ends after Vietnam—seizes upon the demands of the have-nots as evidence that (a) our affluence is immoral in a world where people are starving, and (b) we must avert a "north-south confrontation" at all costs. The password to color-the-U.S.-guilty orgies is "interdependence"; Robert Tucker demolishes such misplaced egalitarianism in September's *Commentary* magazine.

Radical-sheik views will have some effect on the U.S. position in the U.N. We can expect Ford Administration officials to remind the poor nations of their obligations, of massive U.S. aid in the past, and even of the work ethic; but the gentle finger-wagging will be done amid mushmouthed rhetoric of interdependence. (Our real position is to call their demagoguery "dialogue," and hope that poor nations will get frustration off their chests at a series of meaningless conferences.)

Some frankness might be refreshing, however. Like this: Do you realize, poor nations, that OPEC's oil-price rise has added a total of $12 billion to your own import bills?

Poor nations of South America, why not demand that Venezuela pay back what she took from you? Poor nations of Africa, why not demand that oil-rich Nigeria ante up the money that her oil-price rise took directly out of your pockets? Poor nations of the Indian subcontinent, why not have a chat with your neighbors, Saudi Arabia and Kuwait, about reparations due you? Cartels only help those who help themselves.

We are not talking here about vague social costs due past generations. The amount owed to the poor nations by the oil producers is specific and unarguable at this U.N. session; we should urge that the bill be presented.

Even more to the point, the U.S. should pay the poor nations the compliment of telling them the truth: that the U.S., which has shared its wealth more generously than any other nation in the world, will not be coerced out of a thin dime by threats of monopoly, nor will be shamed into giving our hard-earned wealth away by protestations of morality from nations too proud and impatient to make it—as we did—the hard way.

Let those who wish to share the fruits of free enterprise try the method of free enterprise. It works. And its workers enjoy their Labor Day holiday in freedom.

Let those who wish to share the abundance of socialism try the method of socialism. Its economic system sometimes works, too, and when it doesn't, we provide the grain. But poor nations who choose socialism should learn from Mr. Nehru's mistake; it mixes poorly with freedom.

Perhaps poor nations can work out ways of their own. But the way of the arrogant mendicant is demeaning, and the way of the impotent confronter is foolish. They would be better off picking one of the ways that work.

Such straight talk loses flavor in diplomatic translation. But we should pass the message that having rejected the Welfare State, we are not about to embrace the Welfare World; "a decent respect for the opinions of mankind" does not mean that the United States owes the world a living.

PROFIT WITHOUT HONOR

February 19, 1976

PITTSBURGH—Even in the slowest-to-recover metals and mining industry, the feeling is that 1976 will turn out to be a very good year. But along with the warm glow of anticipation that suffuses most businessmen comes the defensive chill: The only thing harder to do than to apologize for no profits is to explain away profits.

The adjectives used by populist politicians to describe profits these days are "swollen" and "bloated"; profits never rise, they "skyrocket" to "unconscionable" peaks; and when they reach a healthy level—say, over 5 percent of sales or 10 percent of invested capital—profits are described as "obscene."

Every fresh breeze brings a "windfall"; Nast-y cartoonists portray profitmakers as profiteers, on the theory expressed by 16th-century essayist Michel de Montaigne: "No man can profit except by the loss of others. . . ."

In a year in which television newsmen will be reporting percentage leaps in quarterly profit figures, looping their vocal cords into a noose for capitalists, a few words in praise of profits may be in order.

First an appeal to simple greed: We are all full partners in those rising profits. One-half of corporate earnings goes to the Government in taxes; as profits rise, revenues rise, and the budget deficit narrows. More tax revenues from corporate profits mean less pressure for personal tax rises.

Next, an appeal to logic: More profits mean more real wage increases based on productivity, and more investment in plants and new equipment that will generate new jobs. Only one-twentieth of profits is paid out in dividends, and over 30 million stockholders plus another 30 million indirect investors cannot all be fat cats.

Finally an invitation to compare: The profit motive, even if you ascribe to it a greedy base in human nature, works out for the public benefit. Our standard of living doubles each generation because of, not in spite of, the discipline of the marketplace. Under reasonable regulation to increase competition, the profit system far outpaces centrally controlled economic systems—and produces the added value of free choice.

In the current Book-of-the-Month, *The Russians*, Hedrick Smith shows how much more is produced by Soviet farmers on small sections of "private" land than on collectivized land. No scientist can come up with a chemical superfertilizer that works nearly as much magic with soil as the profit motive.

But even defenders of the profit system, with its fair reward for risk and its efficient allocation of resources, find profitable an examination of that process. At the John Diebold Lectures at Harvard next week, questions will be asked about "good" versus "bad" profits, "social costs," and the terrible risk of removing the risk from corporations dealing with the Government.

Economists and orators might ponder these Ten Commandments of profit:

1. *Thou shalt have no political gods before me.* No golden idols called "the public interest," dictated by elitist goo-goos, shall replace the individual decisions of people in the marketplace.

2. *Thou shalt keep the Sabbath day and other fringe benefits.* Corporations must remember that labor's profit is not only expressed in dollars but in job satisfaction and in more leisure time more creatively spent.

3. *Thou shalt not take the name of profits, thy system, in vain.* Before anybody denounces capitalism as the institutionalization of greed, he ought to consider with what other incentives—or coercion—it would be replaced.

4. *Honor thy father and mother, and other dependents, but not one food stamp to an able-bodied loafer.* Countercyclical benefits improve the free enterprise system, but when we remove incentives for productivity, we kill the goose that lays the golden eggs, which is not to be confused with a golden idol.

5. *Thou shalt not steal thy competitor's secrets, nor kill his markets, nor covet his stockholders lists; neither shalt thou bribe local politicians nor pay off foreign customers,* as business morality varies from place to place and changes from time to time.

6. *Whosoever eschews risk shall forgo profit.* The businessman who seeks loan guarantees or wage and price controls should be driven from his corporate tent with shouts of "Abomination!"

7. *Thou shalt not adulterate thy product nor unduly pollute thy environment, nor fail to disclose thy every weakness* (nor continue to ten commandments when space permits but seven).

The lust to make money, the desire to get ahead, the shame of failure, the pride of achievement—this amalgam of motives, some of them igno-

ble, powers a system that produces more public good with personal freedom than any other.

That personal freedom is the political soul of our body politic. It is what
the profit system puts first and what socialism—the nonprofit system—
puts second, well after material things. Although I have been irreverent
here, the antimaterialistic question posed by St. Mark ought to be taken
most seriously by those who do not think that personal freedom is all that
important:

"For what shall it profit a man if he shall gain the whole world and lose
his own soul?"

Foreign Policy

I'M A HAWK. I believe Cold War II has been on for years. I think America's war-weariness in 1973 and 1974, coupled with the staggering of the Presidency, led to disaster for millions in Southeast Asia and danger to the United States in the 1980's.

These essays spat into the prevailing winds at the time of America's Asian rout. That was the era when all the demonstration signs read "Stop the Killing": In fact, after we withdrew, the killing began in earnest. Readers who disagree will find a forceful presentation of the contrary view in the letters selected from a pile of angry and often eloquent mail.

One selection—"Perdicaris Alive, or . . ."—relates to the *Mayagüez* incident. It should be read in the light of the Iranian experience five years later, as should the "Declaration of Cold War II" in the group of pieces about our Soviet policy.

VIETNAM AND CAMBODIA

STICKING WITH IT

February 10, 1975

WASHINGTON—A Communist rocket, fired with the intent of killing civilians in the capital of Cambodia, exploded in a school and slaughtered a score of children.

Shocking pictures of the bodies of the children appeared on nightly television news and on front pages, bringing all the horror of war once again into the American living room.

Had the rocket been supplied by United States' aid, or fired by recipients of United States' aid, the anguished uproar would have been heard in the halls of Congress and in every cranny of the land to "Stop the Killing" and deny the murdering attackers one more round of ammunition.

But it was a Communist rocket, financed in Peking or Moscow and launched by the Khmer Rouge who are trying to overthrow a non-Communist government. Therefore, after a humanitarian wince of pain, the reaction here is muted. We shudder and turn away.

That is because we are bored with Southeast Asia's endless warfare, frustrated by our inability to end it once and for all; a large Congressional group now seriously proposes to let it end by cutting off supplies to our allies so that they will lose and be quiet.

They tell us that our allies are at fault for the killing that comes with their continued resistance to overthrow; that our word is our bondage, and the United States is somehow to blame for the continuance of warfare, since we are unwilling to dictate a surrender; that our allies are more evil than the enemy they are fighting.

That final assertion—that President Thieu is a "corrupt dictator" unworthy of our aid—is made by longtime doves with a vested interest in his downfall, because they predicted his collapse the moment we pulled our troops out of Vietnam. But there he stands, two years later, an obstacle to takeover by North Vietnam and—worse yet—a reproof to those who were so certain he had no indigenous support.

One basic fact stares us in the face: There are no South Vietnamese troops killing anybody in North Vietnam; there are over 100,000 North Vietnamese troops fighting today in South Vietnam. It is still the South that is defending itself from sustained attack from the North.

Forget about that, says a weary majority; America did its bit. If the South Vietnamese cannot defend themselves by themselves now, we cannot be expected to support them forever. That goes for the Cambodians as well.

Foolishly, responsible officials in the United States repeat the light-at-the-end-of-the-tunnel argument; just another year's aid, just a billion or so more, and we'll win. That's misleading, as is President Ford's desperate promise to end all aid in three years, no matter what.

We should know by now that Communist aggressors, financed and supplied from outside, are prepared to fight on for decades until they win. The non-Communist majority in those countries seems prepared to fight on just as grimly for just as long, provided we match the supplies from outside. Our allies may be weary, but they are not bored; shall we now tell them we are no longer willing to match the Soviet contribution to their enemies, and they should plan for defeat?

Moreover, there is the possibility that we will be embarrassed by the severity of the local consequences of Communist victory. This is that hoary chestnut, the "bloodbath argument": When Nelson Rockefeller raised it recently, he was roundly denounced by people who are absolutely certain that no wholesale executions will follow Communist victory. Such certainty must be comforting, since it runs contrary to much experience.

The reason why the United States should continue aid to people fighting Communist takeover is because we are on the side of human freedom. Not because we lost 50,000 men in Vietnam; or because the Congress authorized current aid; or even primarily because our support tells the world that our word to our allies is at least as good as the Soviets' to theirs.

Why are we so afraid to assert that what we are doing to help others defend themselves against Communist-sponsored aggression is the right thing to do? Costly, painful, nerve-racking, and when Mr. Thieu jails journalists, infuriating—but essentially moral.

The measure of our success is not in making peace, since the Communists want victory and not peace, but in helping our allies to continue to resist as long as the pressure is on.

As Senator Jackson begins to waffle on Vietnam, just as Senator Percy finds it expedient to waver in support of Israel, we ought to ask ourselves what kind of a people we are becoming. Do we stand ready to help allies help themselves, or do we let them go hang after a certain length of time?

Much more is at stake here than the fate of one regime, or the expenditure of several hundred millions, or the justification of past positions. Either America will remain a strong force against worldwide totalitarian coercion or she will turn inward and head downward.

EUPHEMISM FOR SURRENDER

March 13, 1975

WASHINGTON—When South Vietnamese troops moved in 1970 to destroy Vietcong supply bases in Cambodia, the necessary and useful attack was called an "incursion." Infuriated doves in the United States insisted the foray against bases used by North Vietnamese in a neutral country should have been termed an "invasion."

It turned out to be an incursion; the South Vietnamese forces ended the use of much neutral Cambodian territory as a Communist resupply and staging area, and returned within a few months. "Incursion" was not a euphemism after all.

Now, however, we are being treated to a tender phrase to hide a very harsh recommendation. As if by unwitting orchestration, on a single day this week, the delicate wording appeared in three places:

A dispatch from Phnom Penh to a Washington newspaper quoted an unnamed diplomat as saying: "It might not be fair, but the only logical outcome now is a *transfer of power* to the other side."

A story coming out of a television interview with Hubert Humphrey quoted that potential candidate as demanding we cut off military assistance and "try to arrange for a *transfer of power*."

And in an Op-Ed column of *The New York Times*, a colleague of mine suggested that the choice of pivotal figures in Congress is "to help in the orderly *transfer of power*." (All italics mine.)

To Americans, the orderly "transfer of power" is that marvel that takes place in our democracy when a member of one party is elected to succeed a member of the other party. A President-elect pays a courtesy call on the lame-duck President; the aids of both confer; and the process called "the transfer of power" takes place.

But that is not the process Senator Humphrey and the others are talking about. The word that they are so laboriously straining to avoid is "surrender." In plain words, they want to force the Cambodian Government (which they now call a "regime") to run up a white flag and throw itself on the mercy of those Communists who are now deliberately firing rockets into schoolyards.

That is properly called "surrender," not a "transfer of power." Changing the name does not add bravery to the advice. But the very reluctance of the euphemizers to use the harsh word, "surrender," is tacit admission of shame—at suggesting we cravenly force such an action, or at the shame Americans would feel at denying supplies to an ally that is willing to fight.

But wait, say the power-transferers: Our aid only prolongs the agony. Since the non-Communist forces are doomed, why try to help a loser?

Perhaps surrender will turn out to be the Cambodians' only choice, but the decision to fight on or give up should be theirs, not ours. Many of those here who now wish to speed up the "transfer" were absolutely certain that South Vietnam's "corrupt, dictatorial regime" would collapse as soon as the last American troops pulled out. That was over two years ago.

Those defeatists do not like to be reminded how wrong they were about the ability of the South Vietnamese to defend themselves, using our weapons against Soviet weapons. Incredibly, our allies are blamed for breaking peace agreements, despite the plain evidence of tens of thousands of North Vietnamese troops steadily moving down across the border to launch a new offensive.

News reports from besieged Phnom Penh continually stress how unhappy the people are with their Government; how hard it is to enlist soldiers; how palindromic Lon Nol has not taken Thomas Jefferson as his model. Thus victims become villains; where are the reports of the courage of the defenders or denunciations of the sustained brutality of the Communist attackers?

No; that would hardly serve to speed the "transfer of power" or to assuage our consciences for refusing to supply any more bullets to people trying to defend themselves against well-supplied Communists.

You see, we are supposed to believe that the war in Cambodia is our fault; that we corrupted those peaceful Cambodians. But were the Khmer Rouge troops, now slaughtering children, indoctrinated by our Green Berets? Hardly; they are local Communists bent on seizing control, using rockets supplied by Hanoi, Peking, and Moscow to kill their Cambodia countrymen.

Our visiting Congressmen, who felt the cold fear of the people surrounded in Phnom Penh, are less inclined than Hubert Humphrey and Hugh Scott to demand surrender. A sensible idea has been put forth to "index" aid—that is, to key continued American support to the level of support other outside powers provide local Communists.

Indexed aid to help people fight for their survival against Communist takeover is more in our foreign policy tradition than adoption of the old "better Red than dead" line.

The defenders of Phnom Penh may offend some of us by having the temerity to die all over our television screens, but we must not be the first generation of Americans to force the surrender of a beleaguered people in a fog of bloodless phrases.

                                                                13 March 75
William Safire:

Your use of the "palindromic" to describe Lon Nol is incredibly nonsensical, misconstrued and obviously some blatant attempt to mind-boggle the reading, yet dictionary-less public to thinking that Lon Nol is some far-out, outtasight weirdo who either masturbates in public or suppresses and kills children with despotic rage in order to maintain power. Your speech writing background with its enlarged vocabulary of nothing words is showing. . . .

"Palindromic"—good bad!!!—I've clipped out the paragraph and put it on my wall as an example of journalistic abuse!

                                                                Van Talmage
                                                                Red Hook, New York

WHAT WENT WRONG?

April 23, 1975

WASHINGTON—In 1969, President Thieu met with President Nixon on Midway Island to announce the beginning of America's troop withdrawals from Vietnam. In private conversation before the two leaders went out to face the cameras, Mr. Nixon told General Thieu: "I would not like to be breaking the umbilical cord to your people."

The South Vietnamese leader moved to reassure the American President, who obviously felt guilty about doing what he knew was necessary, and replied: "No, we have been saying for years we have been getting stronger. And if that is the case, then we have to be willing to see some Americans leave."

In that spirit, "Vietnamization" began; a half-million U.S. troops were replaced by South Vietnamese soldiers and a peace accord was signed; now, with all lost, the departing President Thieu speaks of the United States as "inhuman" and "untrustworthy."

What went wrong in Vietnam? Why are guilt-edged doves pointing fingers of blame at resentful hawks who point fingers of blame back at them?

The first thing that went wrong in Vietnam was when we decided that there was no way to "win" without starting World War III. As we later learned from the Soviet lack of response to the mining of Haiphong harbor and the bombing of Hanoi, the Goldwater strategy of 1964 made a lot of sense and the Johnson strategy of gradual escalation was disastrous.

The second thing that went wrong was that the Nixon Administration assumed in good faith that the North Vietnamese would settle for anything less than total victory. A week after the 1973 peace agreement, I asked Henry Kissinger what he would have done if we had the four years to live over, and he replied: "We should have bombed the hell out of them the minute we got into office." More thoughtfully, he added: "The North Vietnamese started an offensive in February 1969. We should have responded strongly. We should have taken on the doves right then—started bombing and mining the harbors. The war would have been over in 1970."

The third thing that went wrong was that the American President who was capable of keeping the North Vietnamese peacefully intimidated became impotent in 1973, and was unable to marshal public support to resist the tide of American isolationism which ultimately invited the final North Vietnamese assault.

Despite the foregoing, South Vietnam had been given what America had promised it: a "reasonable chance to survive." True, the announced intention of the United States not to intervene to enforce the Paris peace accords was a weakener; and the cutback of military aid that had been promised and announced in early 1973 did not help.

But the collapse of South Vietnam's anti-Communist Government was not induced by United States perfidy; the central fact about Mr. Thieu's downfall—what suddenly went wrong—was that he committed a strategic blunder which led to a panic and then to political disintegration. The army—which had been a pretty good fighting force for a long time—was not good enough to roll with a blunder, to recover confidence in the face of mysterious orders and uncertainty at the top.

So the Government of President Thieu came apart. Against a determined and well-supplied enemy, the South Vietnamese could not "hack it." But we were not wrong to hope they could.

As our allies surrender, we would do well to put aside the inclination to hate the losers, or to discuss their leader as a "corrupt dictator" as bad as the invading Communists, or to take cheap shots at a distraught human being lashing out in his bitterness.

Though we went about it in the wrong way, we were right to try to help South Vietnam defend itself against invasion. We were right, too, to extricate our troops honorably, over a period of time, for the purpose of giving an ally its "reasonable chance."

What we could not give them was the good generalship and the fierce discipline of their enemies, or a firm guarantee of unwavering support, and so they lost the war. The South Vietnamese read as much strength as possible into our pledges as we left, just as we read as much strength as possible into their army.

In sifting "what went wrong," we need not flagellate ourselves as imperialist aggressors or mad bombers, or make President Thieu our scapegoat. For 15 years, we were the umbilical cord to a people fighting to resist takeover, at enormous cost in blood and treasure; must we berate ourselves now for not having been sensibly selfish?

Every umbilical cord, by its nature, is temporary; it is ironic that Mr. Nixon chose that metaphor. We did almost all we could; a twist of political fate here and a military blunder there intervened. In the end, it was up to the South Vietnamese, but after a generation's bloodletting, they were just not up to any more.

April 24, 1975

Dear Mr. Safire;

Usually I admire your work, a fact which makes your "What Went Wrong?" column in today's *Times* all the more dismaying. I am sorry that the best newspaper in the country or one of its best columnists *still* doesn't know the final, basic causes of the tragedy in Viet Nam. Please let me hasten to enlighten you. Here are some of the enormous mistakes:

(1) The United States should not have associated itself with France on the Viet Nam issue in the first place. We used to be a revolutionary power, not a colonial one.

(2) We let ourselves be sucked into the giant blunder of fighting a land war in Asia. There are many reasons why the United States should not try to fight an infantry war in Asia, and almost everybody understands them except our secretaries of state, defense, and, of course, the generals. I am sorry that columnists are now added to this list of blindfolded leaders.

(3) We forgot the fact that we do not have a moral right to take sides in another nation's civil war.

(4) Sounding almost like Senator Joseph McCarthy, our leaders tried to drum up hatred and fear of the Communists in Viet Nam. Meanwhile back at LBJ's ranch and Nixon's palm-shaded homes, we tried to explain to the Russian and Chinese Communists how much we love them. This was confusing to some of the troops in the field who occasionally worried about the problem of telling which Communists to kill and which ones to ask to dinner.

(5) It is a law of nature, I believe, that one moral disaster leads to more. The United States leaders occasionally sounded like Nazis as they boasted of body counts and all the rest. Soon they began to lie a lot. Thieu was candidly called an anti-Communist because no one could figure out what he was *for*. It took increasing courage, if not deceit, for our leaders to present Thieu as a champion of the press, the humane president who wouldn't hear of anyone being tortured.

(6) The jolly hawks liked to point out that Russia would never interfere with our fun in Viet Nam. Some even were sure that the Chinese would not interfere. Only a few dreamt of bugle calls in the morning fog, of a million quilted infantrymen, many of them riding horses, charging at the first light of day. This of course could never happen. Ask the ghost of General McArthur. He said it would never happen in Korea.

(7) Our final error was to be heedless of life, both ours and theirs. That is what went wrong in Viet Nam.

As ever,
Sloan Wilson
Ticonderoga, New York

GET OUT OF TOWN

May 12, 1975

WASHINGTON—What if every man, woman, and child who lived on Manhattan Island were told: "Get out of town. Today, on pain of death. No excuses. Start walking and don't stop until you get to farmland upstate or in Pennsylvania. When you get there, if you do, you're on your own."

Manhattan mothers would give their babies to strangers who had some chance of escape or survival; Manhattan doctors, at gunpoint, would put down scalpels in mid-operation and begin the long march to nowhere; occupants of nursing homes would push wheelchairs in the direction of the Lincoln Tunnel; proud and law-abiding Manhattanites would learn to steal and beg to get the towers of the city far behind them.

That is roughly what is happening to the three million people of Phnom Penh, capital of the newly Communist Cambodia. In all human history nothing has taken place quite like the emptying of Phnom Penh.

Sennacherib destroyed Babylon, the Romans sacked Carthage, and Hitler's bombers leveled Guernica, but in every case the attacker was destroying a particular city, not the idea of a city itself.

The new rulers of Cambodia are doing something original. They have taken the "classless society" of Marx and put it together with the "natural selection" of Darwin. Cities breed civilization, they are saying; civilization differentiates between people, creating classes; therefore, we will drive the populace out of the corrupting cities, back to the purifying land, where only the fittest will survive.

This is social engineering on a scale that would make a Stalin blush: creating a society of equals by making everybody a refugee.

Since you can't make an omelette without breaking some eggs, the Cambodian leaders wish to conduct their experiment in private, which is why foreign newsmen have been deported. In the United States, that leaves us to a fruitless debate about how many thousand executions make a bloodbath.

Many commentators have long been saying that the Cambodians are a gentle people who would return to peaceful ways if only we were not there; and they have been deriding predictions of mass executions as merely scare tactics to justify our propping-up of corrupt dictatorships. These voices will now be saying that the reports we hear of killings are probably exaggerated: What kind of bloodbath is it, after all, that goes on unrecorded by videotape?

Contrariwise, a great many other Americans, myself included, will be tempted to ask: What happened to all that moral outrage about "stopping the killing"? And how come the Jane Fondas and Ramsey Clarks are not focusing our attention on the shortcomings of those who brought this bloody kind of peace to Indochina?

Such justification of past positions may be satisfying—we all like to insist we were right all along—but there is a reality to the emptying of Phnom Penh that should cause us to agree on a fundamental: that the difference between "freedom" and "slavery" is not a relic of cold-war rhetoric. Communists in every region are serious about remaking the world, and we must stop pretending that the death sentence pronounced even temporarily on city life in Cambodia is some form of "agrarian reform."

To the Khmer Rouge, the elimination of classes requires that tens of thousands, perhaps many more, die by the wayside; this is no Cambodian aberration, but the path always taken by new Communist parties as they take power. As they become sophisticated, later generations act more subtly, in civilized trappings from great cities, but the mental set of the ideology sees the individual soul as a building block and not a citadel.

People try to fight Communism, or to run away from it, because they do not want to be absolutely controlled by the most modern tyrants. They fight or run not because democracy has won their "hearts and minds," but because they sense that only Communism is capable of driving a population of three million out of their homes and into the countryside so as to indoctrinate those hearts and minds.

How do some of us receive the people running from death? A trendy cartoonist here portrayed a shocked Statue of Liberty looking at a parade of slant-eyed pimps, prostitutes, and politicians, which fairly well sums up the view of those—like Senator McGovern—who came to hate our Southeast Asian allies.

Most Americans will recoil from this prairie-populist cruelty, as the decapitation of a capital city sinks in. A city is civilization; civilization is diversity and creativity, which needs personal freedom; Communism is by its nature anticity, anticivilization, antifreedom.

The Khmer Rouge understand this; too many Americans do not. If we are unwilling to help people fight for their freedom, if we pretend that the victories of Communism are local options of little concern to us, then the order to "get out of town" may be repeated. And someday it could cause quite a traffic jam in the Lincoln Tunnel.

May 10, 1978

Dear Mr. Safire:

Recently you, as other conservative writers, have condemned those who protested against the war in Vietnam for failing to similarly protest the mass murders in Cambodia. As one of those who marched against the war, I wish to respond.

I must first make the obvious point that, in protesting against the war, I was opposing the action of my country, the United States, for which action I bear some responsibility, and not that of some other country. Our present Cambodian policy, regrettably, is inaction, which is not quite as morally objectionable.

But that is not the whole story. I am a child of the 50's, raised to respect authority. I protested the war, knowing full well that the protests were destructive to the social order of the country, and hence a most serious action, but required by the gravity of the offense. Such protest was against my inclination, but I did not want to be a Good German. . . .

I saw the anti-war movement taken over by radicals whose opposition to everything mocked the seriousness of my own. Those who supported the Viet Cong (somebody must be the "good guys") had no comprehension of what I was protesting against. Those who declared feminism an equal issue trivialized a more serious issue: namely, that to kill for a cause (which is what war is about), one must be absolutely certain that the cause merits so drastic an action. And finally I worked for George McGovern and the Great Referendum, only to watch McGovern get persuaded by the press that being a one-issue candidate bespoke shallowness, so that he threw away the referendum on a mess of liberal pottage. Then came the Christmas bombing.

After all that killing, I then had to watch the triviality of Watergate drive Nixon from office, and I had to watch our leaders who had told us lie after lie after lie finally believe their own lies to the point that they could not take the action that would save the Vietnamese who had stood by us from being captured by their conquerors. And while this may have been the final proof that we never really cared about the Vietnamese, it was still bitter beyond tolerance. Am I then supposed to get upset because America betrayed the Kurds?

So now you want me to protest Cambodia? Well, my numbed moral sense dimly understands that Cambodia today is a horror that matches the Turkish genocide against the Armenians and the Nazi death camps of Adolph Hitler. And I know the world stood by and watched both. But I guess if you can roust up a protest demonstration with someone other than the hardcore anti-Communist right, I will go put my body on the line with you. I don't know whether my heart can make it.

Sincerely,
William A. Baker
New York, New York

PERDICARIS ALIVE, OR ...

May 15, 1975

WASHINGTON—On the eve of the Republican Convention of 1904, a Moroccan bandit named Ahmed Raisuli kidnapped an American citizen, Jon Perdicaris, who had been living near Tangier. American and British warships were rushed to the Moroccan capital, three Marines went ashore to assert our serious intent, and President Theodore Roosevelt demanded that the Sultan force the bandit to release the American.

This demand took the form of a telegram from Secretary of State John Hay which set a standard for succinctness in ultimata: "We want Perdicaris alive or Raisuli dead."

Read aloud at the convention nominating Teddy Roosevelt as candidate—he had moved up from the Vice Presidency but had not yet been elected in his own right—the tough telegram was received with roars of patriotic enthusiasm.

And it worked, not just for Perdicaris, who was ransomed by the Sultan and released, but for Roosevelt, who showed the world and the American voter that he was not a leader to be trifled with.

After the election, it turned out that Mr. Perdicaris might not have been an American citizen after all, and that he had probably been released before the dramatic message was delivered, but the diplomatic point was made: The United States would protect its nationals anywhere in the world.

Three generations later, another unelected President faced a somewhat similar challenge in the *Mayagüez* affair. A cocky new Communist regime had kidnapped 39 Americans and a ship, possibly for barter or some other reasons, and triggered a military response. But times have changed, and what is in the national interest may not be in the President's political interest.

America's opinion leaders—especially old hawks, like Senator Jackson, who needs some dovish support—are likely to turn on the victim rather than on the pirate. They will ask: What was that merchant ship doing over there in the first place? Can we be sure it wasn't a spy ship? Wasn't it under military charter? Did we provoke the incident to get ourselves reinvolved in Southeast Asia or to assuage our injured machismo?

Unless our military action is stunningly successful right away, the central theme of the President's critics will be (a) we were not really consulted, and (b) what harm would it have done to wait and ask everybody else to help?

But the responsibility to protect American lives is the President's and cannot be abdicated, and waiting could have caused great harm. We are not dealing with a superpower, where diplomacy is the only route and hot lines are in place; we are dealing with a minipower whose leaders have shown no concern for human life and are not susceptible to the normal pressures of politics and economics.

America is no longer a world power whose will to use its strength is undoubted. Not long ago, we could afford to overlook provocations like the *Pueblo* and the "flying *Pueblo*" because our resolve was not in doubt. Now, however, with foreign affairs too much in the hands of Congress, the President is forced to assert U.S. strength to dispel the doubt that does exist.

This is not the way it should be. Retreat is dangerous, and the steady retreat of American willpower in the past two years invites the kind of incident we face off the shores of Cambodia now. As a certainly-great power, we could afford to be patient and long-suffering about these incidents before; as a maybe-great power, we have to react lest our inaction invite every nation to strike at our interests everywhere.

"National honor" may be a phrase that invites derision these days, but a reputation for strength has been protecting Americans abroad for some years; hesitation and handwringing in the face of this latest provocation pose the greatest danger. A long delay, presented as caution, is most incautious: It causes other powers to line up pro and con, and could elevate an incident into a searing decision between war and knuckling-under.

President Ford is not thinking of nuking anybody back to the Stone Ages, or starting the Southeast Asian involvement all over again. He cannot even threaten Phnom Penh, because nobody is home. Our attack on the Cambodian gunboats was a measured response to piracy; the hostages were in great peril, but if we acquiesced in this technique of international relations, we would encourage the seizure of many other Americans elsewhere in the world.

Decisiveness should not be equated with hotheadedness, nor national honor with jingoism. Perdicaris was released and Raisuli met no harm. This is the first test since an isolationist Congress took charge of American foreign policy, and if the President can hold the country with him in stepping up to it courageously, we can deter others from testing our resolve in much more serious ways.

COLD WAR II

ON IRREVERSIBILITY

July 4, 1974

MOSCOW—The central fact of the third Nixon-Brezhnev summit is that the two leaders tried—and failed—to establish a momentum that was intended to make it impossible for their successors to change the direction of their policies.

The magic word in all Communist rhetoric these days is "irreversible." Today's joint communiqué speaks redundantly of "the imperative necessity of making the process of improving U.S.-Soviet relations irreversible." Both leaders envisage the snowballing of the peacemaking process as the only way to influence the men who will come after them.

To this bandwagon effect of peacemaking, "personal relationships" are trivial, Mr. Nixon's protestations to the contrary notwithstanding. More to the point is the creation of what the President calls "a positive stake in peace"—a web of mutually profitable enterprises that a renewal of tensions would jeopardize. In relentlessly weaving that web, the President aims to protect his successor from the need to pander to the isolationist impulses that periodically afflict the American people.

Leonid Brezhnev also seeks to reach into the future, past the present Politburo, whose members now average 65 years of age. If he were to leave the stage suddenly, his place would probably be taken by Andrei Kirilenko, a capable manager who has followed Mr. Brezhnev up the ladder but is hardly a generator of momentum. The General Secretary hopes, instead, to outlast his contemporaries and to deliver the reins to a man at least fifteen years younger, one accustomed to the achievement of Communist goals by subtle and patient means.

That is why this was a summit concerned mainly with summits to come. Having a summit merely to have a summit seems an odd notion, unless the purpose of both men is taken into account—in this case, to make unbreakable the habit of meeting and meshing.

Does this "regularization of normalization," as one zation-happy explicator put it, make unstoppable the future of détente? Or is there a public opinion requirement that dramatic forums be used only for dramatic undertakings?

A summit is expected to be a mountaintop event, not a regular gathering at the crest of a Crimean foothill. But this summit, like the first, was a gamble. Mr. Nixon did not win on arms control and so, wisely, he refrained from making an agreement in which American security would have suffered.

The trouble with summitry-every-summer is that it draws thousands of diplomats and reporters together in what Churchill called "vast, cumbrous array" and confuses atmosphere with policy.

The Russians see détente as an atmosphere, in which long-term policy can best be conducted. Americans see détente as a policy, and the best hope for the avoidance of war. Four eyes are looking at each other, but only two eyes meet.

Only a month ago, when the President was washing his hands of responsibility for "transforming" other societies with which we must deal, the chief Soviet theoretician, Mikhail Suslov, was boasting of "the strengthening of those public forces that are destined by history to play a revolutionary role of transforming society on the basis of progress and socialism."

The other day in Minsk, while the President was eloquently paying tribute to the millions who died at Nazi hands, I walked through the city in which my grandfather was born, dripping those tags and correspondent's credentials that make too many of us look like modern displaced persons. A Soviet youth who spoke some self-taught English sat next to me on a bench and, with considerable courage, after a while asked me the question that was most on his mind.

"Will the visit of the Americans make things better for us here someday?"

Granted that an American essayist would never be walking alone through Minsk without Mr. Nixon's diplomacy. But as we work for processes of constant contact, the Russians talk détente and resist compromise on the matter of arms control, talk friendship in prepared toasts, and brazenly censor American television reports of dissent in the U.S.S.R.

Anything that Soviet propaganda declares to be irreversible is eminently reversible. On our side, Mr. Nixon's noble motive of building a generation of peace cannot bind his successor to the détente-first tolerance that encourages repression. On Independence Day, we would do well to remember that the only genuine "irreversible" in this world is the inarticulate but inexorable demand for more human freedom.

ENDING WORLD WAR II

April 14, 1975

WASHINGTON—In case you hadn't heard, World War II will soon be coming to its official end. The Russians won.

In Helsinki and then Geneva, delegations from 35 nations have been meeting for the past two years at the European Security Conference, preparing for the grand summit finale this summer at which the heads of state are to gather and make legitimate the Soviet conquest of Eastern Europe.

Naturally, the Soviet Union has long been looking forward to this triumph. To get the conference started, it agreed in 1971 to a four-power arrangement on Berlin, and in 1973 to exploratory talks on a mutual reduction of troops in Europe, which have led nowhere but seemed hopeful at the time.

Since the Soviets have been salivating at the chance to make their Iron Curtain a permanent division of Europe, one might think that the United States is extracting great concessions in return.

But all the Russians have been offering is "confidence-building measures," such as prior notification of military maneuvers, which have no real military meaning, and economic and scientific cooperation projects that the Soviets need more than we do. No quid pro quo there, unless you consider détente an end in itself.

The British, the Belgians, and the Dutch—with some belated interest on the part of the United States—have been pressing for freer movement of people between East and West, placing in the basket freedom of contact between creative artists, specific guarantees of credentials for journalists, the opening of "reading rooms" to insure access to foreign periodicals, and agreements to make available television time for the airing of other countries' documentaries.

The Russians are turning aside demands for specifics, instead offering flabby language like "nations shall endeavor to encourage" human rights, which already exists in the United Nations Charter and permits the Communists to interpret it any way they choose.

When the West Germans wanted a provision saying that border changes could be made by peaceful agreement in the future—reunification is still their goal—the Soviets artfully put that in the "Sovereign Equality of States" section of the draft document, and not in the part about the "Inviolability of Frontiers" where it might have had some meaning.

The United States delegation is demoralized. Since our position has been to denigrate the importance of the whole conference, the United States delegation in Geneva is half-headed by our Ambassador to Czechoslovakia, who has his hands full in Prague; his deputy in Geneva has returned to Washington and not been replaced, and the rest of the frustrated staff passes along this story:

When the American Secretary of State met in Geneva two months ago with Soviet Foreign Minister Gromyko, the European Security Conference was discussed at length; afterward, Mr. Gromyko gave a detailed briefing to the Soviet delegation on what had transpired. But the United States delegation was left in the dark and had to ask their Soviet counterparts what had gone on. That close-to-the-vest technique is exactly what led us up the garden path on the SALT negotiations.

President Ford, who plans to attend a NATO meeting soon, did not refer to the European Security Conference in his State of the World address; perhaps he felt that ignoring the problem—as he did Portugal—would make it go away. But if he is serious about making détente a "two-way relationship," Mr. Ford should put a high price on any legitimization of Soviet victories.

First, no European security summit conference should be convened until the Soviets agree to much more than a token reduction of troops in Europe and a timetable for future withdrawals.

Next, a subject we should insist be put on the agenda for debate is the Brezhnev Doctrine, under which the Soviets claim the right to put in their tanks to crush uprisings against their puppet regimes. If that is not a matter of concern to "European security" and relevant to the "inviolability of borders," what is?

Finally, the Soviets should be made to understand that their deeds—in providing North Vietnamese with the means of victory and extremist Arabs with hopes for a "final solution" to the Israelis—speak louder than any protestations of détente. Linkage should live again: no deal in the Middle East, no deal in Europe.

Would demands for these quids pro quo scuttle the Helsinki summit? Perhaps; at a time when the Soviet Union is riding high and the United States' President is helpless against a large group of willful men in Congress, a two-year postponement of the biggest gathering of heads of state since Queen Elizabeth's coronation might not be a bad idea.

Thirty years have passed since V-E Day. America's power has dwindled from days of dominance through an era of parity to a stage of uncertainty. Why, at this worst moment, are we allowing ourselves to be drawn into a supersummit at which the only purpose is to declare the Russians the victors of World War II?

COLD WAR II

WASHINGTON—As 1975 draws to an end, détente is dead. The Second Cold War is under way.

Every partisan of peace wishes otherwise—that the spirit of superpower cooperation could be revived quickly—but it is dangerous to act as if our wishes were reality. The moment in history in which one set of leaders might have turned the world permanently from war has slipped away. It serves no purpose to pretend that the moment is still with us; on the contrary, we must adopt a new policy that will make such a moment possible soon again.

What evidence do we have that Cold War II has begun?

After solidifying World War II gains at Helsinki, the Soviets promptly reneged on their vague promises of increased human freedom, and increased their demands for ideological discipline among Communists everywhere. They pressed for a takeover of a NATO country, Portugal; when that failed, the Soviets hired this century's Hessians—Communist Cubans—to help the U.S.S.R. replace Portugal as the colonial power in Angola.

As to strategic arms limitation, supposedly the main course of the love feast, the Soviets have violated our understandings of their limitations, corroding the trust that might have made progress possible.

Who caused the death of détente?

Our senatorial protestations of weakness in 1973, followed by the collapse in Southeast Asia, helped speed détente's demise. The hubris of American doves commingled with the suspiciousness of American hawks to make it politically unwise to take more risks for peace; we had no leaders capable of overcoming both the weariness of the left and the wariness of the right.

But the victim cannot be made the villain. Détente was killed by the Soviet inability to refrain from exploiting our weakness. In pressing their strength, the Soviet leaders revealed that détente meant, to them, a cost-free method of "normalizing" the world into Russian-dominated Communism.

How will Cold War II be different from Cold War I?

The kind of edge-teetering confrontations that took place in Berlin and Cuba are no longer tolerable. Although wars of national liberation will be supported by expansionist Communism, less brinksmanlike maneuvers can be expected. As Cold War I was political, creating a neutral third world, Soviet strategy in Cold War II will be economic, absorbing the third world into an alliance against the maverick Chinese and the dwindling democracies.

Was our initial response to the Soviet probe in Angola good Cold War II strategy?

Absolutely not. Our knee-jerk reaction—to supply arms to the local opposition to the Soviet clients—was a Cold War I response, out of sync with today's drummer. Henry Kissinger never really understood the Nixon doctrine; instead of responding in Nixonian global terms (which led to détente), the Cold War I warrior responded in Truman-Kennedy local terms (which led nowhere).

Should we then ignore the Soviet-sponsored aggression and subversion in Cold War II?

No; appeasement rarely appeases. But we must not be trapped into responding at the time and in the place our opponents choose; we must apply pressure in a way that gains the initiative and gets results. The strategy that ended the last cold war and brought about the recent détente was this: to up the ante of local challenge; to link arms control advances to economic reward; to negotiate from strength; and then to make a deal at the summit for parity with a respectful Communist world.

But Mr. Kissinger is not doing that now; he is putting out fires, or trying to, in the Cold War I way, which will never lead us to a new détente. He clings to the idea that the old détente—"his" détente—still exists, and needs only a little patching up.

What weapons do we have to fight Cold War II through to a new détente?

Our new weapon: Both the opposing superpower and the third world are desperate for one commodity our system produces in abundance—food. Our old weapon: A technology capable of proving we cannot be outstripped in the ability to "win" a nuclear war. Our forgotten weapon: The yearning of human beings in the strangest places for freedom, which democracy permits and Communism prevents.

Wouldn't it be easier to patch up the old détente than to go through a second cold war?

Certainly, if the choice were ours—but it is not. What currently passes under the name of détente is the Soviet's opening offensive in Cold War II. If we respond intelligently and firmly, with the most up-to-date linkage, we can establish a fresh and genuine détente—to give the next set of leaders that moment of power parity and mutual respect needed to begin again the process of peace.

CHINESE PUZZLE

A few years after the Nixon opening to China, that nation underwent its post-Mao upheavals. Americans found it hard to read the tea leaves—who was up, who was down, what this meant to the embryonic Sino-American relationship. Here were a couple of thoughts from a pundit with a nagging worry that some of the most important events in the world were not being understood.

KUNG FU-TZU

February 25, 1974

WASHINGTON—Two centuries before the birth of Christ, the first emperor of the Ch'in dynasty in China came to the conclusion that the only way to break out of feudalism into nationhood would be to strike at the followers of the philosopher Kung Fu-tzu.

Accordingly, book-burning was invented, along with "scholar-pitting"—the burying-alive of hundreds of scholars in pits—a campaign that can be safely described as anti-intellectual.

A couple of millennia later, Chairman Mao Tse-tung has launched a fresh campaign of vilification against the teachings of Kung Fu-tzu, whom Westerners call Confucius. A question arises: Why do the forces of change in China, then and now, initially find the teachings of Confucianism so subversive?

First, Confucius was a preconservative, teaching methods of weaving a social order in which men accepted a given role in life. A man obedient to his ruler could demand obedience from his son, creating stable, if rigid, hierarchies.

But where Confucius said "accept," Mao says "struggle"; where Confucius said "not more surely does the grass bend before the wind, than the masses yield to the will of those above them," Mao preaches the opposite.

Second, the style of Confucianism is abhorrent to Mao: "The man of superior mind is placidly composed," said the Master, "the small-minded man is in a constant state of perturbation." Mao, hardly small-minded, considers regular turbulence essential to revolutionary purity.

In a fascinating series of dispatches by reporters Fox Butterfield and Joseph Lelyveld in Hong Kong, another possible reason for the current campaign denouncing Confucius is suggested: that it may be an oblique attack on Chou En-lai, an outward-looking and urbane man, signaling a retreat from the "Ping-Pong diplomacy" that led to summits and cultural exchanges.

But when a national demigod like Mao, near the end of his life, turns fiercely on a figure revered by his countrymen for 2,500 years, there must be more to it than a backing off from a probe to the West, or a matter of palace intrigue.

In taking on Confucius, Mao cultivates a mighty opposite, and challenges the centuries ahead to judge him on the highest level of confrontation.

When history's judgment is made, Mao is likely to fare well on several counts: He upset an unduly placid acceptance of poverty and immobility that stemmed from Confucianism; he ended the subjugation of women; he broke the primacy of allegiance to the family, which had spawned the world's worst nepotism and guaranteed corruption of government.

The idea put forth by Confucius that will ultimately prevail in the Chinese future is the "rectification of names," expressed in four cryptic symbols: "Father father, son son." This is expanded to mean that a father, or a ruler or leader of any kind, can be called by that name only if he accepts all the duties that go with that name. Should he reject the path of virtue that the name implies, he ceases to be a father, son, king, or friend.

A marvelous irony in the confrontation between the Four Books of Confucius and the Little Red Book of Chairman Mao is this: Not only has Mao adopted Confucianist principles in shunning the idea of God, but he has been forced to follow the Master in dealing with one of his toughest ideological problems.

To a Maoist, Lin Piao is the ultimate traitor, the man who tried to grab power and sell out the revolution. And to a Maoist, Mao is a leader who is an infinitely wise judge of men.

Problem: How can a good Maoist reconcile the treason of Lin Piao with the good judgment of Mao? The answer of a Western dictator would be a good aide, wisely trusted by the top man for years, who became corrupted and went off the deep end.

But, strangely to Western eyes, Mao does not contend that Lin was ever any good. On the contrary, he claims that Lin was bamboozling his comrades all along, tacitly admitting he was not such a good judge of Lin's character during all those 40 years. Why does a man who likes to appear infallible grant his fallibility when he doesn't have to?

Because "Confucius say" that a man's character determines his conduct, and the only way Lin Piao could have tried to depose Mao was for Lin to have been a bad apple right from the start. Thus trapped, Mao must blacken the name of Lin Piao even if it means making Mao look less than all-wise.

This concession by the modern leader who presumes to defy his teachings might bring a smile to the placidly composed face of Kung Fu-tzu.

The old sage has seen how the dynasties that began by throwing his followers into pits went on to preserve their power by adopting his ideas of social order. He will see it happen again, as the men who come after Mao select traditions of ancient mandarins to freeze in the results of Mao's revolution.

PEKING TOO SOON

April 15, 1976

WASHINGTON—I have a vested interest in Hua Kuo-feng.

It was in this space that Hua's name as a potential prime minister first saw the light of Western print. Making a list of fearless forecasts for 1976, I came to the question of the successor to Chou En-lai; everybody was saying Deng Xiaoping had it in the bag, but there were those who looked at his picture on the cover of *Time* magazine and said to themselves: "Funny, he doesn't look like a prime minister."

By iconoclastic reckoning, the next No. 2 man to Mao had to be a new face, a Chinese Jimmy Carter; somebody of the generation younger than Mao who was clearly Mao's choice, not a selection of Chou. But who?—or as the Pekingologists say, Hu?

I turned to a *Times* Washington bureau colleague, Joseph Lelyveld, an experienced China-watcher, for a name of some dark horse with a good outside chance on a muddy track. Without hesitation, he chose Hua, then head of internal security. I named Hua in my prediction list, to general snickering from friends at State and C.I.A., and now—just look at him. As solidly ensconced as No. 2 as Lin Piao or Liu Shao-chi used to be.

Having thus helped put Hua over the top, I am obliged to try to explain what brought about the events at Peking's Tien An Men Square last week. As the official Chinese account stated, "a handful of class enemies" and "a few bad elements sporting a crewcut" (Haldeman left his imprint), accompanied by 100,000 passers-by, beat up Maoist students, smashed bicycles, overturned cars, set fire to a barracks and—getting serious—recited "reactionary" poems.

Why did it happen? Conventional China-watching wisdom holds that the succession struggle within the world's most populous nation pits the ideologically pure "radicals" under Mao against the pragmatic "moder-

ates" supposedly protected by Chou and later led by Deng. In this ideological view, my friend Hua rose to the top because he was not clearly
identified with either group.

Less conventional wisdom, put forward by Japanese observers, deals
with power groups: the party, the army, the police. When the party began
to lose its revolutionary zeal in the 60's, Mao turned to the army to spear-
head a cultural revolution. After that, he made a villain out of the head of
the army, Lin Piao, to strike a new power balance. Hua, head of the police,
is neither ideologue nor soldier, and is a natural—in this view—to maintain the equilibrium.

In the former hotel on Connecticut Avenue that now serves as the Chinese liaison office, officials chuckle merrily at such outlandish theories of
outsiders. A recent dinner guest there tried not to stuff himself with the
delectable finger-sized egg rolls and tried to puzzle out the answer to a key
question: Why was the riot at Tien An Men Square given such a big publicity play by the Chinese?

If Russians had rioted in Moscow's Red Square, Soviet leaders would
have suppressed the news; *Pravda* would have ignored it and the jamming
of outside newscasts would have doubled, lest a riot give ideas to dissidents in the countryside. But the official account of the Peking disturbance ran over 2,000 words, with copious quotes from the inflammatory
poems of rioters and detailed descriptions of beatings.

The Chinese account was anxious to tell the countryside and the world
about the damage done to army barracks and to describe the bloodied
heads of soldiers. In a style that may choreograph the next epic propaganda ballet, the report closed on the way the "people's police perse-
vered."

The decision of the Chinese Central Committee seems to have been to
take advantage of the riot, to incorporate it into folklore, to use the event as
the beginning of a new catharsis. This boiling-over may be what Mao and
his followers have needed: big enough to trigger a nationwide purification,
but not too big—they hope—to be genuinely counterrevolutionary.

"Struggle is progress," say Chinese officials; "there can be no progress
without struggle." When one asks about the deposed Deng, the response
is denunciation; when one asks about Hua, however, there is no compen-
satory buildup—the answer is to praise Mao.

"There is no middle of the road," the officials insist. Communists are on
one side, arrayed against "social imperialists"—the Soviets massed on the
border, along with "class enemies" inside China. It is not in their interest
to admit to moderation.

To paraphrase de Gaulle, China cannot be Communist without turmoil. The aging Chairman has selected a fresh villain in Deng, and named
Hua as the new heir, to keep the pot bubbling. As of now, Hua is the dark

horse with the anti-Soviet colors—which is why all of us may have a vested interest in his career.

THE MIDEAST

In the mid-70's, under a conservative Republican President, America stopped being a staunch ally of Israel. While professing unwavering support for the only democratic power in the area, the United States sought the role of broker between Arabs and Jews, which caused the threat of—and soon the fact of—a "reassessment" of our relationship with Israel. With the rise of Arab oil power came the rise of concern for evenhandedness.

"Evenhandedness" is one of those unassailable words that presupposes that both sides are half-right and the way of wisdom is to split the difference. Occasionally, that is right; more often, justice lies closer to one side or the other.

In the Mideast, I think justice lies on the side of the right of Israel to exist within defensible borders—and that includes the Golan Heights and a claim to a share of the sovereignty of the West Bank. Moreover, I think an ally should be readily recognized as an ally; only if Israel is convinced of the steadfastness of America's commitment, would Israelis be justified in taking more risks in making concessions to its radical neighbors.

Despite lip service, this was not the view that prevailed in the National Security Council or seventh floor of the State Department, where the clapping of one even hand could be heard. There, it was felt that America's interest had been overlooked in defending Israel's interests.

I thought then and think now that America's interest is best served by having a friendly bastion of democracy in the Mideast, and in showing the world that the United States is a reliable ally—not a patsy, but not a distant broker, either. This was generally interpreted as incorrigible hawkishness, worthy of the type of essayist who would defend our support of "corrupt dictators" in Southeast Asia. I think of it as consistency.

In this group of calls for reliability is a piece on the two-facedness of Henry Kissinger, which blew a whistle on a manipulation of the press via "backgrounders"; it had, I was told much later, an effect on some coverage.

I felt the need to declare to readers that I am Jewish, and wrote one day that I was "an American Jew." A reader wrote to correct me, pointing out that I am "a Jewish-American." The reader was right: When I pray, I'm an American Jew, and when I vote or write political columns, I'm a Jewish-American.

ARAB COUNCIL OF WAR

October 31, 1974

WASHINGTON—The Arab leaders who gathered in Rabat this week decided that a peace settlement was not a worthy objective, and that ultimate victory over Israel was within their grasp.

Toward that end, the Palestinian terrorists—who fervently pledge the destruction of the Jewish state—have been legitimized by the Arabs as a government-to-be on the West Bank of the Jordan.

Why have the Arabs chosen a course so likely to lead to another war? Several good reasons:

First, the monied Arabs hold Western Europe and Japan hostage to oil power, and these nations have shortsightedly opted for appeasement.

Second, the legendary invincibility of the Israelis went up in the smoke of the Yom Kippur war. Given enough chances and plenty of firepower Goliath now thinks he could take David.

Third, the Soviet Union has moved to supply the most modern arms to the newly confident Arabs with a vengeance; they have lost before, but they have to win only once.

Finally, United States peacemaking has been based on an assumption of good faith by both sides. But the Arab extremists do not want peace, they want Israel, and the Arab moderates let them have their way.

We can now expect a spate of dope stories about how King Faisal of Saudi Arabia and President Sadat of Egypt fought to restrain the hotheads, and hints about how King Hussein will outfox the Palestinians in the end.

But the fact is that the Arab extremists are in the saddle, and war is their solution. The question now is not whether the Israelis can be forced into negotiating with the Palestine Liberation Organization; the question is whether Israel will be pressured into agreeing to the creation of an adjacent nation which professes itself to be dedicated to Israel's destruction. The answer must be no.

Arab moderates can be expected to take over only when it becomes apparent that a countervailing power exists to block the obliteration of Israel as well as the dominance of world trade by Arab oil power.

That means that the United States, in this period, should be less of a broker, and more of a counterforce. As Mr. Kissinger learned in Vietnam, the application of power is an urgent reminder of the need for good faith in negotiations. Deliberate ambiguity has not worked in the Middle East; our "evenhandedness" has had its fingers crossed; now is the time to make clear to the Arab world that the United States insists upon peace without victory.

We can help Arab moderates gain the upper hand again by showing the futility of the extremists' cause. Thus:

1.   We should reaffirm that as long as organized forces are committed to the destruction of Israel, we shall see to it that—in the words of a Republican candidate in 1968—"the balance must be tipped in Israel's favor." We can be a superbroker only by acting like a superpower: The United States should become evenhanded as Arabs become settlement-minded.

2.   The Jews to be permitted emigration out of the Soviet Union are not going to Israel for their annihilation; part of any trade deal with the U.S.S.R. ought to be an agreement that limits Soviet offensive military aid to regimes like Iraq and Syria.

3.   Oil independence should be asserted by the U.S. not only in the limitation of our auto horsepower but in providing incentives to stimulate production. U.S. policy should actively encourage U.S. companies to explore for oil everywhere from the Gulf of Mexico to the Sinai desert.

4.   Someone might observe quietly that the manifest destiny of the Indian subcontinent lies westward toward the Persian Gulf. If oil inflation causes the per capita income of the residents of Kuwait to continue to soar hundreds of times higher than that of the average Indian, then that economic imbalance might likely be redressed by undiplomatic means: A nuclear power won't stand there with its hand out forever.

The Arab power play at Rabat calls for an unemotional, purposeful power response. Israel is the symbol of the Arab bid for dominance throughout the non-Communist world; if the new oil power succeeds in scaring away all support for the Jewish state, it will be used to subdue democratic systems elsewhere.

The Arab leaders are an extraordinary collection of absolute monarchs, skillful demagogues, and ardent nationalists; we have sold their abilities too short for too long. At Rabat, they have shown readiness to exploit Western weakness.

The only way to turn the Arabs away from extremism is to show how it will lead to no progress in regaining disputed land.

The only way to turn Arabs away from dreams of economic domination of the Western world is for the United States to lead in cracking their cartel.

The only way to turn Arabs away from war against Israel is for the United States to make clear to them that Israel would win.

HENRY'S TWO FACES

March 27, 1975

WASHINGTON—Henry Kissinger is still pursuing his favorite tactic: saying one thing in public, and "passing the word" directly to the contrary in private.

Voice cracking in anguish, he tells cameras that he does not blame either Egypt or Israel for the breakdown in negotiations, that this is not the time for "recriminations."

Then, from the ambush of unquotable background, we read in an accurate dispatch in *The New York Times* that the Secretary "was reported to have said in private that he was disappointed with Israel for not being able or willing to take a more flexible position."

Another example: With much fanfare, the United States has announced a "reassessment" of Mideast policy which everybody with his head screwed on tightly took to mean exactly what it was meant to mean: that Israel, not having obeyed our orders, had better watch out. There could not have been a clearer or crueler implied threat.

Not so, says Henry Kissinger, wearing his public face again. Gee, reassessments come naturally; we always strike these matches in gas-filled rooms; we did not mean to frighten the Israelis.

A third example of the two-faced technique: Henry briefs a group of twenty Senators on the failure of the mission. He tolerates their fawning attentions like a lost mountain climber discovered by an overly affectionate St. Bernard, and then passes the word to the most prestigious columnist in America that "he found that the reaction was violently anti-Israel."

Senators who were in that room do not agree; indeed, many were astounded that their troubled reaction was characterized by the Secretary of State as "violently anti-Israel." In such ways does Henry—the private Henry, from the ambush—punish the Israelis for not accepting his terms, undermining their public-opinion support.

This analysis of two-facedness will be hotly denounced as an attack on the Secretary's personal honor, but the facts cannot be disputed: Mr. Kissinger likes to work on two tracks, often going in opposite directions, and the American press lets him.

Let us credit him with the noblest of intentions for his two faces: We can see how he wants to keep himself on good mediation terms with the Arabs, who are not unsophisticated at this game, and cannot be displeased at the background savaging of the Israeli position.

Presumably, Secretary Kissinger figures he can always win back Israeli friendship, and it is useful to keep a foot in the Arab tent for future dickering. But in so doing, he fundamentally misreads the kind of policy necessary for the United States to follow in order to keep the peace in the Mideast.

With the failure of the latest round of mediation, we must stop being the evenhanded nation in the middle, honestly brokering until the final crunch, when we put our pressure where it can most easily be applied, on Israel.

As we approach Geneva—which we should be in no great hurry to do—we should position ourselves enough off-center to counter the Soviet bias toward the Arabs. We ought not to berate Arabs, or even privately blame them for the tension; we must make certain, however, that all the world knows that any force applied to Israel will be met with more than sufficient counterforce.

As Mr. Sadat announces "we have the upper hand," he must be made to understand that any war he starts would be followed by defeat, and so the best course is a gradual lessening of tension. Only a credible United States Secretary of State can make him understand that.

The diplomacy of negotiation is not the diplomacy of duplicity. To replace Mr. Kissinger's two faces, we need three faces: one new face as Secretary of State, another new face as National Security Adviser, and a third new face—perhaps an old face—for roving envoy.

The Israelis do not want supporters to call for Henry's scalp, for fear that they will be blamed for an abortive effort; in addition, Mr. Nixon privately and loyally informs friends (in refreshingly strong handwriting) that he is distressed by attacks on Henry by his former colleagues. Sorry, everybody; it's time for a new team and a fresh start.

If the route is through Geneva with nations present, we need a man whose assurances will be believed and whose public face will at least nearly match his private face. If the route is low-key two-party negotiations with the United States working the middle, an envoy is needed who will not have to bear the burden of not being Henry.

Dr. Kissinger genuinely wants peace, the highest motive of all, but he also wants to be the man revered as peacemaker. The time has come for him to make the sacrifice of the second in order to help achieve the first.

March 28, 1975

To the Editor:

William Safire's attack on Secretary Kissinger ("Henry's Two Faces," March 27), citing his "duplicity" in making conflicting public and private statements on the breakdown in Middle East negotiations, suggests nothing less than that American support for Israel should be totally unqualified.

Mr. Safire quotes Mr. Kissinger as having said privately that he was "disappointed" with Israel, while publicly refusing to blame either Israel or the Arabs. First of all, his carefully chosen word "disappointment" is not necessarily equivalent to "blame," and such a private statement does not render Mr. Kissinger guilty of "duplicity." If in fact Mr. Kissinger does blame Israel for the failure of the talks, he was wise to avoid declaring it publicly: any public statement to that effect, which would only serve to diminish Israel's already minimal resources of international moral support, would surely aggravate the tense Middle Eastern situation.

Mr. Safire thus requires of Mr. Kissinger that he either injure the cause of Israel publicly, or that he should never allow himself to think privately that Israel's intransigence is so great as to be inimical to her own and the world's interests. Otherwise, in Mr. Safire's eyes, he is guilty of "duplicity."

If Israel's intransigence is so great as perpetually to exacerbate the danger to world peace, why indeed should Mr. Kissinger not warn her—in the manner least injurious to her cause, the manner which he chose?

Jere L. Crook III
Cambridge, Massachusetts

P.S. You have my permission to publish this. I'd love to get it published!

THE DIFFERENCE BETWEEN ALLIES AND INTERESTS

July 21, 1975

CAIRO—At the foot of the Mount of Beatitudes, facing the Sea of Galilee, where Jesus delivered his most famous sermon a couple of millenia ago, a Bedouin Arab family now lives in a black tent. The woman of the tent works, the kids and their goats nibble at whatever they can find, as the head of the nomadic family stares at a Syrian broadcast on an Israeli television set.

There you have the Middle East: a TV antenna sticking out of a Bedouin tent, hostile anti-Israel propaganda arriving courtesy of Israeli technology, the medium of today competing with the message of thousands of years ago at that spot. "Blessed are the peacemakers. . . ."

Americans are the peacemakers today, and it might be helpful for us to get our sermon straight. Does our role as broker between Jerusalem and Cairo make us neutrals in our relations with both adversaries? Can we remain a strong ally to one if we are to gain traction with the other?

For years, diplomatists have been insisting that great powers do not have friends, only interests. Professionals in our State Department have been saying that we have been letting "domestic considerations" unduly influence our foreign economic interests.

Since hardnosedness and toughmindedness are much in vogue, Israel's spokesmen counter with arguments stressing America's self-interest in building a strong, independent Jewish state that can act as a bulwark against Communism and resist the vicissitudes of Arab nationalism in a strategic area.

At the risk of softnosedness and tendermindedness, let me suggest that national self-interest ought not to be the sole basis for foreign policy, and that our relationship with Israel and with Arab states is by its nature quite different.

America has an interest in Egypt. We benefit if we can help that impoverished nation straighten out its economy, and not be forced to trade young lives in war to receive subsidies from oil-rich Arab states. We profit by Egypt's turn away from debilitating socialism, and gain from the peace that its stability could bring about. We are right in wanting to establish relations far better than "correct."

America is an ally of Israel. "Ally" is a subjective, emotional word scorned by diplomats who see national attachments as temporary, dictated by economic or geopolitical interest. But to be an ally is neither a sometime nor a wartime thing; it is a valuable and sometimes mystic connection between peoples.

Why is America an ally of Israel? A visit there tells the story: It is a democracy, with an active opposition and a free press, and that spark is one we should breathe on wherever it appears. Although the kibbutz life gets the publicity, the small, private-property co-op makes the money and is growing faster, showing that Israel's economy is powered by—of all things—what we have come to call the Protestant ethic.

Our long-standing recognition in the United States of the Jews' right to a homeland after World War II; our admiration for their willingness to fight for their independence; and, surely, the attachment of many U.S. Jews to the Zionist dream—all this goes toward making a relationship what Winston Churchill would call "special."

The diplomat who derides the introduction of such sentiment into any foreign intercourse—who calls it "unrealistic"—is himself out of touch with political reality in modern democracies. Public opinion counts, and it is not always determined by the neat patterns of immediate self-interest. Cultural affinity, tradition, admiration for pluckiness, common ways for doing politics and business, the expectation of returned loyalty—all this goes into the intangible making of an ally.

Our diplomats err in trying to befriend an Egypt by defriending an Israel. There are other, more complex ways to express our interest in Egypt than to join her in condemnation of our ally. We can act as honest brokers without trying to deceive one side by pretending that we do not know and are not allied to the other side: We might even pick up a point for candor.

"Blessed are the peacemakers," goes the Sermon on the Mount. A less familiar portions goes: "Blessed are they which are persecuted for righteousness' sake, for theirs is the kingdom of heaven."

Israelis have a right to their kingdom with secure borders now, here on earth, and America as peacemaker ought not to be in the least embarrassed to be known as a reliable ally in that cause.

THE KURDS

Anybody who empathizes with underdogs has to be a friend of the Kurds—this, despite the Kurdish proverb, its wisdom proved in every generation for a thousand years: "The Kurds have no friends."

Here is a bloody but unbowed people, now living under at least four flags, desperately trying to cling to cultural identity. I was first attracted to their case because it reflected a too-callous misuse of America's guarantee of honor: We willingly let the Shah of Iran betray them. Next, the irony struck me of the way Iraq pressed claims for "the Palestinian people" that they stringently denied the Kurds living in Iraq. Finally, I met Mulla Mustafa al-Barzani, and admired him more than any man I met whose language I could not speak. For a farewell to him, see the follow-up section on the Kurds in the second half of this book (pp. 330–336).

MR. FORD'S SECRET SELLOUT

February 5, 1976

WASHINGTON—One section of the still-secret Pike committee report especially troubling to the White House is the revelation of a shameful action for which President Ford must be held responsible: the betrayal of the Kurdish people.

The two million Kurds are a distinct ethnic group, Moslem but not Arab, most living in Iraq, who have been fighting for self-determination for forty years. When President Nixon visited the Shah of Iran after his Moscow summit conference in 1972, the Shah asked the United States to help him help the Kurds make life difficult for his enemy and neighbor, Communist-dominated Iraq.

The Shah was quite capable of helping the Kurds by himself, but the Kurds did not trust him; they did trust the word of the United States, however, and as the unexpurgated Pike report says: ". . . the U.S. acted in effect as a guarantor that the insurgent group [the Kurds] would not be summarily dropped by the foreign head of state [the Shah]."

The United States agreed, with Treasury Secretary John Connally carrying the word to the Shah in utmost secrecy. Israel, too, was delighted; the separatist Kurds could tie down the Iraqi Army. But when the Yom Kippur surprise attack on Israel took place in October 1973, and the Kurds were willing to launch an attack of their own that would have won their freedom as well as taken some heat off the Israelis, Secretary Kissinger refused to let his Kurdish pawns move. On October 16, he ordered intelligence chief William Colby to send this message to the Kurds: "We do not repeat not consider it advisable for you to undertake the offensive military action that ['another government,' says the Pike committee, meaning Israel] has suggested to you."

The Kurds obeyed: The United States was the ally they trusted. They (and we) did not know that at that moment in 1973, the Shah was putting together OPEC, the oil cartel—and a crucial part of the inducement to Iraq and other Arab neighbors was Iran's willingness to double-cross the nettlesome Kurds.

Iran and its neighbor, Iraq, embraced, and OPEC price rises stunned the Western world. Through 1974, the Shah of Iran kept the Kurds in Iraq fairly quiet, but still kept them well enough supplied to be "a card to play," as a C.I.A. memo characterizes his views. The C.I.A. then viewed the low-key support of the Kurds as "a uniquely useful tool for weakening ['our ally's enemy's,' says the report, meaning Iran's enemy, Iraq] potential for international adventurism."

Then the Shah, having played Mr. Nixon for a sucker on oil, played Mr. Ford for a double-crosser on the Kurds: In March 1975, with President Ford hopelessly dependent on Henry Kissinger, the Persian rug was jerked. "The extent of our ally's leverage over U.S. policy," continues the suppressed Pike report, "was such that he apparently made no effort to notify his junior American partners that the program's end was near.

"The insurgents were clearly taken by surprise as well. Their adversaries [the report is referring to the Communist-dominated Iraqis], knowing of the impending aid cut-off, launched an all-out search-and-destroy campaign the day after the agreement was signed. The autonomy movement was over. . . ."

Our Shah-forsaken clients, the Kurds, turned to the United States. The C.I.A. chief of station in Teheran felt guilty and cabled Director Colby on March 10, 1975: "Iran's action has not only shattered their political hopes; it endangers lives of thousands"; he made some suggestions for amelioration and concluded "it would be the decent thing for U.S.G. to do."

The Kurdish leader, General Mustafa Barzani, sent a plea to Mr. Kissinger on that same day: "Our movement and people are being destroyed in an unbelievable way with silence from everyone." But on Henry Kissinger's advice, President Ford maintained that silence. Two-hundred thousand Kurdish refugees fled to Iran, and 40,000 of the most vulnerable were forced back to Iraq.

This unconscionable sellout took place without a peep out of us, public or private; no U.S. pressure on the Shah to make a decent deal for Kurdish autonomy in Iraq; not even a dime proposed for humanitarian aid. Gerald Ford was the first U.S. President in such a circumstance to look the other way.

A "high U.S. official," who is trying to keep secret his remark to the Pike committee staff, dismissed this betrayal of an ethnic group that placed its trust in the secret assurances of the United States in these words:

"Covert action should not be confused with missionary work."

That's a tough guy talking. But since when is it United States policy to be tough on the weak and weak on the tough? When did U.S. Presidents get in the habit of encouraging people to fight for their freedom, giving them guns, and then cravenly walking away from the consequences?

The callous, amoral voice may be Henry Kissinger's, but that decision of only 11 months ago is the direct responsibility of Gerald Ford. If the President wants to defend this sellout of the Kurds at the command of the Shah, let him do so; if he wants to disavow this act of American dishonor, let him fire the adviser who urged the dishonorable decision upon him.

Would such a dramatic dropping of the pilot be lacking in compassion for Mr. Kissinger, that selfless aide who longs to become an Oxford don at a time of his own choosing? Perhaps. But Presidential action should not be confused with missionary work.

SON OF "SECRET SELLOUT"

February 12, 1976

WASHINGTON—In this space last week, some new information about the secret sellout of the Kurdish people was revealed: The United States, which had been quietly supplying arms aid to Kurdish rebels fighting for self-determination inside Communist-dominated Iraq, betrayed our allies at the behest of the Shah of Iran.

When it suited the Shah to foment trouble in neighboring Iraq, he invited the United States to help him aid the Kurds. We secretly went along, since trouble in Iraq set back the Soviets and helped the Israelis. But when the Shah made a deal with the Arab world for oil solidarity, he drew the United States along into a double-cross of the Kurdish people: Last spring, when our $16 million aid to the Kurds was cut off and the revolt was smashed, Iran forcibly returned 40,000 refugees to Iraq, and there is no telling how many were executed.

A State Department spokesman reacted to my column with a statement approved by Secretary Kissinger: "We look upon that piece as a collection of distortions and untruths unsupported by any documents or the record. Frankly, I find it too contemptuous for further comment." (The spokesman meant to say "contemptible"; it is Mr. Kissinger's attitude toward Congress that is "contemptuous.")

Okay; let's look at some documents.

1. Two years ago, on March 23, 1974, Soviet Defense Minister Andrei Grechko went to Iraq to help that Soviet client make a deal with its rebellious Kurds. On the advice of Iran and the U.S., General Mustafa Barzani, the 74-year-old Kurdish leader, refused. Here is a C.I.A. memorandum of March 22, 1974—the day before Marshal Grechko arrived in Iraq— showing our policy had been to help the Kurds just enough to keep them bothersome but not enough to win: "Iran, like ourselves, has seen benefit in a stalemate situation . . . in which Iraq is intrinsically weakened by the Kurds' refusal to relinquish its semi-autonomy. Neither Iran nor ourselves wish to see the matter resolved one way or the other."

2. One year later, the Shah made a deal with Iraq on oil. He then cut off supplies to the Kurds, and the Iraqis attacked. On March 10, 1975, the stunned Kurds sent the following message to the C.I.A.: "Our people's fate in unprecedented danger. Complete destruction hanging over our head. No explanation for all this. We appeal you and the U.S. Government intervene according to your promises. . . ."

3. On that same day of infamy, March 10, 1975, the C.I.A.'s chief of station in that area cabled Director of Central Intelligence Colby in Washington: "Is headquarters in touch with Kissinger's office on this; if U.S.G. does not handle this situation deftly in a way which will avoid giving the

Kurds the impression that we are abandoning them they are likely to go public. Iran's action has not only shattered their political hopes; it endangers lives of thousands."

4. Again on that fateful March 10, 1975, while Secretary Kissinger was shuttling about the Mideast, Kurdish General Barzani sent him this letter: "Our hearts bleed to see that an immediate byproduct of their agreement [between Iran and Iraq] is the destruction of our defenseless people in an unprecedented manner as Iran closed its border and stopped help to us completely and while Iraq began the biggest offensive they have ever launched. . . . We feel, Your Excellency, that the United States has a moral and political responsibility towards our people who have committed themselves to your country's policy. . . . Mr. Secretary, we are anxiously awaiting your quick response. . . ."

5. Twelve days later, on March 22, 1975, the Director of Central Intelligence received this cable from his chief of station: "No reply has been received from Secretary of State Henry Kissinger to the message from Barzani. . . . If the U.S.G. intends to take steps to avert a massacre it must intercede with Iran promptly."

6. One day later, Secretary Kissinger—furious at the Israelis for their "intransigence"—suspended his shuttle diplomacy and flew home. The Kurds, whose revolt had long been tying down the Iraqi Army, were crushed in a few weeks. On April 10, the C.I.A. chief of station cabled Director Colby: "Only a few Kurdish leaders knew that until recently they had our secret support for their military resistance because it diverted Iraq from Israel. If senior Americans like Kissinger . . . do nothing to help the Kurds in their present extremity, we may be sure that they will not lie down quietly to be buried without telling their story to the world. . . ."

Now the documents that tell the story of American dishonor are finally leaking. Henry Kissinger—whom President Ford, if elected, is determined to continue in office for four more years—has coolly dismissed the Ford Administration's betrayal of an ally with a line classic in its amorality:

"Covert action should not be confused with missionary work."

OF KURDS AND CONSCIENCE

December 13, 1976

WASHINGTON—According to some of our best doctors, Mulla Mustafa al-Barzani, 74, leader of the Kurdish people, should have died of cancer about six months ago. On the assumption that his illness was terminal, and with the tacit understanding that he would not try to enlist public support for the Kurds in his waning days, General Barzani was permitted to undergo treatment here at the Mayo Clinic.

To the amazement of his doctors and the embarrassment of our State Department and C.I.A., the old rebel got better. His iron-gray hair has grown back, his eyes are bright and fierce, and though he looks awkward in Western civilian clothes, the grip of his hand is strong and purposeful.

Four months ago, the State Department—uncomfortable at the presence of this living reminder of our most amoral diplomatic double-cross—told him to return to Iran, where 38,000 Kurdish refugees from Iraqi vengeance dwell. Mustafa al-Barzani said no, that if he were forced to leave the United States, he would go to Iraq and face his execution.

Nobody at Foggy Bottom wanted nonsecret blood on his hands, so our guilt-ridden diplomats backed off and let him stay. The reason he stays, and the reason he is so grimly determined to live, is to prick the conscience of the next Administration to redress the wrong that a few Americans secretly did to his people.

The Kurds—perhaps 16 million of them, in Iran, Turkey, and Iraq—are a distinct ethnic group, a mountain people with their own history and culture who live under three flags. When it was in the interests of the United States and Iran to annoy the Soviet-dominated Iraqis, we encouraged the Kurds to revolt, and supplied them with arms; but when Iran and Iraq made a deal, the United States and Iran left their Kurdish clients high and dry.

Since the aid to the Kurds was in secret, the power-politicians at State did not have to explain this unprecedented betrayal. The sordid story came out in Daniel Schorr's publication of the House of Representatives' Pike Report on the C.I.A.

The consequences of our double-cross are what might interest a new Administration, one presumably more interested in America's moral position. The Iraqis have begun their own solution to the Kurdish problem, by executing several hundred leaders of the abortive revolt, and by "Arabizing" over 300,000 of their three million Kurds—moving them out of their homes to the Arab south, dispersing them and denying their culture. Iraqis are being offered bonuses to marry and assimilate Kurds.

Here is a culture being systematically demolished, a people being destroyed, and the United States—partially responsible for the Kurdish plight—has raised no voice in protest.

Let us not picture the Kurds as democrats, or Mustafa al-Barzani as James Madison. A generation ago, when the Soviets planned to use the Kurds to harass the Iranians and Turks, General Barzani abided in the Soviet Union a dozen years, learning Russian and befriending Marshal Grechko. Even today, if the Soviets were to switch their policy toward

Iraq, and offer to support the Kurds, the mountain people would gratefully turn to them. Although General Barzani now forcefully asserts his
anti-Communism, his people—first and foremost—want to survive as
Kurds, and could be expected to take help when it came.

What do the Kurds want? Not independence, not a new nation carved
out of three existing nations. They want to be let alone, as an autonomous
region of Iraq, loyal to Baghdad but living their own lives. If that were all
the Palestinians wanted—autonomy under Jordan—an instant Mideast
settlement would be possible.

How can a newly moral American foreign policy help bring Kurdish
autonomy about, and erase the stain of betrayal?

First, we should send a signal that we are interested by accepting some
600 refugees, mostly young and activist and threatened, to join the 400
here now.

Next, put Kurdistan on the agenda for our bilateral discussions with the
Russians. They supply and dominate Iraq, controlling the largest air base,
Shaibe, and Umm Qasr (a well-named naval base). As in the past, the
Soviets could mediate between the Kurds and the Iraqis.

Next, lean on the Iranians and the Egyptians. General Barzani is anxious not to offend the Shah, who has taken in so many refugees fleeing execution and "Arabization" in Iraq, and I will explore the Iranian position
in a future column. But the United States is not helpless in dealing with
Iran and Egypt.

Finally, put the Kurdish question before the United Nations, and use
the spotlight of publicity to stop the killing of a culture, while reminding
other cultural groups that identity can be sought in a larger, diverse nation.

Will it work? Who knows? But America owes such an effort to her conscience. Mustafa al-Barzani takes the plastic-tipped American cigar out of
his mouth and says: "We do not want to be used to destroy relations between Iran and Iraq. We do not want to be anybody's pawn. We are an
ancient people, we want our autonomy, we want *sarbasti*—freedom.

"I do not know who will take my place one day. But they cannot crush
us."

CANADA

Some people think it is not our business to tell our neighbors how to run their countries. I think Canada is in danger of coming apart and we ought to tell our friends up there that such a split would be bad for them and worse for hemispheric defense.

54-40 AND NO FIGHT

November 22, 1976

WASHINGTON—At a small reception following a state dinner in Paris in February 1969, I found myself standing next to President Charles de Gaulle. Anxious to appear knowledgeable in world affairs, I mumbled something about how he had really stirred Canadians up a couple of years before with his cry of "Vive le Quebec libre" to a crowd in Montreal.

He looked at me through eyeglass lenses thick as Coke-bottle bottoms with eyes that seemed to wonder why a President of the United States would bring along such a simpleton as a member of his staff. "One day," de Gaulle stated, with absolute certainty, "Quebec will be French."

The ghost of *le grand Charles* must have smiled imperiously last week when the Province of Quebec astounded Canada and the world by electing two-thirds of its representatives to the National Assembly from the Separatist Party.

Many worried Canadians, pointing to public opinion polls in Quebec that do not seem to favor independence, say that the regional election was only a rejection of the Liberal Party leadership on other issues. They insist it cannot be interpreted as a vote for separation of Quebec's six million French Canadians from the 16 million English-speaking Canadians across North America.

But movements gathering momentum lend respectability to ideas previously held to be unthinkable. Prime Minister Pierre Trudeau, himself a French Canadian, was thought to be a symbol of a unified Canada's ability to accommodate minority desires. However, Mr. Trudeau—with his praise of Castro, his rejection of Taiwan, and his foolhardy manipulation of Canada's economy—is losing control.

The head of the victorious Parti Québécois, René Lévesque, plans a provincial referendum on independence two years from now. Since a chance exists that any separatist referendum victory would be followed by secession, the federalists who believe in one Canada will probably put the issue to a nationwide vote before that time. Separatists, who might be a majority in Quebec, would still be a minority in the nation—and such a decision is the whole nation's to decide.

What does this mean to the United States? The possibility now exists of an argument to our immediate north on the subject of "self-determination" v. "nationhood." Such national arguments have a way of encouraging hotheads and becoming fierce (in our own case, it took the South over a century to triumph).

As a neighbor, the United States must refrain from poking its nose in. But as fellow Americans, we can hope that the much-maligned spirit of nationalism—even including its prickly anti-United States manifestations—will prevail over separatism.

The reason is that the breakup of Canada would not create two strong nations, but two—and perhaps more—weak and quarrelsome bordering states, each inviting exploitation from abroad.

If Canada were to acquiesce in its own dismemberment, a modest proposal would be recalled that was put forward in the 1844 victory of James Polk—"Fifty-four forty, or fight." At that time, the United States angrily disputed British ownership of part of the Oregon territory leading up toward Alaska, to the longitude of 54-40.

President Polk, however, preferred to fight Mexico for the annexation of Texas than the British for the Canadian province now called British Columbia, which is why the northern border of the United States is the 49th parallel. We did not get to 54-40, nor did we fight.

But if Canada divides, would there not be pressure from above and below the 49th parallel to merge Canada's western provinces into a United States of North America, with our "Manifest Destiny" marching unvexed from Oregon to Alaska?

If separatism succeeds, would not a Saskatchewan Statehood Party press for admission to the United States, citing our common language, common democractic tradition, common western frontier culture, and—above all—territorial contiguity?

A Canada that tolerated the separation of its largest province would start down the road of further subdivision, resolving regional differences by further Balkanization and—in some cases—affiliation with the United States.

We would be better off with one Canada. Canada would be better off with one Canada. The Canucks are not like the Kurds, a separate people decimated and dominated by oppressors; nor is Canada a New World Yugoslavia, five nations held together by the legend of an aging leader.

Canadians ought to stop pretending the separatist threat is not serious, and start making it clear that whatever autonomous and culture-respecting arrangements are made for the Québécois, they flow from the font of one diverse but unified nation.

Charles de Gaulle, with his incitement to a "liberated" Quebec, was wrong. I only wish I could think of another occasion in which de Gaulle, in the long run, was wrong.

November 22, 1976

The New York Times
New York, N.Y.

Gentlemen:
There is much drivel at times in your paper, but the effrontery of Wm. Safire in today's paper takes the cake. Why should sitting next to General de Gaulle at a dinner some years back qualify Mr. Safire as an expert on Quebec and its separatist movement?

Any country or province with a colonial past, or a country with a dual culture, must present complexities beyond the scope of such simplistic mouthings as you allow Mr. Safire to write for two columns of your editorial pages. This is not an argument against free speech, but a plea for competency and responsibility.

Whether it is Northern Ireland, Quebec, or even the Northwest of our own country, *The Times* will always find a no-nothing to plead for solutions based on the primacy of ignorance rampant on Manhatten [sic].

Sincerely,
(Mrs.) Frances Doyle
White Plains, New York

HENRY KISSINGER

Henry and I were fairly close friends in the old days; I was the only White House colleague he invited to his 50th birthday party in New York in 1973. But then I zapped him for encouraging the illegal wiretaps, including the one on me; he retaliated with demands that *The Times* fire me (the publisher never passed on the heat); I seethed at his backstabbing of the falling Nixon; then I differed with him on policy toward Israel. I took after him with some zeal on the Kurds and later on human rights.

He thought mistakenly that all our policy differences were motivated by my personal grudge, as a result of the wiretap.

How could a man who was so wrong about so many things, I wondered, be so right about the need for American resolution and stability in Southeast Asia and in resisting Soviet expansion? Frankly, I had trouble with that anomaly.

My problem with Henry is that there is nobody with whom I agree more on certain essentials and nobody with whom I disagree more on other essentials. That is why I criticize him with such fervor while resenting some of the fervid criticism he gets—unfairly, in my view—from others.

Ultimately, we established a cautious communication; David Mahoney gave me a 50th birthday party in 1979 and invited Henry, who came and made a gracious speech, not giving an inch. So did I, and neither did I. We're civil these days; I generally get along with people out of power.

THE DÉTENTE-FIRSTERS

December 17, 1973

WASHINGTON—For about 5,000 years, Jews have been confronting each other and the rest of mankind with irritating moral questions. In that tradition, the two moral dilemmas of today's international affairs center on Jews:

1. Should the United States condition its trade policy with the Soviet Union on a relaxation of emigration restrictions now applied to Soviet Jews—or should we place détente ahead of a campaign to pressure a totalitarian system into granting some of its people what we consider to be their human rights?

2. Should nations follow their obvious economic interests by supporting the Arab states' war against Israel, and thereby avert sacrifice and discomfort by people who are not "involved"—or should they indulge their guilty consciences and support commitments made two Mideast wars ago?

Because these moral questions are on the world's front burners today, we can ask an even more fundamental question: What part should morality play in the foreign affairs of a nation like ours?

Henry Kissinger, after making all due obeisances to morality, motherhood, and the spirit of laws, would say that it is not the business of the United States to seek to influence the way other nations live—that the action of moralists like Senator Henry Jackson harms the establishment of a "world order" without war.

The Kissinger position, while essentially amoral, is defensible. He would point out that wars are always started in the name of morality; crusades were undertaken that savaged infidels in the name of God; world wars were begun in the name of a righteous "place in the sun," and throughout history, moralizers from Patrick Henry to John Foster Dulles place themselves squarely against the normalizaton of relations between different systems.

To the peace-seeking amoralists now shaping our foreign policy, the moralists are the mischief-makers, the obstacles to change and the unwitting disturbers of the peace. Why, asks our Secretary of State, should we impose our standards of freedom on others—why should not every nation and every ideology seek its own destiny, in peace with its neighbors? Haven't the moralists been able only to achieve a bloody war in every generation?

The détente-firsters have a potent argument, even if—in deference to old value systems—they do not make it in such stark, amoral terms.

In truth, however, they ask the moralists to set aside the troublesome questions of right and wrong, or freedom and slavery—and instead consider the necessity of survival in a nuclear age, and think about the freedom to live in an "order" that at least does away with world war.

The first trouble with "détente first" is that this new amorality is inconsistent with the Nixon doctrine. We proceeded in Southeast Asia on the notion that "our word" was good and that a great power would lose its stabilizing influence throughout the world if it were to renege on a commitment anywhere. We did not expend all that blood and treasure in Vietnam, turning back a military challenge to "our word," to succumb to a diplomatic temptation in the Mideast to sell out an ally.

The need for consistency in policy does not impress the amoralists. When a challenge was made to Henry Kissinger at a White House meeting two years ago that some move was "not consistent with the Nixon doctrine," Mr. Kissinger's heated reply was: "We wrote the goddamn doctrine, we can change it." But it is hardly a good idea to swap doctrines in midstream.

The greater difficulty with "détente first" as a substitute for the Nixon Doctrine is this: Even such a noble end as a stable world order does not justify any means for attaining it. Our foreign policy must have a moral basis, upsetting though that may be.

We cannot close our eyes to Communist injustice in the Soviet Union or to Fascist injustice in Greece. That does not mean we return to those halcyon days of gunboat diplomacy, or demand that everybody adopt our system or else, but it does mean we use our considerable influence—and our economic muscle—wherever we can to encourage human freedom.

A realistic *realpolitik* would recognize morality as a force in international affairs; no genuine pragmatist can overlook the debilitating effect on the national character of the amoralists' policy of détente-first.

The irony is that the American people, in the last election, chose a leader whose past performance and every current instinct is in the direction of a basically moralist foreign policy, with a practical overlay.

But the President has turned his foreign policy formulation over to the number one détente-firster, who—in both the trade-emigration issue and the Mideast situation—has shown his every instinct to be in the direction of a basically amoralist policy, with an endearing overlay of the rhetoric of moral anguish.

DOBRYSSINGER

September 16, 1974

WASHINGTON—"Anatoly, I have the bottle of brandy you sent," said Henry Kissinger to Soviet Ambassador Dobrynin on the telephone a couple of years ago. "The Secret Service is going over it now for hidden microphones."

After some more friendly banter of that sort, the two men got down to business, which on that day was the quick and quiet exchange of captured spies. Together, they formed a unique international force: Dobryssinger.

These days, Ambassador Dobrynin and Secretary Kissinger, men so alike in reach of intellect and grasp of power coming from nations at such variance in the tradition of freedom, are working closely on a plan to change Soviety emigration policy in exchange for trade concessions.

The good idea is to induce the Soviet Union to stop discriminating against people, particularly Jews, who want to emigrate, by ending the United States policy of discriminating against the Soviet Union on matters of trade.

The Russians are now willing to go for this deal on a grand scale, which proves that Senator Henry Jackson has been right all along, and Secretary Kissinger has been underestimating the power of positive pressuring. The Soviet Union is far more willing than Dobryssinger ever indicated to set aside objections to "interference with its internal affairs" so as to advance its economic interests.

But the way the arrangement is being made uses a false notion of practicalities to put over a fundamental change in the method of conducting United States foreign policy.

As it stands now, Dobryssinger has come to an understanding, but no agreement is to be written down between the two countries. Instead, our idea of the understanding is to take the form of a letter from the President of the United States to several individual Senators who have been insisting on an emigration *quid pro quo* before passing a trade bill. The United States would have an unwritten agreement with the Soviet Union, and the President would have a letter-treaty about it with the U.S. Senate.

What's going on here? Our Secretary of State is supposed to represent the whole United States Government in foreign policy dealings, not the executive branch; he is not the middleman between certain U.S. interests and certain Soviet interests. The U.S. Senate is supposed to advise and consent on treaties made by the President, not to enter into treaties with the President about its understanding of unwritten understandings with foreign powers.

Undoubtedly, this warping of the American foreign policy process is rationalized as a necessary device to make a humanitarian deal work, to help the Soviets save face. It also flatters the Senators, who can brandish a document with their names on it to voters.

But that excuse is only what Dobryssinger gives us today. Three months ago, word from the amalgam to Senators Jackson, Ribicoff, and Javits was that the Soviet Union was reportedly ready to make a written agreement; three years ago, Dobryssinger was saying that even the mention of emigration put détente and arms control in serious jeopardy.

In fact, when the Soviets decide on the substance of a deal, the form is not all that significant. They have been denying the harassment of would-be emigrants all along; in a controlled press, it would hardly be humiliating for the Soviet Union to issue a pronunciamento condemning harassment as contrary to Soviet law.

At stake here is not the substance of an agreement—a deal is in the works because it is clearly in the interests of both superpowers—at stake is a tradition of U.S. foreign policy.

Will policy be set by a supernational force called Dobryssinger, thinking of itself as acting in the interest of world survival, dickering with what it considers militaristic or moralistic elements in the U.S. and the U.S.S.R., treating the essential conflict as being within each system rather than between the two systems?

Or will we return to those simplistic days of yore ("I'm the American Secretary of State and I'm on our side"), when the President's principal agent for foreign policy would hammer out our national position and then negotiate with a foreign power for an agreement to be signed and published?

The Dobryssinger amalgam is intoxicated by its mountaintop juggler's role; the Senate preens with its new and extraconstitutional power; moral men are excited by the prospect of using economic muscle to contribute to human freedom. And nobody notices what a wrench to our system is in the works.

SECRETARY KISSINGER'S "MALICIOUS CANARD" ROTI

February 17, 1975

WASHINGTON—Just before leaving for the Middle East, Secretary of State Kissinger took a few hours of his schedule to write a three-page letter to the editor of *Harper's* magazine denouncing an article of mine in its current issue.

The charge that caused this latest attack of Salzburg fever was this: I wrote that in Vladivostok three months ago, it was Henry Kissinger who orchestrated the touting of President Ford at the expense of President Nixon, enlisting Press Secretary Ron Nessen in the dissemination of the phony line that the SALT agreement was "something that President Nixon could not do in three years, but Ford did it in three months."

Of my statement, the Secretary of State writes: "That statement can only be described as a malicious canard, which in an earlier day—when journalistic standards were higher—would have merited a retraction and apology."

Dr. Kissinger then sets forth proof of his noninvolvement in the episode: "Mr. Nessen's statement was made on Air Force One on the way back from the Far East; I was in Japan, preparing to go to China and therefore thousands of miles from the event. When I learned of the statement, I immediately asked that the White House issue a retraction, which it did." He then goes on to pat Mr. Nixon on the head for his assistance in years gone by.

In looking at the record, I am forced to break a "deep background" rule or two. Mr. Kissinger frequently works from the ambush of nonattribution, and reporters eager for information or afraid of retribution tolerate it; but when a writer is accused of a "malicious canard" by the most powerful person in the world, there is some excuse for lifting the lid.

The opening note of the Kissinger orchestration began on the Anchorage-to-Tokyo leg of the flight to the Far East. Aboard Air Force One, Henry Kissinger told reporters that in terms of personality, Ford and Brezhnev are better matched than Nixon and Brezhnev." Under the rules, that opening cut could not be attributed to any source, nor did Secretary Kissinger make much of it; but it was a start.

While in Vladivostok, Ron Nessen extended the theme in conversation with a few reporters. At 2:00 A.M. Sunday morning in the press hostel, Nessen said that "Nixon could never look Brezhnev in the eye" as Ford could. When asked how Nessen, new to international diplomacy, could be aware of this, the Press Secretary replied: "I dunno—that's what Henry tells me."

This Kissinger line, dutifully unsourced, appeared in *Time* magazine later as "While Former President Nixon was often nervous in summit negotiations and had trouble looking his adversary in the eye, Ford . . . never wavered from eyeball-to-eyeball contact."

Subsequently, while still in the Soviet Union, the Presidential party rode Siberian rails from Vladivostok to a Soviet air base. In the dining car, obviously acting on instructions, Mr. Nessen said on the record that Ford had done in three months what Nixon could not do in three years. Mr. Kissinger was on the same train, not "thousands of miles from the event."

Reporters I have talked to make no secret of the fact that Henry Kissinger was the source of most of the Ford-Nixon comparisons, though they are careful to stay within "deep background" rules.

Even reporters who had no liking for former President Nixon could not stomach this manipulation of the truth—and of the press secretary—by Dr. Kissinger. John Osborne, writing in the *New Republic*, slid past the "deep background" barrier to nail the perpetrator: "Secretary of State Henry Kissinger initiated the operation at the expense of his former President for the benefit of his new President. Messrs. Ford and Brezhnev were still in Vladivostok when Kissinger recalled defects of Mr. Nixon. . . . This was strange and ugly stuff, coming indirectly but authoritatively."

As the press backlash began, the "deep background" source sensed this reaction to his overkill, spun around on a dime, and ostentatiously rode to the rescue of the former President's reputation. The Kissinger campaign had gone too far to be credible so he scotched it.

Mr. Nessen learned his lesson from this, and apologized to the press corps in withdrawing his unsalable line. But Henry Kissinger has said nothing about this until now.

In fury, he denounces any charge of his participation in this unsuccessful media-washing as a "canard" (from the French *vendre des canards à moitié*, to half-sell ducks, hence, a deception). Worse than that, he calls my protest at his easily demonstrable smear attempt "a malicious canard, which in an earlier day—when journalistic standards were higher—would have merited a retraction and apology."

Journalistic standards are higher now, despite the willingness to tolerate subversion by "deep background" campaigns of denigration. It is diplomatic and political standards that require elevation, especially when a senior official insists that black is white because he says it is.

The saddest part of this dreary episode is that it shows how little Watergate has taught some of our men at the top. Mistakes are bad enough, but they can be dealt with when faced up to. It is when men in high places cover up mistakes with blustering deceit that they get into terrible trouble.

THE DEAD-KEY SCROLLS

January 15, 1976

WASHINGTON—A "dead key," in Washington parlance, is a receiving extension built into a telephone to permit a secretary to listen in to her boss's conversations without the caller suspecting that everything said is being overheard by a third party.

As soon as they entered the White House, and a full two years before the secret Nixon taping system was installed, Henry Kissinger and his deputy, Al Haig, made certain that relays of secretaries on "dead keys" made verbatim notes of all that was said to them over the telephone. The callers—reporters, colleagues, Presidents—were never told that their words were always taken down.

But within the White House it was no big secret; aides could see the secretaries outside Henry's door, extensions to their ears, taking shorthand silently.

In 1971, my then-colleague and friend Henry showed me the transcript of a conversation with a reporter for *The Christian Science Monitor*, in which the National Security Adviser chewed him out for a less-than-adulatory article. Since he was planning to send the transcript to President Nixon, the rough draft had "corrections" marked by Mr. Kissinger, adding to the fierce loyalty of his own remarks.

Even with the self-serving emendations, these transcripts are an invaluable, irreplaceable part of the record of the Nixon Presidency, predating as well as paralleling the White House tapes. What has happened to them? The other day, we began to find out.

In a sworn answer to a question submitted to him by Morton Halperin, who is suing Mr. Kissinger for his part in ordering illegal F.B.I. wiretapping, the Secretary of State writes: "Business telephone conversations from my White House office during this period [January 21, 1969 to February 12, 1971] were usually monitored by my personal secretaries and records prepared, in accordance with routine Government practice, in order to facilitate implementation and follow-up of business transacted."

And where are all his records kept? Appointment books, correspondence, schedules of his White House years, says Mr. Kissinger, have remained where they belong: "All such records, with the exception of the records of my telephone calls, are in the White House. They are in the custody of the N.S.C. [National Security Council] staff. The telephone records are in the State Department, in custody of Mr. Lawrence S. Eagleburger."

Hold on a minute: When Mr. Kissinger left the White House, he left everything behind—*"with the exception of the records of my telephone calls."* Those are not mere logs of calls, of which he took a copy—those are substantive, verbatim transcripts of conversations, of which he took the only copy. Some questions arise:

1. *When were the dead-key scrolls removed from the White House N.S.C. files?* According to Mr. Eagleburger, within a month after Mr. Kissinger's appointment as Secretary of State in 1973. (But Mr. Kissinger continued as National Security Adviser at that time, and left behind his other N.S.C. files—presumably he wanted to get these supersensitive files out of the White House, fast).

2. *Under what authority did he take them?* Mr. Eagleburger claims he needed no authority—that these four years of records were considered "working papers that can accompany him wherever he goes, as long as he's in Government." And afterward? "I presume he would leave copies behind, but that's a legal question."

3. *Why didn't he leave the originals where they belonged at the N.S.C. and only take copies, if all he wanted was access to "working papers"?* No answer to that. Did Al Haig walk off with his telephone transcripts, too? General Brent Scowcroft, the present National Security Adviser, will not return calls on these matters; he has probably offered no objection to having the N.S.C. files denuded of all these transcripts.

4. *Who owns these transcripts?* The Justice Department last week won a decision in the Court of Appeals in which Congressional seizure of the papers of the Nixon Presidency was held constitutional. If N.S.C. transcripts are Presidential papers—as they surely are—then, as of now, they belong to the public and not to Henry Kissinger.

5. *Why have these transcripts never been subpoenaed?* Ah, that's the big one. The Special Prosecutor's investigation of the wiretaps was a joke; the Senate Foreign Relations Committee look-see was a Kissinger whitewash from start to finish; the Church cover-up committee is afraid of what a subpoena might turn up, and the woebegone Pike committee knows that the House won't back up any subpoena.

One ray of light: By removing the dead-key scrolls from the White

House, leaving no copies behind, and by dint of the tacit White House approval of the removal to a Government department, Mr. Kissinger has made his years of conversations subject to the Freedom of Information Act. Citizens may rush in where solons fear to tread.*

GIVE HENRY THE CHAIR

May 23, 1977

"There is no place at Columbia for Henry Kissinger," cries that university's student newspaper. "The issue is whether this university respects the moral values it purports to represent. . . . A Columbia appointment would reward and legitimize Kissinger's policies. His actions have shown him unfit to teach here, and Columbia should not hire him."

Professor Noam Chomsky, the linguistics giant from M.I.T. who has equated some Nixon "crimes" with those of Kennedy and Johnson, told a rally of Columbia protesters that Mr. Kissinger should head a "Department of Death," and—adding injury to insult—challenged his scholarly qualifications for any academic post.

Should Columbia, or any other great university, offer Mr. Kissinger a professor's chair from which he could never be fired? Or should he—like Walt Rostow and Dean Rusk—be ostracized by much of the academic community for being a part of a policy that many faculty and students found repugnant?

My own anti-Kissinger credentials are in apfel-pie order: I was the first on my block to oppose his 1973 confirmation as Secretary of State, and I recently joined the group of plaintive plaintiffs seeking to make public his "private" papers, which were assembled at a cost to the taxpayers of over $400,000.

But I believe Columbia was right to have offered him the post. Let's analyze the objections:

1. *The university is making the offer purely out of fund-raising and celebrity motives.* True. The Rockefellers and others would cough up a fat endowment, and Columbia would have a "star" for other fund raisers.

2. *Between writing multimillion-dollar books, starring on NBC, and advising the Chase Manhattan Bank, he would have little time to teach.*

* The Reporters' Committee for Freedom of the Press sued for access; in 1980, the Supreme Court ruled in Kissinger's favor.

Also true. But since when are big-name professors required to teach? He would be a kind of absent "presence."

3. *He is being hired secretly, circumventing the normal procedures applied to other professors.* Come, now: Public disclosure of the delicate negotiations could abort the entire opening to academia.

4. *He is only seeking legitimacy, sanitization, the approval of the academic community that money cannot buy—and not the freedom to teach, so the academic freedom argument does not apply.* True about what he is seeking, but the academic freedom argument definitely does apply.

Academic freedom is at issue because anti-Kissinger demonstrators would deny him honor and tenure on the basis of "war guilt." But he is not Adolph Eichmann; the bombing was not "mindless"; the war from which he helped extricate us was not imperialist.

Assuming he would show up on campus between board meetings, the former National Security Adviser might open a few closed minds about the most outrageous rewriting of history now going on: that the United States was somehow responsible for the bloodbath in Cambodia.

Truth has been turned on its head by the assertion that our bombing of Vietnamese forces that were using Cambodian territory in some way "brutalized" the gentle Cambodian Communists. In reality, only our abandonment of Vietnam made it possible for the Cambodian Khmer Rouge to take over, and to begin their outside-the-media reign of terror.

Doves in the United States, who had been shouting "stop the killing" for years, needed some alibi for the killing that started and is probably still going on. Hence the nonsense about how we, and not the occupying Vietnamese, "expanded" the war, and how our attacks on enemy supply centers in Cambodia transformed peace-loving agrarian reformers into death-march savages.

If Henry Kissinger were to be denied an academic post because of his role in the war—which is what the students' hollering is really all about—then higher educaton in America would be saying there is no toleration for an unpopular view of recent history.

Higher education would also be saying that the us-against-them passion that used to rule the campus and the White House prevails, and that vengeance and self-righteousness remain the order of the day.

Mr. Kissinger committed some terrible abuses, but he is no war criminal. His eight-year devotion to duplicity makes difficult a defense of the law of return to academic life, but getting even with an individual is not as important as holding firm to a principle: Any educator who serves in any unpopular administration ought not to be barred from returning to campus.

If I can swallow the honoring of Henry, so can the students at Columbia.

The Kennedys

DOUBLE STANDARDS BOTHER ME. (That originally read "Double standards bug me," but I hesitate to risk a double meaning so soon after a section on Kissinger, wiretaps, etc.) For the first couple of years as a columnist, nothing angered me more than the double standard of political morality applied to Richard M. Nixon by old admirers of John F. Kennedy.

I liked J.F.K.'s speeches and I liked his stand-up foreign policy; I even liked the fierce nothing-beats-winning attitude of his political associates and could understand the tight-lipped protectiveness of his intimates in their memoirs. But when Kennedy sychophants, who knew of "hardball" as played by their man, expressed shock at similar tricks of Nixon men, that bugged me; and when those who knew all about the underside of the Kennedy years kept silent about their man while reveling in the exposure of the underside of the Nixon years, that moved me to some reporting.

That was new to me. I used to think that reporting was for reporters, and commentating for commentators, and my job was to read the papers, suck my thumb, and turn out a useful polemic. Occasionally Joe Alsop would run into me at a party and say "You'd do a hell of a lot better with that column if you did some real reporting," but that took a while to sink in.

The first reporting I did—and the beginning of my still-current experiment in investigative commentary—was to read the fine print in the footnotes of a Senate committee report. As an old speechwriter, I could tell when the Church committee report-writer was artfully trying not to say something with the term "the President's friend." Other reporters already had printed the story of J.F.K.'s relationship with the girlfriend of the head of the Chicago Mafia, but not in the "big," attention-getting media. I went with it, *The Times* picked it up and went with it on the front page, and I began to see what a little poking-around could do. The story was not so much the President's relationship with a gangster's moll as it was the deliberate cover-up of the episode by a committee out after different dirt.

Interesting. It made me some new friends and some new enemies, and changed the nature of my work.

THE KENNEDY TRANSCRIPTS

February 20, 1975

WASHINGTON—Benjamin Bradlee, executive editor of *The Washington Post*, was a close personal friend of President Kennedy. In *Conversations With Kennedy*, a book transcribing his notes that is previewed in this month's *Playboy* magazine, Mr. Bradlee makes a few revelations, not all of them intentional.

On Kennedy's seduction of the press: As a *Newsweek* correspondent covering the 1960 Kennedy-Nixon campaign, Mr. Bradlee admits that he "wanted Kennedy to win." After his friend did win, Mr. Bradlee saw nothing improper in soliciting President Kennedy's advice—generously given—about which reporters to hire for *Newsweek*'s Washington bureau. "If I was had," says editor Bradlee in a related context, "so be it"; not all of *Newsweek*'s trusting readers will be so philosophical.

On Kennedy's use of language: Nothing we have read in other Presidential transcripts approaches the frequency and pungency of profanity that Mr. Bradlee unnecessarily ascribes to President Kennedy. Such lines as "they (deleted) us and we've got to try to (deleted) them," with the word I have deleted filled in, may add verisimilitude to the conversations, but are they really a contribution to history? Antedating John Dean by one full decade, Mr. Bradlee quotes President Kennedy directly as saying of steel-executive adversaries: "We're going to tuck it to them and (deleted) 'em."

On the abuse of power: Toasting Attorney General Robert Kennedy at a dinner party, the President referred to a telephone conversation with Tom Patton, president of Republic Steel:

"Patton asked me, 'Why is it that all the telephones of all the steel executives in the country are being tapped?' And I told him that I thought he was being wholly unfair to the Attorney General and that I was sure that it wasn't true. And he asked me, 'Why is it that all the income-tax returns of all the steel executives in the country are being scrutinized?' And I told him that, too, was wholly unfair. . . . And then I called the Attorney General and asked him why he was tapping the telephones of all the steel executives and examining the tax returns of all the steel executives . . . and the Attorney General told me that was wholly untrue and unfair." After what Mr. Bradlee describes as "another Stanislavsky pause," President Kennedy added, "Of course, Patton was right."

On concern for history and tradition: When President Kennedy was told of a rumor that his Air Force aide's girlfriend "had taken a dip in the pool at midnight and had been seen later jumping on the bed in the Lincoln Room," he directed Mrs. Kennedy to "get after" the aide, but not immediately. Mr. Bradlee found it "interesting" that the President did not question the rumor.

On two profiles in courage: President Kennedy confided to Mr. Bradlee that billionaire J. Paul Getty had paid only $500 in income tax one year: Asked about tax reform to prevent this, the President's answer was "maybe after 1964." On another politically sensitive subject, Mr. Bradlee writes: "He said he was all for people's solving their problems by abortion (and he specifically told me I could not use that for publication in *Newsweek*)."

On insistence upon the rectitude of one's running mate: President Kennedy is quoted as saying he felt sure that Lyndon Johnson had not been "on the take since he was elected" Vice President. Before that, he said, "I'm not so sure."

On "hardball" campaign tactics: After quoting a Kennedy remark about Nelson Rockefeller that is unprintable here, Mr. Bradlee delicately drops a clue to the source of the vicious draft-dodger attack on Hubert Humphrey in the West Virginia primary: "It is interesting how often Kennedy referred to the war records of political opponents. He had often mentioned Eddie McCormack and Hubert Humphrey in this connection. . . ."

Nowhere in these early selections from the Kennedy transcripts is there the idealistic uplift and intellectual stimulus that we have been led to associate with the late President. Deploring "kiss-and-tell journalism," Mr. Bradlee says President Kennedy approved of his record of "intimate details," but adds: "I was not convinced he knew how intimate those details might get—though I suspected Jackie did—but that's for another decade."

Think of it—only five more years to wait until the 80's, when Mr. Bradlee will give us names and measurements of all the girls in wet bathing suits who jumped on Mr. Lincoln's bed at midnight.

Conversations With Kennedy proves that if you are President, you do not have to install a secret taping system in order to guarantee the besmearing of your reputation. One trusted confidant who wants to write a gossipy best seller will do.

John F. Kennedy did not need a journalistic "enemies list"; he had Ben Bradlee for a friend.

March 24, 1975

Ms. Charlotte Curtis
Editor, Op-Ed Page
The New York Times

Dear Ms. Curtis:

I respect the desire of *The Times* to offer a broad range of opinion on its Op-Ed Page. I recognize, also, that the pool of conservative writers is limited: for an articulate exponent of that philosophy, where do you go after William Buckley?

To William Safire, obviously. Mr. Safire is indeed a skillful word-monger, articulate enough for any journal, and witty to boot.

Unlike all the other writers whose work I have read regularly in *The Times*, however, Mr. Safire does not play straight with his readers. He uses his verbal skill not to persuade by force or reason, but to manipulate.

I have not kept tabs, but my resentment has been growing. It was brought to the point of protest by last week's column on Benjamin Bradlee's recollections of John F. Kennedy. Mr. Safire appeared to be assailing Mr. Bradlee for dishonoring the memory of a dead President: what he was actually doing was recounting, for an audience most of which would probably never see the book, the juiciest episodes in Kennedy's disfavor. I expect to read the book, and I expect to find that in context, the bits excerpted are far less damaging.

By providing space for this kind of trickery, I think *The Times* demeans itself.

Sincerely yours,
Virginia Franklin
(Mrs. D. S. Franklin)
Thornwood, New York

THE PRESIDENT'S FRIEND

December 15, 1975

WASHINGTON—Senators Frank Church and Gary Hart, acting like a couple of frightened men, have been forcing intelligence committee staff members to sign affidavits swearing the staffers were not the source of leaks of the committee's most closely guarded secret.

The secret was hinted at on page 129 of the committee report on C.I.A. assassination attempts. While straining to show that President Kennedy did not know that the C.I.A. had hired Mafia chiefs John Roselli and Sam

Giancana to arrange the assassination of Fidel Castro, the committee report reluctantly and guardedly revealed a Kennedy-Mafia connection.

"Evidence before the committee," the report reads, "indicates that a close friend of President Kennedy had frequent contact with the President from the end of 1960 through mid-1962. F.B.I. reports and testimony indicate the President's friend was also a close friend of John Roselli and Sam Giancana and saw them often during this same period."

The report footnotes that "White House telephone logs show seventy instances of phone contact between the White House and the President's friend whose testimony confirms frequent phone contact with the President himself. Both the President's friend and Roselli testified that the friend did not know about either the assassination operation or the wiretap case. Giancana was killed before he was available for questioning."

There the Church committee hoped the matter would rest. But the reason for the "plumbers'" operation—complete with threats of perjury and warnings of lie-detector tests—was the investigative reporting of Dan Thomasson and Tim Wyngaard of the Scripps-Howard Washington bureau.

According to their sources, which they say include F.B.I. documents, "the President's friend" was a beautiful girl who divided her time between the Chicago underworld leadership and the President of the United States. The President's secretary, Mrs. Evelyn Lincoln, is reported to have testified that the purpose of the almost twice-weekly calls over a year's time was to set up meetings between the President and his friend.

The private life of any public figure is nobody's business but his own, and salacious gossip of White House kennelkeepers and self-described intimates can be dismissed as offensive. But when the nation's Chief Executive receives even a few calls from the *home telephone* of the leader of the Mafia in Chicago, that crosses the line into the public's business.

That is particularly the case when—of all Mafia leaders around—the one with whom the President shared a close friend turns out to be the one whom the C.I.A. selects to handle arrangements for the assassination of Fidel Castro, and the one who is murdered just before testifying.

F.B.I. documents show that J. Edgar Hoover, whose agents were watching "Momo" Giancana and John Roselli as part of Attorney General Robert Kennedy's war on organized crime, discovered the link between the President and the Mafia leaders. On February 27, 1962, Mr. Hoover alerted Robert Kennedy and aide Kenneth O'Donnell to the associations of the President's friend, and on March 22, the F.B.I. director took another memo on this subject to a luncheon meeting with President Kennedy. After that, the relationship was abruptly broken off. That must have been some lunch.

But substantive questions remain: (1) Since gangland figures are concerned about the liaisons of their girlfriends, did the Mafia figures encourage the girl's White House relationship, and if so, to what end? (2) Did Director Hoover's obvious concern with Mr. Giancana's White House connection suddenly cut off just short of knowledge of the Giancana-C.I.A. plot to get Castro? (3) Why did Mr. Hoover check in with the C.I.A. and then tell a Las Vegas sheriff to stop prosecuting Giancana for wiretapping an unfaithful girlfriend—right after his luncheon showdown with President Kennedy?

Too many coincidences here. When Mafia leaders and a President share the same girl's attentions; when those two Mafiosi are chosen to make the hit on a foreign leader by our C.I.A.; when the delivery of poison pellets is made to one of them on the weekend the President is with the girl in Florida; when the F.B.I. is listening in, and cautioning the President—and when the President winds up murdered by a supporter of Castro, target of the aborted C.I.A. assassination plot, the matter is worth a thorough public examination.

The Church committee has attempted a cover-up from the Government's end; the Mafia, by silencing Giancana forever, has clamped down the lid from its end.

Thanks to the Thomasson-Wyngaard reporting, however, the story of the President's friend gives us a useful clue to a related mystery: why the Kennedy men were so ready to acquiesce in the wiretapping and bugging of Dr. Martin Luther King.

The clue: After that luncheon in March 1962, when the F.B.I. director laid out the evidence of the Mafia connections of the President's friend, the Kennedys must have been prepared to do anything and everything J. Edgar Hoover wanted.

MURDER MOST FOUL

December 22, 1975

WASHINGTON—The revelation that the President of the United States had regular access to a woman who may have been controlled by two Mafia gangsters hired by the C.I.A. to kill Fidel Castro has had the expected reaction: prurient interest, compounded daily, in the logistics of White House sex, whether Jackie knew, etc.

Forget all that. The serious issue in the Kennedy-Mafia connection is murder—"murder most foul, as in the best it is. . . ." Not hanky-panky, not graft, not abuse of civil liberty—but murder and attempted murder at the highest level that spans 15 years.

The first murder target was Prime Minister Castro, against whom the Kennedy men and the Mafia shared a hatred. The second might have been President Kennedy himself, in retaliation or self-protection. The most recent, only six months ago, was Sam Giancana, the Chicago mobster who failed to carry out his mission to hit Castro, and who presumably encouraged one of his girls to nourish a White House-Mafia liaison.

Sam Giancana was shot dead in his Oak Park, Ill., home, after the Church committee had decided to subpoena his testimony. He is the only person in American history to be murdered just before he was to appear in front of a Congressional committee.

What was the reaction to this unique event? Church committee sources, Mafia sources, and Chicago police sources (who share an interest in forgetting Mr. Giancana) all put out the line that the murder was probably an old Mafia grudge fight, unrelated to any impending testimony. Senator Church's colleague in cover-up, Senator John Tower of Texas, promptly declared that Giancana would not have been "a particularly valuable witness."

I don't believe any of that pap. I suggest that two and two makes four: that Sam Giancana took seven .22-caliber slugs in his body for the same reason that Prosecutor Thomas E. Dewey's witness, Abe Reles, was thrown out of the window of the Half Moon Hotel nearly four decades ago—to keep him from telling all he knew.

And how has the Senate, so sensitive to contempt, reacted to the first murder of a witness to be called before a Senate committee? Did Chairman Church demand that the F.B.I. enter the case to explore this most effective obstruction of justice?

No. An F.B.I. spokesman informs me that nobody has asked the F.B.I. to investigate, and not one agent has been assigned to the case. Sam Skinner, United States Attorney in Chicago, adds that murder is not a Federal crime, so he's out of it. Chicago police reply that the murder took place in the suburbs, outside their jurisdiction, and they're out of it. (The two Chicago policemen who had been parked outside the Giancana house, and who suddenly left their post just before the murder, will probably get a medal.)

That leaves the investigation of the murder of the only Mafia hood who might have penetrated the White House in the hands of Cook County State's Attorney Bernard Carey, a good man doing the best he can, but life in Cook County is a struggle: A local judge was able to block search of the dead Giancana's safe for several months. (When it was finally opened, the judge's name appeared on a list of those who gave generous wedding presents to Mr. Giancana's daughter.)

The Cook County grand jury is not thinking in terms of national, or

Mafia-wide, implications, and has not even called John Roselli, Giancana's lieutenant. "We've had difficulties," admits Carey, "we get a runaround from Federal authorities."

A couple of local cops in suburban Oak Park still show an interest, and have found the murder weapon. Unlike Senator Church, at least one cop on the scene thinks the mobster's impending testimony was the cause of his demise.

"Giancana had something to say," says Lieutenant Donald Corkle of the Oak Park police. But what of Giancana's fabled willingness to sit in jail without talking, which he had done before? Why should the Mafia worry about him spilling secrets of a White House penetration to the Senate committee?

"He just got out of the hospital the day before he was killed. He sure didn't want to go to jail, not in the shape he was in. They knew that, and they got worried about him."

Not an important witness, Senator Tower assures us. Not relevant, Senator Church insists. Forget it; just a gangland "termination with extreme prejudice."

But the dead body of Sam Giancana lies across Frank Church's path to the Presidency. Only the appointment of a special prosecutor at the request of the Senate—a new "untouchable" with full powers to explore the White House-Mafia connections that led to Giancana's murder and cover-up—will uncover a potential scandal that most Washington politicians and journalists wish would go away.

Senator Church cannot slam the lid of Pandora's box back down now that he has glimpsed the evil that lurks therein. As that great matchmaker of Mafia hoodlums, good-looking women and a President of the United States used to croon: "All—or nothing at all."

PUT YOUR DREAMS AWAY: THE SINATRA CONNECTION

January 5, 1976

WASHINGTON—In a recent essay about the way Senators Frank Church and John Tower were trying to conceal a connection between the Kennedy White House and the Mafia mobsters assigned to kill Fidel Castro, I concluded:

"Senator Church cannot slam the lid of Pandora's box back down now that he has glimpsed the evil that lurks therein. As that great matchmaker

of Mafia hoodlums, good-looking women and a President of the United States used to croon: 'All—or nothing at all.' "

A Beverly Hills attorney, Milton A. Rudin, has kindly sent me a copy of a letter he wrote to *The New York Times*, which reads in part:

"There is no question in the minds of many readers that the last sentence refers to my client, Frank Sinatra."

After objecting to my "yellow journalism" in general, Mr. Sinatra's lawyer underscored the "e" in "women," and suggested that readers might infer from that word that his client had been acting as a procurer. He says he is not filing a libel action because of "the horrendous state of the law" on that subject, and because:

"Our client has not issued any statement concerning the stories which have appeared in the press concerning President Kennedy and Judith Campbell because he refuses to join in the chorus of ghoulish scandalmongers. A libel action would have the same effect. Even the printing of a retraction continues this shameful episode in the history of the American press."

At the risk of such shameful continuance, I concede one point: "Women," plural, should have read "woman," singular. The Church committee's interim cover-up reported only one instance of a person introducing a friend of unspecified gender to Mr. Kennedy and also introducing that same friend to Mafioso Giancana.

Committee sources cited in many publications have identified that introducer as Mr. Sinatra, which charge he has not denied. Nor does his attorney deny it now, and it is logical to assume that he would have refuted the charge in his letter if Mr. Sinatra had not been the middleman, or matchmaker, in this particular White House-Mafia connection.

Accordingly, we in the ghoulish-scandalmonger set would like to know why the Church committee never called Mr. Sinatra to testify under oath, nor even had an investigator call him up. One man, presumably Mr. Sinatra, brought together a mobster and a woman, and a President and that same woman; the mobster was the one hired by the C.I.A. in that President's Administration to murder a head of state; as an investigation began in 1975, the mobster was silenced permanently with seven bullets. And Senator Church decided not to hear from the man who probably built the original bridge.

Here are a few of the questions Senators Church and Tower were duty-bound to ask Mr. Sinatra. I regret the innuendo necessarily burdening these shots in the dark, but in view of the Senators' craven reluctance to ask them, and Mr. Sinatra's stated unwillingness to "issue a statement," I know of no other way to set the questions forth.

· When did you introduce Sam Giancana to Judith Campbell, if you did, and at whose request? When did you introduce Miss Campbell to either of the Kennedy brothers? Do you know if the Kennedys were ever aware of Miss Campbell's close association with the mobster Giancana and his lieutenant, John Roselli? Did the mobsters ask you to introduce her or anyone else to the Kennedys?

• Did you ever see Judith Campbell and John Kennedy together, or Messrs. Giancana and/or Roselli and Miss Campbell together? Did you make available premises controlled by you to any of them? Did Sam Giancana or John Roselli ever boast to you about Miss Campbell's calls and trips to the White House?

• To your knowledge, Mr. Sinatra, were any recordings made of any meetings between Judith Campbell and John Kennedy, or were any pictures taken of them that could have been used by organized crime for blackmail purposes? Were you aware of any communications between the President and the men hired to kill Fidel Castro through the woman you introduced to both? Did Sam Giancana tell you how he persuaded the C.I.A. to bug a Las Vegas hotel room on his behalf?

• What was the content of your last conversations with Sam Giancana, John Roselli, and Judith Campbell? Was Mr. Giancana fearful, and if so, did he tell you why?

• Did any member of the Kennedy family, including in-laws, tell you about the plot to kill Fidel Castro? Did Sam Giancana or John Roselli mention it to you?

• Was your association with Sam Giancana, which cost you the right to own part of a casino in Nevada, the cause of your break with the President? When President Kennedy changed his plans to stay with you in Palm Springs, and switched to the home of Bing Crosby, did Robert Kennedy give you the reason why? Did he mention a visit to the President by J. Edgar Hoover?

• Did you ever intervene with the Kennedys to get the Justice Department to stop an investigation?

• Before or after the Kennedy assassination in Dallas, did Sam Giancana or John Roselli ever mention the name of Jack Ruby to you?

Mr. Sinatra, who admirably refuses to abandon friends after their popularity fades, might emerge from such an interrogation with honor bright.

But we can put our dreams away for another day; Frank Church, dart-gunning for the Presidency, needs Kennedy support and has accordingly aborted any future hearings of his cover-up committee. We are left to ponder what might have been learned if only "Ol' Blue-Eyes" could have been required to sing.

ALL IN THE FAMILY

January 26, 1976

WASHINGTON—Mafia mobsters and Kennedy mythkeepers can heave sighs of relief; Frank Church's cover-up committee has decided not to question Frank Sinatra on his role in making possible the first penetration of the White House by organized crime. Nor will Senator Church ask the F.B.I. to investigate the first murder of a prospective Senate witness.

The reason can be found in the way the committee staff was organized. Frank Church first asked John Doar, fresh from impeachment triumphs, for advice. After peopling the committee staff with members of the Kennedy Protective Society, Mr. Doar recommended Burke Marshall (the lawyer Ted Kennedy called in panic from Chappaquiddick), who told Senator Church he would serve as a consultant recruiting suitable lawyers, and who recommended F.A.O. "Fritz" Schwarz 3d to be staff chief.

Count the connections. Mr. Schwarz is a partner of Cravath, Swaine and Moore, the New York law firm that represents IBM; Burke Marshall, a Kennedy Assistant Attorney General, was IBM general counsel from 1965 to 1970; Nicholas Katzenbach, Kennedy Deputy Attorney General, followed him as IBM general counsel, working closely with Mr. Schwarz at Cravath. Roswell Gilpatric, Kennedy Deputy Defense Secretary, is the top man at Cravath.

Now count the cover-ups.

1. *The Ramsey Clark-John Doar cover-up.* As the Church committee blamed J. Edgar Hoover for abuses under Presidents Kennedy and Johnson, no spotlight was focused on the infamous September 27, 1967, memo from Assistant Attorney General John Doar to his boss, Ramsey Clark.

In the Doar plan, approved by Mr. Clark, snooping on dissident groups was raised to a fine art; Mr. Doar urged that the I.R.S. be used, especially its alcohol unit in ghetto areas, and went on: "The Narcotics Bureau is another possibility, and finally, my experience in Detroit suggests that the Post Office Department might be helpful." Mr. Doar was never called; Mr. Clark was never asked to explain. But C.I.A. men are facing grand juries now about their postal "experiences."

2. *The Katzenbach cover-up.* Robert Kennedy's deputy and successor angrily demanded a retraction when I suggested he condoned the scandalous wiretapping and bugging of Martin Luther King Jr., but he professed to amazement when later confronted with his initials and handwriting on scurrilous eavesdropping reports. An aggressive committee lawyer could have forced out more of the truth about the worst abuse of police power in our time—but Mr. Katzenbach easily ducked the committee's marshmallows.

3. *The Roswell L. ("Dearest Ros") Gilpatric cover-up.* In the cases

of his partner, Mr. Gilpatric, and his client, Mr. Katzenbach, Church counsel Schwarz scrupulously "rescued" himself, but the staffers who worked with him got the picture.

Although Mr. Gilpatric was the highest-ranking Kennedy aide working on "Operation Mongoose," the undeclared war on Cuba, the Church interim cover-up plays down his role. And a "Mongoose" plan for "incapacitating" Cuban sugar workers by spraying chemicals on them is dismissed by Church staffers with: "After a study showed the plan to be unfeasible, it was canceled. . . ."

The Church staff chose not to make public the memorandum in its possession that casts a different light on the matter. "In the office of the Attorney General," to use a recently favored term, a plan was seriously discussed to launch a chemical attack on Cuban workers (the chemical had a mortality rate of "only 3 percent") and it was postponed for two specific reasons: (1) Harvesttime was past, and (2) the Kennedys could not get their hands on enough of the chemical at that time.

4. *The Kennedy tainting-of-evidence cover-up.* Senator Church has touched gently on wiretaps approved by Attorney General Robert Kennedy on "at least six" American citizens.

This has not been revealed: One of those taps—and the reason for Senator Church's "at least six" fuzziness—was on a Washington law firm. One imagines that a firm of lawyers has more than one client; those lawyers sometimes work on more than one case.

As we have seen, even inadvertent intrusion taints evidence, and Kennedy Justice Department lawyers were duty-bound to tell every court on every case handled by that tapped law firm just what if anything was overheard. Did they? Did Senator Church ask?

The law firm has requested that the Church committee withhold its name, as I have done, to protect a victim's privacy, but the Churchmen went on from there to conceal the fact of the tapping of a law firm entirely, which only protects the perpetrator's privacy.

Perhaps the tap was so surgical it involved no other clients, and never picked up legal advice—that's for the American Bar Association to demand to know. But of one thing we can be sure: Any lawyers overhead talking to their clients in 1962 did not belong to that well-connected, all-in-the-family firm of Cravath, Swaine and Moore.

Jan. 26, 1976

Editor,
New York Times

Dear Sir,
The politically wanton misdeeds of the Kennedys, Katzenbachs, et al., whines William Safire, should not be swept under the rug. Amen.

But does their misbehavior make the Nixon-Mitchell frolics any less odious? Safire cries, if they could do it why couldn't we?

Why this childish pap should appear in the august columns of *The New York Times* escapes me.

Ralph J. Appleton
Douglaston, New York

ALL IN THE FAMILY: II

January 29, 1976

WASHINGTON—In our last episode, readers were left breathless by revelations of an interlocking directorate of Old Kennedy Hands who set up the Church committee staff in a way that makes easy the cover-up of abuses of power in the 60's.

In today's episode, we go from cozy relationships to actual relatives.

1. *The brother-in-law.* Rule 6.4 of the Church committee calls for the committee to "endeavor to obtain voluntary counsel" for witnesses.

Sounds like an admirable service for indigents. In practice, this is how it worked: A Kennedy appointee named Daniel Rezneck, of Arnold and Porter, then head of the D.C. Bar Association, was asked to draw up a list of attorneys with top-secret clearances. His friend, John Denniston—a Government contract man at Covington and Burling—came up with a secret list of lawyers to receive the business (for a fee—"voluntary" has not meant free).

When Judith Campbell Exner was called, her lawyer also represented Robert Maheu (interesting lead) and begged off; a Church staffer then called the handful of approved lawyers to see who was available quickly. No volunteers.

Then, with the approval of F.A.O. Schwarz 3d, chief Church counsel, the woman who was President Kennedy's Mafia link was put in touch with a member of the law firm of the Kennedy brother-in-law, Sargent Shriver. Such referral is improper on its face; no investigating body can ethically recommend specific lawyers to witnesses. The Shriver firm did represent her at the committee and did discuss fees for future representation.

But the committee insists its staff did not know Mr. Shriver was in that law firm it told Mrs. Exner to call; Mr. Shriver insists the lawyer on his staff who took the job didn't clear it on high. If you believe all that, give my regards to the Tooth Fairy, but remember this incident when Mr. Shriver delivers his delegates to Mr. Church at the convention.

2. *The son-in-law.* One of the four "task forces" of the Church committee concerns itself with military intelligence abuses, and has been investigating the Defense Department and the National Security Agency.

Naturally, a key witness has been Robert McNamara, the Kennedy-Johnson Secretary of Defense whose computerlike mind has emptied its memory bank of all recollection of assassination plots.

Whom did Frank Church select to be the deputy chief of this military intelligence section? Answer: Barry Carter, a former Kissinger protégé, a brilliant mind, a likely future leader of the national security establishment, whose experience qualifies him in every way for the job. One small problem: For seven years, up to two years ago, he was Robert McNamara's son-in-law.

"Not one scintilla of evidence," to use John Tower's favorite phrase, suggests that Mr. McNamara's former son-in-law was not fervent and relentless in his pursuit of any transgressions by his former wife's father. Mr. Carter asserts he avoided the assassination area entirely, and points with justifiable pride to his work on the "Shamrock" intercepts of cable traffic. We shall see how the final report treats Kennedy-Johnson intelligence abuses in the military area.

But is this not what Senator Church would call in others "the appearance of conflict of interest"? The rough equivalent would have been for Leon Jaworski to hire Ed Cox or David Eisenhower to investigate Richard Nixon.

3. *The son.* From the very nave of the Church committee, sources report that when staffers went up to the Kennedy Library in Waltham, Mass., suspicious gaps were discovered in the telephone logs of the President's calls. Nor was there any record of a private telephone, installed in a tiny room just off the Oval Office, where Mr. Kennedy made private calls outside the White House switchboard.

One Church staffer, however, who has tried unsuccessfully to link President Eisenhower to the Lumumba assassination, was especially warmly received at the Kennedy Library.

He is Peter Fenn, and he is the son of Dan Fenn, the former assistant to President Kennedy who is now the director of that same Kennedy Library. Mr. Fenn the younger was given free access to the files of Robert Kennedy there by Mr. Fenn the elder, and cynics will question whether a vigorous search for Kennedy wrongdoing was conducted.

Now, if Frank Church—who needs Kennedy support in his Presidential candidacy—wants to do Ted Kennedy a favor by putting a 25-year-old kid at the public trough for $400 a week for six months, that's politics. But isn't it a bit unfair to young Mr. Fenn, who is Senator Church's son's best friend, to start him off in a situation with such an apparent conflict of interest? Let's assume he's a nice, honest, idealistic young man—why break him in on a cover-up?

Old-fashioned nepotism is not at issue here, nor are the young staffers culpable. Instead, we see what happens when a Certified Good Guy is convinced he has the press in his pocket: Arrogantly, brazenly, Frank Church has turned his investigation into a relative thing.

FRANK AND JACK AND SAM AND JUDY

June 13, 1977

WASHINGTON—In late 1975, a fascinating story that had been carefully buried on page six of *The Washington Post*, ignored by the national media when covered by the Scripps-Howard newspapers, and brushed aside in a footnote by the Senate committee investigating the C.I.A. was given serious treatment in this space.

The story was about the close relationship between President John F. Kennedy and a beautiful woman who was also the friend of Sam Giancana and John Roselli, Mafia bosses who had been hired by the C.I.A. to murder Fidel Castro.

Now more details of that hard-to-believe connection are available in *Judith Exner: My Story*, a Grove Press book I picked up the other day over the counter in a bookstore.

Mrs. Exner's self-serving confession, as told to Ovid Demaris, will be dismissed as distasteful, seedy, unnecessarily sensational, unfairly selective, salaciously gossipy, perhaps psychologically sick. All of which it is.

But there is a core of checkable truth to this story that exposes—for the first time from near the inside—the cancerous connective tissue that exists, apparently to this day, between the underworld, show business, and politics.

Mrs. Exner, then Judy Campbell, says she first met Frank Sinatra on November 10, 1959, upon his invitation to spend a weekend with him in Hawaii. For more than a year, she was one of Frank's girls, part of the rat-pack section of the Hollywood crowd. On February 7, 1960, she was invited to Las Vegas by Mr. Sinatra, and in Dean Martin's hotel suite found herself being introduced to Presidential candidate John F. Kennedy. Mr. Sinatra was evidently not possessive; Mrs. Exner says her affair with Mr. Kennedy began in New York on March 7, 1960, the eve of the New Hampshire primary.

The following week, Judy Exner flew to Miami at Mr. Sinatra's invitation. In his room was "Joe Fish"—Joseph Fischetti, brother of dead Mafiosi Charles and Rocco Fischetti, and cousin of Al Capone. She says that Mr. Sinatra, aware of her new Kennedy relationship, advised her: "Get with it. Swing a little."

On March 27, as she was still puzzling over Mr. Sinatra's admonition to "wake up and realize what you've got in the palm of your hand," the singer introduced her to a man he called "Sam Flood," one of the aliases of Momo Salvatore "Sam" Giancana, a mobster who in 1960 was undisputed boss of Chicago's underworld, with extensive gambling interests in Cuba.

Thus, with Mr. Sinatra as matchmaker, began the most startling dual relationship in the history of crime and politics: For almost two years, one woman was simultaneously seeing the nation's most powerful mobster and the nation's most powerful political leader.

From the start, mobster Giancana knew exactly with whom he was sharing the young woman's affections. Since the appearance of power is a form of power, he was able to use his girlfriend's access to the Presidential candidate—and later to the White House itself—to make a lasting impression on his gangland associates.

Kennedy myth-protectors can no longer deny the relationship documented in dreary detail by Mrs. Exner and Government records, but insist that it was pure coincidence that the Mafia chief chosen by the C.I.A. to assassinate Fidel Castro was Giancana, along with another close friend of Mrs. Exner's, John Roselli.

Mrs. Exner denies she was the go-between in this plot but cites other instances where entertainers like Jerry Lewis and Eddie Fisher, terrified of mob power, used her to pass messages to Giancana.

Great fun while it lasted, as the young woman accepted gifts from the Irish Mafia and the real Mafia, one day reciprocating: "They both smoked Schimmilpenninck cigars. . . . I went to a jeweler in Beverly Hills and had two solid gold cigar cases made and gave them each one."

But the piper had to be paid. Thanks to the Kennedys, she became a patient of the notorious "Dr. Feelgood," Dr. Max Jacobson, whose drug injections were exposed a few years ago by reporter Martin Tolchin. Thanks to Sam Giancana, she suffered close F.B.I. surveillance, and says she was sent to lawyer Sidney Korshak, whose mysterious showbiz-underworld links were exposed by reporter Seymour Hersh.

Skip the gossip and study the pattern that emerges: A series of links exist between underworld and political world through the world of show business.

At J. Edgar Hoover's behest, John Kennedy finally dropped her (she denies that); the reader can assume that because her usefulness as a White House link ended, Mr. Giancana and Mr. Sinatra drifted away. Of Judy's friends, Jack Kennedy was shot, possibly in retaliation for Sam

Giancana's Cuban efforts; Mr. Giancana was executed by the Mafia just before he was to testify; John Roselli was murdered afterward.

The lone survivor: the matchmaker, "Ol' Blue-Eyes" himself, Frank Sinatra. Thanks to an introduction by Mr. and Mrs. Robert Wagner, the late Mr. Giancana's friend has been spending much time in the company of New York Governor Hugh Carey, and is being sought for his help in raising funds for Mario Cuomo in his race for Mayor of New York.

The Media

W HEN YOU LIKE US, we're the press; when you hate us, we're the media. Here are the opinions of one member of the press about the media.

ON ESSAYS

May 30, 1974

WASHINGTON—Nothing much is going to happen in June.

A genuine peace could settle over the Middle East, of course, and the Supreme Court could enter the Watergate case; perhaps an arms control breakthrough will avert World War III, or an upheaval in China will bring it closer. The first untimely economic recovery could get under way.

Otherwise, June is doomed to be a dull news month, an interlude Joseph Goebbels would have called a "creative pause" or what the Al Capone mob would have considered to be a time for Nitti-gritti.

The interlude was heralded by the play given to reverse news recently: "The weekend the President did not resign" made headlines as did the fact that the First National City Bank did not raise its interest rate to 12 percent. Unhappenings have become newsworthy: "Man does not bite dog" is news.

Accordingly, I'm going to take my vacation now, before Messrs. Doar, Jenner, and the rest of the impeach fuzz make it impossible to leave town at all, and will resume these essays from wherever the flying White House may be at the end of the month.

After a year's columny, a personal word might be in order. I did not turn in my speechwriter's typewriter (still smoking from the "nattering nabobs of negativism") in order to don the casual cashmere of casuistry. On the contrary, I had hoped to become more of an essayist than a columnist—perhaps a slow Swift or a hazy Hazlitt, a strident Strunsky or a winkin' Mencken—rather than a columnist delivering topical broadsides from his ukasy chair.

A column is a signed editorial, a polemic, some form of opinionated revelation, a view with a sharp point on urgent matters. An essay finds consequence in the inconsequential, seeking new routes to the tops of mountains that have been climbed before.

An essayist uses current events as a springboard into his own world. After looking into President Nixon's transcripts, Montaigne might have written "Of the Affection of Fathers"; David Hume "Of Liberty and Necessity"; Charles Lamb "A Chapter on Ears"; Francis Bacon "On Simulation and Dissimulation"; George Orwell "Inside the Whale," and Richard Steele "On Deference to Public Opinion" or "On Growing Old."

An essayist creates his own world, and confronts reality; a columnist reacts to the real world, and confronts absurdity. (That's an essay-style sentence, perfectly balanced and murky enough to pass for wisdom.) The field of columnists is burgeoning, but it is hard to think of anyone today who makes a vocation out of the art of the essay.

Why, then, haven't I eschewed the crowded field of the columnists and marched to my different drummer? Why, after one essay, do I get drawn into three or four columns?

One reason is that my different drummer has just marched out of Walden Pond and it is hard to catch the beat of his wet drum. Another reason is that we are living through one of the great dramas of the century, picking our way through a constitutional minefield, and to write of other matters often requires an effort of will (good title for George Will's column).

The President derides "wallowing in Watergate," but to wallow is not only to roll about but to take delight and to luxuriate; the use, abuse, and perception of power offer everyone writing today the chance to probe into probity, an unalloyed joy, and my own, seemingly lonely opposition to impeachment affords me a private wallowing pen with hot and cold running leaks.

Small wonder, then, that I have been so often seduced from the ambition of essaying. So are we all seduced, and should not feel guilty about it: The sudden revocation of a mandate, the curious similarity of bloodlust that turns opponents into enemies, the varying interpretations of our malleable Constitution, are like a preoccupying army.

If we are going to have a fixation about government fixing, then let us fix on it—time enough, after the crisis is past, to verify verities with essays On Political Loyalty, On the Art of Swearing, On Egil Ellsberg, On Trusting Lawyers, On Culpa for Mayor and On the Eyes of History Are Upon You.

And so I shall spend the next few weeks trying to fight off periodic attacks of perspective, so as to return unapologetic about dealing with Topic A at least every other time.

Eventually, however, this national convulsion will end, the fascination will fade, the happenings will get more coverage than the unhappenings, and would-be essayists who are now grimly hung up on the timely can go traipsing off in pursuit of the timeless.

ONE OF OUR OWN

September 19, 1974

WASHINGTON—You are the President's press secretary. You are privy to a secret which, if revealed, would force the President into premature action. A reporter with a small piece of the secret asks you about it.

What do you do? You could say you do not know, which is a lie. You could say you know the story is untrue, which is a worse lie. You could become suddenly unavailable, which is a betrayal of your job responsibility. Or you could tell the truth, thereby betraying the President's trust and isolating you from access to private discussions in the future.

Subtler alternatives exist. You could say, "There are no present plans to do that," which is journalistic argot for "plans will soon be announced, but I cannot say so now."

Or you could say, insultingly, "I won't say, and I don't care how often you badger me or how many different ways you put the question," thereby calling down wrath about the arrogance of power. Or you may repeat blandly, "I have no information to give you on that," which will soon be denounced as "stonewalling."

President Ford's first press secretary, Gerald terHorst, saw that the dilemma would soon become intolerable. He probably quit because other White House aides did not tell him the whole truth about pre-pardon negotiations; but if they had, and his disagreement with policy had been noted and set aside, he would then have had the problem of misleading, ducking, or blabbing. This was a truly terrifying prospect to a genuine newsman, and Mr. terHorst wisely stepped out, to universal acclaim, on grounds of conscience.

To come to grips with the problem this illustrates, change roles. You are now the President. You may be reconsidering some foreign problem and not want to face a question that forces you to repeat the old line (which you may change soon) or reveal the fact of your review (which may lead to no change). In next week's press conference, you will be prepared to handle it decisively.

Meanwhile, what do you do about your Daniel, who has to climb into the lions' den twice a day and might face that question? Do you tell him about your secret deliberation, asking him to turn aside those questions in his most guileful way, or do you keep him in the dark, so that he can be honest in his ignorance even if later scorned for not having access to inner councils?

Change roles a final time. You are now The Press. (Playing the hero is more fun.) Do you want a press secretary who is a poker-faced unflappable who knows how to give you so much, lets you pull out an anticipated 20 percent more in questioning, and then skillfully shuts the door in your face as he slips into confidential discussions in the Oval Office?

Or would you prefer one of your own, a respected newsman, who will fight for more openness in the Administration, who will never shade the truth, but who will be treated by the President as an in-house adversary, dealt with but not trusted? He will be a valuable ally, but he will not be much of a source.

Are you better served by a man who knows and cannot tell, but who will not lie, or by one who does not know and may unintentionally mislead?

Though it makes us all feel better to sound off about a press secretary who will "tell the truth," the truth is that his job is often to withhold the truth—never to lie, that is wrong, but to put on a poker face and be less than candid on matters that are half-baked or on the verge of decision.

Why, then, in an assignment that requires the same kind of compromise with principle that reporters make when misleading readers to protect a source, do we yearn for the imagery of a crusty newshawk—in the job of one who must deny information to crusty newshawks? "One of our own" will soon have to cross the street, and on-the-job training is costly: Are newsmen not better off with a professional spokesman who understands the professional needs of journalists?

A good press secretary speaks up for the press to the President and speaks out for the President to the press. He makes his home in the pitted no-man's-land of an adversary relationship and is primarily an advocate, interpreter, and amplifier. He must be more the President's man than the press's man, but he can be his own man as well.

An honest man can take the job and infuse it with his own integrity. We make it harder for him to be honest by demanding he shut his eyes to the shades of gray and pretend to be "one of our own."

REAR WINDOW

September 23, 1974

WASHINGTON—Looking down and across the street from my eighth-floor window at *The New York Times* Washington bureau the other day, I could see a platoon of blue-helmeted policemen in flak jackets, carrying rifles, preparing to rush down a ramp into a garage.

Recalling a mistake made a generation ago, I hurried to the newsroom to make certain the desk knew of the story breaking across the street. The newsmen were ahead of me; reporter Linda Charlton was already on the scene and she filed an account of the death of D.C. Police Officer Gail Cobb, the first policewoman in the United States killed in the line of duty.

The intrusion of a real news event can come as a jolt into the lives of some of us who pontificate about trends and furnish the fillip of flip philippics. Nor is that disturbance of routine unique to the news business: Everyone has had the experience of dutifully doing one's duty and thereby missing what may be more important.

In 1950, I was a reporter for Tex and Jinx McCrary's interview column in *The New York Herald Tribune*. In a cubicle in the back of my boss's office-apartment on East 63d Street, I was doggedly clicking away despite the commotion that was going on downstairs in the lobby of the town house.

One of the beautiful McCrary secretaries (they were all beautiful, that's why some of us would work for $40 a week) poked her head in the doorway, pointed out the window, and breathlessly began to tell me something. I cut her short.

"Look, Jeanne," I growled in an adolescent Hecht-MacArthur voice, "I'm on a deadline. The only way you get ahead in journalism is to make your deadline no matter what the distraction."

Saying that felt good. It stopped feeling good when I walked downstairs an hour later, the deadline of my innocuous interview feature happily met, to discover a crowd of reporters and policemen milling in the lobby.

The reporter who was there from *The Herald Tribune* informed me that thieves had held up the high-fashion jewelry store on the ground floor, in what was easily the biggest jewel robbery of the year. He then asked me what I was doing there.

When I mumbled that my office was two flights up, and that I had paid no attention to the noise because I was working against a deadline, the reporter said: "You mean this was *The Trib*'s first chance to beat *The Daily News* to a police story, and you blew it?"

He may have exaggerated for emphasis, but it was true enough to hurt. After the crowd had left, I sat on the front stoop of the town house and brooded about the kind of fate that would penalize a man for trying to be conscientious.

A lady in a wide-brimmed black hat, one of the jeweler's regular customers, came down the steps, saw me looking desolate, and stopped to ask me if I was all right. I said thanks, lady, just leave me alone, it wasn't something I wanted to talk about. She tried to communicate again, I gave her the freeze, and she went on.

One of the jewelry store managers came out, pointed to her vanishing form, and said he didn't care if they were robbed as long as they kept customers like that. Like who? "Greta Garbo," he breathed.

Immediately after having missed the news story, I had told the number one target for every interviewer—the mysterious, I-vant-to-be-alone Garbo—that I wanted to be alone.

A re-evaluation of my aptitude for reporting news seemed in order. As an interviewer, I had often asked the people I spoke with: "What was the low point of your life?" (Abe Burrows gave the best answer: "I hate to say, kid, but I think this is it.") Missing the big jewel heist and then rejecting the elusive Garbo was the low point for me.

The lesson of that low point sank in: Concentration is fine, and conscientiousness worthy of a pat on the back, but the pretention that causes us to live our lives with blinders on is punishable by extreme embarrassment. That was why, a generation later, I was more inclined to stare out the window to let the emotions of an event wash over me.

Looking out the window, especially undreamily, is not a waste of time. The world inside our heads, and the world inside our cubicles, ought to be affected more by the world across the street: A contempt for the contemporary only sours our examination of all that awaits us.

Right now, I look out at a parking lot where, just a couple of cars away from my car, a suspected killer was apprehended. I see a park-and-lock sign over a ramp on which a brave young woman, doing her job, was shot to death.

The evidence has been photographed and washed away, the story reported and forgotten, the three-year-old child of the dead policewoman passed on to relatives. But the inclination to look out the window will not soon again be resisted, and the view from the eighth floor will never be the same.

THE NEED TO KNOW

October 17, 1974

WASHINGTON—The Chairman of the House Ways and Means Committee, Wilbur Mills, who has long been regarded as one of the hardest working members of Congress, is now the butt of jokes. A minor driving violation uncovered an apparent peccadillo, and the wags of Washington snicker: "The strippers of the Mills grind slowly."

On the same day, another driving violation took place, this time involving Joan Kennedy, the wife of the Senator. This event received press coverage, too; the general reaction was properly one of sympathy.

Great newspapers differed on the way these stories were played. *The Washington Post* assigned a dozen reporters to cover the Mills affair and ran it above the fold on the front page, mentioning the Joan Kennedy story in a back section; *The Washington Star-News* juxtaposed both stories on the front page; *The New York Times* covered the Mills story fully but on an inside page and ran the Kennedy accident as a minor item.

Serious editors gave thought to the play of these stories, and the fact that such different conclusions were reached illustrates one of the dilemmas of our times: How can we protect the individual's right to privacy and at the same time defend the public's right to know? A refinement of that dilemma: What part of a public person's life should remain private? When does the public have a right *not* to know?

The answers cannot be found in law but in custom and taste, which are changing in a way—unfortunately, in my view—that make more acceptable snooping into and gossiping about the habits of celebrated people.

In *FDR's Last Year*, a carefully researched book by Jim Bishop, the President's love affair with Lucy Mercer Rutherford is recounted in more detail than ever before; since the participants are dead, the question of taste gives way to the requirements of history, but if any future President of the United States becomes involved with "another woman," he must expect the relationship to be discussed gleefully and in detail on television.

The drinking habits of Congressmen used to be taboo, but columnist Drew Pearson blew the whistle on old Mendel Rivers, and now nobody can stagger to work in the Congress without running some risk of exposure. That is to the good, but how about after hours, as in Chairman Mills's case? If a private toot affects public service, let him who is without sin cast the first stone.

The reason usually advanced for invading the privacy of public people in Washington is this: The nearer a politician approaches great power, the more respectful of respectability he should be, and the more prepared for probes into his potential weakness.

That is why, for example, the leaking of the personal income tax returns of Richard Nixon, and more recently of Nelson Rockefeller, is not considered violative of individual rights, while the leak of your return or mine would be reprehensible. We are saying, in effect, that public men have no right to privacy, and we assume this application of a double standard will ingrain in them a respect for equal justice under law.

That is why, too, the attention given Mr. Mills recently is causing moral headaches for journalists who believe that certain problems—which should be ignored in most public figures—ought to be discussed in any whose finger may be near the nuclear button.

A couple of years ago, a story appeared in a couple of newspapers about a minor traffic accident involving House Speaker Carl Albert. In those olden times, a story of a Congressman who was said to have had a few and ran into a parked car rated not much space; times and responsibilities have changed.

The Speaker is a good man and a respected man, does his job well, and for all we know drinks no more. But he has been next in line for 60 days now and it appears he will be a heartbeat from the Presidency for quite a while longer; men thrust into those circumstances ought to be examined.

There are gradations of need for the invasion of public people's privacy. I think the editors who buried or ignored the Joan Kennedy story were right: She does not present herself as a candidate and there is no "public right to know" her problems.

The Mills story deserved coverage, but not the whoopdedo it received; an inside page sufficed, a permanent record that could be consulted if he aspired to higher office. As a great and wise man put it the other day: "Who hasn't had a few wild nights?"

Granted, the right to know about a potential President outweighs his right to privacy; in the case of the Rockefeller tax returns, the public benefits from that exposure, violative though it is of the privacy of many individuals other than the nominee. But the Senate could have handled it in a way to embarrass fewer people.

The press has a right to publish or broadcast nearly anything. With that goes the obligation to weigh the need for exposure against the right to privacy, even in times when the safest decision is to let it all hang out.

The right to know is not under challenge; what editors and readers should ask themselves about is the need to know.

                                        August 5—1976

To the Editor:
   Five beautiful words
      [Op-Ed August 5]
   "William Safire is on vacation"
                           Amen.
                           Mary D. Clark
                           Mystic, Connecticut

Nixon

I COULD HAVE done the popular thing, and denounced Nixon when the rest of the press was reviling him. That would have been the easy way. But I would rather be a one-term columnist. . . .

THE MONSTER WITH TOTAL RECALL

July 19, 1973

WASHINGTON—Let's see what happens if we give the President the benefit of the doubt on his decision two years ago to create The Monster With Total Recall.

"Mr. President," Bob Haldeman or somebody could have said, "you're entering a period in which your Chinese and Soviet initiatives are coming to a head. I'll be making notes, and Henry will be making notes, but there will be too much going on to record the decision-making process for posterity, especially about the formation of foreign policy.

"History will be the loser—and let's face it, most historians will do their best to minimize your role in these events. Besides, the Safire types say we don't recognize a good anecdote if it hits us in the head. So let's just run a tape on everything that happens in any of your offices."

"I dunno," the President could have said. "It may not be fair to the people who come in here thinking they can talk in confidence. On the other hand, there's a third party like you always sitting in anyway."

"You would never betray a confidence," insists the seller of the plan. "We would have complete control of the tapes, and nobody would know of their existence. We'd have the Secret Service do it just to be sure the tape is never tampered with."

"It would help in the writing of memoirs," the President admits. "It took a lot of time, you know, to reconstruct events for *Six Crises.*"

"The tapes would be strictly private source material for you. You could still talk frankly, or cuss, and just be yourself—because the tapes would be buried in the oral history section of the Nixon Library, and after you've used them for memoirs you could have them locked up for 50 years, so no living person would ever be embarrassed."

"But if it got out we were taping everything," the President says, "we'd be criticized, though of course I would not be the first President to do it. Foreign visitors think we're eavesdropping anyway—they do it to us over there. And just about everybody in Government has a secretary on a 'dead key' making notes when I call."

"Not only is there precedent going back to F.D.R.," the seller presses, "but you'll have a helluva time listening to the tapes privately in your old age."

"Let's do it," the President says. "Hold it to a need-to-know basis. No discrimination—keep the activation of the recorders out of our hands entirely. It'll serve the truth, serve history, serve the country, and embarrass nobody."

And so the President, with honorable intent, proceeds to make a horrendous blunder.

Turning the "presence of the President" into a movable feast of snooping profoundly offends and saddens those, like this writer, who have long espoused—with Richard Nixon—the right of privacy, and the cause of individual liberty against unnecessary Government intrusion.

In creating The Monster, the President was not betrayed, ill-advised, or badly served—Richard Nixon's own judgment was bad, and in this case he deserves the heat he gets.

"You do not build confidence," President Nixon once said, "by breaking confidences." When Mr. Nixon caused a switch to be flicked that turned a confessional into a secret broadcasting booth, he let down his visitors, his aides, and his principles. On the President's orders, even the "Berlin Wall" had ears.

Presidents set examples. When a President has an inspiring family life, as Mr. Nixon does, that is good for American family life; when the President comports himself abroad with dignity and diligence, as Mr. Nixon does, that reflects well on all Americans.

But when the President walks around with an invisible Recording Angel on his shoulder, he suggests that it is permissible for businessmen and labor leaders, husbands and wives, reporters and sources to secretly tape each other's conversations as well. That's setting a terrible example.

Public exposure has breathed premature life into The Monster With Total Recall. Posterity is upon us: How can the President emerge neither impeached nor impaired?

The President should let his Monster's voice be heard, in all its ambiguity, just once, in a non-Congressional forum. That would settle nothing, since those longing for a guilty President will claim the tape was tampered with; but it would be a constructive form of penance for the sin of contributing to the eavesdropping epidemic.

Then, to re-establish the confidentiality of the Presidency, Mr. Nixon should drive a stake through The Monster's heart in a public bonfire of tapes on the White House lawn.

SMOKEY THE BEAR

April 21, 1975

WASHINGTON—Twenty-five years ago, a ranger investigating a forest fire came across a black bear cub with burned forepaws clinging to the stump of a tree. Brought to the nation's capital, he was dubbed "Smokey the Bear" and became the living symbol of the campaign to save our forests from fires.

Smokey the Bear has served the cause of fire prevention well. When he first came to Washington during the Truman Administration, some 30 million acres per year were being lost to conflagrations started by unthinking campers and drivers; but after a generation of Smokey's cold war against fire, less than three million acres are now lost each year.

Smokey's pleasant but concerned expression, under his ranger's hat on the posters, have earned him more fame than any other animal of our time, eclipsing even Elsie the cow, but what has gone unnoticed is Smokey's frugal attitude toward the taxpayer's dollar: Merchandising royalties paid to the United States Government by manufacturers of T-shirts, barbecue equipment, toys, and tie tacks have made Smokey a paying proposition, filling the Interior Department coffers with $1.5 million over the years.

At Washington's National Zoo, Smokey was the top attraction for many years. Children flocked to see the celebrated bear. They wrote him 5,000 letters a week, and when ZIP coding was introduced, Smokey became the only individual to receive his own number: 20252. In short, for most of his life Smokey was lionized.

Today, Smokey Bear (in the heights of fame, one often drops the middle initial, and Smokey dropped the "the") sits largely ignored in his small compound of cage and play area. Arthritis has stiffened his hind legs and Smokey has become fairly grumpy, even for a bear. He doesn't work the fence for the crowd anymore. He sleeps a lot.

One irritant to Smokey is "Little Smokey," his putative replacement, who lives in a nearby cage. Little Smokey is the same kind of black bear, with the same background and presumably the same hopes and dreams as old Smokey, but keepers say he is friendlier, with a more open personality, and zoo visitors like him better.

A more significant irritant to old Smokey—and to little Smokey as well—is the tourist competition provided by Hsing-Hsing and Ling-Ling, the zoo's two pandas from China. In zoological society, traffic is power, and all the traffic these days is over at the panda pavilion, where the Government has built a magnificent home for the denizens of détente, who have not yet produced an offspring.

Since the National Zoo's center of power has shifted to the caucus of pandas and their proud keepers, the habitat of Smokey and his replacement is understandably depressed. All branches of the zoo are supposed to be equal, but as animal farmers have noted before, some animals are more equal than others.

No wonder old Smokey Bear is grouchy. On occasion, he will put up a good front for visitors, sniffing curiously at their foreign apparel, but mostly he sleeps in the sun. Sometimes his nostrils twitch and his oft-burned paws quiver, as he dreams of days of zoo glory and of what might have been—of all that he could have done to use his power to bring about an end to bearishness.

But when he awakes to reality, he sees that not even little Smokey pays him any attention. And who can blame the little replacement bear, because it was Old Smokey's surliness in his later years that lessened the attractiveness of the Bear House, and now nobody pays any attention to him, either.

Oh, Smokey Bear! Perhaps you try to puzzle out why you were chosen out of the ashes to become the most celebrated animal in all the world. In matters anthropomorphic, it matters little whose ox is allegoried, but do you ever wonder, Smokey, why you rose so high to fall so far?

Probably not. Smokey Bear is a fatalist. He comforts himself with the fact that while the pandas get all the media coverage and the tourist traffic, Smokey still gets his 5,000 letters a week from loyal fans who are no longer children. He is convinced that one day the zookeepers will remember all he did for the zoo before the pandas came, and will honor him as a near-great bear, even if not a good bear.

So Smokey Bear rests in the sun, sees familiar faces that come to visit, favors his aching leg, works a little at working, and ponders the emptiness of his existence as he awaits the fullness of time.

THE "BANANAS THING"

May 8, 1975

DALLAS—Was Richard Nixon mentally unstable at any time of his Presidency? Did he flip his lid, go bananas, fall off his rocker, become unhinged, demented, looney, or a candidate for a funny farm?

John Osborne, a veteran Nixon-watcher, asserted recently in *New York* magazine that the former President had been "sick of mind," which—if words have meaning—means that the reporter thinks he was mentally ill.

Theodore H. White, in the forthcoming *Breach of Faith: The Fall of Richard Nixon*, writes that the handling of the President in his final days was "the management of an unstable personality" by a staff chief who feared a "personality explosion." Historian White—most of whose judgments of people are right on the mark—sorrowfully predicts that the Nixon story will be written by some future students as "a study in psychiatric imbalance."

Messrs. Woodward and Bernstein have not yet been heard from, but they have been asking: "Is it true he was talking to the portraits on the wall of the family quarters?" The answers have not been wholly satisfactory—there are only landscapes, and no portraits, on the walls upstairs, and not even a crackpot talks to landscapes—but we can expect their Nixon to be virtually swinging from the chandeliers.

Some residents of San Clemente, in bitter amusement, refer to this long-distance amateur psychoanalysis as "the bananas thing." Sensibly, Mr. Nixon says nothing at all: He is not about to follow "I am not a crook" with "I was not a nut."

Why this sudden spate of speculation? First, there is need to come up with a fresh angle, some wrinkle that has gone undetected by analysts on daily deadlines. This pressure affects the most distinguished journalists, who are partly motivated (to use a psychological term) by the urge to come up with a new lead.

Next, logicians abhor a logical vacuum. There is a delicious inconsistency in the Nixon story: How could an intelligent man, a canny politician, blunder so egregiously in covering up a foolish crime—unless he had indeed lost his marbles? The historian who figures this out might earn a niche in history himself.

Spurred by both this need for a lead and itch for a niche, chronicler-analysts turn to the sources closest to the scene. Only two men dealt directly with Mr. Nixon during his final week in office; one, Ronald Ziegler, has contributed nothing to the "bananas thing." The other, not surprisingly, emerges as the national hero in most accounts, the man who gets the hosannas for his easing-out of an "unstable" President before he could explode in madness: loyal, "leak-proof" Al Haig.

Now that we have pinpointed the reasons for—and the source who profits from—the "bananas thing," to the main point: Was Nixon nuts?

Yes, I will have no bananas. From my own observation—admittedly fragmentary, but at least firsthand and buttressed by talks with intimates—I saw Richard Nixon in his final stages as a man harassed, tortured, and torn, but of sound mind coming to a rational decision to resign.

Those who buy Haig's bananas are making medical judgments based on secondhand accounts, which pass along unattributed charges made by men who are not in the least qualified to make such judgments.

A decade ago, when a bunch of alienated alienists were persuaded to declare Senator Goldwater crazy from afar, he won a libel suit—but at least his detractors could claim some expertise. Not so today's bananas theorists.

Secretary Kissinger, who has always been General Haig's closest collaborator, tells Mr. White in direct quotation that Mr. Nixon had been "on the verge of a nervous breakdown" in May 1970. Since practicing psychiatry without a license has become today's indoor sport, let me suggest that Dr. Kissinger was projecting his own anxieties onto a father figure.

The truth, I think, has a Catch-22 quality. A parody of Kipling's *If* goes: "If you can keep your head while all about you are losing theirs— then maybe you don't understand the seriousness of the situation."

In the same way, *if* Mr. Nixon had been serene, calm, and unperturbed during the last white-hot week, *then* he would have been bananas. Instead, he was distraught and upset, as normal minds are under such abnormal circumstances. He cried at his final farewells, which is what sane and strong men do under real strain: Nixon's political crash had nothing to do with a mental crack-up.

At Yale last week, a professor of colonial history presented evidence to show that King George III—long maligned as a mad monarch—was not only not crazy but "was not such a bad guy." It has taken revisionist historians 200 years to give crazy George a clean bill of mental health, and only 200 days to besmear the mental stability of Richard Nixon.

NIXON NEVER DID

June 5, 1975

WASHINGTON—Amid the rash of books and magazine series rehashing all the frightful things Richard Nixon did, it might be useful to recount just a few of the items he has not yet been accused of having done.

1. *Nixon never ordered the murder of a fellow chief of state.* Recent accounts have alluded to the way the Kennedy brothers, fuming over the Bay of Pigs fiasco, might have had a little something to do with C.I.A. and Mafia activity in connection with Fidel Castro. We will never know the full story about this, because no Congressional committee will put a dozen witnesses under oath to testify about their involvement, but enough has surfaced to justify suspicion that President Kennedy did not frown on murder as a tool of national policy.

2. *Nixon never ordered the Justice Department not to prosecute a case that the Internal Revenue Service sent over with a recommendation for prosecution.* The Kennedy brothers did this in the Sherman Adams case, infuriating the I.R.S. professionals; in the post-Watergate morality, such conduct in quashing the prosecution for political gain would be labeled "obstruction of justice."

3. *Nixon never ordered the extended wiretapping of a civil rights leader for the purpose of leaking derogatory information about him to the press.* Certainly the deposed President's eavesdropping proclivities were reprehensible, but his motive was the plugging of national security leaks. The tapping of Martin Luther King Jr., approved by Attorneys General Robert Kennedy and Nicholas Katzenbach, had no such justification, and the deliberate playing of such taped conversations to reporters and Congressmen violated Federal law.

The Justice Department has recently admitted that the purpose of the King tap was "investigating the love life of a group leader for dissemination to the press." As Harvard Law Professor Alan Dershowitz has recently written in *The New Republic*, "The King intrusions involved the taping of as many as 5,000 separate conversations that violated the privacy of hundreds, perhaps thousands, of innocent King callers and visitors." And nobody ever sued.

4. *Nixon never amassed millions of dollars in public office.* One of his aides went to jail for backdating a deed that would have saved his boss a bundle, but Nixon did not enter public life a poor man and emerge a generation later with a net worth over $14 million, as his predecessor did. Fortunately for President Johnson, Senator Sam Ervin was there to cast a ringing vote against a Senate investigation into the activities of longtime Johnson intimate Bobby Baker.

5. *Nixon never used the F.B.I. or C.I.A. to spy on political opponents.* Wrongly, Nixon hired his own "plumbers." But he never ordered the F.B.I. to examine the telephone records of a Vice Presidential candidate, as Lyndon Johnson did with Spiro Agnew in 1968. Nor did Nixon get the F.B.I. to snoop on Robert Kennedy at the 1964 Democratic Convention (no honor among tappers) as L.B.J. did. A *New York Times* editorial referred to one of these taxpayer-supported dirty tricks as "an even graver offense than the original Watergate break-in."

Nor did Nixon order the illegal surveillance of the Mississippi Freedom Party at that well-bugged 1964 Democratic Convention; curiously, nobody seems to want to go to court to discover who did.

6. *Nixon never lied to the people about his health just before an election.* We have known for about a year that F.D.R. knew he was dying in 1944 and concealed that fact from the voting public with the connivance of his doctors. Only recently have we learned from Ben Bradlee that John F. Kennedy referred privately to "my Addison's disease" and fretted about his face appearing puffed up because of prolonged cortisone treatment.

In 1960, when Democratic committeewoman India Edwards charged that candidate Kennedy was afflicted with Addison's disease and that the required treatment called into question his capacity to serve, Kennedy and his doctors put out a misleading statement about a "mild adrenal deficiency." Lying to the people is always wrong, as Mr. Nixon learned, but lying to them about a material fact concerning ability to perform just before voters are called upon to make their decision—as we now find Senator Kennedy did—that has a special poignance.

Those are some of the things that Nixon never did. Of course, we would know a great deal more about other things he never did if Congress were to spend one-tenth the time and money investigating previous Administrations that it expended on Mr. Nixon's. But that is not to be.

So let us smack our lips as we pore over the pages that recount the villainy of the early 70's. We need to reassure ourselves that the Good Guys, who won at last, were really the good guys all along. Isn't that much more fun than forcing ourselves to look at the things Nixon never did?

MEASURING PAST PRESIDENTS

Frank Mankiewicz

June 9, 1975
The Washington Post

William Safire, once my opponent in three debates in these pages during the 1972 presidential campaign and now a columnist for *The New York Times*, wrote a most disturbing column last Friday. It was entitled, "Nixon Never Did," and it listed six non-sins of our ex-President, all of which, according to Safire, other Presidents did commit.

Now Safire, as a literate Nixon bitter-ender, is entitled to claim any virtue he wishes for his former chief, and all this would ordinarily rate would be a sad "say-it-isn't-so-Bill" from his friends. But this particular column is disturbing because it is representative of a well-orchestrated campaign on the part of die-hard believers in Nixon's innocence to make us forget the hard-earned lessons of Watergate by encouraging us to believe that all recent Presidents shared Nixon's genuinely and uniquely low moral standards. It is precisely because of their increasing currency and their patent unfairness to other former Presidents that Safire's apologias for Nixon deserve a point-by-point rebuttal.

Item: *Nixon never ordered the murder of a fellow chief of state.* Here Safire refers to "recent accounts" that John and Robert Kennedy "might have had a little something to do with CIA and Mafia activity in connection with Fidel Castro." That "little something" gives it away; it is an arch way to say "a lot." Safire goes on: ". . . enough has surfaced to justify suspicion that President Kennedy did not frown on murder as a tool of national policy." This is a truly outrageous smear, since *nothing* has "surfaced."

What Safire is talking about is two leaks straight from the Rockefeller Commission, reciting a memo from an old CIA hand, Gen. Edward Lansdale, to the effect that assassination was an option in dealing with Castro. One recent Friday night, Lansdale seemed to tell a reporter he had written the memo in response to pressure from Robert Kennedy, acting for the President. But later the same night, Lansdale took it all back, and wound up by saying that neither Kennedy had ever communicated with him in any way about assassination. Now that Lansdale has retracted and Rockefeller's report has been withheld, one would think the Nixon men would give up the chase. The only evidence to surface so far about the Mafia is that during the Eisenhower years the CIA made some kind of arrangement with two Mafiosi with respect to a contract on Castro, and that Robert Kennedy, when he heard about it, stopped it cold.

Item: *Nixon never ordered the Justice Department not to prosecute a case that the Internal Revenue Service sent over with a recommendation for prosecution.* The reference is to the case of Sherman Adams, spared by President Kennedy so as not to embarrass his predecessor, Eisenhower. The key words are "with a recommendation for prosecution." Nixon men stopped IRS investigations of his friends and urged IRS prosecution of his famous "enemies." There is an old New England saying, "never mention the word 'rope' in the house of a man who has been hanged": If I were a Nixon defender, I would be the last man to use the words "Internal Revenue Service."

Item: *Nixon never ordered the extended wiretapping of a civil rights leader for the purpose of leaking derogatory information about him to the press.* This is a reference to a single wiretap and extensive bugging of Martin Luther King. Since the recordings of some of the bugs were played later to the delectation of some members of the press and the FBI men who furnished them, the matter deserves some discussion.

As Attorney General, Robert Kennedy approved one wiretap on the office of Martin Luther King. The purpose was to attempt to prove or disprove a charge—by FBI Director J. Edgar Hoover—that a secret Communist was working for King. The results were negative, the tap was discontinued, and no recordings were ever played, anywhere. But Hoover—on his own and without *any* authorization (no one has ever claimed any authorization)—had been bugging King's hotel rooms around the country and making the tapes available as part of *his* campaign to destroy King's standing and credibility.

Now, as to Nixon. *He* ordered the wiretapping of newsmen and members of his own staff—including, incidentally, Mr. Safire. And his White House staff—probably with his knowledge—organized, financed and carried out a burglary against an anti-war leader for the purpose of leaking derogatory information about him to the press. Nixon then joined a "cover-up" of that crime. As for Safire's defense that Nixon's motive in wiretapping was "the plugging of national security leaks," he must think we have no memory at all. Most of those tapped (including Safire) had no connection with security, we have all read the transcript of the conversation in which Nixon and his aides created the "national security" defense, and we even have the notation opposite one "enemy" target: "a little scandal here would be helpful."

Item: *Nixon never amassed millions of dollars in public office.* To which, I guess, the short answer is "not for lack of trying." While President, he acquired estates at San Clemente and Key Biscayne (and we don't yet know how or with whose money) and maintained and furnished them largely at government expense. And Nixon's 1969 tax return, based as it was on lies about his place of residence in order to evade capital gains taxes, and a fraudulently dated deed of gift of largely worthless papers, succeeded for a while in sheltering nearly one million dollars of present and future income. He still has the estates, by the way, and he still holds nearly $170,000 of our money he promised to return.

Safire's reference is to Lyndon Johnson, whose wife's net worth increased by several million dollars while he was President, due to the increasing value of a monopoly TV station in Austin. Now it may be true that FCC officials were mindful of the station's ownership when renewal time came around, or conceivably when applications were made for licensing of a competing station. But if LBJ ever intervened, there is no evidence of it. And with John Mitchell and Richard Kleindienst as Attorneys General and Will Wilson and Henry Peterson as Assistant Attorneys General in charge of the Criminal Division, is there any doubt that if a scrap of paper implicating LBJ *could* have been found during the Nixon years, it *would* have been found?

Item: *Nixon never used the FBI or the CIA to spy on political opponents . . . Nor did Nixon get the FBI to snoop on Robert Kennedy at the 1964 Democratic convention, as LBJ did.* Nixon may never have used the FBI for this purpose, but if so it was only because Hoover wanted it in writing and, anyway, John Ehrlichman didn't trust Hoover. But what in God's name was the "plumbers" all about? These were White House assistants, and they did hardly anything *but* spy on political opponents. If Nixon did not spy on Robert Kennedy, it is only because he was never in a position of power when RFK was more than a Senate Committee chief counsel. But to make up for it, Nixon did have his White House gumshoes spy on *Edward* Kennedy, surely a comparable offense.

Item: *Nixon never lied to the people about his health just before an election.* What a sad commentary it is that, in defending an ex-President of the United States, his friends must qualify the phrase, "he never lied to the people," with a particular subject and a particular time. If Nixon never lied to us about his health just before an election, that may well be one of the few things he didn't lie to us about. This is the famous "Maurice Stans defense," in which overwhelming evidence of guilt is met by an assertion that complicity has not been proved in the sinking of the *Andrea Doria.* The things Nixon did lie about were not exactly trifling—for examples, the Paris Peace Accords, the Cambodian bombing and subsequent "incursion" and, most important, just about every phase and aspect of Watergate.

Safire says "that FDR knew he was dying" in 1944 and concealed that fact from the voters. But there is no proof—hardly any evidence—that FDR knew any such thing. He also refers to a pre-convention charge in 1960, by LBJ supporters, that JFK was suffering from Addison's disease, and the Kennedy camp's subsequent reference to a "mild adrenal deficiency." To prove his point, Safire uses a Kennedy remark about "my Addison's disease" in Benjamin Bradlee's *Conversations With Kennedy.* But Bradlee himself believes that Kennedy was making a characteristically wry and facetious reference to a report about the President's health that appeared at that time in *Newsweek* (then Bradlee's employer). This is thin stuff to match up against Nixon's use of the CIA and the FBI to obstruct justice, and then lying about it. But then, if your champion only told the truth in a limited area, it's wise to concentrate on it.

There *are* some things Nixon actually did not do, which other Presidents did. The most important one, I guess, was to maintain our belief in the basic honesty and decency of our leaders. We could start our list with that, and end it with that, too.

June 9, 1975

Editor
The Washington Post
1150 15th Street, N.W.
Washington, D.C.

Dear Sir:

One cannot help but admire the loyal, last-ditch attempt by Kennedy apologist Frank Mankiewicz to save the reputations of his old friends from the ravages of post-Watergate morality.

Always the effective polemicist, he stays on the attack, trying to rivet our attention to Nixon's misdeeds rather than to present a serious defense for the abuses of power we now are beginning to see took place under the Kennedy brothers.

The point of my column was not (as Mr. Mankiewicz distorts it) that Mr. Nixon was innocent, but that we are hypocrites when we apply a double standard to the actions of recent Presidents.

Less admirable than Mr. Mankiewicz's honest partisanship is the *Post*'s reluctant, namby-pamby, double-standardized coverage of Kennedy-Johnson transgressions. Where are the investigative reporters to track down the whole truth to the Kennedy-approved wiretap—and the subsequent bugging and defamation—of Martin Luther King? How long did that "single wiretap" last, anyway, who received the reports, and who in the Justice Department had knowledge of what seem to be illegal acts by government agents? Who closed their eyes to the apparent breaking of the law when it was their sworn duty to enforce the law?

Similarly, where are the ringing editorials demanding exposure of the continuing cover-up of the illegal surveillance of the Mississippi Freedom Party by the Justice Department at the 1964 Democratic Convention? Possible real eye-opener there.

Alas, the *Post-Newsweek* sauciness that helped cook Nixon's goose is not likely to be applied to his predecessors' gander. It is good to have Frank Mankiewicz blazing away in your pages again, but it is wrong for you to make an editorial policy out of President Kennedy's observation that "life is unfair."

Sincerely,
William Safire

NIXON ON HIS KNEES

March 29, 1976

WASHINGTON—Nixon-hatred, that most profitable of media exploitations, reaches a crescendo this week with (1) the glorification on film of reporters-turned-mindreaders Woodward and Bernstein and (2) the publication of their latest journafiction, which purports to be an account of the fallen President's last days in the White House.

What motivates such outpourings of vitriol? "We had to make a lot of it up, but there's two million bucks in it," said one of the writers. (Actually, I doubt whether either of them said that, but somebody once told me that he overheard somebody else say that Woodstein said something remotely like that at a party, which—by the new *Post-Newsweek* reportorial standards—means it can be turned into direct quotation and be accepted as true.)

More important, why is there such a ready market for even the most specious guesswork that Richard Nixon was a drunken, carpet-pounding maniac toward the end of his term?

The answer is the need of many people to cover up their guilt feelings. Now that the nation has learned that the power abuses of the Kennedy-Johnson era were greater both in scope and intensity than even the worst excesses of the Nixon years—and now that there is evidence that the Democratic National Committee knew of plans for the Watergate break-in six weeks in advance—there is a requirement for a heavy dose of reassurance that it was right to strike Nixon down. To anesthetize their consciences they have to keep telling each other that he was Evil Incarnate. They have to insist he was dangerously demented.

Consider the moment that the *Post-Newsweek* set believes proves beyond doubt that President Nixon had gone bananas. In the small Lincoln sitting room, alone with Henry Kissinger, the embattled President is reported to have said: "Henry, you are not a very orthodox Jew, and I am not an orthodox Quaker, but we need to pray." And then, according to this report, "Nixon got down on his knees. Kissinger felt he had no alternative but to kneel down, too."

How square. How cloyingly pious. How insufferably un-Georgetown. Can you imagine any person in his right mind, the target of more intense and extended abuse than any American in this century, turning to prayer?

And worst of all—to actually fall to one's *knees?* That's a bit thick, isn't it? You won't find Katharine Graham, or J.F.K.'s Ben Bradlee, or Woodward and Bernstein getting down on their knees to pray—they're not religious fanatics. To get down on your knees when your world is coming apart must be a mark of mental instability.

Perhaps that incident never happened, but was one of those dramatic

moments put in to hypo sales: In that case, Henry Kissinger is the innocent victim of false attribution. Perhaps Larry Eagleburger, the Kissinger
aide who is made to appear the main source, is telling the truth when he
insists he was present the only time his boss talked to Woodward and
Bernstein, and neither he nor his boss ever said one word to them about
that.

And yet I hope that the Nixon-on-his-knees episode—reported third-
hand, and distorted to fit the authors' best-selling thesis—has some basis
in truth. Even the ending: "Kissinger thought he had finished. But the
President did not rise. He was weeping. . . ."

Pretty nutty, huh? Obviously the man in tears was bonkers: Strong
men who weep are 'round the bend, and in no mental shape to be in positions of power. What we need in the Oval Office are men of real plastic,
with ice water in their veins, who will never shed a tear under any circumstances—cool men, preferably agnostic, who would never embarrass
associates by leaving them "no alternative" but to pray.

Post-Newsweek writers and editors have every right to revile a show of
reverence and claim it as proof that Richard Nixon was nuts. If they were
to present it—as Irving Stone does—as "fictionalized biography" that
would be honest. But what is proper for a dramatist is a rip-off for a journalist.

Who is really sick in this situation? Is it the writers squeezing their last
few million dollars out of Watergate who make a mockery of historical reporting by putting quotation marks around remarks that their secondary
sources never heard spoken?

Is it the reader or viewer, uncomfortable with the mounting evidence
that a moral double standard kissed one Presidency and killed another,
who desperately seeks a fix in film and print to get those hatred juices
flowing?

Or was it the imperfect man who was President, trusting in the decency
and discretion of his closest adviser, who fell to his knees and humbled
himself before God—and, tears in his eyes, cried out for some answer to
why he could not be allowed to fulfill his dream of being the world's
peacemaker?

In judging that man at that moment as worthy only of jeers and snickers, the profiteers of Watergate—and all those addicts who crave a loving
spoonful of fresh hatred—judge themselves.

March 30, 1976

Dear Mr. Safire:

Do you know the German word *schadenfreude?* If my spelling is correct and memory serves, it means taking pleasure—maybe great pleasure—in seeing the downfall and misfortunes of someone that one feels
deserved to fall.

There are those of us who sensed the insincerity in Nixon, if not the venality. There are those of us who were appalled at his voter appeal. There are those of us who waited with monumental impatience during twenty-five years of this man's impertinent and impudent uses of the governing processes that were ours as well as his.

But we had no forum from which to speak, no audience to whom we could write. We did not have access to the facts nor a chance of finding them. Our friends and acquaintances were bored.

Now, we wallow in the books, the columns, the articles and now a motion picture; and reflect how smart we were, how keen our judgement was, and how deep our frustration ranged.

To a large degree the Nixon Men are still there and what are we to think of them? All we have is a group of reporters telling us what took place then, and another group telling us what the first group is telling us.

Schadenfreude.

Sincerely,
Leonard Connor
Milford, Pennsylvania

Thumbsuckers

IN THE TRADE, pieces about political philosophy are called "thumbsuckers." They are mother's milk to some, and a change of pace for me; I usually prefer direct engagement, writing on top of the news, rather than exhibiting a Lippmannesque longheadedness, which I do not have.

Once in a while, however, the opposing finger twitches, and the best source becomes a blank wall.

TRUTH IN LABELING

January 24, 1974

WASHINGTON—One of Fred Allen's radio characters was an amnesiac who kept trying to remember who he was by the process of elimination. "Bduh, I don't carry an umbrella," he would muse, "so I can't be Neville Chamberlain."

Few of us at that time caught Mr. Allen's subtle sociopolitical message—that people tend to identify themselves in terms of what they are not. Thus, many of us apply political labels like "liberal" or "conservative" to others, resisting the application of either label to ourselves, or permitting only a sister-kissing label like "moderate," which is a better description for drinkers than voters.

There are those of left and right who proudly wear a label: For example, the true believers of the right are gathering in Washington this weekend at a political action conference. The conference is to be addressed by such right-wingbacks as Governor Ronald Reagan and Senator James Buckley.

The trend toward self-identification as "conservative" has not been stopped by the decline in the President's popularity or the Agnew scandal: When *The New York Times* surveyed New Yorkers in 1970, those who called themselves liberal outnumbered self-described conservatives by 33 percent to 27 percent, with 31 percent moderately sister-kissing. The same poll conducted only two months ago showed crime-conscious New Yorkers flip-flopping those figures, with conservatives now decisively on top.

Because the best way to sell candidacies is to attack the opposition, even people who accept the label "conservative" define it in terms of what they are against: coddling criminals, raising taxes, or what have you.

Rarely do conservatives define their label in terms of what they are for, and for a seemingly good political reason: A fundamental split is built into conservatism.

One side of conservatism emphasizes traditionalism, permanent moral values, respect for institutions, and order in society. The other side stresses libertarianism, individuality, and holds personal freedom to be the great value.

These two sides of conservatism will agree on the need for self-reliance, diversity, and for halting the growth of big government, and will feel comfortable sallying forth together against the centralization of power.

But the two sides of conservatism will tear up the turf in great doctrinal battles of their own: Most traditionalists will take positions against pornography, prostitution, drug usage, and abortion, while many libertarians will argue those are matters for the individual to decide, not government.

That is why William F. Buckley, in a fascinating new book, *Four Reforms*, can look at the increasing number of victims of crime and call for an end to what he considers the abuse of the Fifth Amendment by the accused—while a minority of other conservatives march in the opposite direction, calling for more protection of individual rights and an end to the growth of Federal police power.

Conservatives in conclave have frequently derided the "zigzagging" of the New Federalists, who try to decentralize administration with one hand and to centralize welfare with the other. But the right has not faced up to the challenge, and the opportunity, of examining the divergent forces inside conservatism's tent—which can be a great source of strength.

Might it not be useful for conservatives to open up their "movement," to recognize conflicting causes within it, and encourage inwardly the same kind of diversity it espouses outwardly?

In that spirit, like mothers sewing labels in clothing to accompany kids to camp, we could identify our political positions in the specific way that invites acquaintance and discussion.

Labels could then cease to be onerous or fuzzy. "Libertarian conservatives" would then be able to gauge what they held in common with

"Great Society disillusionees" and Malthusians could dance with Marcusians. Oxymorons would abound, as moderates exchanged their meaningless tags for something like "egalitarian élitist" or "pragmatic moral absolutist" or "principled opportunist."

Names are not things but nameless things do not communicate ideas: Political labeling can serve a useful purpose, if we specifically identify our own line of thinking along with that of our opponents.

My own label? I'm working on that, by identifying and eliminating alternatives. Conservative traditionalism is not for me, nor Galbraithian liberalism; New Federalism with an underpinning of libertarianism has its attractions.

Sometimes I like to carry an umbrella. Maybe I'm Neville Chamberlain.

THE GHOST OF LOCKE

January 13, 1975

WASHINGTON—John Locke, an English philosopher, stirred controversy three centuries ago with the notion that societies were organized and ruled not by divine right, but by what he called "the consent of the governed."

Choosing his words carefully so as not to offend the King, Locke held that men left the wild state of nature by their own volition, making a social contract in order to protect "life, liberty and property."

When tyrants snatched away the protection of a citizen's natural rights, the government was breaking the contract, and the time came for men to "appeal to Heaven." Locke's reverent phrase was taken from the practice of biblical generals of praying before battle, and actually were code words—widely understood at the time—for armed rebellion against tyranny.

Such ideas fired up young Thomas Jefferson a century later, and he filled the Declaration of Independence with Lockeian ideas and phrases, even to "the pursuit of happiness."

How do I know this? Because I took a course on Locke's second treatise on government just a couple of years ago, conducted by a professor at St. John's College. The seminar was a skullcracker and the handful of students included Alan Otten, David Broder, and Robert Novak, columnists; Herman Wouk, author, and David Ginsberg, lawyer; Marilyn Berger, reporter, and Katharine Graham, newspaper publisher.

The teacher who guided this high-powered agglomeration of opinion molders through the sources of political freedom—expertly shaming class-cutters and homework-skippers into line—was Robert Goldwin, 52, who popped up in the news recently as a special consultant to the President.

Dr. Goldwin, who served with Donald Rumsfeld at NATO, was the man behind the widely acclaimed session of academics with President Ford last month. His job is to "assure the flow of information, ideas and suggestions" to the President from outside government: Such salutary sessions with men who live the life of the mind were described by departing Len Garment as a *"coup de tête."* That play on "coup d'état" may be the only pun in French of the Ford Administration, but it felicitously praises the new green light on a necessary two-way street.

The new White House adviser resists the title of "Intellectual-in-Residence" or "The New Garment Center," preferring to act as a kind of free safety in the Ford secondary: one day lending a hand on speeches, the next day sitting in on Domestic Council discussions, soliciting unorthodox ideas like those of Harvard Professor Martin Feldstein, watching over the interests of the arts and humanities, setting up more skull sessions with the man in the Oval Office.

Locke's treatises, of course, are close at hand; the occasional ghost of Mr. Ford is inspired by the pervasive ghost of Mr. Locke. For the pressure is on—led by those who were so recently decrying Caesarism—for the President to seize control of a free economy, or to do something dramatic to gain the illusion of leadership.

What the President and all his advisers are learning is that the public must be pandered to, at least to a certain extent, even when wrong: Locke's "consent of the governed" has its drawbacks. Dr. Goldwin is working on an equation: "Action in a democratic society equals wisdom divided by consent."

How best can consent be won? Often by indirection, by muting the arguments that appeal most to yourself and appealing instead to the self-interest of others. For example:

Englishmen of the 17th century who believed in freedom of expression sought the removal of the licensing of printing. To advance this cause, John Milton, the epic poet, wrote *Areopagitica*, which stands today as the greatest prose work in denunciation of censorship. But the licensing of printing stayed in effect.

Later in that century, John Locke addressed himself to the same subject. He argued, in dull and plodding language, that licensing of English printers drove up the price of books and was causing the industry to move to France. The economic cost of censorship was too high; Parliament, for less than noble interests, then acted to free the press.

As President Ford labors over his State of the Union Address, wondering now to enlist consent in our time, it is comforting to know that the ghost of John Locke still stalks the corridors of power. An appeal to self-interest is more useful than an appeal to idealism, and even more helpful than an appeal to Heaven, in coaxing the governed to consent.

"MAYDAY" AND *PLAYBOY*

January 27, 1975

WASHINGTON—In May 1971 the hard core of the militant protesting set descended on the nation's capital, determined—as its leadership put it—to "stop the government" by bringing auto traffic in Washington to a standstill.

These rioters were not gentle souls carrying candles, but largely the toughs and crazies who marred the peace movement. As they proceeded to slash tires, terrorize motorists and pedestrians, and roll cans of garbage into the streets, the District of Columbia police moved to prevent anarchy.

Unlike the reaction in Chicago in 1968, there were no police charges to crack skulls; nor was there any panicked use of firearms as in Jackson State or Kent State. Instead, the D.C. police rounded up some 14,000 of the rampaging terrorizers and made them guests of the city in a football stadium overnight.

The real threat of mob rule had been averted with a minimal application of force. The civil liberty of the law-abiding citizen to walk on a public street or drive to work had been protected.

However, in making "mass arrests," the police had infringed upon the civil liberties of the demonstrators. Under our system, arrests for other than individual acts are wrong; a man cannot be jailed for what the man next to him in a crowd may have done (unless we apply the conspiracy statutes). Quite rightly, the local courts threw out the arrests as illegal and the Mayday tribe went home, never to be heard from again.

Until now. Not content with the way the police had protected the civil liberty of most Washingtonians and the courts had then protected the rights of those mass-arrested, the American Civil Liberties Union sued the taxpayers of Washington for damages to those arrested, and one of our sensitive local juries just popped for $12 million.

Twelve hundred of the demonstrators will now each receive about $10,000 for the indignity suffered, and former full-time demonstrators all over the country are coming out of the woodwork to make their claims. This decision, unless reversed on appeal, will turn justice on its head.

But no editorial cannons boom; since the forces of "repression" are trounced, the award of $10,000 to each of these participants in an effort to plunge a city into anarchy is met with equanimity. Who dares to short-change the new heroes?

Ah, says the A.C.L.U., but think of the principle: Local governments will quail before making any more mass arrests. That is simply not so. If the forces of law erred, as they undoubtedly did, official reprimands ought to have been sought, new regulations to meet such a situation proposed and debated. But that would have required hard legal and political action.

If it is difficult to punish the law, and unpopular to punish the provocateurs of repression, who is there to punish? The answer is clear: the taxpayers.

The local citizen in the District of Columbia who was forced to endure a night of terror now must pay for the entertainment in $12 million out of the General Treasury to a group of those who threatened that terror. Perhaps the protestors' payoff—Mayday's payoff—can be squeezed out of day-care centers or policemen's salaries.

Civil liberty cannot stand many more such victories that stand justice on its head. The A.C.L.U., quick to defend the fashionably disreputable, is slow to react to the clear and present danger of "the new torture," far more important to the cause than yesteryear's demonstrations. Which takes us from "Mayday" to *Playboy*.

Recently, a woman employee of Hugh Hefner, *Playboy* publisher, was convicted of a drug offense and given a "provisional sentence" of 15 years. If she had told the prosecutors what they wanted to hear—obviously, by involving a prime publicity target—she would have been treated leniently. If not—she faced a lifetime in jail on a minor charge and a first offense.

What clearer invitation to perjury can there be than such a "provisional sentence"? It is one thing to give a cooperative witness a break, entirely another to threaten to let a defendant rot in the slammer until he or she tells the story the prosecution wants.

The woman who worked for *Playboy*, Bobbie Arnstein, committed suicide under the new torture. We don't know all the facts in that case, but in terms of relevant principle, isn't it more important for the A.C.L.U. to try to stop increasing use of a modern rack by prosecutors and judges across the nation than to belabor the point about mass arrests that the courts made cogently four years ago?

Some sense of proportion is needed. Protecting the right to protest is necessary, but carrying it to the extreme of lavishing great bundles of the public's tax money on aggrieved protesters is an excess of zeal that is against the public interest.

In the "Mayday" case, civil libertarians won their case and justice has miscarried. In the *Playboy* case, civil libertarians have not even come to grips with what the case is about, as justice again miscarries. Perhaps the jubilant young lawyers who ripped all the rest of us off for $12 million should give that some thought as they seek to press money into the hands of the crew who came to slash a tire for peace.

January 27, 1975

Dear Bill:

For once I do disagree, and enough to write. Your characterization of the 1971 protest is silly. Those so-called "terrorizers" included some stuffy Boston lawyers and a number of my pastoral neighbors on Martha's Vineyard.

Maybe it looked like terror from inside the White House. But then, as we know, Mr. Nixon was determined to find that whether it existed or not.

Best—
Tony
[Anthony Lewis]
The New York Times

January 29

Dear Tony:

I know you feel strongly about the Nixon White House's response to protest and I'm glad you wrote.

When you think of "terrorizers," you think of your pastoral neighbors, who undoubtedly were there. But I wasn't looking at it from inside a bunker-style White House that night. I was in Georgetown, I saw people being chased by young hoodlums, I saw—with my own eyes—the garbage cans being dumped in the streets by what we used to call "Fascist bully-boys." Ordinary people were scared. It wasn't a concoction of some law 'n' order nuts. The Mayday tribe, which ran that "rally," and the one in Dupont Circle that I also saw, was a group of people who took delight in what they were doing.

In some situations, we have to respond not by what we read or want to read, but by what we live through. God knows the Nixon men overreacted to protest groups on many occasions, but on that particular one—as in San Jose in 1970—the terror came from the mob and not from the police. And I didn't want people to rewrite history; the hoods I saw were not the friends of yours who might also have been there.

I only wish you had been with me that night; your reaction might have been like that of Pat Buchanan's in 1968, when he saw the Chicago cops charge out to crack skulls—sometimes you don't want to be on your own side.

Best—
Bill

Dear Bill:

Thanks for your letter. I am pleased and grateful at the trouble you took.

As it happens, there is nothing in it with which I disagree at all. I would have felt just as outraged and frightened as you if I had seen those hoodlums, and ashamed of my "side."

My objection is to sweeping everyone who was there in 1971 under the classification "terrorizers." I think that is a mistake as a matter of journalism or law. Our whole constitutional premise is that guilt is individual. The fact that hoodlums dumped garbage cans in Georgetown cannot justify John Mitchell's ordering thousands of peaceful people outside the Capitol arrested without any probable cause for thinking that *they* had committed a crime.

> Best—
> Tony
> [Anthony Lewis]
> *The New York Times*

THE SWITCHER ISSUES

February 23, 1976

MODESTO, CALIF.—Talking to people in smaller towns, one is struck by the blossoming of "switcher issues," which will assume inordinate importance during the coming Hundred Days of primaries.

A switcher issue is not so broadly influential as a bread-and-butter issue, nor so universally visceral as a gut issue. A switcher issue is limited to a single subject's effect on a limited number of people—but the effect of it is decisive, and can even cause a young, liberal, wealthy voter to go against every other inclination to support an old, conservative, poverty-stricken candidate.

Most politicians tend to discount the switcher issues, since only a small percentage of the electorate is moved with such intensity to change all other habits on one overriding matter. But in the Hundred Days when small, dedicated groups can make a big difference, the switcher issue comes into its own.

The best-known and most significant switcher is abortion. The campaign to overrule the Supreme Court decision by constitutional amendment is well organized and carries a powerful moral charge; to many, abortion is nothing less than legalized murder. Taking a leaf from "right to work" and "truth in advertising," this campaign has put a positive message in its name, "pro-life."

Politicians who used to hide behind "local option" now face a tough choice; if they go with anti-abortion switchers, they will lose the votes of pro-abortion switchers in the general election. President Ford has fallen into a unique straddle: He frowns at the Court decision while his wife enthusiastically endorses it.

Another switcher is gun control. In a media contest, the campaign to curb handguns wins hands down; but in the Congress, legislation has been stalled since 1968. Few Congressmen want to risk the ire of the people to whom gun control is enough to switch a voter from support of the incumbent to support of any challenger.

That is why we see liberals abandoning the ranks on this one, and their confreres nodding in understanding: Political survival comes first. On the stump during the Hundred Days, most candidates will answer questions on this subject by denouncing criminals and praising sportsmen.

Switcher issues can range from price supports to Federal control of questionable cancer cures. In many rural areas, you can spot bumper stickers calling for "no helmets," which is not an antimilitary campaign, but a perfect example of a switcher issue.

Many free-spirited motorcyclists like the feeling of the wind and the rain in their hair. But safety-conscious regulators, citing the public cost of picking injured motorcyclists off highways, insist that cyclists wear protective helmets. The easy riders—who like a vroom with a view—retort that this is a Government intrusion into their civil liberties.

Before dismissing their argument, consider the uproar of motorists who resented buzzers that could not be silenced until seat belts were fastened. That was a Government intrusion on behalf of safety, too, but there were enough motorists to get the Government to back down, and now unbelted seats do not buzz. On principle, if you are against buzzers, you should be against helmets.

Woe betide the candidate who walks into a press conference in Kentucky or Tennessee unbriefed on the helmet issue; wild bunches of votes are ready to fall off his tree.

The common denominator of these switcher issues is the role of Government in the decisions of individuals. Here is where one conservative libertarian comes out on all three:

1. Abortion is a personal moral decision that Government ought neither to forbid nor require; thus, in the first trimester, I'm not pro-life, I'm pro-freedom.

2. Handguns are more often used to intrude upon personal freedom than to protect it; I'm not for mild limits or registration, I'm for absolute confiscation of concealable guns, making it a crime to own one. But if a man wants to sit in his living room with a double-barreled shotgun in his

lap, that's his business and the Government has no right to ask if he owns one.

3. On helmets, if a cyclist has little interest in keeping his head together, he has the same right to his folly as the smoker has to court cancer. The question ought to be: When does an individual's action hurt somebody else? The unhelmeted cyclist ought to be forced to pay a higher insurance premium, and the smoker limited to spaces not offensive to nonsmokers. But among a person's rights is the right to take a chance without Government fussing over him all the time.

However, a candidate who disagrees with me on all three of those cases might still get my support. That goes to show that the power to switch comes not from the subject matter, but from the intensity of feeling with which some political activists infuse their switcher issues.

February 26, 1976

Mr. William Safire
NEW YORK TIMES

Dear Bill:

Bear with me while I deliver a forty-five-second lecture.

On your abortion position: you are against abortion in the last two trimesters but in favor of "freedom" in the first. But whose freedom? If the fetus is a member of the human species (and, of course, genetically and biologically it is) during the last six months what structural genetic or biological changes occur that make it different from the being that was conceived and grew during the first three months? Unless there is a biological or genetic change (there are none), on what basis (other than whim) do we say that the fetus at, say, twelve weeks has *absolutely no rights* (the Court's position, by the way, for the *nine*-month period), but at fourteen weeks does?

At the heart of the abortion controversy is this question: either the fetus is a member of the human species and therefore deserving of protection at every stage of its existence or it is *not* a member of the human species and, therefore, is of no (or very, very little) concern. One cannot have it both ways: you can't say it deserves protection *after* three months unless you are willing to show why it deserves *no* protection for the first trimester.

The point is this: we *can* have law that at once protects the fetus and at the same time does not ban IUDs and morning-after pills, because *law can deal only with that* which we know and which can be shown to exist. There is no way the law can determine if the action of an IUD or pill destroys human life. Therefore, the law must remain silent on this issue (I think). But once pregnancy is medically determined we must ask hard questions. What is this "other" that exists in the womb? Every bit of medical, scientific, genetic, fetological and biological evidence demonstrates beyond a doubt that it is a unique, genetically identifiable, member of the human species. It is, in short, a being which is human, i.e., a *human* being. That it doesn't *look* like a human being to some is irrelevant.

The Court asked the wrong question and gave the wrong answer. The question has *never* been "When does 'life' begin?" That is an unanswerable question and is totally irrelevant to the issue. The real question (not asked by the Court . . . Why?) is this: what does all the available scientific (not religious) evidence (not "belief" or "feeling") tell us about the fetus? An irony: for the first time since Galileo, the orthodox churches have science on their side—yet the beclouding of the issue has brought us to this state of affairs.

If, as you put it, you are for "freedom" (and you are), the next question must be asked: "*Whose* freedom?"; and then another: "When two rights to freedom conflict, what do civilized human beings do—what should they do?"

Science, the history of this country and common law going back to Blackstone and beyond demonstrate that *wherever there is knowledge that human life exists it deserves full protection.* Don't let the abortion propaganda fool you: the only reason some of the early law decisions seemed to go easy on abortion was the primitive scientific knowledge of the times: no one was quite sure when a fetus was "human." But the genetic revolution of the past decade has forever cast such doubts into the trashbib of history. The fetus is human or it is nothing.

Sincerely,
Bill Gavin
Washington, D.C.

ON EXPORTING MORALITY

August 14, 1975

WASHINGTON—An American aircraft manufacturer has just asserted in a forthright way that it paid at least $30 million over the past five years to foreign politicians.

The payoffs paid off, says Lockheed; part of its $2 billion in sales to foreign nations over that period came as a result of doing as the Romans do. No United States laws were broken, the company acted to meet foreign payoff competition, thousands of United States workers owe their jobs to Lockheed's willingness to follow local customs, and the United States taxpayer—who keeps the company in business by guaranteeing some of its loans—has the guarantee protected by the success of the bribery.

"Sorry, Charlie, business is business," Lockheed seems to say to the hell-bent hounds of publicity in senatorial and media pulpits, who now howl their horror at practices common to overseas trade since Marco Polo's time.

I sat down to write an essay defending corporations against the politically inspired application of *ex post facto* morality. But a lust for philosophical consistency brings me out on the side of the goo-goos, bleeding hearts, and Frank Churchgoers who will be as uncomfortable with my support as I am to be in their ranks.

The question at issue is: Should the public policy of the United States be to export its ideas about what is right and wrong to the rest of the world? Put another way, do we have a mission to sell our ideals of freedom and virtue in the far corners of the earth?

The answer is yes. Our Founding Fathers rebelled against tyranny "not just for ourselves, but for all mankind"—a fairly pretentious notion, unmatched in the world until the onset of Communism.

America has a mission to perfect her own freedom and to encourage the growth of her ideals everywhere. Not every American believes that, but those who do can make five points about current affairs consistent with that principle:

1. We are right to pressure the Soviets to permit more human freedom within their borders in return for trade.

2. We are wrong to tell Portugal's anti-Communists that we are powerless to assist them because our President is fearful of criticism if he uses the C.I.A.

3. We are right to help democratic nations like Israel to survive and prosper in a region of one-man governments, just as we were right to try to help allies in the past to resist totalitarian takeover.

4. We are wrong to maintain official silence about the rape of freedom in India, and cowardly to accept Secretary Kissinger's slur that speaking out in criticism of Mrs. Gandhi would merely "satisfy our self-esteem."

5. We are right to try to impose our standards of morality in doing business abroad, and to refuse to condone bribery from now on. That's being consistent. The trouble is, few Americans will subscribe to all five applications of that missionary principle. Most of us will be moralists in politics and pragmatists in business, or vice versa.

For example, the political pragmatists who say "We cannot impose our ideas of Western culture on societies totally different from our own" are likely to be in the vanguard of business moralists who say exactly the opposite—that we must impose our most recent ideas of business ethics on the brothers-in-law of Arab sheiks and the campaign managers of sitting dictators.

Sorry, but rationality does not permit us to choose one from Column A and one from Column B. It is not possible to sally forth carrying the

American message of freedom and virtue on political matters, and then suddenly to adopt the business-is-business argument on the conduct of businessmen abroad.

Frankly, the pragmatists have all the fun. In the sunshine of détente, they can shrug off conquest by Communism in Portugal and, in the cool of detachment, they can tacitly watch the conquest by coup in India. And if some businessman is to grease a few palms under the palm trees, what's the big deal?

Moralists, on the other hand, are pests. Economic freedom is a bother; meddling in other people's business leads to friction; bumbling democracies are harder to maintain than efficient dictatorships; honesty is the most troublesome policy and morality our least desired export.

And yet America, to be herself, must be a force for good. Ethics in business is a part of the American Dream, even if we have fallen short often enough; America stands for competition on the basis of quality, price, and service, and not on payola. If, in the short run, this costs us jobs and money, that's the price we pay for setting standards.

Holier-than-thou? Sorry about that, but democracy and honest competition are holier than totalitarianism and bribery. American ways and ideals should travel arm-in-arm with American trade and power, and that goes for allies, détente, and Lockheed.

People

$\mathbf{A}$N OCCASIONAL SALLY into philosophy is permissible, and frequent dips into policy are expected, but a column that overlooks personalities soon becomes a column without personality.

I began as a "people" columnist in 1949, doing the interviewing and writing the rough notes for a "Close-up" column by Tex and Jinx McCrary in The New York Herald Tribune syndicate. "Reading a column about people is like eating peanuts," Tex used to say. I could never get the rest of the message because his mouth was full of peanuts, but I think he meant it was hard to stop doing.

It's easy to be wrong about people in politics: Spiro Agnew was a pleasure to attack "permissiveness" with, and to coin "the nattering nabobs of negativism" for—and what a letdown he gave those who defended him. On the other hand, unlike most, I'll always have a happy recollection of "Lucky" Luciano.

People columns bring good mail. After Henry Kissinger was given his second hat in 1973—becoming Secretary of State while continuing as National Security Adviser—I predicted that one day the man to fill the N.S.C. slot would be Zbigniew Brzezinski. On January 2, 1974, under the letterhead of "The Trilateral Commission," came a letter from Zbig, kidding, but only half-kidding: "On further reflection, I have decided that I would rather be Secretary of State—our predecessor proved that you need not apply yourself too hard to the job and our incumbent is proving that it is possible to hold it concurrently with another full-time job!"

SPIRO AGNEW

ON MISTER AGNEW

October 11, 1973

WASHINGTON—The man who carried the standard against "permissiveness" copped a plea today, and in return for his resignation, the judge and the Justice Department permitted him to go free.

The prosecutors must have had the evidence, as they say, and they must have had it cold. Assistant Attorney General Henry Petersen deserves congratulations for the confidence he showed in his case, though it can be hoped he will exercise more care in the number of people he expresses his confidence to in future cases.

People who believed the former Vice President's ringing protestations of innocence feel betrayed and shaken; people who felt the lash of his tongue over the years feel vindicated. But his friends and his foes would be mistaken to take the fall of any man to mean the end of all he said and all he stood for.

What was it that Spiro Agnew came to mean in American life, for good and for bad?

He was the man who made "élitism" famous. The "impudent snobs" he inveighed against were often unnecessarily impudent and certainly snobbish. There had always been a disdain for what used to be called "the great unwashed" by a social or intellectual élite. Agnew, as the voice of the "silent majority" (a phrase he coined six months before President Nixon used it), spoke out for egalitarianism, and was promptly, and unfairly, attacked for being a know-nothing or an anti-intellectual.

He stood up for the establishment against "those whose lifestyle has neither life nor style"—the professional aginners who all too often did not know what they were for, who wanted only to reject all forms of authority and treated dissent as an end in itself. This is where he smote "permissiveness," deriding the parents who produced a "Spock-marked generation" and fell for "demand feeding up to the age of thirty."

The rise of Agnew put a crimp in the growth of adversary journalism, causing many writers and reporters, even while angrily wrapping themselves in the First Amendment, to wonder if they had not lost touch with their readers or viewers, and to ask themselves if objectivity were not a more important goal than persuasion.

As often happens, in the good, there was bad. Mr. Agnew's antipathy to the "media"—that's the sinister word for "press"—which he acquired under the press's bludgeoning in the 1968 campaign, became a kind of obsession with him: Even last week, when he had a chance to strike a blow for individual liberty against prosecution-by-leak, he could not resist the chance to subpoena reporters instead of concentrating on leakers.

In his anti-élitist posture, he went beyond the expounding of egalitarianism, beyond the dignifying of the brow-beaten will of the people, to the unnecessary provocations of the "rotten apples" as he stood before audiences that demand what politicians call "red meat."

He recognized his own excess; after the campaign of 1970, in which the President designated him the "cutting edge" to keep Democratic candidates away from the economic issue, he restrained his rhetoric and gave evidence of thinking more deeply about those sociological matters he had raised.

As an articulator of unspoken issues, Mr. Agnew was good, certainly surprising to the man who chose him: Late one Miami night, after his 1968 acceptance speech, Candidate Nixon said to me about his running mate: "He can't make a speech worth a damn, but he won't fall apart."

But as a personal symbol, as the embodiment of a type, Agnew was more than good: He said what he meant, with no folderol. He stood for principle, even though it was popular; he stood for character, at a time when charisma was going out of style. And now he stands for hypocrisy, which he so effectively denounced, because he cannot say he was not once on the take.

According to his own antipermissive precepts, the people who believed in him were wrong, but the people who believed in the message he carried are not wrong: This is a time to believe in "measures, not men."

I'll remember this saddened man for his sense of humor: As we came into San Diego in 1970, he noted how the reporters were picking up his alliterative phrases, so he asked his writers to come up with the biggest, self-mocking whopper we could think of to slip into a speech about undue pessimism.

We gave him a choice of "hopeless, hysterical hypochondriacs of history" and "nattering nabobs of negativism." The Vice President laughed, said: "Hell, let's use both," and—tongue in cheek—sailed them into the political language.

It's a good thing he quit; he would never again have been a happy warrior.

12 October 73

Editor, Letters Column
N.Y. Times

Dear Sir,

Mr. Safire's apologia (in the issue of Oct. 11) for Spiro Agnew's recently exposed chicanery was just about par for the course in Administration-Excusers. In essence, his message was: "Sure, he was a crook all along; but he never made a speech against Patriotism—Home & Mother, and we should all pattern ourselves after what he *said*, not what he did." That fits in well with the current White House dogma.

As for Mr. Agnew's "egalitarianism" . . . it was the Animal Farm variety. The "some of us" who are more equal than others, spake Spiro, are those who agree with Dick and me. All others are suspect and let's have Preventive Detention all around. Mr. Safire asks us to forget that while Agnew was foaming away at the press, at the young, at the peace-lovers and anything else in view to the left of center, he was collecting pay-off money in his office at the Tattle-tale grey House. We are also asked to forget that the "authority" some of us wanted to reject consisted—beside Mr. Agnew's own nefarious self—of an Executive mansion full of (at best) shady characters, and a Cabinet that has lost two of its members to indictment on various charges.

Mr. Safire asks us to forget one hell of a lot: I suppose he wants us all in training for the big push for political amnesia in 1976.

Sincerely yours,
Mrs. Irving Berler
Syosset, New York

October 12, 1973

To the Editor:
The New York Times

Dear Sir:

Mr. Safire stands truth on its head in his October 11th piece expressing continued admiration for Mr. Agnew because he stood for "principle" and "character," and opposed "Spock-marked" permissiveness.

Agnew was elected Governor of Maryland as a liberal who supported civil rights and then quickly betrayed that cause. Now he's resigned before a barrage of criminal charges.

I never advocated permissiveness or demand feeding, as parents who've used *Baby and Child Care* agree. Agnew, in accusing me (like the Rev. Norman Vincent Peale, Nixon's New York pastor, who was the first to preach this), showed that he had never read the book. He simply resented the opposition to the Vietnam war by me and the young and tried to discredit us all in the same shotgun blast.

Benjamin Spock, M.D.
New York, New York

SPIRO AGNEW AND THE JEWS

May 24, 1976

WASHINGTON—The anti-Israel lobby has a new champion: my old friend and former colleague, novelist Spiro T. Agnew. Up to now, the anti-Israel lobby was made up of these dissimilar elements:

¶Hawkish columnists and longtime Arabists at the State Department who honestly believe that support of Israel undermines our influence in the oil-strategic Arab world and thus is against America's self-interest;

¶Dovish writers and longtime liberals, including many Jews, who are uncomfortable with positions of solidarity and strength, and who urge the beleaguered Israelis to adopt appeasement under the labels of "accommodation," "flexibility," and "risks for peace";

¶A Secretary of State and his sycophants who grind out propaganda on background to chastise Israel as "intransigent" for not giving up its security to make a quick-fixer look like a peacemaker;

¶The usual assortment of anti-Semites, envious of the status earned by many individual Jews, who share one conviction: that the Jews control and manipulate America, and are the secret cause of most other people's individual failures.

To the head of this powerful and disparate conglomeration rides Ted Agnew, plugging his novel, on media that wants to give him access so as to prove his accusations of one-sidedness are wrong. His message: Jews in the media make up a "Zionist lobby" leading us to disaster in the Mideast.

As one who wrote many of Mr. Agnew's speeches in the 1970 campaign; as one who attacked his prosecution-by-leak in 1973, going out on a limb in this newspaper even as he was sawing that limb off with his "nolo" plea; and as a Jew in the media today, let me offer some sad reflections.

The Ted Agnew of 1970 was neither anti-Zionist nor anti-Semitic. On the contrary, like most Nixon men, he shared an admiration for the patriotism and courage of the Israelis—"moxie," it was then called in the Cabinet room—and throughout his political career, many of his associates and staff members were Jews.

Nor was he anti-intellectual, as many liberals tried to picture him. His blasts against permissiveness, élitism, quotas, and bureaucratic intrusion into individual lives have been reduced to slogans and adopted by most candidates today. Mr. Agnew labored over those speeches, pouring more thought and work into them than most fuzzy stump speakers do today.

What turned him around—business associations with the Arab world? I doubt that. Former Agnew staffers tell me his anti-Semitic cracks first began when the Jewish businessmen he had known in Baltimore County sought immunity by turning state's evidence against him. He became embittered at a handful of Jews, which might well have turned him against Jews in general.

This new prejudice fitted neatly into an old and fruitful hatred: the media. Mouth-filling diatribes against the press (no, I didn't write those) were what made him famous; now he has a fresh angle, a newsworthy slant. Not only was the media too powerful, as he has long said, but it is Jewish-dominated. That's how novels are publicized and disgraced politicians are able to get off the defensive.

Shrewdly, he points out that his assertion that Jews dominate the media and the media dominates America will get him labeled a bigot, while he is only trying to be constructive. The man who twitted liberals for anti-merit affirmative action quotas in 1970 now warns of a group whose influence is "far out of proportion" to its numbers.

Hating individual Jews does not make you a bigot. Being anti-Israel does not make you a bigot. But undertaking a crusade to persuade the American people that they are being brainwashed and manipulated by a cabal of Jews who sit astride most of the channels of communication, and thereby encouraging an irrational hatred of Jews—that makes you a bigot.

The growing anti-Israel lobby, most of which is not bigoted, may be embarrassed by its new cheerleader. But it will find him an articulate spokesman, with an angry following ready to join the cause for all the wrong reasons.

The tragedy of Agnew is that he had the talent and the opportunity to lead those angry people, along with a great many others who felt powerless and unrepresented, toward a satisfying respect for law and tradition, toward greater self-reliance and more personal freedom, and toward a new sense of pride and affirmation in international affairs.

Instead, as he has confessed, he cheated on his taxes. It wasn't the "national-impact media" or any Zionist conspiracy that brought him down: It was only the law.

That is why it saddens old friends to see the former Vice President on television these days reduced to the bitterness of bigoted backbiting. Frustrated and vengeful, he has become what we all once took some joy in deriding: a nattering nabob of negativism.

WILLIAM PALEY

BILL PALEY'S BIG SECRET

March 1, 1976

WASHINGTON—CBS board chairman William Paley has been looking for an excuse to discipline correspondent Daniel Schorr for two years.

Mr. Schorr may be the best television newsman in the field today, figures Mr. Paley, but he is not a "team player." Not only does he refuse to follow the news judgments laid down by the major morning newspapers, but he has been known to criticize network actions at college lectures.

More important, Mr. Paley needs his own Big Enchilada to toss to local affiliate owners who reflect the resentment of what used to be known as the silent majority.

Does the opinion persist that CBS was the fiercest pursuer of Mr. Nixon and even today has a distinct liberal slant to its campaign coverage? If so, figures Mr. Paley, getting rid of Daniel Schorr will help the network "get well" with Middle America, while removing a burr from under the CBS saddle.

As usual, Mr. Paley is out of touch with the way a great many people on the right really feel. When Mr. Nixon was riding high, it is true that correspondent Schorr was a vigorous inquisitor; but after the Nixon power began to wane, and many other reporters rushed in savagely when it became the journalistic fashion, Mr. Schorr was regarded by most of the "Nixon people" as eminently fair in his reports. With no need to suddenly establish anti-Nixon credentials, he covered the news hard, straight, and clean.

Conservatives have also noted how Mr. Schorr's curiosity does not desert him, as it does so many others, when it comes to the power abuses of liberals. He has a way of following a story wherever it leads.

I suspect that CBS plans to use the current furor over the publication of the Pike committee report in *The Village Voice* as its excuse to publicly chastise Mr. Schorr.

Other journalists have provided Mr. Paley with necessary cover. *The Washington Post* (which still preserves its *Deep Throat* fiction about sources) smoked out *The Voice*'s source, and covered its embarrassment about being beaten by making the story about the story more important than the story itself. And a *New York Times* editorial unfairly accused

Mr. Schorr of "laundering" funds—when, as it turns out, he was trying to prevent any commercial publisher from profiting in the publication of the suppressed report.

But wait: Mr. Paley's apparent excuse may evaporate. Reporters have learned that the attorney recommended to Mr. Schorr by the Reporters' Committee was also the attorney for *The Village Voice*, and did not reveal this to him. And it is safe to assume that a reporter, looking for a place to get a document into print, first offers it to his own employer, who happens to have a book subsidiary.

Soon the truth will dawn: Mr. Schorr's "last straw" was not in publishing Mr. Pike's report in *The Voice*, but in exploring Mr. Paley's big secret on CBS.

Here's that story: A few weeks ago, former CBS News president Sig Mickelson told reporters of a time Mr. Paley called him into a meeting with two C.I.A. men to discuss C.I.A.-CBS cooperation. That was a sensitive story; Mr. Schorr did not turn discreetly away, but directed a query to the chairman of the board for his reaction.

Walter Cronkite, to his credit, put the Schorr report on his evening news program, including the Paley reply calling Mr. Mickelson's statement "absolutely untrue" and, in Mr. Schorr's words, "Mr. Paley said he never called news personnel into his office for any discussion with C.I.A. officials."

To me, that little-noticed report was one of the great moments of television news. But the airing of the charge, and the daring of the reporter to penetrate his privacy, must have caused Mr. Paley to burn. It is my guess that from that moment, Mr. Schorr's future at CBS was decided; next day, the Pike report was printed, and soon CBS News made it ominously clear that after its press freedom issue had been defended, it would deal with the impertinent Mr. Schorr in its own way.

That's Mr. Paley's privilege, since he owns the controlling stock. If he should censure Mr. Schorr, he would be following his grand tradition of forcing out Edward R. Murrow and Howard K. Smith, other CBS newsmen who became too uppity.

A pity, though; a prickly conscience is useful for a news organization. We cannot expect Roger Mudd, Dan Rather, or Bob Sheiffer—each one carefully picking his way through the corporate minefield to become the successor to Mr. Cronkite—to burst into the board chairman's office with an imaginary question like this:

"Look, Mr. Paley, we all know that Sig Mickelson is not crazy, and sooner or later the whole story of any involvement CBS has had with the C.I.A. will come to light. The only way we'll lift this cloud that now hangs over every CBS reporter is for us to dig the story out ourselves and lay it out in front of our viewers. Now, how about it, Mr. Paley—on the record and in detail, what did the C.I.A. want us to do and what did we do and who did it?"

Fat chance of that. If and when Daniel Schorr gets Mr. Paley's heat, every newsman in every network will get the message: Rock all the boats, except your own boat; tell the people the truth, except when the truth hurts.

NELSON ROCKEFELLER

SAUCE FOR THE GANDER

September 26, 1974

WASHINGTON—Nelson Rockefeller told the Senate this week that he paid not one shiny dime of Federal income taxes for the year 1970.

How could a man who had an income of two and a half million dollars in 1970 find a way not to pay any Federal income taxes for that year? Answer: He deducted a million and a quarter given to charity, deducted another half million paid in nonincome taxes, and went on to deduct another three-quarters of a million dollars in "office expenses."

What happens when a media favorite like Mr. Rockefeller reveals publicly that he signed his name to a Federal tax return declaring he owed nothing on an income of $2,413,703?

The admission creeps into paragraph seven of *The New York Times* account of the confirmation hearings; *The Washington Post* buries it at the end of its 15th paragraph on page eight, swaddled in a qualifying clause about how he paid lots of state and local taxes that year; the television news from studios in Rockefeller Center mentions it not at all; editorial writers shyly avert their gazes.

Of course, when it had been revealed some years ago that Governor Ronald Reagan, acting within the tax laws, had paid no California taxes, there was a big story and much embarrassment; a similar story brought down Senator Howard Metzenbaum of Ohio.

And when Richard Nixon's tax returns were first revealed, showing that he paid Federal income taxes on a quarter-million income comparable to a man earning $15,000 a year, the furor shook the land at the inequity—even before the legality of Mr. Nixon's deductions came into serious question.

Remember how shameful and damaging it recently used to be for a public figure to use tax loopholes to avoid paying his "fair share" of income taxes? Where are the outraged editorialists now, or the caustic television reporters, or appearances-count columnists who so enjoyed whipping up Populist resentment by shedding crocodile tears for the "little man" who didn't have smart accountants?

Editorial cheeks are dry because, you see, Mr. Rockefeller gave half his income to charities of his choice rather than pay taxes that would have gone to programs of the people's choice. Because he is a Rockefeller, nobody who was incensed about tax avoidance in other politicians bats an eye at his three-quarter of a million dollar "office expense" deduction, or asks about which part of his earned income it was applied against.

When this double standard is called to their attention, the Rockepologists will claim that Rocky was generous and Mr. Nixon a skinflint, Rocky's deductions proper and Mr. Nixon's shady, which may be very true but has nothing to do with the point: Public figures in these times must consider their public relations in figuring out their tax returns, and failing to pay any Federal income taxes at all is hardly setting a good example.

The tax avoidance that was so hateful in the *nouveau-riche* Nixon has suddenly become tolerable in the old-rich Rockefeller; obviously, what is sauce to cook the goose of a Nixon is not sauce when taking a gander at a Rockefeller.

How come? The Eastern Establishment Conspiracy Theory leaves me cold; journalism is not ordinarily afflicted with rampant hypocrisy. Perhaps, in the presence of the superwealthy, we make the same assumptions of wisdom and sensitivity we used to make in the presence of the superpowerful.

The political power of Rockefeller wealth is not, as the Vice Presidential nominee would have us believe, a "myth"; it is a hard fact, as in the spending of ten million dollars in a state campaign, as well as a subtle presence that makes us assume uprightness because there can be no motive for anything else.

When CBS broadcast a laudatory two-hour television special on the Rockefellers, the network did not feel the need to disclose that 12 percent of CBS stock was then in the partial control of the Chase Manhattan Bank, headed by a Rockefeller. No hint of pressure was brought to bear. But our modern reverence for the probity of great wealth often causes otherwise alert guardians of public morality to fail to see even the potential of conflict of interest.

Equal treatment under press is as elusive a goal as equal justice under law, but it is usually worth a try. Richard Nixon's unsuccessful attempt at tax avoidance was stupid, selfish, arrogant, and technically illegal. Nelson Rockefeller's 1970 Federal income-tax return was stupid, arrogant, probably technically legal, and—for a billionaire in politics—reprehensible.

Press favoritism that ignores this blunder will not help Mr. Rockefeller to be a better Vice President. He should be confirmed; but what is being confirmed at his Senate hearings right now is the suspicion that double-standard-bearers are all too ready to overlook in a man "too rich to steal" a mistake that drove them to frenzied fury in a man who had been too powerful to care.

ON CLOSING HURLEY'S BAR

October 16, 1975

WASHINGTON—A generation ago, as a producer of radio and television programs on NBC's New York stations, I worked at the RCA Building in Rockefeller Center. At the end of each celebrity-stricken day, I would wind up—and wind down—having a drink at a little bar on the corner named Hurley's, and it was there that I became a Republican.

Hurley's was a place that respected tradition in a fast-changing neighborhood, having dispensed booze on that spot for more than a century. It had even survived Prohibition, by turning its front window into a flower shop while operating a speakeasy in the back, until the big-government "drys" came to understand that Americans did not want their personal habits legislated.

But the greatest source of inspiration at Hurley's was that tavern's rare display of courage and family pride in the face of monied power. When the Rockefellers bought up all the houses and establishments on the block to knock down and make way for the RCA Building, the Hurleys refused to give up their lease. As a result, the perfect symmetry of Rockefeller Center was spoiled, and its 70-story central edifice had to be built around a rickety 3-story building and bar.

Individualism had triumphed; power was not everything. The Hurleys had thumbed their noses at the Rockefellers and had won; their lease on that old building gave us all a new lease on life.

But leases, like lives, run out. Last week Rockefeller Center took control of the property, ousted the nettlesome Hurley successors, and announced that the century-old bar would be gutted and replaced by—get this—"a real old-fashioned 19th-century tavern of wood and copper."

So the Rockefellers are tearing down the old to make way for the imitation old. Such are the authentic-reproduction signs of the times; you can't even buy real tinsel any more.

That's the Rockefellers for you: big projects on the boards, big intellects on the payroll, big power on display—and none of the street-smartness so necessary to earn the trust of ordinary people.

These thoughts come to mind as the first rift develops in Mr. Ford's White House: On the subject of aiding New York, Mr. Rockefeller, the appointee's appointee, has double-crossed his Administration.

The President is trying to minimize the Vice President's defection, but centrist Republicans elsewhere, who originally supported the Rockefeller appointment, are reviewing the past year's Rockefeller record and wondering if he is somebody they want to stay in national office.

Some conservatives who are concerned about the "tyranny of the majority" remember how Mr. Rockefeller, against the President's wishes, used the most highhanded tactics to break the ability of a minority of Senators to delay majority-demanded legislation. The filibuster is dead; any individualists in the Senate must make way for majoritarian progress.

A few other conservatives have been nagged by an ethical lapse that came up at his confirmation hearings: the $50,000 "tip" he gave to Henry Kissinger after that former Rockefeller hand had been named National Security Adviser. Together, Rockefeller and Kissinger have controlled the makeup of the Foreign Intelligence Advisory Board since 1969 and obviously the oversights were underset.

Many Republicans—and not the clutch-fist crowd, either—were stunned by Mr. Rockefeller's single "bold new initiative": a $100-billion off-budget Federal Energy Authority to guarantee risky loans with public funds, while the people who run it are immune to public opinion.

The "authority" route, an American form of fascism popular here in the 30's and 40's, may be efficient but is hardly in tune with either conservative or progressive Republican principles. When asked about the opposition to this scheme by other Administration financial men, Mr. Rockefeller said, in effect—let 'em resign, the President's already made his decision.

That strong endorsement of team play may haunt Mr. Rockefeller in his sudden conversion to the cause of using Federal money for city financial support. On this, the Vice President has left the reservation. If Mr. Ford wants to pretend there is only a "minimal" difference between them, then the President (a) has changed his own mind, (b) does not understand what the Vice President said, or (c) is trying to be all things to all men.

Those are the reasons Mr. Ford's first big appointment has become his first big albatross. Democratic candidates (everybody and his brother-in-law is running for President) will charge that Rockefeller is being dumped to "placate the right wing."

But it is more accurate to say he is likely to be dumped because some Republicans are offended at his big-spending energy scheme, some are dismayed at his flip-flopping on bailing out New York, some are vengeful at his decision to let the steamroller roll in the Senate, some are worried about the pervasive Kissinger connection, some are leery of his tendency to forget that he's only number two.

And some of us will remember the closing of Hurley's bar.

JOHN CONNALLY

CROSS HAIRS ON CONNALLY

April 7, 1975

WASHINGTON—"Ah wouldn't trust that feller," John Connally used to say about untrustworthy characters, "any further than Ah could throw a chimney by its smoke."

Today, a jury will listen to Jake Jacobsen, a former Lyndon Johnson aide, being cross-examined by Defense Counsel Edward Bennett Williams, and will form its impression about whether to trust Mr. Jacobsen's accusation that he bribed John Connally.

Leaks from the Special Prosecutor's office for the past year have hinted at additional circumstantial evidence that would clinch the case; no such "smoking gun" has been produced so far, however, and now we are being told that the case boils down to which man is to be believed—the accuser or the accused.

That is not strictly true. Put yourself in the jury box. You are not merely asked to believe Mr. Jacobsen, a confessed perjurer who is testifying in order to escape prosecution for alleged felonies in Texas. You are also asked to believe The Good Guys—the Watergate Special Prosecution force—who have been hailed and sanctified over the past two years as avenging angels combating the Forces of Evil.

Now put yourself in the shoes of the typical juror. You are a black and poor Washingtonian, being asked to overcome natural prejudices in judging a rich and white Texan. You do your best to set aside ingrained animosities, just as a Catholic juror tries to do in an abortion case, or a Jewish juror in a case involving an Arab terrorist, or a white juror in a case involving a black defendant.

But that is not easy to do, which is why the Special Prosecutor likes to try big cases strictly within the District of Columbia.

It is no coincidence that every Watergate case brought to trial in Washington, D.C., has resulted in a conviction, and the only Watergate-related case tried before a non-D.C. jury—in New York—resulted in an acquittal. The prosecution's "edge" here is so enormous as to be scandalous.

In this recession-proof, political capital, the local media has devoted far more attention to Watergate than anywhere else; Mr. Nixon "and his henchmen" are hated here with an intensity unmatched elsewhere in the nation; and any fair-minded observer would list this city at the very bottom of a list of a thousand places where a trial should be held in order to be fair.

Serves 'em right, people say; a taste of their own medicine; what did those Nixon men care about individual rights when they were in the saddle? Thus, prosecutions soaked in prejudicial publicity before partisan juries are accepted as a kind of poetic justice at a time when our law courts could use more justice and less poetry.

Of course, this jury could upset the odds and find Mr. Connally innocent. If the charge-dropping bribe paid to Mr. Jacobsen by the prosecution is too galling; if the jurors are not shown incontrovertible evidence to corroborate the central part of the accuser's story; and if—above all—Ed Williams can separate John Connally from the guilt-by-association aura of Watergate, then perhaps conviction of former Nixon officials in the District of Columbia will prove to be nonautomatic.

One antidote does exist to counter the poison of Nixon association, which is why Mr. Connally has a slim chance. His attorney, the Clarence Darrow of this generation, needs no instruction from the sidelines, but he would stand a better chance if he could counter the Nixon tape with the Zapruder film.

John Connally has been the target of two different kinds of assassins. One took aim from the Texas School Book Depository on Nov. 22, 1963, and drilled a bullet into his back while he was accompanying President John F. Kennedy. Lee Harvey Oswald nearly succeeded in assassinating Governor John Connally as well.

Whether or not a different kind of assassin—a character assassin, if such he be—will succeed in terminating Mr. Connally's political life is up to the jury. The analogy is not all that farfetched. At least Mr. Jacobsen has a rational purpose for seeking to strike down Mr. Connally: The accuser is freed from prosecution of criminal fraud in an unrelated case.

Mr. Connally's tragic association with President Kennedy may balance the local antipathy to President Nixon; his counsel's reputation may compete with the never-miss-in-D.C. luster of a prosecution that will dwell on the word "Watergate" at every chance.

Whichever way it goes, it's jake with Jake. Thanks to the Special Prosecutor, Mr. Jacobsen is out of his big Texas fraud trouble, and has pleaded guilty only to giving a bribe. If the jury does not believe that he bribed Mr. Connally, and sees him as a false accuser—then no bribe was given, and Mr. Jacobsen has his freedom and a good, long laugh.

CHARLES "LUCKY" LUCIANO

I REMEMBER LUCKY

December 23, 1974

WASHINGTON—Charles "Lucky" Luciano, king of the underworld in the 30's and 40's, may now be enjoying the last laugh from beyond the grave.

His *Last Testament*, supposedly dictated to a movie producer just before the gangster's death in 1962, is being published by Little, Brown, has been chosen as the Book-of-the-Month, and—for a while, at least—seemed to command a paperback resale of close to a million dollars.

Then Nicholas Gage, a reporter for *The New York Times* who often covers organized crime, blew the whistle, calling into question the validity of the book. The events recounted can be found in other published works, even to the extent of picking up other errors; no tapes or notes of Lucky Luciano have been produced as yet in support of the *Testament*'s authenticity; and there is the strange case of how Lucky got his nickname.

In the book the writer, working from the notes of the movie producer who is supposed to have taken it all down from Luciano himself, relates an incident in 1929: The young mobster was "taken for a ride," stabbed and beaten, but—fortunately—not murdered. Hence the nickname "Lucky."

But reporter Gage dug up the contemporary newspaper account of that beating, which began "Charles (Lucky) Luciano," showing that the gangster had been known as Lucky before that incident. Does this mean that the *Last Testament* is spurious, a product of pastepot and clippings—or was Lucky himself telling that phony story of the origin of his nickname in the final years of his exile?

Perhaps I can be of some assistance. In 1954, as an Army corporal assigned to the American Forces Network in Europe, I was covering some dull NATO maneuvers out of Naples and decided to try to record some interviews with local personalities.

My first target was Ingrid Bergman and Roberto Rosselini, at the time a controversial couple trailblazing today's marital mores for celebrities. "The United States Army is down in the lobby and wants to interview you" was an unorthodox approach that worked. Encouraged after getting them for an hour on tape, I looked up the other most-famous resident of Naples, Lucky Luciano.

That cautious, polite, swarthy gentleman did not want to speak into a microphone at first, but he was fascinated by the tape I had just finished making with Miss Bergman, a woman he worshiped from afar. Had they ever met? "Of course not," the considerate racketeer replied, "she shouldn't associate with me."

In the lobby of the Albergo Vesuvio, with a Federal narcotics agent quietly observing us from a corner, the gangster put on earphones and listened, enraptured, to Miss Bergman describe her role in *Joan of Arc*. But when movie director Rosselini appeared on the tape, an expression of embittered outrage, and then of pure malevolence, crossed Mr. Luciano's face.

"Can you imagine," said the man who had been imprisoned for heading the prostitution racket in the United States, "any guy takin' advantage of a woman like that?"

In that spirit of moral indignation, the man described by Thomas E. Dewey in *Twenty Against the Underworld* as "the greatest gangster in America" consented to a few mild questions with a recorder spinning.

"They're all lies," he said of the accusations against him. "How can you fight back, when the press is against me? Some of them try to give me a fair shake, but they can't get it in print." Mr. Luciano felt strongly that he was the target of a media conspiracy; later in life, I was to run across an identical attitude elsewhere.

Since the story of how he came by his nickname has fresh relevance this week, I dug up the old recording (try to find a needle that plays 78 RPM) and refreshed my recollection.

How did he get nicknamed "Lucky"?

"Bein' that my right name was Luccania," he said matter-of-factly, "it was cut short when I was a young boy, and made it 'Lucky.' "

But what about the famous story about the time in 1929 when he was taken for a ride, and miraculously escaped and was called Lucky afterward?

"Not true." Even after 20 years and on a scratchy record, Lucky's resounding "Not true" comes across as the irritated denial of a legendary figure who is not pleased with that part of his own legend.

I must have looked disappointed; curling a lip, he added, "all newspaper talk." He hated the press, and delighted in shooting down whatever reporters liked to build up.

Would this man, some years later, recounting his life to a biographer, change character and meekly accept the "newspaper talk" as the truth? Hardly; and the fact that reputable publishers have swallowed that concoction must be causing Mr. Luciano paroxysms in purgatory if not hilarity in hell.

January 23, 1975

Dear Mr. Safire:

Your remembering Lucky made me remember Molly. When I came to live and work in New York straight out of the Yale Law School in the early '40's and post-Luciano prosecution period, I had the opportunity to talk on many occasions with a very efficient and humanizing secretary who had once been, as I recall it now, the secretary to Thomas E. Dewey or at least one of the secretaries who participated in his crusade to the governorship through the New York District Attorney's Office.

This crusade rolled along the Appian way of criminal convictions of sundry big-name crime figures, who no doubt needed convicting, including Lucky Luciano. But the thing which niggled my young lawyer's mind as I went about being a deputy assistant district attorney in the office of Mr. Dewey's successor was the attestation of that secretary, whom I remember only as Molly, that a prosecutor with the noble ambition to be governor of New York would lean under the high ideals of prosecutorial noblesse to frame a defendant to the end that the conviction of Luciano should fall in place among the others.

For Molly told me that while Lucky had been involved up to his hair roots in crime of every sort, she was told by reliable police sources and even the prostitute witnesses who perjured themselves to make the "frame" stick, that the only thing Lucky Luciano never involved himself in personally was the procuring of participants for the age-old profession nor the acceptance of one cent of tribute from that particular endeavour.

Hence, it comes as no great surprise or amused commemoration as it did to you, Mr. Safire, that Mr. Luciano reacted as he did to the mistreatment of Ingrid Bergman by Roberto Rosselini and could not "imagine . . . any guy takin' advantage of a woman like that. . . ." If Molly was accurate, Dewey got Luciano, but he didn't get him right, and that might explain Mr. Luciano's ability to assume moral outrage at the desecration of womanhood. I garnered other information, solely for my own curious inquiry, into the ways and means of ambitious prosecutors, which corroborated Molly. I felt even a racketeer should be convicted only for that which he did criminally. And it would seem that his conviction for the prostitution racket was just as "strange" as the case in which he got his nickname. And Charles "Lucky" Luciano may now be laughing from beyond the grave at both Reporter Gage and Essayist Safire.

Very truly yours,
S. Allen Early, Jr.
Detroit, Michigan

On Language

LIKE MOST WRITERS, I don't live to write, I write to live. But I enjoy what I do, and take a certain delight in examining, sharpening, and playing with the tools of my trade.

Lexicography has been a sideline of mine since the mid-60's, when I turned out a worst seller, titled (or entitled, if you wish) *The New Language of Politics.* Writing about the words used in political discourse led me to writing about writing generally, and some of my most enjoyable afternoons have been spent celebrating Webster's birthday or pricking the balloons of legalese.

After enough of these essays, it occurred to A. M. Rosenthal, executive editor of *The New York Times,* that I might launch a nonpolitical column for the Sunday *Magazine.* ("Eureka!" he shouted, explaining to the others in the meeting: "That means 'I've found it.'") That has resulted in a book of its own—nothing is wasted in this business—but here is a sample of what got me my assignment as a Dr. Jekyll on Sunday.

THE POLITICS OF LANGUAGE

May 7, 1973

WASHINGTON—Back when we had a half million troops in Vietnam, an irate citizen wrote a letter to the White House addressed not to the President but to his speechwriters. Why did the President keep warning about "precipitous withdrawals," the writer wanted to know, when the correct adjective was "precipitate"?

Heatedly, the citizen correcting the President pointed out the difference: while both words come from "precipice," or brink, precip*itous* means steep (as in "a precipitous slope") and precipi*tate* means abrupt or headlong (as in "precipitate action").

Accordingly, a "usage alert" was distributed throughout the White House four years ago, and from that day on we all inveighed against "precipitate withdrawals."

When the President spoke on television recently about Watergate, and cautioned, "I was determined not to take precipitate action . . ." at least one viewer out of the 73 million who were watching said to himself: "By George, he's got it!"

Words, words, words. Attention to the use of language betokens a concern for orderliness and precision, and the people who write to Presidents or essayists to set them straight about the use of a word are a hardy bunch, good-humored about being stern, like traffic cops at school crossings.

Occasionally, appreciators of English blow their cool: After four years of listening to the metaphor of the computer favored by Press Secretary Ron Ziegler—input, programmed, time frame—his use of "inoperative" in withdrawing past statements set a great many teeth on edge. That was understandable, but why did the use of "compassion" by Henry Kissinger, about those who may be involved in acts of zealotry, stir such passionate response from Administration critics? Mario Pei's *Double-Speak in America* reports that the word compassion "has now become a shibboleth of the moderate left . . ." and as such, its use on Nixonian lips drove long-standing compassionaries up the wall.

Nor were they the only ones to take offense in the linguistic crossfire over Watergate: Every time the call went out for a special prosecutor of *unimpeachable* integrity, Nixon men took it as a not-too-subliminal affront, and silently seethed.

By and large, however, word watchers introduce a note of good sense and good grace, of interested disinterest, to the action and passion of their times. The word for a thing is not the thing itself—a pig is only a marking of letters on paper and not a flesh-and-blood animal, or a slang derogation and not a real police officer. The sense of dealing with a subject once removed from reality gives the lovers of language both their balance and their self-image of proud eccentricity, as they try to brush back a flood with a whisk broom.

In that spirit of respect, I must disagree with the gentleman who chastises me for using "proven" when Fowler's *Modern English Usage* says the proper word is "proved"; on that usage, the great book is outdated. I take issue with the lady who categorically rejects all euphemisms, because that would have denied F.D.R. and J.F.K. the use of "quarantine" to soften the diplomatic impact of a blockade. Nor will I dispense with "élitist" until convinced "racist" and "sexist" will sink with it.

What is more (it's easy to get worked up over this), nothing is wrong with the acceptance of colorful, if transitory, metaphors like "to blow your cool" or "to drive him up the wall," just as nothing is wrong with chewing gum in public, provided you do so quietly and dispose of it in a suitable wrapper. However, the advertising community's slavish following of the youth culture's "into"—as in "to be into Bach"—turns me off, conveying the image of a violated composer. ("Turns me off," by the way, turns me on—but it is a similarly foolish affectation, with drug-related overtones, and I'd better cut it out.)

There is a point to all this: The language of politics has much to learn from the politics of language.

In the language of politics, the apt alliteration of an Agnew competes with the colorful imagery of a Connally ("Ah wouldn't trust that feller further than Ah could throw a chimney by its smoke," he once expostulated), which is healthy; but there also exists a sinister tendency to deceive, to make the fluffy ponderous and to make the heavy light, and worst of all, to exaggerate and inflame, making a difference of opinion appear to be a difference of principle.

In the politics of language, the prescriptive school (don't say different *than*, say different *from*) is different from the descriptive school, which holds that general usage dictates "correctness." One is strict, the other permissive, one conservative and the other liberal, and they clash. But they go for each other's minds, not for each other's throats. They sally forth in civility and come home in compromise.

"English is my native tongue," writes a man who does not like my prose style at all, complaining rationally about a piece in this space. "I read the article twice. I still have no idea what Mr. Safire is trying to tell me." And then he concludes: "In fairness, I have a head cold."

May 8, 1973

Dear Mr. Safire:

A man who tacitly presumes under the heading of "Essay" to emulate in matter and manner his eighteenth-century predecessors should be careful not to dangle his modifiers so provocatively before "appreciators of English"—especially in an essay on usage.

In "The Politics of Language," which appeared yesterday in *The Times*, the modifier "After four years of listening to the metaphor," etc., modifies something incapable of listening, namely, Ron Ziegler's "use of 'inoperative.'" It is not just misplaced for "teeth"; even a "great many teeth" are similarly incapable of listening. No matter how many years pedants have listened to danglers, this one is going to set their teeth on edge, as a great many may already have told you.

In the third to the final paragraph, with an inexactness of syntax typical of commercial and political obfuscators, the relative phrase "which is healthy" is relative, at best, to the entire preceding clause. But pronouns are designed to take the place of nouns, not clauses. It is not Connally "which is healthy" (certainly not the quoted "chimney"); it is the linguistic competition between him and Agnew "which is healthy."

Let's keep it that way.

Sincerely,
(Mrs.) Ruth Ann Lief
Bronx, New York

WEBSTER'S BIRTHDAY

October 15, 1973

WASHINGTON—Tomorrow, on October 16, lexicographers the world over will celebrate the 215th anniversary of the birth of Noah Webster.

The writers of dictionaries will face toward West Hartford, Conn., his birthplace, and affectionately retell the apocryphal story of the time that wordy worthy was embracing the chambermaid when his wife unexpectedly burst into the bedroom.

"Noah, I'm surprised!" Mrs. Webster expostulated. Whereupon the great definer coolly responded, "No, my dear. You are amazed. It is we who are surprised."

But October 16 must not be only a day of anecdotage and merry puns: It is a day, too, for thoughtful second soberings. This has been quite a linguistic year.

Ron Ziegler has much to answer for in the coinage of "the President misspoke himself"; his computer program terminology, from "input" to "time frame," came a-creeper with "inoperative."

This essayist stubbed his pencil on "centered around," which several readers circled and sent in with "There's a neat trick," and on another occasion I threw down a gantlet instead of a gauntlet. (I miswrote myself.)

Watergate writers made the long leap from "caper" to "horror"; the "plumbers" gained a meaning beyond that of George Meany's profession; and the metaphysical cliché of the year became "at this point in time."

The most frequently misspelled new word at the Senate hearings was "misprision," a precise legal word rooted in the French *méprendre*, to err, and quickly replaced by the easier-to-spell "coverup," which soon lost its hyphen and thus its virginity.* (Why am I impelled to point out here that "Senator" and "senile" come from the same root?)

"Hardball" is probably the most useful new coinage in politicalingo, to differentiate between the tough but legal activity that our side engages in, from the "dirty trick" that your side perpetrates.

The translation error most frequently made in the last year was that the name "Segretti" means "secret" in Italian: No less an authority than Mario Pei, America's leading vocabularian, writing in the quarterly *Modern Age*, held that "Segreti (single t) is the term for 'secrets,' and the single or double 't' gives the two words different pronunciations and derivations." (Mr. Pei is of Italian descent; he is sometimes thought to be Chinese when his name is confused with I. M. Pei, the architect, who is.)

The most furious inter-columnar battle over the meaning of an Americanism took place between David Broder and Mike Royko, on the word "clout." Washington's Broder used the word as defined in my dictionary—"power, or influence"—and Chicagoan Royko clobbered the "brazen misuse" of a word he takes to mean not power, but purely influence: "Clout is used to circumvent the law, not to enforce it," wrote Mr. Royko. When Mr. Broder sent this to me with "I relied on your goddam book and look what trouble I'm in," I turned to the ultimate arbiter, Arthur Krock, down the hall.

"Clout means impact," said Mr. Krock, disagreeing with all of us. "If I say something, it has an effect on public opinion, it has 'clout.' If you say it, it does not." That's it, gentlemen: Mr. Krock was probably a personal friend of Noah Webster.

The most brilliant pun of the year (there are a few of these awards envelopes still to open) was in a *Wall Street Journal* headline about a solvent developed to clean oil slick off sea gulls, harmless but temporarily befuddling: "Leaves no tern unstoned."

The most profound punster was Dan Rather of CBS, with his assessment of the energy crisis, which began: "You can fuel some of the people all of the time . . ."

The best new word that fills a gap in the language was minted by architectural writer Ada Louise Huxtable to describe a happy marriage of form and function: "beautility."

The best political derogation was Governor Ronald Reagan's characterization of the expensive medical program put forth by Senator Edward Kennedy: "Teddycare."

And the grammatical error most frequently made reflects a sad state of affairs: indictments are never "handed down," they are only "handed up."

---

* Throughout this book, "coverup" is hyphenated, which conforms to *New York Times* style. Only in language can a frequently-violated term regain its virginity.

Indictment grammar and etymology are worth studying because they metaphorically preserve truths too soon forgotten: An indictment is an accusation handed up to a high bench where a judge sits, for further adjudication. The Latin derivations in oldest dictionaries give us the most up-to-the-minute political guidance: An indictment means "the writing down of a charge," and only a verdict means "the speaking of the truth."

Happy birthday, Noah.

Oct. 15, 1973

Dear Bill Safire:

I enjoyed your Noah Webster/word/phrase column today (being so constituted that such matters interest me far more than the state of the Union).

The story you tell about Noah being surprised and his wife amazed I had always heard as being attributed to Dr. Johnson. With it, I always heard, went this one:

Dr. Johnson was, of course, notorious for not being overfond of clean linen, or bathing. At a dinner party once he sat next to a young lady who, after a while, couldn't help remarking: "Doctor, you smell."

"Ah, no, my dear," says Dr. Johnson. "*You* smell. *I* stink."

Totally apocryphal, no doubt, but it does—like your Noah Webster story—illustrate the nice distinctions between words which keep getting lost, to everyone's loss.

I was also interested in the business about indictments being hand up and not down. I've noticed that error repeatedly, and sometimes in *The Times*. Still—venturing to quibble—is that a *grammatical* error, as you say? More a mistake in usage, I should have thought.

Regards,
Dick Hanser
Mamaroneck, New York

October 15, 1973

Op-Ed Page, The Times

Gentlemen:

Certes this point in space has endured "quite a linguistic year" (William Safire's "Webster's Birthday"), perhaps a whimper compared with the brutal bangs of the Eisenhower years, when a generation was taught to split its infinitives, interchange like and as, say finalize when it meant finish and directive when it meant order and learn to love bigger, better noo-kew-ler weaponry.

And the hyphen—ye gods, the hyphen! If Safire now sees cover-up losing its virginity, how many of our maidens were laid waste in those hurryup years? Where are any more, all right, business man and teen-ager (the latter barbarous enough before it was welded into oneword)?

Among other syntactical vandalism 1973 may whimper about is the introduction to urbanity of the term "track record" in persistent impropriety. A track record, as any Aqueduct Special rider knows, is the fastest time recorded for a particular distance over a particular track; what the jet-setters and "newscasters" are trying to say is Past Performance, as the *Daily Racing Form* designates such history in inch-high letters every day.

In the interest of history, Mr. Safire's boudoir anecdote was the more apocryphal because it was not Noah Webster who was surprised in the bedroom with the chambermaid, but another lexicographer, Samuel Johnson. (The consensus of off-the-record historians is that Dr. Johnson's wife caught them in the pantry, but no matter.) And he told his wife that she was astonished, not amazed. Had the happening happened to Webster's wife, she well might have been what Noah defined as amazed (greatly astonished) or at least astounded (stunned with bewildered wonder). But Mrs. Johnson was, Dr. Samuel advised her, merely astonished. She was aware of his Past Performance, which may have included a track record or two.

John A. Mann Jr.
McLean, Virginia

THISTLEBOTTOMISM

December 24, 1973

WASHINGTON—"Miss Thistlebottom's Hobgoblins" was the name of a delightful book about word usage written by Theodore Bernstein of *The New York Times* two years ago.

"Miss Thistlebottom" was a mythical English teacher, and her hobgoblins were fussbudget rules that—rigidly applied—obfuscate rather than clarify meaning. It was a Thistlebottom who insisted that Winston Churchill not end a sentence with a preposition, to which he thundered, "This is an impertinence up with which I will not put!"

Recently, a group of Thistlebottoms has been formed by the National Council of Teachers of English into a "Committee on Public Doublespeak," charged with finding and exposing what the teachers call "lying in public places," which could mean reclining in libraries but probably refers to the use of euphemisms by public officials.

"We need to point out to kids," says Walker Gibson, president of the teachers' council, "that they are being conned in many ways by powerful, rich forces." (The use of "rich" in that statement tends to foster class hatred; as used by some teachers today, "rich" has a pejorative connotation, like "political.")

The Public Doublespeak Committee will "combat semantic distortion," it says. An example of the distortion it will expose: "protective reaction," a Pentagon term for air strike, which is a dragon that has frequently been slain.

But where does "semantic distortion" begin? In the halls of academe, that's where, as malleable little minds are worked over by pretentious Thistlebottoms.

Who took a chubby little boy named Ronny Ziegler, bombarded him with computer terminology at a tender age—even to the point of using "program" as a verb—until, years later, "inoperative" sprang unbidden to his lips?

Who took the words "contemporaries" and "equals"—that convey honest meanings—and cast them into the ashcan, to be picked up by garbage men, now called sanitation engineers, semantically distorting them into the harsh and pseudoscientific "peer group"? The pedageezers, that's who, not the politicians.

Physician, *spiel* thyself. In spoken discourse, who has elevated the verb "to orient" to the acme of academic vogue, and not by occident? The "peer-group-oriented" child hardly knows where his head is at, and one Far East expert at the State Department described himself as "Orient-oriented."

Have you ever tried to pin a Thistlebottom down to specifics without getting back a fistful of Pablum he or she calls an "overview"? How come the "underview" is not part of academic jargon? Bel Kaufman, in *Up the Down Staircase*, defined "interpersonal relationships" as a fight between kids, and a request for "ancillary civic agencies for supportive discipline" as a frantic academic euphemism for "Call the cops!"

Wading through the meaningless "meaningfuls," the irrelevant "relevants," the cancerous "viables," and the madness of "methodology," it is not hard to see how the jargon-fed graduates of our school systems turn into the jargoneers of the Pentagon, cranking this in and phasing that out, exacerbating, quantifying, proliferating as they were taught to do. They were weaned on hegemonized milk.

The scenario-oriented general, gruffly barking "What are the options?" is the pupil who started to say "choose" one day when his teacher came back with the voguish "opt"; that child swore never to be one-opt again.

I'm not really angry at English teachers; I was started on my way with words by Miss Ruth Goldstein of the Bronx High School of Science, and hardly a typewriter clicks whose pounder does not owe a debt to some Miss Thistlebottom somewhere.

And it is a great idea to combat semantic distortion, so long as one begins at home and never pretends that an "Orwell Award"—named after the essayist who held that political speech was "largely the defense of the indefensible"—is limited to men seeking political power.

For with all the doublespeak spoken by teachers and politicians who would like to consense us, we can also hear the vivid phrases that inspire, inflame, or infuriate: from the apt appellation of leak-pluggers as "plumbers," to the cruelly evocative "twisting slowly, slowly in the wind," to the use by John Mitchell of Joseph P. Kennedy's immortal line: "When the going gets tough, the tough get going."

That enlivens and bespirits the discourse, and calls for toppers, not stoppers: Teachers of English should not just be pointing to the manipulative use of language but hailing the birth of colorful phrases.

Examples are everywhere. Sprayed on the side of a New York subway car was a Latin student's social comment: "Gloria mundi is sick of transit." And across a table in a Washington restaurant, Presidential counsel Leonard Garment summed up the Administration's energy policy with a paraphrase of St. Matthew: "Many are cold, but few are frozen."

Tell that to your peer group, Miss Thistlebottom.

THE WORD-WATCHERS

August 15, 1974

WASHINGTON—In Cottondale, Ala., I. Willis Russell, professor emeritus of the University of Alabama, sifts through newspapers and magazines looking for new words, or new uses of old words. He is the dean of America's word-watchers.

But Professor Russell is growing old, and to make certain that new words do not go unwatched, he has trained a younger colleague, Professor Mary Gray Porter, to take his place. Together, they kneel among the neologisms in *American Speech*, the most leisurely quarterly magazine published anywhere in the world, now ambling along toward the publication of its Spring, 1971 issue.

But an even more deliberative publication, the Oxford English Dictionary, makes *American Speech* look like a deadline-happy daily rushing to hit the streets with its bulldog edition. Every forty years or so, the "OED" publishes a supplement to its monumental 13-volume work.

The word-watcher in the United States who does his thing for the Oxford University Press is Peter Tamony of San Francisco. Mr. Tamony's hallmark is early derivation, while Professors Russell and Porter excel in discovering citations of current usage. All three are on guard against treating as permanent the "nonce words" that whiz through the language like Kahoutek's flop comet.

"Nonce words" and phrases that marked the Nixon years, for example, were descriptions of events such as "Saturday night massacre" or "third-rate burglary." These will fade, like "(expletive deleted)," "inoperative," and "smoking gun," which are linguistic barnacles of an event limited in time.

More likely to last, but in a technical rather than general vocabulary, are locutions like "plumbers" (to plug the leaks of news) or "black advance," (to disrupt a political opposition's rallies). Some word-watchers feel that "tilt"—as in "tilt toward Pakistan"—may be with us to stay, but new words in order to last must fill a vacuum in vocabulary; "tilt" is merely a synonym for "lean," and we need not worry about renaming Pisa's tilting tower.

The lexicon of business, which contributed "lame duck" (a bankrupt broker) to politics a century ago, has been frequently heard in square Government circules recently: But "bottom line," which is more vivid and less redundant than "end result," is not likely to replace the more established phrase. Similarly, nitso on "net-net."

"To bring up to speed" was used occasionally in the Watergate hearings, meaning "to brief." Tom Brokaw of NBC wondered if this had a television derivation, and his suspicion was well-founded: Mr. Tamony tracks the phrase back to early radio broadcasting, as a technique to avoid the "wow" sound of a recording's start. A warmed-up turntable was considered "up to speed," or ready for use.

Of all the words of tongue or pen (the saddest are these, it might have been, but life goes on) the single most useful new word to come out of the early 70's is the verb form of "stonewall." No other word exists to describe its meaning: "filibuster" (from the Dutch word for free booter, or pirate) means to delay, or talk to death, but to stonewall has come to mean something else—to rigidly resist inquiry, to make obfuscation a policy.

"Stonewall" as a verb originated in the game of cricket, as a term for playing solely on the defensive. Australian political slang picked it up in the late 19th century, and it was adopted quickly by British politicians.

In America, stonewalling was rarely used: The citation in Webster's New International Unabridged Dictionary is a James Reston column of the late 50's, "stonewalling for time in order to close the missile gap." But then Henry Kissinger picked up the term: I first heard him use it in late 1969 as, "the North Vietnamese are stonewalling us."

As a needed figure of speech, the word's usage increased; more stones were added as a strategy of silence was adopted by the Watergaters, and when the President's tapes revealed him to have said "I want you to stonewall it," the word was sealed into the language.

Stonewalling has a pejorative connotation today. But long before its scornful use by cricketeers, politicians from Down Under and up above, the figure of speech was used in admiration during our Civil War about one of the Confederacy's greatest generals: "There stands Jackson, like a stone wall!"

Might it be possible, someday, for stonewalling to regain an admirable connotation? The word-watchers will be watching.

ON POLITICAL SIMILES

February 27, 1975

WASHINGTON—The art of the simile is as dead as a doornail.

Here we are, making do with expressions like "smart as a whip," "blind as a bat," "happy as a lark," and "sound as a dollar," which were coined centuries ago.

The simile's less explicit cousin, the metaphor, is constantly being renewed and updated. The economy is treated as a metaphoric automobile, slamming on brakes and overheating its engine. The political system, still a word-picture ship of state, charts "new directions" while critics charge it is "off course."

But the simile—the specific, daring insistence that an idea is similar to a symbol—lies there, flat as a pancake, with none so pure to do irreverence.

A generation ago, tough-guy fiction writers like Dashiell Hammett and Raymond Chandler revived the art for a short time; Chandler's classic of the genre was a description of a heroine "blonde enough to make a bishop kick a hole through a stained-glass window."

American discourse, however, is reflected by—not determined by—novelists. Pervasive figures of speech are invented or popularized by political writers and speakers. The "cold war" was coined by Herbert Bayard Swope for Bernard Baruch; "iron curtain" by Churchill out of the Earl of Munster; "eyeball to eyeball' by Dean Rusk, and "hawks and doves" by Stewart Alsop and Charles Bartlett, political commentators all.

Why, then, have today's political people given similes no more of a chance than a snowball in hell? There are exceptions. Historian William Manchester wrote of a fateful day that dawned "as clear and crisp as a Kennedy order." And Daniel Patrick Moynihan—it seems so long ago—talked of programs "as evanescent as the mists over San Clemente."

The easy way to create similes is to play on the characteristics of famous people, along the lines of "rich as Croesus" or "blameless as Epictetus," both of which are easier to write than to pronounce. Today, "relaxed as Mondale," "self-effacing as Rockefeller," and "overscheduled as

Reagan" spring to mind, as well as "unassailable as Nader" and "unavailable as Kennedy."

More imaginative are the categorical similes, such as "poor as a church mouse." This spawns "lionized as an investigative reporter," "inexorable as a bicentennial," "leaky as a Senate committee," or "fresh as an impeachment."

The rhyming simile—"snug as a bug in a rug"—can be approached as "cheeky as a chic sheik," but the lost art of the specific metaphor is best illustrated in its situational form, on the analogy of "busy as a one-armed paperhanger."

This gives rise to "as anxiously revered as a freshman at a caucus," "as greasy as a public opinion poll," or "as lost as a moralist in a fogbank of détente."

Situational similes come into their own on purely political matters: "as confident as a Ways and Means chairman on a tax-cut vote" and, contrariwise, "as nervous as a WASP, male, Nixon holdover in the Ford Cabinet."

On the rainy, rainy, days ahead, let a simile be your umbrella. The inventive, wholesome activity enriches the language and enlivens turgid speeches, and it need not be as convoluted as some of the examples here.

Last week in Katmandu, Nepal, for example, a young man was crowned absolute monarch of that high-rise Himalayan land, and the words he spoke were royal in their simplicity.

"For the welfare of the people, I am ready to be the king," declared Birendra Bir Bikram Shah Dev. Just before the high priest of the kingdom placed the crown on his head, the 29-year-old ruler-to-be made this pledge:

"I will be popular like the raindrop. I will be friendly like the sun."

Where are you going to beat a speech like that these days? Back to the fundamental device of the simile, with two original twists that turned a political promise into a mystic evocation of water and light, crowning his coronation like a rainbow in the sky.

SECRETS OF "AMERICAN ENGLISH" MAY YIELD TO DIALECT GEOGRAPHY

September 28, 1975

In Bernard Shaw's *Pygmalion*, Professor Henry Higgins was able to pinpoint the district of origin of a Cockney flower girl by listening to her accent and vocabulary. Could that be done today by an American linguistics expert and a local Eliza Doolittle?

Thanks to a growing branch of language study called dialect geography, the answer may be yes.

Since the early 30's, when dialect pioneer Hans Kurath began gathering data for his linguistic atlas of the eastern United States, language researchers in other sections of the country have been working on regional atlases to discover how words, usages, and accents have traveled from one locality to another, as well as between social classes.

Dialect geography is not yet a full-fledged academic discipline, but Professor Harold Allen of the University of Minnesota estimates that there are now 25 specialists active in the field. Much of their work dovetails to make possible a coast-to-coast study of the way "American English" came to be.

One set of clues is in word usage: Do you *pick* cotton or *chop* cotton? Do you *take* cream or *use* cream?

Other clues are in vocabulary: A *hero* in New York is a *hoagy* in Philadelphia and a *sub* in Washington, D.C.

Still other footprints of language movement can be found in pronunciation: A California *oar-inge* is shipped east to become an *ar-ringe*, as New England *grease* turns to *greaze* as it dribbles south of Trenton.

Most geographers of language agree that the information gathered so far indicates that several dialects of British English landed along the American Eastern Seaboard. These became spiced with Americanisms borrowed from traders, Indians, and slaves, or coined to describe freshly discovered situations, and the speech styles trekked westward in traceable patterns.

"Take *pail* and *bucket*," says Dr. Kurath, professor emeritus of the University of Michigan, author of *Studies in Area Linguistics* and, in active retirement at 83, regarded as the father of dialect geography. "In New England, through the upper Midwest to Seattle, a container made of metal is called a *pail*. But from Pennsylvania west and southward, the same container is called a *bucket*. There's a complication: If it's made of wood, the New England and northern word would also be *bucket*, taken from ship's buckets and fire buckets. You have to be careful."

Years of selective sampling have led to the drawing of dialect dividing lines, and a dozen dialect areas have emerged. Dr. Kurath stresses that dialect differences exist within each area, in social gradation from folk speech to cultivated speech, and that constant migration commingles American dialects.

Pronunciation patterns show the spoor of the mobile language. "Mary married Harry," for example. East of the Alleghenies, all three words are pronounced generally alike; in the West, says Dr. Kurath, all three are pronounced differently, and Mary can be *may-ree, mair-ee, marry*, or *merry*.

General linguist Mario Pei points to another East-West difference in pronunciation: In most of the East, there is no difference between *horse* and *hoarse;* in the West, the *oar* sound gets hoarier treatment. (New York's mounted police, however, ride *hawses.*)

A typical North-South difference is *wash* (North) and *wush* (South); the nation's capital is called *Wash*ington in New England and *Wush*ington, or *Wursh*ington, in the South and Southwest.

Sometimes a pronunciation that is outside the normal stream of dialect migration can identify the speaker. For example, the *ou* in "about the house" has a round sound in the speech of Maryland and Virginia—more "*abowt* the *howse.*" When this sound is heard in the discourse of a person who otherwise speaks like someone from the northern Midwest, the speaker is usually Canadian.

Unique to Utah is the reversal of the *or* and *ar* sounds: As one Salt Lake City resident said: "Here we praise the *lard* and put the *lord* in the refrigerator."

Tracing the westward trek of America's earliest dialects, trying to find out how and where the eastern *bag* became the western *sack*, language geographers must cope with three other migrations: the movement of blacks from South to North; the retirement migration to Florida and southern California, and the move from rural to urban to suburban within all American regions.

When people move about this way, language cross-pollinates, and local dialects are enriched. The Forty-Niners of California, who coined words like *splurge* and usages like *strike it rich* and *pan out* from their mining experience, reached back into early English rural archaisms to reintroduce *gumption* and *deck* (rather than pack) of cards.

However, these movements tending to localize and enliven dialect are opposed by the two centrifugal forces of language and enemies of dialect: the mandatory public school, which attempts to enforce "standard" speech, and the national communications media, which have favored a "general American" accent.

In the past, television was seen to be the homogenizer of the language, producing a national speech like that used by Walter Cronkite and John Chancellor—nationally understandable and "correct" but inhospitable to philological flavor or originality. Of late, language geographers have been cheered by three developments:

· The practice of networks of hiring reporters with regional accents.

· The ability of mass media to popularize local dialect or occupational argot on a national scale, resulting in a language that becomes more uniform but changes more quickly.

· The demand of some local advertisers to present their messages in local dialect, with a "down home" touch, which is a countervailing influence to most television network speech.

Can linguists predict which direction the American English language will take—toward more centralization and standardization, or toward an increase of local dialects in communities within different cities?

Dr. Pei sees "pockets of strong resistance" within a general trend toward standardization: "Good Brooklynese and good Ozarkian are not likely to be obliterated, even in a historical period of centralization. It was the same at the height of the Roman Empire, when Latin was insisted upon, but the Iberians and the Gauls held on to their local differences."

A specialist in dialect geography, such as Dr. Kurath, is more reluctant to project his data into the future: "Variations in speech reflect differences in ways of life. That's what makes the historical study of usage so fascinating."

In that case, could he—like the fictional Professor Higgins—listen to a person's speech and be able to identify birthplace, social class, and itinerary through life? "I could make a very good case for my guess. But not on television—I'm usually too slow to make a decision," he says.

PARDON MY LANGUAGE

November 13, 1975

WASHINGTON—In the use of language in this space, I have occasionally erred. Here is a rundown of bloopers and goofs of my own, along with observations of mistakes by other hapless miscreants.

Media Rare

"The local media has devoted . . ." When Thomas Luskin of Bayside, N.Y., saw such abusage in this column, he wrote: "Media is now a singular—I wonder why?" Henry Anatole Grunwald, of Rockefeller Center, was also dismayed at such neglect of pluralism, and sent along an essay he wrote in *Time* magazine: "On all sides, ostensibly well-educated people in full command of the English language talk about the media in this singular fashion. 'The media is to blame.' . . . Webster's, that horror of permissiveness, allows the usage. It is, of course, illiterate: 'Media' is the plural of 'medium,' hence the media *are.*"

Lexicographer Alma Graham agrees; nine out of ten members of the American Heritage Dictionary usage panel sternly disapprove of media as singular. Okay; henceforth, "The media are to blame." The data are conclusive. (Are?)

Cotton-Choppin'

In a piece about regional dialect, I wrote that "Mary married Harry" rhymed east—rather than west—of the Alleghenies. Worse, I did not see the difference between "chopping cotton" and "picking cotton." The Atlanta correspondent of *The Times* points out that "cotton-choppin' " is the hoeing of the young plants, which precedes cotton-picking by a full season, and he wisely suggests I keep my cotton-choppin' fingers off Southern dialect.

Cockamamie Criticism

Somebody complained about my use of the slang term "cockamamie." According to the new and valuable Bernstein's Reverse Dictionary, "cockamamie" comes under "crazy," specifically "absurd."

The word has a delicious onomatopoeia, bouncing along in its cockeyed, crackbrained way. Sidney Landau of the Doubleday Dictionary traces its etymology to "decalcomania"; the new supplement to the Oxford English Dictionary cites a 1945 Arthur Kober usage: " 'Cockamamies'—painted strips of paper which the kids applied to their wrists and rubbed with spit until the image was transferred to their hands."

American Heritage gives the best version for the meaning: Tattoos produced by a decalcomania process are imitation, hence counterfeit, worthless, and trifling. (The French *decalquer* is to transfer by tracing.)

Therefore, I intend to continue to use "cockamamie" in this space whenever some future Nelson Rockefeller comes up with hundred-billion-dollar, off-budget financing concoctions to enervate our energy program.

Getting Into "Into"

Transcendental surgery has grafted a simpering fuzziness onto the language of late. To be "in touch with yourself," to "get your head together," to be "into a whole different headset" is the argot of wretches, concentered all in self, who write books celebrating the dysphasia of determined daydreaming.

The time has come to think twice about meditation. Its vogue words are vague words, its imprecise message is glazed in candied candor. *Harper's* magazine labels it "the new narcissism"; R. D. Rosen calls it "psychobabble" in *New Times* magazine, its practitioner a "victim of his own interminable introspection . . . the victim of his own inability to describe human behavior in anything but platitudes."

Rippling Rhythms

A man who monitors vogue words, C. D. Bonsted of Syracuse, has latched onto the new, universal appellation for a recluse: "a very private person." Forget "introvert"; when a celebrity won't grant an interview, he's a "very private person."

Remember how "de-escalate" was the big new word in the late 60's, which wound up as "wind down" when everybody became bored with de-escalation? Today, the "domino theory" has been so discredited that the new vogue phrase is "ripple effect." New York City's default, we are repeatedly warned, will have a "ripple effect" on municipal bond financing elsewhere. Recently, Birch Bayh's campaign manager announced that endorsement by the New Democratic Coalition would be "the beginning of a ripple effect."

The pseudoscientific phrase is coined on the analogy of "Doppler effect," the appearance of change in light or sound waves from a moving source. Watch the way it spreads through learned discourses on late-night television; meanwhile, don't make ripples.

Top Kick

The word "topless" has been part of our language since poet Christopher Marlowe in the 16th century wrote of the "topless towers of Ilium." The modern meaning—nudity above the waist—has become so firmly fixed in our consciousness that it is in danger of causing confusion.

Around the corner from *The Times*'s Washington bureau, a massage parlor displays a large sign: "Topless Shoeshines." I have been in my closet all morning searching for a pair of topless shoes.

April 7, 1975

Dear Mr. Safire:

Although I do not always agree with your views, I always read your editorials or essays in *The New York Times* because I do enjoy your use of the English language. But today I was singularly disturbed by your using the word "media" as a singular. I quote: "In this recession-proof, political capital, the local media *has* devoted. . . ." How is it possible that a highly educated man, as you undoubtedly are, does not know that medium is the singular and media the plural? From now on, please, write that the "media *have* devoted. . . ."

With apologies for correcting you,

Sincerely yours,
Fritz Jahoda
New York, New York

NEWSWORDY EVENT

December 25, 1978

WASHINGTON—When *The New York Times*, which publishes about 75 million words a year, chooses a new dictionary to serve as its primary guide for meaning and spelling, that's big news in the world of words.

Up to 1961, the established authority was the great Second Edition of Webster's New International Dictionary of the English Language, Unabridged (Merriam). But the permissive Third Edition—a flexicon that tossed linguistic standards to the winds and allowed slang to lie down with formal English—put *The Times* in a quandary (a jocular pseudo-Latin word for predicament).

Liberal editorialists revealed themselves as conservatives in language, and the decision was made to lay in a stock of Second Editions for use until the dictionary-makers came to their senses. But, as a decade passed, the stock of Second Editions dwindled; erudite reporters thumbed copies into frazzles, and used-book dealers charged up to $100 for copies in good condition.

Meanwhile, an explosion of neologisms had taken place: from sexist astronaut to racist overkill, from watershed to waterbed to Watergate, the tide of words could not be stonewalled. At *The Times*, consulting editor and Elder Wordsman Ted Bernstein passed the word that a great new dictionary had been born.

News editor Lewis Jordan and assistant foreign editor Allan M. Siegal, at work on a new stylebook (formerly the Style Book) became convinced that the occasion of the publication of *The New York Times Manual of Style and Usage* was the right time for the big lexical decision.

And so, the other day, Webster's New World Dictionary, published by Collins-World, made its appearance on newsroom desks as the new authority. But rival Merriam-Webster can take heart: Its 450,000-entry Third Edition has held its own at *The Times* as an unabridged back-up for those words not defined in the 160,000-entry New World. (If you are worried about a "kakistocracy," you must turn to the unabridged.)

Kudos to David Guralnik, new rex of lexicography. (In Merriam-Webster, "kudo" is accepted as a singular back-formation from "kudos," perceived as plural; but in Mr. Guralnik's New World, "kudos" is defined as "credit or praise . . . sometimes wrongly taken as a plural of an assumed 'kudo.' " Dictionary warfare, though genteel, is fierce; for myself, "kudos" is a word like "praise," and one "kudo" is as nonsensical as one "prai.")

Of the more than 70 dictionaries on the market, most of which use "Webster's" in the title the way hotels use "Ritz," The New World, in my opinion, has the edge in identifying and showing the roots of Americanisms. The venerable Mitford Mathews (whose grand-nephew is now

Secretary of H.E.W.) is responsible for that contribution, and 14,000 words are starred as Americanisms, including Noah Webster's only coinage, "demoralize."

When it comes to usage, however, I would turn to The American Heritage Dictionary, which also has the best citations, and an important auxiliary to any writer is Merriam-Webster's New Dictionary of Synonyms, the most useful book in this field since Hester Piozzi began splitting hairs.

Usage; now we're in trouble. Once you accept the idea that the current status of a word in current speech should be set forth in a dictionary, the prescriptive-descriptive argument subsides; but usage decisions often must be arbitrary, and can be seen as dictatorial. That is why *The New York Times Manual of Style and Usage* is awaited with narrowed eyes.

Will employes resent being referred to as employees? Will staunch Republicans hail the prospect of no longer being labeled as stanch Republicans, or will there be blood on the floor to be stanched? Will we fling down a gantlet and run a gauntlet, or vice versa?

Already, the word is out that the new stylebook (what a slim, chic new word for the pompous old *Style Book*) will change most of the "premiers" in the world to "prime ministers," which may come as a blow to Chou En-lai. And the decision to treat all nations as neuter gender will ring *La Belle France.*

In most cases, The New World Dictionary will nestle comfortably against the new stylebook but there is at least one instance of trouble. The dictionary defines "Ms." as "a title free of reference to marital status. . . ."

But the soon-to-be-issued stylebook staunchly—perhaps stanchly—refuses to recognize "Ms." and also throws a pox on "chairperson," "chairwoman," and much of the other feminist propaganda.

Right on! (*adj.* [slang] sophisticated, informed, current, etc.)

LEGALESEY DOES IT

July 28, 1977

WASHINGTON—Why do lawyers write the way they do? Why must wills "give, devise and bequeath," or leases caution "without let or hindrance," or contracts convey "right, title and interest"—and all the rest, residue and remainder of legal archaisms?

"Sir, the law is as I say it is," replied John Fortescue, chief justice of the King's Bench in 1458. ". . . we have several set forms which are held as law, and so held and used for good reason, though we cannot at present remember that reason."

Thus, for more than five centuries, have lawyers kept and maintained their special argot, cant, and slang. Such legalese confuses laymen, making lawyers more necessary, which may be why some shun and avoid the new and novel.

Comes now Peter Sullivan, an assemblyman from Westchester, N.Y., with a revolutionary bill that has passed both houses of the state legislature, and awaits only Governor Hugh Carey's signature to become final and conclusive.

The bill would require all leases—those agate-typewritten instruments long out of tune—to be "written in non-technical language and in a clear and coherent manner using words with common and everyday meanings."

What's this? A radical assault on necessary precision? To some lawyers, a lease without a whereas is like a complaint without a plaintiff, a null without a void.

Before lovers of plain English climb on their white allegators, it is fit and proper we heed and attend the attorneys who love their old language and urge reformers to cease and desist.

Some legal language, including but not limited to terms of art, has such case law behind it that the very words discourage litigation. Also, some argot shortens argument between learned counsel: "This case is on fours with the case at bar" can save a judge's time. And some of the old language of law is beautiful, like the sonorous, majestic King James translation of the Bible.

For example, my favorite legalese is "anything herein to the contrary notwithstanding." Such phrasing excites delectation, its lilt evoking an ancient minuet, its rhythm comparable to e. e. cummings' "with up so floating many bells down."

With those stipulations, the approval of the legal profession to the language-reform bill should not be unreasonably withheld. With David Melinkoff's classic *The Language of the Law* as our guide, we can mutually agree (Why "mutually"? Why not simply "agree"?) to strike from our contracts some meaningless terms for the rest of our natural lives (Why "natural"? For good reason: to allow for the legal idea of "civil death," as when a monk enters a monastery).

Whereas. The word means everything and nothing. Pettifogging lawyers often use it to mean "since," or "considering that," while most of us use it (rarely) to mean "while on the contrary." "Whereas" has become a useless sound, a legal-sounding murmur, good only as a verbal dingbat in the recitation of lists.

Aforesaid. This is a grandfogging lawyer mumbling "I already told you about that." If it refers to more than one antecedent, "aforesaid" is confusing; if not, it is unnecessary. Lawyers use this construction to lend the aura of precision to fuzzy thinking, whereas its use was condemned centuries ago by Sir Edward Coke.

Forthwith has a nice, regal feeling, doesn't it? Off with his head, forthwith! But does it mean "instanter" (the same day) or "immediately" (at that moment) or "without unnecessary delay" or "with all convenient speed"? No, the aforesaid "forthwith" is indeterminate; better put down a date certain.

Hereby. That old legal window dressing was the precursor of "at that point in time"; it has no position in space or chronology. If it means "by means of this," fine—but does it mean "by means of the whole document" or part of it? "At this moment" or a little later? "I revoke" is more precise than "I hereby revoke," which only sounds more legal.

Herein, hereinafter, heretofore. Forget 'em all. "Herein" can mean in this sentence, or essay, or newspaper. "Hereinafter" is similarly uncertain as to time—for the rest of this contract, or for the term of the agreement, or what? "Heretofore" may or may not include the date of the document containing it, and ambiguity begs for litigation: Better use a good verb in the past tense and abandon aforesaid legalese.

A good bill—nay, an opening blast in a war on Fortescue-ism—lies on the Governor's desk. Of course, the bill is shot through with "hereby designated" and "void or voidable" (some legal draftsmen just never get the void). Assemblyman Sullivan is sheepish about the language of his own legislation: "You see, um, there are lots of lawyers in Albany."

The Governor should strike a blow for clarity and sign the bill forthwith, anything herein to the contrary notwithstanding.

TO WHO IT MAY CONCERN

October 31, 1977

Be it ever so humble, there's no word like "whom."

I continue to get it wrong, and in this salute to readers who care enough about precision and accuracy to have taken me to task over the past year, I propose to get it right.

My first lapse was fairly simple: "Mr. Carter," went the errant line, "—after a three-year run for the roses—knew pretty much who he wanted and who he had to repay." The word should have been "whom" in both cases, since it was twice the object of verbs. And, as Miss Goldstein of the Bronx High School of Science laid it on me 30 years ago: Who is a subject, whom is an object.

Rattled by the above experience, I wrote in another piece that a State Department man had "leaked to whomever would listen. . . ."

Wrong. The misuse of "whomever" drew fire from a veritable "whom's whom" of grammarians.

"Your grammar is as disagreeable as your politics," wrote William Smyth, chairman of the English Department of the Trinity-Pawling School in Pawling, N.Y.

"As I have explained to my tenth-graders only today, 'whoever' is the subject of the verb 'would listen' and the noun clause, 'whoever would listen,' is the object of the preposition 'to.' "

That did not help me. Chauncy B. Ives of Kingston, N.J., with an acerbic "teachers have enough troubles without columnists adding to them," instructed: "The pronoun should be *whoever*, subject of *would listen*. The object of the preposition *to* is the clause *whoever would listen.*"

That helped the message sink in, but the most effective explanation came from an itinerant lecturer and author who has a special understanding of leakage: Daniel Schorr of Washington, D.C.

"The way my grammar teacher tried to make me understand such constructions was thus," he explained, clearing the air.

"*Verb:* leaked.

"*Preposition:* to.

"*Object:* whoever-would-listen.

"The last three words read very fast, and sort of run together."

By George, I've got it. And now to etymology, where part-time lexicographers are on safer ground. Recently, I reported that one of the insider's locutions of the Carter Administration is "behind the power curve," used to mean "not up to date on the decisions from the top." In the White House, to be "behind the power curve" is to be out of it.

The source of "power curve" was suggested in this space to be a 1960's statistics-graph test for alternatives, but George E. Burns of New York City writes: "Being behind or on the backside of the power curve is an aviation expression. It's a condition where flying slow takes more energy than going fast, and most things you do produce a result opposite what you'd intended."

The "power curve" appears on a graph of the power an aircraft needs to overcome wind resistance. Normal "drag" increases as a plane speeds up, but a certain type of "drag" increases as a plane slows down, which is why you hear a fresh surge of power when a jet is landing. To be "behind the power curve," to an aviator, is to be on the way to a crash.

Such phrase origins are fun (does anybody know the first use of "bargaining chip"?) but watch out for sloppy sourcing. Seeking symmetry in a column that began and ended with derivations of phrases, I used as a fulcrum the point that *Thunder On the Left* was the title of a 1925 book by G. K. Chesterton.

Wrong. "It was Christopher Morley, not G. K. Chesterton, whose *Thunder On the Left* was published in 1925," writes Lee Culpepper of Croton-on-Hudson, a town with a word missing, adding the tart advice: "Avoid volunteering unnecessary information."

This correction was topped by Irwin Stark of Hillsdale, N.Y., who writes from that oxymoronic village that he has found the origin of that passage in Sir Eustace Peachtree's 17th-century tome, *The Dangers of This Mortall Life:* "Among the notionable dictes of antique Rome was the fancy that when men heard thunder on the left the gods had somewhat of special advertisement to impart. Then did the prudent pause and lay down their affairs to study what omen Jove intended."*

Cocking an ear to that thunder, and with all the chargin of a Cheshire cat, I pledge here and now to get out front of grammar's power curve no matter whom I offend or whoever objects. (Who? Whomever?)

---

* That turns out to have been a hoax perpetrated by Mr. Morley, who was a mischievous editor of the eleventh edition of Bartlett's *Familiar Quotations*. The fictional "Eustace Peachtree" was expunged from subsequent editions.

American Life

A *column*, in my lexicon, is a group of facts or beliefs given meaning by a point of view; a *polemic* is an angry man's attempt at persuasion, not quite a *tirade* and easier to take than a *harangue*; an *investigative commentary* is a presentation of new information designed to make a point and get action.

I do all five. Occasionally, when reflecting on a fact of life rather than a piece of news, I try my hand at an *essay*.

ON CHARITY

September 20, 1973

WASHINGTON—Arthur Goldberg, the former everything, used to tell the story of the rescue party that approached some trapped mountaineers in a snowy ravine, yelling to them, "It's the Red Cross!" To which the desperate men yelled back, "We gave at the office!"

The Ervin committee's look into political fund raising, scheduled for the coming month—which could lead to specific legislative reforms—opens up a related subject that is rarely discussed: the element of coercion in much of today's fund raising for charity.

Gifts by corporations to political parties are against the law; similar gifts by corporations to organized charities are within, and even encouraged by, the law. This is what happens:

Charity X comes to the public relations man for a large company and says, "Let's make a philanthropist and a civic demigod out of that old skinflint you have for a chairman of the board. We'll give a dinner in his honor."

Chairman Tightwad coughs up a few thousand dollars to the Fund for Free Computer Access for Precocious Children, which makes him a "founder," and then hands over what the charity really wants: the corporation's list of suppliers.

Soon after, any company that sells raw materials or any kind of service to Tightwad Industries gets a letter from the dinner chairman, known to be a crony of their important customer's top man, inviting its executives to come and do homage to this lifelong philanthropist.

The charity-wise suppliers—the ad agencies, unions, architects of the corporate headquarters—make no immediate commitments but wait for the next step: the telephone call from the professional fund raiser "on behalf of" Chairman Tightwad, telling them how many tables they are expected to buy.

In case the corporate cousins do not get the word, the presidents of those companies find themselves appointed "vice chairmen of the dinner committee" and invited to a cocktail party at which Old Tightwad in person watches with beady eye as they pledge to pass the pressure on to their subcontractors. Thus, a little viggerish is added to price, quality, and service as the criteria for doing business.

At the dinner in the grand ballroom, where the entertainer in the hotel's nightclub makes a "free" appearance (that's the hotel's kickback for the dinner business) some upright people extol Tightwad's career while his suppliers and industry associates sit grim-faced on the dais and junior executives fill up the tables and listen to the speeches.

And a substantial amount of money goes to "charity." The donations had nothing to do with the spirit of charity: They were coerced, given at the direction of corporate officials to protect business currently done or to curry favor with a good prospect, or given by competing corporations who have the right to demand an equal "contribution" when their chairmen need ego massages.

Business is business, one might say—after all, isn't the money for a worthy cause? If we did not permit this little element of self-aggrandizement through corporate coffers, would not innocents suffer and diseases go uncured?

Perhaps. But consider who is doing the contributing. Not Tightwad Industries and its suppliers and banks and dependents. Corporate contributions are deductible up to 5 percent of taxable income, which means that one half of that "contribution" out of corporate profits would have gone to the U.S. Treasury—and deductible corporate charity currently adds up to more than a billion dollars a year.

The other half of the corporate contribution is ordinarily tacked on to the price the suppliers charge Tightwad Industries, which it in turn passes on to the consumer. (If this is not done, then the money has been taken out of the profits and dividends of millions of stockholders.) Old Tightwad and his dais guests are not especially out of pocket.

Hold on, now—what is really being done? Even if the money "contributed" comes from taxpayers and consumers and stockholders, isn't it better that the money be channeled through privately run charities rather than through the Government bureaucracy? Doesn't this guarantee diversity?

Answer: Private charities are and have been enormously important to the American spirit and are often more innovative than Government. That is why some tax deductions should continue to be permitted on personal contributions by individuals.

But charities should be truly privately supported, not publicly supported, which means we should make corporate charitable contributions as unlawful as corporate political contributions.

And let's cut the coercion out of charity. Creative fund raisers should be able to come up with the most heartrending appeals, or rational and sensible motivations, to get people to give—which they will do only if they are denied the corporate or union power to twist arms.

The spirit of generosity dies when the practice of corporate extortion is tolerated. We can discover more faith in ourselves and hope for our fellow man if we shake off the hypocrisy in our daily lives—and among the greatest of these is much of what goes on under the name of "charity."

September 26, 1973

Editor
The New York Times

Dear Sir:

Mr. Safire's recent Op-Ed essay, "On Charity," overlooks the full dimensions of giving in America. In a reasonably accurate way, he does portray the "bite" that some corporate executives put on people and firms "beholden" to them. But to make perfectly clear the nature of philanthropy in our nation, it must be underscored that corporate giving is a minor—unfortunately, very minor—part of the nation's charitable sector.

A few brief facts give proof of this. Total philanthropic giving for the 1960's was approximately $125 billion. Of this, $97.5 billion was donated by living individuals, $10 billion through bequests, $10 billion by private foundations and only $7 billion by corporations. In other words, the core of philanthropy—individual giving—was upwards of 78 percent, while the corporations "exposed" by Mr. Safire accounted for only 5 percent.

The basic danger implicit in his column is that it gives a bad mouth to philanthropic giving. It casts doubt on the intrinsically generous response of Americans to the needs of schools, hospitals and health organizations, religious and cultural institutions.

All of these are dependent on the generosity of the private sector, individuals and foundations. This is particularly true when the response of government is not keeping pace with the needs of our public service and social welfare institutions. If it be true that "charity begins at home," Mr. Safire could well take a more eleemosynary look at the men and women of America who give from their hearts and are gratified to see their dollars go directly to the charity of their choice.

> Sincerely,
> Jack Herman
> New York, New York

ON COHABITATION

September 24, 1973

WASHINGTON—Eight times as many couples are living together today without being married as cohabited ten years ago.

That judgment—it's really my guess—is based on a new study being made by Dr. Paul C. Glick, the Census Bureau population division's senior demographer. (Census Bureau people are either Democrats or Republicans.)

In 1970, 143,000 unmarried persons told the census takers they were living with a partner of the opposite sex, compared with 17,000 in 1960; obviously, there are millions more who do not volunteer this information to strangers, but a trend toward cohabitation outside of wedlock is discernible.

What's the reason for it? When the subject of singlehood is explored, it usually centers on the swinging blessings of the bachelor existence, but let us narrow the question to those couples who are not single but who are not about to get married.

Lauren Hutton, who wears the mantel of the "nation's most-celebrated model," which over the years has graced the perfect shoulders of Jinx Falkenburg, Jeanne Paget, and Suzy Parker, told a *Time* magazine interviewer that she had been living with a male friend for eight years and considered marriage "great for taxes, necessary for children, abominable for romance."

I have no cheekbones to pick with Womannikins Lib, but I think the matter of a change in the mating procedures of the human race deserves a little discussion before being hailed, winked at, or tut-tutted.

Many couples who will neither marry nor kick the cohabit say that their in-between status perfectly suits their needs. They usually do not want children (the birth rate has been declining, partly because of the acceptance of contraception) and they often want independent careers (the biggest increase in the labor force in the last decade has been women).

Moreover, parental pressure on daughters to marry early seems to have abated: The number of women in their twenties who remain single has risen by over a third since 1960. Time was, girls would dread the moment when the nagging question, "How come you're not married yet?" would subtly change to a mildly curious "Why is it you never married?" Local cultures differ, but that moment seems to come later today if it comes at all.

Proponents of living together singly say, with Miss Hutton, that it is good for romance: That is, the lack of a legal document enhances a relationship, keeps both partners on their toes, staying together because they prefer to, rather than because parting would be too complicated and expensive. People who settle down soon settle up. Thus, to them, the absence of legal ties helps strengthen emotional bonds.

Unmarried cohabitors never say they maintain their status because it's daring and chic and "in," and they are under pressure to conform to the nonconformist life-style, or because they want to flaunt their sophistication by flouting morality. But sometimes that enters into it.

Conservatives find it hard to react to this cohabitation trend; they are torn between traditionalism, which sternly condemns any assault on the sacredness or permanence of the family unit, and libertarianism, which holds that people not hurting anybody by their actions should have the personal freedom to do what they want.

People who want to live together outside of matrimony (the word's root is "motherhood," which says a lot about the purpose of marriage) should neither be stigmatized nor applauded. If no children are involved, that's the couple's business; if they are young, it can be their tragedy, if they are old, their happiness. (If they are very poor, they have been doing this for years, but this is not today's subject.)

There is this weakness in the cohabitation argument: If a "piece of paper" should not be needed to hold people together, why must that marriage certificate be permitted to become a license for mature people to drift apart?

The unmarried state of people living together is less a mark of independence than a mark of uncertainty; less an expression of the strength of mutual respect than a confession of the weakness of people to commit themselves to each other; and less a challenge to society than a refusal to rise to the greatest individual challenge of all—symbolically to make permanent a union with another independent person.

Sept. 24, 1973

To the Editor:

Why does William Safire pretend that marriage is what it is not?

He could not name a great writer, artist, or scientist who shares his view that marriage is "the greatest individual challenge of all—symbolically to make a permanent union with another independent person."

Why does he pretend that marriage can be "just a piece of paper"? It fulfills many roles, but for the largest number of participants it is economic protection for mothers and children, and other material benefits for fathers, with the law backing up "good faith."

Some people do not need or want this protection. It is pretentious for Safire to decree that they should be neither "stigmatized" nor "applauded." Instead, he should try to analyze why so many people find cohabitation a more suitable framework for their needs and goals than the legal protection of marriage.

> Sincerely,
> Betty Marshall
> (teacher, wife, mother, and
> baker of apple pie)
> Brooklyn, New York

FOUR-DAY WEEK

November 22, 1973

WASHINGTON—The four-day work week—a quiet revolution in American life—could come to pass a decade before its time, hurried along by a sustained fuel shortage.

This does not mean four days' work for five days' pay, which is a labor dream and a management nightmare; it does mean a rearrangement of working hours to give a worker an incentive to produce as much in four days as he now does in five.

Up to now, organized labor has looked askance at dividing the 40-hour work week into four days instead of five, for health and safety reasons. Most businessmen are leery of the four-day week, too: They wonder how customers would react, and what such a change would do to their web of relationships with suppliers.

But in fact, most people do not work a regular 40-hour week today—instead, the 40-hour mark is a convenient mark at which to start paying overtime rates. In reality, the 37½-hour week is here already; the next step could be to a 36-hour week made up of four nine-hour days.

Such a rearrangement would please most workers, and experiments have shown it possible to maintain or improve productivity in a four-day week. The idea is not to abolish Friday as a business day, but to stagger weekends: some people off Fridays, others off Mondays.

In terms of conserving energy, there is not much doubt about the impact of a 20 percent reduction in the fuel Americans now expend in getting to work, especially if coupled with Sunday driving restrictions.

Moreover, traffic pressure would be reduced as the "weekend" would mean different days to different families, and most gasoline is wasted by cars stuck in traffic jams at weekend rush.

The four-day week has an appeal to the social scientist and the conservationist, but does it make business sense? Former Assistant Secretary of Labor Jerome M. Rosow, now a long-range planner for Exxon, thinks it could—if approached on a community-wide, or government-wide, basis.

The enormity of such a change in work habits on American life is only beginning to be considered. For example:

1. More time would be available for consumption, which would mean increased spending on leisure activities, from recreation to study to staring dully at the television set. More consumer spending is what powers the economic engine.

2. Moonlighting would be transformed, as the second job at night would be discouraged by the longer work day. But some ambitious workers would seize upon the extra free day to extend their income or open up a new career.

3. Working women, now 40 percent of the work force and the fastest-growing segment of the new entries into the labor market, would be encouraged by the extra day off, since the four-day week would permit more time to shop, housekeep, and spend with children.

4. The breakup of the five-day pattern would probably lead to "flextime," an experiment meeting with some success in Europe that permits a worker to choose what time he wishes to work, provided he is on the job between 10 A.M. and 3 P.M., and his total time adds up to a full day.

Production engineers, union leaders, and politicians used to consider all this to be blue-sky stuff, but work time—which has trended downward by a half percent a year throughout this century—can be arranged to meet the combined conservation and productivity needs of the economy.

Daring? Imaginative? Scary? You bet. No movement resists movement like the labor movement, and some businesses will find the switch unproductive: The whole idea deserves debate and much more analysis. The real question, however, is not "if" but "when" and "how"—which is why

Labor Department officials and some White House aides are thumbing through a paperback titled *Four Days, Forty Hours* by Riva Poor.

For the Federal Government is considered the "model employer": If the 2.5 million Federal employees were to go to a four-day week, they would soon be followed by 15 million state and local employees, and then the rush would be on. (This will not happen tomorrow, but never underestimate the willingness of an embattled Administration to punt and pray.)

Americans are cautious about speeding up trends in an economy now laying golden eggs, but conservatives especially—rightly concerned about the loss of personal freedom that energy rationing would bring about—are wondering if in the four-day week there is an answer that adds to, rather than subtracts from, the sum of individual liberty in our society.

The four-day week, inexorable in the future, is worth a close look today. I can hear it now: "Thank God it's Thursday!"

November 23, 1973

Dear Mr. Safire:

I thought it rather sad that you should still be laboring under the assumption that working women were in some way responsible for the household shopping, housekeeping and children. It may well be true, and I think it is, that most of them by far still think they are and think, too, that their husbands are being quite generous to them in "allowing" them to work.

Point four might better have been that the four-day week would make it easier for women *and* men to both work and take care of the numerous household chores they rightly share when both work, as well as having more time to spend with *their* children.

Yours, for all of us,
Catharine Howe Kelly
New York, New York

THE NO-FAULT SOCIETY

February 4, 1974

WASHINGTON—"No-fault" auto insurance has gone into effect in many states; no longer will drivers, insurance companies, and attorneys be haggling in too-crowded courts about who was to blame for wrinkling that fender. The companies will pay up without a fight and the only people to suffer from the new system, we are told, are the lawyers.

If this pioneering form of the idea of "no fault" lives up to its promise of lower insurance rates, it will give impetus to the adoption of the same idea in another form: "no-fault divorce," which already strikes terror into the hearts of divorce lawyers.

Strange things are happening here. Having removed the element of blame for accidents, if we then go on to strip the stigma of one side's guilt from the separation of couples, consider the consequences:

The trend toward a no-fault society will undermine our time-honored tradition of blaming the other guy, to react to adversity by becoming righteously irate, to shuck responsibility that might be partly our own to a "guilty party."

What might happen if we were to apply the no-fault principle to other matters in our lives? Take that trendy topic, the energy crisis. As television newswatchers are aware, we have begun a national orgy of oily recrimination. Citizens clear their throats and demand to know: "Who's responsible for this?" Small children can say: "Why wasn't I informed?"

Otherwise sensible Senators like Henry Jackson line up quavering oil-company executives as a tartarus of villainy, berating them publicly in a hearing designed less to get at the facts than to get at the sympathies of the voters, less to see what can be done than to discover on whom the rap can be pinned.

The President, not to be outdone in the finger-pointing department, blames Congress for not passing his energy legislation years ago; William Simon becomes a household word by denouncing as "blackmail" the kind of economic pressure Americans have been using since William Howard Taft defended "dollar diplomacy."

In a no-fault society, all this irrelevant fault-finding would give way to fact-finding and solution-finding: Oil men, politicians, and consumers of energy would stop fishing for carp and start providing incentives for new supplies and reductions of demand.

Granted, there would be less shining exposure for demagogues, publicity nuts, and crisis faddists, but the ordinary citizen would soon have more gas in his tank and more tanks for his memories.

How would the inflation issue fare in the no-fault society? Financial page headlines would shrink: The White House could not blame Congressional spenders, Congressmen would not blame Mr. Nixon for not making unworkable price controls work, and the dismal scientists of economics would have to stop cost-pushing and demand-pulling each other's hair out.

In the no-fault economic world, politicians would be forced to decide whether to promise more inflation and more jobs, or less inflation and fewer jobs. Such imperfect packages could be clearly labeled because politicians would no longer be blamed for not delivering what is presently beyond the state of the economic art: price stability with full employment in peacetime.

With no fault as his guide, the man with the muck rake might, at long last, look upward to behold the wonders in the sky; instead of lingering lasciviously over the peccadillos of the past, he might pass stringent campaign-financing legislation to prevent abuses in the future, and he might stop tsk-tsking about invasions of privacy long enough to legislate an end to warrantless wiretaps once and for all.

Obviously, a no-fault way of life would free great chunks of time now spent on a fixation about the affixation of blame.

But there are dangers, of course: Without blame, there is no shame, and without an abiding sense of guilt, no purifying conscience to become our guide.

Worse yet, the blamelessness would take some of the fun out of sin, and almost all the fun out of punishment. Seesaw politicians would be deprived of the spotlighted fulcrums on which they move their worlds. As thin-ice treaders like to say, these dangers must be fully explored and openly debated before we embrace the no-fault world of the future.

As we recognize these real dangers of no fault, let us not flinch from its opportunities. Criticism would have to become constructive. The floo-floo bird, which flies backward because it is more interested in where it has been than where it is going, would become extinct. Satchel Paige, who counseled "Never look back, something might be gainin' on you," would replace backward-glancing Rod McKuen as our poet laureate.

Only the lawyers, who have been slowly taking over the world, would lose. The story is told in London's *Observer* of a solicitor who was nearly given a will to challenge that, as he put it, "would have raised the law to the level of poetry." Unfortunately for the lawyer, the family members settled their dispute about the legacy out of court, and—in the unhired attorney's embittered words—"the entire estate was frittered away among the beneficiaries."

OF TWO CITIES

March 25, 1974

If you want to compare New York City with Washington, D.C., as a symbol of civilization or a center of power, a good place to stand is the corner of Fifth Avenue and 59th Street.

There, amidst the traffic's din (score one for Washington) you can see New York's Plaza Hotel, 67 years old and going strong, a tribute to the marriage of free enterprise and good taste.

In Washington, by way of contrast, the equally famous Willard Hotel—the work of the same architect, Henry Hardenbergh, at about the same time—stands empty and desolate, thanks to some arrogant goo-goos and timorous bureaucrats.

A decade ago, a grandiose Pennsylvania Avenue plan was bruited about in the nation's capital, which blighted any renovation prospects for the historic Willard; now, with Caesarism on the wane, the city fathers want to preserve the hotel, but the owners are not sure enough of the bureaucracy's steadfastness to invest several million dollars in turning the Willard into another Plaza Hotel. (Score one for New York.)

Still on the corner of 59th and Fifth, one can be impressed by the equestrian statue of General William Tecumseh Sherman, his horse being led by the winged figure of the goddess of victory. (Visitors from Atlanta often say "Isn't that like a Yankee to ride while the lady walks?")

As a work of art, the Sherman statue is not much; the sculptor, Augustus Saint-Gaudens, did far better for Washington with "Grief," a small classic of a woman in a hooded cloak, located in Rock Creek Cemetery. John Galsworthy placed one of his Forsyte Saga characters in front of the mysterious memorial and wrote: "It was the best thing he had come across in America; the one that gave him the most pleasure, in spite of all the water he had seen at Niagara and those skyscrapers in New York." One for Washington.

Scraping the sky, of course, is a hallmark and a glory of New York; when Boston put up the tallest tower in New England, Fate treated the city like Icarus and made the windows fall out.

No such presumption could take place in Washington: the Capitol dome stands a nicely proportionate 130 feet and no commercial structure can look down upon it. Only the obelisk to Washington towers over the Capitol, as the executive one-ups the legislative, and the result is a city built to the scale of people rather than giants.

The Federal city's bursting into cherry blossoms this week while the trees in Manhattan's side streets still hang lifeless on the crutches that hold them up. Washington is graced with an Italianate spring and New

York suddenly lurches into summer, tempting Washington columnists to wax lyric about their gardens, yet John Kennedy added a necessary astringency to the assessment of the Government town: "Filled with Southern efficiency and Northern charm."

New York is still the communications capital, but Washington has become the news capital; listen to the way Walter Cronkite on CBS News rushes through the names of the reporters who will be giving the Washington stories and lingers on the names and datelines of stories from anywhere else.

Local television announcers in Washington are most often black, dress conservatively, and maintain a certain dignity; their counterparts in New York are most often white, dress flashily, and try to maintain an aura of youthful irreverence.

New York has had a subway for 70 years, and riders grimly tolerate it; Washington is finally digging itself up to have a subway of its own. New York talks about the stock market; Washington rarely does, because there can be no economic recession in the nation's capital; if hard times hit, the bureaucracy will grow ever faster.

New York is too diverse to have a "mood"; the life of the mind is livelier there, the social crosscurrents swifter, the intellectual fashions more demanding of conformity but of shorter duration. One-industry Washington's mood, on the other hand, is discernible: Right now, muscular Christians are tearing apart toothless lions in the arena, and the crowd is titillated by the roars of the martyred beasts.

Standing on the corner, watching a pothole grow in the street that leads to Bergdorf's and Tiffany's, a former New Yorker gets the feeling that the big town is a university, a tumultiversity, while Washington is a well-endowed college on the make.

An affection for both is not a sign of fickleness. Both places of learning are "at the center," because the symbol of our civilization at this stage of its development, and the center of power in our time, is not a city but a state of mind.

Thank God for the shuttle.

March 26, 1974

To the Editor:

It's trying enough to endure William Safire's frequent apologias for White House machinations. It becomes intolerable when he turns to something really important: the realm of art.

Delivering himself on Saint-Gaudens' equestrian statue at the corner of 59th and Fifth Avenue, your Op-Ed contributor declares: "As a work of art, the Sherman statue is not much." Well, as a critic of art, Mr. Safire isn't much either. I can only hope that no one will be put off by his casual dismissal.

Having spent several years in Italy assimilating the equestrian master-pieces of Donatello and Verrocchio, and after poring over hundreds of statues while preparing a book on New York sculpture, to be published by Scribner's next year, I can assure Mr. Safire's readers that the Saint-Gaudens "Sherman," with its vital rhythms and dramatic composition, is unquestionably one of the few great equestrian monuments to have been created since the Renaissance.

Joseph Lederer
New York, New York

DON'T SLAM THE CLOSET DOOR

April 18, 1974

Ordinances prohibiting discrimination against homosexuals have been passed in Minneapolis, Detroit, and the District of Columbia recently; the matter comes before the New York City Council this morning.

To the reasons why a person cannot be denied employment or hous-ing—"race, color, creed, national origin, ancestry, sex or physical handi-cap"—the proposed amendment to New York's civil rights law would add "sexual orientation."

Should homosexuals—"gays," to use the word they prefer to the dozens of slang derogations used by "straights"—be given a legal means to combat a social stigma?

I think so. But not for the reasons advanced in most of the writing on this subject.

As homosexuals have gained the courage to come "out of the closets and into the streets," many have proceeded to overstate their case. No longer do gays say "live and let live"; they suggest that criticism of homosexual-ity is bigoted and psychologically outdated, and assert that their way of life is fulfilling and morally unassailable.

Psychiatrist Robert E. Gould, writing in a recent *New York Times Magazine*, holds that if social taboos were lifted, "most humans would be functioning bisexuals ... pathology might very well consist of exclusive interest in one sex."

Flat assertions like that, with no empirical evidence to back them up, go unchallenged. It is one thing for the American Psychiatric Association to decree that homosexuality is no longer considered a category of mental illness, but to say that in the future the heterosexuals will be considered the deviates steps over the brink.

To be gay is to be abnormal, whether or not that abnormality extends to one-tenth of the population. To be gay is to be engaged in an activity that both moral absolutists and moral relativists would label "immoral," with both Scripture and sociological statistics on their side.

The majority who consider homosexuality to be a mental problem to be corrected, or a moral decision to be castigated, are not to be dismissed as a bunch of benighted bigots.

Homosexuality should be discouraged; the prospect of universal bisexuality is infinitely depressing. The question then becomes: How can this abnormality be contained in a way that does not abridge personal freedom? To that fine, philosophical question can be added this practical note: How do we deal with gay militants so as not to make heroes out of them?

The answer is to treat gays as people who are different, who are becoming unashamed of being different, and who have every right to be different. People who are "normal" (the etymological root of that word is "square") have every right to disapprove, to discourage, to dissuade, but not to coerce.

Does this high-sounding concern for civil liberty mean that we should pass laws allowing gays to teach small children in public schools? I'm afraid so. As long as a teacher does not teach homosexuality, he's entitled to be gay; we can hope that gay leader Ronald Gold is right when he says, "It isn't catching."

That is a painful stretch, but there is a practical side: Better a forthright homosexual teacher than a secret one.

Certainly there is danger in toleration being taken for approval, but the greater danger is the invasion of everybody's right to privacy. The adult homosexual's right to be let alone must not be invaded by a majority seeking to make unlawful what it regards as sinful.

If society does not like what it sees, society should remove its eye from the keyhole; now that gays want to come out of the closets, it is not right for the majority to slam them back in.

Is our morality so tepid, or our heterosexuality so enervated, that the majority must find petty ways to discriminate against homosexual men and women? In sexual competition, the male-female connection needs no legal or social edge: Let the straights play it straight.

Repression and intolerance (as well as a tone of condescension I cannot comb out of this essay) demean all of us and cloak a psychological problem in the guise of a "cause." Homosexuality should be neither a cause nor a crime, but as long as we treat it as a crime, we will be giving its practitioners a cause.

The New York City Councilmen who shy away from offering homosexuals the full protection of antidiscrimination laws worry about backlash on Election Day (or worse, support from gay liberation groups) but they should worry more about each citizen's personal freedom.

We can treat the gays as people with mental problems, or counter their new proselytism with some missionary work of our own, or gratify our consciences by railing at them as sinners; but when we fail to give them the equal protection of the law, then it is the law that is queer.

April 18, 1974

To the Editor:

It's thanks, but no thanks, to William Safire for his grudging advocacy of "gay rights" (Essay, April 18).

Safire is right when he says we gays deserve equal protection of the law; he is wrong in labelling homosexuality "immoral" and something that "should be discouraged."

Discouraging homosexual tendencies is not only futile, it is hell for the person in the closet. Until I was 21, I tried to suppress my gayness—and I lived a scared, uptight life.

But since I've come out, I've felt fulfilled (apologies to Safire) and have been ready and able to help other people realize their human potential.

That's why gay liberation is more than just a passive "live and let live."

I want to be out front taking gay liberation one step farther: to a "human liberation" in which all of us—straight and gay—are freed from the classic masculine male, feminine female stereotypes that confine our personalities.

Sincerely,
Allen W. Kratz
Lansdale, Pennsylvania

April 21, 1974

Dear Mr. Safire,

This is to congratulate you on your excellent essay, "Gay Rights," in *The Times* of April 18. I do not often agree with your opinions or admire your writing, but this is the clearest writing on homosexuality that I have seen in a long time. If your reasonableness is condescension, then I'll take condescension any day over the dishonest hysterics of the homosexual militants. But I do not think they are entirely to blame for their extreme views; they have learned the lessons of contemporary public life very well, and who can fault them at this date for putting those lessons to work for themselves? For at least ten years, we have lived in a period of the most astonishing intellectual irresponsibility, and Dr. Gould's pronouncement is but a mild example.

I am myself homosexual and at least old enough to know that I cannot rid myself of guilt anxieties by projecting them onto others. The Gay Lib Movement doesn't know this and attempts to tag the rest of society with precisely those labels they themselves fear most: thus an exclusive interest in the opposite sex isn't really normal, and criticism of homosexuality is bigotry. Of course, on the deepest level, the gay militants believe that the old derogatory slurs justly belong to them after all; otherwise, there would be no need for the desperate reversal of verbal aggression that we now witness. This, in my view, is the true sorrow, and the pity. Thanks for your fine article; I'm sorry I must remain—

Anonymous

ON KEEPING A DIARY

September 9, 1974

Diaries are no longer dear; as the invention of the telephone began the decline of letter-writing, the invention of the tape recorder has led to the atrophy of the personal diary. Many of us record our words but few of us record our thoughts.

Why is a diary stereotyped today as the gushing of a schoolgirl or the muttering of a discontented politician, unworthy of the efforts of a busy person? Perhaps because we are out of the habit of writing, or have fallen into the habit of considering our lives humdrum, or have become fearful of committing our thoughts to paper. When I urged a White House friend to keep a diary through the fall of a President as a service to history, he sadly replied that he had better not—notes and diaries could be subpoenaed.

But the fear of Nosy Parkers and Pepysing Sams ought not to deprive us of the satisfaction, nor history of the benefit, of keeping a fairly regular account of our personal observations. Consider what diaries do:

Diaries remind us of details that would otherwise fade from memory and make less vivid our recollection. Navy Secretary Gideon Welles, whose private journal is an invaluable source for Civil War historians, watched Abraham Lincoln die in a room across the street from Ford's Theater and later jotted down a detail that puts the reader in the room: "The giant sufferer lay extended diagonally across the bed, which was not long enough for him. . . ."

Diaries relieve us of our frustrations. William Inge, Dean of St. Paul's early in this century, said that diaries permitted "the repressed self to stretch his legs." When G. K. Chesterton blasted him in print, Dean Inge said nothing publicly but "I retaliated in my diary by hoping that the public would soon get tired of the elephantine capers of an obese mountebank. These flowers of speech happily did not find their way into print. . . ."

Diaries can be written in psychic desperation, intended to be burned, as a hold on sanity: "I won't give up the diary again," wrote novelist Franz Kafka; "I must hold on here, it is the only place I can." Or written in physical desperation, intended to be read, as in the last entry in Arctic explorer Robert Scott's diary: "For God's sake look after our people."

But what of people who are neither on trial nor freezing to death, neither witnesses to great events nor participants in momentous undertakings? To most of us, a diary presents a terrible challenge: "Write down in me something worth remembering," the neatly dated page says; "prove that this day was not a waste of time."

For people intimidated by their own diaries, here are a handful of rules:

1. *You own the diary, the diary doesn't own you.* There are many days in all our lives about which the less written the better. If you are the sort of person who can only keep a diary on a regular schedule, filling up two pages just before you go to bed, become another sort of person.

2. *Write for yourself.* The central idea of a diary is that you are not writing for critics or for posterity but are writing a private letter to your future self. If you are petty, or wrongheaded, or hopelessly emotional, relax—if there is anybody who will understand and forgive, it is your future self.

3. *Put down what cannot be reconstructed.* You are not a newspaper of record, obligated to record every first time that man walks on the moon. Instead, remind yourself of the poignant personal moment, the remark you wish you had made, your predictions about the outcome of your own tribulations.

4. *Write legibly.* This sounds obvious, but I have pages of scribblings by a younger me who was infuriatingly illiterate. Worse, to protect the innocent, I had encoded certain names and then misplaced my Rosetta Stone; now I will never know who "JW" was in my freshman year at college, and she is a memory it might be nice to have.

Four rules are enough rules. Above all, *write about what got to you that day*, the way a parched John Barrymore did during a trip to Mexico in 1926 when he discovered a bar that to him was an oasis:

"The beer arrived—*draft* beer—in a tall, thin, clean crystal of Grecian proportions, with a creamy head on it. I tasted it. . . . The planets seemed to pause a moment in their circling to breathe a benediction on that Mexican brewer's head. . . . Then the universe went on its wonted way again. Hot Dog! But that *was* a glass of beer!"

That is the art of the diarist in its pure form, unafraid, intimate, important in its insignificance, ringingly free. Who can compare Barrymore's frothy recall with the insecure jottings-down of most of us on little expense ledgers?

Wish I still kept a diary. But you see, I get very tired at the end of the day, and besides, nothing interesting happens anymore. And so to bed . . .

September I2, I974

Dear Mr. Safire:

I have read in this morning's *Oregonian* your column on Diaries. It prompts me to write you this letter.

The Surrender Speech of Chief Joseph, the famous Nez Perce Chief, was as follows:

"Tell General Howard I know his heart. What he told me before, I have it in my heart. I am tired of fighting. Our chiefs are all killed. Looking Glass is dead. It is the young men who now say 'yes' or 'no.' He who led the young men in battle is dead. My little daughter has run away upon the prairie and I do not know where to find her. Perhaps I shall find her, too, among the dead. It is cold and we have no fire, no blankets. The children are crying for food and we have none to give. My people—some of them—have run away to the hills and have no blankets, no food. No one knows where they are; perhaps freezing to death. I want to have time to look for my people and see how many of them I can find. Hear me, my Chiefs; my heart is sick and sad; from where the sun now stands Joseph will fight no more forever."

The only reason it is preserved is because my father, a First Lieutenant and aide to General Howard, took it down in his pencil notebook at the time. It was thus preserved for posterity and is known to many, but not to enough.

Sincerely,
Erskine Wood
Portland, Oregon

GOING TO POT

November 2I, I974

WASHINGTON—Through the local United States Attorney here, the Department of Justice has made known that the crime of possession of small amounts of marijuana will no longer be prosecuted.

Because this announcement comes as a welcome relief to many who do not like to see young people "busted" for participating in a prevailing custom, nobody takes notice of a remarkable precedent being set.

The executive branch of Government, through its Attorney General, has just arrogated to itself power formerly held by the judicial branch and the legislative branch.

What right does any law enforcement officer have to decide which laws, passed by local or Federal legislatures, shall be labeled null and void? What right do prosecutors have to usurp the function of judges in deciding that the holder of five marijuana cigarettes shall go free and the holder of six shall be prosecuted?

The right, of course, is the discretion placed in the hands of law enforcement officials; in practice, not one of ten crimes of almost any nature is aggressively prosecuted, because courts and jails are already overcrowded.

But this discretion, or latitude, is given to prosecutors on the assumption that they will act discreetly; it is grossly abused when lawmen publicly announce which laws they have decided not to carry out. The Department of Justice is not in business to make new laws or repeal old laws—that is for Congressmen and councilmen alone—and the final decision to mete out justice should remain in the hands of judges.

Our off-the-wall U.S. Attorney here has gone to the extent of assuring policemen that they will not be prosecuted for failing to carry out the law. What has happened to the concern so recently expressed about the sinister assumption of power by the executive branch? The concern vanishes when the power is usurped for a purpose popular with most liberals.

The decision on the legalization of marijuana is a matter to be faced squarely by elected officials, not fuzzed up by the fuzz. "Decriminalization" is a foolish euphemism for crime without punishment: If we are not prepared to exact a penalty for the commission of an act, then we should stop calling it a crime.

I think marijuana smoking is harmful and should be legalized. Liquor and tobacco are harmful and legal; a libertarian conservative view is that government should get out of the business of telling people how to conduct themselves when their conduct does not harm others.

At least 20 million Americans smoke pot; the grass has roots. Since prohibition has not worked, regulation should be given a chance. The only effective curb on marijuana use will come from the left, not the right; from the force of health faddism and social pressure, not the force of law.

This week, as elected officials permitted appointees to walk off with their power to legislate under the banner of "decriminalization," the Department of Health, Education and Welfare was coming at marijuana use from its vulnerable left side.

A new H.E.W. report warns that habitual use may depress the male sex hormone, possibly leading to birth defects; it also may lower resistance to disease; and in a classic non sequitur, the report adds that intoxication may lessen the ability to concentrate. As with H.E.W. data on cyclamates, the report plays on fears more than facts—pot has not been proven to be a gaseous thalidomide—but fear does more than evidence can to justify God's ways to man.

In a coming, short-lived era of the cannabisinessman, this is what we could expect: the legal importation, growth and sale of marijuana, heavily taxed by each level of government ("soak the young" is the slogan, but prices should be kept high as a work incentive).

Advertising would be regulated; as with liquor, TV and radio would be banned, and as with tobacco, warnings would be required on all print media. Tests would be developed to measure marijuana intoxication, and the crime of driving while stoned would be vigorously prosecuted.

Most important, the social protest connection would be broken. Smoking pot would be viewed not as "our thing," forbidden fruit, but as a combination of booze and butts, harmful to the human body; substitutes would be sought for mind expansion that are harmless, like exercise, meditation, self-hypnosis or—who knows?—gargling.

Tests will continue; not to determine whether marijuana is addictive, which was yesterday's argument, but to show whether it is harmful. And it is in the very nature of "scientific tests" to show that the ingestion of anything is ultimately harmful.

Tomorrow's young people, already suspicious of smoking tobacco, will read the scary label of the legal packet of grass: "The Surgeon General warns that smoking pot may cause sexual impotence, birth defects, and lower resistance to colds."

Wouldn't that be more effective in curbing the use of an artificial escape from reality than the present method of unenforceable law, or the abdication of legislative responsibility to the Department of Justice?

BECAUSE IT'S THERE

December 19, 1974

The search for the Northwest Passage—a water route from Europe to Cathay, across the frozen wastes of North America—was one of the great adventure stories of all time, the vain quest of Sir Francis Drake and Henry Hudson, finally discovered at the turn of this century by Arctic explorer Roald Amundsen.

With a prosaic thud, the commercial consequence of this adventure was covered on the shipping-news pages recently under the headline "Waters Off Jersey Will Become Terminus of Northwest Passage." Icebreaking supertankers will one day be bringing millions of barrels of Alaskan crude oil down through the bays and seaways of Canada to offshore terminals near Cape May.

Once again we see the pragmatizing of a dream, the glory of exploration ending up in a big tank in New Jersey. But the search for the Northwest

Passage always had a commercial impetus; what has happened to adventure for adventure's sake, the sweetening of life by risk that rejects the practical application of exploration or the commercial embodiment of Evel Knievel?

Sir Edmund Hillary, who led the expedition that conquered Mount Everest, spoke of adventure the other day delivering the Frank Nelson Doubleday lecture at the Smithsonian Institution. "I have often resented the way that science has sometimes been introduced to justify an interesting adventure—particularly if a lot of money is required.

"Adventure is worthwhile for its own sake," said the man who had just come back from scaling some peaks in the Antarctic. "How many of us have been stimulated by some glorious effort that had no conceivable economic or scientific reward?"

Not many of us. The remnants of America's space program, a great adventure drowned in the sinking of America's national spirit after Vietnam, is today justified merely on military, diplomatic, and applied-science grounds.

When John F. Kennedy said: "America has tossed its cap over the wall of space"—and what a beautiful figure of speech that was, of a kid presenting himself with a challenge—he did not say that spacefoods designed for astronauts would be great in school lunch boxes, or that satellite reconnaissance would make possible future arms control agreements.

Essentially, the object was to shoot for the moon, which would not only enhance our national pride at beating the Russians there but lift our spirits at the thought of what puny man could do. But then we became self-conscious about our success, and embarrassed at spending so much money on pure adventure when there were mouths to feed on earth.

Accordingly, our space program today is justified on practical terms. The link-up of Soviet and U.S. space capsules scheduled for July 17, 1975, is said to be important for détente and to show other nations who the real superpowers are. The probe of the solar system by Pioneer 11 is said to be finding useful data on radiation belts and whatnot mumbojumbo.

The reason we have poked a hole in the sky with a rocket is that we are as curious as hell to find out what is out there. Adventure is danger faced for the sake of curiosity, the rise to a challenge "because it's there." Such self-testing ennobles the human spirit.

Why, then, is there not great public fascination with the half-billion-mile flight of Pioneer 11 to Jupiter, wonderment at its grazing the Jovian clouds, and then using Jupiter's gravity to "crack the whip" and head for Saturn, a half-billion miles beyond?

The answer, of course, is that there are no human beings aboard and there can be no adventure without danger. But one day there will be men aboard (and women, and blacks, and young people, and ethnics) and this whole world will hold its breath as the human spirit reaches up and touches another whole world.

Viewed from centuries hence, these explorations will be the big news of our time, and our descendants will be amused at our self-consciousness at heavy costs of adventure without practical payoffs. Why couldn't we see that such contests and heroics provided the necessary moral equivalent of war?

That is why we can hope that NASA's publicists do not equip next year's astronauts with link-up messages like "this is a giant step for détente" or "the march of scientific progress is irreversible."

Let our adventurer crawl through the passageway, stick out his hand, and say something more appropriate to the gloriously impractical spirit of the occasion. Like: "Dr. Livingstone, I presume?"*

THE INWARD GENERATION

March 6, 1975

Americans may be the only people who fail to see the importance of poetry in politics.

In the Soviet Union, dissident poets are treated with the utmost seriousness; their work is suppressed by a state that worries about the latent power in the most free form of literary expression.

Yevgeny Yevtushenko, who had been a rebel until he was impressed with the Communist cause, is used by Soviet authorities to write inspiring lines that transmit the general line. Criticizing the Peking Government, for example, he pities the regimented Chinese "cheated of his human existence from his diapers," and writes:

The young—spiritless confusion.
And the wisdom of the old who are still alive
Is nearly illegal.
What have you done with a human being?
Limiting him by harsh veto to your—uncited thoughts?

There is irony in the use of a regimented mind to complain about another culture's regimentation, but it underscores the new freedom and self-discovery that is making itself heard in American poetry, especially in the voices of the women poets.

* Henry Stanley's immortal line contains a solecism: he meant "Dr. Livingstone, I assume?"

"Poets who are women" is the way most of them would prefer it put, and a rejection of sexism is understandable; yet, as with "woman candidate," a gender-engendered interest exists. Women writing poetry tend to celebrate the emancipation of women, and that theme has become an artistic drive as well as a political fact.

Today, young women seem to dominate American poetry. Although death-obsessed Anne Sexton removed herself from the field with the severest form of self-editing, much of the excitement is about the work of Denise Levertov, Diane Wakoski, Adrienne Rich, Maya Angelou, Nikki Giovanni, and Marge Piercy.

Most widely known of the new generation of women poets is Erica Jong, who casts a lovely light because her candle burns at both its ends: a serious, provocative poet at one end, and a writer of a sexy novel at the other. Her *Fear of Flying* is a paperback hotcake, and even gets a big play at airport newsstands; its shock value centers on the discovery that yes, young women really think that way, and now have the courage to put it in print.

Miss Jong's sure-to-come celebrity and financial success may cause the rest of the poetry establishment to turn on her, for popularity breeds in-group contempt. And woman-poet Lois Wyse, whose *Love Poems for the Very Married* sold 300,000 copies in hard-cover, is now unfairly compared with male sentimentalist Rod McKuen, who is a modern A. E. Housman bewailing his critical rejection all the way to the bank.

For students of politics the significance of the poetry of Miss Jong and her cohorts is in the absence of political or racial protest, which has permeated so much of the poetry of the past generation.

Like the varied carols of the folk singers (Carole King, Carly Simon), the message in much of the "voice music" written by the new women poets flows from an awareness of their liberation. Often using the imagery of the body, they delight in discovering that there is no need to be self-conscious about the consciousness of one's self.

Their message is mainly inward and affirmative, rather than outward and angry, or upward and fearful. The protest, when it appears, is social rather than political, against the remaining bonds of sex, or against the unwanted responsibility of a sudden infusion of education and opportunity. Rebellion is directed at the way we live and not so much at the way we govern ourselves.

Does this attitude reflect the thinking of a self-centered élite group, or does it represent the yearnings and the uncertain freedoms of this generation of young adults—a group that Gertrude Stein might have labeled The Inward Generation?

If the young poets are singing what most of their contemporaries are thinking, then aspiring political leaders would do well to push aside conventional polls and tune themselves in. Instead of dealing exclusively with energy-environment policy, unemployment-inflation trade-offs, and ser-vices-vs.-taxes arguments, political leaders will have to find a wavelength that concerns itself with respect for individuality, the glorification of pri-vacy, the resentment toward society's standard impositions.

This inclination to "do your own thing," as Emerson called it more than a century ago in his essay on self-reliance, is not necessarily enno-bling. It can also be selfish and lazy, corroding young teeth with transcen-dental caries, refusing to pay for the new freedom with the coin of self-discipline.

The social protest of the young women poets is a political fact, ignored by politicians at their peril. The danger to the generation these poets rep-resent is not in going unheard but in falling into the trap Soviet poet Yev-tushenko finds himself in: dutifully conforming to a denunciation of regi-mentation.

PATTY, SLICK WILLIE, AND YOU

June 9, 1975

POSSUM TROT, Ky.—When Master Bank Robber "Slick Willie" Sut-ton was asked why he robbed banks, his answer was a classic in purity of thought: "Because that's where the money is."

Mr. Sutton occupied a place of honor on the F.B.I.'s "Ten Most Wanted" list for nearly four years, from 1948 to 1952, before being picked up in Brooklyn. Not every law-abiding citizen was happy to see him caught, since there is an element in the American character that secretly roots for the fugitive.

In this generation, the fugitive being silently cheered on is Patty Hearst, who has eluded the most intensive search for nearly a year and a half. She is not even on the "Most Wanted" list anymore; like the Duchess of Windsor and Mrs. William Paley, who dominated the Ten-Best-Dressed-Women's list for decades, Miss Hearst has been retired from the F.B.I.'s list and placed in superstar status.

Why do even law-and-order types get a surreptitious thrill out of one young woman's success in foiling the Feds? Why was *The Fugitive* such a successful TV series for so long? Why, when we are protected by the hounds, do we harbor secret sympathies for the fox?

One reason, of course, is that we take a perverse delight in seeing au-thority frustrated by the individual, even when we believe authority is right and the individual wrong. There stands the vaunted F.B.I., with all those computers and eavesdropping devices and laboratories and clean-cut agents, being made to look foolish by one girl and her underground allies.

Underneath that is a turning toward privacy that many of us have—usually unnoticed, seldom admitted—that makes us apprehensive of the hunter even as we demand the apprehension of the hunted.

The United States is the easiest place in the world in which to disappear. No other society in the world gives the fugitive such an opportunity. When Assassin James Earl Ray fled to England, he was picked up within three months; if Patty Hearst is in Kowloon or Timbuktu, she is likely to soon be gathered in.

That is because the United States has not yet become a papers-and-documents society. In many countries, permits are needed to travel; papers are needed to change jobs; identity cards are issued regularly and checked carefully; the arm of the law is long and strong because a person out of place quickly attracts attention.

In the United States, such identification requirements as exist can be circumvented with ease. Want a phony birth certificate? Look in the obituary notices of the year you were born, find a young child who died, and apply for a "copy" of your birth certificate at any one of 15,000 Vital Statistics offices in the country. Because births and deaths are registered separately, you'll get one. More than a million illegal aliens hold jobs in the United States on this gambit alone.

Shouldn't we tighten our identity laws, make it tougher for the fugitives and "illegals" and make it easier for the F.B.I.? The answer is no. Although the benefits to law enforcement are substantial, the cost of requiring "papers"—in freedom and privacy—is exorbitant.

These ruminations occur in Possum Trot, Ky., halfway between the academic center of Murray and the bright lights of Paducah, Popcorn Capital of the World. A fugitive could easily disappear among the upright outcasts of Possum Trot—and live a good life here, with nobody checking closely on movements or background—just as one could in Brooklyn, and more easily than in Kowloon.

As summer takes hold and schools let out, many Americans will be traveling again, fugitives from routine; many will voyage abroad to discover the red tape and documentation that afflicts other societies far more than our own. Every time we turn in our passports to a foreign hotel clerk for a police identity check, we make a small obeisance to tyranny.

I will be among those travelers for a month, since this is the time to "seal up the mouth of outrage for a while, till we can clear these ambiguities. . . ." But one matter is not ambiguous: If protection of every American's privacy causes the F.B.I. to take a little longer to catch Miss Hearst, the delay is worth it.

Why is the United States the best place for a fugitive? Because, as "Slick Willie" would say, that's where the freedom is.

CB: BANDING TOGETHER

June 17, 1976

LAS VEGAS, Nev.—If my rug rats want to send 80-8's around the house, they can get me ears for Father's Day.

Which is to say, in the lingo of Citizens Band (CB) radio, that if my children want to convey their thanks and best wishes, they can get me a transceiver to break into the world of two-way radio.

The Citizens Band combines the fascination of the old-fashioned party-line telephone with the protection of anonymity. Basic equipment to transmit and receive runs $100 or so and anybody over 18 can get a license from the F:C.C. Then with your official call letters and a nickname of your choice, you're on the air.

Curiously, it took the Arab oil boycott to make personal broadcasting a reality. With the imposition of a nationwide 55-miles-per-hour speed limit to conserve gas, and its sensible continuance to save lives, resourceful truck drivers took to the two-way radio to warn each other of speed traps by police cars.

Centuries ago, cockney pickpockets developed rhyming slang to confuse their pursuers: "Money" was encoded to "bread 'n honey" (which is why money is called "bread" in slang today). In the same way, modern "gear jammers" (drivers) frustrated by the unprofitable "double nickel" (55 m.p.h.) worked out an argot to counter the "Smokey's in a brown paper bag" (a cop is a bear, or Smokey Bear, who sometimes hunts his speeding prey in an unmarked police car).

When cops began tuning into the Citizens Band, the law-stretching element of the drivers' communications faded, but a new subculture had been spawned. Country music celebrated it, and Lanie Dills in Nashville ("Sugar Britches" of "Guitar Town") put together a CB slang dictionary. The method of mobile intercommunication merged with the mystique of a Middle-American movement to become a craze.

Miss Dills' dictionary is near the top of the paperback best-seller list; distributors of magazines and books, meeting in convention in Las Vegas, are talking of ways to ride the rise of interest in Citizens Band radio with more books and specialty magazines. Six million CB sets are said to be in use today, F.C.C. applications are nearing a half-million per month, and some auto manufacturers are making CB an option in new models this fall.

Will this CB explosion become another Hula-Hoop or transistorized calculator—another "this year's present" for the country that has everything?

I think not; these ears have no walls. The owners of radio stations are worried for good reason: The Citizens Band will slice the growth out of their sets in use. Telephone companies have already lost a court fight and must face an unexpected source of competition.

The reason Citizens Band radio will not fade is that it answers the need to answer. Newspapers, recognizing this pent-up desire to talk back, have expanded their letters-to-the-editor columns; radio stations have featured listener call-ins on discussion shows; on television, *60 Minutes* wisely makes much of its viewers' comments.

But that is only representative reaction, not the audiences' longed-for two-way communication. The lonely crowd wants company. A human being is not merely a receiver. Behind locked doors in cities, behind locked cliques in suburbs, behind the lock of isolation in rural areas, individuals want to say—with no loss of safety or privacy—"Hello, I'm me; let's talk about something."

In CB language that message could be: "Break 10. This is KHT 1776, the Washington multplug, do you read me?" More likely than not, somebody out there—locally, within a few miles—will answer, and neighbors can have a conversation, knowing that others are listening in. No lonely-hearts club; no singles bar; no intermediary needed.

So far, a down-home etiquette dominates the CB airwaves. People call each other "good buddy" and expletives are replaced with an ironic "mercy sakes." People who talk longer than the allotted five minutes are called "ratchet jaws" and soon get the message. Calls for help are heard and reported to police.

But forget about truck drivers' lingo, the love of a new toy, the sudden exploitation of a new craze. Think about the answer offered to people starved for company by this safe, private, local two-way communication. And not just to the lonely driver, or to the aged or the handicapped—but to all the people who do not meet anybody "new," or who are shy, or who have been told by relatives that they are pests.

Here is a beginning of a personal medium which will—in a generation—be as important as any mass medium is today: for back-fence gossiping; for word-of-mouth selling; for citizen participation in fighting crime without getting overly "involved"; for remote parental control; for two-step opinion formation.

But let me not sail off into "I see a day." Here and now, we will find imaginative new uses for this most democratic intercourse. On Election Day this year, I'll be "on the side" (monitoring the channel) when some woman will say, "I would be voting for Reagan today, but I've got nobody to watch the kids." I'll mash my mike button and say, "Breakety break, this is KHT 1776. I'll be right over, lady—and it's 80-8's around the house."

Whimsey

WHY CAN'T an essayist horse around, like normal people? Because the art of humor is difficult to master and is best left to masters like Russell Baker. On matters of style, however, I've had some fun, and even satirized myself, which hurt.

OF PANDAS AND FIREFLIES

January 14, 1974

WASHINGTON—A world unabashedly hooked on symbolism has—mistakenly, as we shall see—looked upon the two happy, healthy pandas as the symbol of détente between the great powers.

Ling-Ling and Hsing-Hsing: Year of the Panda, a new book by Larry Collins, keeper of the pandas at Washington's National Zoo, and James Page Jr. of the Smithsonian magazine, offers a delightful and astringent look at these gifts to the United States from the People's Republic of China.

Our panda keepers point out, for example, that an elongated wristbone serves as a kind of thumb, giving these black-eyed huggables a manual dexterity denied to most other animals.

Let me add one item to panda lore: The naming of the two specimens sent by Chou En-lai was a matter of top-level concern at the White House. With infinite subtlety, the Chinese had assured us that "Ling-Ling" and "Hsing-Hsing" were only working titles given to the young pandas by their keepers, and that the President was free to name them whatever he pleased.

Special consultant to the President Richard Moore, fresh from his triumph of renaming Air Force One "The Spirit of '76," was asked to survey his colleagues on appropriate names for this historic state gift.

Several White House aides, including John Scali, now Ambassador to the United Nations, lobbied for "Ping" and "Pong," after the game that built the first dramatic bridge to what we used to call Red China.

My own suggestion was "Peter" and "Wendy," on the theory that a beast that would always look like a baby would be well-named Peter Panda. These and other options were duly sent to President Nixon for his decision, along with caveats that Ling-Ling sounded like an unanswered hotline to Peking, and Hsing-Hsing carried an inappropriate, penal connotation, especially since the animals were to be caged.

The President decided to hang tough: Chinese gifts should have Chinese names, he ordered, no matter what everybody said, and so Ling-Ling and Hsing-Hsing remained the names. I registered my vigorous dissent and still feel it would have been wiser to panda to public opinion.

Be that as it may, these two lovable, popular, bearlike mammals have been cavorting together for a couple of years now and nothing has happened; that is, the breeding of pandas in captivity has proved to be as difficult as ever.

If these two representatives from Communist China were to produce an offspring in the very capital of capitalism, they would be worthy of remaining the symbols of détente. But somebody has to say the unsayable: Reproductive results are nil. (I'm not blaming either one.)

That is why we must look elsewhere for a symbol of détente. What living symbol can we find that could stand for the relaxation of tensions, the normalization of relations, better than these unproductive showoffs?

In Harrisburg, Pa., last month, state legislator Frank Lynch of Upper Darby introduced a bill (House bill 1708) to designate the firefly as Pennsylvania's official insect. The suggestion came to him from a third-grade class in his district.

I would like to join the Lynch mob, to make the firefly not merely the Keystone state's official insect but the international symbol of détente.

Most of us think of the firefly as a little airborne beetle bravely lighting its candle instead of cursing the darkness. But recent entomological research by Dr. James E. Lloyd of the University of Florida in Gainesville has revealed the firefly to be a clever trickster, especially in its mating habits.

Did you ever wonder why fireflies seemed to synchronize the rhythm of their glowing? They're not all singing together—more likely, an interloping male is picking up the beat of a courtship so as to confuse the female into flying united with him.

Yes, Virginia, fireflies are phosphorescent foolers. They glow to mislead, seeming to dance to your tune but doing so with duplicity in their hearts.

In the light of Middle East mischief, the betrayal of the spirit of SALT, and the quiet buildup of the North Vietnamese—a couple of cute, unproductive pandas would better be replaced as a symbol of détente by the firefly, the amoral beetle so expert in getting partners to switch.

ON EMANCIPATION

February 11, 1974

WASHINGTON, Sept. 22, 1862—President Lincoln announced today his intention to free the slaves in those states still in rebellion as of Jan. 1, 1863. White House aides referred to the press handout as an "Emancipation Proclamation" and characterized it as a "major statement." A fictional roundup of comment follows:

By a Mary McGrory

So the word finally crashed through the barrier erected by his "Secretaries," Nicolay and Hay, to the wisecracking warrior that cartoonists have come to know and love as "the big baboon," that the Civil War is not about preservation of the Union after all, but about the abolition of slavery. It's about time.

Lincoln's name may be on the document, but the real authors are Wendell Phillips and William Lloyd Garrison, who were out marching in the streets while Honest Abe was doffing his stovepipe to the gang who tried to tab "copperhead" on the people who believe in peace and human freedom. . . .

By an Evans and Novak

At a stormy, secret Cabinet meeting two months before the Emancipation Proclamation, Postmaster General Montgomery Blair—the only man with political savvy still close to the increasingly isolated and morose President—warned Lincoln that the move could spell disaster for candidates in the midterm elections.

By polling bellwether-beaten districts chosen for us by psychologist Oliver Scammonberg, we find four Border states—Maryland, Kentucky, Delaware, and Missouri—are still loyal and highly necessary to the Union cause. But they are slaveholding states. At the urging of vote-conscious Blair, Lincoln watered down his edict to apply only to Confederate states.

Even so, proslavery sentiment in the North is likely to cause a political whiplash. Barring bombshells, insiders say anti-Lincoln forces will sweep New York, Pennsylvania, Ohio, Indiana, and Illinois, all states Lincoln carried two years ago. . . .

By a William Buckley

The rodomontade accompanying the White House statement—"Emancipation Proclamation" has a mouth-filling quality—obscures one of the recherché ironies of this Administration. Here is a President freeing slaves (on paper, at least) and at the same time imprisoning thousands of his countrymen unlawfully, denying them the basic Anglo-Saxon right to *habeas corpus*. Can we expect to hear a mighty roar from liberal abolitionists on that issue, sensitive as they are to the cause of human freedom? As General Nathan Bedford Forrest said only last week, "I told you twicet, Goddammit, no."

Although the assault by central Government on private property is troubling, the constitutional principle of the equal creation of men must control, which is why conservatives can support the restoration of certain muniments, if not the aureate rhetoric, of this "proclamation." . . .

By a C. L. Sulzberger

One must assume that the primary reason for Mr. Lincoln's Emancipation Proclamation was to influence the Government of England not to enter America's Civil War on the side of the South. Antislavery sentiment among England's workingmen is high, and no British leader, much as he would like to encourage a Southern victory that would enhance England's commercial dominance, can afford to oppose it.

Thus the emancipation is seen by observers here in Ulan Bator, strategic nervecenter of Outer Mongolia, as a diplomatic-military masterstroke. . . .

By an Art Buchwald

Now that emancipation is here, everybody wants to be a slave. My friend Simon J. Legree, who has just become a management consultant to Little Eva Industries, thinks now that slavery is on the way out, nostalgia for it will grow. "Chains and flogging turned a lot of people off for awhile," says Simon. "But now they're coming to see the advantages: no taxes, no responsibilities, no jury duty. . . ."

By a James Reston

The trouble with Mr. Lincoln's proclamation is that it deals with the politics of the problem and not the problem itself.

The President, in seeking a compromise, has freed the slaves in only those states in which his Government has no power to enforce emancipation, and has not freed the slaves in those states where his Government does have the power to enforce it. That's why the mood pervading this capital today is somewhat cynical, holding that the proclamation is a lot of weak talk, and this is especially difficult for the wives.

The problem has not lent itself to a political solution, which is why we're fighting a civil war. "Preservation of the Union," a worthy goal, is a political abstraction. Slavery is another matter—a profound moral issue—and it can no longer be ducked, compromised about, or postponed. Mr. Lincoln will soon have to take an unequivocal moral stand.

As the yet-unborn Walter Lippmann will one day write. . . .

MR. LINCOLN'S COVER-UP

February 16, 1976

A long-sealed box preserving the contents of the pockets of Abraham Lincoln on the night he was killed was opened last week by the Librarian of Congress, Daniel J. Boorstin. The box contained 11 favorable newspaper clippings and a $5 Confederate bill.

One can imagine the following commentaries:

Newsweek's "My Turn," by Kenny O'Sandburg

The Confederate $5 bill proves nothing. I handed him his wallet every morning and I vividly remember there was never any Confederate $5 bill in it. I think it was palmed and slipped in the other day by Dr. Boorstin, who never gives President Lincoln the proper reverence. As to the clippings in the wallet, they only go to show the President's high regard for the media.

And let the record show that President Lincoln went to Ford's Theater that night at the insistence of his wife, Mrs. Lincoln. Abe, we hardly knew ye. . . .

By a Mary McGrory

The Case of the Tucked-Away Fin only shows that Mr. Lincoln knew the South would rise again, which was what Reconstruction was all about. Before the Nixon-wasn't-so-terrible crowd tries to turn this into a new Hughes loan, maybe we ought to turn the matter over to the most Lincolnesque of the Democrats on the scene, Frank Church. This sensitive and eminently fair, if jowly, Senator is owed a doffing of our stovepipe hats for his even handling of the reports of the subcommittee on multinational assassinations. . . .

By a *Washington Post* editorialist

Why can't we have done, once and for all, with all this unseemly poking into the past? Although Presidential payola can never be condoned, this sort of raising of eyebrows in a post-humous impeachment strikes us as— well, excessive.

We would extend this spirit of amnesty to Allan Pinkerton, long at the helm of Mr. Lincoln's intelligence agency, who—although consistently mistaken in his estimates of Confederate troop strength throughout the war—was, after all, a dedicated American in a job once considered the role of a patriot, and ill-deserving of harassment today.

As we were telling our investigative reporting team, Redford and Hoffman, now that the Big Deed's been done, perhaps the most constructive course for journalism in the future is to expose those who print leaks rather than join the irresponsibles who betray our nation's secrets. . . .

By a Jack Anderson

The reason why not one of the 11 clippings in Mr. Lincoln's wallet included a column by this reporter can now be revealed: I was in the vanguard of those denouncing the civil-liberties abuses of Lincoln Secret

Service Chief Allan Pinkerton while that cooper-turned-snooper was at the peak of his power.

My associate, Les Whitten, reports that the mysterious Confederate $5 bill discovered in Mr. Lincoln's billfold was linked to a Pinkerton-White House plot to poison me.

To be fair, when an associate of Mr. Whitten's called the Lincoln family for comment, he was told that Mr. Lincoln had "malice toward none," including this reporter, despite some irritation over my publication of the minutes of his "tilt toward Emancipation" Cabinet meeting.

Further checking was done by Mr. Whitten's associate's associate, whom I have yet to meet. . . .

By a William Safire

Five score and 11 years too late, we're finally being permitted a peek at the evidence that Lincoln mythmakers have been covering up.

Now, long after marble temples have been built to his memory, we're being allowed to discover the way Abe Lincoln, that secret egotist, pored over favorable press clippings, hoarding them as they yellowed and frayed, just as Lyndon Johnson cherished his rave reviews and sycophantic polls.

The trail is a little cold, but there is still time for a special prosecutor to ferret out the details of the un-breathed-about Lincoln-Jefferson Davis connection.

Some questions arise: (1) Why did Mr. Lincoln feel the need to take the unprecedented step of personally visiting Congress to testify that his wife was not a Confederate spy? (2) Why was Allan Pinkerton, hero of the Georgetown dinner party set, left completely out of the Church cover-up committee's select report on multi-assassination corporations? (Pinkerton's corporate symbol, an eye with "We Never Sleep" inscribed below, was the etymological origin of the term "private eye.")

That's not all: (3) Why, when it is well known that Lincoln wrote the Gettysburg Address on the back of an envelope, has nobody demanded to know what (or how much) that envelope originally contained? (4) Why was John Wilkes Booth gunned down before he could be brought to trial? (5) Why did Lincoln's manipulative Secretary of State, William Seward, secretly sell out Kurdish rebels in the hills of Tennessee? (6) . . . .

ON PUFFERY

May 16, 1974

WASHINGTON—Carmine DeSapio, boss of Tammany Hall a generation ago, abolished the smoke-filled room during his tenure as leader because his eyes were sensitive to smoke.

In that sense at least, Mr. DeSapio is regarded as a prophet without honor in his own time by members of a new organization, one fiercer and more self-righteous than the old Tiger of Tammany: the Group Against Smokers' Pollution (GASP).

Across the nation, GASP chapters have been formed to help shame the 52 million American smokers into refraining from indulging their habit in the "breathing space" of nonsmokers.

"Nonsmokers have rights too" is the slogan of GASP and in its "liberation guide" there are tips to members about methods to discomfit those who discomfort them. Some ideas are forthright—"Speak out against smoking!"—while others are maddening, such as "Discourage smoking by not providing ashtrays."

So far, so good: In an enclosed space, people who are annoyed by tobacco smoke should make known their irritation to smokers, who should then have the courtesy to desist. Unfortunately, that is not the last GASP: Buoyed by their success in getting airlines to segregate smokers, the nonsmokers are pressing their attack with demands for Government regulation of "breathing space."

From Barry Goldwater's Arizona to George McGovern's South Dakota, states have passed laws prohibiting smoking in museums, concert halls, theaters, libraries, and elevators. This morning, New York City's Board of Health is scheduled to act on a proposal to compel the segregation of smokers from nonsmokers in most public places, including restaurants.

This is a good example of the tyranny of the minority. A little group of willful persons, representing no opinion but their own, has rendered the great smoking public helpless and contemptible.

Where a fire or health hazard exists, nobody disputes that smoking should be prohibited. But despite the fuming of former Surgeon General Jesse Steinfeld, no evidence exists to suggest that the exhaled smoke of other persons poses a health hazard to nonsmokers. A tiny minority is acutely allergic to smoke, and its wishes need to be considered, but public policy ought not to be set to accommodate today's Carmine DeSapios.

The cigarette smoker is already the target of too many Government agencies. He cannot be advertised to on television; he must carry around on every pack a dire warning about killing himself; he is taxed regressively and punitively.

Yet the smoker continues to smoke; in the United States last year, 588 billion cigarettes were puffed, dragged upon, and choked over, and thanks to the growing interest in smoking by teen-age girls, the market continues to grow.

This perverseness—the refusal of people to do what is good for them— activates the antismoking brigade, I think, even more than the annoyance caused by the exhalation of the coffin-nailers. If smokers do not respond to reason, to warnings, to the silencing of advertising, to tax disincentives, then perhaps the only way is to make it more difficult to find a place to light up.

"You are not denying the smoker's right to smoke," GASP assures its members, "only his/her right to smoke in your breathing space." Not true; any harassment, especially harassment by executive regulations, is part of a process that infringes our liberties and pollutes our statute books.

Today the smoker, tomorrow the onion-eater, and the day after tomorrow the person who prefers cheap perfume to the taking of baths: Once Government gets its nose under the tent of social intercourse, there will be no privacy for anyone.

The bossism of the do-gooder is intolerable, even when he/she (fight linguistic pollution!) cloaks paternalism in the guise of selfishness. Not every social inequity needs a legal cure; social, not government, pressure is appropriate to curb the smoker. A glare, a sniff, and if necessary the green-gilled appearance of the onset of motion sickness, should be enough to get a smoker to stub out his butt in a hurry.

I gave up smoking two years ago and it is like losing a friend. I don't feel any better, and am not inclined to badger others into sacrificing one of life's little pleasures. What incenses some people is incense to me; blow some my way.

But the abuse of the power of health agencies to put a governmental fist into the glove of social courtesies is worrisome. A new law separating smoking from nonsmoking areas in restaurants would invite a smoker's sit-in at a nonsmoking lunch counter, turning the civil-rights clock back by decades.

In their zeal, the people from GASP have gone too far; we can now look forward to the formation of "People United to Fight for Freedom by Fighting Fire With Fire" (PUFFFFF).

ON THE HUSTLE

August 4, 1975

WASHINGTON—"If a man were permitted to make all the ballads," wrote Scottish rebel Andrew Fletcher in 1704, "he need not care who should make the laws of a nation." This sentiment was echoed by Artemus Ward in 1863: "Let me write the songs of a nashun and I don't care a cuss who goes to the legislater."

On that theory, the most profound political development on the American scene in recent months has been the success of a new song and dance called "the Hustle."

The word "hustle" is rooted in the Dutch word for "shake"; in underworld lingo, a hustler was one who shook up, or jostled, a victim while an aide picked his pocket. In the United States, the word gained a connotation of nervous go-getting, and recent usage has centered on hard-working prostitutes.

Despite the sleazy lineage of the name, the dance form of the Hustle offers hope to aficionados of grace, sex, and discipline. To the solid beat of the bass guitar—the sound is called "disco," after discothéque—dance partners take two long steps on the beat, followed by three quick steps of a half-beat each.

Some will dismiss the Hustle as a fad, just another craze, but political observers attuned to public moods and the changes foreshadowed in the youth culture are convinced that this new dance is as revolutionary as the Twist, and as politically portentous.

1. *The Hustle must be learned.* Throughout the Vietnam-Watergate span of the past 15 years, dance-floor gyrations required no instruction. The dancer would lurch into action doing whatever jerk, bump, wiggle, slide, and grind came to mind or hips, and the only measurement of success was the degree of enjoyment that such frantic self-expression achieved.

The advantages of such a choreographic free-for-all were (a) no investment in lessons was required and (b) no embarrassment would accrue to the beginner. The disadvantage was that there was no satisfaction in becoming a "good" dancer.

The Hustle changes all this. Suddenly, attention must be paid, steps must be learned, as the free lunch is swept off the dance floor and dancers can once again be rated as smoothies or stumblers, born leaders or hopeless cornstompers. A standard is set; one must study, practice, and work to achieve success in doing the Hustle. The political ramifications of such a conservative trend are mind-boggling (which is why some Young Republicans call an advanced form of the dance "the Boggle").

2. *The Hustle requires mental communication with a designated dance partner.* In Vietnam-Watergate era dancing, the opposite was the case: Following a grimly inward-turning philosophy of doing one's own thing, dancers would deliberately ignore whatever one's partner was doing. To be in step was to be out of step.

Not so with the Hustle. Oh, apologists for the old ways claim that Hustle dancers "share their own thing," but this is a contradiction in terms, designed to lull aging rebels-without-a-cause into thinking no decisive break with the past is taking place. The political fact is that the absolute-freedom days of the dance are over. When you are committed to considering what your partner will do next, and must signal your own intentions so that the "team" of which you are a part can stay in step, then you have embraced not only a dance partner, but responsibility.

This means that turning inward is no longer "in"; that personal isolationism has peaked and may already be on the decline. Transcendental meditation will soon lose its numbing fascination as people find it more exciting to communicate with other people than to lollygag in the ever-expanding recesses of ever-narrowing minds.

3. *The Hustle involves holding one's partner in one's arms.* Body contact, which has been denied to the dance in recent years, has been limited to professional football. The enshrinement of detachment, the glorification of "cool," has resulted in forced loving to achieve mental balance.

Fortunately, the rise of the Hustle provides a socially acceptable way for people to get their hands on members of the opposite sex. Now people no longer have to leap into bed together to discover if they are physically compatible; they can dance together first.

After a terpsichorean era of confrontation, we are entering an era of negotiation. The geopolitician who fails to see this social phenomenon is out of touch with his time. As dancing requires instruction, genuine standards become the fashion; as eyes focus on and arms enfold a partner, responsibility and humanity come into vogue.

Hail the Hustle, with its studied discipline, its communicative style, and its honest passion! At long last, the "cool" war is ending.

The Campaign of '76

A PRESIDENTIAL CAMPAIGN is like a symphony: subdued beginnings, great crescendos, distinctive movements, a sense that the orchestra is leading the conductor.

The 1976 primaries that led to Ford versus Carter, and the television debates that led to President Ford's self-destruction, were the first campaigns I covered as a registered pundit. In the past, I had sailed as a participant: in 1952, organizing a rally in Madison Square Garden for General Eisenhower; in 1960, joining Jackie Robinson in a plea to Richard Nixon to make a phone call to Martin Luther King in jail; in 1964, hauling a sign that said "Stay in the Mainstream" through San Franciso's Cow Palace to the jeers of the Goldwater enthusiasts; in 1968, churning out cheer lines for speeches aboard the campaign plane, and in 1972, left curiously outside the CREEP organization, for which I thank the angel on my shoulder.

But it is not necessary to be a participant to be a partisan. I was for Reagan over Ford, and then for Ford over Carter. I got in the habit of losing graciously that year, and in consoling my fellow disappointees, but that was a position I had been prepared for: As a speechwriter, it had always been my lot to prepare the concession speech.

FRESHETS ARE RUNNING

September 4, 1975

WASHINGTON—The political freshets have begun to run; soon, streams of press releases will be coming from various camps and factions, each purporting to represent the mainstream, culminating—nine months from now—in two mighty rivers of conventioneers, flowing vexatiously to the sea.

One freshet is the Citizens for Reagan headquarters here, presided over by lawyer John Sears, 35, who thinks "it's more like '52 than '64—and this time Taft's a good-lookin' guy."

Since political wisdom holds that the electorate tunes out politics between Thanksgiving and New Year's, the Reagan campaign plans to get under way in late October or early November. The White House professes to be aloof and unconcerned, but the political operatives there are concerned and have reason to be.

That's because Reagan and his men swing easy, with little to lose and much excitement ahead. One of the first men brought aboard is a lawyer, Loren Smith—who prepped on James St. Clair's White House staff—to make sure nobody runs afoul of the new campaign laws, and a direct-mail money-raising expert, Eberle Associates. (In the old days, the first aboard would be a speechwriter and a press agent.) They've just signed up a full-time pollster, Richard Wirthlin, whose California firm has one of those dynamic-sounding titles: Decision-Making Information.

Maybe it will all go nowhere, maybe it will go all the way. The glory of American politics is that nobodies become somebodies, somebodies become has-beens, and everybody gets another chance someday.

Consider John Sears. Few men of his years have ridden the roller coaster so far up and so far down. He began in the mid-60's in the law firm of Richard Nixon, a studious conservative volunteering to work on speeches and position papers, later moving into the field of buttonholing delegates.

An easygoing and likable young man, his illusions about king-making and its rewards were shattered when a hard-eyed crew took over in the late 60's. As a member of the Price-Buchanan-Garment set who actually engineered the beginnings of the Nixon comeback, Sears found himself on the outside when John Mitchell and Bob Haldeman became the In's.

Mr. Sears' friendly dealings with the press especially raised the ire of John Mitchell, who found such fraternization intolerable. In the White House, as it later was revealed, Sears was most egregiously wiretapped, and without the most remote justification of "national security."

When he became fed up enough to walk out of the White House, Mr. Sears could not have faced a bleaker political future. If Nixon stayed for eight years, as seemed so likely, Sears had no Republican opportunities; if the Democrats ever got in, he was not one of them; and the third-party route had no appeal. Sears was all washed up before he was 30.

Now, in one of those turnings of the wheel that typify American politics, Mr. Sears lunches at Washington's Sans Souci restaurant, guest of a series of high-powered pundits, sprinkling his conversation with those delicious "not-for-attributions" and "deep backgrounds" that we all lap up with the sauce *meunière*.

I will go to my grave before revealing who told me this, but I have it from a "key Reagan strategist" that the secret plan of the former California Governor is to "manufacture momentum in the primaries" of New Hampshire, Florida, and Wisconsin and win going away in the California primary, thereby capturing the nomination from a sitting President.

All this may sound like the usual political hot-stove-league stuff, but such talk is mother's milk to Sears and young men like him, who share an excitement that drags otherwise sensible people into the arena. They are no Kamikaze pilots, either; if the effort aborts, the usual procedure is for the winner to pick up the best of the loser's staff to heal party wounds.

The impermanence of defeat, the turnings of the wheel, the possibility of a comeback help make politics attractive. That was what was suspended in Watergate times, when the politics assumed a savagery and its reaction a hate-filled retribution alien to the system, but it seems those days are fading and some of the fun may come back.

For politics ought to be a place for "happy warriors," and men like Hubert Humphrey are not to be reviled by cynics for having spoken of the "politics of joy." Serious business, yes; intense emotion and furious debate, of course; but after the battle, the blood should turn out to be catsup and some of the roundhouse punches only what Willkie called "campaign oratory."

To latch on to the latest teen-age cliché, "put it this way": as the Democrats most talked about for the nomination, it's good to see two men whose political obituaries have been issued time and again: Hubert Humphrey and Edward Kennedy.

And it is good to see John Sears, a comrade in taps, working the media fences with good humor and good sense, playing the long shot he believes in. Even if he loses, he's not wasting his time; and if he wins—who knows?—the earnest young man who was all washed up before thirty could wind up Attorney General of the United States.

As the freshets begin to run, young politicians everywhere hear them whispering: "Get a horse! Get a horse!"

CORN AND CARTER

November 10, 1975

CEDAR RAPIDS, Iowa—"I honestly believe I'm going to be your next President," says former Georgia Governor Jimmy Carter.

His style is low-key, what Madison Avenue likes to call "sincere," and his message is strictly middle-of-the-road: "There is no inherent conflict between careful planning, tight management, and constant reassessment on the one hand and compassionate concern for the plight of the deprived and afflicted on the other."

That safe-and-sane message is going over well in Iowa, which will become a closely watched state in a couple of months. On January 19, a nonprimary primary will take place: In each political precinct, Iowa's Democratic and Republican voters will meet in caucus to choose their delegates to next summer's party conventions.

Parenthesis: Since that word will be bandied about a great deal, an etymological note might be helpful. Some say "caucus" is an Algonquin Indian word, from "*caucauasu*" or "counselor" and belongs with Indian contributions to politics like "mugwump," "sachem," and "high muckamuck"; others find it rooted in the Greek "*kaukos,*" or drinking vessel, alluding to the convivial nature of Boston's Caucus Club, frequented by the revolutionary John Adams. End parenthesis.

Four years ago, an indication that Ed Muskie's front-running was an illusion came in Iowa's caucus, when George McGovern's organizers first displayed their talents. Today, similar talk about effective organization centers on the Carter people; the television salesmen here say the first queries about time availabilities for a TV blitz right after New Year's are coming from Carter's headquarters.

Although Carter leads the polls at the moment, Hubert Humphrey shows his strength as a write-in on straw ballots, and no support is more impressive to polls than write-ins, which show an intensity of feeling.

Scoop Jackson shares labor support with Carter, but his campaign shows a lack of savvy: Denouncing the "Nixon-Ford Administration" (much as Nixon denounced the "Johnson-Humphrey Administration" in 1968, though Johnson was not running) Jackson told an Ames audience the nation had witnessed the worst mismanagement of the economy since Herbert Hoover. The Democratic audience sat on its hands; Herbert Hoover's birthplace is only a few miles away, and a certain local affection for him exists.

On the Republican side, one might think that former Des Moines radio sportscaster "Dutch" Reagan would be moving hard and fast to exploit his local background and grab the spotlight here, but the Reagan talk is muted. This is Ford country, at the moment; his Cabinet shakeup was not seen as all that important here, and those who noticed thought it showed the President to be a take-charge executive.

On both sides, the size of the "undecideds" in polls and casual conversation is enormous: Cedar Rapidians are getting as cagey as the overinterviewed residents of Concord, N.H.

Does the forthcoming national interest in Iowa make sense? Is this caucus really important? The answer is yes, because this first test of strength will be *treated* as important by national media, which—like it or not—makes it important. And after the McGovern experience, which caught most of the press grassrootless, rest assured Iowa's "first" will be swarmed over.

We will be hearing reports from a generally happy land. Thanks to the weather, the corn crop is in early this year, and farmers are having a more leisurely November than usual. No recession took place here, and though farmers grumble about the increased assessed valuation of their thousand-an-acre farmland, the biggest problem Iowans seem to face is what to do with the $200-million surplus that came in from the state sales tax.

Though candidates abound, nobody rides through the cornfields with a flaming sword. At Coe College in Cedar Rapids, nobody's dander is up. With Midwestern interest so closely tied to grain sales and détente, the traditional isolationism has become a self-interested internationalism. Iowa's voters display their bipartisanship by choosing two United States Senators who are Democrats along with a Republican Governor, Robert Ray, who is the most popular man in the state.

In Iowa, prosperity is on the side of the man in the White House. What does an opposition candidate do when he has good times going against him? He organizes his troops, spends time meeting the folks, stresses his trustworthiness, and fuzzes up any issues.

That is why Democratic campaigners in the middle of America play the politics of the 50-yard line. Jimmy Carter's message is calculated to offend nobody: "Waste and inefficiency," he straddles in all sincerity, "never fed a hungry child. . . ."

BOOTING SILKY HOME

July 26, 1976

WASHINGTON—Silky Sullivan was my favorite horse. He never won the Derby, or took home the kind of money Secretariat did, but he is remembered by racing fans for a certain exciting quality.

Silky would dawdle out of the gate and lumber along for a while, wondering where he was and why all those guys up ahead were running so fast. Then, rounding the far turn way behind, he would come on with a whoosh on the outside—surprising himself, amazing fans, and infuriating handicappers.

Sometimes he flashed past the front-runner in the nick of time, sometimes not. But with Silky in the race, the favorite never looked like such a sure bet in the home stretch.

Metaphorically, horse racing has been generous to politics: dark horses and running mates, shoo-ins and bolters, front-runners and also-rans. Which is why it may be apt to consider Ronald Reagan as this year's Silky Sullivan.

Like Silky, Ronnie showed no early foot in the first primaries. But he hit his stride coming around the Texas turn and now has the panic-stricken handicappers shredding their tip sheets, explaining how he cannot possibly beat the odds.

One reason Reagan might win by a nose at the finish line in Kansas City is that delegates want what those who play horses want: a chance at a winner. By showing he could come from behind in the primaries, Mr. Reagan has fed the hope that he could come from behind to win the general election.

The Republican nominee will be a long shot. The question before the convention will not be "Which is the lesser long shot?" but "Which long shot could spring a surprise in the stretch?"

Ford supporters will insist that their horse has the best upsetter qualities, citing the White House as the place where surprises can originate, and recalling Mr. Truman's "turnip day" challenge to a do-nothing Congress.

Reagan supporters will stress their entry's upsetter qualities in a handful of ways:

1. The favorite has now become the Establishment, embracing the traditional power brokers, pictured at "21" soothing business leaders on taxes, and handing over to Mr. Reagan the most successful baton of the year: the anti-Washington, anti-politics-as-usual, anti-Establishment issue.

2. The favorite's aggressive religiosity, and the way he gave the back of his hand to the Democrat's leading lights who are Catholic—Senator Kennedy and Governor Brown—opens a new vista to the center right for reaching voters who are traditional Democrats. Mr. Reagan, who has been quoting Popes and addressing Catholics on a cultural basis, has an edge over the President, who now cannot be so pleased with his wife's outspokenness on abortion. Most of the people who applauded her for it are now for Carter.

3. The favorite is vulnerable to the "fuzziness" charge. Mr. Carter, who supported the Vietnam war, now says it was "racist"; Mr. Carter, who telephoned the accused Vice President Agnew urging him to hang in there, now professes to have disapproved of the Nixon pardon. Reagan on the offense, better than Ford on the defense, can make the case against such phony, retroactive popularism.

4. The favorite's delayed debut as a liberal—who finds the forthright heavy-spending votes and pro-busing stand of Fritz Mondale "compatible"—invites an upset by a candidate who presents a clear contrast.

5. The favorite cannot honorably duck a debate, and Reagan proved to be a surprisingly adept debater against Robert Kennedy a decade ago and Ralph Nader last year. Reagan is more likely than Ford to swiftly narrow the gap with debates—as John Kennedy did in 1960—and would issue the challenge in his acceptance speech.

"Upset potential," then, will be the crucial factor in Kansas City. This is a more focused form of "electability," evoking a gambling instinct not reflected in preconvention interviews with uncommitteds. Hidden Reagan strength exists in several delegations, while—as Murray Kempton has perceived—the rarest form of political life is a closet Fordite.

The whirring and buzzing of tabulators and the claims and counterclaims of delegate-hunters can safely be set aside: Nobody knows the answer, because there is as yet no answer. A contested convention has a life of its own. The intensity factor will get full play—and this will be a whooping, wheezing, wheeling, never-sine-die convention.

We cannot preview the finish through media binoculars, or work it out from the form chart, or put credence in whispered tips from the stables. We must look at the first of this year's two close finishes with the naked eye, remembering that the track record of the Democratic favorite is to fade toward the finish.

Which would you choose, if you wanted a fast-closing long shot? *C'mon, Silky!*

RICHARD REDUX

May 13, 1976

WASHINGTON—Those who still defiantly wear Richard Nixon tieclasps—a slim bar terminating in a trained Presidential seal—can find much to admire in the campaign techniques of Jimmy Carter.

More than any candidate in either party, Mr. Carter is following the precepts set down by candidate Nixon in his 1968 campaign.

1. *Stay fuzzy on the issues through Labor Day, then inundate the press with complex stands in lengthy position papers and radio speeches.* Little is to be gained, and much to be lost, in spelling out positions in the primaries. Mr. Carter has made his necessary concessions to the specific—the obeisance to labor in opposing Taft-Hartley's 14-B, the sop to the liberals with support of the makework job bill, the muted appeal to blacks with his

whispered call for repeal of the Byrd Amendment that permits importation of Rhodesian chrome—but these are doled out sparingly, without hoopla.

The Carter position on the Panama Canal is a perfect expression of the Nixon rule: He opposes "relinquishing actual control" of the canal to Panama, which pleases the silent majority, but is willing to remove the word "perpetuity" from the treaty, which pleases the Establishment responsibles.

2. *Keep a tight circle of young, longtime advisers, and trust nobody else.* Mr. Carter's inner circle of Hamilton Jordan, Jerry Rafshoon, and Jody Powell are even younger than were Nixon aides Haldeman, Ehrlichman, and Ziegler. In both cases, the inner circle is made up of men whose lives are totally dominated by their leader's long quest for the Presidency. In both cases, the press secretary has had the advantage of no previous experience as a reporter.

And in both cases, the campaigns were burned by the breaching of this rule. In 1968 conservative outside speechwriter Richard Whalen stormed out of the Nixon camp on principle, and in 1976 liberal outside speechwriter Robert Shrum gagged when he was offered a spoonful of Carter's political pragmatism.

"I don't want any more statements on the Middle East or Lebanon," Mr. Shrum says Mr. Carter told him privately. "Jackson has all the Jews anyway. It doesn't matter how far I go, I don't get over 4 percent of the Jewish vote anyway, so forget it. We get the Christians." That's not anti-Semitic, that's pro-politic; candidate Nixon thought the same way, although—perversely—he went on to espouse the pro-Israel view he proved later he held.

3. *Damn your opponents with faint praise.* "Never go after them personally," Mr. Nixon used to instruct Mr. Agnew; "Say 'my wife likes them,' or something." Carter carries this out well; he often says, "My opponents, they're good people, I don't want to criticize them."

But even as Mr. Carter doesn't criticize, he does what playwright Arthur Miller calls "acting against the words"—saying one thing in a way calculated to cause the audience to believe the opposite. Mr. Nixon would do this with a rather heavy hand; Mr. Carter has a lighter, more devastating touch.

4. *Keep your eye on the ball, and remember only the In's are guilty.* Singlemindedness is required. While Governors Rockefeller and Reagan were busy running their states, Mr. Nixon spent full time pursuing the Presidency, and won it in the primaries; while Messrs. Humphrey, Jackson, and Udall were phumphing around in Washington, Mr. Carter was out organizing in the primary states.

Mr. Nixon was among the first to see that running against Washington would be profitable, and that the American people did not want to be blamed for the Vietnam war. Mr Carter, uniquely among present candidates, has a way of absolving us all from Vietnam—and Watergate—and blaming it on a scapegoateed "them." Guilt is a loser; pride goeth before the fall campaign.

Of course, there are differences between the 1968 Nixon and the 1976 Carter. While Mr. Nixon had a lifelong interest in foreign affairs, Mr. Carter is picking his up as he goes along. While Nixon had a few close personal friends, Carter has none. While Nixon downplayed his Quaker fatalism, Carter parades his piety.

And one precept of Mr. Nixon's is not being followed by Mr. Carter: *Try never to let the cruelty and ruthlessness show.* If wounded, a candidate must never let the voters see him bleeding ice water; if Mr. Carter wants to go into a general campaign with his party behind him, he would do well to choke back his inner rage at "those who" would stand in his way.

When Humbert Humphrey refused to lead the charge, shedding a tear as he let his last chance go, the gracious reaction one might expect from the front-runner was absent. Instead, Jimmy Carter allowed as how he was sorry Hubert didn't enter the New Jersey primary; the loss of the opportunity to personally humiliate the old warrior seemed to distress him. The Carter staff must warn him about letting such cool vindictiveness show.

But taken as a whole, the similarity of the '68 Nixon and '76 Carter campaigns is startling. Some of us polish our tieclasps and smile at the way today's candidate holds up a triumphant index finger as if to say: "Carter's the One."

CAMPAIGN CLICHÉS

June 3, 1976

WASHINGTON—The late Frank Sullivan's cliché expert, Dr. Arbuthnot, has given this brief interview at a hastily called press conference:

Question: In this late stage of the campaign, what are delegates?

Answer: The name of the game.

Q: What is the object of the game?

A: The magic number.

Q: And what is that?

A: For Democrats, 1505; for Republicans, 1130.

Q: Does one add them up?

A: No, one counts them down.

Q: What must a candidate have to reach the magic number?

A: Momentum.

Q: What must he avoid at all costs?

A: Erosion.

Q: What must campaigns be nowadays?

A: Issue-oriented.

Q: Is this true of Chinese elections as well?

A: No, Chinese campaigns are issue-occidented. Politicians there must take care not to be occident-prone.

Q: Back to America. What is the burning issue?

A: Sexual favors.

Q: How are they to be handled?

A: They are always bestowed, by the lady in question, in return for.

Q: Do sexual favors exist in the spoken language?

A: No, the phrase can only be found in journalese. No real person has ever said: "Do me a sexual favor."

Q: What are they, anyway?

A: Sexual favors are the hats, bonbons, noisemakers, and other souvenirs one takes home from an orgy.

Q: What are they called if bestowed by a society matron?

A: A romance.

Q: By a powerful lady publisher?

A: A personal relationship. But that's part of my memoirs—goodbye, and keep your eye on that magic number during the media blitz.

Surro-advocates

Semantic de-Nixofication, which began with the expunging of the word "détente," is progressing nicely with the elimination of the word "surrogate," which was the old definition of aides of a President speaking in his place. Mr. Ford's campaign calls these ex-surrogates "advocates," which has a Clarence Darrow connotation, and is not as apologetic as "apologist." The new cliché for White House mouthpieces, then, is "advocate"; smaller big wheels have spokesmen.

Adult-erated

"Adult unemployment," say the spokesmen for the Humphrey-Hawkins bill, must be reduced to 3 percent. This clever new cliché, spoken quickly, is intended to suggest that unemployment can be brought lower than those halcyon employment days of the Vietnam war. But it knocks out the unemployed teen-agers, with their 19 percent unemployment rate.

When you hear the "adult unemployment" dodge, add another half point or so for the real unemployment figure.

I See, I See . . .

Political speechwriters know that one sure-fire way to hypo a speech with visionary uplift is to use what the pros call "the 'I see' construction."

Jimmy Carter's new ghost, Patrick Anderson—a fine writer whose most recent ghosted effort was Jeb Magruder's book—used the tried-and-true lifter-upper last week, and must have been amused when it was described as an "ambitious new text" by a commentator with a heart too soon made glad.

Said Mr. Carter, staring off into space: "I see an America that has turned its back on scandals and shame. . . . I see an America that does not spy on its own citizens. . . ."

Richard Nixon in 1968, that same dreamy look on his face, said: "I see a day when Americans are once again proud of their flag. . . . I see a day when our nation is at peace. . . ."

And then one of them—Carter or Nixon, it's hard to tell which, this speech is interchangeable—said: "I see a day when the President of the United States is respected and his office is honored because it is worthy of respect and worthy of honor."

Back in 1969, I confessed to F.D.R. speechwriter Samuel Rosenman that I had borrowed that effective repetition of "I see's" from a speech that he and Robert E. Sherwood wrote for President Roosevelt in 1940.

"I see an America where factory workers are not discarded after they reach their prime," F.D.R. said, that dreamy, far-off look gripping the labor audience. "I see an America where small business really has a chance to flourish and grow. . . . I see an America devoted to our freedom . . . a people confident in strength because their body and their spirit are secure and unafraid."

Judge Rosenman smiled, and as one speechwriter to another, suggested I check into the speeches of Robert Ingersoll, the man who gave the so-briquet "Plumed Knight" to candidate James Blaine.

I dug around, and sure enough, there it was: "I see a country filled with happy homes. . . . I see a world where thrones have crumbled. . . . I see a world without a slave. . . ."

That was back in 1876, oratory for the American Centennial. Wonder where Ingersoll's writer got that "I see" construction from?

BAN THE BALM!

July 12, 1976

Around the beginning of this century, the Democratic Party in convention assembled followed its heart and chose William Jennings Bryan with his philosophy of populism. Three times, Bryan and his populist dream of the redistribution of wealth went down to defeat.

This is the week that the Democratic Party embraces and exalts a wholly different philosophy with a similar name: popularism. Here in New York—a city tingling with the one-two-three stimulation of the tall ships, the gracious Queen, and the Democratic coronation—popularism is seen as the path to victory.

Popularism turns on its head the old method of political appeal, which used to say "Here are my beliefs, and if you agree with them, follow me." Popularism says "Tell me what your beliefs are, and I will agree with them, and then you can follow me."

That is Jimmy Carter's way, and he makes no bones about it. In a prepared speech, he said recently that he had listened to the voters in his long campaign and "what we learned we gave back to them in a political program that reflected what they wanted, not what we wanted for them."

That is popularism, stark and candid. Nor is it especially original: Four years ago, a candidate for President whose name slips even John Connally's mind said: "On matters affecting basic human values—on the way Americans live their lives and bring up their children—I am going to respect and reflect the opinion of the people themselves. That is what democracy is all about."

Reflecting the popular will is what democracy is partly about. Democracy is also about leading and shaping the short-term popular will so that we act justly and accept a great nation's responsibilities. Most political leaders of past years have sought to reflect the popular will in most areas for a particular purpose: to strengthen their base, enabling them to lead in some other areas that might not be popular.

Not so Mr. Carter. For the first time, we are confronted with popularism not as a means to an end, but as the end in itself. If we are to believe what he says, and we have no reason not to, it is his goal to do what most people want all of the time.

That is why he spends a great deal of money on polls; he adjusts his position to his perceived consensus. Unconcerned with the hobgoblins of consistency, he believes whatever is unpopular is "divisive" and thus wrong. As Charles Mohr has suggested, in politics Mr. Carter is remarkably nonevangelical. Like the lost firebrand in the French Revolution, he has to find out where his people are marching, "for I am their leader."

Is popularism pernicious? In theory, nothing could be more democratic:

a government doing what the people want, with those desires scientifically measured, and not burdening the people with "what we wanted for them." Imagine: a four-year floating referendum.

In campaign practice, popularism is proving to be effective. To Democratic delegates who lived through two self-torturing conventions, there is no inclination now to ban the balm. When winning is all, Scoop Jackson's lion will lie down with Frank Church's lamb, and a platform will be adopted that lambastes ol' debbil inflation and proposes huge government employment—as if no contradiction existed.

But that's where popularism fails. The people, being human, want everything: more employment and less inflation, more services and less taxes, more respect and less defense. Although nothing is wrong with trying to give the people much of what they want, everything is wrong with pretending you can give the people all they want.

Real life involves choice, and choice involves pain, and the last thing Democrats want this week is the pain of "divisiveness." So the symbol of the Democratic Convention is not the tear gas of 1968, not the flowers and beads of 1972, but the Great Forced Smile of 1976. They have determined that the overriding issue of our time is that the Out's should be the In's.

Far be it from this lover of politics to burden the euphoria of Democrats who think they will be running against a sitting Presidential duck.

On the contrary, I will drape a bright yellow press pass over my tarnished tieclasp, go to the new Madison Square Garden, and whisper the secret question: What's the first name of Hawkins in Humphrey-Hawkins? That will get me on the convention floor during a spontaneous demonstration.

Not because I am a Democrat, a Carter supporter, a popularist, or a seeker after truth, but because I get an inexplicable kick out of the carefully choreographed hoopla of spontaneous demonstrations. Such a feeling is both of and above politics.

"A convention feels about demonstrations," wrote William Jennings Bryan, "somewhat like the big man who had a small wife who was in the habit of beating him. When asked why he permitted it, he replied that it seemed to please her and did not hurt him."

THIRTY QUESTIONS

July 19, 1976

WASHINGTON—Eight years ago, in an acceptance speech, a nominee used a device that speechwriters call "the train whistle," as he spoke of his childhood: "I see another child . . . he hears the train go by at night and he dreams of faraway places."

The other night, the train whistle blew again: "Years ago, as a farm boy sitting outdoors with my family on the ground in the middle of the night . . . listening to the Democratic Conventions in far-off cities . . ."

Such comparisons of Nixon and Carter campaign and rhetorical techniques touch a sensitive nerve among Carter men. On a street outside a convention party given by *Rolling Stone*, the newest Democratic house organ, a Carter insider felt called upon to excoriate this essayist, as is his right.

What infuriated Patrick Caddell, 26, the Carter campaign's chief pollster and one of the half-dozen men closest to the candidate, was any suggestion that the Carter staff formed a snap-to, self-righteous "Palace Guard" around their man comparable to the one regularly denounced in the Nixon years. Missing the point, Mr. Caddell snaps: "We're not a bunch of convicted felons."

Let's approach the same point in a different way. On March 8, 1976, Cambridge Reports Inc., which is 35 percent owned by Mr. Caddell, signed a contract with the Royal Saudi Arabian Embassy in Washington.

For $50,000 per year, paid in advance, the Saudis receive four quarterly reports on American public opinion. This is two and one half times the rate to others of what Mr. Caddell calls a "subscription" to this service. The contract calls for "an oral presentation of the data," which was recently conducted by Mr. Caddell for the Saudis, and "personal consultations to assist sponsors to understand and employ the information contained. . . ."

For an additional $30,000, the Saudis have contracted with Mr. Carter's pollster for thirty questions of their choice to be added to their "report."

In addition to the total of $80,000 from the Saudis, Mr. Caddell's firm receives $80,000 from four American oil companies for his report: Exxon, Arco, Shell, and Sun. Main business-getter for Mr. Caddell is his McGovern campaign associate, Fred Dutton, who is himself on a Saudi annual retainer of $100,000.

The fact that Mr. Caddell is an agent for a foreign principal (let us not use the sinister "foreign agent") is duly filed at the Department of Justice. Anticipating some conflict-of-interest criticism, Mr. Caddell wrote a letter which was forwarded to the Anti-Defamation League, making it appear that all he was selling was a subscription to a report, available to any buyer.

On the basis of that self-serving letter—which Mr. Caddell will not make public—Arnold Forster, general counsel for the A.D.L., last week said he saw "nothing in this that would disturb us" when called by a *New York Post* reporter obviously anxious to put the story in a light least damaging to Democrats.

A few things disturb me:

1. Mr. Carter's pollster claims his relationship with the Saudis long predates his identification with the Carter campaign. The documents show otherwise: The Saudis knew they weren't hiring just another pollster.

2. Mr. Carter's pollster claims he is performing an "educational function" in teaching Arabs about American attitudes, and insists no Middle East politics are contained in his questions. In fact, the information could well be purchased to help lay the basis for Arab propaganda in America, which is precisely why the law requires his registration with the Department of Justice.

3. Mr. Carter's pollster insists his $160,000 in oil money in no way influences the questions posed or areas covered in his report, which the Presidential nominee reads. I am ready to believe him, since Mr. Caddell was ready to let me see the report on a restricted basis, which I would not accept—but is there no potential for abuse apparent?

4. Mr. Carter's pollster says "the confidentiality of my client situation" keeps him from revealing the 30 questions his Arab clients hired him to ask. Can you imagine the editorial roar of "Cover-up!" if a Nixon aide used that excuse?

5. Mr. Carter's pollster—off with the candidate and the staff on vacation this week—asserts forthrightly that his Carter colleagues know all about his Arab business arrangements, and even approve his plans to solicit other foreign clients.

Think about that: Jimmy Carter knows about the foreign representation of his pollster-aide-confidant, and he sees no potential conflict of interest. He can spy no possible use of the Carter association by a consultant to sell a service. He accepts his aide's explanation that poll-peddling for exorbitant fees to Arabs and others who may want a Carter connection is not "representation," because the press has not yet hollered about it. So much for "moral leadership."

Mr. Carter cannot see the appearance of impropriety because he knows his aides and himself to be honest, truthful, God-fearing, upright men who do not intend to do wrong. And that is why I blow the sad train whistle of recent experience: The bright young men most likely to fall into the greatest error are those who are certain they are holier than thou.

July 23, 1976

Editor
New York Times

Dear Sir:

Don't you think it's about time you ended the sham of having William Safire pose as your house reactionary?

That this man could call Jimmy Carter's aide, Patrick Caddell, an "apologist" should be *prima facie* evidence that he has lost his sense of perspective. Isn't he the character you hired several years ago to placate the conservatives and provide "balance" to your own liberal philosophy? Isn't this the same character who has since made a mini-career of apologizing for Richard Nixon?

The preceding complaint is actually niggling, a minor sin to what followed in his column of July 22.

It is one thing to present a reasoned, intelligent analysis of the men surrounding Carter but vicious innuendo is quite another matter. I refer you to his item 5 in which he accuses Carter of balancing off one Jew against an Arab lobbyist and then follows with the observation that Carter "ought" to make his foreign policy decisions on the basis of what is right and in the U.S. interest. His obvious implication is that Carter will *not* make foreign policy decisions on those criteria.

But he saves his most masterful piece of deceit for the last. By placing the phrase "hang tough" in juxtaposition to Carter's name he knows he is transferring the sinister connotation that phrase earned as applied to his old buddy Nixon.

His last conclusion is so blatantly vicious that it borders on the libelous ... that foreign agents will have an opportunity to "buy" Carter.

In the interest of preserving the integrity of *The Times*'s editorial voice, I urge you to send this sick man packing to join his equally sick friend in San Clemente. There certainly must be a vacancy for a valet or receptionist that his talents could master.

> Cordially yours,
> John R. Simon
> San Juan, Puerto Rico

CARTER BLANCHE

July 22, 1976

WASHINGTON—In our last installment on the moral leadership of Jimmy Carter, it was revealed here that one of the members of his inner circle, Patrick Caddell—Carter pollster, strategist, and apologist—was not only on the payroll of the Saudi Arabian royal embassy for $80,000 per year but provides poll answers to questions submitted by them and "personal consultations" to help them "employ the information" he gathers in their behalf.

Here is Mr. Carter's public response: "I don't have anything to conceal about it, and I don't think that because we have a contract with Mr. Cad-

dell to do political polling that he should have to give up all his other subscribers where most of his income is derived. . . ."

Mr. Carter continued: "Mr. Caddell does not fulfill a role in our campaign of establishing policy concerning the Middle East, or even the analysis of issues concerning the Middle East.

"As a matter of fact," Mr. Carter went on, "the person who is in charge
of our issues analysis is Stuart Eizenstat, who happens to be Jewish and
who I might say is a very strong proponent of a strong state of Israel. So
I'm the ultimate one who makes decisions about policy concerning international affairs and I do not see anything wrong or improper about Mr.
Caddell serving Saudi Arabia or other nations in the Middle East."

Fascinating response. Let's look at it:

1. "*I don't have anything to conceal about it. . . .*" Evidently Mr. Caddell did. Worried about Jewish reaction as he was closing his deal with the
Saudis, Mr. Caddell wrote a friend a letter about how the Saudis would
merely be "subscribers" to an innocuous poll.

That letter was duly forwarded to the Anti-Defamation League, as Mr.
Caddell intended it to be, and was the basis for that usually vigilant organization's whitewash when asked about the matter later. The letter—
which Mr. Caddell insists on concealing—did not, as A.D.L. officials recall, mention the whopping fee or the central facts that both proprietary
polling and personal consultations were involved.

2. "*. . . that he should have to give up all his other subscribers. . . .*" Mr.
Caddell's relationship with Mr. Carter began in earnest last November,
and he was frequently identified as the Carter pollster early this year.
After dickering with Mr. Caddell for months, the Saudis did not sign the
$80,000 deal with Mr. Caddell until five days after Mr. Carter won the
New Hampshire primary.

The issue here is not "all his other subscribers," as Mr. Carter seeks to
fuzz it up; the conflict of interest is with one client, the foreign power that
enforces the anti-Jewish boycott, which Mr. Carter's pollster signed up
after the Carter bandwagon had begun to roll.

3. "*. . . where most of his income is derived.*" Mr. Caddell is not going
to go hungry without his Arab fee, as Mr. Carter suggests. The pollster's
firm received "hundreds of thousands of dollars," in his own words, from
the Carter campaign to date; he draws $1,500 a month personally as a
consultant to Carter as well; and Mr. Caddell says his two firms' revenues
are nearly a million dollars a year.

This is not an issue of making great financial sacrifice to come to work
for a candidate (although such sacrifice is called for in the case of some
foreign clients). This is greed, plain and simple, in the face of an obvious
conflict of interest—and Mr. Carter's insistence that it is not "wrong or
improper" tells us what to expect in a Carter Administration.

4. "*Subscriber.*" That word is a deception. Mr. Caddell is not selling a

product, or a magazine; he is selling a personal service, tailored to his client's demands. As a representative of the Saudis, he recently traveled to Saudi Arabia to report to his clients. His polling is as much a part of their propaganda effort as market research is a part of marketing.

5. *Mr. Carter's some-of-my-best-analysts-are-Jewish response.* This is what one expects now of Spiro Agnew. If the able Mr. Eizenstat has been placed in charge of Israel policy because he can be pointed to as window dressing, he should be the first to resent it.

The notion that Mr. Carter blithely presents of balancing one Jew against one Arab lobbyist on his staff—for him to then make Middle East decisions—is repugnant. He ought to be making his foreign policy on the basis of what is right and in the U.S. interest, with staffers providing facts, not representing other interests.

Mr. Caddell may be no more capable of changing Mr. Carter's mind about Israel than Marion Javits's attempted representation of Iran could have turned around her husband. But surely the potential here for a conflict of interest—and the precedent being set for an inner-circle member to also be a foreign representative—should shock a few moralists.

But not hang-tough Jimmy Carter. His Carter-blanche to his pollster to "serve Saudi Arabia or other nations in the Middle East" is an open invitation to Syria, Egypt, Libya—even Israel—to buy their way into the Carter campaign.

A LOT TO LEARN

November 4, 1976

WASHINGTON—How come I cannot work myself up into feeling really miserable about the outcome of the 1976 elections?

How come my Democratic friends are not pounding each other's backs in triumphant glee, as in 1960?

Here are a few reasons why the losers are not desolate and the winners are not delirious.

1. *Accountability has arrived.* No longer will flowering fields of Congressional alibis be watered by executive branch water. The Democrats are in charge, and since the buck can no longer be passed, perhaps the dollar will be treated with more respect.

2. *The land did not slide.* The language of natural disaster—landslide, avalanche, snowed under, tidal wave—so often used to describe political movements is out of place today. President Ford's strong campaign results in his leaving office with far more respect than he was given in it, and

leaves those Republicans for whom he was second choice feeling that he carried their banner most honorably.

3. *Henry will be gone.* This delights the losers, as much as it worries the winners.

4. *The quality of the Senate is improved.* Three Democratic duds were retired—Hartke, Montoya, and Tunney—and a couple of the Republicans turned out, Beall and Taft, lacked luster. The saddest conservative moment of the night came with able Bill Brock's defeat. But I want to be in the Senate gallery when Professor-Senators Hayakawa and Moynihan light up that sleepy place with linguistic fireworks.

5. *The center-right has held.* Except for one brief period of leftward lurching—promptly corrected as his ratings slipped—candidate Carter showed he knew where the political action was: "inevitable" tax reduction, budget balancing, strong defense posture, and postponement of social spending that interferes with those. Liberals worry that Mr. Carter might have meant what he said, while conservatives intend to rivet him to his rhetoric.

6. *The back-up quarterback is good.* For all his liberality, Walter Mondale is a man of character, intelligence, and good humor. To many, Carter-Mondale was the classic "kangaroo ticket"—stronger in the hind legs than in the front.

7. *The commitment was never intense on either side.* The winners were mostly Democrats, far more organized laborites than "Carterites"; the losers often those who sided with the President because of their distrust of his opponent, who reminded them of Dr. Fell. The financial journal, *Barron's*, shrewdly diagnosed the reason for the long-sinking market: Investors were worried that either Mr. Ford or Mr. Carter would win.

8. *The South Will Not Rise Again.* The states of the South, having solidified to put one of their own across for the first time in a century, will soon come to understand that their man must lean against them, and toward the suffering Northern states, in dispensing Federal funds. After Carter, Southern solidity will vanish, making possible a two-party system there for the first time.

9. *The West Was Won.* A hopeful lesson to the losers is the formation of the Winning West as the future alternative to the Carter Solid South. With such a base, a conservative candidate could aim for added "heartland" support.

On balance, then, the people on the losing side are disappointed but not devastated. Our first natural reaction, to growl "Don't treat a squeaker as any kind of a mandate" at President-elect Carter, should be set aside. A one-vote victory is a mandate to lead.

Another temptation for losers to resist is the tendency to look for justification of previous suspicions. Cartoonist Herblock, who had always drawn Richard Nixon with a sinister five o'clock shadow, greeted the

Nixon Presidency with a drawing announcing that his department always treated a new President to one free shave.

And so this "Essay" department will put free mental dental caps on those Carter incisors that only yesterday looked so much like fangs. For a little while, the urge to holler "Aha! Worse than Nixon, and you're letting him get away with it!" will be wrestled to the ground. (The match is not fixed; the urge may occasionally win.)

The reason, in all seriousness, is that he is my President-elect as much as he is Jody Powell's President-elect. Supporters of the loser may wish Candidate Carter had not won, but we must wish President Carter will do well.

Of the last four occupants of the Oval Office, one has been shot out, one scared out, one thrown out, and one voted out. It would be very good for all of us to have a President serve a full, successful term.

In his victory remarks, the next President spoke of a "new dawn," a hackneyed phrase from both Hubert Humphrey's and Richard Nixon's 1968 acceptance speeches. (Why am I sniping already?) But he also struck just the right note with this line: "We have a lot to learn about each other." If he means that—and we should assume he does—then Presidential success might just be his, and ours.

Nov. 4, 1976

dear sirs;

in answer to mr. safires question as to why he doesnt feel miserable about the outcome of the election it is my opinion because in spite of being a jerk first class he still has a job. i mean to say here we have a clown who has steadfastly proved that he doesnt know what the hell he is talking about and yet able to continue spouting his half wit ravings and getting paid i presume for it. i recall his describing sam ervins watergate comittee as a dead whale rotting on a beach or some such thing and that the american public was tired of it; the snotnose decribed franklin roosevelt as leaving office feet first; and of late this silly ass went into details describing first how ronald reagan was going to beat ford (i believe it hinged upon fords snub of solzenitsen an atrocity that the american people would never forgive; after all wasn't this the man who exposed the soviet slave labor camps for what they were. prior to this expose we all thought that the soviet slave labor camps were a riviera type vacation spot with fun and frolics for all). and then the moron explained in detail how ford was going to beat carter. i have yet to see this oracle say anything that made sense and i believe that this inability to cope with reality, his lack of talent naturally assures him of a job on your august paper. about the only humorous remark this cluck ever made was his comparing himself in the same breath with herblock and his assuring us that he would give carter a chance before he unleashed his fury against him. the simpleton is oblivious to reality and actually believes that the american public gives a damn or cares about any of his idiotic drivelings. i could continue but i am running out of names

yours truly,
Arnold Verosloff
Freehold, New Jersey

IF ONLYS AND WHAT IFS

November 8, 1976

WASHINGTON—"Of all sad words of tongue or pen," gloomed the poet Whittier, "The saddest are these: 'It might have been.'" To which Bret Harte responded: "More sad are these we daily see: 'It is, but hadn't ought to be.'"

After close elections, such rhymes of rue are indulged in by the losers, who enjoy their melancholia by playing the game of "if onlys," while the winners heave sighs of relief and play their own game of "what ifs." Some examples:

If only Mr. Reagan had not discovered the foreign policy issue in North Carolina, Mr. Ford would have turned aside his challenge easily and not have had to alienate independents by protecting his right;

If only Mr. Ford had been able to persuade Mr. Reagan to be his running mate, the Republicans would have carried Texas and Mississippi and won the election;

If only Mr. Reagan had been the Republican candidate, the first debate would have been such a rout that the Democrats would never have been able to recover their early lead;

If only Earl Butz had fallen asleep on that plane flying home from the convention;

If only Ladybird Johnson had gotten her dander up publicly about Mr. Carter's derogation of her husband;

If only Attorney General Levi had been gutsy enough to investigate a false accusation with standard Justice Department procedures, and not nervously tossed the hot potato to the Special Prosecutor;

If only it had rained in New York City on Election Day;

If only Ford had chosen John Connally as his running mate, which would have turned around Texas, Florida, Mississippi, and Ohio;

If only Senator Dole had not, in his debate, revved up organized labor's troops to go out and fight for George Meany's choice;

If only House Judiciary Committee Chairman Peter Rodino had asked the Ethics Committee to pinpoint which liberal Democrat broke the law by leaking Ford income-tax reports (I erred in blaming a former Special Prosecutor staffer for the 1976 campaign's dirtiest trick, and apologize—the lawbreaker is probably on the Rodino committee);

If only the judges on New York State's Court of Appeals had permitted Eugene McCarthy to remain on the ballot, he might have won 4 or 5 percent of New York's vote, which would have delivered New York to Mr. Ford and changed the results of the election;

If only Richard Nixon had come out for Carter.

Meanwhile, in the winner's circle, the wondering "what ifs" are heard.

What if Frank Church had realized how important the Iowa convention was, and announced early enough to nip the Carter campaign in the bud?

What if Fred Harris and Sargent Shriver had not run for the exercise in the early primaries, splitting the liberal Democratic vote and never letting Morris Udall emerge?

What if Mr. Udall had won the nomination, and then the nude body of his aide was found in that park frequented by homosexuals in Arlington, casting a pall over the Democratic campaign?

What if there had been no debates—would Ford have been able to energize his campaign the way he did with the first debate, or would Carter have been able to capitalize on the Eastern Europe blunder in the second?

What if Jody Powell had opened his mail from *Playboy*, gone over the manuscript as submitted, and crossed out a few lines?

What if the press had forced Mr. Carter to release his 1970 contributors' list earlier, so that the full story of the Rabhan connection might have broken before the election?

What if only 8,000 voters in Hawaii and Ohio had gone the other way? (The President would have won.)

What if 2 percent of the voters in eight states had gone the other way? (Then Mr. Carter would have come roaring into office with a 420 electoral vote landslide.)

What if Hubert Humphrey had listened to the importunings of organized labor, gone into the New Jersey primary, won easily, and—choosing Jerry Brown as his running mate—been nominated at the Democratic Convention?

To follow that last "what if" to its conclusion: Then what if the Democratic nominee was stricken with cancer, had to go to the hospital for an operation in the middle of the campaign, turned the choice of the replacement nominee to the Democratic National Committee, which picked the convention runner-up as the nominee, and that little-known candidate—with all factions of the Democrats enthusiastically behind him and no time to be scrutinized—asked for and received the nation's trust?

If that string of "what ifs" had taken place, then—and this stretches credulity—a peanut farmer from Georgia that nobody ever heard of a year ago "might have been" the President-elect of the United States today.

11/8 (76)

Sirs:

If only President Ford had not forgiven ex-President Richard Nixon . . .

If only President Ford had chosen Howard Baker or Nelson Rockefeller or any one else other than the one he chose . . .

If only President Ford had not told New York City to "drop dead" . . .

If only Congressman Ford had not tried to impeach Justice William O Douglas . . .

If only the President had vetoed a few bills less . . .

If only President Ford had consulted Henry Kissinger on Eastern Europe before he took part in the Second debate . . .

If only President Ford had a better company of speechwriters and supporters than William Safire . . .

Who knows, add a few more "ifs" and "buts," he would have won.

M. T. Antony
Brooklyn, New York

PART II

★

1977–1980

The Lance Affair

THE FIRST APPLICATION of post-Watergate morality—so ringingly invoked by Jimmy Carter in the 1976 campaign—was in the case of the financial maneuverings of Mr. Carter's best friend and closest associate in office, T. Bertram Lance. On a smaller scale, many of the same elements were there—the potentially illegal activity, the agreement during the interregnum to sweep it all under the rug, the six-month delay before the trouble surfaced, the investigative reporting, the indignation at "smears" of respectable men, the firm Presidential support for a friend, and the long, slow, terrible unraveling until the indictment.

I became interested in the affairs of Bert Lance when the White House sent the Senate a letter asking to be let out of an agreement Bert had made to divest himself of some stock. The letter was artful—I remembered that kind of writing—and had, to me, the unmistakable clang of falsity. The first few articles reprinted here were not too well received: Lance was likable and accessible, the Carter Administration was on its honeymoon, and it appeared that an old Nixon apologist was out to prove that "they're all the same" and, in so doing, somehow rehabilitate the felons of Watergate.

The low point was a meeting of the Senate Committee on Government Operations, chaired by an irate Senator Abe Ribicoff, who was extraordinarily sympathetic to Lance and scornful of those who found his story unbelievable. I was present that day, at the press table, and felt no sense of support from any of the Senators responsible for oversight or from most press colleagues. In his testimony, responding to softball questioning, Lance seemed to demolish the points I had made about his finances. I felt sick.

But I was convinced he had broken the law: His testimony was a tissue of evasions. I hung in there, annoying some people with a "single-standard" argument, encouraging some whistle blowers to do their thing.

After a few weeks, A. M. Rosenthal, executive editor of *The Times*, asked me what specific law I thought Lance had broken. "18 U.S. Code 656," I replied, "misapplication of bank funds. Abe—the President's best friend could be going to jail." He walked out into the city room of *The Times* in New York, called an investigative team together, and I no longer felt alone.

The report of the Comptroller of the Currency, John Heimann, contained the basic information that was later used to indict Lance. That investigation was called for, almost as an afterthought, by the Senate committee that had only wanted to provide Lance with a forum to "clear himself" from the nasty charges in *The New York Times*. President Carter, who read the summary of the Comptroller's report and bravely said: "Bert—I'm proud of you," finally had to face the music and let his friend go and let a reluctant Justice Department proceed.

As an appreciator of rogues, I came to like ol' Bert, and took a continuing interest in his attempts to use his "Georgia mafia" influence. After a time—a long time—he was evidently told to stop being an embarrassment; as this is written, he awaits a decision about a retrial after a jury could not decide on a couple of felony counts. Whatever happens, I hope he makes a comeback in politics—he's got a lot of gumption, and he's done a lot for me.

CARTER'S BROKEN LANCE

July 21, 1977

WASHINGTON—Jimmy Carter is trying to sell the Senate a dubious bill of goods about his longtime friend, Office of Management and Budget Director Bert Lance.

The Georgia banker should be excused from conflict-of-interest divestiture promises, the President has asserted, because his promise to sell his stock has depressed its market value.

That is a deception. The reason that National Bank of Georgia stock has slid from 16 to 11 this year has little to do with the "overhang." The stock has dropped because of the revelation that Mr. Lance tolerated bad loans on his books. The man who inherited the mess has had to write off the bad loans and suspend dividend payments.

The truth is that Mr. Lance's departure for Washington did not cause his financial embarrassment. On the contrary, we now see how his willingness to carry questionable loans as assets may have artificially maintained the price of his stock.

Mr. Carter is intimately familiar with Mr. Lance's affairs. On June 19,

1975, only a few weeks after borrowing $2.7 million to finance the purchase of his stock, Bert Lance brought Jimmy Carter to the Manufacturers Hanover Bank in New York to meet Lew Jenkins, the bank officer responsible with Bruce Broughm for making the Lance loan.

Purely a social call, insists Mr. Lance, nothing to do with using the former Georgia Governor to shore up his reputation as a borrower. But Mr. Jenkins was the only banker to whom Mr. Lance took the new Presidential candidate that day.

Bankitician Lance, who was Governor Carter's highway commissioner, also claims to have had nothing to do with the infusion of the Teamsters Central States pension fund money into his bank in early 1976, as Mr. Carter's star began to rise. At the time, the Lance bank's three-person trust department had no account over $2 million to manage; for no apparent reason, the politically sensitive Teamsters fund put into the Lance bank $18 million that has since grown to $23 million.

Not my doing, says the modest Mr. Lance today. Bank officials want us to believe that Atlantans John Spickerman, Teamster employer trustee, and Robert Pollar, Teamster fund lawyer, initiated the deal with King Cleveland, Mr. Lance's colleague, now retired.

But after Mr. Carter's election, on the very morning Mr. Lance's picture was front-paged as the first Carter Cabinet likelihood—November 24, 1976—Mr. Lance met in his bank with Teamster pension fund executive director Dan Shannon, John Spickerman, and Teamster lawyer William Nellis of Chicago. Mr. Lance sees no impropriety in a Cabinet designee helping to line up some future business with the fund that the Labor Department says corruptly bankrolls Las Vegas mobsters.

Just before leaving Atlanta six months ago, Mr. Lance must have had cause to worry about his financial house of cards. He turned to another Democratic bankitician, J. Robert Abboud, the go-go boss of the First National Bank of Chicago, who has replaced his mentor, the late Mayor Daley, as the city's most powerful man.

Mr. Abboud must have been delighted to bail out a man who would be part of the President's quadriad, and whose ambitions include becoming chairman of the Federal Reserve. On January 6, 1977, prior to his January 11 trip to Washington, Mr. Abboud refinanced the $2.7 million Manufacturers Hanover Loan that enabled Mr. Lance to own his stock—adding another $725,000.

Why? Mr. Lance (give him credit, he answers his phone) says: "First Chicago is moving aggressively in the Atlanta area."

I see a more sinister motive. First Chicago's Abboud knows all about bad real estate loans, and should have known that Mr. Lance's assets would shrink when the bad loans were audited by a successor. Here was Mr. Abboud's chance to gain life-and-death financial control over the man closest to the President.

The central question, which Senators Ribicoff and Percy do not see, is this: Was the President's most powerful Cabinet member given a "sweetheart loan"? Did Mr. Lance's assets include his closeness to President Carter? And why did he need that extra money in the refinancing?

Here we have a situation in which the man in charge of the nation's books is deeply, dangerously in hock; who goes home every night not knowing whether the Labor Department will find out about his Teamster connections, or the S.E.C. will look into his assurances to 45 people about a stock issue, or the bank examiners and First Chicago stockholders will expose a sweetheart loan, or the man on whom he depends for financial solvency will exert some subtle pressure for political advantage.

Jimmy Carter's Broken Lance is a walking conflict of interest. The complaisant Senate subcommittee now glancing at his wheeling and dealing should stop making an exception and start making an example.

BOILING THE LANCE

July 25, 1977

CHICAGO—When Sherman Adams made a phone call to inquire of a Federal official about the status of a Bernard Goldfine request, outraged Democrats pointed to a vicuna coat and demanded the scalp of President Eisenhower's chief of staff.

When Howard "Bo" Calloway was accused (falsely, as the current *Harper's* magazine reveals) of using his Government job to help along a private project, editorial voices boomed and President Ford's campaign manager was forced to resign.

But they were Republicans. Since Democrat Bert Lance, President Carter's most influential adviser, was revealed to have used his public job to line his pockets, the trumpets of rectitude have been muted.

Lest loyal Carter men complain that a charge of using public office for private gain is excessive, let us count the ways the President's chief financial man cut his corners:

The sweetheart loan. Mr. Lance's bank put $200,000 of its depositor's money in the First National Bank of Chicago, at no interest. Within three months, and after being appointed to the Carter Cabinet, Mr. Lance turned to Democrat Robert Abboud, who runs the Chicago bank, and personally borrowed $3.5 million.

First Chicago's spokesman at first told reporters that officials of Lance's bank "came to us as a result of the correspondent banking relationship" to borrow Mr. Lance's money. Evidently every lawyer in the bank landed on that harried fellow's neck, because he tells me his words were "misinterpreted"—but an investigator from the Comptroller of the Currency spent all day Friday at First Chicago to determine whether an illegal "compensating balance" can be proved.

Despite denials, the full record will show that Bob Abboud's loan was one sweet deal for Mr. Lance. One hopes Senator Ribicoff's committee will insist on a detailed, comparative analysis of that loan's terms—and its underlying collateral, which a prudent bank is obligated to examine—by the Comptroller of the Currency, else why did not the original lender— New York's Manufacturers Hanover—"Manny Hanny"—compete for the business?

The Teamster connection. How can an itty-bitty bank, with a tiny trust department, latch on to $18 million in Teamster Central States Pension Fund money in a Presidential year? By flexing political muscle, as detailed in this space last week, that's how.

The Butcher appointment. Thanks to the investigative reporting of John Berry, Jack Egan, and George Lardner Jr. of *The Washington Post*, who also broke the no-interest deposit story, a vivid picture emerges of the way Mr. Lance uses his political clout to shore up his financial house of cards.

The Butcher brothers, Jake and C. H., own a few banks in Knoxville and Nashville. Their old friend Bert Lance is into one of their banks for $443,466 on terms not likely to be available to the average borrower.

Now that their debtor has the run of the White House, the Butcher boys thought it would be a dandy idea to get on a first-name basis with the Secretary of the Treasury, Michael Blumenthal.

So they called friend Bert. "We asked for the appointment," blurted C. H. Butcher, not realizing how the truth would hurt, "because we had never met him [Blumenthal] and he does regulate our business as Treasury Secretary."

That candor caught Mr. Lance in the middle of a cover-up. He had enlisted his press spokesman in concocting a story that gave a quasi-public purpose to the Butchers' meeting with Secretary Blumenthal: some folderol about promoting a Knoxville exposition, which is, of course, of enormous concern to the Secretary of the Treasury.

But Mike Blumenthal knew nothing about the exposition, or why he had been asked to glad-hand these particular two bankers. Mr. Lance had never confided the real reason to his Cabinet colleague: He owed the Butchers $443,000 (skip the change), and wanted to show them he could put them on a first-name basis with the man who, in C. H.'s phrase, "does regulate our business."

Yet here is Bert Lance using his office to protect and improve his personal fortunes with impunity. Worse than that: One week ago, the President of the United States sent the Senate a letter about Mr. Lance's finances that was patently misleading. Who drafted that letter?

The unhappy Government Affairs Committee wants to "confront" Mr. Lance with a few newspaper clippings, let him make ringing, self-serving denials, and then claim the Senate has discharged its responsibility.

But Mr. Lance's appearance should be the beginning, not the end, of a serious investigation. Illinois Senator Percy, who will come under great pressure from well-connected Chicagoan Abboud, bears a heavy burden; he should insist the G.A.O. be assigned to audit the truthfulness of the asset statements Mr. Lance submitted at his confirmation.

On the other hand, Senators and editorialists can agree that Mr. Lance is too amiable a guy, and Mr. Carter too new and clean a President, to charge with such tawdry abuse of power. In the event of such a whitewash, let the Senate at least vote a single-standard resolution of exoneration for Sherman Adams.

THE LANCE COVER-UP

August 1, 1977

LOS ANGELES—"You have been smeared," clucked Senator Abe Ribicoff to O.M.B. Director Lance last week, declaring no investigation was needed. Republican Charles Percy, ranking Republican on the "millionaire's committee," solemnly agreed. President Carter reaffirmed his faith in his old friend's "impeccable integrity."

Editorial writers on *The New York Times* and *The Washington Post* tut-tutted gently at this brazen whitewash, awaiting only a report from Mr. Carter's new Comptroller of the Currency. By not asking the President a single question about his first scandal at his press conference last week, the White House press corps completed its transformation from hound dog to lap dog.

A few questions that Senators and reporters did not see fit to raise:

1. Mr. Lance has sworn that the reason he switched his $2.7 million loan from the Manufacturers Hanover Bank in New York to the First Chicago was that he had assured "Manny Hanny" repayment when he left the presidency of his own bank. Was that really a condition of the loan? Does it not suggest collusion to make the personal loan because of the correspondent bank relationship, and not on its merits?

2. When Mr. Lance refinanced his loan after the election, switching from "Manny Hanny" to First Chicago, he borrowed an additional

$725,000. He swears this was primarily for "debt service." Does that mean he was in arrears on his New York loan? On any other loans? Was this extra money to help pay future interest? Did Manufacturers Hanover want to continue its loan—or was that bank delighted to see First Chicago take it over?

3. Mr. Lance's longtime pattern has been to use a "correspondent bank" relationship to borrow money personally. Is the Comptroller looking into all those double deals, or has his inquiry been limited to the Chicago sweetheart loan?

4. When Senator Heinz (R.-Pa.) asked the only cogent question of the hearing—about Mr. Lance's collateral on his Chicago loan—the witness suddenly could not remember such trifling details. Mr. Lance had previously sworn, however, the loan was "fully collateralized"—with what? Why can't we know?

5. On the assumption that most of his Chicago loan was collateralized by his Georgia bank stock, what happened at First Chicago when the stock's price dropped from 16 to 8? Did First Chicago call the loan, or demand more collateral, as it surely would do with normal borrowers on non-sweetheart loans?

6. What are the terms of the loan made to Mr. Lance by the Butcher brothers of Tennessee, whom Mr. Lance then introduced to Secretary of Treasury Blumenthal? Will the Comptroller look for a triangular relationship between Mr. Lance, Manufacturers Hanover, and the Butcher brothers?

7. Under 18 United States Code 656, and after the 1975 decision in *United States* v. *Brookshire*, the United States Attorney in Atlanta began an investigation into misapplication of funds in Lance banking operations. On December 2, 1976—*one day before President-elect Carter named Mr. Lance to his Cabinet*—U.S. Attorney John Stokes ordered the investigation quashed, over the objections of his investigators. Mr. Stokes, a Nixon appointee, was then continued in the U.S. Attorney's Office by Mr. Lance's friend, Griffin Bell. Mr. Stokes denies a quid pro quo, and quit last week. Did a deal fall apart?

8. The F.B.I. prepared a report based on the aborted investigation and submitted it to the White House before Mr. Lance's Senate confirmation hearings. Robert Lipshutz, the President's counsel and Mr. Lance's Atlanta friend and associate, improperly withheld this disturbing information from the Senate.

Has Mr. Lipshutz passed on this evidence of an earlier pattern of misapplication of funds to Comptroller John Heimann—or is he still trying to contain the inquiry to the Chicago loan (the modified limited hangout)?

9. Since questions were raised about Mr. Lance's wheeling and dealing, Carter fund raisers have launched a frantic angel hunt to find an "investor" to buy the Lance bank stock at about $1 million over its market value.

In my opinion, at the inflated price, the sale would be a fraud, since it would not involve control stock.

What of the other investors, who cannot, like Mr. Lance, get $17 a share for a stock selling at $11? Is the Securities and Exchange Commission asleep? Will Team Player Blumenthal's I.R.S. not consider the payoff premium to be ordinary income?

10. *Time* magazine led the way into this story, with *Newsweek* aggressively following up; the Atlanta *Constitution* must have resisted pressure from Mr. Lance to suppress this column, but almost everyone else is "waiting for Proxmire," the only Senator to have voted against the Lance confirmation.

Which leads to the question sure to be asked after the truth has been forced out: Where were you during the cover-up of the first scandal of the Carter Administration?

THE SKUNK AT THE GARDEN PARTY

September 8, 1977

WASHINGTON—"Nobody wants to be a skunk at a garden party," said job-hungry Robert Bloom, explaining why his Comptroller's office concealed Bert Lance's shady past from Senator Ribicoff, who didn't want to know anything about it.

Rather than sift through year-old chicanery, let us focus attention on the original charge, which deals with this year's venality—committed quite recently by a leading member of the Carter Administration.

My charge was that after his Cabinet appointment, Mr. Lance received a sweetheart loan from Democrat Robert Abboud's First Chicago Bank— so favorable a loan that one could only conclude Mr. Lance was using his position of public trust to line his private pockets.

A crucial test of whether a loan is corrupt or legitimate is collateralization. On July 25 of this year, under oath before the Senate, Mr. Lance was asked: "Was it fully collateralized, or was it just a personal loan?" His sworn testimony: "No, sir, it was fully collateralized."

Let's see how true that was.

According to the report of the Comptroller, Mr. Lance signed two notes to First Chicago on January 6, 1977: "a secured note for $1.8 million and an unsecured note for $1,625,000." The word "unsecured" means that no collateral was required as security.

Even the secured note was defective: For some time Mrs. Lance would not provide the stock powers necessary to make the collateral salable.

On its face, Mr. Lance's sworn testimony was untrue. That explains why, when asked by Senator Heinz to describe his collateral, Mr. Lance had a sudden attack of forgetfulness—as if any banker would forget the collateral he has pledged on his biggest outstanding loan.

In an effort to tone down that "fully" assertion, Mr. Lance's trustee responded to the Senate query in an August 12 letter lumping together the two notes and trying to stretch the collateral over both: "When the loan was originally made there was provided as collateral 162,920 shares of the National Bank of Georgia with a value of $2,932,000, 9,422 shares of the Calhoun First National Bank with a value of $235,000. . . ."

That's a total of $3,167,000 in collateral, a quarter million dollars short of the total loans. Straining, Mr. Lance's trustee throws in a life insurance policy (which, documents show, First Chicago never considered as collateral). But there is no way to consider the politically motivated loan to Mr. Lance "fully collateralized."

Indeed, the First Chicago loan officer wrote on the day a $4 million line of credit was extended to Mr. Lance that "approximately $3 million in other securities" was "to be pledged." But they were never put up, and First Chicago did not demand the missing "full" collateral until the inadequate collateral was sinking.

The key point is that "fully collateralized" meant that far more than 100 percent of the value of the loan must be put up: On listed stocks, banks and brokers must demand 200 percent collateral. Bank stocks are unconscionably exempt from regulation, but on thinly traded stocks such as those put up by Mr. Lance, any prudent banker would ask for an even higher percentage of collateral.

However, on July 7 of this year, when the two notes were combined into one $3.4 million loan, First Chicago priced its Lance collateral at $1,717,611. That's 50 percent collateral.

Curiously, on July 21, Mr. Lance's trustee raced to First Chicago with an additional $1,150,000 in collateral (using First Chicago's strange computation of $15 a share for stock selling at $11).

What happened on July 21 to prompt Mr. Lance's trustee and his favorite bankitician to shore up the woefully inadequate collateral? Answer: On that Thursday morning, a column appeared in this space charging Messrs. Abboud and Lance with a sweetheart loan. On that same morning, according to the Comptroller's report, Treasury Secretary Blumenthal told the Comptroller "that the President expected me to take such action as was appropriate. . . ."

The hurry-up collateralization was hardly the action of innocent men. First Chicago refuses to say if William Wood Prince, chairman of its audit committee and responsible to its stockholders, has approved this grossly improper and imprudent banking practice.

The plain fact is that Mr. Lance's First Chicago loan was not fully collateralized when he signed the two notes in January; it was not when he testified under oath in July; and it is not today. The only reasons he was given such preferential treatment are (1) Carter fund-raiser Jack Stephens made sure "it would be difficult to refuse the relationship" and (2) Robert Abboud wanted a friend in the Carter White House.

Will our suddenly vigilant Senator Ribicoff send the Lance testimony to the Justice Department for examination for perjury? If so, it would be left to Lance crony Charles Kirbo's former correspondent lawyer, Criminal Division chief Ben Civiletti, to handle with care. The cause of justice would be better served with a special prosecutor to be the skunk at the garden party.

STONEWALL

September 22, 1977

WASHINGTON—In announcing Bert Lance's resignation, Mr. Carter did not give an inch: "I don't think any mistake was made."

My colleague Russell Baker has rightly called the Lance affair "a crisis without a theme." Here is the theme: the abuse of governmental power after the election of 1976 by the President-elect and a clique of cronies who may well have conspired to end a cease-and-desist order, to stop a criminal investigation, and to deceive the Senate—in other words, to obstruct justice.

During the corrupt interregnum, three cover-ups took place:

1. *The Comptroller cover-up.* On November 22 there is reason to believe Bert Lance asked Donald Tarleton, the official responsible for supervising his bank, to "lift the agreement on Calhoun," and thereby save him from embarrassing disclosures. Although Lance and the official swear to the contrary, the attorney who has just reported this adds that he was told that, in return, Lance offered Mr. Tarleton a "back channel" right to the top of government.

A quick check at the Justice Department tends to substantiate the charge. On January 31, 1977, Mr. Tarleton wrote to Mr. Lance at O.M.B. asking for help in speeding up Justice on opening a grand jury inquiry into a banker. The Associate Attorney General—Michael Egan, an Atlanta friend of Mr. Lance's and a co-director and stockholder with him of Modern Fibers Company—admits receiving a call about that time from Mr. Lance, or one of his Atlanta assistants, paving the way for that message from Mr. Tarleton. Mr. Egan, following Mr. Lance's unconscionable intercession, assured Mr. Tarleton February 16 by letter that a grand jury would soon be empaneled.

The cover-up of the cease-and-desist agreement was effective: Mr. Tarleton cut it off within hours of Mr. Lance leaving his office on November 22, 1976. The then-acting Comptroller, job-hungry Robert Bloom, swears that Lance "preferred that the enforcement agreement not be disclosed to the F.B.I." and it was not.

2. *The criminal investigation cover-up.* Less than a month after the election, the United States Attorney in Atlanta—desperate for a job in the new administration so he could get his pension—grabbed the criminal investigation into Mr. Lance and, over strong objections from aides, closed it out.

This curious decision did not go unnoticed at Mr. Ford's Justice Department. At high levels, it was reviewed and approved—quite wrongly, as it turned out—and that is now the subject of another investigation.

Criminal division chief Richard Thornburgh evidently wanted the job as head of the F.B.I.; after being interviewed by the Shapiro committee screening applicants, he inquired of his friend Peter Flaherty, whom he had introduced to Mike Egan and who wound up as Deputy Attorney General, if he was in the final five; but Mr. Thornburgh was not.

3. *The house-of-cards cover-up.* At year-end, the banks were closing in on Mr. Lance, seeking unpaid back interest and the split-stock collateral. He turned to his law firm, top members of the Carter circle: Philip Alston and John Moore.

The bank that Mr. Alston dominates, Citizens and Southern, loaned a Lance campaign committee $140,000, which was used to pay off personal loans of Lance's wife. An intermediary was found to buy some of Mr. Lance's stock and was loaned $180,000, which was paid to Lance. (He had to wait for the money to clear, which explains the backdated checks; it enabled him to have a "clean" year-end statement to show the Senate.)

Mr. Lance was then taken off the hook temporarily by a loan from Robert Abboud's First Chicago bank—the sweetheart loan declared "substandard" by the Comptroller. John Moore, who served two masters as Mr. Lance's lawyer and Mr. Carter's "ethics" chief, was Mr. Abboud's Harvard College roommate. Reached in Tokyo, he says he learned of the loan after it was made.

Mr. Moore was rewarded by Mr. Carter with the plum of president of the Export-Import Bank, which dispenses $8 billion a year in loans; he flew to Chicago on September 7 to speak to a group of Mr. Abboud's bank customers and prospects and to recall his lifelong friendship with their host.

Mr. Alston was rewarded with the embassy to Australia.

At the Justice Department, which is supposed to be investigating these three cover-ups, Attorney General Bell has properly disqualified himself;

Associate Attorney General Egan sees "no impropriety" in taking instructions on grand jury matters from his friend at O.M.B.; Criminal Division chief Ben Civiletti will not step aside although he owes his job to his correspondent lawyer, Lance-Carter crony Charles Kirbo; and the job is being handled by Deputy Attorney General Peter Flaherty, who owes his introduction to Mr. Egan and later Judge Bell to the man whose review of the criminal investigation-quashing he is supposed to be investigating, Mr. Thornburgh.

Only a special prosecutor can look at the abuse of power, as Lancegate enters its more serious phase. The stonewalling President says Mr. Lance "exonerated himself completely." We'll see.

MR. CARTER'S CONFESSION

September 26, 1977

WASHINGTON—President Carter, in his much-delayed 15th press conference, made an admission that seemed to confirm the worst suspicions of a few of us: that during a corrupt interregnum, the President-elect and others conspired to lift an embarrassing cease-and-desist order, kill a criminal investigation, and "clean up" Bert Lance's financial affairs so that Mr. Lance could become the new President's key aide.

In the previous press conference, Mr. Carter had responded to a question by James Wooten of *The New York Times* about inquiries soon after the election in this way: "If there are any people who worked in the transition time who made an inquiry about Mr. Lance's affairs, they did it without my knowledge and without my authority, and it would have been contrary to my expectations."

Thus did Mr. Carter then deny any part of impropriety. We now know that not only was a restrictive Comptroller's disciplinary agreement lifted within minutes after a visit by Mr. Lance on November 22, 1976, but that a criminal investigation of Mr. Lance was aborted on December 2, one day after a Lance lawyer telephoned the U.S. Attorney in Atlanta to get him to stop the investigation. Mr. Carter nominated his friend on December 3.

Up to last week's press conference, then, the situation was developing like this: The men around the President were being implicated in a cover-up, but the President was being kept out of it.

But Press Secretary Joseph L. Powell insisted that the President-elect was not informed in December of the criminal investigation, that it was a matter Powell, Hamilton Jordan, and counsel Robert Lipshutz knew but did not think the President had any need to know.

On December 1, Mr. Lance, his lawyer Sidney Smith, and Mr. Smith's law partner John Moore—the Alston law firm's man in charge of "ethics" on Mr. Carter's transition team—telephoned the President-elect in Plains about a press release minimizing Lance's problems. This conversation took place on the same day Smith's approach to kill the probe was made to the U.S. Attorney.

In last week's press conference, Mr. Carter recalled he had met with Bert Lance on November 15 in Plains, when—according to Lance's sworn testimony—Lance had briefed him on problems concerning campaign overdrafts. But the President's story differs significantly from Lance's and Powell's:

"The first time I heard about it [campaign debt overdrafts] was when Bert mentioned it to me in Plains about two weeks later—I think the date now determined to be the first of December." Then the President let the cat out of the bag. "I was called from Atlanta and told that the matter had been resolved by the Comptroller's office and by the Justice Department. On that date was the first time that either Bert or I knew that the Justice Department had been involved at all."

As *The New York Times*'s Nicholas Horrock wrote the next day: "Mr. Carter's version at the news conference carried startling implications. It meant that he knew before he formally announced Mr. Lance's appointment that the nominee had been under criminal investigation. Moreover, the President's version implied that he had been assured that the criminal investigation of Mr. Lance by the Justice Department would be dropped the day it was terminated by the United States Attorney in Atlanta."

The President had not followed the Lance-Powell cover-up script: Instead, in his tearful and distraught state, he may have blurted out the truth. The next morning, Joseph L. Powell rushed out with the agreed-upon version. "At no time prior to the December 3 announcement [of the Lance nomination]," corrected Mr. Powell, "was he aware, of course, of the existence of a Justice Department referral on this matter. . . ."

But reconstruct that moment on December 1. In Atlanta, on one end of the phone, is Mr. Lance, his lawyer Sidney Smith, and Smith's partner John Moore. They swear they were informed on that day of a criminal investigation in the Lance activities.

Do you suspect they discussed that shattering turn of events with the President-elect, on the other end of the phone, in Plains? Can you imagine them *not* telling their leader of their distressing discovery? Can you conceive of John Moore, representing Mr. Carter, withholding from his client the news of his close friend's vulnerability and its happy ending?

No wonder John Moore swore he "does not recall" telling Mr. Carter on December 1 about the criminal investigation, avoiding a perjury charge by carefully adding "but it is possible." No wonder Mr. Powell is frantically trying to get the President to forget what he heard on December 1. Because if what Mr. Carter said last week is true, then his statement in his previous press conference was false, and he may be involved in an obstruction of justice.

Which Presidential spokesman do you believe? I believe that Jimmy Carter—too upset by the forced resignation of his friend to stick to the cover-up script—told the truth in his press conference. In his own unforgettable phrase: "I don't think any mistake was made."

LOVE THY ENEMIES LIST

January 9, 1978

WASHINGTON—Bert Lance sent me a friendly note the other day from Calhoun, Ga. In a firm hand, he wrote: "The Bible says, 'Love those who despise you.'" In that spirit of forgiveness, he sent holiday greetings.

My friend Bert is the only politician who has compiled an "enemies list" for the purpose of loving those on it. But he's wrong about me: Far from "despising" him, I salute the President's best friend in awe, wonderment, and gratitude. Consider his current contributions:

1. *He is providing the White House with a direct link to Saudi Arabia.* By prevailing on a group of Saudis to buy (for a generous $20 a share) stock in the National Bank of Georgia that had been recently selling for $11 a share, he has given that government good reason to believe that the President of the United States is obligated to them for bailing out his best friend.

Although the front man in Bert's bail-out is Ghaith R. Pharaon, that Saudi contractor is merely the go-fer and agent of Sheik Khaled Bin Mahfouz, deputy general manager of the National Commercial Bank of Saudi Arabia. The Sheik sits on two billion, seven hundred million in deposits in Jeddah, with instructions from his King to buy control of selected United States banks which have useful political connections.

The man who made this deal is John Connally, who may say nasty things about Mr. Carter in public but who is now the White House's darling in private. "Big Jawn" was Sheik Mahfouz's partner last August in buying control of the Main Bank of Houston. The young law partner in Houston's Vinson & Elkins who put together the Lance-Mahfouz deal is Frank Van Court, who sits outside Mr. Connally's law office and handles his deals.

Although the United States Government makes a fuss about who buys government-licensed television stations, it cares not what foreign interests buy government-chartered banks; thanks to this anomaly and to Bert Lance, Saudi Arabia now has close financial-political ties to both a United States President and a Republican Presidential hopeful.

2. *Bert has made it possible for middle-level professionals to redeem the highly politicized Justice Department.* (Attorney General Bell has properly recused himself from all Lance matters; the value of Mr. Bell's 2,000 shares of the National Bank of Georgia rose $18,000, thanks to the Saudi offer.)

Since Deputy Attorney General Peter Flaherty quit on December 9, a troika of aides has been pursuing the Lance investigation without supervision. That is because the next Deputy A. G., Ben Civiletti, faces Senate confirmation hearings and wants to be able to plead ignorance of the Lance investigation.

Thus unencumbered, the troika—Cono Namaroto, John Kenny, and Richard Beckler—are creeping laboriously ahead. Though they have let one statute lapse, they have been using an Atlanta grand jury to subpoena—and will take sworn testimony from—First Chicago, Manufacturers Hanover, and National Bank of Georgia officials to determine if Lance collateral was real or fictitious, a subject never dealt with in the Senate hearings.

Also, the Lance troika has been laden with material from S.E.C. investigators about securities and money manipulation involving other people's assets, as well as the file from the Comptroller's office that has to raise the question of perjury.

As the case builds, other Justice pros wonder why the troika has not yet impaneled a special grand jury. Perhaps they worry about an Atlanta jury's "hometown call," or are awaiting pressure from Baltimore Democratic politician Civiletti. But the chance to redeem a soiled departmental reputation is theirs.

3. *Bert is making it possible for the Republicans to pick up an extra 20 House seats this fall.*

The "Southern Salute to the President" will take place at the World Congress Center in Atlanta on January 20. The dinner, which aims to raise $650,000 for the Democratic National Committee in $1,000-per-couple bites, will feature Bert Lance as dinner chairman and emcee, impressing friends in Georgia and Jeddah by embracing John White, the new Democratic chairman, and hearing the President say: "Bert—I'm still proud of you."

The Democratic fat cats brought together by Lance (and Vice President Mondale, who last week was hustling tickets to this dinner in Florida and North Carolina) will feast on roast duck à l'orange with sauce bigarade, topped with Georgia peach tarte chantilly.

But come this autumn, if and when a potential Lance or plea-bargaining begins, Republican candidates will be feasting on the special-treatment diplomatic passport still granted to Lance, the nights spent in Mr. Lincoln's bed at Jimmy Carter's invitation, and—most of all—the fact that every Democratic candidate who gets money from the party's National Committee next fall will be campaigning on "Lance money."

That's why I sent friend Bert an answering note with cordial greetings, along with another biblical saying that motivates journalists: "Ye shall know the truth, and the truth shall set you free."

BERT LANCE

12-20-77

Dear William :

The Bible says "
Love Those who despise
you ".

May you + yours
have a Merry Christmas
& a Happy New Year —

THE FIRST TO KNOW

January 30, 1978

WASHINGTON—At 4:45 P.M., Wednesday, December 28, the Dow-Jones ticker thudded out the news that known quantity Arthur Burns was being replaced by unknown quantity William Miller as chairman of the Federal Reserve, a fact of enormous importance to anyone interested in money. The White House press office confirmed the fast-leaking story, and at 5:07 P.M., President Carter made the official announcement.

In the financial world, where knowledge is power, anyone who knew this information in advance was in a position to profit from it.

"Government bond prices fell moderately late yesterday afternoon," reported John Allen in *The New York Times* the next day, "in reaction to newswire reports, later confirmed, that G. William Miller, chairman of Textron Inc., would be named . . ."

On another financial front, Paul Lewis of *The Times* wrote in the lead of his report from Paris the next day that the Carter decision "helped send an already weakened dollar sharply lower on world currency markets today." *The Wall Street Journal* reported that the President's decision "prompted a further late spate of selling in New York" on the afternoon of the announcement.

I have no evidence that anyone profited in any way from advance knowledge of the President's decision, or even passed it on to someone who knew how to make a killing. But it is interesting to note how good news was passed from Ghent to Aix, even if it only gives us a glimpse into the way the White House seeks to mold public opinion.

Let us begin with a man who did not get the message. Gabriel Hauge, chairman of the Manufacturers Hanover Bank in New York, acknowledges receiving a telephone slip reading "Washington call on the upcoming appointment." The caller left a number. Mr. Hauge says he got the message the next day, threw the slip away since the point was moot, and does not recall the number. The time on the slip was between 3:45 and 4:15 P.M.

Walter Wriston, chairman of Citicorp, which used to be known as the First National City Bank, was reached at a meeting and took the call around 4:30. The news was about the imminent appointment. The caller was Bert Lance.

Earlier that eventful day, Hamilton Jordan, the White House non-chief of staff, summoned the Chairman of the Council of Economic Advisers, Charles Schultze, into his office and went over the list of calls to be made to ensure a good reception to Mr. Carter's announcement. Both were aware the news was "market-sensitive," which is why the announcement was scheduled after the 4 P.M. closing of the New York Stock Exchange. Vice President Mondale had been dispatched to Florida to bring Dr. Burns back to the White House to be given his departure news and to appear at the announcement.

Economist Schultze took the agreed-upon list from Mr. Jordan. Schultze thinks he waited until about 3:30, and started calling. Robert Roosa, at Brown Brothers Harriman, who had been a candidate for the job, was informed, as was John Connor at Allied Chemical, an old friend and former Secretary of Commerce.

First, however, Mr. Schultze reached Treasury Secretary Michael Blumenthal, on vacation in Florida, who already knew that the President had accepted his recommendation of Mr. Miller, to pass on his assignment list of calls.

Secretary Blumenthal recalls making no calls before the public announcement. Afterward, he called Henry Ford, Tom Murphy of GM, Alden Clausen of the Bank of America, Donald Platten of the Chemical Bank, John Perkins of the Continental Illinois Bank, former Treasury Secretaries Henry Fowler, George Shultz, and William Simon (not John Connally)—about 25 calls in all, not all of which were completed. But Gabriel Hauge of "Manny Hanny" was not on the Blumenthal list. Bert Lance wanted him.

Nothing is wrong with calling business leaders, post-announcement, to get their support. Moreover, it is entirely proper and often vital for governments to inform each other's central bankers of moves that might affect financial markets before the news breaks. It is simple courtesy to tell seriously considered candidates that someone else has been chosen before they read it in the papers, and it is the business of the press to respect reasonable embargoes.

But for Bert Lance, a private citizen who the President knows is the subject of criminal investigation, and whose former creditors at the Manufacturers Hanover bank are now appearing before an Atlanta grand jury—is it right for him to be tipping off other business leaders (and perhaps his Arab financial backers, who know all about trading against the dollar) with the President's blessing?

I don't blame ol' Bert, who was born to hustle. I do blame White House slotmen Jordan and Stuart Eisenstadt, and team players Schultze and Blumenthal, who knew in *advance* that Mr. Lance would be making pre-announcement calls to the men he most wanted to impress, and who were too fearful of Mr. Carter's wrath to object to what they knew was wrong.

X-000065 STRIKES AGAIN

February 20, 1978

WASHINGTON—On the inside front cover of every black diplomatic passport is this bold statement: "The bearer is abroad on a diplomatic assignment for the Government of the United States of America."

Of the 24,000 diplomatic passports issued since the beginning of the Carter Administration, only 151 are made out to Americans who are private citizens. The State Department—untruthfully, in my opinion—claims that no list of these 151 non-Government "diplomats" exists. Therefore, the public has no way of finding out which friends of Mr.

Carter and Mr. Vance get waved past the normal barriers and never have to suffer the indignity of having their baggage searched.

The holder of special-privilege passport X-000065 (in passperks as in license plates, low numbers are coveted) is the President's Best Friend Bert Lance. He also has been issued a regular passport, which he may use, but the one that impresses his overseas contacts in the Arab world is X-000065, a status symbol that beats any private aircraft or limousine perks.

In our last installment on the adventures of the President's Best Friend, Bert was busily telephoning bankers to give them advance information about the President's choice for chairman of the Federal Reserve. The message was loud and clear: Bert was still "in" and the bank vice presidents testifying before a grand jury about unlawful loans had better remember it. (G. William Miller's nomination is now in doubt because his testimony on overseas payoffs is being contradicted; Bert may have another chance to call with a new name.)

In today's installment, the man with two passports is more "in" than ever. He has returned from London, Pakistan, and the Middle East with the go-ahead from Agha Hasan Abedi, whose Bank of Credit and Commerce manages billions in Arab funds, to take control of Financial General Bankshares, which owns a dozen banks in the Washington, D.C., area.

This is a much bigger deal than selling a Georgia bank to the Arabs. Financial General is a $2.2 billion company, with banks in a market that serves Congressmen, Government officials, the top military and naval brass—a bonanza for those who might want to influence our nation's opinion leaders and lawmakers. If I were a sheik, the advantages of knowing the intimate financial details of many United States leaders' lives— and the ability to make loans or deny them—would impel me toward moving in on the Washington banks.

Ol' Bert—you have to give him credit, as Henry likes to say—takes care of his old friends. The local Washington agent Bert used to buy the stock (and who denied it all last week) is Eugene Metzger, once a lawyer for the Comptroller of the Currency. Judith Miller of *The New York Times* reported last week that Mr. Metzger had recently offered a job to Robert Bloom, the job-seeking Atlanta Comptroller who suddenly removed embarrassing restraints from Bert Lance just before Mr. Carter appointed him. Mr. Bloom, who could be a witness against Mr. Lance, may soon owe his livelihood to him.

But what of the S.E.C., and its fearsome enforcement chief, Stanley Sporkin—weren't its investigators swarming all over the Lance affairs? Well, you see, Bert is represented by Clark Clifford's law firm, which knows the power levers; next month, Mr. Lance will consent to a civil cease-and-desist order, which amounts to a light tap on the wrist. Like Victor Posner and David Begelman, he will have to pay back what he took in tax-free perks. Bert will agree only to refrain from taking a title, but he will not be denied the fun and profit of taking control of banks for his clients in the Mideast.

And that grand jury in Atlanta causes no fluttering at Butterfly Manna. The three Justice officials in charge of the Lance case—Cono Namaroto, John Kenny, and Richard Beckler—have nobody to report to, and have let key statutes of limitations run out. They cannot but be influenced by pictures of the President with his Best Friend at an Atlanta Democratic fund raiser. They have mouths to feed, and getting tough on Bert is no way to get ahead at Justice.

That's why Jack Stephens, Mr. Carter's biggest fund raiser and the near-billionaire behind the attempt to take over the Washington banks for the Arab investors, has never been called to testify; nor have the bankitician Butcher brothers of Tennessee. The bank that financed the Carter campaign, Atlanta's C and S, has skipped its dividend (as predicted here in November); its officers are counting on Bert's influence in Washington and Araby to bail them out of trouble.

Bert might just bring it off. Hail to thee, X-000065—piker thou never wert. Hang on to that diplomatic passport, take care of those prospective witnesses, use the President to impress the grand jurors and intimidate the prosecutors, tip off your banking cronies and dollar speculators with the inside poop from the Oval Office—as the bumper stickers in Georgia say "Nobody Drowned at the Calhoun Bank."

"BERT—I'M PROUD OF YOU"

March 20, 1978

WASHINGTON—After promising the Senate under oath that he would not engage in banking activities, and after taking the oath of office as Jimmy Carter's most powerful Cabinet member, Bert Lance broke his promise and dishonored his oath: He met two men in the Metropolitan Club in Washington, D.C., last spring to discuss the takeover of a company that owned a dozen banks in Washington and New York.

So says the Securities and Exchange Commission, in charging that Bert Lance and a collection of Washington wheeler-dealers, Carter fund raisers and Arab sheiks—including the former head of the Saudi Arabian C.I.A.—violated Federal securities laws which are on the books to prevent investors from being cheated.

Bert Lance and his partners have signed a consent decree, not contesting the S.E.C. charges. And what will Bert's punishment be, for misleading the Senate, abusing the power of his public trust, and breaking the securities law? Only this: He and his friends are directed to give back the money they have bilked from unsuspecting investors, and Bert has promised he will not break that particular law any more. End of Draconian punishment of the President's Best Friend.

This farce is typical of the special treatment given Mr. Lance by the S.E.C., the Department of Political Justice, and the White House. Consider:

1. The S.E.C. The Enforcement Division's Stanley Sporkin, who strikes terror in the heart of corporate executives, has been dilly-dallying for ten months on his Lance investigation.

If Mr. Sporkin's men had been on the job, the full report of the Lance doings would have been issued, and restrictions put upon his activities, before the long-planned takeover attempt. The S.E.C. is expected to slam the barn door next week with great rhetorical fervor, but if this week's wristslap is any indication, Mr. Lance will be able to laugh at S.E.C. "enforcement."

2. The Department of Political Justice. The Lance case—such as it is, after more statutes of limitations have been allowed to run—is under the jurisdiction of the Namaroto Trio, which has failed to play its song to the chief of the criminal division since December 9, when Deputy A. G. Peter Flaherty ran away to run for Governor of Pennsylvania.

No special grand juries have been empaneled in Washington, New York, or Chicago, where some of the activities sent to Justice for prosecution by the Comptroller's office took place. Only in Atlanta, where ol' Bert will get the friendliest treatment.

At Justice, conflicts of interest abound. The Attorney General, Atlanta's Griffin Bell, owns 2,000 shares of stock in Lance's old bank, but— Ben Civiletti tells us at his confirmation hearings—has not recused himself from other Lance decisions. The United States Attorney in Atlanta is such an obvious Carter political debtor that he has had to take his office out of the case after publicly denouncing a potential witness against Lance. The Associate Attorney General, Michael Egan, was a partner of Lance's in Modern Fibers Corporation.

Nor is that all: Mr. Civiletti, the putative Deputy Attorney General, is the hand-picked former correspondent lawyer of Charles Kirbo, Lance's local Atlanta protector and Griffin Bell's senior law partner. Mr. Civiletti has told the Senate with a straight face that he saw no danger of any grand juror in Atlanta being influenced in any way by publicity of the President of the United States appearing in that city arm-in-arm with the target of a grand jury investigation.

3. The White House. Mr. Carter's continued closeness to Mr. Lance— house guest and favorite fund raiser—has enabled the Arabs' most effective agent to style himself as "special envoy of the President," complete with black diplomatic special-privilege passport X-000065.

Some questions not likely to be asked at the next Carter press conference: Did Mr. Lance, while in office and secretly negotiating the purchase of bank stock, do anything wrong? Did you approve of his tipping off bankers about a new Federal Reserve chairman before that news was publicly released? Does Mr. Lance have your permission to call himself your "special envoy"—and if not, why does he carry that diplomatic passport? Has Mr. Lance ever discussed the Mideast with you, and espoused the cause of his Saudi and Abu Dhabi partners?

I hate to be a Johnny One-Note, but few others seem to care. The double standard has never flown higher: If banker Lance were named B. B. Rebozo, or fund raiser Jack Stephens were named Maurice Stans, then editorials would thunder and the Senate would demand—as the price of confirmation of the Deputy Attorney General—the appointment of a nonpartisan special prosecutor.

March 22, 1978

Dear Safire:

I have to question one sentence in your column in this morning's Kansas City Times on Lance and his crowd. "The double standard has never flown higher."

It has—starting with Franklin Delano Roosevelt . . . and the Kennedys.

Best—

Alf M. Landon

Fort Collins, Colorado

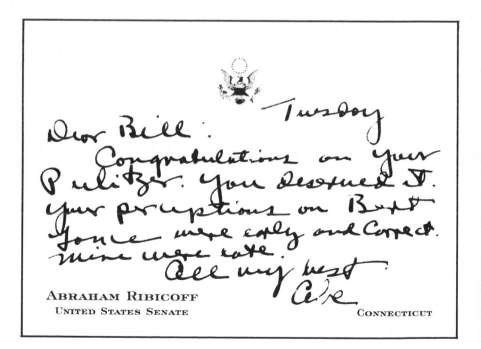

ABRAHAM RIBICOFF
UNITED STATES SENATE   CONNECTICUT

COVER-UP SCORECARD

WASHINGTON—Philip Heymann, chief of the Criminal Division of the Department of Justice—who boasts of his experience as a special prosecutor investigating Republicans—has been leading the Carter Administration fight to prevent the appointment of special prosecutors to investigate Democrats.

The thin-skinned ex-Harvard professor has been derogating the Ethics in Government Act, which mandates court-appointed independent prosecutors to handle charges against high officials. Mr. Heymann wishes us to believe he can do better. His record:

1. The Vesco bribe accusation. A fugitive financier paid $10,000 to a crony of Hamilton Jordan's to get President Carter to intercede in his behalf. When a Carter aide made the approach, President Carter—instead of blowing the whistle on an apparent bribe—wrote his Attorney General a note directing him to see the possible fixer.

Because it could not ignore columnist Jack Anderson's revelations, Justice grudgingly convened a grand jury. After 11 months, the grand jury foreman went public with charges of "cover-up." He was disgusted with Justice's foot-dragging to protect the White House.

In a meeting called to allay suspicion that Justice prosecutors were obstructing the grand jury, Mr. Heymann admitted that he considered the sworn testimony of a key White House aide to have been untruthful.

When this admission was accurately reported by Edward Pound of *The New York Times*, Mr. Heymann issued an artful statement claiming he had never actually used the word "perjury" in connection with Mr. Carter's aide. With the narrow denial, Mr. Heymann tried to placate the White House and mislead the public, but the truth is that the chief criminal law enforcement officer of the U.S. led several witnesses to believe that a special assistant to the President had lied under oath.

2. The Lance case. Exactly two years ago—in September 1977—Justice was handed the evidence of Lance wrongdoing by the S.E.C. and Treasury's Comptroller of the Currency. Result: The Treasury Secretary fell from favor, the S.E.C. enforcement chief's career has been blocked, and all the Justice officials forced to work on the case have fled.

The indictment was returned in May of this year, breaking little new ground. The politically embarrassing trial is not scheduled until late January of next year, and is likely to be postponed further, until after the early primaries. The venue will be most favorable to the President's friend.

3. Koreagate. This case hinged on the ability to convict former Congressman Otto Passman of taking over $200,000 in bribes, and then to turn him into a witness against a dozen other Congressmen. But Mr. Heymann's Criminal Division—to the amazement of the District of Columbia judge—permitted the bribery charge to be tied to an income tax charge, which automatically enabled Mr. Passman to change the venue to his hometown in Louisiana.

As predicted here, Mr. Passman was promptly acquitted, and—thanks to the ineptitude of Mr. Heymann's "Public Integrity Division"—twelve bribe-takers now sit safely in Congress.

4. The Marston affair. When corrupt Congressman Joshua Eilberg called President Carter to demand that he fire the Republican prosecutor who was closing in on him, the President told Justice to do just that. Mr. Heymann has suppressed the F.B.I. report on this suspected obstruction of justice. Inquiring Congressman Bob Walker (R.-Pa.) is told only that the President has been "exonerated," but the embarrassing report must remain secret because it "contains information that is inextricably intertwined with other current criminal investigations."

5. The Carter warehouse-money laundry. Only when prodded in this space to "follow the tangent" did Mr. Heymann permit Lance investigators to follow leads into questionable fund raising by the Carter family. The Ethics in Government Act was circumvented, because cover-uppers at Justice did not want a panel of judges to pick an aggressive, independent prosecutor; under pressure the Carter men chose amiable Paul Curran, and sought at first to restrict his powers, with his acquiescence. Press agitation stopped that nonsense, and now the probe is ambling along. (The long delay in the related Lance case, however, means that no heat is being applied to Lance to induce him to cooperate in the Carter warehouse case.)

6. The Jordan cocaine charge. Last year, when Presidential Drug Adviser Peter Bourne was caught fraudulently prescribing drugs, he told newsmen that illicit drug use was frequent among Carter staffers. But Philip Heymann decided not to send a single F.B.I. investigator to question Mr. Bourne; his apparent crime was shrugged off.

Were it not for the new Ethics in Government Act, that is exactly how Mr. Heymann would be handling the accusations of cocaine use against the President's Chief of Staff. D.C. drug sleuths conduct well-publicized busts against newsletter writers, but have no inclination to follow the white stuff into the White House.

The record of the Carter Department of Political Justice has been a series of grudging investigations, unconscionable foot-dragging, suspicious ineptitude, and self-righteous posing. No wonder Philip Heymann resists the appointment of special prosecutors now required by law: They might even investigate, prosecute, and convict a Democratic public official.

Sept. 11, 1979

Editor
The New York Times Company

Dear Sir:

Fresh from the Nixon Administration reunion last month at the California redoubt of his mendacious mentor, indeed a program of celebration of the character and service of former Attorney General Mitchell, Wm. Safire (column 9/10) professes to give instruction on morality in governmental service with the article entitled "Cover-Up Scorecard," aimed specifically at the current Department of Justice which he calls the "Department of Political Justice," mindful surely of the fact that that would have been an exceedingly charitable characterization of that unit in 1971–73.

Aside from the fact that a "scorecard" in those days would have been useless owing to the number of players and their prestigious positions on the very First Team, it would appear that one of the concluding resolutions at the aforementioned reunion must've read something like "misery, along with massive, admitted, administrative felony conspiracy, loves, seeks and insists upon company laced with sour grapes." And all this from one who authored speeches of the master of misrepresentation and "high crimes and misdemeanors"!

Mr. Safire frequently forgets to take to heart the ancient truisms about rocks and glass houses, etc., and should grind those old saws a bit rather than his biased axes.

R. Thomas
Westport, Connecticut

Inflation and Jimmynomics

P**UNDITS** are blessed with not having to run for office. This enables us to say the unsayable, which in economics is "It would be good to have a recession soon, because that's the only way to slow down inflation." Such an unpalatable idea is denounced as "simplistic" by savants who cannot tolerate the simple.

The phrase "double digit inflation" was popularized in the United States by *New York Times* editorialist Leonard Silk; the pun "double digitalis," while not exactly a thigh-slapper, plays on the stimulant effect of the drug digitalis to make the point that a stimulating deficit cannot be taken too long before the economy gets too excited and the dollar collapses.

SOFT-NOSED BUSINESSMEN

December 16, 1976

WASHINGTON—Meeting Bert Lance, who is to be the Carter Administration's chief budget officer, for the first time last week, I narrowly resisted the impulse to reach out and squeeze his nose.

The reason for this odd urge is that Mr. Lance has been invariably described—by reporters, profilists, editorialists, and pundits—as a "hard-nosed banker."

In an earlier day, bankers were known as "fishy-eyed," a term intended to be pejorative. Now, however, fishy-eyedness has become popular, which has spawned "hard-nosed" as the required adjective for Democrats anxious to assure taxpayers they are not about to be sloppily compassionate.

Why do Democratic politicians now want to appear "hard-nosed" and why do we all play along with their desire? The reason is that liberals think that most businessmen are conservatives, and politicians believe that the way to a businessman's heart is to make self-reliant noises, touch all the zero bases of efficiency, and squirt nose-hardener into their nostrils.

Wrong, wrong, wrong. The big businessman who thrives on competition, who actually lives with the work ethic is a myth. He no longer exists. Some small businessmen have those crusty qualities, and now and then a big-business manager shows certain entrepreneurial tendencies, but these are regarded as throwbacks. In today's top corporate echelons, to be really hard-nosed is to be hopelessly old-fashioned.

Consider price controls. Jimmy Carter has publicly eschewed them, thinking thereby to win the affection of "the business community." But he is at least a generation out of phase. Most managers up in their eerie eyries do not despise controls; they like controls. It is the labor leaders who despise controls.

Which is natural. All too many top business managers are hooked on stability, certainty, order, long-range plans; controls, to them, mean playing by the rules, settling for a predictable profit margin, minimizing risk. Top labor leaders know that controls means wage controls, an end to collective bargaining, and an end to the need for labor unions.

Eschew that over, Mr. Carter. One of my major sins in life was to write the August 15, 1971, Presidential address freezing wages and prices. When Mr. Nixon worried privately about it being a double-cross of his business supporters, John Connally assured him—quite rightly, as it turned out—that "big" businessmen were fairly panting for the security blanket of controls. George Shultz, who hated the suspension of economic freedom, went along only because he was certain America's free labor movement would bust any control system before it became permanent.

The myth of top-management hard-nosiness can also be observed in the way some businessmen seek to eliminate competition in the aircraft industry.

Eastern Airlines president Frank Borman, a hard-noseconed former astronaut, is a scrappy, likable, go-getting executive who probably considers himself an economic conservative. But he has put forth some wistful wondering if it would not be more efficient for airlines to buy our next generation of commercial aircraft from a "single source" rather than have the present three manufacturers make big investments in prototypes and then compete for sales.

Colonel Borman's intent is to lower the cost of the aircraft, which is laudable, but his method is the Big Government "Apollo project" way—the negotiated bid with the single supplier—and that monopoly philosophy is pernicious.

Some airline executives are tired of the "old" Boeing 727 or the Lockheed C-130, which are relatively cheap now because their development costs have long ago been recovered. They wish they could have a more perfect plane, suited exactly to their needs, and are uncomfortable with the economic discipline of having to accept yesterday's design.

How easy it would be, they think, to have a single source, a Government-protected monopoly, to buy the newest planes at whatever cost, which would then be passed on to the consumer. Easy, but anticompetitive. No sweat for the executive; more control for the bureaucrat; ultimately higher cost for the air traveler.

The secret desire of so many top-level managers for controls and regulated monopoly is never openly stated; on the contrary, the rhetoric is always for "stopping the wage-push by monopolistic unions" or "helping us to buy more efficiently so we can compete better." But today's managerial trend is not toward accepting risk. It is toward getting Government help to avoid risk, thus becoming socially responsible, or "soft-nosed."

The irony is that liberal politicians still think that businessmen think that hard-nosiness is next to godliness, and so the pols pretend to be toughminded when the managers have long ago become tenderhearted. It is as if we have reached some universal halftime, and Big Government and Big Business are now marching toward each other's former goals.

SAVE THE SQUIRRELS

October 17, 1977

WASHINGTON—The A.P. reported last week that the National Park Service trapped more than 100 squirrels in Lafayette Park, across the street from the White House. Officials explained that a drop in park attendance caused a peanut shortage for the squirrels, which have since gone on a rampage through the geranium plants, triggering the Park Department's reprisals.

That depressing item sent me to the Bernard M. Baruch Bench of Inspiration, located in the middle of Lafayette Park near Andrew Jackson's statue, to discuss the cruel pogrom with a group of my furry friends, long considered symbols of thrift. To me, squirrels have been like small investors, wisely depositing acorns in safe trees against the possibility of a cold winter.

"High interest rates are doing it," chirped one, looking over his shoulder for a park attendant. "Always makes me want to disintermediate."

"The depreciating dollar is doing it," insisted a second. "Whenever the dollar drops, and I have a bunch of nuts in a tree, I feel as though I have to check my cache."

"The collapsing stock market is doing it," said a third, angrily waving a chart from a branch. "An 18 percent drop in the Dow means we're in the 'Crash of '77.' "

An older squirrel, named Pujo, who had taken peanuts from Mr. Baruch himself, shook his head from his perch on the railing and dismissed all these plaints as effects, not causes.

"My panic-stricken colleagues are wrong," he observed. "Only short-term interest rates have gone up since April, in order to hold down the rise in the money supply and to combat inflation. The long-term rates have held steady—consumer installment loans, mortgages, municipals—which means that long-term inflationary expectations have not gone up. It makes sense to raise the short-term rates in order to protect the long-term rates."

His young associates fell silent, largely because they never knew what he was talking about. "As for the drop in the dollar, as valued against other currencies, that's not such a hot idea. It's what they want"—Pujo pointed to the Treasury Department, on one side of the park—"because they think it will curb imports and reduce our trade deficit, but it will only make imports more expensive and fuel our inflation."

But what of the stock market—wasn't the 180-point drop the cause of the peanut-feeding tourist disappearance and the panic among the squirrels?

"Confidence is not lost because the market drops," Pujo stated slowly. "The market drops because confidence is lost."

And why has confidence been ebbing? The other squirrels came in close; they wanted to hear this, too.

"Very surprising," said Pujo, veering off. "The economy has vitality and dynamism. Since the spring of 1975, we've generated seven million new jobs, at a greater rate than ever before."

Then why was investment of capital in plant and equipment relatively weak?

"First," said Pujo, with a sigh, "managers discovered that the Government cannot stop business cycles; that was a shock, so they're cautious, and don't know what to expect on tax policy. In turn, that reluctance to invest in new plants hurts productivity, which makes it harder for us to compete abroad, which adds to the trade deficit, which weakens the dollar, which makes everybody nervous."

"That's all very well," interrupted the young squirrel who was angrily ripping up a geranium plant, "but I'll tell you why the rest of us have lost our confidence." He pointed to the White House. "It's him. I don't think he likes us."

Pujo blinked. Mr. Baruch would never say that.

"One week, he says he's going to kill the capital gains incentive, and there goes investment," said the angry young squirrel. "Next week, he appoints every fresh-air fiend in the Nader stable, and that's got to mean more regulation and be bad for business. Then when he doesn't get what he wants from the Senate on energy price controls, he goes into a temper tantrum like Nixon after Carswell and calls us profiteers."

"There is that populist strain," admitted Pujo. "What worries me most is the way he leaps on his horse and runs madly off in all directions. One week tax reform, next week energy reform, next week welfare reform—I wonder if they've added it all up."

"What we need is reform-reform," said the young squirrel, furiously stripping the bark off a beech tree. "And a feeling that we have a few friends over there. Blumenthal zapped Lance—at least that big guy used to come across the street and feed us—and now Blumenthal is zapping Burns. And who's Blumenthal? Only the guy the U.A.W. wanted to run for the Senate. That's no friend of the thrifty squirrel."

"Don't knock the Treasury Secretary," said the shaken Pujo. "He's the only one who's not giving the President what he wants on punishing people for making money."

The dreaded park police began a squirrel sweep, scattering the group; I threw my raincoat over Pujo, hiding him until the danger passed, and later offered him a peanut in my palm.

He placed a tiny paw over his wildly beating heart. "Just set the bag on the bench and I'll get it when you leave," he squeaked. "My colleagues are right—we can't trust anybody anymore."

THE NEW POOR

June 1, 1978

WASHINGTON—If you are making more money now than you ever made before, but inflation and the "tax-bracket creep" have reduced the purchasing power of your take-home pay, then you are a member of The New Poor.

If you used your life savings to buy a home, and rising property taxes are forcing you to sell and move to a neighborhood where houses are cheaper, you are a member of The New Poor.

The growing resentment of The New Poor will make itself felt next week in a taxpayers' revolt in California; a chain reaction is likely to follow in other states, as voters turn on their bureaucratic tormentors.

The source of this resentment is a combination of furies. Not only do The New Poor believe that Government programs have become too bloated and expensive, they also believe that Government policy is directed against their interests. Carternomics stimulates the economy to reduce unemployment and help The Old Poor, while it causes runaway inflation that creates legions of The New Poor.

The Consumer Price Index released today, showing a 10.8 percent yearly rate of inflation, will be explained away as temporary, caused by flukes or greedy capitalists or bad weather. But double-digit inflation (a phrase coined in March 1974 by *Times* economic writer Leonard Silk) is wiggling its victory sign, and the Administration in power cannot pass the buck.

Although Government statisticians claim that the cost of living has risen by only 28 percent in the past four years—an average of 7 percent a year—they are living in an unreal world. Raymond DeVoe Jr. of Loeb Rhoades Hornblower has compiled a half-facetious "trivia index" that shows what has been going on beyond the price of hamburger:

Since 1974, the cost of a can of Coca-Cola has doubled, from 20 cents to 40 cents; in that time, a milkshake at McDonald's has risen 47 percent; Band-Aids are up 75 percent, dog biscuits up 67 percent. Laundering a shirt cost 50 cents then, 91 cents now; a Beefeater martini that cost $1.75 then is $3.00 now, and a dime's stay at a parking meter is now a quarter. (Panhandlers now ask for a quarter instead of a dime, a 150 percent increase.)

The price of *Time, Newsweek, Playboy, TV Guide,* and the New York *Daily News* has gone up 100 percent since 1974, as has a stein of beer in a singles bar and a packet of Kleenex in which to cry. (*The New York Times* has risen 33 percent, but now offers new sections and a conservative columnist.) New rubber heels cost twice as much, as do basketball tickets, and a check bounced by your bank now costs $5.00 instead of $3.00. (The salary of the chairman of the Council of Economic Advisers has risen 35 percent in two years.)

The point is that the "real" cost of living—including all those non-necessities that we cannot do without—has risen at a rate twice that of the official inflation rate. And not because of the weather, or corporate greed; the reason is that public policy demands stimulation to reduce unemployment.

How do we stop double-digit inflation and the creation of tens of millions of New Poor? At the local level, as in California, force the reduction of the bureaucracy and accept fewer services; at the Federal level, cut non-defense spending and tighten money to put the brakes on the rise in the cost of living.

But Mr. Carter has not the stomach for this. When he replaces his token woman in-house liberal, Midge Costanza, he keeps her on the bloated White House payroll; to make way for her successor's staff, he puts the unneeded Costanza crew on the Labor Department payroll for over $100,-000 a year. When the latest save-the-cities boondoggle was announced, it included a budget to employ the President's son at $26,000 a year; to off-set this sort of petty patronage graft, Mr. Carter's budget calls for 495 fewer F.B.I. agents.

Instead of attacking Government-caused inflation, Mr. Carter seems destined to take the Nixon route: He will exhort for a while, perhaps add his own antibusiness finger-wagging, and then—in the third year of his Presidency—impose wage and price controls, which will be popular and make him seem activist.

The controls may come in the form of the Wallich-Okun scheme, using the tax system to subsidize "reasonable" price and wage increases. This is wage-price control in sheep's clothing, and might hold down the lid until the 1980 elections, after which organized labor would blow it sky-high.

To deflect the resentments of The New Poor, Mr. Carter will jawbone at selected villains until failure is apparent, and then will treat only the symptoms of inflation with disguised or direct controls.

That's a sad scenario. If the Carter men had the courage to apply the brakes now—and thereby gain the productivity increases that a mild recession brings—we would be able to avoid a crippling inflation this year, a loss of economic freedom next year, and a major recession after that.

June 1, 1978

Dear Sirs,

I am deeply touched by Mr. Safire's lamentations on the plight of "The New Poor" (Op-Ed, June 1). The tragic rise in the price of a Beefeater martini—from $1.75 in 1974 to $3.00 today—is a poignant symbol of inflation's menace to affluence. The 150 percent increase in cash demands by panhandlers (was a dime, now a quarter) is further evidence of debilitating economic pressure on the New Poor, whose wealth and prestige have been eroded by "Carternomics" and big government. Mr. Carter rightly advises a reduction of costly federal bureaucracy (excepting Defense and the F.B.I.) and a turning away from public policies that demand economic stimulation to reduce unemployment. The burden of inflation, carried with weakening patience by Mr. Safire, can be lifted by the return of high unemployment, which affects only the Old Poor who do not drink martinis. Furthermore, by increasing the ranks of panhandlers, market forces would almost certainly restore the ten-cent handout.

I drink to you, Mr. Safire. Gallo today, Beefeater tomorrow!

Sincerely,
Frank B. Gorin
Port Washington, New York

THE KRATZ CLAN AND THE DREAD DOUBLE DIGITS

September 14, 1978

EARTH . . . long, long ago, in a galaxy far, far away, there existed a race of humanoids led by a family called Kratz.

The head of the Kratz clan, a man named Demo, possessed a remarkable father image, considering he was only a little lorne-green man. Paternally, he guidelined the destinies of his two handsome sons—the stodgy Buro and the studious Techno—and his élitist daughter, Aristo.

The Kratzes had governed the humanoids for eons, it seemed, occasionally turning the chore of running the government over to "Me-2-Me-2," a perky little robot programmed to provide a change of face but not a change of pace. The Kratz empire grew and grew, taxing and spending, until it had beneficent control of every nook and cranny of the galaxy.

Then, one day, before anybody could prepare for it, the happy galaxy found itself invaded by the Dread Double Digits. Silently, invidiously, the microscopic economoids infested everything of value in the Kratz universe: Cosmic thoughts, formerly a dolloid a dozen, shuttled out to ten dolloids a dozen, and the thoughts were smaller, too.

"This is a disgrace to the humanoid race," said Demo Kratz, "causing disharmoniousness and incompatibility, and it's not fair."

"I know who's causing it," volunteered his snooty daughter, Aristo. "The Double Digits were sent to afflict us by our arch-enemy, that Char-asthmatic media-wizard."

"Darth Garth!" ejaculated Buro and Techno, shaking in unison.

"Which means," put in the wise, white-haired Demo, "we're under attack by the family that wants to take over the galaxy."

"The Outz," nodded Aristo, curls bobbing.

"Here's my plan," said Buro. "We set up a vast, four-phased organization to administer the Double Digits . . ."

Demo shook his head. "That didn't even work for the Outz."

"Here's my plan," said Techno. "We utilize the tax system to reward or penalize the greedy producers or unions who . . ."

"Get off it," snorted Aristo, "we couldn't even sell that to the Moynihoids."

"Only one person has the answer," Demo decided paternally.

"I'll ask her," he said.

In a quick match-dissolve, Demo strode into a murky intergalactic barroom, peopled by—or thinged by—a motley assortment of brawling harpies, hydras, and monsters. Behind the bar, under a sign that read "The Sauce Be With You," was an immense barmaid, Elaine "Battleaxe" Galactica.

"One draft myrrh," ordered Demo.

"That'll be a thousand dolloids."

"A thousand dolloids for one glass of myrrh?"

"When your galaxy has double digits," retorted Battleaxe, "your dolloid falls into a black hole."

"It's the work of Darth Garth," Demo insisted. "To fight him, we've hired our own wheezing media wizard."

"Forget all that," said the oracular barmaid, drawing the sepia suds and knocking the head off a monster. "The media is not the message. Your enemy is within, and if you don't control him, the Outzes will come and take over."

"You mean . . ."

"Yes. Your own son, Buro. Unless Buro Kratz is cut down to size, the Double Digits will drive your galaxy into the hands of those guys in the corner."

Demo glanced over; with his eyes accustomed to the gloom, he could make out the grizzly nucleus of the Outz.

There were the no-necked jarvis monsters—spawned in the mudslides at galaxy's edge—grunting, cackling, scratching their thick-pack scales with their lawn signs. There were the fast-swiveling jerrybrowns, fawning on the jarvae.

There, too, in the corner—slightly apart from the roaring jarvae—were the high-domed kristoloids, the obscure wanniskis, and the curving laffers, backs aching from constantly checking the intellectual underpinning of the upsetting jeffbells and kempt kemps.

Demo Kratz recoiled in horror. Were these the waivers of the future? Would the humanoid galaxy be seduced by the Outz, and demand the expulsion of Buro Kratz to end the plague of the Double Digits?

Join us Tuesday, November 7, when even the intergalactic bars are closed, for the beginning of the answer on (Crash! Clatter! Zunk!) Battleaxe Galactica.

JIMMYNOMICS

November 16, 1978

WASHINGTON—This essay is intended for the eyes only of professional speechwriters; its purpose is to illustrate the latest techniques in weasel-wording.

Whenever a political figure inserts a slightly awkward or out-of-sync phrase into a speech or press conference answer, or when he slips a last-minute qualifier in front of what is seemingly a ringing pledge, members of the old profession know he is weasel-wording.

Jimmy Carter is getting good at it. Observe:

1. *The six-month pushback:* Your object is to minimize your budget deficit for the coming fiscal year, thereby creating the impression you are not a big spender. The trick: Find a time when the deficit was at a high and make it seem as if that was when you entered office.

That accounts for the careful wording of his goal as "a budget deficit less than half what it was when I was running for office." Why "when I was running" instead of the more natural "when I became President"? Because that wording pushes the comparison back eight months, to June 1976, when sensible economics demanded a high deficit to bring down high unemployment.

Mr. Carter's pushback to mid-1976 also removes the embarrassment of having to compare with the $68 billion deficit he presented when he became President—adding $11 billion to the budget submitted by the outgoing President Ford. By this neat pushback trick, Mr. Carter can present himself as less a deficit-projector than his predecessor, when the opposite is true.

2. *The $12 billion "about":* In trying to appear to be cutting spending, he has hitched his wagon to a soaring standard of comparison—the gross national product. The trick is to say you are "holding" the Federal spending rate to 21 percent of G.N.P., which gives you room to spend more, since the G.N.P. must rise.

But, at the last minute, Mr. Carter inserted the key weasel word in his White Paper—"about" 21 percent. Since each one-tenth of 1 percent equals about $2.5 billion, that "about"—still under 21½ percent—gives him a $12 billion cushion.

3. *The firm percentage of the amorphous subject.* This is a Carter innovation, and deserves close study by aspiring weasel-wordsmiths.

Object: to appear strong on defense matters, and to assure allies that we will keep our increased-spending end of a bargain without having to spend the money.

Here's the wording: "We have encouraged our NATO allies in particular to increase their expenditures for a joint defense of Europe, and therefore us, by 3 percent a year above the inflation rate. I intend to honor that commitment."

Sounds like a commitment to a 3 percent real increase in military spending, no? Ah, but you've missed the weasel words: "for a joint defense of Europe." He's only committed himself here to a 3 percent increase in money we spend to defend Europe, which is a minor portion of the U.S. defense budget—does not cover the Navy, or strategic arms, or the Pacific. That zipped past everybody.

Of course, we all know what the budget is going to be after the coming three-month charade is over. Take today's level of $490 billion, add 7 percent for inflation, add a smidgin for NATO, chop a few billion from Western states for the appearance of hardheartedness at little political cost, and you have $530 billion of spending; figure tax-bracket creep to filch an extra ten billion from taxpayers (some "cut") and you come up with a projected deficit of $29.2 billion—as promised.

In that way, you rely on high interest rates, which you can start denouncing next year, to trigger the housing recession; meanwhile, you are able to adopt the stern demeanor of budget-cutter without actually having cut the budget.

Thanks to this use of weasel words, you have avoided taking the painful step of using genuinely restrictive fiscal policy to brake the boom. Comes the recession, blame the damn bankers and the greedy businessmen. You can, half-truthfully, insist that you toughmindedly reduced the deficit "to less than half of what it was when I was running for office," that you "cut" spending to "about" 21 percent of G.N.P., and that you have "honored" your commitments on military expenditures to (mumble, mumble) "3 percent a year above the inflation rate."

EASY OIL ANSWERS

July 2, 1979

WASHINGTON—Some straight answers to questions being asked by slow-burning motorists:

Why didn't our Government protect us from the oil shortage and the price gouging?

Because Government "protection" has long been the prime cause of the oil shortage. Years of domestic price control lowered the incentive to produce, making us more dependent on foreign sources. At the same time, that artificially low American oil price encouraged waste and made a mockery of Presidential pleas for conservation.

What triggered the current crisis?

The obvious immediate cause was the slight drop in world production caused by the fall of the Shah, which Mr. Carter's dithering helped hasten. The less obvious cause was the inability of the Saudis to continue to pick up the slack in world production, owing to extensive water seepage into many of their wells. When Aramco informed the royal family that a production increase was inadvisable, the Saudis concealed this fact and claimed they were holding back production to support the Palestinians.

Why did this relatively small drop in world production make a desert out of Self serve Island?

Because our Government bureaucracy, rather than an efficient free-market system, decides on fuel allocations, we have the spectacle of gas availability in Cleveland and Detroit while the citizens of New York and Washington and elsewhere are gas-fuming. Congressman Jack Kemp put it succinctly: "The only reason we have gas lines in parts of the country is that it is illegal today to match up willing suppliers with willing consumers of gasoline."

Granted that nobody is for what is frowned on as "a quick fix"—but can't we have what is smiled on as "speedy relief"?

The Administration was in a dilemma: to risk motorist fury this summer, as Mr. Carter's popularity rating sinks to that of Mr. Nixon's upon his sudden retirement—or to risk the anguish of New Hampshire and Pennsylvania homeowners next winter, as the primaries begin. The decision was made to direct oil supplies to the Northeast for the coming winter, at the expense of the motorists across the United States, because hell hath no fury like homeowner huddled in an overcoat in his living room.

What would be the worst step the Government could take now?

Precisely the step that is most likely to be taken: gas rationing. Because Government "protection" on price has put us in the bind we are in, the answer put forward by liberals is to go further down the road of controls to rationing. This will not only continue to depress United States production, it would encourage waste through a proliferation of black markets. Well-placed distrust of Government would make rationing in peacetime as unpopular in three months as it seems popular today.

Is there no hope for an end to the gas shortage?

Certainly there is hope: a hair-curling recession is on the way. At the end of the tunnel, there is another tunnel. The coming "hard landing" will not be caused by the oil shortage (though that will be the political excuse), but by the Administration's unwillingness to curb inflation for the past two years. With the real decline of economic growth, demand for oil will plummet, a glut will develop, and punditry will be awash in the word "awash."

How can we make that probability of a recession work for us now?

By promising to retaliate in hard times against the foreign suppliers who especially torment us now. For example, when the Nigerians use their supply as blackmail to affect our foreign policy, or when the Libyans lead the pack in seeking to disrupt our financial markets and finance a Moslem H-bomb, the Congress could officially name them "Least Reliable Suppliers." When the worldwide pinch begins to be felt and our oil imports decline, those unreliable suppliers would be the hardest hit. Such a prospect could be sobering.

What should we do right now to make sure we don't find ourselves in permanent bondage to the radical sheiks?

The President has let the situation deteriorate to a point at which even he can look like a leader. The easy answers are the best:

1. Better a quick fix than no fix at all: End all controls now, accept the agonizing wrench of realistic prices cold-turkey; that will curb demand and encourage supply.

2. Break the environmentalist stranglehold on coal, and then guarantee purchase of energy from coal and shale at prices that will later help break the oil cartel.

3. Adopt the plan being quietly urged on the White House by Arthur Burns and Felix Rohatyn, to involve the former Axis powers in a $50 billion international finance corporation that would underwrite the development of synthetic fuels.

The outline of an inspiring television speech springs to mind, but the car ahead of me has begun to move.

July 14, 1979

To the Editor
The New York Times

I can't help wondering at the apparent contradiction between William Safire's "Easy Oil Answers" of July 2 and the news article "Critics Assert Oil Price Decontrol May Not Spur Production in U.S." of June 17.

Mr. Safire says "years of domestic price control lowered the incentive to produce" oil in America. Yet the news article says oil companies are "typically reaping returns of 20 percent and more from their investments in domestic exploration and production ... as against 13.3 percent for manufacturers generally."

I get the feeling that either Mr. Safire isn't reading the rest of the paper, or that he doesn't suppose other people are.

Sincerely,
Mike Shenefelt
New York, New York

ECONOMY IN MELTDOWN

October 8, 1979

WASHINGTON—The impossible is happening: the soaring rate of inflation (an 18.5 percent annual compound rate in the latest producer price index) is intersecting with the plunging rate of support for the President (19 percent in the latest A.P.-NBC poll).

One is the logical consequence of the other. As President Carter proves himself helpless to stop the pain most directly felt by most Americans, he deservedly loses more of their support. All the secondary reasons for the growing desire to get rid of Mr. Carter—weakness in foreign affairs, foot-in-mouthism, incipient scandals, Teddy-mania—pale before the primary cause: his incompetence in dealing with a runaway inflation.

Mr. Carter offers the alibi of the increase in oil prices. However, energy costs—direct and indirect—account for less than 3 percent of the leap in the cost of living.

The real reason we are beginning to look like the Weimar Republic is the unwillingness of Democratic politicians to bear responsibility for any kind of recession. For more than two years, a President who came into office pledging to balance the budget has run resounding deficits, stimulating the economy away from dreaded recession and into higher inflation.

Worse, the monetary policy of Mr. Carter—endorsed by Senator Kennedy—was designed, during the blundering tenure of William Miller at the Federal Reserve, to do too little and too late for two years.

Mr. Miller began by resisting higher interest rates, which made him a hero at the Carter White House and on liberal editorial pages, but which proved to be a mistake. Then, after it became apparent that political cowardice on the budgetary front left only the Federal Reserve to resist inflation, Mr. Miller allowed interest rates to creep upward, reacting always too slowly to the inflation rate.

That compounded his mistake. Higher interest rates are themselves inflationary, and can be justified only by their overwhelming effect on the economy—slowing it to the point where recession bites, inflation slows, and interest rates themselves can be lowered, which in turn reduces the cost of living.

But by raising interest rates piecemeal, Mr. Miller added to the cost of living without the overwhelming effect of turning the economy downward. As we now see, such Jimmynomics made the problem worse: We now have both high interest rates and higher inflation, more than triple the rate prevailing when the Democrats took office.

What to do now? In the next week, with Paul Volcker at the Fed, and with the unsuccessful Mr. Miller still talking of painless austerity at the Treasury, we will probably see some financial legerdemain to "save" the dollar again. Mike Blumenthal did the same thing a year ago and it looked fine for a few months, but the dollar is worse off now than ever.

The only thing that can turn this inflation around is a recession. No politician of either party will say that, but everyone knows it is true. Delaying that needed recession (and fueling inflation) is our current $30 billion deficit—as well as our inadequate interest rates and too-loose money supply.

To kick inflation in the head, to trigger a recession and to let the world know we mean business, we should do two things: (1) Slash nondefense spending to balance the budget now, with all the pain that it implies, and (2) break out of our "negative interest rates" and establish a positive interest rate. That means jacking up short-term rates by three full points— whammo. Cold turkey.

That sounds draconian. Yet a 3 percent interest rate rise today corresponds to a rise of less than 1 percent in the 60's, when rates were less than a third of today's. And, like castor oil, it would do the trick.

The alternative is to continue a policy that preaches austerity and practices profligacy, which has led to the worst inflation in our history. Those who have been calling for an induced recession have been proven right, while the Carter economists and Kennedy-school optimists have been proven consistently and egregiously wrong. Their public rejections have been phony, and even their private predictions have been unrealistic.

Today's spiral, unchecked, would lead to disaster. If we are not willing to take a recession, we are in danger of a crash and a depression. If the tone of this essay seems apocalyptic, it is to counter the complacency of our economic ostriches: They talk smugly of "underlying" rates of inflation increasing, and secretly like the idea of the ensuing demand for controls because they envision themselves as economic dictators.

Get angry. Demonstrate. Picket, before the rising price of signs makes picketing prohibitive. An inflation that wipes out savings, bankrupts pensioners, and rewards high rollers is more poisonous to our system than radioactive waste, more dangerous to our personal freedom than the Soviet threat. Our economic engine is in a state of meltdown, but our Government is still adding more heat.

October 8, 1979

Mr. William Safire
c/o New York Times

Your polemical blasts have always seemed more than a little hysterical to me, but few more so than your column in today's *New York Times* called "Economy in Meltdown." The title suggests you are seeking to become the economy's Jane Fonda.

I ordinarily react with as much detachment as possible to such columns, but have become increasingly concerned over the past year or so about the growing sentiment expressed in a number of newspapers in New York and Boston that a kind of raging aggression toward "THEM," i.e., government officials, elected and otherwise, is the answer to all of our social, economic, and political ills. It has become the new fad. Criticism of government, of course, is nothing exactly new. What seems to be gaining acceptance, however, is the belief that, like the characters in the film *Network,* all that is needed for a solution is for everyone to throw their windows open at once, stick their necks out, and yell "I'm mad as hell and I'm not going to take it anymore." You prescribe "get angry. Demonstrate." Your final sentence blames only "our Government."

I am criticizing your column only because, while you are doubtless an intelligent man and know better than to accept your own simplistic advice, there are many people who may take you at your word. And no one with a memory for European history of the 1930's can ignore the real danger that inflation will once again produce fear, frustration, anger, and the demand for a "strong" government, even a fascist one, that will "DO SOMETHING ABOUT IT." I believe that your type of column, in suggesting that simple solutions are available, and could be put into effect except for the stupidity of the government, and will be put into effect if everyone gets mad enough, contributes to such a potential.

Yes, inflation seems to be a major problem, at least we are told it is, after, I guess, our military/defense posture in the world, and after such problems as world population growth, the availability of food, the threat of nuclear destruction, racial conflicts and injustice, economic underdevelopment and lack of employment, etc. At the same time, as I read it at least, there is a growing consensus among economists that a recession is no longer the simple cure to inflation it was once theorized to be (and perhaps never was in reality). Recessions do not really much decrease the demand for energy, food or housing, the biggest segments of our costs and expenditures. They do not do much to reduce the "cost-push" factors in inflation, as opposed to the "demand-pull" ones. The real drive that seems to be needed now is toward ways of dealing with cost-push. Greater productivity. Simpler distribution networks. Fewer middlemen. More basic, no-frills levels of products, better and more realistically designed to meet essential needs. Yes, we need to express our anger. But then it needs to be guided by our intelligence in search of solutions.

Sincerely,
Wayne H. Sherwood
Boston, Massachusetts

October 13, 1979

To the Editor,

The parody, "Economy in Meltdown," of economic reasoning based on the overheating analogy is one of the finest pieces ever to appear on the Op-Ed page. It is a pity that it was mistakenly attributed to William Safire, although it is the obvious work of Russell Baker. The pronouncement that "The only thing that can turn this inflation around is a recession" can only be compared to Col. Blimp's circa 1938 thought that "The only way to ensure peace is to give everybody plenty of arms and let them fight it out."

Richard Sacksteder
New York, New York

Foreign Policy II

ISRAEL, THE ARABS, AND CARTER

MR. CARTER came on the scene deploring the "reassessment" of our alliance with Israel put forward by the Ford-Kissinger Administration. In office, he came under the Brookings Institution-Brzezinski influence, seeking a swift, "comprehensive" peace by convening the Geneva conference and permitting the Soviet Union to lend its support to the most radical Arabs.

With the United States off on this tangent, Egyptian President Sadat made his historic move to establish bilateral relations with Israel. A year later, with the "comprehensive" approach safely sidetracked, Mr. Sadat and Prime Minister Menachem Begin came to Camp David to enlist the United States in a massive economic underwriting of their démarche.

These essays reflect a long-held belief that the best way to bring peace to the Mideast is to give our democratic ally a sense of permanence, and the Arab world evidence of our steadfastness. In a world newly conscious of the power of oil, and in a post-Vietnam America that flinched from accepting overseas responsibilities, this became a minority view.

LET US BEGIN

May 19, 1977

WASHINGTON—A couple of years ago, in the elevator of Jerusalem's King David Hotel, I mentioned to a bellman that I was on my way to meet Menachem Begin, leader of the hard-line Likud Party.

The bellman smiled. "A generation ago, when the King David was British headquarters, he blew this place up."

Mr. Begin, winner of this week's election in Israel, who may become the next Prime Minister, is a terrorist who made good. As head of the Irgun, Mr. Begin was branded an "outlaw" by David Ben-Gurion; after Israel won its independence, civil war was narrowly averted.

Through a long generation, Mr. Begin became a permanent opposition to the establishment Labor Party. To visitors, the man with a reputation as a firebrand was, on the contrary, soft-spoken and precise; one received the impression that he believed that one day his route to peace would be chosen, but that he never expected to be Prime Minister himself.

Now, at 63, with heart trouble and running against a strong Labor Party candidate (who promoted Peres?) Menachem Begin has emerged as the chosen leader of the Middle East's only democracy. Why?

Thunderstruck Labor Party members—the new "outs" who have never been out before—grumble that the Begin victory was merely the result of a split in Labor ranks, plus a public desire for change after a series of scandals.

Dazed United States officials, who had hoped to present the Carter plan for Mideast peace while disclaiming any intent to "impose" the plan on the parties, are hurrying to put out the line that the expression of popular will in Israel was rooted in economic troubles and did not reflect any hawklike tendency among the majority.

Both explanations are true, to an extent, but leave out the gut issue: Israelis worry more about survival, personal and national, than about scandal or prosperity. As the United States shows signs of weakening in the world, and as the new American President speaks in favor of a "homeland" for hostile Arabs on the Jordan River's West Bank, the Israeli voter turns toward the candidate least likely to trade security for unstable peace.

For Menachem Begin does not even use the phrase "West Bank"; he prefers the ancient "Judea" because he sees that crucial area as an integral part of Israel. In building a coalition to govern, he may have to give up the idea of annexing the West Bank, but the center of Israel's bargaining position has undoubtedly shifted toward trading away less land.

As might be expected, Syrian radio says the Begin victory "will push the Middle East close to a new war." And other dictatorships and monarchies call the newly elected leader a "notorious terrorist" (our "guerrillas" are your "terrorists").

But the free election of a hard-liner in Israel cannot be permitted to become an excuse for Arab violence, or for a new round of attacks by State Department Arabists on our Mideast ally as "intransigent." If the Carter Administration is looking for opportunities for success rather than alibis for failure, here are some reasons why the election upset could advance the prospects of a secure peace:

First, Mr. Begin is likely to try for a coalition that Mr. Ben-Gurion called *me kir el kir*—"from wall to wall"—a wide gathering of the center and right. He is using Lincolnian bind-up-the-wounds rhetoric, suggesting that his more moderate campaign tone will be his policy.

Next, an outspokenly hard line on territorial defense happens to be the best approach. For example, the Israelis will never let themselves be enticed into handing over the Golan Heights, from which they have been attacked so often, and it is helpful to understand that position going into a negotiation. U.S. "guarantees" of indefensible Israeli borders would be impractical and should not be taken as serious: In the crunch, the Israelis have to depend on themselves to bear the first brunt of battle.

Finally, the man in office is never the man in opposition. That's not hypocrisy, that's government in a democracy. As it took a de Gaulle to extract France from Algeria ("You are not the army's army, you are France's army") and as it took a Nixon to tranquilize hard-liner reaction to the opening to China, it might just take a Begin to assure Israelis that the chances that must be taken in negotiation are well-calculated risks.

Menachem Begin's goal, as expressed in that interview years ago, was a secure peace, not conquest. He will have to be more flexible than he has been, but he will not panic at the first withholding of American arms. He gave his visitor a copy of his book, *The Revolt: Story of the Irgun*, and it included this line:

"If you have the anvil (love of country) and the hammer (the ideal of freedom), you will indubitably find the iron from which to fashion the weapons for the struggle."

THE ALTALENA *DOCKS*

July 14, 1977

WASHINGTON—They tell a story in Israel these days about the *Altalena*, a ship carrying guns to the Irgun in 1948 that was sunk off Tel Aviv by David Ben-Gurion's Haganah, in a demonstration of who was running the newly independent nation.

Since the election victory of Menachem Begin, who had been an Irgun leader, to have been on the *Altalena* is now considered equivalent to an American socialite having ancestors on the *Mayflower*.

"Why did the *Altalena* sink?" goes the question.

The answer: "Because 200,000 people were aboard."

Suddenly Prime Minister Begin has a great many longtime supporters. That is because (1) he won; (2) he has said that everything is negotiable; (3) he has appointed a familiar face, Moshe Dayan, as Foreign Minister; (4) he has reappointed the trusted Simcha Dinitz as Ambassador to the United States; (5) he has sought advice from Golda Meir on the eve of his departure to the United States to meet President Carter.

Instead of being a right-wing exterrorist kook, as he was suspected of being by State Department Arabists who find democratic election upsets distasteful, the new Israeli Prime Minister has proceeded with restraint.

As Mr. Carter revealed in his press conference this week, the Egyptians recently withdrew 1,000 troops that had been violating the 1975 Sinai accord. When Mr. Begin called a United Nations official's attention to the breach of agreement, the Israeli leader did it in a way that seemed to assume a misunderstanding by the Egyptians rather than a deliberate provocation. The polite manner of the objection permitted Egyptian withdrawal with no loss of face.

Mr. Begin comes to America with a surprising initiative in mind. Until recently, the Israelis paid lip service to the idea of a Geneva conference: They did not want to seem to oppose an attempt at a comprehensive settlement, but they much preferred "a piece of land for a piece of peace," or a step-by-step, approach. In that way, a settlement requiring a big security risk was less likely to be imposed, and Arab-Israeli direct negotiations would be generated.

A bolder course seems to have been chosen by Mr. Begin. If the United States will agree not to present the parties with a prearranged deal (which would permit Arabs not to deal directly with Israel), then Israel is ready, even enthusiastic, for Geneva. Mr. Begin has gone so far as to suggest a date: October 10. (Why October 10? Look at a calendar, and diplomacy loses some of its mystery: It's a couple of weeks after Yom Kippur.)

With Israel suddenly embracing the U.S. suggestion for an attempt to make a package deal at Geneva, the Carter Administration is just as suddenly suspicious. Why, we wonder, should anybody agree without a price? What is this, some kind of trick?

That was why Mr. Carter told his State Department to put out a harsh statement demanding Israel weaken its West Bank position before Mr. Begin arrived. When that pressure backfired, the weather-vane President began saying he does not want the Palestinians to have an independent state, which has now confused everyone.

One imagines that Mr. Begin will try to clear up the confusion on three fronts, and in a constructive way:

First, on what "peace" means in the Mideast, the United States and Israel are in fairly close accord. Peace is not just the temporary absence of war; any package deal must include diplomatic relations, and any long-term negotiation must be face-to-face. The Arabs do not want this, and talk of "steps toward" peace. But a little step would deserve only a little land; a package requires the total peace both Mr. Carter and Mr. Begin have in mind.

Second, the "Palestinian homeland" that Mr. Carter talks about can be worked out, if the accent is on the home rather than on the land. Despite propaganda, Egypt, Syria, Saudi Arabia, and Jordan do not really want a radical Arab state, probably Soviet-dominated, in the area; like the Jews, they would prefer the Palestinians contained as an "entity" within Jordan.

Third, on borders, the United States should stop demanding only "minor" modifications of the 1967 lines. The United Nations most specifically, and after debate, did not insist that Israel give up "all" territory it won; the United States should not insist on Israeli pullbacks to impossible-to-defend positions. On the contrary, the United States should move the Arabs off their all-or-nothing recalcitrance—or better still, let the parties work it out in direct negotiation.

Even the West Bank issue is manageable. Israel has both historic claim and possession; instead of returning to Jordan what it took by force in 1948, why not a semiautonomous region, civil affairs run by West Bankers and Jordan, defense policy by Israel?

The point is that Mr. Begin's emergence might be a *mitzvah* for Mr. Carter, offering a chance of success or at least a quick calling of Arab bluffs.

After 29 years, the *Altalena* has docked; Menachem Begin has a relatively short time to make an impact on his country's future and would like to be remembered as the man who laid the basis for a secure peace.

SELLING OUT ISRAEL

October 6, 1977

WASHINGTON—If, as he claims, our Secretary of State had been "somewhat surprised" by the reaction of fierce dismay to the Soviet-U.S. statement giving the Arabs what they want before the Geneva conference begins, then the Secretary of State would be a fool.

But if, as is more likely, President Carter's foreign policy advisers are feigning surprise in order to pretend that the deal conferring "legitimate rights" upon people pledged to destroy Israel is "not a new policy," then Mr. Carter takes the American public for fools.

For the selling-out of Israel is definitely a departure from the policy of previous U.S. Presidents. Mr. Carter has shown he is determined to take land lost by Arabs in wars against Israel, and to force the creation of a Palestinian state.

"Sellout" is a strong word. Mr. Carter's motive is not to abandon Israel but to make peace in the Mideast, and acquiesce in a new presence by the Soviet Union in that area in return for progress on arms limitation. But the effect of his policy would be to make Israel vulnerable, which is why Mr. Carter disclaims the very policy he pursues.

For example, the code words for a Palestinian state on Israel's border have long been "legitimate rights," just as the code words for not returning lands won in 1967 are "defensible borders." These are not diplomatic niceties; to many the phrases carry the same force as "final solution."

Under Soviet pressure, Mr. Carter has announced his embrace of the "rights" to a state demanded by the Palestine Liberation Organization. He knows exactly what he is saying; his nervousness in taking that step was revealed in the Freudian slip in his speech to the United Nations, calling for "the legitimate rights of the Panamanians—uh, Palestinians."

Every step Mr. Carter takes is to create that state or "entity" or "homeland." The Israelis cannot tolerate it; the Saudis and the Egyptians and other moderate Arabs do not really want it; the P.L.O., after its defeat in Lebanon, is too weak to demand it. But Mr. Carter is pressing hard for it, with the cooperation of the Soviet Union, which undoubtedly will provide arms.

A second example of a Carter policy in force that is always disclaimed is that he is "imposing" a settlement. The Israelis resist this for a simple reason: They hold lands that the Arabs want back, and want to deal directly with Arabs who cannot pretend that the party they are dealing with is not a nation.

To avoid this direct dealing, Arabs turn to the United States for brokerage. The more we intervene on substance—as in the recognition "rights"—the better for militant Arabs, the worse for Israel. Consequently, as Mr. Carter rigs the outcome of the Geneva conference with the Soviets, he goes out of his way to insist that "we do not intend to impose a settlement." He protests too much.

In the face of the "not-new" Carter Mideast policy, what can supporters of Israel—and opponents of the extension of Soviet influence—do to restrain a missionary whose misguided zeal could lead to war?

First, we can call for an end to duplicity. If Mr. Carter has a deal in his back pocket he plans to spring at Geneva, putting all the pressure of the superpowers and the third world against Israel, then we ought to know its outlines now—in time to urge Israel to wait a year or two.

Second, we can expose the campaign to isolate and weaken Israel. This includes the Carter decision to withhold antimissile-bunker weapons; the Israel-is-a-burden philosophy that afflicts the Joint Chiefs under General George Brown; the plants by the Carter press office about a "Jewish lobby" that portrays as sinister any call for the U.S. to honor its commitment to its only democratic ally in the Mideast.

Third, we can lean back on those who lean on Israel. The President has shown, above all else, how susceptible he is to pressure. No better example of that could be found than in his abandonment of the subject of human rights in his U.N. speech on the day the Belgrade conference opened.

After the infamous Soviet-U.S. agreement, Senator Hubert Humphrey rose from a sickbed to reach the President and his Minnesota colleague, Vice President Mondale, and is said to have stunned them with the force of his argument and the depth of his feeling.

As a result of the mini-firestorm, Mr. Carter held a late-night meeting with Foreign Minister Moshe Dayan to work out a way for the Israelis to avoid recognizing the representatives of terrorism in the working sessions at Geneva, so that a Palestinian presence does not force Israel to negotiate a Palestinian state.

That's not much, but it puts our Arab-tilting President on notice that Israel will not accede to one man's notion of their needs for survival. If the deck is stacked at Geneva by the Carter plan to impose a settlement that turns the West Bank into a Soviet staging area, Israelis will find a great body of public opinion in the United States supporting their refusal to walk meekly to their doom.

"THEY CAME SO FAR"

October 27, 1977

WASHINGTON—"They have never recognized the right of Israel to exist," said President Carter of the Soviets, explaining to an interviewer why he was proud of the joint U.S.S.R.-U.S. statement on the Mideast.

The President's assertion is demonstrably false. If he believes he has wrung this concession out of the Soviets in return for agreeing with them to give the Palestinian Arabs "legitimate rights" to a state of their own, then Mr. Carter has been grossly misled.

Let us look at the President's statement in context, as reported last week by Saul Pett of The Associated Press. Mr. Carter had just observed how surprised he was that something "completely innocuous" could grab the attention of the nation, such as the Soviet-U.S. statement. He sought then to show how far the Russians had come toward our position:

"In the past," President Carter said, "the Soviets have been just a complete obstacle to progress. They have been recalcitrant. They have never recognized the right of Israel to exist or that an absence of complete peace was an obstacle to a solution of the Middle East. They came so far.

"We looked upon that as a great political achievement to remove a major obstacle."

Mr. Carter's "great political achievement" No. 1: "*They have never recognized the right of Israel to exist.*"

Not only has the Soviet Union repeatedly recognized the right of Israel to exist, the Soviets were the first to recognize the state of Israel on May 15, 1948, beating the Americans to that honor by 24 hours.

Through two breaks in diplomatic relations, the Soviets have continued to recognize Israel as a state, and therefore its "right to exist." Andrei Gromyko, in a December 21, 1973, speech to the United Nations, declared: "Israel was granted that right [to exist] by the very fact of the creating of that State by decision of the United Nations. Possession of that right was confirmed by the establishment in due course of diplomatic relations with Israel by many states, including the Soviet Union." What could be more clear?

In pitching for a Palestinian state, the Soviets have always stressed Israel's right to exist even as they supplied the Arabs with arms: On February 10, 1976, the publicly announced Soviet plan for the Mideast included "the right of all countries involved in the Middle Eastern conflict for independence and secured existence, namely the Arab states bordering Israel and Israel itself."

Even in the famed Security Council Resolution 242 (which was delicately ignored in last month's joint statement), the Soviets had previously acknowledged the "territorial integrity and political independence of every state in the area."

How, in light of 30 years' continuous recognition, and with hundreds of Soviet restatements of Israel's right to exist, could President Carter say "they have never recognized the right of Israel to exist"?

Okay. Now the Official Correctors will explain that, um, you see, the President "misspoke." But he does not misspeak; he misthinks. His foot is not so much in his mouth as in his mind. Mr. Carter really believes he has bargained the Soviets into recognizing Israel's existence.

Mr. Carter's "great political achievement" No. 2: "*They have never recognized . . . that an absence of complete peace was an obstacle to a solution of the Middle East.*"

That shows the President has been led to believe that he induced the

Soviets into accepting, for the first time, the goal beyond armistice, an end of the state of war. But Leonid Brezhnev, in a March 21, 1977, speech, said specifically that "there would be put an end to the state of war between the Arab countries involved in the dispute and Israel, and there would be established relations of peace." And Resolution 242, with Soviet agreement, calls for "termination of all claims or states of belligerency." Again, what could be clearer?

The stark fact is that the President did not know what he was doing, and to this day is inexcusably misinformed. When he caved in to the Soviets' "legitimate rights" demand, and thus rigged the Geneva conference to force Israel to accept a Soviet-armed radical state on its border, he was told he won two concessions, two "great achievements." He is thankful to the Soviets: "They came so far."

Neither David Aaron at the White House nor Anthony Lake at State has the inclination to explain to the President that he is using false justifications for his blunder, that what he calls "great achievements" are no concessions at all. It is as if he traded away the cruise missile in return for a restatement of our clear title to Alaska.

The Mideast does not lend itself to quick study. Next year, when our President is better informed, is soon enough to convene the parties at Geneva.

VISIONS OF ZACHARIAH

November 21, 1977

WASHINGTON—Both the Egyptian President and the Israeli Prime Minister chose Zachariah, a minor prophet, for their biblical text in their speeches before the Knesset.

An apt choice: Zachariah was a visionary who had to break away from formalism to achieve his people's goal, the rebuilding of the second Temple. The historic Sadat visit is a break with diplomatic formalism to surmount what Mr. Sadat called "the Psychological Wall." That wall not only separates Arab from Jew, but it divides moderate and extremist Arabs.

The Israelis in his audience knew that the man before them had just been marked for assassination by one radical Palestinian, while a head of the P.L.O. had just said "Sadat will go down in history as one of the founders of the state of Israel." The official Syrian radio was calling on Egyptians to overthrow their leader.

In that context, the leader of the moderate Arabs could have said just about anything and been applauded in the Knesset. But the Egyptian President went beyond what might have been expected in the way of national recognition: not only "We accept to live with you" in the Mideast, but "We welcome you among us." That is the speech of a man who knows exactly what history he is making.

The positions set forth in his speech were, as predicted, elements of a standard public Arab line: demanding every inch of land taken in 1967, finding the annexation of Jerusalem "unacceptable," and calling for the creation of a Palestinian state. Mr. Sadat drove the final point home by noting that "even the United States" had recognized "legitimate rights," and thereby skillfully used the Carter position to support the demands of the most radical Arabs.

All these extreme positions he was required to lay out, and the Israelis fully understood his requirement. Mr. Sadat also had to say that he had not come to sign a separate peace, which other Arabs rightly take as a warning that a separate peace is possible should the Sadat lead not be followed.

Mr. Begin's response was not, as some American commentators evidently hoped, "It's a deal." A sense of the occasion required him to say a few things for the record, too.

That was why the Israeli leader—entirely in character—took advantage of the opportunity to tell a worldwide audience about the historic right of Jews to their homeland, and to remind this generation of the Holocaust. Many people, including many Jews, become impatient as a review of that past; Mr. Begin sees it as essential to an understanding of Israel's reason for being.

He then treated Mr. Sadat's hard-line pan-Arab proposals as openings in a discussion, and not as non-negotiable demands. Mr. Begin repeated his own position that "Everything is negotiable," and solicited an invitation to Cairo and elsewhere, assuming that the Sadat visit was the beginning of the peace process and not an our-way-or-else position.

The weakness in the Begin response was his too-abrupt dismissal of Palestinian needs. It was fortunate that Simon Peres, the Israeli opposition leader, was there to add "We are alert to Palestinian identity" and to sketch a solution within a Jordanian state.

But Mr. Begin has not come this far—despite Carter intransigence and the growth of Arab oil power—to give away Israeli security on a surge of emotion in response to a bold move by an extraordinary, brave Arab leader. He is right to treat the Sadat initiative as a historic beginning of serious negotiation.

Because this meeting was arranged by television, there is a danger that it will be judged by the need for a fresh lead every night. If stunning progress is not made, the meeting will be called a failure, and a refusal by

Israel to meet the most extreme Arab demands would be deemed un-
sportsmanlike conduct in the great new game of media diplomacy.

The presence of Mr. Sadat at the Knesset is a major concession in itself.
It requires not a quick, blockbuster comprehensive agreement to top it,
but a forthcoming attitude by the Israelis about territory claimed by
Egypt. As that takes place, the understandable sense of insecurity of Israelis will diminish, and other Arab nations will be encouraged to negotiate
on such matters as the access to Jerusalem and a solution to the Palestinian
problem.

We ought to take Mr. Sadat at his word that his trip is "a new start,"
and not a take-it-or-leave-it publicity stunt. Americans, observing, can
help by refraining from the measurement of peacemaking in terms of a
football team's momentum.

Peace, as the Egyptian leader eloquently put it, is a struggle. The only
peace that can last is one—to repeat the biblical reference made today—
where peace and justice embrace.

BARBARA'S DINNER PARTY

December 22, 1977

WASHINGTON—Barbara Walters gave a dinner party in Washington
recently to bring together the Ambassadors of Egypt and Israel, who had
never officially acknowledged each other in the past. The evening turned
out to be memorable, even though reports about it have a Rashomon-like
quality.

Art Buchwald, drawing on an old Jack Kennedy quip, praised his
ABC-TV hostess "for bringing together two men who have been ideologically miles apart, who fought each other over the years—Hamilton Jordan
and Bill Safire."

As it turned out, both Ham Jordan, who is President Carter's non-chief
of staff, and I got into trouble that night.

My social stumble was in making notes of the speeches. Whenever
present at a historical occasion, I like to write down everything I hear.
The editor of *The Washington Post*, who was under the impression that a
private dinner was off the record, took umbrage at my note-taking, and
later prevailed upon the hostess to point out to me that what I had written
down was not for publication. Under this peer pressure, and blushing at
my journalistic pushiness, I pocketed my notes.

Ham Jordan (he pronounces his name Jerden to differentiate himself from the river) did even worse. Seems he made a vulgar crack that some at his table took to be insulting to the lady next to him, who happened to be the wife of the Egyptian Ambassador.

An account of this episode appeared in the gossip column of *The Washington Star*, which evidently moved the editor of *The Washington Post* to rethink his previous insistence that Barbara's dinner for 40 was all off the record. So Sally Quinn of *The Post*, in her vivid style and in italics, recorded Mr. Jordan's crude behavior and earthy announcements. *The New York Times*, with decorum and reporting appropriate denials, covered the story in full.

Since the entire press corps followed this up by serenading Press Secretary Joseph L. Powell with "See the pyramids along the Nile" (in a heavy-handed reference to Mr. Jordan's crack), I feel somewhat lonely in my adherence to off-the-record strictures and will therefore print some notes.

Sorry, the Jordan incident took place at another table, and I have no lip-smacking details to add. On the contrary, my impression was that the Carter Administration was tastefully represented: Zbigniew Brzezinski came to the pre-dinner cocktails, stood properly silent as the two Ambassadors greeted each other for the first time, and then gracefully took his leave so as not to upstage Henry Kissinger, who is now upstageable.

Henry entered, embraced both the Egyptian and the Israeli Ambassadors, and said in a friendly way to the departing Mr. Brzezinski, "You I won't embrace." After dinner, when it came time for him to speak, the former senior official got off a good, self-deprecating line: "I have not addressed such a distinguished audience since dining alone in the Hall of Mirrors."

Then he turned serious, and the evening's mood reflected the wonderment so many of us feel at the Sadat-Beginning. Henry described the breakthrough as "more than a political act, a spiritual commitment," adding that he was "convinced that peace in the Middle East is inevitable—neither side can possibly miss this opportunity."

Israel's Ambassador Dinitz, with a sense of the occasion, paid tribute to his Egyptian colleague "for his ability and professionalism—and sometimes I wasn't too happy about it—but I always hoped the day would come when I could tell him that." He praised Mr. Sadat's "bold act" after which "the Middle East cannot be the same anymore." In lighting the Chanukah candles in his home, he recalled the smiling faces of the children he had watched on television welcoming the Egyptian President, and said it was "incumbent on us to give them a reason for their smile."

Ambassador Ghorbal rose. "For the first time," he said quietly and with feeling, "Ambassador Dinitz has spoken for both Israel and Egypt." The small, articulate diplomat changed the pace with an anecdote about Henry's shuttle diplomacy, and then told the television people in the room how the world watched "with fixed eyes and deep emotion" the warm greeting in Israel of President Sadat.

To the hushed room, the Egyptian pledged on behalf of his nation to strive for a full, comprehensive settlement "and not leave it to the next generation." He reminded his audience of the aspirations of the Palestinians, and raised his glass to the prospect of peace, to the Ambassador of Israel, and to President Carter.

There, in that room, at that moment, not even the most cynical media satrap present could help but be touched by the drama of the beginning of communication between two strong spokesmen of nations that have spent a generation at war.

The moment passed, the dinner ended, and we all fell to squabbling about ground rules for coverage and murmuring about the earlier behavior of a White House aide. But long after gaffes are forgotten, the warmth and graciousness of the first meeting of the two ambassadors at Barbara's dinner party will be remembered.

SILENCE IS GUILT

April 24, 1978

WASHINGTON—NBC-TV performed an enormous public service in showing a dramatic version of *The Holocaust* to a generation that wishes that memory would go away. That service is being nitpicked by viewers distressed at the need for commercial interruption; by people who might have preferred a "pure" documentary that might have reached a fraction of the audience; and by a minority of Jews who still fly the battle flag of "don't make trouble."

The nitpicking ignores the central question driven at least into nearly half of America's homes: Where the hell was the rest of the world when a part of the world was a Hell?

The best way to find the answer about a previous generation's lack of concern is to examine the turning-away from horror prevalent in this generation.

1. *The Soviet slave labor camps.* A former high official of the C.I.A. tells me that he vividly recalls a briefing of several years ago showing the extent of the Soviet slave-labor program, with a map pinpointing the scores of camps in Eastern Europe and throughout the U.S.S.R. This was not guesswork: As the Soviets know, we have high-altitude photographic surveillance detailing the barracks and work areas of each one of those camps.

Why do we tacitly condone this slave-labor practice by helping the Soviets keep it a secret? None of our intelligence-gathering sources and methods would be compromised by making public the pictures and details we know of camps and "asylums."

Not even Soviet dissidents know as much as we do about the logistics and location of all the camps. The publication of the photos and maps would hardly contribute to the spirit of détente, but might remind the world that the Soviet system has some festering sores to hide.

2. *The slaughter in Uganda.* Taking the low side of the best estimates, Idi Amin, butcher of Central Africa, has murdered at least 150,000 tribal dissidents. As a result, other leaders of Africa are slightly embarrassed but none want to say so publicly.

Does the White House, so ready to undermine internal settlements in Rhodesia, publicly excoriate the murdering Amin and urge sanctions to help topple him?

Hardly. A United States company, Page Airways, sells Uganda its commercial jet aircraft and helps supply its pilots and crews, thereby helping build Mr. Amin's power. Who runs Page Airways? James Wilmot of Rochester, New York. Who has long been the chief fund raiser for House Speaker Thomas P. O'Neill? James Wilmot. Who has been a most significant contributor to and fund raiser for the campaigns of Daniel Inouye, Democrat of Hawaii, until recently chairman of the Intelligence Committee, and a leading light on the Transportation Committee? James Wilmot.

The Speaker of the House—from John F. Kennedy's old district, one of the most liberal in the nation—is rarely even asked about his close association with the man who helps one of the bloodiest dictators in the world stay in power.

3. *The harassment of the Kurdish people.* The Communist-supplied government of Iraq has been systematically uprooting and destroying the culture of the non-Arab Kurds, who only want a degree of autonomy so as to continue their civilization.

But the United States, which secretly joined with the Shah of Iran to guarantee help to the Kurds in return for a 1973 agreement not to revolt, has washed its hands of the affair. One of the men who acquiesced in the sellout, Harold Saunders, is our newest Assistant Secretary of State, and will not permit the dying leader of the Kurds, General Barzani, to make a personal appeal to President Carter.

4. *The bloodbath in Cambodia.* In terms of numbers of people murdered, this generation's rival to Adolph Hitler is the leader of Communist Cambodia, Pol Pot. A population of two million was death-marched out of Phnom Penh. Many of the Cambodians being killed are of "mixed blood," marked for death because they are part Vietnamese.

Where are all the people who used to march around with those "Stop the Killing" signs? Untelevised death does not inspire them. At the United Nations, only one Ambassador—Israeli's Chaim Herzog—speaks against the genocide in Cambodia. The United States Ambassador, Andrew Young, cannot bring himself to upset third-world colleagues by demanding investigation and condemnation of the slaughter; to the shame of this nation, he sits silent as hundreds of thousands of human beings die.

Therefore, ask not how a previous generation could tolerate the murder of six million Jews; on a smaller scale, this generation is doing just dandy along those lines. The world still sees victims as pests, which should help us understand why Israelis are not about to let themselves become victims again.

April 24, 1978

Editor
New York Times

Dear Editor:

Your William Safire's criticism of April 24th of the insensitivity of today's world to the acknowledged brutality by people and government is quite justified. The comparison between today's savagery and the Holocaust is one of degree. But it does seem unfair to suggest that Speaker O'Neill's failure to condemn the atrocities in Uganda springs from the fact that James Wilmot is a fund raiser for the Speaker and the owner of Page Airways whose best customer is Idi Amin.

I want to defend Speaker O'Neill. He needs no inducement to remain silent about tyranny and oppression. Witness his reluctance to ever mention the performance of the British Army in Northern Ireland, or Amnesty International's findings or Great Britain's recent conviction by the European Court of Human Rights in Strasbourg of torture of Irish prisoners in Northern Ireland. "The people are silent," charges Safire, about Soviet slave camps, slaughter in Uganda, harassment of the Kurdish people and savagery in Cambodia. But then, Mr. Safire couldn't find space in his column to include Great Britain and Northern Ireland. So you see, O'Neill is not the only one guilty of silence. Yet I can't blame Safire either—it is O'Neill's relatives who are being gored.

Sincerely yours,
Paul O'Dwyer
New York

WORD OF DISHONOR

May 1, 1978

WASHINGTON—President Carter is reported to be icily furious at the Israeli Prime Minister for having the effrontery to object to the sale of the most lethal United States weaponry to Saudi Arabia. Mr. Carter suggests he is only carrying out a commitment made by his predecessor, making good America's "word of honor."

That turns both truth and honor on its head. Let's look at that secret deal:

According to an unpublished Senate Foreign Relations Committee study, in the late summer of 1976 "the Saudis received strong support in their bid for an advanced fighter aircraft from the State Department, especially from Secretary Kissinger and the Near East Bureau [Atherton] ... President Ford accepted the State Department recommendation."

Think about that: In the midst of the United States Presidential campaign, while President Ford was publicly making new commitments to Israel's defense (since repudiated by Mr. Carter), he secretly sends word to the Saudis through Mr. Kissinger and Deputy Secretary William Clements in October 1976 that the United States will break precedent and sell the Arabs the means to destroy America's ally.

Mr. Ford said to me this weekend: "I did approve a commitment that we would favorably consider a sale to the Saudis of a fighter of their choice, with a right to veto that choice if we thought their decision was militarily wrong from our point of view."

The truth is that Gerald Ford deliberately withheld the facts from the American people about Arab arms sales in October 1976. Mr. Carter, who publicly opposed such arms sales in the campaign, has seized upon that secret agreement-in-principle and has constructed an enormous "commitment"—now quite specific and throwing away our veto right—to attribute to his predecessor.

On Friday of last week, Senator Howard Baker told Secretary Cyrus Vance to tell the President to stop claiming the Carter plan to sell 60 F-15 attack jets was a commitment made by President Ford: Instead, the Carter proposal is a vast escalation of a general promise made to the Saudis in secret, and stripped of the balancing pledges made in public to Israel.

The time is long past when any American President or Secretary of State can pledge America's "word of honor" in secret, withheld from the Congressional review and contrary to public opinion in the United States. Born in secrecy, this Carter escalation and distortion of a Kissinger bribe ought to be dishonored forthwith.

Contrast the secret deal with the open, publicly debated commitment to

Israel. Withdraw from the strategic passes in the Sinai, Israel was told, and the United States will provide these aircraft to compensate for the loss to your security. The agreement was in writing, filed in the Congress. That is a commitment, a "word of honor"; and what has happened to it? Mr. Carter has now added a big "if," by linking the jets due to Israel with approval of the first lethal arms sale to the Saudis.

In coming weeks, Congress will change the Carter package around, giving some more planes to the Israelis, fewer to the Saudis, fiddling with delivery schedules. This entirely misses the point.

Selling Arabs the means to destroy Israel is a moral disaster for America. Let's stop kidding ourselves: The F-15 is the best airplane we build, and can park its missiles with uncanny accuracy in downtown Tel Aviv.

Oh, but that won't happen, we are told. The Saudis want the plan to match the planes we sell the Iranians, or to stand up to the advancing Cubans. Baloney: The United States can easily guarantee the Saudis against invasion by Cubans, without handing the Arab world the weaponry it needs to wipe out Israel.

The weakest justification is the Carter Morality-In-Arms-Sales Doctrine, which goes "if we didn't sell it to them, the French would get the business." The answer: Let them. If Frenchmen should decide to run the risk of having Israeli blood on their hands in any future war, that need not be the decision of Americans.

As long as the Saudis refuse to negotiate directly and as long as they are the financial backers of the P.L.O., it ought to be repugnant for any Congressman to sell them American weapons. Israel is safe only so long as the Arab world thinks Israel cannot be beaten.

If moderate Arabs are sincerely concerned with the Soviet military threat in Africa, let them make the peace that is readily available to them with Israel by: (1) resuming the peace talks broken off by Egypt after only 36 hours; (2) expanding the talks to include Saudi Arabia and Jordan; (3) making the agreement that both sides know is possible.

After the Congress sees that progress, after we can be assured that the weaponry would be used for self-defense, then—in public with Congressional consultation, and in writing—the United States can give, and live up to, its "word of honor."

"FIRST PEACE" FIRST

November 13, 1978

WASHINGTON—President Carter spent more than a year trying to bring about a Geneva-style "comprehensive" peace agreement in the Mideast—with Soviet representatives present and the radical Arabs having veto power over Egyptian actions—and failed.

At Camp David, by acceding to the noncomprehensive approach that both Israelis and Egyptians wanted—a "first peace" between those two nations, with another, separate, agreement for West Bank autonomy—the President started to succeed.

Today the completion of that "first peace" is threatened by Mr. Carter's renewed attempt to go "comprehensive," to force the Israelis to give up the West Bank and thus to establish the homeland for Palestinian Arabs that Israelis see as a knife in their side.

Here is how the preliminary accords have been endangered. President Carter sent State Department Arabist Harold Saunders (you remember him—he arranged the sellout of the Kurdish people at the behest of Mr. Kissinger and the Shah) to assure Jordan's King Hussein that his hope for the ultimate removal of Jewish settlements from the West Bank was not misplaced.

News of that Saunders-Hussein meeting, with its suggestion of withdrawal from an area the Israelis have no intention of abandoning, caused the Israelis to make a point of "thickening" their West Bank settlements with new settlers, as they had every right to do.

Those West Bank settlements are vital to Israel's security. Jordan claims that area by right of conquest in 1948; Israel claims it by right of history and in repelling an aggressive war in 1967; the P.L.O. claims it, too. Israel, by asserting its claim with the presence of Jewish settlers, makes possible a living-together compromise in that area under an autonomous local government—an effective neutralization. Even a hint of abandonment of Israel's claim would insure creation of a radical state capable of shelling Tel Aviv.

The Egyptians understand that. Mr. Sadat has tacitly accepted the West Bank settlements, just as he refused to accept Israeli settlements in Egypt's Sinai, where Israel does not claim sovereignty and has agreed to leave. That was why Mr. Sadat's reaction to the "thickening" of West Bank settlements was at first muted.

But the Carter Administration went through the roof at Israel's public reassertion of its right to settle in the face of the Saunders provocation. Since Mr. Sadat could not allow himself to be seen in the Arab world as any less militant on behalf of the Palestinians than Mr. Carter, he was drawn into upping the ante. The Egyptian called for the stronger tying-together of the specific first-peace agreement between Egypt and Israel with the general "framework of peace" agreement about the West Bank, adding his demand for a deadline on Israeli withdrawal of military forces from lands retaken in 1967.

That "linkage" of a solid deal with an ephemeral deal is a trap into which the Israelis will not step. Neither Egyptians nor Israelis have control over how soon an agreement can be reached with local Palestinians or King Hussein on West Bank autonomy. By tying that "iffy" West Bank negotiation with the Egypt-Israel peace treaty, Mr. Sadat and Mr. Carter would achieve exactly what Israel is determined to avoid—a "conditional" peace treaty.

Here's the trap: By its Egyptian treaty, Israel would be required to dismantle its bases in the Sinai and begin to turn the territory back to Egypt. But if that treaty were made conditional on a West Bank agreement, then unless Israel caved in to radical Arab demands, the Egyptians could *legally* claim that its treaty requirements have not been met; Mr. Sadat could then call the peace off. That's why Israel's desire for a clean first peace, unencumbered by "ifs" and loopholes, is so important. The "linkage"—the loophole that would allow Egypt to keep the Sinai without a peace if Palestinians, in terror of Mr. Arafat, refuse to cut a West Bank deal—is a central issue.

Amazingly, it is not Mr. Sadat who has reintroduced the issue that was successfully finessed at Camp David. The heat to write in the loophole comes from Mr. Carter, with his born-again "comprehensive" scheme, endangering the first peace by trying to force Israel to tie that treaty to the abandonment of its West Bank claims.

Evidently Mr. Carter has forgotten why Camp David succeeded: only because Mr. Sadat and Mr. Begin agreed to the principle of a solid, stand-by-itself first peace. By turning the clock back to 1977, the President is undermining everyone's best recent efforts.

White House insiders hint that the reason for the "linkage" pressure is to placate the Saudis, who have turned thumbs down on Camp David; this leaning on Israel is supposed to be in our interest.

But think about our strategic position: With 4,000 Soviet nationals now running Afghanistan; with the Shah of Iran seriously weakened; with Pakistan about to send a man to Moscow to negotiate an accommodation; with a powerful Cuban military force in Ethiopia capable of moving on the Mideast oil fields—would it not be a sound strategic move for the United States to establish reliable bases in the only democracy in the area?

CARTER BLAMES THE JEWS

December 18, 1978

WASHINGTON—We now know that the Camp David summit—that pre-election public relations extravaganza that halted for a time the crumbling of confidence in Mr. Carter's competence—produced no genuine agreement at all.

The two "accords" that were signed with smiles and hugs on prime-time television were (1) a separate peace between Israel and Egypt and (2) an independent "framework" for working out autonomy for the Palestinians if and when they wanted it. Mr. Sadat was evidently assured that the Saudis—whose cooperation Mr. Carter thought he had won with an agreement to deliver them our most sophisticated attack jets—would come around.

But Mr. Carter made a fatal miscalculation: The Saudis, with their arms deal already approved (thanks to Senators Byrd, Baker, and Ribicoff) double-crossed the Americans and supported the radical Arabs against the one-piece-at-a-time approach. The radicals want the Egypt-Israel treaty to contain an enormous "gift": to be valid only if Israel makes a deal to permit a militant, Soviet-armed state to be created on its border.

Mr. Sadat knew that the Israelis would be crazy to give up their main defense buffer—the huge, oil-producing Sinai—in return for an iffy treaty. But with the Saudis against him, the Egyptian leader began pressing for strong "linkage" between the two separate agreements.

On November 11, the Israelis agreed to a draft treaty put together in Washington under the benign eye of Secretary Vance. Israel complained about a side letter, not part of the treaty, that asserted a little more iffiness—but accepted the treaty.

Mr. Sadat figured that if Mr. Carter could not get the Saudis to stop pressuring Egypt, the U.S. President could at least get Americans to further pressure Israel. He then tore up the draft treaty and demanded anew all that he had been denied at Camp David.

The new Arab demands made a mockery of the "accords." If Israel did not accede to Palestinian demands by a deadline date, then Egypt—with the Sinai in its grasp—would not have to abide by its treaty. If Syria were to invade Israel again, then Egypt's treaty with Syria could take precedence over the iffy peace treaty with Israel. By no stretch of imagination could these and other new Arab demands be construed as being in the letter or the spirit of Camp David.

At that point, with Israel accepting and Egypt rejecting the draft treaty submitted by the Americans, Mr. Carter showed his pro-Arab tilt: Coolly, deliberately, he betrayed the Israelis.

He sent Secretary Vance to Cairo to characterize the Egyptian treaty rejection and fresh demands as "new ideas," and to hail the Sadat attitude as "forthcoming." Meanwhile, in a display of arrogance and petulance wholly alien to any "evenhanded" mediation, Mr. Carter in effect publicly endorsed the return of the Egyptians to their original hard line even before the proposals had been presented to Israel.

Secretary Vance in Cairo helped prettify some of the iffiness. The deadline was renamed a "target date," and the basic changes gutting the treaty draft were called interpretations "annexed to" the treaty—but still an integral part of the treaty, voiding the illegality of an Egyptian attack on Israel to support Syria.

Mr. Carter then blamed the crash of his Camp David effort on the Israelis. White House leaksters pointed to Carter's man, Vance, in Cairo getting marvelous cooperation; if Israel did not embrace the new U.S.-endorsed Sadat proposals, then the Jews would be guilty. Incredibly, the Senate Democratic leadership, in the person of Senator Robert Byrd, participated in this crude attempt to put the onus on Israel.

Even Cy Vance was embarrassed at being used as a "take it or leave it" messenger, too busy to stay for further discussion. He knew that the basic changes would be an abomination to all Israelis, and to present them as an ultimatum from Carter would force an angry rejection. But a job is a job; Mr. Vance does not argue with the boss.

The blame-the-Jews orchestration from the Carter men will continue while the President himself refrains, Kissinger-style, from saying so publicly. Joel Sherman, the U.S. spokesman most despised by the Israelis, is expected to let it be known on background that Mr. Begin is a liar; White House aide Ed Sanders will dutifully bring in groups of Jewish leaders to be told that Jimmy knows best about the survival of Israel; and news manager Gerry Rafshoon will arrange for foreign policy announcements—like the accommodation of China's wish for us to terminate our Taiwan defense agreement—to distract attention from the failure of the last big stunt.

Curious about that: We now know that the choice of December 15 as Chinese recognition day was made three months ago, at Camp David, where the date of December 17 was fixed as the moment for Egyptian-Israeli treaty signing. Do you suppose Mr. Carter was thinking that if one of his juggler's plates came crashing down about now it would be nice to have another plate sailing high in the air?

THOSE "ILLEGAL" SETTLEMENTS

May 24, 1979

WASHINGTON—As Israel and Egypt begin negotiations this weekend on the degree of autonomy to be given Palestinian Arabs, the central question is this: To whom does the West Bank belong?

Our State Department has no position about who owns that land, except to say that it does not belong to Israel. Although Secretary Vance admitted in 1977 that it is "an open question as to who has legal right to the West Bank," his spokesmen lose no opportunity to label Israeli settlements in that area as "illegal."

When a reporter asks for the legal opinion on which such condemnation is based, the best the State Department can come up with is a six-page letter written to House Foreign Affairs subcommittee chairmen on April 21, 1978, from legal adviser Herbert Hansell.

In that letter, Mr. Hansell pointed out that the U.N. partition of 1947 was "never effectuated"; that's a lawyerly way of saying that Trans-Jordan (the name meant "across the Jordan") grabbed the West Bank by invading the new Jewish state in 1948 and became the occupying power.

In 1967, Jordan's King Hussein saw a chance to take the rest of the land west of the Jordan River and joined the Syrian-Egyptian attack on Israel. The Arabs lost, and the West Bank—previously occupied by Jordan's troops—was then occupied by Israel.

Here the Hansell Doctrine takes its curious leap. Never mind that the West Bank was taken by force and occupied by Jordan in 1948, or that it was retaken by Israel while defending itself in 1967, or that its sovereignty was murky. Simply because Israeli troops went in, says Hansell, "under international law, Israel thus became a belligerent occupant of these territories."

From that pronouncement, all else flows: ". . . territory coming under the control of a belligerent occupant does not thereby become its sovereign territory," and under Article 49 of the 1949 Geneva Convention (intended to prevent displacement of populations) the "occupying power shall not transfer parts of its own civil population on to the territory it occupies." Hence, settlements are "illegal."

But the Israeli settlers are not displacing Arabs, and do not threaten to. Moreover, those rules were never applied to Jordan when it was the occupier. Oregon Senator Bob Packwood attacked the "illegal" charge in a speech last week: "From 1949 to 1967, Jordan held the West Bank. No second Arab-Palestinian state was ever created in those 18 years. No country except Great Britain and Pakistan ever recognized Jordan's sovereignty over the West Bank. No Arab country has ever conceded Jordan's right to the West Bank."

Sovereignty—who owns the land—is the key. Jordan claims it; the P.L.O. claims it; and Israel, through its continued settlement policy, asserts its own claims. The moment Israel gives up its right to settle, it gives up that claim to sovereignty. If Israel were to admit it is not at least part owner, an independent Palestinian state would be born, which—in this decade, at least—would be an intolerable threat to Israel's security.

That's why Mr. Carter, blind to the danger of a radical Arab state nestled in Israel's vitals, calls the settlements "an obstacle to peace"; in reality, they are an obstacle to the P.L.O.

At Camp David, when Menachem Begin presented his plan for self-government by Palestinian Arabs, he made clear that at the end of five years, if anyone else claimed sovereignty, Israel would also claim sovereignty: Israel was not giving up its interest in that West Bank land.

That's what the big flap in the Israeli Cabinet was about last week, as Israel and Egypt prepared initial positions. For openers, Mr. Sadat announced he would be calling for his extreme: a sovereign Palestinian Arab state. As promised, Mr. Begin countered with his own extreme: local autonomy of the people, but Israeli sovereignty over the land.

Defense Minister Weizman blew his stack at that; he felt such an honest laying of the cards on the table would distress Mr. Sadat. Foreign Minister Dayan patched things up by treating the position paper as "guidance" to the Israeli negotiators and as a paper to be handed the Egyptians.

That provides some more room to maneuver, but illustrates the essence of the negotiation: It's about sovereignty. If the negotiation succeeds, nobody will emerge the clear-cut sovereign power. Nobody—not Israel, not Jordan, not some autonomous entity—should wind up with *exclusive* sovereignty. National ownership can be shared; there can be no final settlement that does not include the right of Jewish settlers to settle.

We should be on our guard against phony Administration claims that only by pressuring Israel to give up its settlements policy can we induce the Saudis to embrace the Egyptians again. Mr. Carter should stop insisting Israel has no rights of sovereignty in the West Bank, and start urging the negotiators to find a middle ground—one that will enable Jews to live peaceably among Arabs in that Arab-populated land just as a half million Arabs live peaceably in Israel.

May 25, 1979

The Editor
The New York Times

Sir:

Mr. William Safire's essay published on May 24, 1979 should be awarded the National Award for Sophistry. In marshalling an impressive array of arguments and counterarguments regarding the West Bank, he overlooks in his rather convoluted article the basic principle of self-determination.

The dilemma of Mr. Safire and the State Department as to whom does the West Bank belong can be resolved by simply stating that the West Bank belongs to the West Bank people.

Who are the West Bank people?

Mr. Safire and the State Department share with us the fact that the West Bank people are Arab Palestinians who actually live on the West Bank; whose history unfolds there and who were born and die there. The West Bank, Mr. Safire, is not claimed by the P.L.O.; it is claimed by its Palestinian population. The P.L.O. speaks for them.

The argument of the sovereignty over the West Bank can be referred to the principle of self-determination which all civilized nations subscribe to. If the West Bank is populated by indigenous Arab Palestinians, and if we apply the principle of self-determination to those people, we will have no difficulty labelling the Jewish settlements as illegal at any given time in history. It is in the context of this concrete reality and in the context of the universally recognized right of self-determination, not because of Mr. Hansell's argument, that the Zionist settlers on the West Bank are illegal intruders and invaders.

Mr. Safire's suggestion to his President to stop insisting that Israel has no rights of sovereignty on the West Bank is tantamount to the U.S. divorcing herself from the stream of civilized, law-abiding nations, and to subscribe to the Zionist principle of creating borders wherever Jewish people settle.

Sincerely,
A. Hadi Toron
Director of Information
The League of Arab States
Arab Information Center
New York, New York

OF BLACKS AND JEWS

September 27, 1979

WASHINGTON—"The only thing necessary for the triumph of evil," wrote Edmund Burke, "is for good men to do nothing."

Secretary of State Cyrus Vance is generally considered a good man. No great shakes as a foreign policy expert, perhaps, but cool-headed, loyal to his boss, discreet, honorable.

Yet at the moment of truth in his tenure at State, he put loyalty and discretion ahead of honor and decided to do nothing about stopping the evil of racial-religious hatred from spreading through our body politic.

When Ambassador Andrew Young was forced to resign, the question that swept through the black leadership was: "Who got Andy? Was he fired because he offended the Israelis by meeting with the P.L.O., or was he fired because he lied to the State Department and made a fool out of the Secretary of State?"

If that question had been answered truthfully and promptly, much of the animosity that has developed between black leaders and Jews since that time would have been nipped in the bud.

The central facts are not in dispute. Mr. Young asserted he did not tell "the whole truth" to his superiors about his planned contravention of an American commitment. Shortly after that admission, Mr. Vance spoke to President Carter, with a State Department note-taker on an extension. Then Mr. Young's resignation was accepted.

The simple truth: Mr. Vance coolly pointed out that our Government had been placed in an impossible situation, putting out an untrue story supplied to it by an Ambassador operating on his own; unless Mr. Young did "the proper thing," Mr. Vance could never again be trusted to speak for the United States.

When asked about this, the departmental spokesman denied that there had been any "him or me ultimatum," adding that "the Secretary behaved in a gentlemanly fashion." That was surely factual—Mr. Vance is not the sort to bang his shoe on the table—but surely misleading. What really happened is that with great dignity and deference, Mr. Vance let the President know that he could not continue to serve along with Mr. Young. That's why Mr. Young, who did not want to leave, had to leave.

The subsequent outbreak of black anti-Semitism, and the impassioned embrace of the P.L.O. by some black leaders, could have been muted by a simple assertion of the truth: It was a betrayed Secretary of State, and not the Israelis, who "got" Young.

When a few White House aides realized the damage being done to American society, they urged Mr. Carter to set the record straight. The

President could not bear to do that: In his August 30 speech in Atlanta, his continued silence on the real reason for the Young resignation encouraged black distrust of Israel.

That left it to Secretary Vance. On September 5, he was asked twice, in the most precise terms: "Was the Young resignation brought about in fact by the American Jewish community, or the Israelis, or was it brought about as a result of his own actions?"

Exercising great lawyerly care, he absolved Jews in America but not Jews in Israel: "It was not the result of actions by the Jewish community." By selection, he seemed to be blaming both the Israelis and Mr. Young.

That stunned the Israelis, who had not sought the Young resignation; worse, it did not deter any black leader from believing that the Israelis "got" their Andy, which in turn encouraged the pilgrimages to Yasir Arafat.

Mr. Vance probably thinks to this day that he was merely being a good soldier, backing up the President, who did not want to offend his black support. But a half-truth can be as bad as a lie. Mr. Young's half-truth deliberately misled the Secretary of State, and Mr. Vance's later half-truths—that he didn't actually issue a "me or him" ultimatum and that he could not absolve the Israelis—deliberately misled the American people.

The whole truth will come out in memoirs years from now. In the meantime, Mr. Young's half-truths—on top of President Carter's craven evasion of responsibility—are fomenting bigotry and backlash.

Mr. Vance's refusal to speak the whole truth means that an Ambassador, fired for lying, has been treated to a free tour of Africa to help establish his private import-export business. It set up the media events of Jesse Jackson in Jerusalem, and of Mr. Young's meeting today with an ill and seriously debilitated Israeli Foreign Minister.

Sometimes, "for reasons of state," a U.S. official must button his lip. But when the reason for misleading Americans is purely political, and when the consequence of silence causes lasting harm, a good man will tell the whole truth.

Mr. Vance—long known as "the man who leaves no footprints"—has decided to let the racial hatred spread. Long after the "Georgia-Texas gang" joins the Harding "Ohio gang" in the pages of perfidy, the decision of this good man to do nothing will be remembered.

September 28, 1979

Editor
New York Times

To the Editor:

William Safire's vituperative attack on Cyrus Vance (Sept. 27) can only serve further to exacerbate racial difficulties between Jews and blacks. Safire's efforts to "get" Carter and his "gang" do nothing either to bring out the truth or to encourage less hysterical attitudes.

Safire calls Vance a liar on the basis of detailed knowledge of conversations at the highest levels of government. Even when he worked at the White House, Safire by his own admission hardly knew what was going on. He simply reveals his own lack of political sense. Of course the Israelis cannot be absolved of any part in the departure of Andy Young. Israeli politicians view any direct dealings with the P.L.O. as support for the enemy; they did not try to get Young because he was black, but because he was pulling American policy in a direction unacceptable to Begin's government. On the other hand, some of the strongest support for the radical states of the Third World comes from American blacks, who support the P.L.O. and therefore see Israel as a political foe.

The point which must be made is that there is no reason for American blacks and Jews to engage in racial quarrels because some members of their communities support opposing political forces. The solution is not to heap personal abuse on our government, but to encourage both sides to act more sensibly in resolving political differences.

Sincerely,
Steve Hochstadt
Instructor of History
Bates College
Lewiston, Maine

JOHN CONNALLY AND ISRAEL

October 15, 1979

WASHINGTON—For the first time, a candidate for President has delivered a major address which he knew would disturb and dismay every American supporter of Israel.

John Connally dusted off the old Brookings Institution "comprehensive" peace plan and told the Israelis (*a*) to get out of the West Bank completely, perhaps leaving it to "an entirely independent entity"; (*b*) to give the strategic Golan Heights back to Syria; (c) to give up Israel's exclusive sovereignty in Jerusalem, its capital.

In return for thus laying its head on the block, Israel would get "ironclad" promises of peace and the "strong military presence" of the United States.

Throughout this forcefully delivered speech, there appears an un-Connally-like fear of Arab oil power: "The oil of the Middle East is and will continue to be the lifeblood of Western civilization for decades to come. . . ." "There hovers over our nation the awful specter of economic upheaval. . . ." ". . . if, through a catastrophe in the Middle East, America's economy is gravely weakened, so too will be our ability to defend and support Israel." In other words, an oil embargo would so terrify us that we might let Israel sink.

Who encouraged this bellicose timidity? Connally sources insist that Henry Kissinger, who recently appeared at a Connally fund raiser and was all but anointed by the candidate as the future Secretary of State, "reviewed a draft." The man who began the U.S. "reassessment" four years ago added a paragraph hoping that West Bank Palestinians would choose to live in an autonomous area within Jordan—a pious wish that would hardly be the choice of the P.L.O.—and then gave his approval.

The part of the speech that would strip Israel of its present control of its own capital was the work of James Akins, a former U.S. Ambassador to Saudi Arabia who now represents companies doing business there. The speech contained some sound ideas: Scott Thompson, a Tufts College professor, stressed our increased presence in the Indian Ocean, and Richard McCormack, adviser to Senator Jesse Helms, had a hand in the suggestion of a regional development bank to pay off angry land claimants. The speechwriter was Sam Hoskinson, an ex-C.I.A. analyst who until recently was the hawk on Zbigniew Brzezinski's staff.

Rita Hauser, a veteran of Javits, Rockefeller, and Nixon campaigns who has been winning friends for Connally, was politely listened to but not heeded; more in sorrow than anger, she quietly resigned from the Connally campaign this weekend.

No adviser sold John Connally a bill of goods—this was exactly what he believes is in the long-run interests of Mideast peace. Nor was it a political aberration: For an oil man and a gambler, a get-tough-with-Israel posture may make sense.

First, the corporate managers who are sold on Connally, and who have helped make his campaign the best-financed of all, agree with his assessment of our dependence on the Saudis. Most corporate executives and bankers worry about Arab economic muscle, and want to be persuaded that if we were only to pressure the Israelis to go back to 1967 vulnerability the Arab oilmen would respond by not trying to drive a hard bargain on oil in decades ahead.

Second, some Republican county chairmen, and many of my fellow right-wingers who work in Republican primaries, have been looking for a scapegoat other than Jimmy Carter and the amorphous OPEC. When that jab-Israel message came from Jesse Jackson, they blanched; when a more responsibly phrased message came from John Connally, they perked up.

Therefore, Governor Connally did not speak, as he claimed, "without concern for political consequences." The challenger had to break from established policy ranks, show gutsiness, and shake loose some of those county chairmen. "So he loses the Jewish vote," a friend of his says. "In Republican primaries, that's not losing much."

Credit Mr. Connally with candor; unlike Jimmy Carter, he has made his "comprehensive" proposal before, rather than after, Election Day. Credit him, too, with sincerity: This is not only a political gamble, but has the added advantage, as the approving Henry would say, of being an expression of the candidate's genuine beliefs.

I think he is mistaken on both politics and policy. Voters here will not like the idea of first making Israel vulnerable and then endangering American lives; most would prefer, as the Israelis prefer, for America to help Israel defend itself.

Hard-liners in foreign policy are more likely to heed Ronald Reagan's stiffly phrased but sensible warning of a month ago: "Only by full appreciation of the critical role the State of Israel plays in our strategic calculus can we build the foundation for thwarting Moscow's designs on territories and resources vital to our security and national well-being."

After John Connally's speech last week, supporters of Israel—along with many others concerned with noisy U.S. weakness in the face of Soviet military and Arab economic threats—made a reassessment of Ronald Reagan and decided he looked ten years younger.

22 October 1979

Dear Mr. Safire:

Your piece on John Connally revealed your rabid, pro-Israeli, Semitic (anti-anti-Semitic) bias! Why?

Respectfully,
Wayne Sheeks
Professor of Philosophy
Murray State University
Murray, Kentucky

KURDS II

MY ACQUAINTANCE with the Kurds is explained in the first part of this book (pp. 82–88); these essays continue that interest into a time when the ethnic minorities of Southwest Asia suddenly gained recognition as a force to be reckoned with.

OF KURDS AND KISSINGER, CARTER AND CONSCIENCE

December 19, 1977

WASHINGTON—In last week's press conference, President Carter made a welcome reiteration of his concern for human rights. Let us examine a case in which recent American policy led to the loss of human rights by a people called the Kurds, and see if Mr. Carter is willing to help right a wrong.

Some history: In 1972, the Shah of Iran wanted to irritate and occupy the Soviet-supplied army of his radical neighbor, Iraq. He offered to help the Kurdish people—a non-Arab ethnic group, nearly three million of whom live in Iraq—in their long struggle for autonomy.

The Kurdish leader—Mulla Mustafa al-Barzani—understood the Shah's selfish motive, and suspected the Shah might encourage the Kurds to revolt and then pull the Persian rug if he wanted Iraq's help in world oil politics. So the Kurds asked the Shah for a partner in their support—the United States, which they trusted.

Accordingly, the Shah asked Mr. Nixon in Teheran in 1972 to join him in supporting the Kurdish uprising. Since it was in the American (and Israeli) interest to tie up a radical Arab Army in Iraq, the United States President agreed.

The Kurds sent Mulla's son and another Kurdish leader to Washington, to spell out what supplies would be needed. They met at C.I.A. headquarters with Richard Helms as well as a White House representative: Colonel Richard Kennedy, then Henry Kissinger's top N.S.C. deputy.

People who sat on both sides of that table agree that the Kurdish request was "sympathetically received," and within two months the C.I.A. station chief in Iran delivered to Mulla the United States commitment to help their fight for local self-government. Only supplies were promised, never any troops, and the cost—expected to be about $5 million worth of captured Soviet equipment—channeled through Iran.

The Kurds fought well for their homeland. During the October war in the Mideast in 1973, with the Iraqi Army looking two ways, their big opportunity came for an all-out attack. But the Israelis had turned the tide, and Mr. Kissinger did not want to further weaken the Arab cause. Word went to the Kurds from the United States and the Shah: Do not attack.

The Kurds obeyed, trusting the Americans. They paid dearly for that misplaced trust. In the spring of 1975, the Shah made a deal with Iraq, and sold out the Kurds, cutting off all supplies and telling them to give up. When the Kurds turned to the Americans, Mulla Mustafa (and the C.I.A. station chiefs) were amazed to find Mr. Kissinger washing his hands of the whole affair.

An ex-senior official maintains that we had been told by the Shah's men that a continued Kurdish rebellion would require two Iranian divisions, at a cost to the United States of $400 million; such a post-Vietnam covert investment was impossible. Maybe that's what Henry was told by Iran; it bore no relation to reality, as the last thing the Kurds expected or wanted was Iranian troops taking over their fight.

Whoever was to blame, an American guarantee was dishonored. An ethnic group that wanted only to speak its language and pursue its cultural traditions, as an autonomous region under the Iraqi flag, has since been systematically uprooted and dispersed.

The totalitarian state of Iraq has driven hundreds of thousands of Kurds out of their homes. Thirty thousand Kurdish Pesh Merga ("forward to death")—Mulla Mustafa's followers—were reported to be in concentration camps. Amnesty International has the names of 389 hostages—innocent wives and children of rebel soldiers now fighting once again in the hills—who have been jailed by Iraq, without medical care, in defiance of anybody's idea of human rights.

Mulla Mustafa, now 75 and ill, is in America trying to call Mr. Carter's attention to the plight of his people, to get world opinion to shame Iraq into halting its political executions, and to induce the United States President into mentioning his people's name to the Shah. But Mr. Carter is too busy making statements about human rights, and supporting entities for Palestinians, to see the old man.

Instead, the Kurdish leader was coldly received last summer by the former Kissinger aide who was in charge of first supplying the Kurds with supplies, and then cutting them off: none other than A. Leroy Atherton, now in Cairo as Mr. Carter's Assistant Secretary of State for the Mideast.

Making certain the Kurdish pleas are not heard by President Carter is the man who took over covert connections with the Kurds from Colonel Kennedy in 1973, and who then personally handled the supply and cutoff decisions for Mr. Kissinger: Harold H. Saunders, whose reincarnation in the Carter Administration is as Director of Intelligence for the Department of State.

As he focuses on the Mideast, President Carter would do well to consider the only human beings in that area currently being harassed, and their leaders executed, for daring to demand the kind of internal autonomy now being offered to Palestinian Arabs, and rejected by Iraq's rejectionists.

The Kurdish sellout was a stain on the Nixon–Ford years; by turning away, by refusing to rectify a wrong, Mr. Carter tacitly makes that disgrace his own.

"FORWARD TO DEATH"

March 12, 1979

WASHINGTON—Mulla Mustafa al-Barzani, veteran leader of the Kurdish people, received me for the last time a couple of months ago in his small but well-guarded house in Virginia. Since we shared a fondness for pistachio nuts, he put a large bowl of the Iranian nuts between us, and as we shelled, he talked.

The Kurds, he pointed out, are an ancient people, Moslem, but not Arab, with a history, culture, and language distinctively their own. Although Kurdistan covers a large area, it is not a nation; 16 million Kurds live in Iraq, Iran, Turkey (where they are called "mountain Turks"), a few in Syria and Russia. Because the stiff-necked Kurds refuse to be assimilated, they are oppressed almost everywhere.

Mulla Mustafa, whose father was hanged by the Turks for leading an independence struggle, continued to fight in northern Iraq.

In 1972, the Shah of Iran wanted to cause trouble for his neighbor, Communist-supported Iraq. He offered the Kurds arms to support a rebellion which would tie down the Iraqi Army. Mulla Mustafa al-Barzani—ready, as usual, to accept help from any source—did not trust the Shah, but he did trust the Americans. He told the Shah that the Kurds would take the arms (mainly Russian guns captured by Israel in 1967) and launch guerrilla war, *provided the Americans guaranteed that the Shah would not suddenly cut off the supplies.*

The Shah asked President Nixon for this U.S. participation when the President passed through Teheran after his 1972 Moscow summit. Nixon and Kissinger later sent Treasury Secretary John Connally to the Shah with our agreement to help supply the Kurds. To seal the deal and assure the Kurds they would not be double-crossed, a Kissinger aide met with a Barzani son at the C.I.A. in Washington.

With the Americans firmly if secretly behind them, the Kurds began their fight in earnest. In October 1973, after Arabs launched the Yom Kippur surprise attack against Israel, and while the Iraqi Army was looking south, Barzani saw his big chance to start a decisive uprising.

Henry Kissinger said no. On October 16, 1973, he directed C.I.A. Director William Colby to send General Barzani this message: "We do not consider it advisable for you to undertake the offensive military action that another government [Israel] has suggested to you."

Trusting the United States, the Kurds obeyed, which was the greatest mistake of Barzani's life. Unknown to him and to the U.S., the Shah had an oil cartel to be called OPEC in mind, and needed the Iraqis. The Shah struck the new deal: Iraq would follow his lead on pricing and production, while the Shah would cut off the Kurdish revolt.

In March 1975 the Shah signed a friendship pact with Iraq; one day later, the Iraqi Army moved against the Kurds. General Barzani, his fear of double-cross realized, turned to the Americans, whose guarantee he had taken and whose orders he had followed.

In what was surely the most shameful foreign policy act of the Ford Administration, the United States—in the persons of Henry Kissinger and his closest Mideast aides, Alfred Leroy Atherton and Harold Saunders—turned its back on the Kurds. To the amazement of the C.I.A. station chief in Teheran, no U.S. diplomatic pressure was put on the Shah to remind him of his—and our—pledges of support to the Kurds.

The Kurdish fighters were slaughtered. Following their defeat, the Kurds were systematically dispersed and their culture shattered. When U.S. Congressional investigators sought information on this secret betrayal, they reported that they had been told by Henry Kissinger: "Covert action should not be confused with missionary work."

In the vain hope that the Carter Administration represented a change in moral climate, Mulla Mustafa al-Barzani came to the United States to plead for humanitarian aid and United Nations backing to stop the destruction of his people. But the Mideast specialists chosen by Carter turned out to be Kissinger's men—the same Atherton and Saunders—who refused to give Barzani access to the White House.

So his mission failed, Barzani said, shelling the pistachio nuts. Arabs, who talk of "legitimate rights" of Palestinians, fall silent at the mention of the Kurds, who want only the autonomy that Palestinians have already been offered. The Israelis, too, are silent, having done nothing for Kurds who smuggled 3,000 Jews to freedom. And the U.S. State Department has been waiting for Barzani's long-promised quiet demise.

The fiercely proud old man obliged them last week, dying at 75. In our last talk, he remarked that the name of his guerrillas, the Pesh Merga, means "forward to death," and that after him would come others—in Iran, Iraq, and elsewhere in Kurdistan—until Kurds achieved *sarbasti*—freedom.

He pushed aside the small mountain of shells between us and handed over a napkinful of small green kernels; for the past hour, the old desert chieftain had been shelling the nuts for his guest.

14 March 1979

Dear Mr. Safire:

I was moved by your article on Mullah Mustapha al-Barzani, and saddened.

In the Fall of 1973 my younger brother and I drove an old Volkswagen across Asia, just before I went to work for Senator Henry Jackson in Washington. We came in touch with many Kurds: tough, fascinating, fiery people. I am still captivated by them.

A few years later I was sitting in the Senator's front office, talking to a group of constituents, when a short stocky man walked in, followed closely by two tall swarthy companions. When the short fellow sat down, he looked at me and I him. The fiery look in his eyes made my spine tingle. Moments later another member of Senator Jackson's staff, Richard Perle, came in and took him into the Senator's office.

As they walked in, I grabbed Richard and asked him who that man was. "Barzani," he said. So that was the man. I'll never forget that look, or the man behind it.

Thank you for writing that article.

Sincerely,
Jere Van Dyk
Washington, D.C.

THE KURDISH QUESTION

October 20, 1979

WASHINGTON—One of the reasons the price of gold has been jumping is the belief held by many wealthy Middle Easterners that a coup or a
civil war will soon take place in Iran. The gold buyers guess that whatever
the result—a Soviet-supported regime or a scorched-earth guerrilla war—
the amount of Iran's oil available to the West will decline, and the price of
oil (usually followed by the price of gold) will rise.

The shakiness of Ayatollah Khomeini's government was underscored
by the surprisingly strong uprising of the Kurds, who drove off the Ayatollah's militia and had to be driven into the mountains by the F-4's and
helicopter gunships of Iran's regular armed forces.

The Kurds are a remarkable people. They are a distinct ethnic group—
non-Arab, Sunni Moslem, with their own language, customs, and dress—
who live in Kurdistan.

For a thousand years, Kurdistan has been a place but not a country.
Saladin, a Kurd, fought the Crusaders, but Kurds have always lived—and
grimly maintained their cultural identity—under other nations' flags. The
area called Kurdistan is now carved up by Turkey (which calls its six
million Kurds "mountain Turks" and outlaws the Kurdish language);
Iraq (which has depopulated several Kurdish regions and seeks to assimilate its two million Kurds); and Iran (where four million Kurds are
threatened with what Ayatollah Khomeini calls "a feast of blood").

The Kurds in Iraq were pro-Western, under the late Mulla Mustafa
Barzani, but he was double-crossed by the Shah, whose perfidy was
blandly countenanced by Henry Kissinger and his aide, Harold Saunders,
in an American disgrace previously recounted in this space. The Kurds in
Iran are mainly pro-Soviet, except for Barzani's son, but ideology is not
the prime motivator: These bloody but unbowed people are "for" whoever will help them achieve autonomy.

The Kurds are not talking of "self-determination," though that was
what they were promised at the Treaty of Sèvres in 1920. Nationhood is
too wild a dream; all they want is the right to live—*as Kurds*—under
whatever flag happens to be flying overhead. They seek autonomy, not
sovereignty. They want to be let alone, to have their culture respected.

That reasonable quest has provoked the greatest series of hypocrisies in
the world today.

P.L.O. leader Yasir Arafat, who wants not only sovereignty in the West
Bank but claims all of Israel, has embraced the Ayatollah in Iran, even as
that old revolutionary crushes a distinct ethnic group that wants autonomy in that country.

The Soviet-supported Baathist regime in Iraq inveighs against Egypt for not fighting for independence of the Palestinian Arabs, while Iraq scatters the non-Arab Kurds who dare to hold on to their identity in Iraq.

Drafts of resolutions blow through the halls of the United Nations in New York, presaging the establishment of a separate state for a new "people" called the Palestinians, while no voice is raised in that entire establishment for the legitimate rights of an ancient people now being denied by Iraq, Iran, Turkey, and Syria.

Here in Washington, Assistant Secretary of State Harold Saunders (the man responsible for denying the dying General Barzani access to the Carter White House to press his plea) treats the Kurds as an embarrassment as we seek to curry favor with the Ayatollah.

The Carter human-rightists are not only silent about the Kurds, but quietly worked to defeat them: Eight times this year, an Iranian 747 cargo jet came to the United States bearing the household goods of ejected U.S. citizens, and returned to Iran with previously purchased spare parts for the F-4's and gunships that strafed Kurdish mountain redoubts.

That arms delivery could have been cut off with a word from Mr. Saunders. (Presumably, we needed the returning furniture.) Mr. Saunders reserves his objections to the use of U.S. equipment by Israelis preventing terrorists in Lebanon from launching attacks on Jews; no word or protest is raised about using U.S. spare parts to keep jets and gunships on missions to massacre Kurds in Iran.

Kurdish rights are ignored wherever P.L.O. supporters are lionized for a simple reason: Every day the Palestinian leaders are turning down the offer of autonomy that Kurdish leaders are fighting and dying for. If Shiite Moslem Iranians and Iraqi Arabs were to give the Kurds the degree of self-government that the Israelis are today offering the Palestinian Arabs, the Kurds would happily accept the *sarbasti*—freedom—they have been fighting for.

In their travels in the Mideast, men like Harold Saunders, Andrew Young, and Jesse Jackson might ask their hosts the Kurdish question: Why do national leaders who loudly demand a sovereign state for the P.L.O. ruthlessly—and now bloodthirstily—suppress the legitimate rights of autonomy of an ancient people on their own territory?

THE SOVIET THREAT

THE mid-70's were not good years for hawks. The intellectual fashion in foreign policy was set by President Carter in 1977, when he derided the "inordinate fear of Communism" that had characterized our previous dealings with the Soviet Union.

Détente, which had been sought from a position of strength and realism in the early 70's, was pursued with more naïveté and greater weakness as the decade wore on. Those who warned of a tolerance for this shift in the balance of power were named "cold warriors" by Soviet propagandists; Radio Moscow excoriated those "unreconstructed hawks" who wanted to rescind the misbegotten Helsinki Agreement and put some muscle in our arms control negotiations.

That American drift into defenselessness was arrested as the 80's began, after the Soviet invasion of Afghanistan; suddenly, it became hard to find a dove in any aviary. These essays were written during the hard years of softness.

ARMS AND THE MAN: PATIENCE AND FORTITUDE

April 4, 1977

WASHINGTON—"Barbaric!" an infuriated Leonid Brezhnev shouted at the President of the United States and his three advisers. He thumped the table, complaining bitterly and at length about American actions on a less-than-strategic matter that threatened détente. "Just like the Nazis," he charged, and railed on uninterrupted for 15 minutes.

The date was May 24, 1972, the place was the Brezhnev dacha outside Moscow, and the subject of Mr. Brezhnev's ire was the mining of Haiphong Harbor in Vietnam just before the summit conference. After the American President heard him out, refusing to shout back, the Soviet anger subsided and the work of détente went forward.

Five years and two American Presidents later, Soviet leaders are once again roaring their rage. This time the provocation was, first, the needling they have been given on the suppression of human rights; and next, the temerity of Americans to come up with an arms control proposal that did not acquiesce in future Soviet nuclear superiority.

That the Russians are angry does not in itself mean that President Carter is doing something right; in fact, by floating out the details of his proposals in the newspapers before discussing them with Soviet officials, the President unnecessarily insulted the Soviet Union. The aw-shucks, I'm-an-open-book approach is out of place in some diplomatic negotiations.

Nor does Secretary Vance and his traveling party look all that professional this week. His first mistake was to steam up the press with "high hopes" as he entered Moscow; his second to breathlessly hang on such clues to the Soviet reaction as Mr. Gromyko's presence at the Bolshoi Ballet; and his worst mistake was to have somebody on his staff say, in effect, "Boy were we a bunch of dopes!" when the Soviets lowered the boom.

Those are the tactical errors of an Administration with a heart too soon made sad and of a President not confident enough of his support.

But neither do the Soviet denunciations mean that Mr. Carter has done anything substantively wrong. On the contrary, the arms control approach designed by National Security Adviser Zbigniew Brzezinski is considerably more toughminded and sensible than the détente-first compromises offered by Secretary Kissinger a year ago.

The first thing Mr. Carter did right was to inform Soviet Ambassador Dobrynin of the essence of the American approach in February. The recent profession of shock and amazement by the Russians is a negotiating ploy, and the President should not help it along by agreeing his proposals were turned down because they were "radically new."

The next thing Mr. Carter did right was to seek to cut down the Soviet lead in missile size, or "throw-weight." If parity is the goal, it makes little sense for the United States not to challenge the Soviet superiority in this area.

Most important, Mr. Carter snatched off the table some United States concessions of last year regarding the one weapon that is giving the Soviets fits—the cruise missile, which at the moment is the greatest single incentive we have to bring about arms control.

That upsets the Russians, whose negotiating technique is to assume all concessions offered as final, with no possibility of withdrawal. But we need not play into their hands. The cruise missile has not been negotiated away, and before it is, we should make certain we achieve effective equality in other strategic areas.

"They say to us, don't develop the cruise missile, and don't develop the MX missile," a Carter aide points out, "and they say what a threat to world peace those weapons would be. If we say O.K., we won't, what'll you give us for not doing it? they reply, We won't pay you for them, you never developed them. Well, the hell with that."

Such talk is good to hear, because the public opinion crunch will begin in about a week, after the first flush of support for any United States President being denounced by the Russians fades, and the second-guessing begins.

The hand-wringing in Secretary Vance's traveling party is a preview: If only we had cooled it on human rights, the chorus will soon begin, or if only we had gone the route of Kissinger détente, or if only we hadn't been so beastly about hanging on to our cruise missile.

Pressure will build on Mr. Carter from dovish supporters who think that if the Soviet Union turns down a United States offer, then there must have been something wrong with the offer. It never quite dawns on them that the Russians may be turning it down cold because it is an eminently fair offer, or one designed to elicit a reasonable counteroffer.

Then will Mr. Carter's resolution be tested. He will be griped at from abroad and sniped at from home, and anxious to show some kind of progress. If he is patient, and keeps his cool, the anger of the Soviet leaders will subside and the work of genuine détente can go forward.

IN FRANCE: "THE NEW PHILOSOPHERS"

October 10, 1977

PARIS—The word "Eurocommunism," I am informed by Flora Lewis of *The New York Times*—who learned this from Artigo Levi of Italy's *La Stampa*—was coined by a Yugoslav named Franj Barberi, who invented the phrase in one of his articles in Milan's *Il Giornale*.

The catchy label describes what purports to be a new form of Communism—not that nasty kind practiced in the Soviet Union, but wearing a "human face"—a kind of Marxism that claims to be independent, indigenous, and willing to obey the rules of democratic elections. Such a benign Communism, we were told, would pose no threat if it were to share power in the Western European nations.

That notion of a peacefully evolutionary Communism, led by French-men or Italians who profess to scorn the "proletarian internationalism" line from Moscow, was given a swift kick in the head recently by the decision of the French Communists to say to their socialist partners on the left: "No more Mr. Nice Guy."

Why, with electoral power just around the corner, has the French left split wide apart?

First, the Communists would rather be first in opposition than second in power. They do not trust their Socialist ally, François Mitterrand, and want to be certain he publicly buys the Communist line of nationalization before they help put him on top. The Communists are quite willing to ride to power in a moderate socialist vehicle, but they want their seat in the ideological driver's seat secure.

Second, Communist leader Georges Marchais responded to Soviet party discipline. A few weeks ago, he told a journalist friend he expected no problems in the "common program" with the socialists. Days later, Moscow pulled the strings, probably through the head of the French trade unions, and Mr. Marchais suddenly blossomed in his true red colors, demanding that Mr. Mitterrand subscribe to the nationalization of over 700 specific companies.

Moscow has made known its approval of this hard line. Not only does this send a stern signal to every Eurocommunist in Italy and Spain who might be starting to believe the rhetoric of compromise and independence, but it strengthens French President Giscard d'Estaing, who has been a firm economic and diplomatic ally of the Soviets, and who is preferred by them to either the Socialists or the right-wing Gaullists. Until the Communists can really take over in France, Moscow much prefers dealing with the center; Lenin always reserved his fiercest loathing for the Socialists.

What does all this "thunder on the left" teach the United States? Essentially, it drives home the fact that the "human face" of Eurocommunism is merely a mask: that Communism remains, as 27-year-old former Maoist Bernard-Henri Levi calls it, "barbarism with a human face."

Mr. Levi is one of "the new philosophers," a group of young and articulate activists who have rejected ultra-left discipline, and whose best-selling criticism—using the language of the left in the cafes along the Seine's left bank—has been giving the Communists fits.

"The new philosophers" were double-crossed by their Communist leaders in the student riots of 1968, and were revolted by the proofs of Communist brutality in the Gulag, as recounted by Solzhenitsyn. This has left them both anti-Communist and anticapitalist, fuzzily pro-ecology and pro-do-your-own-thing; what preserves them from intellectual hippyism is their clear insight into the nature of Communism.

For generations, idealistic youths have excused the totalitarianism of Communism as a necessary means to a good end—as Russian aberration, its cruelty not needed in Western societies. But "the new philosophers" warn that Communism everywhere relies on brutality and repression as central to its process.

Across a coffee in the Twickenham Bar, Levi explained: "Some friends were going to take an ad that said 'The Soviet Union is not a truly Socialist country.' Usual thing, the Russians were spoiling Communism. But I said no, we should take an ad that says—'The Soviet Union *is* a Socialist country.' The brutality is not on the way to the system, the brutality is a part of the system."

That is a point one hopes will get across to befuddled United States diplomatists who think Eurocommunism is more a problem to the Soviets than to the West, or who are unwilling to tell European friends that a turn toward Communism would mean the end of the United States defense of Western Europe. The disunion of the Left in France should send Mr. Carter a message: The Communists are not playing to participate in democracy, they are playing to win power in the long run.

"The new philosophers" know that. And how was that phrase coined? "I was doing this collection of pieces in a newspaper," says the engaging Mr. Levi. "And I was tired, and it was 2:00 A.M., and there was a deadline, and there was this girl waiting, so I said to go with 'the new philosophers.'"

THE SALT SELLERS

November 14, 1977

WASHINGTON—Customer comes into a grocery store, sees the shelves loaded with huge bags of salt, barrels of salt blocking the aisles. Says to the grocer: "You must sell a lot of salt." Grocer replies: "I hardly sell any salt, but the salesman from the salt company—can he sell salt!"

The man President Carter has placed in charge of his campaign to sell the Senate and the public a treaty coming out of the Strategic Arms Limitation Talks is David Aaron, the ex-Mondale aide who is now our Deputy National Security Adviser.

As every merchandiser knows, a new product needs a marketing plan, an advertising agency, big-name endorsements, and a way of discrediting the hard-line competition.

(a) *The master plan.* This was circulated on July 26 by Les Gelb of the State Department, formerly a colleague of mine at *The Times,* who likes to use phrases like "the intrinsic fungibility of cruise missile technology" to describe the ease with which we could break down and trade away our most useful new weapon.

The crucial part of the 18-page plan has already worked: Congress has been kept out of approving the extension of the first SALT agreement, which ran out last month. "We should plan to extend the Interim Agreement," wrote Mr. Gelb this summer, underlining this sentence, "preferably through parallel, non-binding declarations, avoiding formal extension that would legally require Congressional approval." The Soviets went along; Congress was cut out, and will not fully learn the details of the U.S.-Soviet agreement until a treaty is submitted next year.

(b) *An ad agency.* The group formed to take full-page ads hailing the virtues of SALT no matter what the agreement is calls itself "The American Committee on East-West Accord." It is run by old Fulbright hand Carl Marcy and partly bankrolled by General Motors heir Stewart Mott.

On August 5, the East-West accordianists received a letter from Assistant Defense Secretary Thomas Ross bemoaning the fact that the law prohibits the Pentagon from producing "sexy propaganda footage such as that put out by the Soviet Union" and "I'm afraid we must leave it to interested private groups such as yours to produce films in this area."

(c) *Expert, big-name endorsements.* The long-abandoned advisory committee on arms control—a group that used to be fairly balanced between hawks and doves, all experts—is now being set up by Hamilton Jordan's office.

One carry-over expert is Harold Agnew (no kin to the novelist) of Los Alamos, who earned his way back on by signing a letter of support for the disarming Paul Warnke, who then turned our disarmament agency into a dovecote. The "Charles River Gang" will be represented by Paul Doty of Harvard and Jack Ruwena of M.I.T. One or two hard-liners will be included for window dressing. Also chosen are Democratic fund-raiser Arthur Krim of United Artists, who can advise on SALT because he once distributed a war movie; Paul Austen of Coca-Cola because he's the re-ul thing; and what White House wags call a "three-fer"—someone who can give the group balance by being black, a woman, and a cleric simultaneously.

The SALT lobby's prime catch will be Brent Scowcroft, Gerald Ford's National Security Adviser. He will be used to give a Kissinger flavor to the SALT agreement, while Henry publicly temporizes.

(d) *Discrediting the competition.* To make certain Congress is given no embarrassing material on weakening United States defenses, David Aaron sent a memo on October 18 to State, Defense, A.C.D.A., the Joint Chiefs, and C.I.A.: "All responses to requests from the Congress for such material [SALT data and analyses] should be cleared through the SALT Working Group."

To stop the leaks about planned concessions that might disturb the public, the job of Chief Plumber has been given dovish Iowa Senator John Culver. Last week, he demanded an investigation into the way fungible columnists like Evans and Novak get their stories. This, if pursued seriously, would mean lie-detector tests for Congressional staff and ultimately would lead to surveillance of suspected leakers and their press contacts. Here we go again.

We are witnessing an amazing anomaly. In the past, secrecy was demanded by those interested in protecting national security; today, secrecy is being demanded by those who are unwittingly undermining national security. Meanwhile, men who took seriously their clearances for top secret—from defense expert Paul Nitze to yours truly—find that the cause of national security can be served only by forcing into Congressional and public view the concessions being kept secret from the American public but not from Soviet negotiators.

Will the White House merchandisers be able to sell their SALT? Not with this plan, and not with their current product. It takes only 34 senatorial customers to say no "and can they un-sell salt!"

RESCIND HELSINKI

May 29, 1978

WASHINGTON—"Okay, so our Africa policy has turned out to be a disaster," says a Carter supporter heatedly. "And okay, we look a little desperate blaming Congress now for constraints that we supported all along. But what do you want us to do to discourage the Russians in Africa—send in U.S. troops? Break off the SALT talks? Blockade Cuba?"

American diplomats who would like to find a way to penalize Soviet expansionism without resort to brinkmanship might consider a proposal that is beginning to be discussed in hard-line circles: the renunciation of U.S. approval of the 1975 Helsinki Agreement.

That misbegotten 35-nation accord, which does not have the force or status of a treaty ratified by the U.S. Senate, marked the high-water mark of Brezhnev diplomacy. The Helsinki "final act" fulfilled a generation-long dream of Soviet leaders: to have the Western nations ratify and implicitly endorse the Soviet conquest of Eastern Europe. The U.S. was roped into the negotiations leading to this Soviet triumph during the heyday of détente. In 1972, we agreed to negotiate toward a European Security Conference in return for a Soviet promise to negotiate toward a Mutual and Balanced Force Reduction (MBFR) agreement, which we believed would have lessened the danger of war in Europe.

Both negotiations began, as agreed. But as the Soviets planned, the MBFR negotiations led nowhere—they are still dragging on hopelessly—but the border-fixing negotiations that the Soviets wanted to succeed were crowned with success.

After conservatives in the United States began to wonder about the wisdom of giving the Soviets the border approval they wanted in return for nothing, the Ford Administration—in need of a summit—came up with a reason to go to Helsinki: "Basket Three," an addition to the accord that promised human rights to the oppressed, human dignity to the dissidents, and a new openness in communication across the Iron Curtain.

Some accommodationists swallowed this line; when hard-liners gagged at the empty promises, a final sweetener was put in the deal to convince conservatives that the Soviets would be held to account: A follow-up conference was to be held in Belgrade in 1977 in which progress on the human rights "basket" was to be carefully reviewed.

The Soviet Union began ignoring their human rights promises the day after the Helsinki Agreement was signed. Immigration was restricted; refuseniks were harassed; dissidents were jailed in a new crackdown.

The Belgrade review conference which ended a few months ago was a mockery; U.S. representatives whimpered a bit for the record, but the Carter human rights crusade turned out not to apply to Communist countries. Our executive-Congressional commission fretted and then voted itself a new junket in a few years so the newly hired staffers can fret some more.

What did we get for agreeing to negotiate the agreement the Soviets wanted so badly? Nothing. What did we get for our pains in writing in human rights guarantees? A horse laugh from Moscow. And what are we doing to retaliate? Just going along with what the Soviets wanted, recognizing the inviolability of their European borders.

We are not required by international law to go along with this charade. Since the Helsinki Agreement is a "declaration of intent" and not a treaty, what a stroke of the Ford pen has done can be undone with a stroke of the Carter pen.

Would this be going back on our "word"? Just the opposite: It would be assessing, as we had promised, Soviet performance on human rights. They have broken their word; therefore, we should notify the world that the United States signature is nullified.

A resolution of the Congress asking the President to consider this action would surely cause consternation in the Kremlin. Informal discussions of this idea among NATO diplomats now in Washington might induce a couple of our allies to stop complaining about lack of U.S. leadership and to follow our lead.

The hard-liners know that serious discussion of formal rejection of the Helsinki "final act" would be a bargaining chip itself. Previous U.S. Presidents were able to use the Mansfield Amendment (calling for the return of U.S. troops from Europe) as a lever in getting our European allies to share more fairly in their own defense; in the same way, this President could use a "rescind Helsinki" action to dramatize to the Soviets that adventurism has specific diplomatic costs.

This is no parlor game: Mr. Brezhnev is proud of the pledge to honor Soviet conquests extorted from the West at Helsinki. And Kissingerians will react contemptuously to a move to rectify their blunder.

But a move to cancel our approval of the agreement that the Soviets have already broken would be legal, nonbelligerent, and cost-free. It would send a message to the Kremlin that their continued duplicity will make the "final act" no act at all.

June 7, 1978

To the Editor:

In his May 29 column William Safire recommended that the United States should denounce the Helsinki Agreement and refuse to recognize the inviolability of the Russians' European frontiers, in which he sees a unilateral Soviet advantage from this accord. He thereby places the United States, one of the winners in the war, in the tragicomical position of a revenge-seeker not accepting its results.

The whole of Europe represented at Helsinki recognized the inviolability of postwar frontiers on the old continent, both to Soviet and all-European advantage. If the United States follows Mr. Safire's recommendation, it will make the entire world get out of step, and only the United States will be keeping pace.

As the reason for crossing out the U.S. President's signature on the "final act" he mentions American remarks concerning the implementation by the Soviet Union of the "third basket" part of the Helsinki Agreement and the Soviet position at the negotiations in Vienna. He fails to take into consideration the fact that the Soviet side also has remarks regarding the U.S. fulfillment of the obligations arising from all the three "baskets" and the position of the West at the Vienna negotiations.

One of them is the elementary commitment assumed in Helsinki to make the text of the agreement widely known to the population.

Your newspaper could publish an interesting report on the difficulties one may encounter in trying to get the full text even at the New York Public Library. I, for one, have published such a report. Your respected newspaper did print "excerpts" from the draft of the agreement, yet it is little read in Peoria, Ill.

I am constantly surprised at how Americans venture to judge the fulfillment of an agreement whose text is inaccessible to them. In the Soviet Union the text of the agreement has been published in an edition of 20 million copies.

The main idea of Helsinki is the materialization of détente. Of course, efforts, the good will of participants, and compromises are needed, but intimidation by denunciation is not. It is necessary to continue the game rather than to overturn the chessboard with its pieces.

In order to cure the cold Mr. Safire claims to have diagnosed, he suggests, in fact, removing the head.

Just think of the consequences for détente.

Gennady Gerasimov*
Moscow

SOVIET LAYER CAKE

July 10, 1978

WASHINGTON—What are the Russians up to?

One week, they arrest an American businessman on trumped-up spy charges, and the next week, they hang a medal on an American cellist for the way he plays Tchaikovsky's "Variations on a Rococo Theme."

One week, they expand into Afghanistan and increase the pressure in Africa, and the next week, they stun the West with a constructive proposal on the reduction of tanks and troops in Europe.

Next week, in the midst of Stalinist show-trials to shut up dissidents and uppity Jews, they serenely sail into another round of the Strategic Arms Limitation Talks with a thoroughly flummoxed American Secretary of State.

Is there a pattern to their moves? Or is some internal convulsion going on between the Kremlin's expansionist neo-politicians and ideological purists, similar to the foreign policy dissension in the troubled Carter White House?

To give coherence to recent Russian conduct, diplomats put forward the "layer cake theory": that in its external relations, the Soviet Union deals on different levels, each with its own priority. Within each layer, counterpressures are expected, but they are trying to convince us not to link apples and oranges, not to mix one layer with another.

The top layer is called *mutual national interest* and includes ingredients that benefit both superpowers: The Russians need our grain and computer technology, and our producers can use their markets. Even

* The writer is a political observer of Novosti press agency.

more important to them, now that the Soviet Union is achieving military and naval superiority, is strategic arms limitation.

The middle layer is *geopolitical competition.* In a long-term battle for domination, here are the usual arenas: the Middle East, where the Russians support radical Arabs and are trying a pincers movement up from the Horn of Africa to control the Nile headquarters; Africa, where the Russians and their mercenaries are making good progress in taking over a continent whose mineral resources could determine world industrial supremacy; and Europe, where the Russians hope to seduce the West Germans away from the North Atlantic Treaty Organization.

The bottom layer is *ideological warfare.* For two generations, the Soviet Union has been on the offensive; however, a decade ago, the Chinese began challenging Russian ideological leadership within the Communist world, which makes Mr. Brezhnev most sensitive to our playing of the "Chinese card." He is even more sensitive to the American encouragement of Soviet dissidents, who the Soviet leaders believe may be sowing the seeds of the destruction of Communist society.

According to this layer-cake theory, Soviet diplomacy is prepared to deal within—but not between—the top and middle layers.

Thus, in the top layer of mutual interest, the Russians are willing to encourage cultural exchanges and are willing to talk about the spirit of détente as they pursue a Strategic Arms Limitation Treaty. Similarly, though they would never admit it publicly, Russia expects some American economic leverage to be applied in the context of strategic arms limitation negotiations.

In the middle layer—of competing for world domination—the Soviet Union is willing, if pressed, to make a few deals: If we continue to acquiesce in the takeover of Africa, they may lessen the military threat in Europe. If we bring them back into the Middle East with a Geneva conference, they may ease the pressure on Saudi Arabia from South Yemen.

What the Soviet leaders will not do is permit the trade of a middle-layer item for a top-layer item: That is why we cannot get them to help SALT along by cutting out the rioting in Africa.

And what the Russians are most determined about is never to mix the third layer with anything—or even to deal within the third layer of ideological warfare, which they know could erode all their gains elsewhere.

This explains why—on the eve of a crucial SALT meeting—the Soviet leaders consider it not in the least inconsistent to deliver a personal insult to the President of the United States, and to thumb its nose at world opinion, by bringing to trial for espionage a man for whom Mr. Carter has specifically testified.

Will this layer-cake principle prevail? Or will United States policy demand some linkage between the layers? The appeasing answer was given over the past weekend, when our Secretary of State reacted to the calculated human rights repression with the wrist-slap cancellation of a couple of junkets, and declared meekly he would go to the meeting to discuss strategic arms limitations with Mr. Gromyko as scheduled.

The United Kremlin knows exactly what it is doing. The divided White House may get a Russian medal for its variations on their rococo theme.

SHAKING THE RED TRAIN

June 25, 1979

PARIS—Where will Leonid Brezhnev rank in the pantheon of Communist heroes?

A pair of French Communists, Nina and Jean Kehayan, spent a year in the Soviet Union and came back with this allegory of disillusion:

Generations ago, a train crossing Russia suddenly stopped. The engineer turned to Lenin for aid in getting the train rolling again. "Let's all get out and push," said Lenin in an inspirational address, which everyone did, and the train rolled.

When the train stopped a few years later, the engineer turned to Stalin. "Shoot half the passengers," Stalin directed, which lightened the load, "and tell the other half they'll be shot if they don't push hard enough." The train rolled again.

Next time the train stopped, the man in charge was Nikita Khrushchev. Informed by the engineer that the track out ahead had been stolen by enemies of the people, he offered an ingenious solution: "Tear up the track behind us, lay it ahead of us, and we'll roll again." And so they did.

The other day, when the Red train—its engine worn out, its cars seedy, and passengers dispirited—stopped again, the engineer appealed to Leonid Brezhnev. "Pull down all the shades," replied Leonid, "tell the passengers to grab hold of their seats and to shake as hard as they can— *and it will seem as if the train is moving!*"

Too laden with meaning to be a thigh-slapper, that little tale tells half the story of Leonid Brezhnev's place in the pantheon. The Soviet economic system is a resounding failure. Under Mr. Brezhnev, productivity—the essence of a nation's real growth—has stagnated. The Soviet Union must turn to the West not only for grain but for computers, oil-drilling equipment, and technical innovations that its anti-incentive system has failed to produce.

The other half of the Brezhnev story is a truth that the West does not like to hear: He brought his nation from a position of strategic inferiority to equality, and soon to superiority.

That is Mr. Brezhnev's legacy: economic failure, military supremacy. To apply some basic logic, this combination of results sets the stage for Mr. Brezhnev's successor to use the military power to extort from other nations what the Soviet economic system has failed to deliver. To argue otherwise is to hold that the most massive buildup of arms in world history—requiring enormous consumer sacrifice—took place for no reason.

The dovecote in charge of United States foreign policy during the final stages of Mr. Brezhnev's military buildup cannot avoid this logic. To justify our SALT concessions, the dovecote produces this conventional wisdom: Leonid Brezhnev is a conservative, nonbelligerent force in the Kremlin. We must agree on SALT with him quickly, say our doves, before he dies and the "hawks in the Kremlin" take over.

That wisdom is nonsense. No hard-line bogeyman is in the closet; the hawks in the Kremlin have been in charge ever since Mr. Brezhnev took over. Mr. Brezhnev sent the tanks into Prague and reasserted the "right" of the Soviet Union to dictate who rules its Eastern European neighbors. Mr. Brezhnev supplied the North Vietnamese invasion of South Vietnam in the 60's and Cambodia in the 70's. Mr. Brezhnev hired the Cuban mercenaries who took over Angola and intimidated Africa.

Under the banner of "détente," Mr. Brezhnev has been winning Cold War II. Whoever his successor turns out to be—the Carter men pick Konstantin Chernenko, so I'll guess Vladimir Shcherbitski, 61, of the Ukraine—he will press the advantage Mr. Brezhnev is now negotiating for him.

Because Mr. Brezhnev is the devil we know, too many Americans accept the notion of a nice Uncle Leonid holding off the hard-line hoards.

But it is good old Uncle Leonid, not some hard-line bogeyman, who is the only support of Communist Vietnam as that savage nation undertakes its latest atrocity. While the Russians get a Far Eastern foothold at Camranh Bay, Hanoi drives hundreds of thousands of refugees into the sea. This also serves Soviet purposes by punishing and embarrassing China while weakening and demoralizing the nations of Southeast Asia.

Must the niceties of summit protocol force us to close our eyes to this obvious Soviet complicity in mass murder? If Mr. Brezhnev did not want Hanoi to engage in the genocidal exportation of its Chinese minority, he could apply the leverage to stop the plan overnight. But the Soviet interest is not to intervene; on the contrary, it is in the Soviet interest for its client, Vietnam, to traffic in Chinese lives. So instead of leaning on Hanoi to stop the killing, Mr. Brezhnev plants a big kiss on Mr. Carter's cheek.

In the end, this latest Soviet leader will be remembered for more than "shaking the red train" to give his failing system the illusion of movement. Unless Americans wake up, Leonid Brezhnev will be revered by Communists for making his successor the most powerful man in the world.

June 28, 1979

To the Editor:

In William Safire's essay "Shaking the Red Train" (June 25), he states that the Russians have been building up their military forces to make up for economic problems. Yet America has continued to expand its arsenal, and this has done little to relieve American economic worries. The things that Russia needs most for its economy—grain and technology, according to Mr. Safire—can best be acquired through cooperation with the West rather than by belligerence and militarism.

The United States has justified its arms buildup on the basis of fear of the Russians. This happens despite the fact that the United States has a history that encourages cooperation with foreign powers, leaders, and a society who have been encouraged to think with an open mind about other nations, and the friendship of most of the other powerful nations in the world.

On the other hand, Russia has a history of being invaded by foreign powers, leaders, and a society who have accepted close-minded dogma about other countries, and the enmity and opposition of almost every other important nation. These conditions would tend to make Russia much more paranoid about us than we are of them.

Therefore, when one considers that the primary motivation of the United States in participating in the arms race has been paranoia about Russia rather than possible economic benefits, it follows very logically that Russians have been building up their arsenal also because of paranoia rather than because of economics.

David Shapard
Poughkeepsie High School
(Senior in 79–80)
Poughkeepsie, New York

CHINA-WATCHING FOR FUN AND PROFIT

T HE ONLY PLACE my Nixon Presidential tieclasp gets any respect is in China. Thanks to my old connections, along with my hardline-to-ward-the-Soviet views, I was the first American newsman permitted into the People's Republic of China after the fall of the "Gang of Four."

These reports from China, including an article for *The New York Times Magazine*, are by what the Chinese call "a foreign friend"—not a supporter of their ideology, but an enemy of their enemy.

Chinese Government officials operate differently in press relations than do their American counterparts. After one interview in the Great Hall of the People, the official told me firmly that the interview—even the fact that it was held—was "between friends," off the record. Next day, a report of the interview, complete with picture, was in Peking's *People's Daily*. I figured that released me from the bonds of background.

THE TREES OF PEKING

March 21, 1977

PEKING—A columnist given the opportunity to wander about the For-bidden City is tempted to try his hand at reporting.

To American eyes, a good story would be an indication of the consoli-dation of power by the new leadership of Hua Kuo-feng. For nearly six months, since the downfall of the "Gang of Four," China-watchers have been asking why the National Party Congress has not been called into session to place a seal of approval on the new leadership.

In particular, Westerners wonder why Chairman Hua felt it necessary to retain not only the posts of Chairman of the Party and Prime Minister of the country, but also his original power base as Minister of Public Security. The beginning of such appointments would be taken as evidence of increasing stability.

Before probing this weighty matter, it seemed a good idea to try reporting about the commotion that took place in front of the Peking Hotel the other night.

When I went to bed, Chang An Boulevard—the long, wide avenue that becomes part of Tien An Men Square a couple of blocks down the road—was lined on both sides with 30-foot tall trees just about to bud for spring in Peking.

At about 2 A.M., an impressive display of manpower came around with ropes, saws, and trucks. Amid much shouting of Chinese heave-ho's, the tireless workers spent the rest of the night tearing out all 200 trees by the roots.

It was as if a Communist-style Howard Hughes had driven down the avenue, did not like what he saw, and said "I want every one of those trees out of here by 8 o'clock in the morning."

The next day, crowds of Peking residents came by to pick up the small branches that had been sawn off, and carted them home on bicycles for firewood. At nightfall, trucks arrived to haul away the large tree trunks.

Nobody thought the event was in the least noteworthy. Here was the main thoroughfare of the nation's capital, with a line of craters on each side making the center of the city look like the smile of a man who has just had all his teeth extracted, and not a soul to ask why.

So I asked why, and learned something about reporting in China.

The first answer, from a semiofficial source at the scene, was: "Insects." Some tree disease had been detected, similar to our Dutch elm problem, and the trees were ordered destroyed.

Sounded logical, until I heard from a second source, who said that he was only guessing, but that the trees had grown to a height where they were blocking the street lighting as well as the view from the hotel and offices, and would be replaced by shorter trees.

A third explanation was put forward by a cynical Western observer: The trees had grown to maturity and were simply being harvested for timber, which is scarce. They would be replaced by saplings, which would be harvested in a decade, when they reached full size. In a Communist state, trees were not only for looks, but for wood.

By this time, my patient and polite hosts were beginning to wonder why I pushed for answers on the trees. Factories, communes, and neighborhood committees were there to be visited; what was so important about sifting through the various theories about the mystery of the trees?

It was hard to explain that in interpretive reporting nothing is more important than a metaphor; and if I could understand the uprooting of the Chang An trees, I would parlay that into a theory about the uprooting of the "Gang of Four," whose following was being ripped out for "criticism" throughout Chinese society.

But there was no information available. All I had to show for two days of badgering was the unrelated fact that Chairman Hua had vacated the office of Minister of Public Security, and that Hsinhua news agency would announce one of these weeks that the man chosen to replace him was named Chao Chang-pi, whose name is not exactly a household word but who is described as "a long-tested, veteran cadre."

Someday it would be good to interview Minister Chao Chang-pi. Not to ask about the size and scope of China's public security operations, or how he intends to keep order in what may be the last stages of a great political transition; but I would like to get the straight story of the trees.

"WHERE WOULD THEY GO?"

March 28, 1977

CANTON—What about human rights in China today? American visitors often think it might offend their hosts to ask about the massive campaign to "re-educate" dissidents, or assume it would be impossible to get a straight answer.

Surprisingly, that is not true. Chinese at several levels, when questioned about the human rights of a large number of their second-class citizens, seemed forthcoming and not in the least apologetic. The replies tell us much about their values and our own.

A Peking diplomatic official, asked first about President Carter's criticism of the Soviets for their crushing of dissidents, was unexpectedly frank: "A few intellectuals deprived of free speech is only a minor question. In the Soviet Union, the workers, the peasants, and the intellectuals are all being oppressed."

At the moment, with Secretary of State Vance visiting Moscow, the Chinese are testy about the United States resolve. The official went on: "China is the country where human rights are best observed. Over 95 percent of the population enjoy human rights, and the other 5 percent, if they are receptive to re-education, they can also enjoy human rights.

"On the contrary," the official bantered, "in the United States, only 5 percent of the population enjoys human rights, and 95 percent don't have them. So if you criticize China on this point, we think it is ridiculous."

Five percent of 800 million Chinese was 40 million people—wasn't that a significant number of dissidents, a long generation after the victory of Communism in China?

He ticked off the five components of those Chinese denied human rights: "About that figure—that includes landlords, rich peasants, bad elements, counter-revolutionaries, and bourgeois revisionists." Mostly young? "Both old and young. Mainly old." He gave some more thought to his earlier assertion and cautioned: "Maybe that figure is less."

Let's assume that figure to be roughly accurate because a different official outside Peking judged the five components needing re-education in his area to be 3 percent: "Less than the national average." Let's assume further that this does not include the many erring brethren who were said to be understandably confused by the "Gang of Four" led by Madame Mao, which until recently controlled the media.

Who, then, are the dissident 40 million? To "landlords and rich peasants" add the word "former"; to have been propertied and to have exploited the masses before the 1949 liberation, say the Communists, is a sin not yet forgiven. The "bad elements" category usually refers to thieves and rowdies; the "counter-revolutionaries and bourgeois revisionists" are those who march to the wrong political drummer.

Are these people in jail? Most, I was told, are not; they are under "mass surveillance"—ostracized, watched, and reported upon by all other Chinese, who are described as disciplined, dedicated, and politically conscious.

A 22-year-old Canton farmer, selected almost at random, said: "We have only one rich peasant in our production team. I am one of those chosen to watch him closely, and report if he is not working hard or is taking a bourgeois line." Are the children of that once-rich peasant required to report on their father, and do they? "Of course." How is he reformed or punished? "He is criticized, in front of everyone. We don't beat him."

In another province, a mid-level bureaucrat explained that a house in a commune had bars in the windows "to keep out thieves." Wasn't it a jail? "No," he replied. "Our jails don't have bars, or locks on the doors."

If that's so, don't the prisoners escape?

The veteran cadre found it hard to understand my lack of understanding. "All throughout China, we have mass surveillance," he said. "Where would they go?"

It is a measure of the gulf between our societies that Americans cannot comprehend the pride the Chinese take in the coercive remodeling of 40 million recalcitrant minds, and that the Chinese cannot comprehend the chill Americans feel at a question as disturbingly revealing as "Where would they go?"

CHINA BY THE NUMBERS

June 19, 1977

The Chinese like to number things.

The message of the late Chairman Mao that is being most closely studied in China today is "On the Ten Major Relationships," one of his more down-to-earth blueprints for the way competing interests should get along on the road to Communism. Emphasis on "The Ten" shows that the present Chinese leadership under Chairman Hua wants to stress that part of Mao's thought which seems most sensible to most Westerners.

The sinister villains characterized as opposing this pragmatic line are lumped together as the "Gang of Four," a catchy enumeration said to have been coined by Chairman Mao himself, who, his successor Hua now relates, told his ambitious wife, Chiang Ching, a couple of years ago: "Don't be a gang of four."

In the same numerical vein, in Shanghai, where the "Gang of Four" had its greatest strength—and was expected to launch a civil war if it could not otherwise take control—the radicals' downfall was greeted by what has been called "the three emptinesses": Stores were emptied of both firecrackers and liquor to supply the celebrants; and the hospitals—where opponents of the radical line were often incarcerated—were emptied of their "patients."

In keeping with the numerological spirit so familiar to a quarter of the world's populace, here is a series of impressions gathered on a recent trip to China by a "foreign friend," who was given fairly free access to officials in the Great Hall of the People and to people in the communes of Nanking and factories of Canton.

The Two Chinese Astonishments

1. "Dig tunnels deep," cautioned Mao, and the Chinese have been building tunnels under all major cities to enable them to survive atomic attack. In Peking, I was conducted through a maze of well-ventilated concrete-reinforced tunnels, which the official in charge said remained undamaged throughout the recent earthquakes. Today, the streets of Peking are made colorful by the ramshackle one-family shelters thrown up in front of the mass-produced housing at the time of these catastrophes; Chinese officials cannot explain the reluctance of the citizenry to use the tunnels. A puzzled air-raid warden says ruefully: "Somehow, during an earthquake, it is impossible to get people to come down underground for protection."

2. The average Chinese, who gets his news from a radio loudspeaker on

the farmhouse wall or from a television set in a commune's meeting hall, has been taught to regard Americans as harmless barbarians. But high-level Chinese, in Mao jackets of fine gray gabardine, expect Americans to understand the subtleties in Sino-American relations. For example, what makes a "foreign friend"? When I asked why I—who have often warned against selling out our friends around the world, including Taiwan—was given a coveted newsman's visa to visit China, a high Chinese diplomat shook his head in wonderment at such American lack of subtlety, replying that "international considerations"—toughmindedness toward the So-viets—"were more important."

The Three Western Head-Scratchings

1. A city with enormously wide boulevards and few cars, Peking has more traffic noise than New York. That is because the rivers of privately owned bicycles compete with the few state-owned cars and army trucks and the motorized drivers just keep leaning on their horns. The Westerner may cringe in the back of the car as the driver plunges into a stream of bicycles, honking furiously, but the intrepid Chinese bicyclists seem to pay little attention to the noise. The purpose of the horn is not to say "get out of the way" as much as "this is where the car is, don't swing out front or you're dead."

2. Godless Communism? You bet—but the antireligious system is curiously religious. Scripture is Mao's writings, and 200 million copies of Volume Five of his teachings are being printed—that's one-tenth the number of Bibles that have been produced in 2,000 years. Statuary of a benign Mao is everywhere, more frequently seen than statuary of Christ in the West. The godlike leader is quoted constantly, with reverence; his name is never taken in vain; his sayings are murmured for reassurance and benediction. The party is the church hierarchy; the "leading member" of the revolutionary committee is the village priest; the "Long March" the weary suffering up the Via Dolorosa; the Central Committee is the Col-lege of Cardinals, and the new chairman a kind of Pope. The Devil is regu-larly reissued: first Chiang Kai-shek, then Liu Shao-chi, then Lin Piao, now the "Gang of Four."

3. Westerners find it shocking when Chinese officials blandly speak of "the 5 percent" who are second-class citizens. These some 40 million Chi-nese who are denied human rights are labeled "bad elements" (crimi-nals), "landlords and rich peasants" (people who were well off before 1949), and "counter-revolutionaries and bourgeois revisionists" (dissent-ers or individualists). Since the "Gang of Four" had a following large enough to challenge the present leadership, the number of people outside the pale is probably much larger than what officials are admitting to, but they want to keep the villainy to a "tiny handful"—enough to denounce

and serve as examples, not so many as to constitute a threat. When Western eyebrows go up at even the 5 percent figure, the response is: "In the U.S., 95 percent of the people have no human rights."

The Five Sensible Old Things

1. The Western traveler in not-so-modern China is struck by the use of items of comfort or conservation that our own civilization has foolishly zipped past, such as the *endboard* of a bed. Instead of tucking the sheets and blankets in at the end of the bed with precise hospital corners, the Chinese loosely drape the bedclothes over the endboard. Americans accustomed to sleeping with their feet splayed, or curling up on their sides to get the blanket pressure off their toes, are astonished to find they can lie on their backs in a Chinese bed, feet sticking up in comfort, except when the bed is too short.

2. If any Westerner's memory should be honored by the Chinese, it is that of Sir James Dewar, the Scottish physicist who invented the *thermos bottle.* No Chinese home, Politburo member's palace, or peasant's hovel is without at least one. In Chinese department stores, the shelves near the entrance are always stacked with them—all sizes and colors. The Scotsman's invention, which is used mainly in the West to keep fluids cold and retard spoilage, is primarily an energy conservator in the Far East, employed for the purpose of keeping the tea water hot—and makes you think of the fuel we waste reheating water.

3. The mopping of one's brow with *a hot, moist towel* is an ancient Oriental custom that makes good sense. But dispensing with a used one is a problem: As I began an interview with an official in the Great Hall of the People, an aide handed me a hot towel. After burying my face in it in suitable form, I looked for a place to deposit it. To the official's horror, I held it over a round, white enamel container at our feet, and just as I was about to release it, another aide snatched it away, saving the "foreign friend" from the ignominy of having dropped his towel into what he later learned was the spittoon.

4. One of the widely emulated old ways of conserving human and natural resources is the Chinese *silkworm trick:* Outside of Canton are fish ponds where carp are raised. The ponds are surrounded by, and irrigate, mulberry bushes. Here's the trick, a kind of ecological *ronde:* The fish droppings and silt from the ponds become the fertilizer for the mulberry bushes; the mulberry leaves are the food for the silkworms; the silkworms' droppings provide the food for the fish.

5. Plodding through the rice paddies, the *water buffalo* evoke the agelessness of China. Will the tractor one day replace these great, gray, curly-horned creatures, erasing this picturesque vestige of China's past?

No, says county leader Lu Kanh: "When we realize mechanization by 1980, there will still be water buffalo, for some delicate plowing, and for the milk." Is sentiment involved? "If war broke out, and diesel oil were blockaded, we would need the water buffalo."

The Four Borrowings

1. In ancient Chinese, certain words were used as punctuation: For example, "ma," at the end of a sentence, pronounced with an upward inflection, was a clue that a question was being asked.

That method has been replaced by Western *punctuation marks*, which have been in use for some time—but because of the need for advertising exhortation have recently been employed with a vengeance. The most common slogan—"Unite, to win still greater victories"—has a big, Western comma after the Chinese symbol for "unite," and Westerners are jarred by the presence of a familiar question mark after a string of puzzling Chinese characters. Subtlety is eschewed; exclamation marks are everywhere: "Deeply criticize the sabotage of the 'Gang of Four'" is given almost apoplectic stress by the addition of three exclamation marks.

2. No neon signs are visible in Peking, a formal and somber capital city. But in more cosmopolitan Shanghai, and in the deep-south Canton, *neon lettering* carries propaganda messages through the night. But in contrast to the flashing and blinking of lights in Tokyo and Times Square, Chinese neon is either on or off—no movement of light allowed.

In British Hong Kong, that no-flashing rule is also followed, at the request of airline pilots who do not like the distraction; as a result, Chinese cities, with their stationary lights, seem quieter at night.

3. Whenever you visit in China, you are offered a cup of tea (green tea up north, black tea down south) and a *cigarette*. The offering of a cigarette has become the single most common expression of hospitality in modern China. I chose a peasant hut at random during a visit to a commune and one of the children of the surprised family was quickly dispatched. In a few moments, he came back with a pack of cigarettes borrowed from down the road. (I don't smoke anymore, but gratefully accepted it "for later.")

Though cancer follows heart disease as the leading killer in China (more stomach and liver cancer than lung, I was told), doctors in a Shanghai hospital still follow the national custom of offering a visitor a cigarette. "In hospitals," they apologized, "we tell patients not to smoke too much."

4. To a visiting reporter in China the dreaded word is *beijing*. It means "background"—not for attribution to a specific person—and it's a privilege that is claimed by everybody in positions of authority. After four hours of furious note-taking, a reporter is gently told, "Of course, all this

was on background, just talk between friends." Chinese leaders are delighted with this Western invention, and use it when they don't need to: After being told my interview with Vice Chairman Yao Lien-wei of the National People's Congress was "background," I was astonished to see my picture with that gentleman in *People's Daily* the next morning. For me, it was background; for him, it was on the record.

The Four Unmentionables

1. You can compliment a Chinese on any number of attributes, but to call a Chinese woman good-looking is a put-down. In a Peking subway car during rush hour, I spotted a tall woman soldier who bore a marked resemblance to Faye Dunaway. "She's beautiful," I told the interpreter; "She's a cadre," he countered, using the word for leader, or officer. How could he tell, since the Chinese pride themselves on no rank insignia? "Count the pockets." Officers have four pockets, enlisted personnel only two. How come? "Cadres need more pockets." But wasn't she beautiful? "She's fit."

2. Premarital sex is frowned on, and not discussed. The Chinese have a population control plan that requires young people to stay single and preferably continent until the late 20's; illegitimate children have as few rights as sons of ex-landlords. A lack of privacy inhibits sex, and forced separations are common: A silk worker near Canton who was married at 23 (to a soldier, for whom the age rules can be stretched) explained that she and her husband, who are stationed 25 miles apart, see each other one month a year. She seemed resigned to this.

3. Jails are admitted to—for the "bad elements"—but are not on the tour, and always seem to be "in a nearby town." Veering off the road in a commune, the traveler comes across a house with bars on the windows: The explanation is that the place is being defended against thieves, or hooligans. A chilling note is the boast that the never-seen jails have no locks on the doors: "Where would they go?"

4. The question that draws the hardest glance from polite hosts has to do with the whereabouts of fallen leaders. "Whatever happened to Liu Shao-chi?" a guest asked. "Is he still alive? Was he executed? Rehabilitated?" The answer: "He is politically dead. It doesn't matter if he is physically dead."

The Two Mysteries

1. What happened on the night of April 6, 1976? After a day of severe rioting in Tien An Men Square, the Central Committee met in an extraor-

dinary all-night session and, under enormous pressure of civil war, cut a deal: The Shanghai gang forced out army favorite Deng Xiaoping, the old pragmatist, but gained no power themselves; instead, Hua emerged as the strongman. Investigations of and judgments about the events of that day and night are still going on in China: "A small handful of bad elements did stir up trouble," says a high official. "Others were against the 'Gang of Four.' We are handling each on the merits of the specific case. . . . We do not intend to build our country into a clear-as-crystal country," the official added murkily; the convulsive events, he hopes, will remain a mystery.

2. Why don't the Chinese speak softly about Taiwan? In that way, they could lull Americans into feeling better about cutting their old ally adrift as they "normalize" relations with the mainland. Most China hands in the U.S. are searching the tea leaves for the barest hint that the Communist Chinese would not attack Taiwan so we could abrogate our defense treaty with a clear conscience. The Chinese know this, but strangely go out of their way to stress the opposite. "We have never said we would liberate Taiwan only by peaceful means," a leading diplomat says. "There is a big bunch of counter-revolutionaries in Taiwan who do not want Taiwan liberated, so the only other alternative is to liberate it by force." The Chinese know this threat of military action sets back normalization. The mystery is: Why do they, contrary to their professed impatience, want to go slow on improving relations with us?

The Five Nagging Doubts

1. *Am I seeing only what I am supposed to see?* The traveler to China realizes he is meeting only a tiny percentage of the people, all of whom seem programmed to channel him toward certain propaganda goals. Denials of requests can be revealing—it was "not convenient" to visit Fu Tan University in Shanghai, which probably meant there was still a problem in that former hotbed of radicalism. The surprise, however, is the way a "foreign friend" is permitted to go off the beaten track. I could stop the car where I wanted, take a walk down a side road, enter a country house or an earthquake shelter in Peking without restriction. And my tape recorder insured accurate translation. The people I encountered on my own—often illiterate, usually friendly—all knew the "right" answers, denouncing the "Gang of Four" in similar phrases, showing no resentment at having to limit their ambition to whatever work the party assigned them. After a while the doubt changed: Since this is obviously not all being rigged for me, is it being rigged for the whole country?

2. *Am I being conned?* About ten kilometers outside most cities is a roadside sign, in several languages, warning the traveler not to go beyond

that point without permission. A small all-weather checkpoint is set up where your interpreter shows the proper credentials. Then you get out of the car and have your picture taken next to the sign, to show that you were able to go where Westerners were not usually allowed. But hold on—they expect that; it happens all the time. Could it be that they know Westerners want to pose for pictures next to signs that say "off limits"?

3. *Am I really in the present?* The most eerie feeling one has in China is the sense of stepping back into the past: On the Nanking railway bridge, a black steam engine, belching smoke—"belching" is the only word—roars by, followed by the coal car, and after a hundred more cars, a real caboose. Inside a small apartment, you sit in a chair with the arms and headrest covered with a piece of lace—an antimacassar! Automobiles with clutches; inkwells with pens and blotters; all just produced, only a couple of generations out of sync. You have to keep reminding yourself that the old locomotive may be hauling materials to Lop Nor, where nuclear weapons are being made.

4. *Has Communism been good for the Chinese?* No beggars impoverish the streets; no epidemics ravage the land; no child looks hungry. With great patriotic fervor, workers "learn from Ta-ching" (an industrial experiment) to build factories with their bare hands, and farmers "learn from Ta-chai" (a model commune) to reclaim every available inch of land to wring produce from the soil.

When you suggest that the trains are being made to run on time at the expense of human freedom, an official in Shanghai says: "We were free before 1949—free to starve, and free to be jailed and killed by the Kuomintang." The visitor is urged to follow his visit to China with a trip to India, to compare the squalor of democracy with the material improvements of Communism.

But then you compare Chinese with Chinese, and the doubts grow: The standard of living in Taiwan and in Hong Kong is much higher than in mainland China, and the rate of economic growth much greater under capitalism.

A Westerner born in China tells you that he estimates that one-fourth of the Chinese live better now than they did a generation ago; one-half live about the same; and one-fourth live worse. On the other hand, a farmer, 54, in his peasant hut, insists his sons fare much better than he did at their age—though to compare life today with life in the 1940's is to compare a time of peace with a period that followed a ravaging decade of civil war and Japanese invasion. Hard to tell what is true in these comparisons, but this is certain: The generation that compares today's Communist lack of hunger with the hard times of the 40's is getting older. The young people are comparing their lot with that of the 60's, and life isn't getting any easier.

5. *Was the "Gang of Four" responsible for all the evils the group is*

now charged with? Outlaw Jesse James's gang was blamed for every train robbery in the West; Jesse wasn't that ubiquitous. Surely the "Four," led by Mao's widow Chiang Ching, did try to seize power and used industrial sabotage and slowdown as one weapon: A railroad conductor in Nanking, who brought in a load of crabs to Shanghai for the celebration of the radicals' overthrow, reports that last year vital railroad traffic was cut by a third, causing industrial havoc.

But ask a waitress in the booming Lakeside Restaurant in Canton how the service was last year, and she will say "Terrible—because the 'Gang of Four' told us that good service was revisionist." Hospital officials say the rise of mosquitoes in southern China is attributable to the gang; fishermen say that last year's catch was off because the gang frowned upon working overtime as being part of a bourgeois theory. The highlight of all children's plays these days is the moment when the gang is "smashed with a single blow": Their nefarious crimes supposedly caused schoolwork to founder, and higher education to replace examinations with political cross-examination.

Too much. The campaign to blame all shortcomings in Chinese society on a despised scapegoat is transparent. In Shanghai, a caricature exhibition attracts 7,000 visitors a day, and Tsai Chen-hua, the leading caricaturist, glories in the triumph of the art he learned from *Punch* and the old *Life*. "The 'Gang of Four' only let one flower blossom," he says; "Now that is changed. One hundred and sixty artists are represented here, and all grasp the key link of class struggle." But it's the same key link: The hostility is carefully channeled in one direction.

The One Unforgivable Error

In revolutionary rhetoric, radical means good, which is why the "Gang of Four" is called "so-called radicals." A leading member of the New China News Agency asked me how I would describe the "gang's" political views. When I suggested "ultraleft," the official's visage darkened: I had flunked the test. They don't like to be out-radical'd. "To call them ultraleft is to say the views of 800 million Chinese are for naught," he snapped. "They are ultrarightist, not ultraleftist." To pre-empt the far left, the group in power (who despise being called "moderate") must take the position that the Shanghai radicals were really capitalists in wolves' clothing. To keep this straight, the traveler should remember: *Ultraleft is right, and right is wrong.*

The One Amazing Coincidence

In Washington, D.C., in 1969, the White House was worried about the use of Lafayette Park directly across the street for violent political demonstrations. Accordingly, money was found for its repaving. A fence was built around the site, which was gaily painted by schoolchildren, and nobody wondered why it seemed to take forever to pave the walks. Through the most impassioned of times, that photogenic park was never available for demonstrations—and nobody objected.

In Peking in 1977, Chinese leadership was worried that there would be another demonstration in Tien An Men Square, which a year ago had been the scene of the worst outburst of political violence since the Communist "liberation" in 1949. Mao's mausoleum, to be completed in September for the first anniversary of his death, was still under construction in Tien An Men Square. All the materials—lumber, stones, cement—were stacked up there and much of the square was fenced off. There was no place to hold a demonstration—and, of course, nobody objected.

But, the Chinese went the Americans one better: Around May Day, a time of great tension, Peking Airport was closed, ostensibly to repair the runways. That was a refinement; the idea of closing Washington's National Airport for repairs during a time of disruption just never occurred to the Americans.

CHINA-WATCHER'S GUIDE

May 31, 1979

WASHINGTON—For politicians junketing at public expense this summer, the old "Three-I League" (Ireland, Italy, and Israel) has been replaced by the People's Republic of China. Their constituents must therefore become instant China-watchers. Here are a half-dozen pointers from a not-so-Old China Hand:

1. *Latch on to an anecdote to show your personal contact with a Chinese who has given you a profound insight.* For example, I recently asked a Chinese official to choose the single most important word in China today. Unhesitatingly, he replied: "Stability." From this I was able to deduce that the triumph of pragmatist Deng Xiaoping over the Maoist "Gang of Four" has not produced stability—that, on the contrary, a vast power struggle is now taking place throughout China.

2. *Develop a long-range "overview" that will sustain seasonal theories.* The one I use is "pendulum politics": In the 1950's and 60's, Mao Zedong turned to angry young people to throw out the bureaucracy in the party and the army and to revivify his revolution. Now the aging bureaucrats are in charge again, but the pendulum could swing once more in the 80's to a more radical, inward-looking group.

3. *Put forward a short-term analysis studded with enough names and numerals to make other Pekingologists wonder who your secret sources are.* To illustrate, here is my controversial but hard-to-disprove Theory of the Four Power Groups:

• Weakest power group is symbolically headed by Wang Dongxing, Mao's former bodyguard. Although Wang has been downgraded, he has avoided a purge because he joined Chairman Hua Guofeng at the last minute in arresting the "Gang of Four." His continuing presence near the top shows the need to appease the radical, young, suspicious-of-Deng forces.

• Most underrated power group is headed by Chairman Hua, who was eclipsed by the ascent of Deng. The increasingly confident Hua, only 58, is the bridge between the Inwards and Outwards, between generations, between radical turmoil and pragmatic bureaucratization. (Since Hua was given his first big Western boost in this space, I confess to an interest in his advancement.)

• Deng Xiaoping's power group, assumed by the Carter men to be in charge, may be losing support in the Central Committee. "Mr. Feisty," 74, is a canny professional survivor, and has been the foremost opponent of Mao's closest followers. He "taught the Russians a lesson" in Vietnam, induced the United States to abandon Taiwan, but his "Four Moderniza-tions" economic blitz was overballyhooed and his "liberalization" of human rights (an appeal to non-Maoist youth) backfired when dissidents showed more spirit than he expected.

• The mystery faction, headed by Chen Yun, 76, whose longtime op-position to Mao made Deng look almost like a lichee-polisher. Chen is an economic manager, the architect of the recovery after the disastrous Great Leap Forward, who has taken charge of Chinese economics and finances. He has been criticizing Deng for making grandiose deals and falling in-gloriously short, and—with equal fervor—criticizing Hua for being tied to the past and not showing enough zeal for modernization.

4. *Buttress your tea-leaf-reading with only those facts that support your theory (treat other facts as propaganda put forward by less insightful China-watchers).*

Fact: A "reassessment" of economic plans has been admitted publicly by officials; in the retrenchment, U.S. hotelmen found their presumed contracts to be mere letters of intent;

Fact: The indirect criticism of Mao, encouraged by Deng, has been stopped;

Fact: In spicy Hunan province, birthplace of Mao and power base of Chairman Hua, the official radio has broadcast unprecedented challenges to Deng's policies. The strongly anti-Soviet Maoists resent Deng's favor-able response to a recent Russian olive branch (he seems to have dropped his insistence that the Soviets make territorial concessions before talking).

Even more pointedly, Hunan radio has been urging farmers to "learn from Dazhai"—the supercollectivist collective that Deng no longer uses as a model. Evidently Hua is protecting his hometown crowd from Deng's revenge.

5. *Shape your mental sets and selected observations into a stern warning for U.S. policy makers, whose information is no better than yours.*

My favorite: If the Chinese (all four power centers) do not see a nice balance of firepower and willpower between Russia and the United States, they will gravitate toward the stronger. Already most Chinese leaders are privately contemptuous of the weakness we recently demonstrated in the Persian Gulf, SALT, Africa, and even Taiwan. If the United States looks like a loser, China will ultimately go with the superpower that appears to be winning, and thereby help it win.

6. *Conclude with any cryptic proverb, and leave yourself an out.* Let a hundred gray cats contend: Watch this wall poster.

June 5 [1979]

Dear Mr. Safire,

I've been a long-time admirer of your work as columnist and novelist, and thus was doubly pleased to be able to get some professional tips from your recent column "China-watching Guide." The heathen printers at *Stars & Stripes* messed up the spelling of Wang Donxing, but never mind.

I think I'm doing okay on citing only those facts that support my theories. But your comments have convinced me I need to improve in the area of stern warnings to U.S. policy makers and anecdotes of profound insight.

That was a great column, and I hope you'll continue to do your best to try to stir up our little ingrown fraternity (oops, forgot my wife).

Best,
Jay Mathews
The Washington Post
Hong Kong

FROM PANAMA
TO CAMBODIA

COLUMNS about foreign policy draw fairly heavy mail if the subject is Vietnam and Cambodia, fairly light mail if the subject is Africa or Mexico. Of the following pieces, the most mail was generated by "Who to Root For," a column suggesting which side to support in various scuffles taking place around the world; about 30 angry letters insisted it should have been "*Whom* to Root For."

In a harangue directed at "The Blame Passers" desperate to avoid guilt and blame for our abandonment of Cambodia and the subsequent blood-bath, I inadvertently defended Henry Kissinger. He sent me a ruefully optimistic note: "I am progressing. Yesterday's column was the first in months in which I broke even."

PANAMA'S POLITICAL PALINDROME

March 6, 1978

WASHINGTON—"A man, a plan, a canal—Panama!"

That ringing slogan—stirring memories of an American leader with the vision of exporting the idea of freedom along with technological genius—is not a slogan at all. It is a palindrome, an arrangement of letters that spells the same message backward as forward.

The debate about the way we turn over control of the Panama Canal to a pro-Castro strongman whose family peddles drugs is similarly bereft of substance, useful only as a device on which to neatly arrange our political attitudes. (George McGovern used to denounce "a corrupt military dictatorship" but liberals now consider the quality of our ally "irrelevant.")

The canal treaties will be amended by the Senate and will pass. The people of Panama will be told by their maximum leader, General Torrijos, to vote for the United States Senate amendments and Panamanians will do as they are told. In this way, everyone involved in the debate will have "won."

Here is why the canal debate is a no-lose situation for all three groups: The accommodationists, the pragmatists, and the stalwarts.

The accommodationists, led by President Carter and the traditional foreign policy establishment, will claim victory simply because the treaties will be signed. They will dismiss the amendments as a necessary sop to the right-wing Cerberus, and Mr. Carter will stage a glorious ceremony celebrating the conquest of the hearts and minds of Latin Americans, as we hand over what Lord Bryce described as "the greatest liberty man had ever taken with nature."

The pragmatists, led by Tennessee Republicans Howard Baker and Bill Brock, will be able to say to accommodationists that—were it not for pragmatic efforts—the nuke-'em neanderthals of the right would have replaced sensible foreign policy with unrestrained jingoism; they will be able to say to the stalwarts that—were it not for pragmatic efforts—the craven, lefty giveaway set would have sold out United States security interests because some tinhorn dictator scared them with threats of sabotage.

The stalwarts, led by Ronald Reagan and Senators Helms and Allen, will claim victory with the passage of strengthening amendments like placing United States ships "at the head of the line" in any emergency and a permanent right to defend the canal from any third-party takeover (plus one more not-yet disclosed "deal-maker" amendment). In truth, the stalwarts can say their opposition transformed the inadequate agreements negotiated by Mr. Carter into treaties we can now live with.

The debate has taught us a great deal about Mr. Carter. To keep his South solid during the 1976 campaign, the Democratic candidate took a hard-line canal position to the right of both Mr. Ford and Mr. Reagan; he has since flip-flopped, and pretends he has not.

Worse, he was less than candid about the price of the giveaway; the White House now admits that turnover will cost us over $1 billion, and that is surely on the low side. If a businessman put into a prospectus the kind of computations of worth used by the President, he would find himself in the slammer for fraud.

Worst, by treating these treaties as the very cornerstone of his foreign policy, he has enshrined accommodationism—especially, concession to third-world demands—in the character of his Presidency.

In light of this broken promise, financial flim-flam, and wrongheaded symbolism, how would I vote on the amended treaties if I were a senator?

I would vote for them. The overriding reason: I would not want the world to know that a United States President, even a not very competent one, does not speak for the United States in foreign affairs.

If Mr. Carter's position had been take-it-or-leave-it, like Woodrow Wilson's after World War II, I would have been an "irreconcilable," but if he gives in to opposition Senators on the amendments, as he signals he is willing to do, the hard-liners are out-foxed: Though the treaties weaken our defenses in the Caribbean region, the humiliation of the President would weaken us far more in all international relations. A President strong enough to act weakly is better than a President unable to act at all.

But he gets only one bite at that apple of reluctant accord: If I were a senator, I would remain "undecided" until Mr. Carter offered specific assurances that any SALT treaty would insure verifiable security, that the Senate's lawful right to approve arms sales would not be subverted by a doctrine of executive package deals, and that Cuban mercenaries in Africa would no longer be considered "a stabilizing force" by the ideologue who misrepresents us at the United Nations.

Mr. Carter needs a vote of confidence on Panama. We should give him that, with the proviso that the foreign policy-making strength we are putting back in the Presidency is not the power to appease.

We cannot afford the appearance of a helpless Presidency. By exiling the policies of the three Presidents of the 60's, by deriding national will as "imperial," and exalting a foolish sense of guilt, we have already gone too far down the road of palindromic politics. As Napoleon never said: "Able was I ere I saw Elba."

NOW WE KNOW

January 11, 1979

WASHINGTON—Sometimes a change of circumstances can illuminate a historical truth. The *Vietskreig*—Vietnam's lightning takeover of Cambodia—is one of those changes.

When Elizabeth Becker of *The Washington Post* was permitted to observe the Cambodian Communists recently, she was given a 94-page "Black Paper" detailing Vietnam's abuse of Cambodia over the centuries. "In 1970," the Cambodian document charges, "the figure of Vietcong in Kampuchea reached 1.5 to 2 million."

"The 'Black Paper' also discloses," wrote reporter Becker, "that when former President Richard Nixon ordered the invasion of Cambodia in 1970, there were in fact some 200,000 to 300,000 Vietcong in the northeastern region of Cambodia including the 'Central Committee of the Vietnamese Party'—the long-sought COSVN."

Asked why Cambodia had never before confimed what U.S. intelligence estimates were at the time, her Cambodian hosts replied: "Because we wanted to be in solidarity with Vietnam." With that solidarity shattered, the truth can be seen, and the real "lesson of Vietnam" can be learned.

Cast your mind back to that terrible summer of 1970, when the campuses erupted in violent protest at our "expansion" of the war and guardsmen killed four students at Kent State.

Protesters and dissenters, on and off campus, derided the U.S. intelligence estimates of Vietcong strength inside Cambodia, dismissing the figures as mere rationalization for our expanding the war. Like our "secret bombing" of Cambodia, the antiwar movement cried, our "incursion" was an example of U.S. imperialism and Presidential power run amuck.

But now we know—even if we discount by half the self-serving "Black Paper's" figures—that the war had already been expanded by the Vietnamese to that Cambodian territory, which was being used as a safe staging area for attacks into South Vietnam.

Now we know we were right—in law, in morality, in military tactics—to attack the forces that had already invaded Cambodia.

And what about the "secret bombing"? Since the Cambodians knew their country was being bombed, the dissenters said, why should the attacks be kept from the American people? The answer: Prince Sihanouk, the supreme neutralist, had a deal with the United States: We could bomb the quarter-million Vietnamese who were using the northeastern jungle of Cambodia to attack our troops, as long as we did not say so publicly—which would force him to tell us to stop.

Now we know that the bombs fell not on peaceful Cambodians, as our doves were insisting, but on a powerful Vietnamese fighting and logistical force.

A couple of more "now we knows":

Supporters of immediate American withdrawal, waving "Stop the Killing" signs, pooh-poohed the notion of a bloodbath to follow our departure. Now we know the killing intensified after we washed our hands of Southeast Asia, as the Cambodian Khmer Rouge caused the deaths of hundreds of thousands—perhaps millions.

The advocates of cutting off military aid to Saigon assured us that the "falling domino theory" had long been discredited. Now we know what happened after Congressional doves pinched off the lifeline: South Vietnam collapsed; Laos soon became a Vietnam puppet; Cambodia fell first to the savage Khmer Rouge, and then to Vietnamese regulars; now real fear is felt in Thailand and Malaysia. The domino theory, in Asia as in the Mideast, is not all that discredited anymore.

The purpose of this essay is not to blame war-weary Americans for the savagery in Asia. The purpose is to use new evidence churned up by the changed circumstances to better understand, in historian Leopold von Ranke's phrase, "how it really happened."

The United States did not invade Cambodia in 1970; on the contrary, we now know that the Vietnamese invaded Cambodia and we struck their positions with some success. The United States did not brutalize Cambodians with our bombing; on the contrary, we now know that we bombed an aggressor—which, now that we are gone, today overruns that country.

The "lesson of Vietnam" that defeatists have drummed into us for five years has been that American power is so limited that we cannot help imperfect allies who are far away resist subversion or takeover.

But the real lesson of Vietnam, being driven home today, is that the perception of America's weakness of will invites aggression; that Moscow is willing to use its client states to bring about a Pax Sovietica; and that there is no turning away from our allies anywhere without the danger of a cost in lives and human freedom everywhere.

January 11, 1979

Dear Mr. Safire:

In order to understand the background for President Nixon's decision to authorize the invasion of Cambodia by U.S. ground forces on April 30, 1970, I would like to refer you to a recent book by the Australian journalist Denis Warner, *Certain Victory: How Hanoi Won the War* (Kansas City, Sheed Andrews and McMeel, 1978). The main events were as follows:

1. On March 11, 1970, anti-Vietnamese demonstrations in Phnom Penh wrecked the embassies of North Vietnam and the Provisional Revolutionary Government of South Vietnam. The Cambodian authorities gained possession of a secret document setting out a contingency plan for the occupation of all Cambodia by the North Vietnamese.

2. On March 18, 1970, Prince Sihanouk was deposed as Chief of State, and replaced by his prime minister, General Lon Nol.

3. In the first two weeks after the March 18 coup the Lon Nol Government pushed on with its ultimatum to the North Vietnamese and the Viet Cong to vacate Cambodian territory. In early April the North Vietnamese attacked, and the pivotal Cambodian town of Krek fell, so that at one stroke about a fifth of Cambodia, including most of its rubber plantations, a principal source of scarce foreign exchange, passed into Communist hands. Along the border areas everywhere the North Vietnamese forces began to move deeper into Cambodia.

4. Alarmed by this development, General Abrams, the U.S. commander in South Vietnam, reported to Washington that Cambodia's fall

to the Communists would destroy all chances for the Vietnamization program and the solution President Nixon sought for the war. By mid-April the situation was so serious that Cambodia's collapse appeared imminent. The Yugoslav ambassador gave the country only ten days. No one thought him unduly pessimistic—until U.S. forces crossed the border.

I trust that this information will be helpful to you. Let me once again thank you for your excellent article, "Now We Know." It was tip-top. Do keep up the good work.

Yours Sincerely,
Edward D. W. Spingarn
Washington, D.C.

January 18, 1979

Dear Mr. Safire:

I read your essay on Cambodia with great interest. For those of us who were there at the time, it seems that the daily struggle to stay alive interfered with our ability to look at the Big Picture. Fortunately, we have learned journalists such as yourself to tell us what it was really like.

I can assure you that I do not consider myself shrill or apoplectic, and I was not anywhere near a college campus in 1970. Instead, I was retained at the time by Uncle Sam as a Fire Direction Officer at a firebase on the Vietnam-Cambodian border between the Fishook and the Parrot's Beak. The area may sound familiar to you; it was part of the jungle that was allegedly "cleaned out" in May of that year. I believe the phrase you used was that "We struck their positions with some success." It's too bad someone forgot to tell those little fellows who had a nasty habit of dropping mortar rounds and satchel charges in our laps.

"Bomb the aggressor," you say. Simple enough, once you figure out who he is and where he is. But what if he disappears into triple canopy jungle or mixes in with the local civilians? Maybe you have the ability to tell the good guys from the bad guys from your vantage point 10,000 miles and eight years away. If so, you are to be complimented. You are much more talented than those of us who were there at the time. Sitting behind a desk in Washington has a way of working wonders for one's visual and mental acuity.

Your talents in military intelligence are exceeded only by your ability to mangle the English language. Your description of the Thieu government that we bled and died for as "imperfect allies" is a masterpiece of understatement. If our Mother Tongue survives the likes of you, it can survive anything.

Maybe I'm just naïve for trusting my own eyes and ears instead of trusting people like you to tell us what really happened. Or maybe I was a little naïve for trusting people like you in the first place.

Our world being what it is, there will probably be situations requiring the use of military force for a long time to come. On the other hand, there will probably be situations where the use of military force will be counter productive or down right stupid. It's too bad that after all that has happened, you still don't know the difference.

Sincerely,
William J. Shkurti
Columbus, Ohio

WHO TO ROOT FOR

February 26, 1979

WASHINGTON—To a public uncomfortable with the feeling that America does not count for much in world affairs, Mr. Carter last week offered an Orwellian theme: Weakness Is Strength. It takes guts to cave in everywhere with equanimity, he argues; to assert our national interest, as those jingoistic cold warriors suggest, would be Taking the Easy Way. In rafshooned halls, a 1980 slogan is bruited about: Keep Cool With Carter.

But Americans need more than to be told to count the blessings of restraint. One reason for the current uneasiness is that we have not been told who to root for. In a series of choices between the lesser of evils, we need more than a fine impartiality. Americans need a global tout sheet that the President has been unwilling to provide.

Here is a handy guide to the Friday-night fights around the world, to help us know when to cheer and when to boo. First to the prelims:

1) *Tanzania* v. *Uganda.* This border war in Africa began in November, when Uganda grabbed a 700-mile chunk of Tanzania. President Julius Nyerere got off the floor and is now belting Uganda's Idi Amin all over the ring; most of the fighting is in Uganda now, and may soon threatten Kampala, the capital.

Root for: Tanzania. Idi Amin is a butcher, of use only to crossword-puzzle writers seeking two short names. President Nyerere is no democratic bargain, but the leader he wants to set up in Amin's place—former Ugandan President Milton Obote—would have to be an improvement.

2) *Yemen* v. *South Yemen.* At the bottom of the Arabian Peninsula, just across from the Horn of Africa, Saudi Arabia's ally, Yemen, is reported to have attacked the Marxist state of South Yemen. Since we have promised the Saudi's to supply arms to the northern Yemenis, we are embarrassed by their bellicosity and hope it does not bring the Cubans across

the Red Sea from Ethiopia to help South Yemen, and then to move on up to grab Saudi Arabia.

Root for: Yemen—that is, north Yemen (which is west of South Yemen). They may be the aggressors, and our State Department will tut-tut at that, but the Communists in South Yemen are the danger to us.

3) *Khomeini's Iranians* v. *Brezhnev's Iranians.* Communists in Iran, who rode with the popular support of the Ayatollah in ousting the Shah, are likely to try to wrest power from the mullahs, thereby achieving in Iran what fellow travelers achieved in neighboring Afghanistan.

Root for: the Islamic anti-Americans, who are less dangerous to us than the Communist Iranians. In the event of a future civil war—in which the Russians would not hesitate to help their supporters—root for a right-wing military coup.

4) *Vietnam* v. *Cambodia.* This has been a mopping-up operation until recently. But Vietnam's new worries will mean fewer Vietnamese troops available for invasion duty, and a resurgence of Khmer Rouge activity in Cambodia.

Root for: Vietnam, because Pol Pot's Cambodian regime was the most tyrannous in the world. Any puppet government would be better than the bloodbathers of Pol Pot. (In a war between Idi Amin and Pol Pot, a lesser-of-evils tout sheet would face its toughest decision.)

5) *China* v. *Vietnam.* Since the purpose of the Chinese incursion (good word) is to force Hanoi to quit Cambodia, the path of consistency for this scorecard would be to support Vietnam. But there is a strong emotional pull to see Saigon, now renamed Ho Chi Minh City, re-renamed Teng Hsiao-pingville.

Root for: China. Its motive is to demonstrate that it is a more reliable ally, in its own sphere of influence, than is the Soviet Union. China intends to bring back a Sihanouk-like regime to Cambodia, which would be a face-saver all around.

6) *China* v. *the Soviet Union.* The U.S. State Department has assured us that the U.S.S.R. will not react against China militarily. But if it should happen—

Root for: China. Even though we now know that Mr. Deng took Mr. Carter to the cleaners by timing normalization to his secret invasion plans, the fact remains that the enemy of our main adversary is our ally.

Though Mr. Carter's main claim is that he has not led us into war, much fighting seems to be breaking out during his watch. Perhaps the need for this brushfire-war scoreboard has to do with his Weakness-Is-Strength philosophy. Winston Churchill, in 1936, described what is now the Carter approach: "Decided only to be undecided, resolved to be irresolute, adamant for drift, solid for fluidity, all-powerful to be impotent."

Dear Mr. Safire:

Your essay "Who to Root For" (*The New York Times*, Feb. 26) was, as usual, provocative, witty, and informative. I was only sorry that you omitted *Rhodesia versus the guerrillas* from your list. This is a war about which Americans have been inadequately informed (even misinformed) by the press and confused by the strange attitudes of our government. As John Burns pointed out in the Sunday *Times* (Feb. 25) the guerrillas are proclaimed communists, heavily financed and armed by communist nations. Should the current transitional government be replaced by either the Mugabe or Nkomo factions, a disastrous civil war would ensue in which the blacks would be the ones to suffer by far the most.

In the face of this situation how is it possible for the United States to maintain its present policy? It is incomprehensible why our government is so short-sighted as to meekly follow the wishes of the bordering Marxist African states which have nothing resembling free elections, and pay no attention to human rights. By refusing to remove economic sanctions against the Rhodesian government, we virtually guarantee that a bloody conflict will occur. Above all, it is certainly not in the interests of the western world to allow Rhodesia to fall to communist dominance. . . .

Sincerely yours,
Dorothy M. Horstmann, M.D.
New Haven, Connecticut

JEFFERSON DAVIS LIVES

April 5, 1979

MONTREAL—On New Year's Eve of 1776, General Benedict Arnold stormed the fortress of Quebec with a force of Americans to drive the British from Canada. He failed. In 1976, separatist René Lévesque challenged English-speaking dominance of the largely French-speaking province with his Quebecer Party. He succeeded.

From the moment he was elected Premier of Quebec, the short, energetic, chain-smoking Mr. Lévesque, 56, has been on a campaign to make French Canada more French and less Canadian. The official language is now French, and only French; English is permitted but not encouraged.

His next step will be a referendum, probably late this year, asking Quebecers' support for negotiating "sovereignty association," an oxymoronic phrase suggesting a declaration of interdependent independence. Once Mr. Lévesque has that fishing license in his pocket, he will probably be rebuffed by English-speaking Canada, because nations are not in the habit of letting large sections float away. Then he will call another election in Quebec, treat his re-election as a mandate to declare independence, and unilaterally fulfill his dream of separation.

To Americans, Mr. Lévesque likes to recall our own Revolution, throwing off the foreign yoke; he most emphatically does not like the analogy of our Civil War, which it took the South a century to win. But one man's "self-determination" is another man's "secession"; the Francophone's George Washington is the Anglophone's Jefferson Davis.

I see him as a modern Jeff Davis with this difference: Lévesque is likely to win. No stubborn Abe Lincoln sits in Ottawa with an oath registered in Heaven to preserve the Union.

Mr. Lévesque is surely the world's most likable revolutionary leader. He is personally honest, sometimes dramatically so: He once heaved a bag of currency back in the face of a man who came to buy a liquor license. And he is intellectually honest: Though the amiable former journalist sugar-coats separation with promises of economic union, he makes no bones about his ultimate goal of an independent nation.

"Rearranging institutions isn't the end of the world," he says, as if the breakup of Canada were no big deal. "Canada is a country that never quite jelled. Inhabited Canada is a loose ribbon that runs across the continent, not the kind of amalgamation you managed in the States. The reaction of more and more Canadians—not so much the politicians, but the people— is that we have to find our way out of the French-English quandary."

What about letting all of Canada decide, in a vote, whether Quebec should be permitted to leave the federation? "Quebec would not stand for a pan-Canadian referendum to railroad Quebec into accepting the status quo." But if that comes about? "Well, then the fat's in the fire. But nobody envisions that—it would mean that Canada would be in deeper trouble than ever."

He loses some of his cool when pressed about potential violence if the rest of Canada said "no" to a Quebec decision to secede: "That's a very remote possibility, a senseless thing. Then we're not talking politics anymore. I reject that damn scenario."

Mr. Lévesque points to international support: "Our referendum will have some resonance outside. We have a firm commitment from France— not to meddle, but to accept our decision. That may not mean diplomatic recognition, but they will make known their feelings. Their *confiance*— their support—is assured."

He professes not to worry about a flight of Canadian or American investment capital: "The pressure at first is to get excited, but when the crunch comes, the pressure from the economic community will be to keep jobs and markets, and to arrange things. We're not going to be begging for that much American investment. Hydro-Quebec has a mission in Riyadh, and feelers coming from Iraq. Sheik Yamani of Saudi Arabia has a good relationship with our energy people."

What sort of nation does he envision? "A small democratic republic, with a presidential system tailored on yours, probably. We're left of center, and will remain so, not afraid of state intervention, but not dogmatic. We're not interested in anything Cuban-like. We're moderate socialists, Scandinavian type—for private enterprise, provided it doesn't try to manipulate things."

What of the English-speaking minority in Quebec? "No crazy exodus—their rights are entrenched. The quality of a civilized society is the treatment it affords minorities." But he expects "diminishing numbers" of Anglophones.

After serving as independent Quebec's first president, he says he thinks about returning to journalism as a foreign affairs columnist (there's real power) or as his country's Ambassador to Washington. And after Lévesque? Ay, there's the rub: When the engaging founder steps aside, the rest of Canada and the United States face the unknown except that our St. Lawrence Seaway partner will be socialist, Arab-influenced, and its friendship a question mark.

ARREST OF ROBIN HOOD

May 7, 1979

WASHINGTON—By electing a Conservative Parliament headed by Margaret Thatcher, the British voter has at last arrested Robin Hood: The notorious brigand of Sherwood Forest, Nottinghamshire, has been something of a hero in English-American folklore ever since his mention in the 14th-century *Piers Plowman.* That is because Mr. Hood and his motley crew of early Socialists—Little John, Friar Tuck, Allan-a-Dale, and Maid Marian (the Jane Fonda of her day)—"robbed from the rich and gave to the poor." That is now called "income redistribution" and has had a good press for five centuries.

However, American economist Arthur Laffer, the tax-cut evangelist and ideological father of Proposition 13, has been putting forward a revisionist theory that Robin Hood and his band were villains, well-meaning meddlers who actually harmed the poor they were reputed to help.

Rich merchants on their way through Sherwood Forest, the reader will recall, were hijacked by the Hood gang (called "Merry Men" by apologists) and relieved of the proceeds of their business on a progressive basis—the more the merchant made, the greater the percentage that was taken from him. These taxlike proceeds, less a bureaucratic overhead to pay for the comely Marian's riding habit, were given to the poor for their welfare.

Take the legend a chapter further, economist Laffer suggests: What did the merchants then do? Some hired a legion of guards to ride quiver through the forest; others avoided Sherwood Forest entirely, going the long way round to pick up and deliver their goods. Either way, the cost of doing business increased, since guards had to be paid, or horses hired for extra transportation, to avoid Robin Hood.

Merchants had to add these additional costs to the price of the goods they sold. Thus, the poor were worse off than before Robin Hood began helping them, because the price of necessities went up (inflation) and the distributions from Robin Hood could not keep pace as merchants avoided his forest (shrinking of the tax base). In robbing from the rich (adding to costs, stealing incentive) Mr. Hood and his Piers Plowman pinkos ultimately hurt the poor.

The original Mr. Hood—who was probably the Earl of Huntington in disguise, your typical élitist do-gooder—was bled to death by a woman, the Prioress of Kirkley. Significantly, it has taken another woman, the redoubtable Mrs. Thatcher, to nab the modern Robin Hoods who have been bleeding the United Kingdom since the end of World War II and to roll back the Welfare State.

Prime Minister Thatcher, having arrested the Merry Band, now faces the question of what to do with them. She and her hard-line Tories have the only strong mandate in Western Europe to junk the debilitating Merry Band philosophy: as the Conservative manifesto pledges, to "cut income tax at all levels to reward hard work, responsibility and success." This means a reversal of nationalization, a shift from income taxes to sales taxes, and a curb on the I'm-all-right-Jack power of unions.

Will she be the reformer in office that she was on the campaign trail? Already, English and American election interpreters are suggesting that she will be more "responsible" than "radical"—that is, she will not rock the boat. If she does try to keep her promises, union leaders are primed to charge Thatcher-Tory rape.

The Carter Administration is putting out that same line in foreign affairs, wishfully thinking that the Conservative campaign rhetoric will soon soften. The litmus test will be the policy toward Zimbabwe-Rhodesia: Tories have pledged to "move to lift sanctions" (possible weasel words are "move to"), which the Young-Moose-Solarz set in Washington still opposes. Our State Department assures one and all that the Thatcher Government will do nothing before the august Commonwealth meeting in Zambia in August.

I wonder. To paraphrase Churchill, Mrs. Thatcher did not become the first woman to become the Queen's first minister because she is made of cotton candy. She has the momentum of a resounding victory behind her, and the force of public opinion on her side today. If she is ever going to count for anything at home or in the world's councils, she is going to have to establish a reputation for boldness soon.

If she temporizes on the need for income-tax reduction, or if she tries too hard to accommodate the foreign policy of an American administration already afflicted with terminal lame-duckiness, her monument in British history will be made of vanilla ice cream.

But I do not think that Maggie Thatcher will abandon principle and swerve sharply to the middle. She sees the tide running to the right, on both sides of the Atlantic, giving her Government the opportunity to make a real difference. Robin Hood stands exposed as a villain; in the next remake of the film, a dashing Erroll Flynn will play the good-guy Sheriff of Nottingham.

LOUDER THAN WORDS

October 4, 1979

WASHINGTON—President Carter may have unwittingly over-reacted this week to the combat brigade placed in Cuba by the Soviets during his Administration.

You would never know that by his television address, of course, which was a sorry spectacle of an American President in full retreat. His spoken response to the Soviet rejection of his demands was to announce that we plan to take some very nasty pictures from up high, and that Americans at Guantanamo would soon prance angrily about, firing loud blanks at one another.

His unspoken response, however, was perhaps more far-reaching than Mr. Carter understands: He let it be known "on background" that Defense Secretary Harold Brown will be sent to Peking to meet officially with Chinese defense chief Xu Xiangqian.

That's not just another pol getting his picture taken at the Great Wall. For the first time, about 15 of our top military planning and hardware experts will begin comparing notes with the Chinese, with the usual disclaimers of any intent to sell them weapons at this time. Although most Senators missed the significance of this high-risk move, Senator Orrin Hatch (R.-Utah) called it "rubbing raw the single most sensitive nerve of the Soviet Union."

Within the Administration, there have been three schools of thought about "playing the Chinese card":

1. *The bluff.* This uses rhetoric alone to worry the Russians, and is the posture we have been in until now. It is favored by dovish Walter Mondale and his ex-aide, David Aaron of the Brzezinski staff. The Vice President said in a q-and-a after his August 29 speech in China: "We are not interested in a military relationship," and repeated in Hong Kong: "We do not have and do not contemplate a military relationship with the People's Republic of China." The Vice President was at that moment arranging the meetings between the U.S. and Chinese defense staffs.

2. *The entangling alliance.* This is the plan for the first stage of a military relationship, and is preferred by the Joint Chiefs of Staff: shared intelligence including a classified data link, electronic sensors to detect potential invasion movements, the skeleton for future tactical cooperation. It was first suggested to the Ford Administration in 1975 by then-Professor Brzezinski, and was turned down either by Henry Kissinger or the Chinese.

3. *The arming of China.* This ranges from "technology transfer"—the sale of civilian equipment then can be quickly adapted for military purposes—to encouraging the British and French to sell arms to China, to supplying antitank weapons and interceptor aircraft from the United States. No school goes so far as to suggest supplying China with missiles to help deliver their nuclear weapons.

This set of approaches is discussed in detail in a Department of Defense document that has come into the possession of *The New York Times:* "Consolidated Guidance 8: Asia During a Worldwide Conventional War." Sensibly, the study—which is not a statement of national policy, but has the status of a Presidential Review Memorandum—states that in such a non-nuclear war, "it would be to our benefit to encourage Chinese actions that would heighten Soviet security concerns. Such encouragement could include arms transfers or the employment of U.S. forces in joint operations."

In his letter of transmittal to Secretary Brown, Assistant Secretary David E. McGiffert wrote on May 14 of this year: "The study indicates the participation of the PRC could be the decisive factor in a prolonged conflict. However, it sheds little light on the issue of how the U.S. could increase the possibility for favorable Chinese involvement. I believe further study should be focused on this difficult question. The Joint Chiefs of Staff concur in this judgment."

At this point, the cheap shot, or easy way, is to point to the seeming contradiction between Mr. Mondale's assertion that "we do not contemplate" a military relationship and the Defense Department's avid contemplation of the same, underscored by the public dispatch of the Defense Secretary to Peking soon after the Soviet Union publicly humiliated our President.

Keep in mind, however, that Defense contemplations are not agreed-upon national policy. Before the first stage of the Sino-American military relationship begins, we should ask ourselves—publicly—what is in it for us? Where will "secure communications links" lead, and how soon? Can we calibrate the progression—from "technology transfer" to arms sales— to allow for a Soviet response? Decisions fundamental as these rate a great debate, not bland assurances to Americans that nothing is happening while we threaten the Russians with the move they fear most.

President Carter, by meekly accepting the unacceptable in Cuba, probably feels he has met the Soviet challenge with exemplary restraint. In fact, his public speech was an abject surrender to a Soviet military probe, while his private action takes the first step on a dangerous path of secret commitments secretly arrived at.

STOP THE BOMBING

July 16, 1979

WASHINGTON—Passive humanitarianism is not an adequate response to genocide.

Communist Vietnam is warring on all its neighbors. Its bombs are boatloads of human beings, tens of thousands every month, forced to buy floating coffins and pushed out to sea to drown or to be taken in by other nations.

That military metaphor was used by Foreign Minister Sinnathamby Rajaratnam of Singapore, who stirred the Association of Southeast Asian Nations in Bali two weeks ago: "Each junkload of men, women and children sent to our shores is a bomb," he insisted, "to destabilize, disrupt and cause turmoil and dissension. . . ."

Many here dismiss such talk as the alibi of nations who do not want to accept the refugees. But assume that the Vietnamese leaders are interested in more than the $6-billion-a-year profit made by stripping "undesirables" of their belongings and dumping them into the sea; consider that possibly the world's fiercest Communist power also wants to accomplish these goals:

(1) *Weaken its neighbors.* The overpopulated nations of Southeast Asia can hardly afford great numbers of new mouths to feed. Singapore's spokesman called Vietnam's people-dumping an invasion that follows a familiar pattern: "This was precisely the weapon used by North Vietnam where thousands of refugees fled to South Vietnam, strained security, initiated riots and brought about the collapse of the economy."

(2) *Brutalize its opposition.* "The Vietnamese are ready, unless

stopped, to drive out millions," said Mr. Rajaratnam. ". . . we have no choice but to turn away hundreds of thousands into the open sea to face certain death. Let's not humbug ourselves. We are sending them to death . . . the Vietnamese are compelling us to be as barbarous as they are. . . . If they can convert people who are essentially humane into savages, that is a victory for the savages."

Such guilt is debilitating; nations resisting the spread of Communism become disgusted with themselves. Distinction between attacker and defender, between the imperfectly free and the perfectly totalitarian, becomes blurred in blood.

(3) *Fan racial hatred of the Chinese.* The ethnic Chinese are traditionally industrious, do not usually assimilate, and tend to work their way out of poverty into the target area of prejudice and envy. In Malaysia, Indonesia, and the Philippines, feelings run strong against local Chinese; since the Vietnamese are now expelling mainly ethnic Chinese, these refugees will probably aggravate such bigotry. It suits the pro-Soviet, anti-Chinese Vietnamese Communists to foster racial hatred of China throughout Southeast Asia.

"The massive unloading of Chinese refugees onto these countries," says the man from Singapore, a city-state predominantly Chinese, could "lead to racial warfare which could tear these societies apart quicker and more effectively than any invading Vietnamese Army."

If these three points are at least partially valid, why doesn't the People's Republic of China simply absorb the million and a half rejectees from Vietnam? Because, the Chinese say, such acquiescence would give Vietnam an incentive to profit from the export of millions more of its own people—including the Vietcong, who thought the men from the North were their allies.

That is why, say the nations threatened by Vietnam, Hanoi's leaders are willing to go to U.N.-sponsored conferences to discuss "humanitarian" measures. By arranging for a more orderly deportation of the millions who do not embrace Communist rule, Vietnam could, in effect, extort "reparations" in the form of refugee aid from other nations.

Certainly the civilized world must immediately finance the settlement of "boat people" already in camps and on the seas. But that will not stop the genocide: Vietnam has an unlimited supply of refugees. The answer to the Communist death trade is neither to encourage the coffin-builders to build more coffins, nor to pay increasing blackmail through the U.N. refugee fund. The only adequate response is to force Hanoi to change its murderous policy.

How? Start with economic sanctions by the free world; follow this with diplomatic sanctions and condemnation by the third world; above all, the U.S. must apply superpower pressure on Russia to rein in its client state.

Tight-lipped humanitarianism is what Hanoi demands from the rest of the world. Such accommodation will never be enough to end the death march to the sea. They way to save hundreds of thousands of lives in immediate danger is to attack the policy at its source—in Hanoi.

Now is the time to brand Vietnam a pariah among nations, to excommunicate Hanoi from civilization until it is willing to end its barbarism. Put a bumper sticker on the world: Stop the Bombing. Unless we act forcefully now, we will all be—in the words of the man from Singapore—"unwilling collaborators in their policy of genocide."

7/22/79

Dear Mr. Safire:

Thank you for your cogent column, "Stop the Bombing."

Newspapers write about and people, including the President, talk about "the boat people" as if they came from nowhere.

The indifference of governments and people to the implications of Hanoi's inhuman policy is amazing and frustrating.

"Boat people" is a euphemism which abets this indifference.

Sincerely,
Jed Taylor
Mansfield, Pennsylvania

THE BLAME PASSERS

November 5, 1979

WASHINGTON—Dick Clark, the former Iowa Senator placed in charge of the American program to get help to starving refugees from Vietnam and Cambodia, last week deserted his post with no notice to take a job in the Kennedy campaign helping to round up Iowa delegates.

Here is a man who spent years in the Senate demanding we "stop the killing" and withdraw our support of troops fighting Communists in Southeast Asia; now, when the terrible consequences of our retreat shocks the conscience of the world, he runs from his responsibility to further his political ambition.

This episode illustrates the hypocrisy of the reaction of some—not all—of our most outspoken doves to the organized murder going on in the area they urged us to abandon.

In the early 70's, the most significant argument made for an orderly withdrawal of U.S. troops, and for a continuance of military aide to anti-Communists, was that the massacre at Hue showed that a bloodbath would follow a Communist victory. This was derided as hard-line nonsense and the moral high ground was claimed by those who demanded we "stop the bombing."

After the withdrawal of our support hastened the collapse of the anti-Communists, reports began to filter in that a bloodbath was taking place in Cambodia. At first, this was seen as the alarmist self-justification of discredited hawks; then—to their credit—some newsmen and columnists ignored past positions to verify and condemn the bloodbath.

This posed a dilemma for many people who never imagined that a Communist victory would begin the killing on a huge scale. To admit tragic error was out of the question for some of them; an expiating new interpretation of events was needed to prevent the most self-righteous doves from being inundated in guilt.

Enter the theory that it was the resistance to Communism that "brutalized" Cambodian Communists and turned them into savages. Truth was turned on its head: The bloodbath that followed our retreat, we were now told, was not the Communists' fault at all—on the contrary, it had been America's fault for trying to stop a Communist takeover.

As the evidence of Holocaust II grew, so did the need for embellishing the legend that would pass the blame. A British print journalist provided a bible for the blame-passers; a British television journalist later used that Orwellian newthink to harangue Henry Kissinger. As the human consequences of abandonment became more apparent, the level of stridency of the doves' attack rose.

The blame-passers felt they had a rationale in "we made the gentle Khmer Rouge very angry." But even as they were clothing that absurdity in bombing-tonnage statistics, they were made naked by evidence of a different genocide in Vietnam: The men in Hanoi were pushing tens of thousands of ethnic Chinese living in Vietnam out to sea to drown.

Somewhat daunted, creative superdoves put forward an answer: Hanoi was acting in an uncivilized fashion because America failed to recognize Vietnam and refused to pay reparations for helping South Vietnamese resist. Not until Hanoi's ransom coffers were filled and enough potential trouble-makers drowned did Communist leaders reduce their export of "boat people."

Now still another crime against humanity is in process. Hanoi, which is undeniably in control of most of Cambodia, is enforcing mass starvation. Hanoi has coolly decided not to permit food to reach Cambodia's refugees.

The blame-passers are frantic. No longer can the murder of millions be attributed to gentle Cambodian leaders we "brutalized"; no longer can the persecution of the "boat people" be blamed in any way on American nonrecognition of Hanoi. The order to refuse humanitarian aid is being given in Hanoi by the same hard-eyed militarists who beat the French and the Americans—by the Communist leaders whose only moment of reasonableness was brought about by the "Christmas bombing."

At this point, the blame-passers might do well to stop accusing others. Nobody, not the most I-told-you-so hawk, expects anybody to say publicly, "Look, it was our war-weariness that lead to the collapse of resistance in Southeast Asia, which led to the killing of millions of innocents."

No such soul-searing admissions are required. Let history decide who lost Cambodia and who misread Hanoi's intentions. Too many people fear being blamed by themselves and others for a horror they did not foresee, and are desperately launching a pre-emptive media strike against those they fear will be their accusers.

Cool it. The blame belongs to the murderers, not to those who disagreed about how or when to resist. Doves and hawks can now join—from wholly different mindsets—to pressure Moscow to pressure Hanoi to stop the starving.

Nov. 5, 1979

Dear Mr. Safire:

In your Nov. 5 column you wrote "Let history decide who lost Cambodia. . . ." I don't know about you, but on my map it's still west of Vietnam and south of Laos, just as it always was.

Sloppy metaphors reveal sloppy thinking.

Sincerely yours,
Douglas Cohen
Chicago, Illinois

VOICE FROM THE BUSH

November 8, 1979

WASHINGTON—If the United States were to take over an African nation, round up thousands of its children, and ship them back to U.S. training centers for forced capitalist indoctrination, cries of "kidnapping," "brainwashing," and even "a new slavery" would ring through an outraged third world.

Cuba is doing that in Africa today. Sixteen months ago, an anti-Communist guerrilla leader in Angola named Jonas Savimbi charged that Cuban forces occupying that former Portuguese colony had been systematically shipping African children to Cuba for indoctrination lasting up to 15 years. His accusation was shrugged off.

Last week, a Dutch newspaper reported scenes of weeping parents at

Brazzaville airport in the Congo as 1,200 black children, mostly between 10 and 15 years old and among the most gifted in that nation, were forcibly shipped to what were called "vacation camps" in Cuba. Communist-dominated Congolese officials called the reports "antitruths."

Today, in Washington, Dr. Savimbi brought his accusation up to date. "Six thousand children have been taken away since 1977," he says. "The latest shipment was 1,300 children in September of this year. Two-thirds were under 10 years old."

Has the Angolan Government, a puppet held in power by some 30,000 Cuban troops, acknowledged this system of dominating the next generation of Angolans with Cuban-brainwashed youth? "The regime in Luanda flew about 100 back, to show they had not been physically mistreated," he asserts. "The Government insisted it had not sold them into slavery. They call it a 'scholarship program.'"

But it is a scholarship offer that cannot be refused. According to Dr. Savimbi, the 6,000 Angolan children are being introduced to life in a Communist society at the isolated Island of Pines. After classes on this former penal colony off southwest Cuba, the children are said to work in the sugar fields.

Does anybody care? This forced busing on a grand scale is surely worthy of investigation by children-protectors at the United Nations, by private foundations, and by journalists who find Mr. Castro such a winning figure. If the charge is an "antitruth," Mr. Castro should welcome investigators to his scholarship island; if the involuntary ten-year transplanting is true, such training for Communist rule is even more dangerous in the long run than the recent Carter corollary to the Monroe Doctrine.

Dr. Savimbi is a unique personage: He is the only guerrilla leader in the world fighting and winning a war against Communists. "I have my people behind me," says this fierce-looking intellectual in his rapid-fire English. "We are winning the war with the Cubans."

Though Cuban troops hold the cities, Dr. Savimbi controls the countryside. The Cuban's puppet leader has no background in the wars against colonial Portugal; Dr. Savimbi has spent eight years "in the bush." Dr. Savimbi is confident enough of his popular support to call for a coalition with the puppet leaders and the ejection of all foreign dominance from Angola.

In such a situation, logic suggests that it is in America's national interest to encourage him. Such logic escapes the remnants of the Andy Young brigade in the Carter Administration: You see, in fighting the invading Cubans a few years back, Dr. Savimbi accepted some arms from South Africa, and even worse, some rifles and ammo from the C.I.A. That makes him more intolerable, in Carter eyes, than the Cuban mercenaries running Angola for the Soviet Union.

That is why our State Department is snubbing him on this visit, and why its Human Rights Division averts its eyes from the Island of Pines. He is the worst kind of embarrassment: Without our help, he is winning. With Angolan diamond mines and with French "sympathy," he buys arms to fight the Cubans; his soldiers like the Soviet Kalashnikov assault rifle, and he is said to be in the market for Soviet surface-to-air missiles rather than the U.S. brand (a consumer preference that should send a message to the Pentagon).

Dr. Savimbi has come to the U.S., under the auspices of Freedom House, to ask Americans to stop helping the new colonialists of Africa, the Cubans. If we want to help him, fine—he won't even demand to know which agency of our Government sends supplies—but at least the U.S. officially should cheer him on, and stop giving tacit approval to the Cuban puppet. A diplomatic push from us would open the way to what the Cubans want least: a coalition in Angola with a nationalist hero.

Zbigniew Brzezinski, who defeated the Young-Moose-Solarz-McGovern-McHenry crowd in the Moroccan arms sale, could put appeasement to rout by making a friend out of Dr. Savimbi. Let's see if he tries.

People II

JERRY BROWN

GOVERNMENT BY GURU

April 1, 1976

ARKADELPHIA, Ark.—People here tighten their sunbelts, dodge tornadoes, witness ruefully the decline of George Wallace, and look hopefully toward the likes of Jimmy Carter and California Governor Jerry Brown.

Most of us equate the fading of Wallace with a rejection of racism, but we forget that the Alabama Governor's appeal included an anti-establishment, anti-intellectual element that has deep roots in American history. Messrs. Carter and Brown do not use the "pointy-headed perfessor" rhetoric but inherit the Wallace resentment at "bureaucrats" in far-off Washington manipulating the lives of "plain folks."

While Carter, a Baptist, is the consummate political evangelist, Governor Brown, a former Jesuit seminarian now dabbling in Zen, is the newfangled political spiritualist. Each seeks to give the voter the impression he is in close touch with that Great Campaign Manager in the Sky.

Governor Brown goes out of his way to stress his personal asceticism. Spartan-like, he refuses to live in the Governor's mansion; he drives a small car to work; he spends occasional weekends at Zen and Trappist monasteries, excellent places to think quietly. Most appealing of all, he delivered a seven-minute inaugural address. This makes him "antipolitical," which is this year's role for the smart politician.

Taking advantage of the revolution of lowering expectations, Governor

Brown lingers on the questions and procrastinates on the answers. He murmurs profundities like, "Who knows if there *are* any answers?"

To a persistent interviewer for *Playboy* magazine, Governor Brown said: "I've spent more time with you than on anything this month. And its made me ask myself whether or not I'd ever want to be President. There are just too many issues on which you have to have positions."

Even as this interview appeared, Mr. Brown announced his candidacy for President, hinting broadly that what he really had in mind was the nomination for Vice President. He has entered his own state's primary, and that of Maryland as well, to prove his coast-to-coast appeal.

Governor Brown understands two principles better than most antipoliticians around today: First, he has grasped the Satchel Paige political philosophy—that is, keep running and never look back; something may be gaining on you. Mr. Brown ran for California Secretary of State on the basis of his father's name, won, and then narrowly won the governorship a year ago. Rather than tackling the job he was elected to, he keeps running—not so much for higher office as away from present office.

The second principle, an understanding of which Mr. Brown shares with Mr. Carter, is Charles de Gaulle's axiom that "there can be no power without mystery." This holds that answers need not be specific when trust is the candidate's demand: "Nothing more enhances authority than silence. It is the crowning virtue of the strong, the refuge of the weak . . . the prudence of the wise, and the sense of fools."

Zenocrat Brown and country-slicker Carter have developed the mystic straddle to a high art. Today, "I don't know" is received as a refreshingly honest answer; the follow-up, "Why don't you know?" is rarely asked.

In the past, politicians stuck to generalities because specific positions lost votes; but Brown—and to a lesser extent Carter—stick to fuzzy generalities because they do not have the specifics in mind. In public affairs, honesty is not always the best policy; *policy* is the best policy.

If we were dealing only with the Vice Presidency we might relax about providing a Washington monastic retreat for Mr. Brown. But our last three Presidents have been Vice Presidents, and two of them stepped suddenly into huge responsibility.

Can Democrats be serious about placing a pleasant, engaging man of such limited experience so close to great power—when he admits he has no idea what he would do with that power? When asked about détente, Governor Brown replied: "I'd have to give that one a lot of thought."

Perhaps Democrats should give more thought to the Browning of America. Envision Jerry Brown as President—having refused to live in the pretentious White House like other politicians—surrounded by limousines loaded with Secret Service agents and cops on motorcycles, driving his own little car to work from his bachelor pad. It would vividly symbolize the Spartan life, but it would cost a fortune every morning.

Spiritualism and evangelism have their place, but that place is not in national politics. California, with its wonderful culture of cults, is entitled to a chief executive with sects appeal, but the rest of the country will look askance at government by guru. As politicians say of the mystic pitch: Nobody should seek the Presidency as a stepping-stone to higher office.

THE FUN GOVERNOR

August 8, 1977

LOS ANGELES—Outside the Los Angeles office of Jerry Brown is a large poster of Linda Ronstadt, the delectable folk-rock artist who is occasionally seen with the young California Governor.

At a time when Anita Bryant's "crusade" has every bachelor politician in the nation lustily asserting his masculinity, Governor Brown's well-publicized dating signals the beginning of his 1978 campaign.

So does his new-found interest in space. This week, the space shuttle "Enterprise" will blast loose from the 747 on which it piggybacks, gliding to earth with two astronauts aboard. Jerry Brown, who has made California's "Space Day" all his own, will probably be near the touchdown spot to pump their hands and make a little speech to the worldwide press.

For those who remember Jerry Brown as the limits-to-growth candidate of a few years ago, whose flip charm defeated Jimmy Carter in selected primaries, and whose rejections of the trappings of power gave the President-to-be a few ideas later, the newly spaced-out Jerry Brown comes as a shock.

But there are reasons for the California Governor to abandon government-by-guru and to call for a multibillion dollar Federal space expenditure. California is a technology state, and the loss of the B-1 bomber was a blow. If Mr. Brown is to win next time out, he must keep the no-growth issue from becoming his Achilles' heel.

Besides, the small-is-beautiful routine was getting dull, and the California Governor is a man with a lively mind. When teased about his seeming turnabout, he keeps a straight face as he tells the visitor his logic: "Everything has limits. Environmental concerns have to have limits, too."

What kind of politician is this? He is fast on his feet, inundating interviewers with data about the potential for getting energy from outer space, artful at the answer that turns into a soul-searching question. Now that he is "into" economic growth, he is ready with useful statistics but is unprepared for the questions that go beyond the superficial.

He considers the distinguishing characteristics of his administration to be (1) "Wider participation" in government by divergent groups; (2) A "shared understanding" of limits of government power, and (3) A feeling of being "future-oriented." (In other words, plenty of minority appointments, good public relations, and the recent space angle.)

He has property-tax relief going for him. Because inflation pushes Californians into higher state income-tax brackets, the surplus is there for disbursement. Taking more taxes from wage earners and giving the funds to property owners is hardly progressive tax policy, but Democrat Brown is getting away with it.

One might gather from these impressions that Jerry Brown deserves his reputation as a political dilettante, an ascetic mystic one day and a savvy spender the next, surfing on the waves of public favor.

True, but you have to add the factor of likability. The attractive, slight young man is not in the least pompous and is hungry to learn. He is an irreverent introvert taking a whack at public life, without long-range vision but with good intentions.

Is that enough? Shouldn't the Governor of our most populous state, and the man Fritz Mondale probably sees as his main competitor, have a set of principles to attract serious people to his cause and—at the same time—cultivate great adversaries? When does the moment come when he stops shooting at targets and media opportunity and starts figuring out where he wants to lead the people?

At this stage of his development, Jerry Brown shows signs of becoming a political Gus Lesnevich, a champion light-heavyweight, widely admired for his technique within his class, but never a real danger to the heavyweights.

That could change. Jerry Brown bears watching because there may be no limits to his own growth, which has already taken him from ostentatious humility to a kind of self-mocking advocacy of national greatness.

Perhaps he can marry ecology with technology, first with space—not just in shooting the interview breeze, but in a more demanding synthesis of imagination and homework. If so—and that is one big if—Jerry Brown could become a political force. And what's wrong with Linda Ronstadt for First Lady?

SPEAKER O'NEILL

HOW TO PERPETRATE AN OUTRAGE

February 17, 1977

WASHINGTON—Nearly a century ago, Speaker Thomas B. Reed, Republican of Maine, broke the back of minority rights in the House of Representatives by taking away its power to filibuster. "The right of a minority is to draw its salaries," "Czar" Reed scorned, "and its function is to make a quorum."

Speaker Reed is remembered today for the way he liked to inform the helpless Minority Leaders of his decisions: "Gentlemen, we have decided to perpetrate the following outrage."

The times, they are not a-changin'. In this era of "reform," with its new emphasis on "ethics" and its sensitivity to the rights of minorities, the House of Representatives is run as imperiously as in the days of Reed, with corruption concealed and responsibility evaded as it was in the days of the first House "Czar."

How does the unrestrained power of the Speaker manifest itself? Let us count the ways:

1. *The I-never-voted-for-it-but-I-couldn't-stop-it pay raise.* This is a trick, devised by the House Democratic leaders in 1967, to evade accountability for a pay increase. The charade is for the President to make salary recommendations for Federal employees, which become law automatically unless either chamber passes a resolution of disapproval.

But it would take 218 members of Congress to blast such a resolution out of committee and onto the floor for a vote disapproving the 30 percent pay hike. The Speaker quietly shakes his head; no vote. The Minority Leader introduces a bill to make it possible for House members to vote for or against the pay raise. The Speaker smiles, and bottles that bill in his Rules Committee, where it will die.

Maybe a pay raise is fair; perhaps not. But Representatives are elected to represent, and to vote, and to be held accountable for their votes by the voters. Under Speaker O'Neill, we are witnessing who-me? legislation, sheltering from embarrassment Congressmen too cowardly to vote for the pay raise.

We do not elect men to Congress to spare them embarrassment. We elect them to make a record which voters can then ratify or reject. This nonvoting pay raise trick is a shabby abandonment of that principle, and is opposed futilely by a minority whose right "is to draw its salaries" and shut up.

2. *The anti-dissent organization rules.* Why did every Republican vote against the adoption of the rules of the 95th Congress last month? Because the minority was slammed up against the wall in a display of arrogance that—had it been practiced by anyone but certified Good Guys—would be attacked as dictatorial as "Reed's Rules" by every liberal commentator.

Here's the hook, which has rated no notice but which has helped eviscerate opposition to "Czar" O'Neill: The number of members needed to make a quorum within a committee has been changed. It used to be a majority; now it is one-third. What with the small sprinkling of opposition members, this little trick means that Democrats can hold committee meetings and mark up bills without any Republican participation.

3. *The "forgive and forget" ethics code.* The proposal that "Czar" O'Neill laughingly calls his "ethics code" resolutely forgets the past and calls on solons to be kind, truthful, and reverent in the future. The hot reforming zeal of the O'Neill of 1973 suddenly cooled when it came to probing Democrats.

Minority Leader John Rhodes has proposed a Select Committee, made up of an equal membership of both parties (like the Senate's Watergate Committee), to conduct a thorough audit of all members' accounts for the past six years.

In the light of the quickly shushed scandal in the accounts of Mr. O'Neill's deputy, Democratic Majority Leader Jim Wright, this would clearly be in the public interest. But "Czar" Tip has crushed the minority proposal.

He has denied the public an independent audit because there is a rot in the House, and I suspect that rot extends into the office of the Speaker, in the form of cash payments, which have not yet been revealed, made to House members by South Korean lobbyists. The Speaker appears to have plenty to hide, which is why he is refusing to permit an audit; the pity is that the watchmen in the night have now fallen asleep.

4. *Recess reform.* Lest this department be considered unduly severe on a genial old pol, whose $500 "tips" to obedient Congressmen was in the grand tradition of influence purchasing, and whose intercession with building officials on behalf of fund-raiser James Wilmot recall the halcyon days of William Marcy Tweed, a word in his favor:

Tip O'Neill's forthright and fearless decision to change the name of the time Congress goes out of session from the lackadaisical "recess" to the dynamic "district work period" deserves the approbation of euphemists around the world. (Congressional fence-mending visits are now to be called "incursions.")

When Jimmy Carter, down the street, smiled publicly at the newest linguistic pretension, the Speaker's office let the White House know that our hot Tip was not amused: The President is not to mess with the Speaker when he is about to perpetrate his outrages.

MENACHEM BEGIN

THE AUTHENTICS

August 4, 1977

In Blair House, across the street from the White House—where, a century ago, Robert E. Lee turned down Abraham Lincoln's offer of the command of the Union Army—another man of principle, Prime Minister Menachem Begin of Israel, recently turned down opportunities offered by the superpowers of the media to enter into negotiations with the terrorists of the P.L.O.

The substance of his remarks will not be reported here, since I accepted the rules of background, but Mr. Begin's general demeanor can be examined and is central to my point: He is an Authentic.

One characteristic of Authentics is the way they utilize the press. An Authentic treats reporters neither as equals nor enemies, but as channels.

For example, the new Israeli Prime Minister would not allow himself to be interrupted, or brought back to the point his questioners sought. To one interrupter, he countered: "I am talking about the sufferings of my people"—and continued, with unabashed passion, to review the lessons of the Holocaust and to show how some Jews feel about negotiating with those who threaten Israel with extermination.

An Authentic will also feel free to interrupt the questioner. When the most respected commentator in America started to pose a question, Mr. Begin politely broke in to finish a previous answer. (I felt like plucking his sleeve to whisper: "Interrupt me if you like, or Hugh Sidney if you will, or Eric Sevareid if you must—but not James Reston!")

Some Authentics have the ability not merely to survive, in Faulkner's phrase, but to prevail. Israel's Prime Minister, now 63, was a contemporary—and fierce opponent—of David Ben-Gurion, and was on the scene when international affairs was peopled with Authentics, like Churchill, F.D.R., de Gaulle, Adenauer, and the younger Tito.

Like them, Mr. Begin has a powerful sense of who he is and what he stands for. He is polite but prickly—a waspish Jew, to use an oxymoron.

Curiously, coincident with Mr. Begin's long-delayed rise to power in the Mideast, another Authentic in the Far East is making his stubborn presence felt.

Deng Xiaoping, 74, has made his second comeback to the posts near the pinnacle of leadership of the People's Republic of China.

Less than two years ago, at a private dinner for some visiting Americans, Mr. Deng displayed the characteristic of an Authentic: When other Chinese rhapsodized the radical line then attributed to the dying Mao, Mr. Deng remained sullen. He would not go along. He was soon to suffer humiliation in the name of Mao at the hands of the Shanghai radicals, until they in turn were cast out as the "Gang of Four."

Contrary to most reports, Mr. Deng's battle is not yet won. It has long been assumed in China that Mr. Deng would at least be returned to the positions he held in the past. The real question is this: Will Mr. Deng be promoted to Premier, a position Chairman Hua Kuo-Feng, now bestriding both party and government, would have to give up?

Mr. Deng's return to leadership of the army does not mean greater dominance by the army, but the triumph of that faction within the army-party hierarchy that wants more modern equipment with fewer soldiers—in turn, requiring more trade with the West. Not because Mr. Deng is pro-West, but because he is pro-modern army.

Chairman Hua, 56, must deal with the practical forces represented by Mr. Deng, knowing Mr. Deng's view cannot be changed, but if the old Authentic gains too much prestige, he might pass the critical power mass and take over.

The Authentics, good and bad, do not always make it. William Jennings Bryan, Huey Long, and Barry Goldwater failed, along with Leon Trotsky, Aneurin Bevan, and Chiang Ching. Time and chance have to combine with their combination of arrogance, principle, and passion.

An Authentic does not wet his finger, hold it up to the breeze, and then point the way. At a time when weathervane leadership holds sway in the United States, long on polls and short on principles, we look at the rise of Authentics in other parts of the world and we wonder: Will the day of the Authentic come again for us?

HAMILTON JORDAN

A CASK OF AMARETTO

February 23, 1978

WASHINGTON—When a woman, who refuses to be identified, claims a White House aide spewed a drink down her back at a swinging bar—that's not news.

But when the White House Press Secretary, whose office did not return a reporter's call for comment before the gossip item appeared, issues an 8,000-word, 33-page collection of documents to refute the charge—that's news.

Since criticism of the Carter Administration has occasionally been aired in this space, today's essay will redress the balance by quoting copiously from a remarkable, official White House release.

"I first became aware of this situation to the best of my recollection on Friday," begins the statement by J. Lester Powell, White House Press Secretary, "... when I arrived at the office Friday morning, I received a copy of the [Rudy] Maxa article in *The* [*Washington*] *Post* magazine. Needless to say, I was horrified."

After cross-examining the reporter, Press Secretary Powell tracked down the bartender of Sarsfield's pub: "I then called the bartender and asked him if he would be willing to make a statement to a lawyer from the [White House] counsel's office."

White House counsel Michael Cardozo conducted the interrogation of the bartender, Daniel V. Marshall III, whose boss is a part-time White House advance man. After establishing that White House aide Hamilton Jordan had eaten a steak and salad, the lawyer asked: "What was Hamilton drinking?"

"Amaretto and cream," replied the bartender, "because he wanted something sweet which is. . . ." His voice trailed off. He started again. "The Amaretto we use is only 40 proof so with the cream it is not exactly like putting martinis down. . . . It was very crowded . . . wall-to-wall people . . . there were other girls coming up to Hamilton and 'woo-woo,' you know what I mean?" (The official White House transcript puts the "woo-woo" in quotations.) "Three or four of them just kind of basically hanging around and just hoping that he would turn around and say something to them or whatever."

Bartender Marshall III continued, according to the White House: "And I think Hamilton said something, he pretty much had enough of these girls falling all over him. And he did say something to the point where enough's enough and I don't want to talk to you anymore and I think one of the girls got insulted—I don't think, I know she got insulted."

The White House counsel then handed the bartender the accusatory article. Mr. Marshall III read it and said: "If he did spit all over the girl it had to be an Amaretto and cream which would have been quite a mess and she certainly wasn't wet. . . . I didn't see it and there was no indication of it happening . . . it's not like a scotch and water or something—it's cream."

"Let me get this straight," the transcript released by the White House has the White House counsel saying. "If he did spit, it would have to have been Amaretto and cream. You know he didn't spit the beer." After an extended colloquy establishing the bartender's conviction that the women were tipsy and Hamilton Jordan was blameless, the White House lawyer bored in: "Are you sure that Hamilton was drinking Amaretto and cream? . . . You're positive?"

Bartender Marshall III: "They're a [deletion by this writer, not by the White House] drink to make. You don't forget something like that. You have to get a shaker out, you got to shake it, you have got to clean the cream off the glasses, you don't forget it. It's not like scotch and water. . . . Like I said, we use the cheapest Amaretto—it's 40 proof—for anybody to get drunk they would have to down four dozen."

This strange release is quoted here to show what is happening to two quite different men close to the President.

Press Secretary Powell has evidently lost all sense of proportion. A gossip item, if untrue, is to be curtly denied or contemptuously brushed off. It is ludicrous—worse, unprofessional—to send out Government lawyers to get statements from bartenders and drinking buddies, using White House secretaries to type, Xerox, and distribute a torrent of denials twice as long as the State of the Union address.

For Chief of Staff Hamilton Jordan, however, one can feel a certain sympathy. "I very seldom go out in Washington to public places," he states in one of the 33 pages, "because I am often bothered by well-meaning people who do not respect my privacy."

There, in an odd twist, is a fallout of the Haldeman celebrity: the White House aide as a superstar. Ham Jordan, 33, is now being pushed by his boss into the top-secret foreign policy areas; he must wonder if he is not getting in far beyond his depth; he lives in a crucible, with every word and act subject to criticism; he is separated from his wife and is tasting some of the misery and guilt that goes with the fun at the center of power.

Which is why the White House over-reaction to the gossip item is so revealing and poignant: It shows us the President's closest aide, alone in a crowd of political groupies, looking for a good bar.

RICHARD NIXON

RETURN FROM ELBA

July 26, 1979

SAN CLEMENTE, Calif.—Make no mistake about it: Richard Nixon is looking forward to returning to New York City or its environs this autumn and to pursuing a more visibly active life.

In a final visit to what used to be called "the Western White House," a former associate is struck by the improvement in his health and demeanor. Three years ago he limped, and a permanently pained look shadowed his eyes; that's gone. Tanned and graying, he appears to be in good shape.

Richard Nixon has become a "morning person": Up before five, he works on his latest book until noon, sees visitors and relaxes in the afternoon, swims occasionally, walks almost two miles a day, and has taken to listening to baseball games at night as he answers mail or signs books.

On his work: The new book, 100,000 words as yet untitled, is nearing completion for publication by Warner Books next April. It is an analysis of foreign policy trends, projecting the U.S.-Soviet competition to the year 2000; Ray Price, working with him on it, believes the book will be important and useful. Nixon sees it as toughminded and likely to be controversial. In the back of his mind is another book, on the lines of Churchill's *Great Contemporaries*, about the giants Nixon has known: Eisenhower, de Gaulle, Adenauer, Dulles, and others.

His writing has been successful: The half-million-word memoirs outsold the expectations of the book trade and earned him over $2 million. Nixon did not sell his San Clemente home because he could not afford the upkeep, nor only because Julie and David Eisenhower are moving to Pennsylvania early next year and Pat Nixon wants to be near her two daughters and their families. Nixon is moving, I think, because he needs and is ready for the mental stimulus of city life; the period of reclusion is over. He recalls that Herbert Hoover and Douglas MacArthur spent productive last years in the center of New York.

On his recent meeting in Mexico with the Shah: "He is not sorry for himself," reports Nixon, "he is sorry for his country. He is grief-stricken by the execution of his friends and the suffering of his people under the new regime."

That meeting of Nixon and the Shah—two fallen non-angels—must have been a drama-laden rendezvous. The Shah gave Nixon "a breathtaking and wise" *tour d'horizon* about the aftermath of the retreat of U.S. power. The Shah is bitter about the United States: When his downfall was threatened, he felt he deserved stronger support, which might have averted Iran's takeover by a savage regime; as a deposed ally, he feels let down by America, which has told him he would not be welcome here for fear of reprisals.

On Carter: Former Presidents tend not to knock their successors, and Nixon turns aside questions about last week's apparent Nixonization of the Carter White House. I have the impression that he thought Mr. Carter's speech was well-delivered but indecisive on decontrol; that the firing of half the Cabinet was something a President has every right to do; and that Carter's new antipathy toward the press would not hurt him one bit.

On energy policy: "If Congress is looking for a villain, it had better look in the looking glass."

On the next Republican Presidential candidate: It is no secret that John Connally is one of his favorites, but Nixon is in touch with—and gives his foreign policy views to—other candidates. "Reagan is a good listener, and not just for show," says Nixon with respect. He will neither help nor harm any candidate with his support.

On the significance of the 1980 campaign: The position of the elected candidate regarding U.S. power could well determine which way China will turn in the next 20 years. If the U.S. chooses a President who will not stop the present drift toward Soviet strategic superiority, the Chinese—survival-minded above all—will move toward rapprochement with the Soviet Union, which would be most ominous.

Nixon has been postponing a China trip in deference to President Carter's plans, but now expects to be in Peking for a few days of top-level discussions before the end of the year.

On the SALT II treaty: Will Nixon—architect of détente—support the treaty now before the Senate? Mr. Carter called him months ago to offer a briefing; Nixon, who can read treaties, declined.

I was all set to put this crucial SALT question to him when in walked Julie Eisenhower, my favorite Nixon, with 11-month-old Jennie. The baby reached out for her grandfather, who proudly took her in his arms, and the opportunity was lost.

However, when I wiggled my fingers at her, and said "SALT II?"—as one does with babies—Jennie said "Goo." As an old Nixon-watcher, I took this to mean that the child was trying to tell me that her grandfather will not soon volunteer his opinion. If Uncle Henry makes a statement that seems to come down on both sides of the issue, and if any such equivocation is interpreted to be Nixon's support of the treaty without amendments, then we will hear from grandpa loud and clear and make no mistake about that.

July 26, 1979

Editor, The New York Times:

We must all be grateful to William Safire, that inveterate "Nixon-watcher," as he unrepentantly describes himself in "Return From Elba," for giving us such heartening news of Mr. Nixon's health, cheeriness and general prosperity. But although I like to remember that Napoleon's return from Elba was followed by his downfall at Waterloo, I was under the impression that Mr. Nixon has already had his Waterloo. Is it all going backward now like a stunt scene in the movies? Waterloo . . . Elba . . . then perhaps another shot at Congress . . . this time from New York?

Alfred Kazin
William White Professor of English, 1978–9
University of Notre Dame
Notre Dame, Indiana

HENRY KISSINGER

TIGHTENING HENRY'S BELT

November 29, 1979

WASHINGTON—Henry Kissinger evidently did not like being portrayed as a pessimist at a crucial moment. In Richard Nixon's memoirs, in a downbeat moment after Hanoi's spring offensive in 1972 threatened the

Moscow summit, Nixon quoted himself as saying, "And then we're defeated," and wrote this about Henry's response: " 'Then we will just have to tighten our belts,' Kissinger replied glumly."

In his own memoirs, Kissinger gives a quite different impression. When Nixon mused that our failure in Vietnam might lose the whole free world, Kissinger quotes himself as rebutting that firmly with "No, if it fails, we'll have to tighten our belts and turn the forces around."

Was Kissinger glum, as Nixon reports, or resolute, as Kissinger reports? Why did Kissinger, whose memoirs followed Nixon's by almost a year, go out of his way to correct that quotation and give it a wholly different tone? Such questions about state of mind—and of the accuracy of direct quotations—are important to historians.

Nixon's source, according to former Nixon writer Frank Gannon, was the diary Nixon dictated after an Oval Office meeting on May 1, 1972. Kissinger's source, according to his associate, William Hyland, was the transcript of a telephone conversation held three weeks before, on April 9. Kissinger (especially conscious of his belt that month) used the earlier quotation to change the impression left by the glum comment cited by Nixon.

Spotlighting such a nuance is fair in examining a book replete with nuances, delicious details, and glimpses into the workings of the world of power politics and collegial backstabbing. For too long, a Watergate fixation has blocked an information-laden analysis of the last time the United States had a coherent foreign policy. Some highlights:

Henry, the newsmaker: The most newsworthy chapter deals with Kissinger's secret trip to Moscow before the summit in 1972 (as he tightened his belt glumly or resolutely). The President's envoy disagreed with his elected superior, treated anxious cabled instructions from the White House as "too late and too vague," and refused to press the Vietnam issue nearly as strongly as Nixon directed.

Never in our history has an envoy set his own judgment ahead of the President's in dealing with the head of a superpower; Nixon's memoir says only "there was no gainsaying his performance after the fact." No reviewer seems to care about the extent of Kissinger's amazing presumption. In his memoirs, Henry explains why "I stretched whatever authority I had. . . ." Unfortunately, he withholds much of what he told Leonid Brezhnev about Nixon, which I suspect would be embarrassing for him to reveal today.

Henry, the gentle self-wrist-slapper: He is amusedly apologetic about conspiring with a Soviet leader to deceive our Secretary of State about the drafting of an important document; in fact, that act, though Presidentially approved, was a spectacle for which "Dobryssinger" should be profoundly ashamed.

Henry, the solid historian: The mosaic of the China initiative is pains-

takingly, lovingly presented; he even tells the truth about the desire for secrecy coming from us, not the Chinese.

On Vietnam, his detailed exposition of the maddening negotiations—he
quotes Le Duc Tho's artful "I temporarily believe"—makes a powerful
case for the wisdom and courage of the course taken.

Henry, the settler of scores: He pays back five years of personal slights
by portraying Nixon as the Trilby to his Svengali. Because he was agent
and not prime mover, Kissinger strains to make it appear that Nixon was
merely a ratifier, and stops just short of suggesting that Nixon had been "a
student of mine at Harvard in 1956."

Because Kissinger evades responsibility for his illegal wiretapping; because he missed the boat on human rights; because he dismisses as "excited polemics" the documentation in this space of his disgraceful sellout
of the Kurdish people; and because he often forces me to agree with people whose side I do not like to be on, it pains me to write the following:

He has produced the Moby Dick of diplomatic memoirs. *White House
Years* (which sells at discount for a paltry penny a page) is an astounding
historical resource—lucidly written, passionate, richly textured, absolutely necessary to an understanding of the Nixon years, and a credit to
the mind and energy of the man who brought it forth. If Laird, Rogers,
Mitchell, Haig, and others see events differently, let them invest the effort
in writing as thorough and challenging a book.

This week, Henry is the target of an orchestrated campaign of White
House and State Department abuse for having committed the sin of suggesting, in regard to the admission of the Shah, that our national honor not
be set aside for fear of what a terrorist regime might do.

Out of place, but not out of power, he will slam back in his own way. In
retrospect, I am grateful for my own odd form of collaboration in his
memoirs: As one of those suing for public disclosure of the "Dead Key
Scrolls"—his telephone transcripts—I like to think I had a hand in keeping Henry's belt tighter and his memoirs more honest.

TED KENNEDY

TRANSPARENT FIG LEAF

May 3, 1979

This July will mark the tenth anniversary of man's historic walk on the moon. Mention that fact to a politician and his mind will instantly flash to the other newsmaking event of midsummer 1969: "Ten years since Chappaquiddick? I wonder if the voters have forgotten . . ."

Senator Edward Kennedy is, by any pollster's count, the most popular public figure in the United States today. He seems to be able to take any Republican on the horizon, and in a match-up against President Jimmy Carter among Democrats and independents, Kennedy is the preferred 1980 candidate by nearly two to one.

The other day, before the nation's newspaper editors meeting in New York City, the strong-voiced Senator, turning gray around the ears, popped the President in his populism, where it hurts him most.

Jimmy Carter, faced with the necessity of finally abandoning the populist dream of controlling oil prices, has had nothing to fall back upon but verbal castigation of the oil companies. He was getting away with it fairly well, snarling at "rip-offs" and "windfalls," until Ted Kennedy said out loud that "the oil lobby . . . has intimidated the Administration into throwing in the towel without even entering the ring on the issue of oil-price decontrol."

That must have smarted. Then the Senator blew away the smokescreen the President was using to cover his retreat: "It has also intimidated the Administration into submitting a token windfall tax that is no more than a transparent fig leaf over the vast new profits the industry will reap."

Not even a modestly opaque fig leaf, but a transparent one that makes profits truly "obscene." President Carter later flailed back with "baloney," a weak and uncharacteristic riposte, and added that he wished he had a bigger tax. The House will give it to him; the Senate will take it away. In the end, Jimmy Carter will have been out-populist-oratoried, as hard to do as out-segging George Wallace in the old days.

In the text of his speech distributed to the editors, Senator Kennedy went even further in his denunciation of what he sees to be the new cheapness in American Government. He wondered if the 1980's would be "a time of new action and inspiration, as when America moved from the decade of the 50's to the 60's?" (That's when the Kennedys took over.) "Or will it be a time of continuing reaction . . . ?"

"Continuing reaction"? That says plainly that Jimmy Carter is a reactionary President, or at least one willingly presiding over a time of reaction. But Senator Kennedy, at the moment of truth, gagged at the charge; he dropped "continuing" from his delivered speech and—on his first assault—backed away from confrontation.

But later in the speech, he was able to get his mouth around the charge: "The chronic serious inflation of the 70's has sent"—originally "plunged"—"the nation into a period of reaction . . . the result is an ominous streak of pessimism in our people. An unnatural meanness is threatening to encroach on the basic generosity of our national character."

This is a liberal speaking, proudly and angrily, against the grain of the times, taking issue not only with honest conservatives, but—more to the Democratic point—with those hypocrites who use the language of liberalism and compassion while riding along with the current popular revulsion against big taxing and spending.

Credit Ted Kennedy with the courage of his convictions, at least in theory. To put them into practice, he will have to enter the arena: My guess is that he will wait, as Robert Kennedy did in 1968, for another challenger to wreck the sitting President's wagon and will then step in to revivify the party. He could do so with all proper reluctance on the grounds that he could not let the party fall into the hands of cryptoconservative Jerry Brown.

Then we will see if the Kennedy anomaly can continue. Can a candidate's personal popularity remain high while his views, which are decidedly unpopular, become widely known? How much of the coin of his personal rating will be expended on his high-tax health proposals and troubling antibusiness bias?

Then, too, we will have the answer to the question I put to him after his speech: "Ten years after Chappaquiddick, do you think the American people have forgotten or forgiven—or not?"

The Senator blanched at the word: With eyes dull and voice sounding like the memory wizard in *The Thirty-Nine Steps*, he repeated by rote: "It's up to the people. I hope they make a judgment based on the total record. I'd certainly expect that. I'd expect it in terms of Massachusetts and I'd expect it in terms of the future."

Not much of an answer. He ought to work out a better one, because he has become the authentic voice of the left in America, and that discredited and disheartened position needs forceful articulation.

One year from now, halfway into the primaries, I expect Ted Kennedy to give his waiting troops the green light. And I think he will win—win big—before he loses.

5-25-79

Dear Mr. Safire:

I really would like to know why you zealous reporters and commentators and the media in general have been so easy on Senator Kennedy. You yourself have been obsessed with getting something on Carter. Yet for all your Republican conservatism, I have never yet read a word in your column suggesting that Senator Kennedy might not have all the qualities one expects in a Presidential candidate.

With all the agitation presently going on to promote his cause, this is a source of great puzzlement to me.

All the ingredients are there. No one, not even President Nixon, has ever more blatantly revealed his basic character to the world. Callousness, cowardice, deception, panic—all were revealed at Chappaquiddick—cheating at college, cheating on his wife—good Lord, what more would any investigative reporter—or reflective journalist—want.

Yet never a word. Virtually a complete blackout. A whole generation has come of voting age who have no reason to believe he is anything but a white knight. Why? It bugs me.

Sincerely,
Helen Gregory
Wilmington, North Carolina

PRELUDE TO THE BRIDGE

October 24, 1979

WASHINGTON—The date was March 26, 1958. Deputy Sheriff T. M. Whitten of Albemarle County, Va., was in his police cruiser that evening at the intersection of U.S. 29 and the U.S. 250 bypass when he spotted a car speeding.

The officer gave chase. He pushed his cruiser as fast as it could safely go on dimly lit Barracks Road, but could not catch up. He kept the speeding vehicle in sight, even though the speeder may have cut his lights to elude the trailing policeman.

Sheriff Whitten saw the darkened car ahead duck into a driveway. He caught up and drove in behind it. The speeder's car was parked, engine off, lights out, apparently empty. The sheriff got out of his cruiser, carefully approached the vehicle, and looked in the driver's window.

According to the officer, the driver was lying prone on the front seat, hiding. The officer told him to get up, he was under arrest. The arrested man identified himself as Edward M. Kennedy, 26, a second-year law student at the University of Virginia. Three months later, on June 16, 1958, Mr. Kennedy—president of the Student Legal Forum and in two months to be named manager of his oldest brother's senatorial re-election campaign in Massachusetts—was convicted for reckless driving and fined $35.

So what's the big deal? Don't we all do some stupid things in our mid-twenties? Just because a man runs for President, do we have to rake up muck that's over 20 years old?

This story was first sketched to me a month ago by someone who called it "a psychological prelude to Chappaquiddick." It is worth examining to see if some pattern exists in Mr. Kennedy's life that shows a trait in his character leading him to run from reality in a crisis.

To check the story, I called Senator Kennedy's press aide, Tom Southwick. He recollected "a speeding ticket back in 1958, ten miles over the limit, $15 fine." That was true enough, but it was not the same incident.

Next stop was the files of *The Daily Progress* of Charlottesville, Va. The article about the minor speeding violation was there, but so was a more serious reckless-driving story—without the part about Kennedy hiding, crouched in the front seat.

A reporter from *The Daily Progress*, Doug Kamholz, became curious and volunteered to do some checking with the reporter who originally covered the story, and with the local lawyer for Kennedy and the arresting officer. He did a thorough job.

Did Kennedy cut his lights to shake the pursuit? At the court hearing in 1958, according to a yellowed clip, "Kennedy testified that he discovered later that his taillights had a short circuit. A garage mechanic testified that the short circuit was found a few days after the arrest."

Today, the Kennedy press aide, after checking with the Senator and the local Charlottesville lawyer, E. Gerald Tremblay, informs me they stick to that story: "The judge determined that it would have been impossible to drive down that road without lights."

But T. M. Whitten, the arresting officer who is now a security guard, tells reporter Kamholz: "He cut his lights out on me and tried to outrun me."

Former Sheriff Whitten has no anti-Kennedy animus: "I don't want any part of anything for or against him." Indeed, he took offense decades ago at reporters who tried to sensationalize the incident, and wanted to tell the Kennedy family he would testify in its behalf in any libel trial. But then Rose Kennedy called him "and really got on my butt" to shut up; now he's neutral.

After Kennedy pulled into his driveway, did he hide? The answer from Senator Kennedy's press aide is unequivocal: "I spoke to the Senator and he informs me he was not hiding."

The cop's recollection differs: "He had gotten down in the front seat of the car," Whitten told reporter Kamholz. This was not information freely volunteered; the reporter had asked if "the story about hiding in the back seat is true," and the former policeman reluctantly set the facts straight on exactly where in the car Kennedy had been hiding.

Did Kennedy receive special treatment in court? Magdelene Andrews Poff, *The Daily Progress* reporter at the time, recalls seeing no Kennedy name on the arrest blotter, but discovered five warrants with Kennedy's name in a court cash drawer. The judge, now dead, "threw me out of court."

If you want to believe the Kennedy version of all this, he was innocently driving along, perhaps a little fast, perhaps with his rear lights out, when he was put upon and convicted by a pack of vindictive Virginians.

But if you believe the cop and the local reporters, as I do, a pattern of character emerges: In 1951, faced with flunking a Spanish exam, he panicked and persuaded a ringer to substitute for him, and for that was expelled from Harvard; in 1958, with a sheriff on his tail, he panicked and tried to escape and was convicted; in 1969, when his companion drowned, he panicked and left the scene of the accident for nine hours until someone else discovered his car.

When in big trouble, Ted Kennedy's repeated history has been to run, to hide, to get caught, and to get away with it.

October 31, 1979

Editor
The New York Times

Dear Sir,

William Safire's article villifying Edward Kennedy merely exposed Safire's own vendetta against the Senator. That Mr. Kennedy erred is common knowledge; what is exemplary is the formidable nature of his political growth and maturity, the development of compassion and understanding he has gained, and the extraordinary assessment of the public mood that no other political figure seems able to grasp.

Safire's bitter political reportage shows itself to be unreliable and seems to stem from a need to rehabilitate the shabby exploits of Richard Nixon. In the process Safire has become obnoxious and scurrilous.

Senator Kennedy will make a great president!

Sincerely
Sylvia Day
Woodstock, New York

November 5, 1979

Dear Mr. Safire,

I have never answered a political column of yours before because we are miles apart on our viewpoints and I doubt that we could look at a sunset in Arizona and see it the same way. I read you, however, because it is important to me to see how "the other side" feels; or says it feels.

But the sentence that triggered this letter is the last sentence in a column from *The New York Times* that was reprinted in the *Arizona Republic....* It was the last sentence in the last paragraph. I quote: "When in big trouble, Ted Kennedy's repeated history has been to run, to hide, to get caught, and to get away with it."

I am a Democrat but no great admirer of Ted Kennedy, nor of Jimmy Carter, but I call this to your attention: Perhaps at this time in our sad and sorry history, we need someone who CAN GET AWAY WITH IT.

Richard Nixon, with all his experience and his proven ability, couldn't; Lyndon Johnson, with all the goodwill of the entire world and this nation, couldn't; Gerald Ford, with his past experience in government, with his holding a fragmented and hurt nation together, couldn't; Jimmy Carter, an (alleged) honest, sincere, intelligent, couldn't. Perhaps the time has come when someone who can get away with it should be given the chance to try.... We have nothing to lose, anymore—or have we?

Very truly yours,
Jeannette Multer
Phoenix, Arizona

REJECTED COUNSEL RETURNS

September 24, 1979

WASHINGTON—I am pleased to see that Ted Kennedy has on his staff a Rejected Counsel. That used to be my job in the White House: to go into the President's office before a major decision and say: "Do the popular thing. Take the easy way." Later, in a ringing speech, the President could truthfully say: "Some of my advisers have told me to do the popular thing, to take the easy way. I have rejected such counsel...."

In his speech to the Congressional Black Caucus not long ago, Senator Kennedy said: "Some say that a different tide is running in this country now. They tell us to slow down, to take a rest, to let things be. But I am here tonight to tell you that they are wrong. Our trumpets do not know how to sound retreat."

The Rejected Counsel was surely at work. "Excuse me, Senator, I know you're working on a speech, but I thought you ought to know that a different tide is running, although if I were you I would lay off water metaphors. Slow down. Take a rest. Let things be. Let the trumpet sound retreat."

He did his job well, that Rejected Counsel, stirring the Senator to rhetorical heights, even if the trumpet image is trite-and-true. But in one crucial area the Rejected Counsel has not yet been rejected. When it comes to Mr. Carter's pitiful economic policy, Senator Kennedy seems content to let things be.

He has already suggested that the trumpet which will announce his candidacy (that instrument evidently does not have the keys necessary to blow retreat) will be heard when he finally decides that economic conditions make President Carter's continued tenure intolerable.

This means that Mr. Kennedy expects to have it both ways: By not criticizing the Carter inflation now, he lets the President sink deeper in the soup; by tying his announcement to the salvation of the economy, Mr. Kennedy absolves himself of blame for what Federal spending has done to the consumer dollar.

The Senator rightly sees the need to disagree dramatically with the President on some major policy. He has agreed with Carter policies on SALT II, on selling out Taiwan, on the disastrous energy price control, on refusing to build U.S. defenses, and even on Cuba. He has differed mainly on health insurance, but he cannot oust a sitting President with a heavy-spending program that even most Democrats do not want. That leaves Topic A: the roaring inflation and coming recession.

Mr. Kennedy is mistaken if he thinks the President will hang around waiting for him to put out a position paper in January condemning Carter and proposing a mix of measures that would sound good and would not be disprovable in a campaign.

Logic suggests that some new ideas will be put forward soon—by labor, Government, or business—to cope with stagflation, perhaps along the lines of a social contract that would deliver mutual benefits rather than rely exclusively on patriotic exhortations.

In that event, the Kennedy candidacy could not afford to lie supine for more than a few months on the central issue in the campaign: Who can best lead the economy away from crippling inflation without triggering really whopping unemployment?

Come next spring, Mr. Kennedy will be forced to stop reminiscing about how wonderful those guidelines were back in the days his brother was President. Unemployment will be on the rise; inflation will still be high; no matter what long-range solution may be in the works—squeezing borrowers and Humphrey-Hawking everybody else—the time will be ripe for a powerful piece of demagoguery.

Wage and price controls. The popular thing; the easy way. Unless Senator Kennedy is easily crushing President Carter and Governor Brown in the early primaries, he will feel the need for some display of leadership to show how his Presidency will be different and activist. He will answer the recession with a plan for a huge tax cut and spending increase, simultaneously clamping down the lid of controls. (If Kennedy is crushing Carter, this becomes Carter's course of action.)

This year, of course, all candidates (some Republicans are running, too) will speak of controls with disdain. But liberals and hyperactivists will respond to popular outcry next year. Kennedy is philosophically even more attuned than Carter to Government control of prices, as his anti-business record on oil illustrates.

One of Mr. Kennedy's eminent economic advisers, when in a facetious mood on the subject of incomes policy, likes to recall an aphorism attributed to the gangster Al Capone: "You get a lot more from a kind word and a gun than from a kind word alone." When liberal families clash, the Kennedy clan will not hesitate to go to the mattresses of controls.

In a fight for the Democratic nomination, the 50-yard line is still at that place that F.D.R. called "a little left of center." Ironically, when a recession bites, productivity rises and inflation abates, and the advice of the Rejected Counsel makes sense: "Slow down. Take a rest. Let things be." But that good advice is given only to be scorned.

WATERQUIDDICK

November 12, 1979

WASHINGTON—Last week, that cruelest of cartoonists, Oliphant of *The Washington Star*, showed a brooding Nixon staring at Ted Kennedy on television. Caption: "So, once upon a time he went on TV, and lied to the people . . . so, what's wrong with that?"

The same day, Tom Wicker of *The New York Times* evoked the similarity of two cover-ups subtly but unmistakably, calling the subject of Chappaquiddick "a cancer on his candidacy."

To compare Chappaquiddick with Watergate is to infuriate Kennedy partisans. How can one tragic accident, with no malice aforethought, be spoken of in the same breath with the systematic abuse of power—the use of governmental agencies to tamper with the political process—that was Watergate?

Let us count the ways:

(*1*) *The guilty innocence beforehand.* Nixon did not know in advance of the Watergate break-in, or even of the break-in at the Ellsberg psychiatrist's office; surely, Kennedy did not know he would be going off the bridge. Yet both men were immediately burdened by a guilty conscience: Nixon, because he had created "the plumbers" long before, and Kennedy, because he probably had been looking for a secluded spot to park.

(2) *The immediate reaction.* Nixon did not consider letting justice take its course; he promptly tried to use the C.I.A. to deflect the F.B.I. investigation.

Kennedy, with Miss Kopechne still trapped in the submerged car—possibly alive and suffocating—did not go to the police for help. The diver who later brought out the body claimed that if called, he could have saved her life. Instead, Kennedy consulted two friends—one was former U.S. Attorney Paul Markham—and supposedly enlisted their aid in an amateur lifesaving attempt. He then directed both not to report the fatality and disappeared for nine hours. His friends obeyed his strange order to report nothing, and the Senator did not acknowledge the accident until the wreck had been discovered the next morning by police.

(3) *The early cover story.* Nixon, through spokesmen, derided a "third-rate burglary attempt," and claimed that no one in the White House had been involved. Kennedy's first statement, prepared by Mr. Markham, made no mention of the rescue attempts later claimed to have been made by Markham and Gargan. Kennedy lawyers insisted the inquest be secret, and, using court proceedings as an excuse, refused all other answers until the emotional and uninformative televised speech. No questioning was permitted.

(4) *The cover-up.* Nixon's men arranged for legal counsel and "humanitarian aid" to pay for the living expenses of those arrested; Jeb Magruder reported the damage had been contained.

Kennedy's men made arrangements for $170,000 to be given to Miss Kopechne's parents, though this could not fairly be called "hush money." Party participants were given the line on the time the Senator and his companion left the party: One witness, who had told many reporters it was impossible to say when Kennedy left, changed her story at the inquest to conform to the version told by the Senator. Incredibly, no autopsy was performed to determine whether death was by suffocation or drowning.

(5) *The limited modified confession.* Nixon, in his memoirs and the Frost interviews, admitted mistakes and wrongdoing—but no criminal act. Kennedy, despite the judge's finding that he probably lied under oath, admits "irresponsible, irrational, inexcusable" behavior—but no crime.

(6) *The big picture.* Nixon says he hopes history will see his Administration with Watergate in perspective. Kennedy says he hopes that his career will be judged in its totality, and not just in the light of one tragic flight from reality.

The similarities are there: over-awed law officers, hesitant about grilling a bigwig; team players protecting the top man; the gap in the tape and the disappearing dosier at the Edgartown Police Department; the lofty speeches and the hanging tough.

The dissimilarities are also there: the glee with which the Nixonians were pursued, and the reverence with which the Kennedyites were questioned; the prosecutorial passion of Judge Sirica to get at the truth, and the pettifogging protection of Judge Boyle that let the truth be hidden.

In order of magnitude, Nixon's sins were the greater: As President, he was the nation's chief law officer. Nobody drowned at Watergate, but nobody challenged the Fourth Amendment at Chappaquiddick.

The purpose of this exercise is to remind all those who were outraged at the cover-up of Watergate that at least part of their old outrage might properly be directed at their new hero. An unexpected dividend of this comparison is to remind those of us who were more understanding of human foibles during Watergate that a single standard requires us to apply some of that cynical compassion to the successful cover-up at Chappaquiddick.

November 13, 1979

Dear Editor:

Your token reactionary, William Safire has gone just a tad too far in his latest attempt to prove that Democratic liberals are just as immoral as Republican neo-facists. In the past, Safire had been content to analogize recent scandals to his former employer's whopper by attaching the suffix "gate" to whatever high crime or misdemeanor had momentarily caught the press's attention (Remember Koreagate, Lancegate, Oilgate, Billygate, etceteragate?). Having finally run out of gates, Waterquiddick (Why not Kopechnegate? How about Liberalgate?) plumbs unreached depths of libel. Intimating that Kennedy drove off the bridge because he was too busy making a pass to watch the road is about as cheap a shot as can be taken. The seat-of-the-pants psychoanalysis Safire engaged in when, in a previous column, he pointed to Kennedy's scurrilous "patterns of behavior" is not just a warped use of history; it is a contemptible misrepresentation. I only hope that Kennedy will file a libel suit against him so that some emerging young journalist can coin the next buzz-word: Safiregate.

David L. Lock
New York, New York

12 November 1979

Sir:

Everyone knows you bailed out of the Nixon administration before Watergate, and assumes that you are untouched by it.

It is, however, apparent to a steady reader of your work that you can't seem to leave it alone. You keep coming back to it, as to the scene of a crime. You are like a tongue around a sore tooth. Why have you persistently devoted your not inconsiderable talents to trying to show that Watergate, well, *was* bad, but no worse than *this* or than *that;* that Watergate was, so OK, wrong; but no more wrong than this other thing. *Et cetera. Et cetera. Ad* oh no, not another one of *those* Safires. You're getting to be a bore. If you don't like something, like Korea payoffs of Congressmen or Chappaquiddick, just say so. Please stop dragging this tatty, old, shedding, smelly, stuffed albatross into every discussion. "See, your albatross is at least as big as this one." "Yeah, but, see, this albatross is no bigger, or only a little bit bigger, than that one." (*Et cetera*)

Become again the surprising & witty columnist you used to be!

Judith Economos
Scarsdale, New York

11/12/79

Bravo on "Waterquiddick"—except for the last line, which you don't believe but which some may think you do.

Best,
Nat
[Nat Hentoff]
New York, New York

The Stuff of Politics

SENATOR BOB PACKWOOD, Republican of Oregon, pulls his party together every February for a weekend-long look at The Issues—at least, a look at those on which Republicans can find common ground.

It's always a good occasion for a political philosophy piece: Here are a couple of them, along with related essays on what came to be known as "the taxpayer's revolt."

THE PACKWOOD PLAN

March 7, 1977

WASHINGTON—Here is what is going to happen in Republican politics:

Most of the behind-the-scenes action will begin in Houston, Tex. Such Republican luminaries as Senator John Tower, former Ford campaign manager James Baker, Anne Armstrong, and Bus Mosbacher are soon likely to line up quietly behind Houston's George Bush for President. At the same time, John Connally can be expected to line up behind Houston's John Connally for President.

The Texas donnybrook will include Ronald Reagan, who has more support among Texans than any Texan. Offstage, and up north, Illinois Governor Jim Thompson hopes one day to pit his inexperience against old Establishment insider Jimmy Carter; and in Washington, Senator Howard Baker hopes to stride like Fortinbras upon the bloodied scene at the final moment.

Got that? Watch this space for an update in a couple of years. Now let us look at what *should* be happening in Republican politics.

Republican leaders should not compete solely on the basis of who can complain the loudest about one-party rule, but should start figuring out what makes their political philosophy different and better.

Senator Bob Packwood of Oregon took a crack at a fresh approach this weekend at a conference in Seaside, Oregon. He reminded his Republican audience that the nation had always been made up of "risk-takers and certainty-seekers," and that for the past 45 years the Republicans were on the side of the risk-takers while the Democrats got a lock on the certainty-seekers, who are an overwhelming majority. To become the majority party again, he pointed out, Republicans have to come up with a way to satisfy the certainty-seekers while without removing the necessary incentive from the risk-takers, as the Democrats are wont to do.

Striking such a balance does not require lapsing into wishiwashiness, or adopting the liberal academic's despairing slogan of "anomie-too." On the contrary; since the Democrat's way of providing security is essentially the high-taxing, big-government way, Republicans can deliver security in a noticeably different way. The "discernable alternative" which Senator Packwood proposes is that the Federal Government requires that employers provide social services for their employees, at the community level, rather than taxing both to set up a separate means of providing those services the way we do today.

"Services provided," says Senator Packwood, "could eventually include health care, legal care, day care, educational benefits, loans to purchase a home, employee stock ownership, income security programs, perhaps even auto care. . . . The important thing is that business provide them before the Federal Government jumps into it."

Such a movement is already under way; the Senator points to Ford Motor's health insurance for employees, which delivers more health care than any Federal scheme now being touted would offer.

Unions are alert to this private-sector approach, as well they should be if they want to stay in business. One imaginative union has come up with prepaid legal insurance for its members, paid for by the employer at the rate of $5 a month per employee.

Will mandatory, employer-financed social services come free? Of course not; its cost is added on the price of goods and is paid for by the consumer. And some Government-provided services must exist for people who are not connected with an employer.

But the central idea is to stop the slide toward let-Washington-do-it by introducing an element of competition: The private delivery of services will compete with the Government's, to the benefit of both.

Makes sense, once conservatives accept the notion that security is here to stay and liberals accept the notion that a Government bureaucracy is not the only way to provide that security.

There is partisan moxie in the Packwood message: "In trying to answer the demands for security and certainty, the Democrats will continue to pile Federal program atop Federal program. The inevitable result will be continued unresponsiveness, mismanagement, and eventual collapse. We must recognize and provide the certainty and security that most people covet," Mr. Packwood tells his fellow Republicans, "but we must fulfill those desires within the traditional Republican philosophy which also rewards those who take risks that move this country forward."

Packwood's plan—and it is not yet a plan—exploits the anti-Washington taxpayer's resentment without arousing the receiver of security's fear. The new way would enable Republicans, while complaining bitterly about Democratic mismanagement, to espouse an alternative with positive passion.

In selecting candidates down the road, Republicans will want more than the carbon copy of Jimmy Carter's vague blasts at "national disgraces" and seat-of-the-pants solutions centered on "trust me." We'll trust the men with a coherent philosophy, able to debate it—and not just another toothy grin.

TAXPAYERS' REVOLT

February 27, 1978

SAN DIEGO—Seventy-five-year-old Howard Jarvis, an irascible old coot usually dismissed as a "conservative gadfly," went out and got 1,200,000 Californians to sign a petition that puts a proposition on the June primary election ballot to reduce property taxes to 1 percent of assessed valuation.

That would slash the average property tax bill by two-thirds, and would give the state budget a $7 billion kick in the head. Nearly every "responsible" politician and editorialist in the state is aghast at the consequences: firing teachers, closing schools and hospitals, cutting welfare.

"But the damn thing could pass," says one prominent politician, who like most others is afraid to oppose in public the modest proposal of the aroused property owners. "And if the tax revolt succeeds here, in a fairly liberal state, there's no telling where it could lead."

To do battle with the Jarvis Initiative, state legislators—who did nothing about soaring property taxes last year—are now scurrying about submitting alternative tax-relief proposals. Democratic Governor Brown, studiously silent about Jarvis, supports a different item on the ballot that keeps the power to tax in the state government's hands while vaguely promising some property tax relief.

Meanwhile, to prepare for the possibility of a Jarvis victory, legislators are working on proposals to increase other taxes to keep the state government in business. Mr. Jarvis is aware of this: Muttering about the "senile old men" who oppose him, the agile codger is preparing a proposition for the November ballot to block the state from levying these new taxes.

The national significance of this revolt against taxation-as-usual should be apparent: Talk of tax *reform* is not enough when middle-class people have tax *reduction* in mind. State and local governments, which have ballooned much faster than the Federal Government in recent decades, go after what the taxpayer owns (property taxes) rather than what he earns (income taxes). As a result, the strapped "rich" are lashing back at the well-to-do poor.

Why should this revolt begin in Southern California? The quick answer is that the population is older and the incidence of home ownership higher. But an underlying reason is the surge in the number of *illegales*—aliens fleeing poverty in Mexico—who have been crossing the border by the hundreds of thousands.

Whether they are derided as "wetbacks" or welcomed as "undocumented persons," the newcomers are transforming California life: Los Angeles will soon be the predominantly Spanish town it started out to be, centuries ago.

But the *illegales* do not come to go on United States welfare. By and large, they work harder than most United States citizens, and in the long run will strengthen the country. They are renters, not property owners, however, and their children born here—all United States citizens—require public schools and other services usually financed by property taxes.

As one might expect, property taxpayers see themselves giving much more than they are getting; they see wage earners, both legal and illegal, getting more in services than they pay for in taxes. Thus, led by the apartment-house owners (those despised "landlords"), and supported by the far more numerous homeowners whose children have already finished school, the property taxpayers have rebelled.

If the Jarvis Initiative succeeds, or even if the state of California comes up with a moderate alternative to reduce property taxes, the local tax base will shift from the "havers" to the "makers": A sales tax falls on the purchases made by *illegales* and others, and a local income tax reaches those who most often make use of local services.

Is such a shift good public policy? I think so. The present notion of putting a tax on wealth, so popular with soak-the-rich demagogues, actually soaks the middle class—penalizing the thrifty while profiting the profligate. People should be taxed on what they earn, not on what they had been able to accumulate after taxes, through savings and investment.

By mindlessly jacking up property taxes, we have been discouraging home and apartment ownership, which is a powerful force for personal economic stability and national economic growth. That's the first tax that ought to be reduced if we want to stimulate the economy without generating inflation.

And so I embrace the seemingly radical Jarvis manifesto. A specter is haunting state and county bureaucracy: the spectre of tax revolt. Mortgagees of the world, unite—you have nothing to lose but your liens.

NO MORE MEGO'S

May 4, 1978

EASTON, Md.—A "MEGO," in newsmagazine lingo, is a topic to be avoided at all costs: The acronym stands for "My Eyes Glaze Over." Typical MEGO's are petrodollars, foreign aid, government reorganization; your lids are growing heavy even as you read these words.

The most stupefying political MEGO of our times has been "fiscal responsibility," a slogan behind which Republicans have been slogging for nearly half a century while the rest of the world has gone by. Cut Federal spending; balance the budget; so went the G.O.P. catechism. But that never happened, even when Republicans were elected.

Last weekend, with neither a bang nor a whimper, the new Republican leadership said goodbye to all that. At the Tidewater conference, organized by Senator Bob Packwood and attended by about 50 G.O.P. legislative leaders of all shapes and political stripes, the body of "fiscal responsibility" was gently interred.

Not that irresponsibility was exalted; No, the change was from means to ends. The question was not "How do we balance the budget?" but "How do we spur economic growth?"; not "How do we slice the pie?" but "How do we make the pie bigger?"

The central issue that divides Democrats and Republicans today, it was decided, is tax policy. Although the Carter Administration and the Democratic leadership in Congress pretends to be for a "tax cut," that is a transparent deception. Even if the Carter proposals are adopted, two out of three Americans will pay more taxes over the next two years than they do today. The new Social Security tax is enormous, and the 9 percent inflation drives wage earners into higher tax brackets, even though their purchasing power stays the same.

The Republicans want a slashing of income-tax and capital-gains tax rates, which would have a profound effect on increasing the take-home pay of the middle-income American, and in attracting the capital needed to create new jobs.

When the ghost of fiscal responsibility, dragging its chains, asks if this will not reduce Government revenues and increase the deficit, the answer is shot back (perhaps too quickly) that less can be more: If taxes are substantially cut, the economy will be productively stimulated, and the lower tax rates will actually produce more revenues than today's incentive-strangling high rates. Bigger pie, you see.

A good case can be made that such a cut might lead to the desired result. When talking to Democrats, the zealots of economic neoconservatism recall the results of the Kennedy tax cut in the early 1960's—lower rates and higher revenues, the best of both worlds.

When talking to conservatives, the tax-cutters harken to the days of 1954, when Robert Taft and Daniel Reeves proposed tax reduction to President Eisenhower but Treasury Secretary George Humphrey turned it down, citing a fear of deficits. (John Rhodes, the House Minority Leader, listening to New York Representative Jack Kemp make his dynamic, hunched-forward pitch, could not help interjecting: "But you were in high school." Mr. Rhodes, however, gladly waves back to the wave of the future; he's tired of losing.)

Which brings up the question: Is the real tax-cut idea too good to be true, too obviously a popular proposal to be "responsible"? Can such good politics also be good public policy?

The Republicans in conclave assembled think so. The liberals (Senators Charles Mathias of Maryland, Jacob Javits of New York) did not object; the conservatives (the Senate Minority Leader, Howard Baker; Delaware's William Roth, Idaho's Jim McClure, Wyoming's Malcolm Wallop) were enthusiastic. The promise of stimulating higher revenues choked off the worries of liberals concerned about reduced Government services, and the prospect of greater rewards for those who work and save attracted the conservatives.

But it is old-fashioned to measure reactions along the old left-right scale, with the left pushing big government and income redistribution, and the right pushing private sector and self-reliance. A North-South scale is being put forward by the next generation of leadership, as it seeks the point at which tax rates generate the most revenues to provide Government services while encouraging more personal freedom and individual economic growth.

As Carter populists prattle about simplifying the tax code (while making more Government grants more complex), tomorrow's leaders talk of using the tax code to provide incentives for people to promote the public interest (thereby simplifying and eliminating many Federal grants).

Tidewater may have been a turning point. The language is new, the attitude is constructive, and—who knows?—the ideas may even be fiscally responsible.

FRIEDMAN AMENDMENT

February 5, 1979

EASTON, Md.—A specter is haunting Congress: the specter of a Constitutional convention.

Twenty-four states out of a needed 34 have already passed resolutions calling for a national convention to pass an amendment to balance the Federal budget; Presidential candidates as similar as Democrat Jerry Brown and Republican John Connally have hastened to head the parade.

The convention method of amending the Constitution was provided by the Founding Fathers as a way of lighting a fire under the Congress if the Government in Washington did not prove responsive to the will of most of the states. The threat of a convention has been used before to induce Congress to propose amendments for states to then ratify; but in 200 years, those who proposed the convention method have never needed to go all the way.

Washington has reacted to the recent pressure of the Constitutional budget-balancers with a combination of fear, loathing, shock, and horror: The often-expressed fear is that if those yahoos in the countryside ever got together with Constitutional sanction, they would tear up the Bill of Rights and bring back slavery.

Such a shrill, anguished reaction from Washington illustrates the wisdom of the Founders: A growing central government is unlikely to share its power or curtail its growth without a powerful threat from the states. Lawmakers in Washington will now have to find a way to limit Federal growth by offering an amendment of their own, or will have the initiative to do so legally wrested away.

The movement to curtail Federal growth will not be stopped. President Carter may try to pose as Scrooge with his "lean, tight, austere" rhetoric, but too many taxpayers know that he is increasing Federal spending by $40 billion—nearly 8 percent—which is a far cry from "budget cutting." Worse, any reduction of the Federal deficit will come not because spending is curtailed but because inflation is squeezing more tax dollars out of workers pushed into higher brackets.

Since most people have become convinced that the Government will never willingly stop its own growth, they are demanding a change in the Constitution that will force the Government to stop growing. The stern adjectives of rafshoonery will not suffice; tax-and-spend-a-little-less-than-usual will not do; if spending cannot be restrained by lawmakers, then the lawmakers' spending will have to be restrained by law.

At the second annual Tidewater conference on Maryland's eastern shore, Republican officials convened by Senator Bob Packwood have reacted responsibly to the undeniable grass-roots demand.

Most of the lawmakers who came to Tidewater knew that an amendment requiring a balanced budget, which is what the states have been talking about, is flawed. Not only would enforced balance forbid the Government to lean against the economic winds when necessary, but it would fail to mandate the curtailment of bureaucracy: Tax-bracket creep could still increase the Federal tax take and a bureaucracy could thus grow, even with the budget balanced. What is desired is not so much "balance" as discipline—a handle on increases in Federal spending.

Nobel laureate Milton Friedman—the conservatives' beloved "Uncle Miltie"—had been asked for his answer by the nonpartisan National Tax Limitation Committee. At a small breakfast last week, economist Friedman put forward a Constitutional amendment limiting the increase in Federal spending to the percentage increase in gross national product—with a more severe limitation in times of inflation, and an escape hatch in times of recession.

The Friedman amendment permits Keynsians to stimulate the economy, when necessary, by tax reduction rather than by a spending increase; most important, it imposes a discipline on the Congress and the executive that neither branch has been able to achieve, alone or together.

At Tidewater II, Republican Senator John Heinz announced he would soon put forward the Friedman amendment; in the Senate, on the Democratic side, Senator Dick Stone of Florida is likely to do the same. These men are two of the brightest lights in their respective parties; it is significant that Heinz and Stone are responding while so many of their confreres are wringing their hands.

What began as an inchoate, impractical movement to balance the Federal budget, eliciting Washington's scorn for its form and alarm for its method, has begun to mature: We now have a practical amendment, conceived by an economist of repute, sponsored by the Senate Establishment of the future.

The specter haunting Washington is doing its job: We may never have a Constitutional convention, but the menace of one will bring about some spending limitation much like the Friedman amendment. The people will be heard, even when the Government does not want to hear; the framers of the Constitution found the most ingenious way, two centuries ago, to make sure of that.

More American Life

PORNOGRAPHY, the rights of gays, the rights of straights, topless-ness, prostitution—these are titillating subjects for an essayist in need of a change of pace. The common denominator of those, of course, is sex; the uncommon denominator is privacy.

My political mindset resists the intrusion of Government into the individual's moral decisions. I call that "conservative," but many people who would not be caught dead at a Republican coffee klatch consider that to be vaguely liberal. ("You are a true liberal," wrote Al Goldstein, editor of *Screw* magazine, after I had upheld his right to raunchiness; I sent him a note back saying: "I didn't knock you, why are you knocking me?")

On some other offbeat topics—personal depression, the politics of marriage, looting, punk rock—when I go in, I don't know where I will come out. The essay is concluded with a satisfying "So that's what I think!" Maybe I ought to try that more often, but it's hard getting away from the front pages.

PORN FREE

December 27, 1976

WASHINGTON—A speechwriter in the campaign of 1968 was asked to come up with an indignation-stirring statement to appeal to the voters of Salt Lake City, and promptly drafted a blast at the smut peddlers who were illegally using the mails to send unsolicited obscene material to children.

Unfortunately, the statement was lost in the shuffle of papers aboard the campaign plane. Just before landing, a panic-stricken Nixon aide rushed down the aisle asking: "Who's got the ——— obscenity statement?"

That innocent use of an obscenity to describe a diatribe against obscenity comes to mind as local prosecutors have broken out in a rash of indictments against pornographers.

In Memphis, a 33-year-old prosecutor is angling for the governor's job by getting a dozen hard-core convictions, including the male star of *Deep Throat*. In Wichita, prosecutors are trying to drive New York-based smutineer Al Goldstein out of business by applying local Kansas standards. In Cincinnati next month, a crime-conspiracy statute is being stretched to snare Larry Flynt, publisher of the raunchy *Hustler* magazine.

The first reaction of most conservatives is to share the indignant reaction against the wave of newsstand porn and sexploitation films. Conservatives respect tradition, and want to uphold moral values and standards of good taste. The anything-goes set is not our crowd.

But certain principles are at stake in the way smut is suppressed.

First, Government does not belong in the personal-morality-among-adults business. We should teach morality, we should preach morality, but we should not legislate morality.

Next, the conspiracy statutes that are being used so often to harass pornographers are an abomination. Whether the targets are rioters, White House aides, or even less popular souls, whenever the Government cannot prove a person guilty of a crime, it ought not then be able to jail that person for "conspiracy to commit" that crime.

Finally, Government ought not to intrude on the right of adults to see or read whatever they choose, provided that performance or publication does not include the commission of, or incitement to, a crime.

Surely, a chorus will reply, there are legal limits to free expression—yelling "fire" in a crowded theater, and all that. Doesn't society have the right to protect itself from moral degeneracy?

Yes, but. The Supreme Court has rightly been directing obscenity decisions down to the local level, to "community standards." But its purpose has been to allow local areas to curtail local distribution, and not to stop national publication by jailing editors or actors. Neither New York nor Wichita should impose its standard on the other.

The problem—in any community—is to defend the rights of those who do not want to be exposed to pornography while defending the rights of those who do. Such a balance of rights is not impossible.

The solution is to allow localities to stop pornographers from grabbing all citizens, including minors, by the lapels. Curtail the hard-sell, not the hard-core. Actors should be allowed to prance about naked on stage, where admission is by ticket only, but not down the public streets; similarly, a publication should be able to exhibit its tastelessness on the inside, but not on the cover where people who don't want to see it are forced to see it.

The absolute, anything-goes demand is as wrong as the absolute put-'em-in-the-slammer philosophy; the freedom that needs protection is not so much the pornographer's freedom or the bluenose's freedom as the freedom of the average person to make his own choice.

It's a free country. Let actor Harry Reems do what some people want to pay to see, let editors Al Goldstein and Larry Flynt hustle what many others feel the urge to purchase, and let all the other people who find such products repellent and degrading have the right not to have smut thrust at them against their will.

That seems to this libertarian conservative more sensible than to let legislators decide that anything in the prurient interest is not in the public interest, or to let judges taste the power and pleasure of being editors, or to let pornographers take over the streets and airwaves.

After eight years, I have an answer to the aide who lost my obscenity statement somewhere over Salt Lake City: Let individual Americans make their own ———— decision about obscenity.

NYKTIMES NYK C
IPMTINT NYK
WU07036 FR TDMT NEW YORK NY 96 12-28 1121A EST
WILLIAM SAFIRE
CARE NEW YORK TIMES
NYK
YOUR WELL THOUGHT OUT PIECE IN SUPPORT OF THE FIRST AMENDMENT AMAZED ME CONSIDERING YOUR PRIOR INVOLVEMENT WITH RICHARD NIXON. IT SHOWS I HAVE MISJUDGED YOU AND I COMMEND YOU FOR YOUR COURAGEOUS POSITION. YOU ARE A TRUE LIBERAL.
BEST REGARDS
AL GOLDSTEIN
NYK TIMES NYK C
IPMTINT NYK

December 29, 1976

Mr. William Safire
The New York Times

Dear Bill:

I read with interest your column on pornography. I would like to try to get you to consider a different slant on this problem.

I write as one who can swap dirty jokes with the best of them. I was once something of a collector of Oriental pornography, and so my viewpoint is not that of a bluenose.

Only half in jest I have said that the trouble with the current liberal permissiveness toward pornography is that it has taken all the fun out of porn. The simple fact is that what made the forbidden books of Henry Miller and his colleagues interesting was largely the fact that they were forbidden. In my college days we got as much fun out of reading Malinowsky's *Sex Life of the Savages* as the young people today get from seeing *Deep Throat*—I imagine. Maybe more.

The psychological principle involved is an ancient one. Indeed, it goes back to Genesis. A large element in sexual excitement derives from its "forbidden fruit" aspect. The effort on the part of some misguided souls to make sex as commonplace as drinking a glass of water would, if successful, result in its being only slightly more exciting than drinking a glass of water.

What this tends to do is push those who are victimized by it into a quest for fruit that is forbidden. This results in greater indulgence in various sexual perversions, both heterosexual and homosexual, in extra-marital affairs, including group sex, and ultimately in some cases in some pretty awful things of a criminal nature.

For example, I read the other day that gang rapes are becoming common in Italy. Are we to think that the rapists could not satisfy their sexual urges by finding a willing young lady or a prostitute? This violent act is not indulged in for lack of other opportunity to engage in sex. It is clearly a reflection of the quest for the thrill of the forbidden fruit. It is a result of promiscuity becoming commonplace.

One sees the same thing in even more horrible cases—the brutal sadomasochism that has produced such cases as the Moors murder case in England is an example.

What one is confronted with is the necessity of drawing the line and saying beyond that line lies the forbidden fruit. If you draw it at sadism and child abuse, then you are going to increase the number of cases of sadism and child abuse.

The trends in pornography reflect this. You will recall that not long ago we had a film purportedly showing a young lady being dismembered. This was obviously to appeal to those who could no longer get much thrill from such commonplace things as seeing sexual acts or nonviolent perversion depicted on the screen.

Pornography plays an important role in this progression. In effect, it is largely through permitting or prohibiting these things to be depicted in published material or on the screen that society draws the line. I don't mean to say that society actually permits all the acts that it may permit pornographers to show. The fact is that we still have laws against simple fornication on the books. What permissiveness in pornography does suggest is that public opinion does not condemn many things that the law prohibits and that within certain peer groups there is widespread approbation of conduct that may be both illegal and condemned by general public opinion. The de facto line is moved by what we are willing to tolerate in pornography.

This applies in other areas as well. It is true in the case of attitudes toward drugs. When I was young those who stepped over the line smoked cigarettes and perhaps drank beer. Now that is commonplace. If you want to be wicked today, you smoke marijuana. But with the drive to make that accepted and commonplace, those who want to step over the line will have to go to harder drugs.

Unfortunately, these trends do not improve the quality of life for anyone. There is a flaw in the strict libertarian philosophy. It fails to account for this quirk in human nature. Like anarchism, it assumes that we are better than we are.

I do not think it is a good society that draws the line so far out that one cannot enjoy the pleasure of forbidden fruit without engaging in acts that are disgusting, personally destructive, or socially harmful.

Sincerely yours,
Reed Irvine
Silver Spring, Maryland

THIS HAPPY LAND

February 14, 1977

WASHINGTON—No wars are going on anywhere. The nation is in a time of relative prosperity. Interesting new faces are in the news, and no new scandals or old hatreds poison the public atmosphere.

Nobody wants to be so gauche as to say "these are happy times," but it could well be that in years to come we will look back on the mid-70's and say "those were happy times."

As a people, Americans have more good reason to be cautiously content than at any time since the mid-50's, and yet an undercurrent of fear and despair is running that is hard to identify and harder to explain.

The fear has nothing to do with nuclear Armageddon, or the loss of civil liberties. We are rarely afraid of anything we "should" be afraid of; on the contrary, we are fearful of the unknown and the too-well-known.

The too-familiar fear is that of being attacked by a criminal. Our major-crime rate is double that of a generation ago; discussion ebbs after elections, but the perfectly rational fear continues to grow.

Another fear that must run through our body politic is less well known: the sense of being hunted. We read about the ten million or more illegal aliens that live among us and think of them as "wetbacks" doing the menial jobs that not many United States citizens want to do.

But how does the phantom population feel? One out of every 20 people we pass on the street is an "illegal," who knows that any attention he calls to himself—such as committing a crime, or making a success, or becoming a hungry nuisance—will lead to deportation and separation from family.

Few television shows explore the lives of the illegals because they have not formed a committee to publicize themselves. Notoriety would trigger arrest; the hunters, who are not really hunting, have to look like hunters when their quarry present an embarrassingly public target.

Their presence is at once a compliment and a rebuke. Millions of human beings live in an underground, neither paying taxes nor drawing welfare, risking a great deal to live in a country that the rest of us take for granted. There is more freedom and opportunity here, even for one who has to sneak around illegally, than outside our borders.

The rebuke is that something must be wrong with our laws: They should be enforced or changed. Since we are not about to throw ten million people out, we have to stop pretending they are not here. We will have to welcome that most silent minority, and thereby lower the amount of fear that flows under our society.

As we uncover our fears, we should take a long look at the perverse popularity of despair. Suicide has now become one of the major causes of death among young Americans. The suicide of a young television star last week cannot be dismissed as the mindless act of an actor who had "everything to live for"; it was a dramatic and dangerous manifestation of a trend we have been reluctant to put on the public agenda.

Evidently a great many people are seriously depressed. Telling them to cheer up and count their blessings does not help. Individuality, which is rightly exalted, can be carried to an extreme of personal isolation, and to a philosophy that holds "it's my life, I can do what I want with it, including throw it away." The fear and rage turns inward toward self-destruction.

The possibility exists that the suicide of a television star will be sentimentalized, perhaps even justified, in song and legend aimed at young people. His act will be sung about not as the tragic end of a mental illness, but as a heroic response to the despair that afflicts so many people who are nowhere near poverty.

The death from drug overdose of two leading rock stars a few years ago helped turn many of their fans away from drugs, but the example of celebrated suicide could be far more harmful—unless it awakens us to the national problem that is not just a personal problem.

If depression is on the rise, where is the sense of urgency to understand its causes and develop preventatives? If—in a very similar vein—a fearful legion of illegals live among us, where is the vaunted compassion that would remove their dread and enlist their energies?

We can hear the signals and cries for help from the various undergrounds, but we do not listen. We are locked into our hard-times topics of conversation, our normal bad news budget, our approved list of national concerns drawn from times of war and national crisis.

But these are good times. This is a happy land. Now we must learn to cope with some of the sadness of success. With new eyes, we must look into ways we can help the despairing who are not the poor, and to help the fearful who need not be the hunted.

NOW EASE UP, ANITA

June 9, 1977

WASHINGTON—Militant leaders of the gay rights "movement" cannot minimize the defeat they suffered at the polls in Miami this week.

The gays wanted national publicity on this and got it; they wanted a big turnout at the polls and got it. As a result, Dade County—ordinarily the most liberal bastion in Florida—voted over two to one against the gays and in favor of Anita Bryant's "crusade" against sexual permissiveness.

Homosexuals framed the issue as civil rights versus outright bigotry. The overwhelming majority did not see it that way at all.

Nor was the majority vote a demonstration of redneck power, or machomania, or the unreasoning fear of child molestation by hated "queers," or a wave of fundamentalist morality—although a little of all of those appeared.

Most of the voters framed the issue, as I did, between tacit toleration and outright approval of homosexuality. Most Americans are inclined to let consenting adults do what they like, short of injury, in private; but the gay activists wanted more: The basic "right" they sought was the assertion by society that what they were doing was right.

But they are wrong. In the eyes of the vast majority, homosexuality is an abnormality, a mental illness, even—to use an old-fashioned word—a sin. Homosexuality is not the "alternative life-style" the gay activists profess; it may be tolerable, even acceptable—but not approvable.

This don't-ask-for-respectability judgment is not limited to homosexuality. Adultery is gleefully if guiltily practiced by—who knows?—perhaps a majority of married persons, but if an approving statute were proposed by Activist Adults for Adultery, voters on their way home from trysts would vote it down overwhelmingly.

Hypocrisy? No, civilization—the understanding that certain moral standards are worth recognizing and perhaps even striving for, even in the knowledge that most people, one time or another, fall short.

Gay activists want more than this; they want the seal on their house-keeping to say "good." That is a moral judgment they have the right to make but not to insist upon from the rest of society, which has the right to make its own contrary judgment and to persuade its children of its value.

Part of that persuasion by society takes place in school. Many of us think that gays should be permitted to teach, provided they do not avow their homosexuality. Gay activists counter by asking: "Why lie to the children?" One reason is so that private homosexuals can have jobs. If avowed gays were to be teachers, the example they would set to children might induce some toward emulation of their abnormality, which society wants to discourage.

But the gay militants did not want privacy, they wanted publicity; not content with toleration, they wanted approval. And so the voters reacted the way most of us do—as when war resisters refuse pardons until the U.S. Government admits it was wrong—by digging in our heels.

The trouble with Miss Bryant's victory is that she now intends to treat the Miami landslide as a license to launch a vast national crusade. That means that the ringing answer given to the activists' demand for moral legitimacy might lash back into an invasion of their legitimate civil rights.

No bluenose moralizer should have the power to tell consenting adults of the same sex they cannot live together in public housing. Gays pay taxes; if they want to love each other, society should get away from the keyhole; if they want to profess their love, that's their free speech. As long as "straights" are not forced to underwrite a homosexual sales message in the classroom, the straights have no right to penalize private citizens for their personal behavior.

Let Miss Bryant and her own militant crusaders not misinterpret their victory: No mandate has been given to put the gays on the run, or to repress their right of free expression. She has turned back a danger posed by wrongheaded gay activists, and deserves credit for that; she does not deserve to be the matriarch of a new movement that would pose a new danger to those homosexuals who want only to be left alone.

That new danger would be the justification of the issue as the gay activists originally (and wrongly) framed it: civil rights versus bigotry. If Miss Bryant's nationalized crusade were to take on the trappings of a political party (here comes the Federal funding), and if private homosexuals were intimidated to pay for gay militant demands, martyrdom would be theirs, and libertarians would be forced to their defense.

So ease up, Anita Bryant: You were given a vote of confidence, not a flaming sword. Most people do not want to be pushed too strongly in either direction. A significant part of your support was resistance to gay extremism, and is ready to switch to resist any manifestation of extremism on the part of the straights.

June 10, 1977

To the Editor
The New York Times

To his credit, columnist William Safire is sufficiently principled in his concern for individual human rights to be somewhat uneasy about Anita Bryant and her virulent campaign against gay Americans (*The New York Times*, June 9, 1977). However, in attempting to defend his "middle-of-the-road" position against those who view Ms. Bryant's campaign in much more alarming terms—as an ominous threat not only to a significant minority of Americans but also to the cause of human rights in general—he indulges in a contorted exercise in sophistry marked by misleading assertions and dubious analogies.

Mr. Safire would have us believe that gays in Dade County were seeking a "good housekeeping" seal of approval, when in fact all that was at issue was their right not to be discriminated against or otherwise harassed under a continuing burden of legally sanctioned disapproval. Should every person or group in this country have to be approved by a majority vote before they can exercise their individual rights as citizens?

Mr. Safire then tries to buttress his case by equating gays with adulterers and arguing that gays should keep their sexual preferences and activities concealed as do most adulterers. But this equation is preposterous in both legal and moral terms. It misses the essential point that adulterers stay "in the closet" rarely because—like gays—they would otherwise face institutional discrimination and harassment, but mainly because they are concerned about the reaction of their spouses. The adulterer's burden of deception is quite appropriate, because it arises mainly insofar as the adulterous act has the potential for hurting a third person. The gay act has no potential for hurting anyone, unless it is carried out in an adulterous or brutal manner; but in this respect, of course, it is no different than heterosexual sex. Gay Americans are not asking for the right to harm or to deceive others without repercussions; they are asking only for the right to be free and honest without having to suffer for it.

Thomas E. Weisskopf
Department of Economics
The University of Michigan
Ann Arbor, Michigan

9 June 1977

Editors, The New York Times

Sirs:

I write with regard to William Safire's piece in today's edition, "Now Ease Up, Anita." It is obviously true that Safire and the overwhelming majority do not see Gay Rights as a civil rights issue. But Safire is himself wrongheaded to conclude that "militant" homosexuals err in saying the confrontation in Dade Co. was between civil rights versus bigotry.

The problem is quite literally that so many people "did not see it that way at all." Ms. Bryant does deserve credit, but not for what Safire attributes to her. She has demonstrated to the gay community that they must come out for all to see. Only when people see that we are everywhere and are like everybody will everyone recognize that the fears and ignorance voiced by Safire and Bryant are simply groundless. We are your children, your friends, your relatives, your mayors, your policemen, even your wives and husbands. If our sexuality is a problem, you have made it so, because you cannot yet see that it is no problem for us except if you fear and hate what you do not understand.

The message from Dade Co. is that we ourselves can't afford to be afraid of you anymore. We must be honest with you, "the normal majority," because to be less than honest leaves you with your wrongheaded fears. We don't want you to learn to tolerate your fears and us. By coming out, by flaunting the truth about ourselves, by letting you learn who we are, we may yet convince you that we are fighting not for permissiveness, not for toleration, not for approval, but instead for your own liberation from ignorance, fear and bigotry. We *will* be role-models, Mr. Safire, for you and your children. We have been silent victims of hate and misunderstanding long enough.

Sincerely yours,
Dr. John Terrell
Chicago, Illinois

PUNK'S "HORROR SHOW"

June 30, 1977

Punk is sweeping the country.

In popular music, a raucous, mock-violent sound rapes the eardrum: "Punk rock" it is called—or snarled. "Groove with me in the gutter, girl," is the message of such groups as the Sex Pistols, who blaze their dum-dums through the filigree of old Elvis-the-Pelvis establishment-rock minuets.

In faddist fascist fashion, the apparent new nihilism is expressed in re-vulsion chic: Savage tears in material is *de rigeur*, rusty razor blades jan-gle nervously from catgut string, and a dashing cape made from an old black plastic garbage bag is the *ne plus ultra*.

In politics, too, the trend toward the glorification of supersloppiness has been noted: Writer-in-residence Bob Greene of *The Washington Star* has explored "imperial punk," admonishing professional rednecks Hamilton Jordan and Jody Powell to take their feet off the White House furniture.

Whence this phenomenon? Who are these insects that have been spray-ing themselves with people repellent?

First, to etymology. Slanguist Eric Partridge speculates that punk is hobo lingo to describe very stale bread, perhaps from the French *pain*.

Punk, applied to a person, began as a slang term for a catamite, or boy kept by a pederast, and later was extended to cover young hoodlums. In both substance and person, the word "punk" has always been used pe-joratively, and usually carried the dual connotation of youth and degener-acy.

Now to pseudo-sociology. The success of punk in music and fashion springs from a rebellion against the material success of rebel leaders. On the current cover of establishment rock's *Rolling Stone* (a vastly suc-cessful enterprise that has become a Carter Administration house organ), three rock stars clad in precious white silken polyester, who call them-selves the Bee Gees appear to be very wealthy young people.

The multimillion-dollar contracts of these idols are turning off some of their audience. Today's rebels-without-causes long for genuine grime, not plastic grime. They prefer bloodied local club fighters to rich televised champions, and identify with unsuccessful slobs rather than with million-aire musicians who exploit unsuccessful slobs.

Similarly, in fashion, with respectability now clinging to jeans and ob-scene T-shirts, the young rebs need something of their own, and have moved farther out to the studied kookiness of safety pins and dog chains. En masse, they are scuttling like lemmings to their idea of individuality—that is, the uniform of the nonconformist, in the regiment of the unregi-mented.

We now know where punk came from and why it is here. Now to a crucial question: Is punk good or bad?

Jerking weak knees, middle-agers tend to waggle our heads and say "bad." After all, it is an inversion of values: A punk-head may be attracted by an attention-getting display of offensiveness, but distaste is not taste; violence is not tenderness. To be in revolt, one does not need to be revolt-ing. A new nihilism, excusable among Egyptians, is hardly the American way of life.

But wait: The aficionados of punk, impressing their sourhearts with os-tentatious rags, are invaluable to a new breed of news transmitters known as the trendustry. Students of mass communication now have a barium to trace the flow of a fad. Photo editors weary of Andy Young and Margaret Trudeau now have fresh, new celebrities to feature. The golden-daffodil hosts of talk-show society have different guests to book and a different topic to pick over. The avant-gardians of Seventh Avenue have a new challenge of adaptation and expensification. Every magazine art director is scrambling to his post.

The trendustry will treat punk with condescension, loftily bejeweling the razor blades and subtly altering the revolting sound. Editorialists will deplore the exaltation of sado-masochism in song and dress.

All wrong. For the punk culture is one extended, mocking snicker. The proponents of punk are spoofing the record companies, the clothing designers, the moviegoers who gape at jaws and wiggle their toes in the deep and jog to the exorcist. The satiric punk innovators are flaying the audience that loves to be titillated by violence as well as the trendustry that thrives on the need for a different different drummer every month.

The godfather of punk is England's Anthony Burgess, author of *A Clockwork Orange*, a novel and movie of a few years ago that satirized our love of violence by portraying a future society run by goons. Their violent-looking clothes and makeup are the guiding spirit of punk.

"Horror show" was the goons' favorite adjective, meaning terrific. Most of us thought the irony lay in equating horror with good; but author Burgess, who is also an eminent linguist, had something deeper in mind: "Horror show" was a play on "horosho," the expression for "good" in the Soviet Union.

Only a word play? Perhaps, but the brief and meteoric emergence of punk is rooted in a satiric reminder of the potential for brutality that lurks in every one of us.

CHRISTMAS IN JULY

July 18, 1977

In white letters on a black background, the headline of a New York Spanish newspaper, *El Diario*, demanded to know "POR QUE?" Why?

Why, when the city's lights went out, was there a billion-dollar orgy of looting and pillaging by tens of thousands of the occupants of the city's slums?

Nothing like the rampage of 1977's Bastille Day has happened to an American city before. This was not a race riot: No discrimination was shown between black or white shopkeepers. Race relations have surely suffered—television's projection of exultant black looters wiped out the gains of the televised *Roots*—but no civil rights cause motivated the blackout's glad-to-be-angry opportunists.

Nor was this an example of people driven by desperation to reach out for necessities. They took toasters, not bread; liquor, not milk; more sports shirts for the sporty than shoes for the shoeless. One of the participants aptly called the evil carnival atmosphere "Christmas in July."

Why? The standard liberal answer is that this was a cry for economic help, an expression of despair by society's forgotten people. It is our fault for abandoning the Great Society, for not making certain that each ghetto resident has a job or a welfare payment to keep him content.

The standard hard-line answer is just as foolishly self-flagellating: that the militia was not called out in time to keep law and order, or that the cops were not equipped with shoot-to-kill instructions.

More farfetched answers come from people in the looting area who were neither criminals nor victims. The blackout itself was described as an Act of God, as Consolidated Edison promptly called it, which suspended the rules of lawful behavior. Or that Con Ed pulled the plug on purpose, to dramatize its need for more power plants, and that such a conspiracy justified gleeful participation in its "strike."

None of these answers, nor all together, satisfy; they are excuses, not reasons. People do not become a thieving mob because they cannot afford jewelry, booze, or new couches. They do not refrain from stealing because of the presence of glinting bayonets. They do not break the law because of signs in the sky or anti-establishment conspiracy theories.

The looters looted because of the spreading non-ethic that stealing is okay if you can get away with it, as you usually can; that only a jerk passes up an opportunity to rip off his neighbor; that society not only owes you a living, but the good life.

Millions of black and Hispanic New Yorkers were the worst victims of the looting and arson on Bastille Day, and do not deserve the shudders directed their way in its aftermath. Many of them called the looters "animals," and in a non-racial sense were right: Inhumanly, the looters attached no guilt to their actions. They took what was in the stores as their right; it was free-style Christmas in July.

What is the basis for that newly widespread attitude of a "right" to rip off? Sorry, the economic-despair excuse will not hold up, because poverty in the ghettos was greater in the last blackout, and the standard of living was lower in the past generation.

One reason for the I'm-entitled-to-what-I-want attitude is the philosophy that welfare is a right to be expanded and not a condition to be avoided by the able-bodied.

Another reason is the claim that because minorities have suffered discrimination in the past, they are now entitled to reparations in the form of special treatment—and some carry that claim to extremes.

Another reason is the notion that a job is something to be provided and not searched for, and that menial work is to be spurned as not a "decent" job.

Another reason is the argument that crime is the result of poverty, and that poverty is nobody's fault but the System's; it follows that in this no-fault world, society is to blame for what a poor person does when the lights are out.

Heresy? Of course. Most of us prefer a much more palatable get-tough-with-the-rich exploitation of resentment or a get-tough-with-the-crooks correctionism. Not many are willing to get toughminded about the prevailing political philosophy, and to face up to the consequences of the overweening assumption of responsibility by Government.

Surely there are other and more complex reasons for the suspension of ordinary civility and morality by so many New Yorkers during the city's ordeal. But that's the beginning of the hard answer to *El Diario*'s "Por Que?"

STRAIGHTS' RIGHTS

February 2, 1978

I read in the public prints (there's a good name for a newspaper) that the old Ridgefield Hotel, on New York City's West 92d Street, is to be shut down by the state Supreme Court, testing a New York State law that wants to do away with indoor prostitution.

At the same time, the first pronouncement of the city's new Mayor, Ed Koch, was that the rights of homosexuals would be upheld and enhanced, that New York City would tolerate no more discrimination against gays.

Is it not enough that the city go bankrupt; must it also go bonkers? Whatever happened to straights' rights?

I grew up in the apartment hotel next door to the Ridgefield, which was a fleabag even then. After a punchball game (I was a two-sewer hitter) or a curb-ball game (Cliff Irving used to aim for the point of the curb) the gang used to sit on the stoop of the Ridgefield and watch the girls go in and out, which was a formative experience, and at age 13, a genuine thrill.

All that's over now. The civil libertarians who would rush to the defense of a gay bar feel no brotherly love for the illicit heterosexuality in the Ridgefield tradition.

To redress that imbalance, the Straights' Rights Movement has been launched. Although we have not yet retained Intimate Relations Counsel, our principles are set forth in this personifesto:

1. *Let gays alone.* We do not approve, but we do not meddle. What they do in private is their business, so long as they do not try to sell us an "alternative life-style," and their radical proposal to rename Bryant Park is to be resisted.

2. *Repeal the Mann Act.* By the way, whatever became of the Mann Act? Probably goes under the name of the Personn Act. Anyway, "white slavery" is both racist and sexist and that's no way to regulate interstate commerce.

3. *Legalize prostitution.* If we agree that morality is to be taught and preached but not legislated, why do we persist in treating as illegal a contract between consenting adults to purchase and deliver a service? If this is too much too soon, we have a fallback position:

4. *Decriminalize prostitution.* The word "decriminalize" is in favor, a fact to which all movements are sensitive. Besides, continually arresting women as harassment creates court logjams and deters nobody. It is also unfair, since the buyer is as "guilty" as the seller, and the "John" is never prosecuted. (A graphic description of the fallback position is available in the *Kamasutra.*) Decriminalization would enable us to:

5. *Fire the vice squad.* In any police force, despite periodic clean sweeps, the squad is vulnerable to corruption that weakens law enforcement generally. Our slogan: Get those men out of bed and onto the streets.

6. *Provide advertising safeguards.* Garish neon signs should be subject to local zoning ordinances; even sandwich boards for sidewalk solicitation can be restricted to meet current Supreme Court guidelines. But if the other two oldest professions—medicine and the law—are now permitted to advertise, why not encourage competition via the tasteful advertising of prostitution? The telephone-derived phrase "call girl" certainly suggests the propriety of using the Yellow Pages. (Let your fingers do the street-walking.)

7. *Drive out the crooks and middlemen.* No minors allowed on the selling end; encourage unionization to eliminate middle-management abuses; eliminate the need for corrupt payoffs; get prostitutes off welfare rolls and onto payrolls, griping with the rest of us about taxation.

8. *Bring dignity to the workplace.* Blue-nosed politicians have given prostitution a bad name. So change the name; one suggestion is "courtesanship." Prostitutes who made special efforts to provide services to the shy, the ugly, and to those in remote, sexually deprived areas should be given "good courtesanship awards" by local chambers of commerce.

These first few thoughts only tickle the surface. Readers are urged to create their own local chapters of the Straights' Rights Movement and tie in with other action groups. Demand media access. Be pushy.

One day, we shall all meet at the federally funded White House Conference on Courtesanship, to sing our straights' rights songs and wave our straights' rights banners.

And the headquarters will be designated a national landmark: New York's Ridgefield Hotel.

18 February 1978

Dear Mr. Safire:

I should like to respond to a recent article concerning prostitution. You took a facetious attitude toward its legalization.

You have undoubtedly never lived where prostitution is legal. You are accustomed to having it operate under cover, with payoffs to police, and controlled by organized crime.

I have lived where it was legal. Not according to state laws, but lawful by city codes and ignored by state statutes. Wallace, Idaho, had prostitution many years as most cities do, allowed by the police for payoff. Then a mayor candidate was elected on the platform that the women be licensed and the money go into the city treasurer where it belonged. Since then, for 30 years, it has operated in this way. The women must have a medical test weekly. The "houses" are in one area of the town, are discreet, with no signs or advertising. Ask any taxi driver, any clerk, or resident for a house of prostitution and they will direct you.

The city has no sex crimes. There are no girls hanging out in bars. The streets are "clean." The houses are run in the old-fashioned way, with a "madam," and a half-dozen girls for her employees. Crime does not control it. The girls are not held there through drug addiction. What happens to the girls, you might ask? Most of them marry—their customers.

Some years ago I lived in Butte, Montana, and prostitution was accepted and managed in a similar manner.

ALLOWING does not mean ACCEPTING. There is nothing about legalization that would lead a young man to think it's the thing to do. It's just there and it's tolerated, and controlled in the best possible way.

I doubt that the big cities would agree to this because the city officials make too much money. But it's surely ridiculous, in an age of real crime, to waste police time rounding up girls and enforcing a law that is plainly unenforceable.

Should you wonder what kind of person I am, let me say that I am a middle-aged history (high school) teacher with three teen-age sons and a civil engineer husband. I am not burdened with the strictures of orthodox religion, so perhaps I can think a little more liberally.

Sincerely yours,
Doris Brooks
Spokane, Washington

MARCHING THROUGH SKOKIE

March 27, 1978

WASHINGTON—A year ago, the National Socialist Party of America—a ragtag bunch of Nazis who wear swastikas, shout "Seig Heil!" and last made big news when a member of the group shot their leader—announced plans to march in a grand parade through Skokie, Illinois.

The choice of Skokie was shrewd. More than half of that community's population is Jewish, and 10 percent are survivors of the Nazi persecution in Germany. The American Nazis' object was, and is, to trigger a violent counterdemonstration, thereby making themselves martyrs at the hands of Jews shouting "Never again!"

The citizens of Skokie went to court to stop this deliberate provocation, but lost the case. Undeterred, they passed local ordinances making it illegal to parade about in uniform, without $350,000 in insurance, or to use symbols—such as the swastika—that foster race hatred.

An appellate court tried to split the difference, permitting the Nazis to march but not to wear the swastika, which is termed "a personal affront to every member of the Jewish faith, in remembering the nearly consummated genocide of the people committed within memory by those who used the swastika as their symbol."

The American Civil Liberties Union, on free-speech grounds, appealed the decision on behalf of the Nazis. Essentially, they argued that if we denied the Nazis their symbol we could deny any group its symbol. The case is now on its way up the judicial ladder.

People I respect say that the defense of the Nazis is a perversion of the First Amendment. The Constitution is not a suicide pact, they hold, and it is self-defeating for any society to try to protect the ability of its opposition to undermine or overthrow it.

Moreover, the use of the swastika is so deliberately insulting as to be "fighting words"—incitement to violence—which the Supreme Court has held places the responsibility for violence on the speaker and not the audience.

The civil libertarian counter to that argument is familiar: It holds that the "fighting words" concept is limited to individual encounters, not nonverbal symbols before general audiences. And if you can keep Nazis from marching in Skokie, you can keep civil rights demonstrators from marching in Selma.

I am not an enthusiastic supporter of the A.C.L.U.; during the Watergate hysteria, when the rights of individual defendants like Gordon Liddy were egregiously abridged, that organization managed only one small peep at the nondisqualification of Judge Sirica. Mass murderers, Klansmen, and Nazis get defended; but the A.C.L.U. could not bring itself to defend the civil liberties of those who threatened civil liberties.

But certain libertarians—like Nat Hentoff of *The Village Voice*—spoke up then for the genuinely unpopular defendants, and thus kept credentials for consistent and principled free-speech defense—even of the Nazis to flaunt their swastikas and taunt the Jews of Skokie. ("Jew" is a quick way of saying "member of the Jewish faith.")

The A.C.L.U. has had 2 percent of its membership resign over its defense of the Nazis, which it likes to exaggerate by a factor of ten. But Mr. Hentoff, in a lively-lefty magazine called *Inquiry*, makes the crucial point: "The reaction to the A.C.L.U.'s position by so many who consider themselves liberals and even libertarians has emphasized—as no other case in many years—how fragile throughout the land is support for the still revolutionary notion that the state has no business quashing anybody's ideas or symbols. *Anybody's.*"

Grumbling all the way, I have to agree: There can be no greater affirmation of freedom than ostentatiously to respect the rights of those who would destroy that freedom.

Go sell that pristine principle to the people in Skokie who have seen their families wiped out under the symbol of the swastika. But perhaps another idea might elicit their support:

When Menachem Begin welcomed Anwar el-Sadat to Jerusalem, he made a great point of taking his visitor to Yad Va'Shem, the memorial to the Holocaust.

America has no vivid reminder of the horror of the Final Solution. But we have a reminder that not even Israelis can boast: our own homegrown handful of Nazis.

Let them march through Skokie, and by media eventuality, through every American living room. Let the television cameras focus on the swastikas, and on the faces of the Jews of Skokie bearing silent witness. Let the networks then reach into the film files of the scenes of Dachau and Buchenwald, to which most young Americans have never been exposed.

We need that reminder, not only to understand the concern for survival that causes Jews in Israel to refuse to give their sworn enemies real power, but to teach a new generation of Americans the extreme to which anti-Semitism can lead.

And if this bunch of Nazis ever disbands, let us go out and hire actors to goose-step through Skokie and flash their symbol on the screen: The dramatic, living memorial of the Holocaust is too valuable to lose.

THE POLITICS OF MARRIAGE

July 13, 1978

MINNEAPOLIS—"It is not good that the man should be alone," the Lord is quoted as saying, for attribution, in the Book of Genesis. "I will make him an help meet for him."

The word "meet," in that King James translation, means "suitable." As he drew a rib from Adam to fashion Eve, goes that passage, the Lord created an aide suitable for man, which is the origin of "help meet."

The times they have a-changed. Consider the help some leading political figures have been getting lately:

In Georgia, Senator Herman Talmadge's former wife, Betty, is running for Congress. The Senate Ethics Committee is already reviewing the curious financial habits of her former spouse; Betty appears to be the source of charges that "Hummin'"—who sat judiciously on the Senate Watergate committee—was the recipient of what old-time Tammany pols used to call "honest graft": profits from land speculation based on inside political information, hidden from scrutiny under a wife's name.

In Massachusetts, Senator Ed Brooke's long-estranged wife, Remigia, has gone back to divorce court to further tarnish the name of the Senate's only black. She and her daughter charged that the Senator lied in some sworn statements and improperly claimed tax deductions.

In Alabama, George Wallace's former wife, Cornelia, who was reported to have bugged the Governor's bedroom before divorce proceedings got really ugly, is now considering a governor's race on her own—presumably based on her knowledge of what goes on inside the Governor's mansion.

These three instances hardly illustrate the kind of "help meet" the Bible-writers had in mind. We are familiar with the stereotype of the woman next to the candidate on the platform, gazing adoringly at her pride and joy, listening with feigned intensity to the speech she has heard a thousand times.

Now it's different: The candidate and the voters look at her and wonder, how much does she know? Will she turn against him one day? Could she lacerate him in court? Could she beat him in a primary?

The political wife, if badly treated or scorned, has a weapon few other wives have: Not only can she cause her husband economic damage, she can do much to destroy his career. The businessman can grumble and pay, but the politician can have his career ended by an ex- who wants to mark the spot.

This is not the "divorce issue," which is becoming more insignificant as more voters separate. It is a new problem of the well-informed spouse—male or female—who seeks revenge and can reveal financial peculations.

Or the spouse who has psychological problems that can threaten to break into the media on the eve of an election.

Politicians I have spoken to while kicking about the country lately are wondering what this warfare is doing to the institution of political marriage, which has usually been a combination of genuine partnership and the front of blissful stability that politicians and their families put up for the voters. Paradoxically, the recent warfare is making political marriages at once more circumspect and more honest.

In the future, politicians—including, of course, women candidates— will be more careful about sharing political-financial confidences with their spouses. That's bad.

At the same time, politicians will be urging their spouses to get their skeletons out of their closets. "You got a problem? Bring it out now before you—or my opponents—can use it against me." That's good.

That is why we are witnessing the second most striking trend in political marriages: the pre-emptive confession.

Betty Ford, the former First Lady, has revealed that she was hooked on drugs and booze. Since she has been battling cancer, and has been known for her outspokenness, this has been received with sympathy; it will not be a factor in any future Ford campaign.

Similarly, Joan Kennedy, wife of Senator Edward Kennedy, has announced that she is an alcoholic, which most people knew anyway, and now she is allowed to take credit for candidly fighting a problem that afflicts millions. If her husband is to be drafted at the next Democratic convention, he will have no secret about his wife hanging over his head.

The attitude of a politician toward his or her spouse, then, is in danger of becoming "stay out of my business, but write a magazine article about your problem." The combination of mistrust and forced frankness is saddening; a couple can come closer together while confiding in, and protecting, each other.

But some of the free-at-last new candidates are gleeful at being on their own. Before her divorce, Betty Talmadge wrote a cookbook entitled *How to Cook a Pig*. When *Times* woman Kathie Wellde asked her how she went about killing the object of the roast, Mrs. Talmadge laughed and said: "Real easy, honey. I jes' thought, 'You little male chauvinist, you,' and I went to it."

July 13, 1978

Dear Mr. Safire:

I was disturbed by your article on "The Politics of Marriage" in the July 13th *Times*.

Of course, political expedience has prompted Betty Ford and Joan Kennedy to reveal their medical and psychological problems before their respective mates' electoral gambols (gambles?). But your attitude toward Betty Talmadge, Remigia Brooke, and Cornelia Wallace is biased. Is it your concept of "help meet" that a wife will stick by her husband and suffer silently regardless of how he behaves?

There seems to be an unwritten law, promulgated and defended by men, that (1) a man's life is departmentalized—*une affaire d'amour* has nothing to do with the little wife back home; (2) a politician is so important that the rules for ordinary folk do not apply to him—therefore, his wife cannot hold him to the same rules that mortal men are supposed to abide by; (3) if your politician spouse is a boozer, womanizer, and gambler, whatever you do—don't go public and ruin his career because that's really playing dirty.

I'm sorry to inform you, Mr. Safire (who was so perturbed by the cover-up of the Korean bribe scandal until you and Bruce Caputo publicized it and pushed it to some sort of exposure), but morality is for everyone. No one is so powerful, so intelligent, or so rich that he can behave without regard to the feelings and sensibilities of those whom he once professed to love.

I would not take this position in the case of a truly political marriage in which each spouse is using the other (with full knowledge) in order to get ahead. But, I assume most marriages begin with a profession of love and taking of vows. If a man betrays that love and breaks his vow, I applaud the wife who is strong enough not to let his infidelity destroy her and, in the most heinous cases, seeks to punish her spouse. Perhaps, vengeance is the Lord's, but a little earthly deflation of a politician's ego is oftentimes a blessing.

In case you are wondering who I am, I am single and 32 years of age— no personal axe to grind and not born during the reign of Queen Victoria.

Sincerely,
Laura Millman
Washington, D.C.

THE AIRPORT WORLD

November 20, 1978

EVERYWHERE INTERNATIONAL AIRPORT—The president of American Airlines has just informed the Mayor of New York that his company is doing what it does best: taking off. Announcement of the airline's plans to move its headquarters from the center of Manhattan to the

Orwellian airport complex somewhere between Dallas and Fort Worth came as a shock to New York's commercial hopes.

But a greater cultural shock awaits any portion of those 1,300 executives and secretaries who will move. They are accustomed to running an airline; now they will discover what it is to spend long stretches of time in a brave new airport world.

No longer is an airport a place just outside of town to which travelers run to catch a flight. We are in the era of the Airport World—flying Clockwork Orange—an eerily quiet, climate-controlled series of cantilevered concrete caverns. Molded plastic chairs stare at coin-operated television sets; doors careen open by themselves; escalators never stop and conversations never start.

In the past week, I have traveled from DUL to SFO to HNL to LAX to MIA—baggagetag-ese replacing the real names of what used to be great, proud cities. The suspicion nags that all these flights were simulations, with filmed cloud scenes rear-projected on little jumbo-jet windows.

Here at Everywhere International, the human cargo numbly waits in line, looks for answers on too-high screens, watches luggage disappear behind rubber-toothed curtains, gets electronically frisked, is moving-sidewalked to buses or subways, is directed by tape recordings to a telescoping sleeve, and finally is wedged into a seat in a wide room which purports to be an airplane.

But that is only part of the experience of life at Everywhere International. Thanks to computer-planned disconnecting flights, and to sales agents who demand the passenger's presence at the airport long in advance of flight time, the person inserting himself into the travel cocoon is encouraged to spend enough time in the Airport World to browse in the gift shops, booze in the cocktail lounges, peruse the paperback racks, and enjoy an invigorating sauna and shoe shine in the men's room.

What's going on here? A bureaucrat's idea of the future is going on, I submit, and submission is the name of the game. Most modern airports are built by "authorities," quasi-governmental entities removed from voter accountability. The guiding mission of the faceless authority is supposed to be efficiency but its passion is the expression of a social manipulator's dream: oppressive monuments of architectural Mussolinis determined to transform individual travelers into long, slow-moving streams of consumers.

This is no plea for the rinky-dink aerodrome, with pilots in leather caps and goggles, without needed radar, meteorological devices, and quick-opening air-sick bags. But I suggest that some urban planners' idea of modernity is at least a generation behind the times. Massive scale is now out; regimentation is out; while our dehumanizing airport-builders have zigged, American society has zagged.

Look at the new airport in Portland, Ore.: cushions on the seats, individual stores open early and late. Granted, Portland is not a metropolis, but it has resisted the urge of other mid-sized cities—from Pocatello to Huntsville, Ala.—to build their own versions of Everywhere International.

Airport "authorities" concerned with the character of their communities should make an effort to bring in local private enterprise: a Hurley's bar, a friendly *bodega*, a kosher deli, or a Mom-and-Pop massage parlor would be worth attracting to the spaces now allocated to the multinational concessionaires of Sameness, Inc.

The planners of the next generation of airports should stop trying to add to the distance between airport entrance and aircraft gate. They should strive to combat that proliferation of hotels, office buildings, and shops that turn a way station into an end in itself. Hapless flight attendants and passengers should not be forced to drag their luggage on little "schleppers" for miles just to satisfy some civic booster's idea of grandeur or some tax-exempt authority's lust for nonprofit.

The edifice-complex builders of the Airport World might also remember that life need not be solitary confinement. Last night, I stayed at the Ramada Holiday Inn-Tercontinental, crown jewel of the cookie-cutter hostelry at LAX, and asked the telephone operator to give me a ring at 7:30 A.M.

This morning, right on the dot, came the ring and a cheery "This is your recorded wake-up call."

I asked, "What's the weather like?" and the voice answered, "This is your recorded wake-up call."

"What city is this?" Quoth the wake-up: "This is your recorded wake-up call."

And so enjoy yourselves, executives of American Airlines. You are not moving to Dallas or Fort Worth, which are real cities, but into Everywhere International, the cheerless lair of the monster you helped create.

RIGHT ON TOPS

June 21, 1979

CANNES, France—Only a generation ago, while picking my way along this pebbly beach, I was struck by a phenomenon so European and avant-garde that it seemed certain never to spread to American shores: the bikini. Near-nudity on public display. Shocking!

What sociological pundit would have dared to suggest, back then, that the wispy tops and G-stringy bottoms of the bathing suits sported by defiant young French women would soon become not only accepted but traditional at Malibu, Miami Beach, and Coney Island?

American eyebrows that shot up were as quickly shot down: The brief swimsuits (somehow, "bathing suit" was changed to "swimsuit") were not only attractive on a good figure but sensibly promoted the tanning of a wider area of skin with no telltale strap marks. Easy to pack and quick-dry, the bikini—only slightly conservatized—became respectable. Anybody who objected was a bluenose.

The recollection of this decade-old cultural revolution was triggered by a stroll along the beaches of the Côte d'Azur this summer. Here is the newest phenomenon to strike the pebble-picking ogler: the one-piece bathing suit.

No, I do not mean the one-piece suit with the covered-up front that is all the rage as part of the "retro" fashion. That throwback will soon disappear along with padded shoulders, kewpie-doll lipstick, and hair that seems to be afflicted with terminal frizzies.

The one-piece suit that rates the serious attention of all who try to discern the American future is best described as the bottom part of what was previously a two-piece suit. No top. Near-nudity on public display. Shocking!

Accompanied by other members of the Society for the Defense of the Status Quo, I made a survey of women on the beach. Twelve wore old-fashioned bikinis; ten wore the retrogressive one-piece suits of the days of Neville Chamberlain. But here was the grabber in my bluenose count: Eight of the sunbathers (political posters would call them "a statistically significant minority") were wearing the new one-piecers—bottoms without tops.

They did not appear to be self-conscious; they attracted no stares or snickers; they were not part of a demonstration and did no proselytizing. They just stood there, sat there, or lay there—naked from the waist up— as if it were the most natural thing in the world.

Which it is, which the Book of Genesis teaches us. Then I was assailed by a sense of *déjà vu*, a sense that often strikes people nearing 50. These topless ordinary citizens were the daughters of the same sun-worshipping avant-gardians of a previous generation who first scandalized and soon converted us.

The questions naturally arise: Will swimsuit history repeat itself? Will the monokini, or suit without a top, be as accepted and respectable on American beaches tomorrow as the bikini is today? If "less is more," how much less is too much?

Think about it; this issue will not go away. The sensible argument will be advanced again: More skin gets tanned per exposure, with no unsightly bands of sickly white on a bronzed body. When the Colonel's Lady pioneered the see-through dress, Rosie O'Grady followed with a wet T-shirt.

Each of us will have to decide the topless question: Taboo or not taboo?

The potential for sociopolitical conflict cannot be dismissed. Extremists of the left will burn their bikini tops and display bumper stickers that say "All cover-ups are illegal." Their counterparts on the right will smash into seaside snackbars shouting "Toplessness is next to Godlessness!"

Libertarian conservatives like myself can quickly come to grips with the issue: Local zoning ordinances and other government meddling in private moral decisions should be eschewed; the decision to go to the beach with a pair of tiny trunks or a set of body-length bloomers is up to the individual, subject to her own reaction to the community standards reflected in the admiring smiles or horrified hoo-hahs of her beachmates.

A front is no affront. Toplessness at the beach and see-throughedness at the theater is a privilege in the process of becoming a right, and will lose its controversiality as it loses its shock value.

But there's the rub: Sex appeal is the promise, and not the fact, of revelation. In the South of France today, half-nude bathers are determinedly stamping out sexuality, to the detriment of both sexes.

Here, then, is a vote for the appeal of modesty and the wisdom of moderation. To paraphrase the poet: If toplessness comes, can bottomlessness be far behind?

June 27, 1979

Dear Mr. Safire—

I read your essay of June 21st with interest, particularly your ending "If toplessness comes, can bottomlessness be far behind?"

Having read your essays for years I thought that you were a very "worldly" individual and particularly knowledgable about what's going on. I should like you to know that "bottomless" *is not* far behind; it's here, right here and now at a public beach in the City of New York condoned, endorsed, and encouraged by the National Park Service, the Department of Interior and the Office of the United States Attorney.

For four years now, we have been requesting the Department of Interior and the National Park Service that operate the national parks of the United States to stop nudity on the public beach at Riis Park (owned by the National Park Service) in Queens, New York. At this public beach in full view of men, women and children and families who have come to spend a day at the beach, nude men and women are allowed to walk the beaches, bathe in the ocean and partake in acts of lewdness in full public view.

All of our protests (including those from our priests and rabbis) to the President, on down to the superintendent of the park have been in vain and the United States Attorney refuses to recognize the rights of the majority of families and those of us who wish to spend a pleasant day at the beach without witnessing any nudity around us.

I write to you because perhaps you could bring this to the attention of *The New York Times*. The public morals are at stake here. We all know that morality has sunk, reached the bottom in private matters but can't we at least save our public morals?

> Sincerely yours,
> Allen A. Sylvane, President
> Neponsit Property Owners' Association, Inc.
> Neponsit, New York

6/22/79

Mr. Safire—

Stop wasting precious space on sophomoric humour, re "Right on Tops." Stick to what you do best: political commentary and revelations.

Buckley has become a bore, full of thin, bright affectations parading as wit & brilliance. Please don't join the society of intellectual Beau Brummels.

Your serious essays are probably the best written in this decaying society today. If you need comic relief watch old Laurel & Hardy films.

> Cordially,
> Martha Wehrly
> Bronx, New York

Mr. Safire:

Must disagree with your article asserting that partial concealment is more alluring (women's swimsuits).

This left me breathless when I was a high school sophomore, but for over forty years exposed breasts (nipples and all) and the indescribably sweet patch of pubic hair have replaced partial concealment as the ultimate in joyful viewing.

> Not yet sixty

THE JOHN HOUR

October 11, 1979

The Mayor of New York, eager to prove how ardent a feminist he can be, announced this week that men convicted of patronizing prostitutes would have their names broadcast over the city-owned radio station, WNYC.

"We're going to call it 'The John Hour,' " said this new impresario of public shame. "We're not allowed to put people in stocks anymore, so instead, what I'm going to do is to focus public attention by putting their names in stocks. . . ."

Chew that over. Half a world away, in Iran, the Ayatollah Khomeini enforces his strict notions of public morality by shooting adulterers and beheading prostitutes. Here in New York, the Mayatollah Ed Koch enforces public morality by reaching back three centuries to come up with a broadcast version of a humiliation Pilgrims called "the stocks."

What happens to ordinary mortals when they are put in a position to dictate their personal morality to others? Upon what meat does this our Mayor feed, that he has grown so fatuous?

Prostitution, we can all assert with righteous vehemence, is a sin. Selling sexual services has been castigated as immoral since morality began. It corrupts the individual, offends society, and, worst of all, adversely affects property values. Bad, bad, bad.

But prostitution should not be a crime. The purchase and sale of sex—when it is a private, commercial arrangement between adults—is no business of government at any level.

First, prostitution was a practice of humankind before lawyers were invented, and will be with us after the last lawyer in office has given up making a tort out of a tart. We tried the prohibition of liquor a couple of generations ago, and later admitted our mistake; the time is ripe to do the same with local prohibitions of sex-for-sale.

Second, the laws against prostitution breed disrespect for the law. When people get used to breaking the law on "victimless" crimes, law enforcement itself becomes the victim. Morality should be taught, not legislated; if we scorn a cop misplaced in the pulpit, we are more likely to scorn him on the street.

Third, laws against prostitution breed disrespect by lawmakers for individual privacy rights. Enforcement is based essentially on entrapment or enticement, which is government encouragement of lawbreaking for the purpose of catching the lawbreaker. That perverts and debases the law.

From the libertarian conservative point of view, that last point is the most important. The police assigned to the demeaning job of tape-recording a solicitation from a streetwalker will soon be wiretapping the telephones of call girls, and then of "johns"—customers—who are suspected of calling prostitutes. As electronic snooping improves, vice-squad investigations open a door to massive invasions of everyone's privacy.

The Mayatollah, a liberal Democrat, would express shock and horror at any such intent to violate civil liberties. After all, he is only trying to be nonsexist in his newest campaign; by harassing the male customers of prostitutes, he thereby attaches a kind of affirmative-action fervor to harassment previously limited to women of the profession.

By publicly broadcasting the shame of the customers (including, in order to be nonsexist, the customers of homosexual prostitutes, which should send a chill up Third Avenue), he thinks this will somehow even the score for the female retailers of sex, who have borne the brunt of arrest and embarrassment until now.

But when you have been wronging women, the solution is not to wrong men equally: The answer is to stop wronging both. The worst answer of all is for government, for the first time, to use broadcasting facilities for the purpose of criminal punishment. (Televised executions, anyone? Great deterrent, sure-fire ratings, and—if sponsored Olympic-style—a nice source of government revenue.)

The New York Police Department's vice squad spends $945,000 a year running prostitutes in and out of court. Add to that the portion of the budget spent by the five district attorneys for this useless activity, the burden on the Legal Aid Society to represent the accused, the court time and overhead, and the expenses of the Department of Corrections to spin its revolving door.

Couldn't that taxpayer money be saved or, better, directed at nailing and jailing the major pimps, or in expanding the $410,000 Youth Board budget to help the exploited children now in prostitution?

Hizzayatollah should stop trying to appeal to feminist bluenoses by coercing judges who must deal with real criminals and don't want to waste time on what consenting adults do in private. Commercial sex is recession-proof and politician-proof.

The Communist Government of China has spent 30 years indoctrinating its people to eschew sexual interests: Women wear unisex clothes and face heavy penalties for moral transgression. In Peking, Jay Mathews of *The Washington Post* this week quoted an official of the Chinese Foreign Ministry on the campaign's success: "There is no prostitution in China. However, we do have some women who make love for money."

October 11, 1979

Mr. Safire:

It may well be that Mayor Koch's proposed "John" hour will turn out to be a more effective means of reaching the same ultimate goal that you advocate in your column of 10/11/79—i.e., the decriminalization of prostitution.

Despite current inroads into the legislative arena, men still outnumber women as lawmaking powerhouses. For as long as the penalties for prostitution are applied solely to women, these lawmakers will not be convinced that any change is necessary. (It's not unthinkable that these men see the law as a means of protecting women from their own baser inclinations!) However, if men begin to be harassed about their sexual activities, as women have been since time immemorial, they may well come to the realization that "of course these laws are antiquated and need to be changed immediately."

In this case it seems to me that the means justify the end.

Sincerely,
Cathy Pullis, Ph.D.
New York, New York

October 13, 1979

The Editor
The New York Times

Dear Sir:

The remedy for a bad law—as nobly demonstrated by Henry David Thoreau and Martin Luther King—is public disobedience of the law and public punishment for such disobedience. The punishment is essential. If you and William Safire truly disapprove of the prostitution law and the Mayor's administration of it, your duty is clear.

I look forward to hearing your names on The John Hour.

Yours truly,
Nelle Haber
Brooklyn, New York

Koreagate

THE FINANCIAL CORRUPTION of about a dozen of our most powerful members of Congress by agents of a foreign power is a subject worthy of investigation. The corruption took place—about $1 million in cash passed hands over a seven-year period—but neither the Department of Justice nor the House Ethics Committee was inclined to probe very deeply.

One reason was that Democratic investigations of Democrats is not as zest-filled as Democratic investigations of Republicans; another was a general heartsickness at more venality after the stains of Watergate; a third reason was a suspicion that any uncovering of corruption would somehow diminish the Nixon misdeeds.

I may have been the one who first labeled it "Koreagate," which was a mistake, since it played into the hands of those who did not want any comparison with Watergate. However, the double standard used in approaching this investigation was apparent, and I compared the lack of zeal in this with the wholly different approach a few years back by the same investigator, Leon Jaworski.

The first time I zapped that thin-skinned public servant—on an unrelated matter of avoidance of taxes on his Watergate book—he fired off a letter threatening "to take action as the law authorizes." A *Times* lawyer responded, citing Jaworski's own book as a source for my knowledge of his tax-exempt foundation, and backing my refusal to correct or retract. He must have brooded about that for some time, finally writing about me scornfully in another book of his own. I have not threatened to sue.

The law's delays, and the insolence of office, led to the collapse of the Koreagate investigations; a few wrists were slapped and a key prosecution was botched. Some took this to mean that no corruption ever existed, that it was all the work of muckrakers. I disagree; sometimes cover-ups succeed.

JAWORSKI TAKES A DIVE

June 22, 1978

WASHINGTON—Leon Jaworski, Certified Media Hero, came to the moment of truth in the Koreagate investigation—and caved in.

Now that Korean agent Tongsun Park has testified that 14 present House members (13 Democrats and one Republican) were recipients of his bribes, the most important witness has become Kim Dong Jo, former Ambassador to the United States.

No Congressman who took envelopes of cash from Ambassador Kim can claim he did not know he was taking payment from a foreign power, breaking the law set down in Article II of the Constitution. Mr. Park's bribery was soft-core—often traceable checks and lavish entertainment, possibly within the laws which were then much looser—but Mr. Kim's bribery was hard-core, cash handed directly to the Congressmen who knew they were breaking the law.

House Speaker Thomas P. (Tip) O'Neill, who admits to taking $6,500 in parties and gifts from Tongsun Park, is extraordinarily sensitive to any mention of his Korean largesse. When cartoonist Garry Trudeau, creator of the Doonesbury comic strip, urged readers last week to write the Speaker about his $6,500, the usually genial Tip O'Neill leaned on the Universal Press Syndicate to suppress the strip. Despite the Speaker's frown, Doonesbury's criticism ran in 500 newspapers.

Last month, the Speaker was given a remarkably gentle "interrogation" in secret, with only one House member present, by Jaworski staff members wearing kid gloves. Tip is happy he hand-picked Mr. Jaworski, symbol of rectitude, who now wants to wrap up the Koreagate investigation and go home to write another best seller (profits to the tax-exempt Leon Jaworski Foundation).

But for appearances' sake, the Tip and Leon show has to make a pass at getting the testimony of the Ambassador who handed the Congressmen the money. Tip has to huff and puff as if he is pressuring the Korean Government, and Leon has to make it seem he is demanding useful testimony.

Accordingly, when prodded hard by the press (thank God for Doonesbury!) and by Congressman Bruce Caputo (R.-N.Y.), the Speaker permitted a resolution to pass on May 31 that the House "will be prepared to deny or reduce assistance" to the Republic of Korea unless that nation cooperated in the investigation by producing Ambassador Kim's truthful testimony. Sounded tough; got great editorial applause.

But the House resolution carefully limited itself to the corrupted "food-for-peace" aid, or $56 million; not a word about the $277 million in direct military aid, not including the cost of our troops there. And the Koreans know that the Speaker and the group of takers would be grateful if they remain obdurate; the potential loss of the $56 million in economic aid is insurance that our annual billion-dollar military commitment will continue.

Meanwhile, Mr. Jaworski has joined in the charade being orchestrated by the Speaker. He strikes the pose so much admired by pressycophants: the fierce demander of testimony.

But he has taken a dive. In a letter to Speaker O'Neill dated June 19, thundering his protest at no cooperation from the South Korean Government, Mr. Jaworski writes: "I offered to negotiate, with flexibility and an understanding of the diplomatic concerns of South Korea, the manner in which information would be conveyed by former Ambassador Kim *if* the Committee could be assured in advance that the information would be forthright and not evasive.

"We even offered," added Leon to Tip—and here comes the beauty part—"to permit our written questions to be considered, answered and returned without personal confrontation by anyone representing the Committee."

He is willing to settle for a nice letter, unsworn, recalling a couple of payments to Congressmen no longer alive or in office, with a cover note from the Korean President praising Ambassador Kim for being amazingly forthright. No oath; no follow-up questioning; no getting of evidence that could lead to the arrest and conviction of the Congressional lawbreakers.

Sound strange for the fearless prosecutor who blasted through the "separation of powers" argument to obtain the White House tapes? Alas, the Houston Democrat who scorned "executive privilege" now gives great weight to diplomatic privilege, and in so doing saves a score of venal Democrats their skins. The kind of unsworn summary he would never accept from an aide to the President of the United States, he happily would accept from an aide to the President of South Korea.

John Rhodes, the House Minority Leader, today wrote to Mr. Jaworski: "I was surprised and shocked to learn in this letter that you had retreated from your oft-stated position that any testimony from Ambassador Kim Dong Jo must be made under oath. . . . You have abandoned any hope of receiving meaningful testimony."

The Koreagate cover-up goes on: Tip and Leon are going through the motions of investigation, and the public is bored and bamboozled. Meanwhile, more than 20 felons—a score of what Mr. Carter would call "bigshot crooks" if they were not mostly Democrats—sit comfortably in the Congress of the United States.

June 22, '78

Dear Editor:

I usually do not agree with Mr. Safire's essays, but I must give him a big applause for his courageous and tenacious efforts in exposing the subtle cover-ups of the Congress and the Administration over the Koreagate investigation. His essay, "Jaworski Takes a Dive" (Op-Ed June 22), is a revealing story of the hidden maneuvers between House Speaker Thomas P. O'Neill, who admited taking $6,500 in parties and gifts from Tongsun Park, and Leon Jaworski, who was hand-picked by the Speaker to head the House Ethics Committee's investigation of the Koreagate. It seems to me that the current investigation will die away sooner or later without letting American people know fully who are the present Congressmen who took the cash—after all, American tax money rerouted from the economic and military aid—directly from the South Korean Ambassador Kim Dong Jo, now a special aide to President Park.

Although the repressive regime of Park Chung Hee is refusing to send Mr. Kim to the U.S. to testify, with the support of the State Department, by claiming diplomatic immunity, there is no reason why the former ambassador cannot return to the U.S. voluntarily if that is what's required to clear up the suspicion and doubt between the two countries. Furthermore, it is questionable whether the claim to diplomatic immunity can be justified in this case since the Vienna Convention allows immunity to subsist only for "acts performed by such a person in the *exercise of his functions* as a member of the mission." Certainly the Park regime would not admit that one of the functions of the South Korean Embassy in Washington was to bribe the U.S. Congressmen by handing out cash. Thus it seems that the real reason why the Park regime is refusing to cooperate in the investigation is to save the "big-shot crooks" in the Congress and prolong his dictatorship.

Are we going to allow the investigation to die away quietly? As a Korean-American, I say loud and clear: Hell No! What is at stake is more than the security considerations that some people are using to end the investigation—it is the undermining of the American political system itself as well as the genuine friendship between American and Korean people.

Sincerely yours,
John H. Kim
Woodside, New York

IF YOU KNEW SUZY

May 12, 1977

"*No person holding any Office . . . shall without the Consent of the Congress accept of any present, Emolument . . . of any kind whatever, from any King, Prince or foreign State.*"

—Article I, Section 9, U.S. Constitution

WASHINGTON—Suzy Park Thomson, who has been granted immunity from prosecution so that she can tell what she knows about illegal payoffs to Congressmen by South Korea, is one of the Justice Department's key witnesses before the lethargic Koreagate grand jury.

Those of us who have suspected a close association between the Korean-born Mrs. Thomson and Tongsun Park, the Korean agent who was a paymaster for funds channeled to U.S. Congressmen, have been pressed to come up with evidence that would speed the lackadaisical Justice Department probe.

Recently, a document has materialized in my hand in the handwriting of B. Y. Lee, a close associate of Tongsun Park, dated April 24, 1975. He reports to his boss that he has met with "Mrs. Sew Thompson," who was saddened by the publicity given Tongsun Park when a friend of his committed suicide.

Mr. Lee then passes along Suzy Park Thomson's assertion that she is a "close information source" to five Congressmen. Here is the list given Mr. Park, with the Congressmen's comments to me today:

Lester Wolff, Democrat of New York, chairman of the House Asian and Pacific Affairs Subcommittee: "She was a secretary in my office, not a foreign policy expert, and she left in 1971 when she went to work for the Speaker." Information source? "Hell, no!"

(Mr. Wolff also states that Suzy was checked out by the F.B.I. at that time and given a "clean bill of health," which bears further checking.)

John Brademas, Democrat of Indiana, House Democratic whip: "There was no relationship, period. It is absolutely false, absurd and outrageous." Mr. Brademas has declared he received a total of $5,150 from Tongsun Park in fund raisers from 1970 through 1974, and has known Mr. Park for 15 years.

Albert Johnson, Republican of Pennsylvania, defeated for Congress last year, who did not answer his telephone today.

G. V. "Sonny" Montgomery, Democrat of Mississippi, who says he is "a friendly guy" and single, and has received "not a nickle" from South Korean sources.

Spark M. Matsunaga, former representative and newly elected Senator from Hawaii. He remembers Suzy Thomson as someone who worked for Patsy Mink (the Congressman he defeated in the Democratic senatorial primary) and Speaker Albert. He says he reported a $1,000 contribution in 1972 from an "S. Park," who turned out to have Tongsun Park's address, which was "not then illegal, and I had no idea he was an agent."

So five more names are tossed into the Koreagate hopper, perhaps because one woman falsely bragged about her connections. What's the big deal?

The deal is that the Lee memo establishes a connection between an agent of the Korean Government who was passing money to U.S. Congressmen and a woman who was working for Congressmen dealing with Asian policy, including the then-Speaker of the House, Carl Albert. That was a pretty effective penetration and corruption of our Government, which Article I of the Constitution sought to prevent.

"I think everybody in the House knew Suzy Park Thomson," recalls Democratic Congressman Walter Flowers of Alabama, who was not on the latest list. "She more or less stands out. Obviously Oriental. Small, wide-brimmed hat, very high heels."

Like many others, Congressman Flowers also knew Tongsun Park, having met him at a large party given by Park in honor of Tip O'Neill, who replaced Suzy Thomson's old boss as Speaker. Mr. Flowers recalls that the South Korean agent later visited him in his office but "can't remember" what it was about; he denies ever having taken any money from Park.

An innocent voter might think that Walter Flowers would want an opportunity to declare his absence of taint to the House Ethics Committee, of which he is a member.

Not so. When Philip Lacovara, of Watergate prosecution fame, today supported a minority move to require statements of noninvolvement from members of the Ethics panel which will sit in judgment on others, Mr. Flowers indignantly denounced it as "impugning our integrity." Counsel Lacovara helplessly acquiesed.

The House Ethics Committee and the Koreagate grand jury are trying to out-slow each other. The Democratic politicians in Justice have not questioned Senator Matsunaga. Mrs. Juanita Moody, the National Security Agency operative sitting on a powderkeg of information, will not talk to the House committee because its staff, after all these months, does not have the proper security clearances.

Georgia's John Flynt, Ethics Committee chairman, looks like an unhappy man. "Don't blame John," cautions one of his Democratic friends. "He's under unbelievable pressure from the Speaker to slow this damn investigation down."

THE TIP AND LEON SHOW

October 10, 1977

WASHINGTON—When House Speaker Tip O'Neill was faced by a revolt of young Congressmen embarrassed by the foot-dragging on the Koreagate investigation, he turned to a Certified Media Sacred Cow,

Texas Democrat Leon Jaworski, to put on a big show of prober's probity.

The Speaker's strategy has worked. Nobody criticizes the House Ethics Committee's halfhearted poking around; Republicans on the committee are regularly denied access to information gathered by the Jaworski staff; and as one top Democrat reports, "No sitting member is in trouble."

Former Special Prosecutor Jaworski is not a man who tolerates criticism. At the risk of eliciting another Queeg-like letter from him threatening a libel suit, let me suggest that his misunderstanding of his assignment—as well as his attempt to cut off minority member participation in a scandal affecting mainly the Democratic majority—plays directly into Tip's hands.

The containment strategy became apparent when Sue Park Thomson revealed, at Republican urging, what she had said in testimony: that when people called former Speaker Carl Albert's office, looking for lobbyist Tongsun Park, she would often refer them to Tip O'Neill's office, where Mr. Park could often be found.

Mrs. Thomson had every right to reveal her own testimony. But this caused Mr. Jaworski to demand House Resolution 752, permitting a Congressional staff to take testimony without any Congressman present. This unheard-of "zero member quorum" has passed the O'Neill-dominated Rules Committee, and—if passed by the full House—would make it impossible for Congressmen to know how narrowly Mr. Jaworski interprets his charge.

While this arrogation of power to contain the investigation was going on, a curious charade took place that seems intended to show that Mr. Jaworski is following all leads, and that Mr. O'Neill is an aggrieved innocent. A story was leaked last week that the Speaker's rent records were being subpoenaed; the Speaker gleefully confirmed the story, adding that he was volunteering his canceled rent checks to show Tongsun Park never paid the O'Neill rent.

Something fishy about that byplay: If Mr. Jaworski were serious about following a lead, he would have subpoenaed the O'Neill checks and bank deposit records, which he had not done.

Next week, to give the illusion of relentless progress, Mr. Jaworski will treat the committee to open hearings. As of today, the plan is to limit the hearings to a showing of how Tongsun Park operated on behalf of the Korean C.I.A., mentioning only Congressmen previously named. (No sitting members need be concerned.)

The staff will show what its subpoenas have turned up. The American Express Company and Hilton Hotels have produced travel records; Diplomat National Bank and Equitable Trust Company of Baltimore records will show some of the banking maneuvers of Tongsun Park and former Congressman Richard Hanna; we will examine stock dealings in a company named Spectrostrip.

The related New Jersey firms of the Connell Rice & Sugar Company and the St. John's Maritime Company—represented by former San Francisco Mayor Joseph Alioto—will reveal some of their operations, and may explain contributions by their owners to various former Congressmen.

To liven up the hearings, General Kim Hung Wook will repeat his story of K.C.I.A. chicanery, but the star witness is supposed to be K.C.I.A. defector Kim Sang Kuen, appearing courtesy of the Justice Department, which holds him in protective custody. They will explain what the Koreans did.

But we are not now scheduled to learn how many present members of Congress were on the take. We will never uncover the cover-up until the following heat is applied to Congress by press and public:

Every member of Congress should be required to come before the Ethics Committee—*under oath*—to testify about what, if anything, the Congressman took from foreign agents. Until now, Mr. Jaworski has been satisfied by an unsworn questionnaire that clears no innocent officeholders and worries no guilty ones.

Every member of the Ethics Committee, even Republicans, should be given lawful access to all the information gathered by its staff and forwarded to the committee by Justice and the C.I.A. This would make certain no areas are being overlooked and no Speakers, past or present, are being treated gingerly.

Moreover, the House should pass a resolution now, this week, cutting off all aid to South Korea until such time as that Government produces Tongsun Park and other witnesses—prepared to cooperate and subject to U.S. penalties for perjury—for examination both before a grand jury in secrecy and the House committee in open session.

That is what the House would do if it were serious about exposing the corruption of Koreagate. Instead, its members are more likely to sleep well every night after a warm glass of the milk of the sacred cow.

THIS YEAR'S COVER-UP

July 20, 1978

HOUSTON—The two-year investigations by the House Ethics Committee and the Justice Department into the corruption of the House of Representatives by operatives of the South Korean C.I.A. is ending in a way cynics predicted it would end: with a handful of former Congressmen indicted, and a handful of present Congressmen slapped lightly on the wrist.

Devotees of successful criminal cover-ups doff their hats reverently to Speaker Tip O'Neill, who quietly limited the scope of the probe; to Ben Civiletti of President Carter's Department of Political Justice, who won powerful friends on the Hill by his botching of the investigation; to Special Counsel Leon Jaworski, king of press clips, who just did not have the gumption to go after the key witness who could have put 13 of our most powerful Congressmen behind bars.

That witness is Kim Dong Jo, former South Korean Ambassador, now a private citizen in Seoul. Although the bribe-takers could pretend that gifts and parties from "businessman" Tongsun Park were not illegal, no such pretense is possible when a foreign ambassador slipped them thousands in cash. Such payments violate Article II of the U.S. Constitution, and the men on the take knew exactly what fundamental trust they were selling.

When it was pointed out in this space a few weeks ago that Mr. Jaworski—to Speaker O'Neill's intense relief—would no longer seek Ambassador Kim's presence under oath, a high diplomatic official took me atop the mountain to give me The Big Picture:

More important than putting a dozen lawmaking lawbreakers in jail, went the explanation, was the need to preserve the principle of diplomatic immunity. If the Korean Ambassador could be forced to testify under oath about his bribery of Congressmen, then our own ambassadors around the world would be vulnerable to local prosecution for real or fancied crimes.

This reasoning caused our Justice Department to give up any attempt to bring back the vital witness, and was responsible for the collapse of Mr. Jaworski's investigation.

But that argument—so readily embraced by politicians anxious to get rid of Koreagate before election time—is specious. Nobody is suggesting that the protection of diplomats be radically altered; on the contrary, the return of former Ambassador Kim for sworn testimony is the only way the traditions of an alliance can be upheld.

Our ally, South Korea, committed a grave and provocative act against the United States by inducing our Congressmen to break our laws. Voluntarily, as a good ally, South Korea should now help us determine which of our Congressmen are felons. We do not seek to punish their diplomat-briber—only to get his truthful testimony.

Our troops have been in South Korea for a generation to protect that country from attack. We have a right to expect South Korea to help us protect our own institutions from attack—and the subversion of our Congress is surely such an attack. If the Koreans expect us to turn over to them $1 billion worth of military equipment in the next few years as planned, we have a right to expect their active aid to help us expose and prosecute our Congressional criminals.

Our State Department frets that we must not embarrass our Korean allies. The truth is that the embarrassment is more ours than theirs. If the Koreans would like an apology for our bugging of their presidential mansion—which was how we learned of the bribery—we should gladly make it, turning over to them the fruits of our eavesdropping as part of the general clearing of the air.

None of this is in the cards, of course: A Democratic Justice Department and a Democratic majority in Congress is determined to keep a scandal involving mostly Democrats from being fully revealed.

If Mr. Jaworski were the patriot he has long been cracked up to be, he would ask for prime network television time (which he would promptly get) to say something like this:

"I have good reason to believe that at least 13 of our most senior Congressmen have broken the law by taking bribes from a foreign ambassador. But I cannot prove my case until Congress and the President take the action needed to produce the witness.

"That action, my fellow Americans, is not to trim economic aid, as has been done, which is a weak gesture to make it appear that we want our witness. That action would be to announce our intention to remove all U.S. troops and equipment from South Korea within 30 days unless that nation tells us what we need to know about our crooked Congressmen.

"Write and phone your Congressman today. Tell him you will not vote for him next fall if he is unwilling to get to the bottom of this scandal. Get angry—that's the only way to get action. I can't do this job of exposing the felons alone. I need your help. Tell your Congressman to stop pussy-footing and start demanding that our ally act as an ally."

Beamed into 60 million homes, that message would get a reaction that would crack through the cover-up and brush aside the phony diplomatic niceties that protect the Speaker's friends. Does Mr. Jaworski have the nerve? Don't hold your breath.

We can only hope that someday, when party power shifts, we will have an investigation of all those who abetted this year's successful cover-up.

JUSTICE FINESSED

July 27, 1978

LOS ANGELES—In this space last week, I railed at the way the House Ethics Committee—given media respectability by sacred cowboy Leon Jaworski—failed to get the testimony of the former South Korean Ambassador Kim Dong Jo and thereby let a dozen senior Congressional felons go free. Embarrassed, the House has shown new interest in Mr. Kim.

Now let us observe how the Carter Justice Department did its fumbling bit to contain the scandal. On April 11, 1977, it was pointed out here that former Louisiana Congressman Otto Passman was a prime suspect in the investigation into illegal payoffs. However, at the written request of House Speaker Tip O'Neill, a longtime Passman crony, the Justice Department was helping to defend Mr. Passman on an unrelated case of sex discrimination brought against him by a woman employee.

The question at that time: Why was the Justice Department helping Mr. Passman? To obtain his cooperation? We now know the answer is no, since he still denies everything. The reason that Justice to this day is Mr. Passman's *amicus* is purely to honor Tip O'Neill's request—and Tip is anxious that Passman know who has been helping to defend him.

On March 31, 1978, after a year of horsing around, Justice obtained two indictments against Otto Passman: one, for taking bribes of $223,000 from Tongsun Park, and two, for income-tax evasion. That figure was surely on the low side: Mr. Park said he gave Mr. Passman about $477,000.

The object of the Passman prosecution was not so much to put one 78-year-old man in jail but to get him to talk about which sitting members of Congress got how much. One suspects that Mr. Passman was not only a taker but a distributor: We have evidence that Los Angeles Congressman Edward Roybal was brought into Passman's office for a Park payoff, and can assume that portions of that half-million in cash went to Passman cronies.

Therefore, Justice wanted to put the fear of jail in the old man; he is said to have told friends that if convicted he would talk in exchange for his freedom. His greatest fear: a District of Columbia jury, which tends to convict, as Watergaters know. His greatest hope: a hometown judge and jury, who can be much gentler to a longtime pillar of the community.

Here is how Mr. Passman's defense counsel, James Hamilton and Camille Gravel, made monkeys out of the Justice Department:

After a ruling by a tough D.C. judge that the ailing Mr. Passman was competent to stand trial, Passman's attorneys asked that the two cases (bribery and income-tax evasion) be consolidated.

The Justice Department mulled this over and did not object. You cannot find anyone at Justice willing to take responsibility for that decision today. Since the prosecutors did not oppose the request to consolidate the two cases, the judge did so.

Then Mr. Passman's attorneys pointed to a law that requires that income-tax cases be tried in the defendant's home district and asked for a transfer of the joined cases to Louisiana. The Justice Department lawyers gulped and tried to stop the transfer, but were then in the untenable position of asking for two trials on the combined cases.

Judge Barrington Parker chided the Justice Department for being "temporarily unmindful" of the consequences of coupling cases, adding that Justice may have been "finessed by the defendant's attorneys." He then sent the trial to Monroe, La., which is equivalent to taking the Watergate conspirators away from D.C. to Orange County, Calif., for prompt acquittal, or at most a suspended sentence.

As a result, Justice has no leverage at all on the man who is charged with taking the most money in the Koreagate scandal. All the other satraps in Congress, who just finished heaving sighs of relief at the Jaworski cave-in, now breathe even easier at the narrow escape of Otto Passman, who might have been the source of considerable embarrassment.

Is this stupidity or venality? Paul Michel, of the Justice Department section laughingly labeled Public Integrity, insists "we were aware of the possibility that both cases might end up in Louisiana." He also admits that the original decision to proceed with both indictments was cleared with the politically sensitive Deputy Attorney General, Ben Civiletti.

On Koreagate the Carter record is abysmal: (1) Justice waited until Tongsun Park fled the country before indicting him; (2) Justice made no real attempt to get Ambassador Kim's testimony; (3) Justice withheld from the Ethics Committee evidence found in Tongsun Park's home—evidence that was later found embarrassing to Tip O'Neill.

And now Justice goofs on Passman. That's the way one party's investigation of itself ends—not with a bang, but a whimper.

JAWORSKI AND SINATRA

May 21, 1979

WASHINGTON—Most of the political figures I have criticized over the years have redeeming features.

Bert Lance, who may have conspired with candidate Jimmy Carter to finance an election campaign, has loyally refused to avert an indictment by implicating his friend.

Attorney General Griffin Bell, who has thoroughly politicized the Justice Department and has turned the expanding Federal judiciary into a Democratic plum tree, is a forthright and likable fellow.

These men—along with other favorite recipients of attention like Henry Kissinger, Gerry Rafshoon, Ben Civiletti, and Tip O'Neill—can and should be excoriated for their political and business sins. All know how to slam back, too, in private and in print. But in taking them on, a critic has a sense of dealing with public affairs professionals and worthy adversaries.

Not so with Frank Sinatra and Leon Jaworski. Last week, in lashing out at this critic, both men revealed a rare combination of pomposity and vindictiveness.

First, Ol' Blue Eyes. It was pointed out here that Henry Ford 2d had used Frank Sinatra (who has longtime gangland friendships) to act as a go-between to induce Roy Cohn (who represents gangland clients in court) to scuttle the stockholder suit against Mr. Ford. Mr. Sinatra's vociferous denial was duly recorded here.

To vent his spleen, Mr. Sinatra has taken to financing the mailing of an anti-press tract with his covering letter attacking journalists who "hide behind" the First Amendment, as if he were being put upon by unscrupulous rumormongers.

To establish the facts of the case that caused the Sinatra mailing, I determined from Henry Ford 2d that he had personally visited Mr. Sinatra before a recent concert in Detroit: purely a "social call." But very shortly after that visit, Mr. Sinatra and friends flew to New York and met with attorney Roy Cohn in a restaurant misspelled "Seperate Tables." The names of more than one of those present would ring bells in the organized-crime section of the Department of Justice.

I put it straight to Mr. Cohn, who was not my original source: What did he and Sinatra discuss? The attorney, a longtime friend, could not duck on a matter concerning my credibility: "The meeting was arranged to discuss an offer to settle the Ford suit," says Mr. Cohn, who had not met Mr. Sinatra before. "I waited for the settlement offer, but it turned out that Henry Ford asked Sinatra to ask me to take a dive. I told Frank to stop kidding and I went home." That's the story both Mr. Sinatra and Mr. Ford deny; I think it is rock-solid. For Frank Sinatra to try to cloak his embarrassment in a high-domed attack on the First Amendment is a measure of his pretension.

And now to the sacred cow of the press clips, Leon Jaworski, who made his fame as the special prosecutor of Watergate and let that public trust be used to cloak the Carter Justice Department's cover-up of Koreagate.

Mr. Jaworski will not tolerate criticism. A newspaper with the temerity to print suggestions that his official conduct might have been less effective than his publicity gets strange, rambling letters hinting at legal action.

In his latest book (this second squeezing of the grapes was written by Howard Cosell's ghostwriter), Mr. Jaworski recounts an episode that perhaps reveals more than he intended.

It was 1974, year of prosecutorial hysteria; I was zapping the special prosecutor, sometimes accurately, sometimes mistakenly, but always alone. Individual targets who could not be charged with a specific crime were being run before a grand jury in order to build perjury cases, a practice no longer permitted by the Justice Department.

Al Haig, then White House Chief of Staff (now taking up man-on-horse-back riding), cornered me at a reception to cheerily pass along an incredible threat: "Leon says he wanted me to tell you to get off his back, or else."

I was incredulous—after Watergate, could any public official be so heavy-handed? But now, in his memoir, Mr. Jaworski confirms his improper pressure. He writes that after I wrote a piece demanding to know why John Dean had not been indicted, Jaworski telephoned Haig to implant this chilling thought: "If Safire has other information, I think I'll just subpoena him before the grand jury."

Mr. Jaworski is proud of that attempt at intimidation. Here was the prosecutor who was marching men into a grand jury room, indicting them for so much as an "I don't remember," warning a critical newspaper columnist to shut up or he would have to join that grand jury parade, perhaps to jail and ruination.

The arrogant Mr. Jaworski does not realize, to this day, that his threat was an abuse of power similar to the abuses he was hired to prosecute. Like John Dean this week, he is still profiting from Watergate, missing the point of its lesson.

That's why I think Sinatra and Jaworski are peas in a pod. When criticized, they go for the throat of the institution that made them celebrities, and they make it difficult for those of us with charity in our hearts to discover some redeeming feature.

Jimmy Carter

I THINK Jimmy Carter presented a mask—a false image—to the public. His self-righteousness turned me off; his assurance that his dovish, too-trusting foreign policy was the right road for America worried me. I thought his unconcern at his brother's unregistered representation of radical Libya was a disgrace. And, for a man who made so much of never telling a lie, he was not always truthful.

Perhaps this intolerance of hypocrisy comes through in the pieces that follow. The letters chosen to show the reaction pull no punches, either, especially the last, from the President's embittered lawyer.

I'm not a hater—haters destroy themselves. I'm a relentless disliker, though, and something in the way the Carter men acted, as if they invented purity, stimulated a certain polemical passion in my work. Perhaps it helped him become a better President; I hope so.

THE NEW PRESIDENTIALESE

November 18, 1976

WASHINGTON—At a long-planned news conference, which has replaced the hastily called press conference, the late Frank Sullivan's cliché expert, Dr. Arbuthnot, revealed the parameters of the new Presidentialese to the official translators.

Question: Dr. Arbuthnot, based on your vast experience, what would you say is likely to be considered as the highest virtue in the Carter Administration?

Answer: Compatibility.

Q: And what will be looked upon as the greatest evil?

A: Disharmoniousness.

Q: How would you characterize, sir, the apparent blood feud now taking place between Jack Watson, head of the transition team, and Hamilton Jordan, who served as campaign manager?

A: Their relationship is halfway between compatible and disharmonious.

Q: Which is called?

A: A short-lived rift, to be patched up or papered over, as soon as one or the other is humiliated and destroyed.

Q: By the way, how do you pronounce Jordan?

A: Rhymes with burden.

Q: What is the proper grouping of rifts, as in "a swarm of job applicants," "a pride of elder statesmen," or "a giggle of punsters"?

A: A raft of rifts, which we can anticipate with confidence.

Q: Those job applications—on what basis will they be chosen?

A: Merit.

Q: And what must their appeal be?

A: Broad-based.

Q: Will they include any malefactors of great wealth who have been using tax loopholes?

A: (icily) They are now referred to as "business leaders."

Q: How will they be chosen?

A: Never through patronage, always through a "process" or a "procedure." The latest is called the "Talent Inventory Procedure," or—this is kind of a catchy acronym—"TIP."

Q: How is that acronym different from President Ford's "Whip Inflation Now," or "WIN," program, that engendered such widespread derision?

A: This was suggested by Congressman O'Neill of Boston. He had a lot of buttons left over from his campaign.

Q: Is there any one word to describe an action the next administration will consider stupid, insulting, and morally reprehensible?

A: A "disgrace." In interstate cases, "a national disgrace."

Q: How would the Administration describe a stupid, insulting, etc., action that it might be called upon to avoid commenting about?

A: Inappropriate.

Q: What will Cabinet members be given?

A: Maximum authority.

Q: Does that mean department heads will choose their own assistant secretaries and deputies?

A: That goes beyond the maximum, and has been ruled out.

Q: Have you determined, Dr. Arbuthnot, the proper appellation for the Plains, Georgia, bus depot on the day the chairman of the Federal Reserve Board arrives?

A: The coterminus.

Q: How should the oil-producing nations act vis-à-vis price rises?

A: With restraint.

Q: What is the correct name for a 10 percent oil-price rise?

A: Between now and January 20, an "unconscionable gouging of the consumer caused by lack of cohesive, or coherent, leadership."

Q: And after that date?

A: "Great restraint."

Q: What would the Carter linguistic reaction be to that?

A: This country can be fueled by speculation.

Q: On a loftier plane, how would peace be sought?

A: "Aggressively," which is one step short of belligerently.

Q: In what political period would you say we are right now?

A: The interregnum, in which everything that happens is "during."

Q: And what follows the interregnum?

A: The next regnum, dummy. Oh, I suppose you mean "Inaugural Euphoria," in which the products of the deliberate, unhurried selection process pore through position papers prepared by transition task forces for the man destined to assume the awesome burdens of the loneliest job in the world.

Q: Which leads into—

A: The "Honeymoon Period," truncated or extended, during which it rains a hundred days and a hundred nights, as the steely-eyed Cincinnatus of the South takes a fact-finding tour of the six economic summits, eschewing the disharmonious, fending off the inappropriate, and spreading the gospel of "The New Compatibility."

Q: But what of the arms race?

A: He doesn't intend to lose, and you can depend on it.

PEDESTRIAN INAUGURAL

January 24, 1977

WASHINGTON—Nobody likes to say it, and everybody is trying to be kind, but the fact is that Jimmy Carter's inaugural address ranks slightly above Millard Fillmore's and not quite up to Calvin Coolidge's.

The keynote of the Carter Presidency turned out to be a themeless pudding, devoid of uplift or insight, defensive in outlook, and timorous in its reach, straining five times to sell its "new spirit" slogan in the absence of a message.

Presented with this material, some commentators promptly fashioned a silk purse: "A welcome theme of simplicity," gushed *The New York Times* editorial, "which consciously moved away from the grandiose."

Simplicity would have been a legitimate theme; but being simplistic, as Mr. Carter was, is an evasion of thought. In Lyndon Johnson's 1965 inaugural, written with the aid of John Steinbeck, no flights of rhetoric were needed—plain, understandable words drove home the message. To be simplistic is easy; to be simple is hard.

Curiously, the fact that President Carter made a banal, forgettable speech is interpreted as good news. That is because the three inaugural addresses of the 60's—thoughtful and well-crafted speeches that put forward the essence of each President's vision of America—were delivered by Presidents who are now much derided. Since their subsequent actions are being derogated as "imperial," the fashion in inaugurals today is the muddled presentation of self-deprecating platitudes.

As a result, an inability to organize thoughts into a coherent speech—a failure to use the English language to uplift, to instruct, and to lead—is hailed as "anti-grandiose" by good writers, of all people.

Consider the Carter speech. As in his nomination acceptance, only the opening sentence was memorable. After a gracious thank you to his predecessor, the new President went downhill.

After campaigning for three years on the theme that government must be as good as its people—promising strong leadership to match the national character—he now changes that into an apology that he's no better than us, and therefore we can't expect much.

"We cannot afford to do everything," he says. That might not have been the way he was talking in the campaign, but it's a legitimate direction, which was usually taken by Mr. Ford. Then, on second thought, President Carter ends the sentence by going the other way: "Nor can we afford to lack boldness as we meet the future." What we can afford, presumably, is to not do everything boldly.

Still straddling, he says: "Our Government must at the same time be both competent and compassionate." He probably thought that was pretty nifty alliteration, a line for the historians; more likely the historians will note that "both" and "at the same time" are redundant.

The speech was mercifully brief, not because he strove for brevity, but because he seemed to have not much to say. He appeared to think he was still unchosen, and was reluctant to define his own version of the American dream lest he lose support. Instead, he seemed content to go along with the revolution of sinking expectations.

The whole world was waiting for some clue, some low-profile hint, some sense of direction from the new President. That is what inaugural addresses are for. But—just as he showed when the audio came back on during the first debate—at a unique moment in history, Jimmy Carter had nothing original to say.

Why? One possibility is that he believes that the best kind of leadership is nonleadership, and that he intends to out-Ford Ford. Another is that he wanted to use the language to make his points memorably and quotably—"ever vigilant and never vulnerable" was a good try—but that he just did not know how.

The most likely reason for his keynote to be so low-key as to be no-key is that he has neither a world view nor a philosophy. He has not become President to accomplish his goal, he has accomplished his goal by becoming President.

Now it is up to us, he seems to say—tell him what we want, he'll do as much as he can for most of us. The only thing to which President Carter is committed is commitment itself.

Long after Jimmy Carter's inaugural address is forgotten (a process that began rapidly the moment he finished speaking) the inaugural event that will be remembered is his courageous, precedent-shattering mile-and-a-quarter personal parade down Pennsylvania Avenue. Those who give his speech a fast couple of claps for being un-grandiose like to dwell on his walk as evidence of originality and commonmanliness.

Give due credit: The stunt was inspired, made great pictures, and made his Vice President look like a limousine liberal. It was also a foolhardy display of macho—acting against the words he had just spoken—and Mr. Carter ought to cut it out before he gives encouragement to nuts.

Inauguration Day, 1977, was the day the new President was hailed for being a pedestrian. Unfortunately, so was his speech.

THE MORAL HOT LINE

January 31, 1977

WASHINGTON—Soviet authorities cannot diminish the effectiveness of their leading dissident, scientist Andrei Sakharov, in the same way they handled Alexander Solzhenitsyn—by sending him out of the country.

The reason is plain: Mr. Sakharov knows how to build a hydrogen bomb. He is in Russia to stay. His fate there is of enormous importance to everyone who believes in human freedom.

Recently, Mr. Sakharov met with an American Civil Liberties lawyer, Martin Garbus, in Moscow. Mr. Garbus (with whom I disagree politically, but who once represented me in an unrelated legal matter) believes that President Carter is sincere in his concern for human rights. He volunteered to carry a letter from the leading Soviet dissenter to the new American President.

Mr. Sakharov warned the American lawyer and his wife not to submit to a search when they left his apartment unless a United States consular official was present; with considerable courage, Ruth Garbus placed the letter inside her brassiere and walked resolutely past the K.G.B. surveillance.

Meanwhile, the Carter State Department started acting as if the new President's rhetoric about human rights was to be taken seriously in United States foreign policy. A statement criticizing Czechoslovakia and another praising Mr. Sakharov was issued—declarations expressing ideals of freedom that could never have been made in the Kissinger era.

Then the reaction set in. Soviet Ambassador Dobrynin got on the telephone to complain to Secretary of State Cyrus Vance. In an incredible display of confusion—or in a shabby exhibition of weakness—Mr. Vance claimed he had not been informed of one of the statements in advance, though he did not repudiate it.

When the Soviet news agency Tass blasted the United States for an "unsavory play" in standing up for Mr. Sakharov, the striped-pants set panicked. Before and after the heat came on, the word was passed to the media to "read Shulman in *Foreign Affairs.*" Columbia Professor Marshall Shulman, a détente-firster now an adviser to Mr. Vance on Soviet policy, writes in the current issue of that publication that it is okay for individuals to express their repugnance of human rights violations in other countries, but that governments should remain pragmatically silent.

Then the editorial pages of *The New York Times* and *Washington Post* weighed in with more of the old Kissinger line, tut-tutting at the way Mr. Carter "seems determined to burden his diplomacy with ideals" (*Times*) and warning that "more is involved than the satisfaction of Americans' moral impulses" (*Post*).

Thus is a President taken into camp. The American people may have been repelled by the Helsinki sellout; voters may have demanded a change by electing a leader who promised the rejection of amorality; and Mr. Carter may want to do what he promised.

But is he willing to fight for that approach within his own Administration? We do not know. When his Administration started to speak up for human freedom, the Soviets told him to shut up and his editorial supporters told him to grow up.

The President's reaction to that pressure has been curious: "What he [the department spokesman] said was my attitude," the President allowed, adding "perhaps it should have been said by myself or Secretary Vance." What does that mean? Are Administration statement-writers not supposed to reflect the attitude of the top officials?

Mr. Carter seems to be backing away without backing away. He is leaving the impression that he would have avoided commenting on Mr. Sakharov at all.

The new President has surrounded himself with advisers who will tell him his instincts are wrong, that the American voter was wrong, that more can be pragmatically done for human freedom by "quiet diplomacy" than by publicly calling the Soviets to account for making a mockery of the Helsinki accords. What's more, *Times* reporter Bernard Gwertzman writes today that the Carter choice for SALT negotiator is Paul Warnke, the dove's delight—another voice for détente-first.

In his fireside chat, Mr. Carter will have the chance to send a signal: To the voters, that he did not lie to them about morality in foreign policy; to the State Department, that we surely want to make progress at SALT, but not at the price of the toleration of repression—a price that Mr. Kissinger was so willing to pay, and which lately brought us nothing.

The signal would also be received by Andrei Sakharov, whose very survival depends on the expression of free men's concern. Will the President reaffirm his commitment to human rights? Or will he back down at the first evidence of Soviet pressure?

OH, WHAT A TANGLED WEB . . .

November 24, 1977

WASHINGTON—Many President-watchers are talking about, though few are writing about, the strange case of Mr. Carter's false statements regarding his participation in the decision to plea-bargain with Richard Helms.

On September 29, at a Presidential press conference, Charles Mohr of *The New York Times*—after pointing out that Attorney General Griffin Bell had once said he was going to consult the President about whether or not to prosecute the former C.I.A. Director—asked how the decision was being reached.

Mr. Carter replied: "He has not consulted with me, nor given me any advice on the Helms question. . . . I think he will make a report to me and possibly a recommendation fairly soon, but until this moment he has not yet done so."

The President's statement was untrue. On November 1, Attorney General Bell revealed that he had met with the President about the Helms case on July 25, two months before the President publicly denied any meeting had taken place. Nor was that meeting a casual one: The Attorney General and two key aides were summoned to the Oval Office for a meeting with the President, Vice President Mondale, and National Security Adviser Brzezinski.

"We there discussed the pending Helms investigation and we weighed the factors which I thought were involved," the Attorney General has recently said. After specifying some of the details presented to Mr. Carter at that July 25 meeting, Mr. Bell added: "We were satisfied from our study to date that it was possible to prosecute. We were authorized by the President to determine the possibility and feasibility of plea bargaining, and to keep him advised of any developments in this matter."

Since the President had assured the public that no such consultation had ever taken place, reporters asked the Deputy Press Secretary, Rex Granum, why Mr. Carter had misled them. After checking with the President, Mr. Granum passed along this convoluted explanation: Although the July 25 meeting about Helms did take place secretly, the President believed that some reporters had been told about it. Therefore, Mr. Carter said he had interpreted Mr. Mohr's question to mean: Had the President met with the Attorney General about Helms *after* the July 25 meeting? And the answer to that was no.

That story had such a clank of falsity that the White House soon abandoned it. The phantom "some reporters" never materialized. On November 10, after assuring ABC's Sam Donaldson that public officials had no "right to lie," President Carter was asked by NBC's Bob Jamieson why he had denied consulting about the Helms case when the opposite had been true. The President tried a new tack, implying the meeting was too insignificant to remember:

"The September 25th [he meant July 25th, says the official transcript] meeting was not, in the first place, a thorough discussion of the Helms case," Mr. Carter insisted. "It was a brief meeting . . . there was a general discussion there, fairly brief."

Oh, what a tangled web we weave. Forced to admit participation in a decision he had previously denied, the President sought to make the crucial meeting appear quick and inconsequential. His implication is patently untruthful. Others present attest to the seriousness and extensiveness of the July 25 Helms meeting, instigated by the President at the request of the C.I.A., which the Attorney General has publicly stated concluded with an important Presidential decision to authorize plea bargaining to avoid a trial. For the President to claim that his controversial decision was made without "a thorough discussion" is absurd.

There the matter rests: The President did not tell the truth on September 29, then sent his spokesman forth with a phony story on November 2, and then made a different false implication on November 10.

Why? The charitable explanation is that he simply forgot about the July 25 meeting, when asked the first time. If that were the case, he could have said later: "Sorry, that meeting slipped my mind—it was a busy day." That would have been the end of it.

Instead, Mr. Carter and his spokesmen seem unable to admit one moment's ineptitude. Rather than acknowledge the first false statement as a mistake, they persist in compounding the original error, if that is what it was, with a farrago of falsehoods.

It gives me no pleasure to show my President as deliberately deceitful (see? columnists can lie, too); but the irony is in the fire: As *The New Republic*'s John Osborne has suggested, if the President had said under oath to a Congressional committee what he said to the press on September 29 and November 10, Mr. Carter could have been charged with the misdemeanors that Mr. Helms was charged with, or not charged with the perjury that Mr. Helms was not charged with.

"I'll never lie to you," said Candidate Jimmy Carter, again and again and again. The matter that troubles those who hope he will be a successful one-term President is not so much whether he is lying to us, but whether he is lying to himself.

CARTER'S PILLS

July 24, 1978

SAN FRANCISCO—A press conference was scheduled last week in prime TV time by a President anxious to shore up his popularity by showing how cool he could be under sharp questioning. But then a crisis arose: Mr. Carter's longtime friend in charge of drug abuse was caught abusing the drug laws, fraudulently prescribing a dangerous substance— "quax pills," in the drug vernacular—to a young woman aide.

The President could have met that crisis calmly, saying nothing at his conference until a question arose. He could then have assured his countrymen that no "Dr. Feelgood" was in the White House, administering amphetamines, as had happened among the "Beautiful People" in the Kennedy days. He could easily have limited his answers to matters not directly concerned with a criminal investigation.

Instead Jimmy Carter choked up. For the first time in televised news-conference history, a panicked President declared a legitimate news story to be off limits: "I will not answer questions on the subject."

At that moment, he sought to change the open press conference format into a forum using newsmen as props for the airing of views on matters of the President's choosing.

The response of the White House press corps was agonizingly slow. Amazingly, for 15 minutes, all too many members of the White House press corps meekly accepted the new ground rules. Finally, after seven softballs, Daniel Schorr—columnist for *The Des Moines Register* syndicate—challenged the unprecedented censorship:

"Mr. President, I hope that this doesn't fall within the area of legal issues that you prefer not to discuss tonight, but the health of the President himself has always been a matter of great concern to the country. Can you say whether any of the prescriptions that were signed by Dr. Bourne were for substances that went either to you or members of your family?"

Mr. Carter could not overtly avoid that. He answered obliquely: "Dr. Bourne has never given me any treatment of any kind." That ducked a response about members of his family, and shied away from the precision of the drug question, so Schorr pressed: "None of those substances went to your—" "No, sir," Mr. Carter interrupted and hurried to the next questioner.

After Mr. Schorr had reasserted the traditions of the news conference, the press corps awakened to Topic A. ABC's Sam Donaldson pointed out that his question would not "touch on the allegations" and wanted to know about the political counterpunch—if the President agreed with Bourne's statement that the attacks on him were really attacks on the President.

With no civil liberties excuse to offer, the apostle of an open administration said grimly: "I would prefer not to answer that question."

If a President wishes to take over the airwaves for what is billed as a news conference, then he assumes the responsibility for answering to the best of his ability all questions of news interest. If the President does not know the answers, or if giving the answer would breach national security, impair a diplomatic initiative, or violate a person's rights, he should say so. But if he "prefers" not to deal with political embarrassments or White House scandals, then the press should prefer not to serve up the questions the President wants to hear.

The significance of the fraudulent prescription is not that it will reveal drug orgies in the White House basement. Peter Bourne was originally brought to the White House at the behest of Nixon drug-abuse honcho Egil Krogh. He showed some permissive views and was fired soon after his car was spotted sporting a McGovern sticker. An early Carter enthusiast, he was paid off with one of those double-dip patronage specials that blessed him and his wife with a total of $101,000 a year in salaries. He will neither be missed nor prosecuted—there will be no "Pillgate."

This "unfortunate occurrence" is significant mainly in what it reveals

of the Magnolia Mafia when confronted with an arrest for lawbreaking in
its midst.

The first, oh-so-familiar reaction is to blame police and press for trying
to embarrass the President. The next step is for the Carter Drug Enforcement Council to brush aside the infraction of law with "everybody does
it" (on the very day the Carter parole board announced John Mitchell
would stay in jail six months longer).

And finally, we have a fearful President coming before the nation to
announce he will not face up to any questions on the subject. To the doctrine of executive privilege he has tried to add "Presidential preference."
We were fortunate to have men like Daniel Schorr and Sam Donaldson to
challenge a Chief Executive frozen in the arrogance of impotence.

BILLY THE PROBLEM

January 15, 1979

WASHINGTON—One week ago in this space, the President's business
partner and brother was identified as the greatest source of White House
worry in the Lance investigation. Although he had claimed a Fifth
Amendment privilege in refusing to testify to the grand jury, it was feared
that Billy Carter might one day provide some information damaging to all
Carters—if the Justice Department should "follow the tangent" into some
curious Carter borrowings from Mr. Lance's bank.

Citing his Libyan connection in the course of last week's harangue, I
prematurely characterized the younger Carter brother as anti-Yankee,
anti-press, anti-Republican, and anti-Jewish. A few days later, as I started
to admit to having no hard evidence of an ethnic slur, Billy Carter came to
the rescue with his memorable rationale for a pro-Arab diplomatic tilt:
"There is a hell of a lot more Arabians than there is Jews."

Some people took offense at that remark. Grammarians seethed at the
double mismatching of plural subjects with singular predicates. Arabs
were offended at the use of "Arabians," which, in current American
usage, is applied more to horses and nights than to people. A few Atlantans (aware, as I was not, of the younger Mr. Carter's earlier crack about a
"bastardized Jew") took exception to his determination of morality by
nose count, although it was entirely consistent with Carter Administration policy on treaty abrogation (which seems to say, "There is a hell of a
lot more Chinamen in China than there is Chinese on Taiwan.")

Others took this opportunity to castigate the President's brother for commercial exploitation of his family name, for using dirty words in a *Penthouse* magazine interview, or for not raising his hand before going to the bathroom.

The top brass at the Carter Justice Department—feeling guilty about ignoring, as a mere "tangent," the investigation demanded by the refusal of the President's partner-brother to testify—told its new press agent to make a big show of mailing a foreign-agent registration letter to Billy Carter.

Everyone, it seemed, turned on Billy. No longer was he the nation's favorite redneck, "First Brother," the Southern version of Archie Bunker, the joker they said would start a business with Bert Lance to produce "Overdraft Beer." All of a sudden he became Billy the Problem.

Only in the White House was he not disavowed. Press Secretary Joseph L. Powell, in a careful contortion, allowed as how—to the extent that others construed Billy's remarks as anti-Semitic—the President did not agree.

Jimmy Carter went on to explain to NBC's John Chancellor why he did not even suggest to his brother that he cut it out: "We love each other, but any attempt that I might make to control Billy's words or actions would not be successful at all." Picking up the newsman's offer of a cliché, he added: "I think it would be counterproductive."

Think about that: If the President sought to restrain him, his brother would retaliate. That is Jimmy Carter's publicly stated reason for silently accepting Billy the Problem. And how could any Presidential effort to "control" Billy be "counterproductive?" Why, Billy could get sore; he could stop telling the world what he does not know and he could start telling the grand jury what he knows.

The righteous indignation this past week at the bigotry and tastelessness of Billy Carter is beside the point. I do not care if Billy Carter treats magazine readers to a grand display of obscenities, or if he accepts a silver saddle from a bootless dictator for introducing to the U.S. the supporters of those wonderful folks who brought us the Munich Olympic massacre. I don't mind his cracks about Jews because Billy Carter is giving anti-Semitism a bad name.

What should be of concern is the reason behind the President's kid-glove treatment of his kid brother: What information, potentially incriminating to himself or his family, is Billy Carter concealing from the Lance grand jury?

The public is entitled to know: (a) What questions did the prosecutors ask Billy Carter about the President's pre-election loans that caused the witness to take refuge in the Fifth Amendment? (b) Why has Criminal Division chief Philip Heymann delayed four months in subpoenaing that same information from the senior partner in the Carter family enterprise, the President's brother's brother? (c) If, as Billy Carter has warned, he possesses information about the family dealings with Mr. Lance's bank that could lead to his own prosecution, why has the Carter Justice Department not assigned a special prosecutor to follow this "tangent?"

At some future confirmation hearing before the Senate Judiciary Committee (E. Kennedy, D.-Mass., chairman) those questions may be answered. And then perhaps we will learn why President Carter much preferred to suffer with Billy the Problem rather than take his chances with Billy the Witness.

Jan. 22, 1979

Dear Mr. Safire:

After reading one of your recent columns, I must suggest that you place less emphasis upon your erudition, leave your ivory tower and come join the majority of your fellow Americans whose grammar is on a par with brother Billy.

Please enlighten us poor peons. Was Billy right? Is there more Arabians than Jews?

Sincerely,
W. Howard Reed, Jr.
Alliance, Ohio

MEMO TO RAFSHOON

July 3, 1978

WASHINGTON—Gerald Rafshoon, described as a "darkly handsome media wizard," has been newly installed across the street from the White House in an office that is richly redolent of symbolism; it used to be Richard Nixon's "hideaway office," and as such is the perfect place to plot a comeback in the polls and to do away with all this wallowing in Angolagate.

With Mr. Carter's standing in the CBS-*Times* poll dipping to 38 percent approval, he has brought in his crack media adviser to stop the Carter decline before it reaches an unprecedented single-digit-support level.

Here are a few ideas from one who is not unfamiliar with Mr. Rafshoon's office surroundings.

1. *Bring back the Old Theme Song:* To do away with the need for Mr. Carter to keep muttering "I'm the President," restore some of the familiar trappings of office that were shunned when "imperial" was assumed to be

a dirty word. At Democratic fund raisers, permit "Hail to the Chief" to be played; in time, it may be possible to reintroduce "Ruffles and Flourishes," which is a nice way of tooting the Presidential horn and gives fair warning to assembled guests to cut out the substitution of Carter jokes for Polish jokes.

2. *Get him out among the people:* Full-scale Presidential trips—Air Force One gleaming, press corps gasping after roaring buses, little children holding up hand-lettered signs that read "Achieve Equitable Strategic Arms Limitation"—can dominate the evening television news. (Watch out for the garment-bag-over-the-shoulder gimmick, though—last time he dropped it and embarrassed everybody when it floated slowly to the ground.)

Some of your backstabbing colleagues in the White House may say that the President would be more "Presidential" staying in the Oval Office, getting photographed deploring intervention and denouncing internal settlements, but they are not seized of the latest in-depth poll results: Most Americans would prefer this President to stay as far away as possible from the White House.

3. *"Let's Talk Tough to the American People":* Polls show that Americans, by nearly two to one, prefer we "get tough" and cut out Mr. Carter's tension-relaxing politics of yoga. So the President must make some tough, hard-hitting speeches. Since the Russians get angry at this, and tend to call bluffs immediately, the tough talk should be directed at allies.

It is not enough to talk tough to Israel, to lash out at Rhodesia, or to cut the Taiwanese adrift. Isn't it time to escalate the fight over our right to fish, and fortify our borders with Canada? The St. Lawrence Seaway is ours, we built it, and we're not letting anybody take it away.

4. *Strike terror into the hearts of recalcitrant Democratic Congressmen:* The President can do this by threatening to come into each of their districts to campaign on their behalf. Never underestimate the power of what Democratic candidates call, with a shudder, "the kiss of Carter."

5. *Find a suitable villain:* The blast at the oil companies kind of fizzled, and last week's tirade against millionaires was just too old-fashioned to fly; neither the President's populism nor the First Lady's momulism has yet made it off the ground.

But run this cookie up the flagpole: Zap the media. Turn the white light of pitiless publicity on those sensation-seeking columnists and commentators who want another orgy of "the breaking of the President." Pushes 'em right off balance every time: Next time you want air time for a Fourth of July speech, title it "The Instant Analysis of the Unelected Elite."

6. *Sell the idea that fuzziness is next to godliness:* Instead of overcoming the "fuzziness issue" by running around making decisions—which would

only make more people unhappy—proclaim the glories of ambiguity. Make a virtue out of vacillation. You know all this flip-flopping on détente and human rights, on Africa and SALT? Are we confusing those Russians? The opinion follower who wants to be a leader must get across the impression that the spot he is in is exactly where he intended to be.

Finally, if all else fails, *play the Mondale card.* Put out the word that if the President's popularity falls to Truman-Nixon levels, below 30 percent, he will resign in a huff to accept a lucrative offer to become czar of international softball.

By raising the specter of Mondale, who would try to carry out all those Democratic campaign promises that Mr. Carter is understandably nervous about, the President would please the liberals and strike the conservatives dumb.

In his ghost-ridden office, Gerry Rafshoon must be pondering the paradox of the candidate who charted his course by the polls now doing so poorly in the polls. But be of good heart, darkly handsome media wizard—and welcome to the N.F.L.

THE NEW FOUNDATION

January 25, 1979

WASHINGTON—In the very first words of his previous appearance before a joint session of Congress, Jimmy Carter made a mistake: He addressed the man sitting above and behind him as "Vice President." But on such occasions, Walter Mondale sits there in his Constitutional role as President of the Senate, and the proper salutation from the U.S. President is "Mr. President."

At his 1979 State of the Union address, President Carter got it right. That minor correction suggested to one ex-speechwriter that this time the President was going to try harder, perhaps even to provide what the Germans call *zusammenhang,* a context or cohesiveness, for what he has been doing.

Let's review the speech, not for policy or substance, but as a speech— which is an attempt, through rhetoric, to combine reason and emotion to persuade and rally others to support one's cause.

1. *Structure.* This speech had a shape to it, which has been rare for Mr. Carter. Its three subjects were the economy, the Government, and foreign policy. Observe the crosshatching: On the economy, the specific denounced was inflation, and the underlying message was confidence. On

the Government, the specific discussed was Civil Service reform and the message was trust; on foreign policy, the specific hailed was SALT and the message was peace. Effective organization.

2. *Unifying Theme.* The idea of a "new foundation" is fitting for this President, since the metaphor helps get across the idea of a return to fundamentals, and also helps explain why so few achievements are apparent after two years. (The use of the word "foundation" ten times in a single speech was excessive, but he tried "new spirit" six times in his themeless pudding of an inaugural address in 1977, and evidently believed more repetition was needed.) The building metaphor helped pull the speech together.

3. *Pace.* He opened quickly, with a good passage deriding three "myths"—choosing between inflation and recession, compassion and competence, confrontation and capitulation—which, as in a symphony, introduced themes to be developed later in the work. (And you won't find me knocking alliteration.) His tempo sagged too much in the middle—about six minutes could have been cut there—but on the whole, the President is getting a feel for pacing, and is learning when to move briskly and when to slow for emphasis. "None did and none will," about world dominance, employed the rhythm of Churchill's "Some chicken; some neck."

4. *Prose Style.* Unfortunately, the President is still afflicted with an inclination to use a plodding series of declarative sentences, interrupted by spasms of verbiage that seem out of place: "Towering over all this volatile changing world, like a thundercloud in a summer sky, looms the awesome power of nuclear weapons." Melodramatic; what worked for Everett Dirksen does not work for him.

5. *Delivery.* The President no longer smiles in the wrong places and has learned not to step on his own applause lines. He still looks to both sides too quickly, as if at a fast badminton match, but his posture on the platform is comfortable and easy; this was a well-practiced, well-delivered speech. He didn't even trip over "we are their heirs."

6. *Cant.* The President finally dropped "disharmonious" and "incompatible," and eschewed "adequate," "competent," and "reticent" in this speech. He is still burdened with "in nature"—our problems are "different in nature" and we must understand "the nature of the SALT process." Although he used a stilted locution like "increasingly supportive," he is at last making some effort to avoid his own clichés. ("Unwinding inflation" is a new one.)

7. *Historical Evocation.* Mr. Carter and his writers have a penchant for turning great phrases into banalities. Lincoln's "we must think anew and act anew. We must disenthrall ourselves" degenerated into Carter's "we must change our attitudes as well as our policies." And the Founding Fathers' ringing pledge of "our lives, our fortunes and our sacred honor" be-

came, in Mr. Carter's pallid paraphrase, "their property, position, and life itself."

8. *Uplift.* A great speech swims against the current of events, as did F.D.R.'s challenge to fear and Churchill's challenge to despair. A good speech can ride with the current, offering the audience the assurance that the raft is drifting in the right direction. Mr. Carter's State of the Union address was a good speech, with a gentle and hopeful peroration that suited an occasion which he felt called for neither sacrifice nor innovation.

The chosen slogan invites ridicule (the crumbling foundation, the corseted society); but credit Gerald Rafshoon, Greg Schneiders, and Hendrick Hertzberg with some creative back-planning. Their intent was to impose a philosophy upon, or at least to show a pattern to, the random lurchings of the Carter Administration. To a modest extent, they succeeded.

January 25, 1979

Dear Bill Safire,

As one former speechwriter to another, I mostly agreed with your analysis of the President's state of the union address. But I thought the address as a whole fell flat because of a fatal flaw in the metaphorical theme.

A sidebar story in today's *Times* indicates that the President's speechwriters also were uneasy, and in fact looked for an improvement on their "new foundation."

As well they might have. At least twice he referred to "building" a foundation. You do not "build" a foundation; you "lay" one. As you know, one must be precise in dealing with metaphors. It is impossible to visualize "building" a foundation. "Build on" a foundation would have been acceptable, but would have destroyed his premise that his administration is still working on the foundation.

This is not a quibble. People absorb most language unconsciously and if it is inaccurate or awkward, they may feel uncomfortable without knowing why. It wasn't until I read the speech, after hearing it, that I knew what bothered me about it. If he had not labored it—as you pointed out—he might have got away with it.

So I don't believe that the Presidential speechwriters achieved even the "modest success" with which you credited them. The speech was a turkey.

Best regards,
John Ward Gerber
New York, New York

SILENCE IS BIGOTRY

February 22, 1979

WASHINGTON—A "reefer" is newspaper slang for a short notice on the front page referring the reader to a story inside. Editors use "reefers" when they do not want to sensationalize a story with front-page treatment but do not want to bury it, either.

The following reefer appeared on the front page of *The New York Times* last week: "Billy Carter Insults Jews: President's brother Billy directed an obscenity at the American Jewish community while at a reception for visiting Libyans."

On page 11, the interested reader could discover that—when asked about the reaction of American Jews to his active interest in the radical Arab state of Libya—the President's brother snarled into a microphone: "They can kiss my ———."

The Times does not print obscenities*, and customarily does not give this much detail about them in its news columns, but the rules were broken at the order of executive editor A. M. Rosenthal, who believed that readers should know with some precision what insult the President's brother had directed at all American Jews.

In the past, when Billy Carter complained about "the Jewish media," a White House spokesman ever so gently dissociated President Carter from his brother's remarks insofar as they could "be interpreted as being anti-Semitic." The President's only comment has been that he "has no control" over his brother, and that any attempt at restraint would be "counterproductive."

In this case, however, the White House made no attempt to dissociate itself from Billy Carter's lewd invitation to Jewry. Press Secretary Joseph L. Powell said he would "not comment" on the Carter remarks because he was "unaware of them," a curious reason to give after being made aware of them.

Then, in Atlanta the other day, President Carter finally gave his reaction—a warm, fraternal embrace for his beloved Billy in front of the news cameras.

After his failure to disavow the obscene insult, that Carter hug was profoundly offensive. Perhaps, as a Jew, I am being sensitive; but I like to think that Catholics, WASP's, blacks, women, or hardhats—after having been told to "kiss my ———" by the President's brother—would also take offense when the President's only response to the intentionally rude affront is to clasp his sibling to his bosom.

---

* The word "ass" is considered a vulgarism at *The Times* and is so described in copy. Curiously, "half-assed" is permitted in quotations in news columns.

Is it really too much to ask Jimmy Carter to be President first and brother second? A President-first would state unequivocally that America is not the place for religious prejudice; that he not merely dissociates himself from his brother's insults and slurs, but that he deplores and condemns them.

The central concern here is not the snappish mouthings of a publicity-seeker juggling his drinking problem, his financial problem, and his growing grand jury problem. The concern is with the proper reaction of the President of the United States.

He is not obliged to *control* his brother; he is obliged to *disagree* with his brother. It is the President's silence that has been "counterproductive": In this situation, silence is bigotry. Prompt reassurance was needed that Billy's hatreds were not shared by the Carter in the Oval Office. He should have told his brother—in a loving way, of course—to do his family and his countrymen a favor by trying to keep his foul mouth shut.

Unless, unless. A few weeks ago, it was suggested in this space that the President would not chastise or in any way deny his brother—no matter what Billy said—because Jimmy Carter was worried about what financial information Billy might then share with the grand jury investigating what may be the Carter "money laundry." The President's silence after this latest outburst shows that suspicion to have been well founded.

Why must this President stay on the best of terms with Billy, the man who operated his enormously expanded peanut business, as well as with Bert Lance, the man who poured millions of bank funds through that Carter business during the 1976 campaign?

Because, one day soon, Billy may be notified by the Justice Department (or by a special prosecutor better qualified to handle the case) that he is a target and no longer merely a witness. As the investigation goes beyond election violations to potential income-tax evasion and other crimes, the prosecutors may be offering him immunity in return for testimony against two lawyers, one banker and one brother. At that point, Billy might stop blaming Jews and start blaming Jimmy.

If Billy should crack, the President and his defenders will say publicly all the nasty things they now say privately about Billy's honesty: that all irregularities in the Carter books were Billy's fault, and not his partner-brother's.

Then the President of all the people will plead for our understanding and support in the midst of his personal crisis. I know the answer that will flash through the minds of more than a few members of one ethnic group.

February 24, 1979

Mr. Wm. Safire:

Even though Billy's remarks were tactless and adolescent, there is surely more than a little truth in them. Therefore I suggest you address the issue rather than the man. May I be so bold as to enquire of you the following:

1) Is it not true that Jews do in fact control much of the media, and certainly the big city media in the United States?

2) Is it not also true that Jews have political and economic power out of proportion to their numbers in the United States?

3) For the reasons enumerated above, do you accept that the Arab position(s) in many instances are either distorted or ignored, *e.g.* the partition of Palestine, the West Bank, oil prices, etc.?

Thank you for your consideration.

Very truly yours,
D. K. Smith
San Francisco, California

THE SECRET OF CARTER

April 26, 1979

WASHINGTON—The first full-time White House speechwriter was Judson Welliver, who worked with President Harding on his bloviation and later helped Calvin Coolidge reach his rhetorical heights.

Mr. Welliver put the thoughts of Harding and Coolidge in presentable form, but he failed to do the other job of a Presidential speechwriter: to write a memoir afterward that reveals the secret of a Presidency, that offers some insight into the man in the Oval Office which only a participant/observer, trained in catching the significant detail or the unifying theme, can provide.

For F.D.R., Samuel Rosenman and Robert E. Sherwood wrote the sympathetic biographies, Raymond Moley the acerbic one; Truman had no Boswell, and Eisenhower was observed critically by Emmett John Hughes. For J.F.K., the loving books by speechwriters Ted Sorensen and Arthur Schlesinger Jr. set the tone for historians of that period. In memoirs, Jack Valenti remained sympathetic and loyal to L.B.J., as did Raymond Price to Richard Nixon.

Comes now James Fallows, chief speechwriter for the Carter Presidency until his recent return to journalism. In "The Passionless Presidency," first of a two-part series in the *Atlantic* magazine, he gives us his insider's clues to the secret of Jimmy Carter.

The young writer makes all the proper obeisances: "With his moral virtues and his intellectual skills, [Carter] is perhaps as admirable a human being as has ever held the job. . . . If I had to choose one politician to sit at the Pearly Gates and pass judgment on my soul, Jimmy Carter would be the one."

In praising Mr. Carter's personal virtues, Mr. Fallows is evidently troubled by the President's willingness to exaggerate ("I was a nuclear physicist") and—in a curious note—Mr. Carter's willingness to look a television interviewer in the eye and say he did not personally control the White House tennis-court schedule, which Fallows knew was the opposite of the truth.

Then he sets forth in public what middle-echelon insiders (not the us-against-them "Georgians") have long been saying in private: that the new President "did not really know what he wanted to do in such crucial areas as taxes, welfare, energy and the reorganization of the government." To aides asking for specific decisions, he would reply vaguely: "Be bold!"

One trouble with Mr. Carter, according to his former speechwriter, is that he was enticed by the dash and drama of foreign affairs to forget what he was elected for: "Next on his plate after Camp David was the most pressing domestic issue of all—inflation—but he appeared bored and impatient through high-level deliberations about what to do about it. . . ."

Mr. Carter lost touch, right at the start, with his central campaign pledge that he would be somehow different: "The first jarring note was struck after two months in office, when large pay increases were allotted to the White House staff." Mr. Fallows was 27, earning $20,000 a year in private life; this jumped to $37,000 when he was hired at the White House, and went to $47,000 afterward: "By going along with the pay increases, Carter gave the clearest possible sign that it would be business as usual in his Administration. His later talk about inflation would be forever undermined by this demonstration that restraint did not really start at home."

The main difficulty with the Carter Presidency, writes Fallows, is that it is a themeless pudding, devoid of direction: "I came to think that Carter believes fifty things, but no one thing. He holds explicit, thorough positions on every issue under the sun, but he has no large view of the relations between them, no line indicating which goals (reducing unemployment? human rights?) will take precedence over which (inflation control? a SALT treaty?) when the goals conflict. Spelling out these choices makes the difference between a position and a philosophy, but it is an act foreign to Carter's mind."

Mr. Fallows finds the sin of pride at the core of Mr. Carter's unwillingness to make these necessary choices: "Carter's willful ignorance, his blissful tabula rasa, could—to me—be explained only by a combination of arrogance, complacency, and—dread thought—insecurity at the core of his mind and soul."

These judgments of a saddened admirer cast light on the general disillusionment with President Carter. He offered apparent goodness without effectiveness; the secret of Carter is that he wanted, above all, to *be* President, and had no clear idea of what he wanted to *do* as President.

In his next installment, ex-speechwriter Fallows intends to survey the Magnolia Mafia around Mr. Carter, and I suspect will damn with faint praise the preening mediocrities who mill about the Oval Office. Would that Judson Welliver, first in our line, had done the same: I don't mean to put down Calvin Coolidge, but he and Jimmy Carter, and the men around them, have much in common.

April 30, 1979

Letters to the Editor
The New York Times

Dear Sir:

Although William Safire said, in his column of April 26, that he did not mean to "put down" Calvin Coolidge it was unjust of him to say that Coolidge and Jimmy Carter "have much in common." In fact, they have little in common.

President Coolidge was a man of deep insight, brilliant speech and effective leadership. A few examples will remind those who have forgotten, or who are too young to have known.

Coolidge's fundamental understanding of the American political system was shown by the reply he gave to the statement that there are lots of sons of bitches in the Congress. He pointed out, trenchantly, "Well, there's a lot of them in the country, and they have to be represented."

Similarly, his grasp of the American economic system was revealed by his famous epigram, "The business of America is business." He also went to the heart of one of our most baffling economic problems when he said that when people were out of work there is unemployment.

Probably the most difficult international economic problem of his time was whether the United States should press its World War I allies to repay their war debts to us. He cut through all the complexities by saying, "They hired the money, didn't they."

These and similar utterances of Coolidge will live forever, but the only remark of President Carter that has survived for more than a few days is something about Montezuma's revenge.

Coolidge took office after a period of great political corruption, but there was no Lancegate, no Peanutgate, not even a maple syrup gate, during his Administration. He found the price level stable when he came into office, and it was stable when he left. Coolidge kept the Federal budget in balance while he was in office, whereas Carter only promises to balance it manana.

President Carter could learn a great deal from studying President Coolidge. He might even try out Coolidge's famous declaration, "I do not choose to run."

Sincerely yours,
Herbert Stein
Washington, D.C.

CARTER'S FOURTH OF JULY PANIC

July 9, 1979

WASHINGTON—The hollowness at the core of the Carter Administration was revealed in three events surrounding the panic that gripped Mr. Carter on Wednesday, the Fourth of July.

1. *The self-delusion.* On Monday of the week that stripped bare his Presidency, an exhausted and poll-worried Jimmy Carter told his advisers, within earshot of reporters, to come up with "a bold and forceful program that . . . will be highly acceptable. . . ."

That is the essential contradiction on which his policy foundered: He has always wanted his advisers to concoct plans that fostered the illusion of decisiveness but would still be "highly acceptable." He does not understand that the quality that makes a decision bold is also what makes it controversial and thus unacceptable to much of the public. He clings to the notion that he can make almost everybody happy.

2. *The Fourth of July panic.* His first decision on Monday of the fateful week was to go with the "speak now" advice of his image men rather than the "speak later" advice of his squabbling substance men. But on Wednesday the Fourth, faced with a speech draft that required him to make far-reaching decisions that split his advisers—price decontrol or not—Mr. Carter choked up. In effect, he threw up his hands and quit for a little while. He went fishing.

In a conference call to imageers Powell, Rafshoon, and Mondale, the President said he would not make the decision or the speech. Icily—with all the arrogance of impotence—he refused to offer any explanation. He was the summiteer, the leader of the free world, and he could damn well cancel a speech when he liked and needed to offer no reason at all.

At that point of panic, his closest staff failed him. Miffed that their speak-now advice had been rejected, the image men decided to teach their boss a lesson. They would announce the unexplained cancellation just as the President ordered—and he would see from the firestorm of dismay sure to follow that their advice had been right. Press Secretary Powell put out the stark announcement and then disappeared from the White House, leaving his post to sulk in pollster Pat Caddell's apartment, as the President's reputation twisted slowly in the wind.

What should a loyal staff have done? When a President loses his temper and issues a petulant and stupid order—such as "give no explanation"— loyal professionals do not let him injure himself or share his rudeness with the country. They are expected to swallow their pride and get to someone like Rosalynn Carter or Charles Kirbo to persuade the President to stop acting like a brat in a tantrum lest his private panic become public scandal.

But the image men made no serious attempt to save the President from himself. If the speech cancellation had been accompanied by a statement like "the President believes it is more important to have the speech right than to have it quickly," that would have been readily accepted. But no; if the boss would not respect their feelings, they would let him suffer.

When others in the Administration—inexcusably uninformed by the faithless trio—heard the cancellation news on the radio, they betrayed their leader, too. With the exceptions of Secretaries Harris and Schlesinger, the Carter appointees and White House aides—echoing William Saxbe five years ago—testily told reporters on background that the President had taken leave of his senses. The truth about Mr. Carter's choking-up was spread far and wide, when a staff insistence on a brief explanation accompanying the speech cancellation could have spared the President his shame.

3. *The lies.* Having thus punished the vacillating President for having spoken sharply to them, the Carter imageers two days later tried to sell an obvious lie: that no real disagreements were rampant in the Administration. Joined by Stu Eizenstat (Carter's Ehrlichman), who was a "speak-later" victor, they put out the line that all was orderly in the decision-making process. Never mind that gas lines had begun to appear months ago, that the OPEC price rise was known to be in the works for months, and that energy policy should have been decided well before this crisis struck—the soothing syrup put out toward the end of Carter's worst week was that serenity reigned at Camp David.

Then came a crusher: the leak of the Eizenstat memo of the week before, showing even the "substance man" to be obsessed with style, and confessing to "the confusion and bureaucratic tangling now occurring." Thus the belated Friday explanation was shown to be a lie.

Mr. Carter is a political zombie; his countrymen, including sympathetic critics, must help him through the remainder of his term even if his petty and disloyal staff will not. Better days, and even a turn in ratings, can come when he abandons hope of renomination and learns the lesson of his panic of the Fourth: that a leader can never be "bold and forceful" if he relies on politicians and pollsters to find a path that is "highly acceptable."

READING JIMMY'S MIND

September 17, 1979

WASHINGTON—For me to have to drop out of a foot race, right after Teddy lets the world know he's in the race for my job—that's typical of the way my luck has been running lately.

Meanwhile, in the eyes of the damn media, Kennedy can do no wrong. He opens his campaign with a bald-faced deception—that he will make his great decision next year based on how badly the economy is doing.

Does anybody seriously believe him when he says that? Everybody knows we'll be in a recession next January. With this little trick, he stands aloof now from our Democratic economic policy, so that he can come on later to say he's not splitting the party, he's saving the country from a depression.

Well, shoot—if I had gone with his big-spending health plan, the deficit would be double, the inflation rate would be past 20 percent, and we'd be headed for a huge crash. But the media says nothing about that. They just let him have a free ride until late January, halfway to the convention, without forcing him to say now exactly what he would do differently.

A Kennedy can get away with those little white lies. The establishment press want their Camelot back, and they close their eyes to little deceptions that would cause them to land on my neck. Is this how Nixon felt?

Look at that little episode up in Massachusetts last month. Peter Lucas of *The Boston Herald-American* dug it out, but the national media ignored it. Kennedy went to the office of Governor Ed King—a good, conservative Democrat whom Kennedy despises—to ask for a Superior Court judgeship for Paul Markham.

For "better get Paul, too" Markham! He was the lawyer at the party at Chappaquiddick who helped dive for the girl's body that night. Kennedy told him not to report the accident, which is contrary to law, and that lawyer kept his mouth shut for nine hours until somebody else discovered the car and the body next morning.

That's the guy Kennedy now is so anxious to make a judge. Why does Teddy have to take care of Markham at this time, ten years later, just before he starts to run for President? Is he worried that if he does not make the effort to satisfy Markham—at public expense—Markham will spill the beans, tell the whole story about what happened that night and how they were able to contain the damage later?

Those are legitimate questions. But if I got Jody to get a reporter to look into it, that would be a "dirty trick" and the media would be defending poor Kennedy. Don't they see that every one of the girls at that party, and everybody who was there or who later helped to cover them up, will all want something now that he's running? They'll all have a claim on him for their continued silence.

No, the media don't see, because they don't want to see. So they pay no mind to Kennedy's need to take care of Markham. The only parties the media are covering are the ones Ham Jordan has been to, but nobody drowned at Studio 54. If they force the courts to appoint a special prosecutor, he'll be asking my men questions that nobody ever asked a Kennedy man. The prosecutor may come after my family, even—I ducked a damn-sure question about that during the Bourne drug flap, but a special prosecutor is harder to duck.

It's not fair. Why doesn't somebody stick a microphone in Kennedy's face and ask him what he would do about the Soviet combat brigade in Cuba? Would he try another Bay of Pigs, or would be bring the world to the brink of nuclear war, Kennedy-style? Or would he cave in? Funny, but nobody asks him the hard ones they ask me.

I'd better stop feeling sorry for myself because it's going to get worse before it gets better. Some snooper will find out soon that brother Billy has written to the Justice Department asking for the forms needed to register as a foreign agent for Libya. Billy has been getting paid for his work for Qaddafi, and Justice will have to slap him on the wrist for ignoring the registration laws up to now. Who would have thought, four years ago, that my biggest headaches today would turn out to be Bert, Billy, and Ham?

I had better get ready for a parade of Democrats, starting with Tip O'Neill, telling me I must step aside and roll out the carpet for Teddy for the good of the party. The hell with that—the party never did anything for me. If Kennedy thinks he can win the Presidency without the South, let him try.

The thing for me to do is hang in there, look cheerful and decisive, and play for the breaks. Maybe the Russians will help. Maybe the damn media will surprise us all by going after Teddy, which will begin to turn the polls around. And the unexpected is always to be expected—some nut could take a shot at either of us. Maybe Jerry Brown will do better than anybody thinks in the primaries, splitting the anti-Carter vote. I could luck out.

The Nobel Peace Prize next month would sure help. Think of it—I'm the only U.S. President since Herbert Hoover who has not lost a single serviceman's life from a shot fired in anger. On the other hand, a lot of good that did Hoover.

CARTER, THE INNOCENT

October 18, 1979

WASHINGTON—I suspected that the reason for the secrecy surrounding the President's personal business affairs in 1976 had to do with the financing of his campaign. The report of Special Counsel Paul Curran has allayed that suspicion.

Why, then, has Mr. Carter—who, like all candidates, made public his personal tax returns—stonewalled all queries about the details of his family business for the past three years? Since we have been assured that no crimes were committed, why did brother Billy refuse to answer grand jury questions?

The answer is provided in the sanitized report released this week, and probably given in much more vivid detail in its secret, unexpurgated form to Democratic leaders of the Congress: A look inside the Carter business is extraordinarily embarrassing to a candidate who claimed to be an upright, successful farmer-businessman.

1. *He received financial favors from a former political appointee.* As Governor of Georgia, he appointed Bert Lance to the powerful post of highway commissioner; afterward, Bert's bank—the National Bank of Georgia—provided a $10-million sequence of loans against insufficient—and sometimes nonexistent—collateral. During the politically crucial spring of 1976, a loan of $1.1 million was "unbonded"—not a peanut was in a warehouse backing up the loan. See if your banker will do the same.

2. *The overdrafts that brought down Lance were what held up the Carter business.* Some $2,380,000 in loan-repayment checks went "unprocessed" because the Carter account had no money in it to cover those checks. When the average businessman writes a check like that, it bounces; but not if you're a Carter doing business with a Lance. That helps explain "I'm proud of you, Bert."

3. *While he was running for President, posing as a competent manager, Jimmy Carter was losing his shirt.* By the time he was in the White House, Carter Warehouses was on the verge of bankruptcy: The President's other company borrowed over $400,000 to "bail out," in Mr. Curran's term, the sloppily organized, mismanaged warehouse business.

Favoritism, kited checks, loans asked for one purpose but the money used for another—nothing criminal, but hardly business practice to be proud of, especially when you're calling for high moral standards.

Buried in the initial "cleared-of-wrongdoing" stories is the information that the Carter business misreported purchases and sales over a three-year period in a way that reduced its tax liability. "Additional taxes are due," said Mr. Curran; pressed about how much, the not-my-department investigator said: "I would have to leave that to the Internal Revenue Service."

Trouble is, when the complaisant I.R.S. Atlanta office audited these years of the Carter businesses (a "sweetheart audit," as once described here), it came up with nothing. Now we learn that the auditors were indeed remiss. I.R.S. Commissioner Jerome Kurtz, a Carter appointee, should now have some fast explaining to do to the Joint Committee on Taxation.

Jerry Rafshoon comes out clean, and I apologize to him for suggesting that he went to other Georgia banks to supply his agency with money then used to extend credit to the Carter campaign. Not so; he in effect delayed taking his profit of 15 percent and extended that credit to the campaign, which the Federal Election Commission evidently thinks was fine. Message to candidates: Hire only agencies that regularly carry their clients.

What comes next? The I.R.S. will finally get on the back of its sleepwalkers in Atlanta; the Federal Election Commission will change its rules about the way campaigns can get credit; and the White House and Democrats in Congress will mightily resist making public the additional embarrassments in the secret part of the Curran report, as well as the President's deposition, but sooner or later, it will all come out.

Was it worth it? The investigation—its scope construed most narrowly by a counsel chosen for his personal probity rather than his aggressiveness in probing—turns up no criminality. Mr. Curran, who says "I'm not exonerating anyone" adds: "I hope to be able to handle the skeptics—I don't know about the cynics."

Nobody can be cynical about a government that does this: From 4 P.M. to 8 P.M. on the afternoon of September 5, lawmen faced the President of the United States and his lawyers (Robert Lipshutz, then White House counsel, and Ronald D. Eastman, of Cadwalader, Wickersham and Taft).

There, in the Treaty Room on the second floor of the White House, next door to the Lincoln bedroom, sworn testimony was taken from the President for the first time in our history. (He was deposed in the legal sense, not yet in the political.) He turned out to be a man who should be profoundly chagrined at the ethical corner-cutting and unsuccessful operation of his own business, but no crook. A system that can discover that to the satisfaction of most skeptics is a good system.

October 19, 1979

To the Editor:

Throughout the campaign of President Jimmy Carter, both for the nomination by the Democratic Party and the election to the Presidency, I served as his national campaign treasurer. From the date of his inauguration until Oct. 1, 1979, I served as Counsel to the President.

A few days ago Paul Curran, a special investigator appointed by the Attorney General, issued his final and detailed report, both to the Department of Justice and to the Congress, as a result of his seven-month inquiry. I, of course, am quite gratified with Mr. Curran's findings and conclusions.

For almost three years after the 1976 election, the handling of campaign finances by the President and by myself was subjected to repeated, unsupported and false accusations by irresponsible writers in the national media, to totally unsubstantiated innuendos by political opportunists and finally to a seven-month grand jury investigation led by the special investigator.

Now that the campaigns, the President and I have been totally exonerated of any wrongdoing, as a result of this thorough investigation, I am writing this letter about the reprehensible conduct of a few so-called journalists, and particularly William Safire.

Safire's numerous repetitions of these completely false accusations against the President and against me were made by him in the same way as charges once were made in the public arena by two of the most despicable men of this century: Senator Joseph McCarthy and Nazi Germany's Propaganda Minister, Joseph Goebbels.

McCarthy recklessly accused many decent people by hiding behind the shield of Congressional immunity. Safire tries to hide behind the claim of freedom of the press in his reckless libels.

Goebbels was Hitler's spokesman and used the "big lie" technique. Like Goebbels, Safire repeated his lies in column after column, apparently thinking that the public would believe him eventually, regardless of the truth. Now the truth is known. The 1976 Carter Presidential campaign has been thoroughly investigated and cleared of all these charges of wrongdoing.

The United States Senate finally repudiated Joseph McCarthy. The German people ultimately repudiated Joseph Goebbels and Adolf Hitler. It is my hope that the journalists of America will repudiate the poisonous, libelous pen of William Safire.

Robert J. Lipshutz
Atlanta,   Georgia

The Oil Lifeline

T HE SEIZURE of American diplomats as hostages by the Ayatollah Khomeini's followers seemed to me to be the kind of provocation that called for the projection of U.S. power into the Mideast. Throughout the month of November 1979, the few advocates of such a course—calling for a food blockade leading to an oil blockade—were denounced as disunifiers at a time requiring everyone to rally round the President.

Mr. Carter put the humanitarian concern for the hostages ahead of the national strategic interest, and his paralysis sent what I thought was a signal of weakness. A month later, the Soviet Union invaded Afghanistan.

CHECKMATE

January 4, 1979

WASHINGTON—The word "checkmate," used in chess to describe the end of the end game, comes from the Persian *Shah mat*—"The Shah is dead."

The present Shah of Iran is far from politically dead; his ability to negotiate a new civilian government in the midst of turmoil has astonished the hand-wringers at the State Department. But even if he manages to remain as a constitutional monarch, on extended vacation, the absolute monarchy of the Peacock Throne is surely gone.

The absolutism of that one-man rule manifested itself in ways big and small. In 1972, when President Nixon visited Teheran after his Moscow summit, White House staff members were presented to His Majesty at the state dinner; when the Shah asked if I was enjoying my overnight stay, I expressed my dismay at not having the time to go shopping. He nodded, turned to his grand vizier or whatever, and said, "Have the shops stay open all night." And so they did; at every hotel accommodating the traveling party and press corps, the groggy shopkeepers pushing their wares at 3 A.M. were testimony to the Shah's absolute graciousness or gracious absolutism.

The end of the Shah's one-man rule brings mixed emotions to Americans who like to root for or against a foreign leader.

The Bad Shah was—more than anyone—the man behind the quadrupling of oil prices, helping cause world inflation, and further impoverishing the poorest nations. He has been the greatest proponent of monopoly economic power in history.

The Good Shah was the man who tried to wrench his people out of the Middle Ages and shove them into the modern world, advancing women's rights, raising the literacy rate and the standard of living.

The Bad Shah was the tolerator of corruption in his family and the terror tactics of his secret police, who—when it suited his economic interests to ally himself with Iraq—betrayed the Kurdish people to a kind of genocide, and caused the Kissinger-Atherton-Saunders set meekly and secretly to acquiesce in that international dishonor.

The Good Shah was the embodiment of stability in the Middle East: sternly anti-Communist, a dependable supplier of Israel, a job-creating customer of the United States defense industry, and the strong guarantor of the safety of oil supplies to Europe and Japan.

With good and bad in such a mix, how do we react to the attempt to seize power from the man who has been both our economic enemy and our strategic ally?

We should decide what the alternatives are and act in our national interest. If the Shah's fundamentalist opposition takes over, the United States is likely to have a new enemy along the seam of power. Human rights advocates, who saw the savage Khmer Rouge replace pro-Western Lon Nol in Cambodia, would do well to study lines from a recent book, unearthed last week by Judith Miller of *The New York Times*, written by anti-Shah Ayatollah Khomeini: "We want a ruler who would cut off the hand of his own son if he steals, and would flog and stone his near relative if he fornicates."

If a military junta seizes power, Iran would be a dictatorship in a state of constant rebellion, and an undependable ally.

Therefore, it suits the American interest to help the Shah make a deal with moderate political opponents, shoring him up, giving him confidence, showing his supporters—and our other allies—that the United States is not only a fair-weather friend.

But consider what the Carter Administration has done. After ignoring a warning of impending trouble in Iran from Israeli intelligence, the Administration took one long month to react to a stay-away-from-your-ally threat from Leonid Brezhnev. Next, when asked if he thought the Shah would prevail, President Carter—in somewhat less than ringing, Churchillian tones—replied: "I don't know. I hope so."

Finally, the hawks in the Administration persuaded the President to let the world know he was about to order a naval task force, led by the carrier *Constellation*, to leave the Philippines and be ready for a show-the-flag visit to the Persian Gulf. But then the doves, led by Fritz Mondale, turned the President around because such a show of support for the Shah might alienate whoever follows him into power.

There, churning around in circles in the South China Sea, half a world away from trouble, is the symbol of the Carter Administration's Iranian policy: the first example of no-boat gunboat diplomacy. We showed a naked flagpole.

The Shah deserves better than that. Not because he is our friend; only because, on the international chessboard, his checkmate by the bishops of reaction and the pawns of the K.G.B. would be a blow to the interests of the United States.

TO RESTABILIZE IRAN

November 15, 1979

WASHINGTON—When one nation deliberately infringes on the sovereignty of another, and seizes prisoners in the bargain, that is by definition an act of war.

Since we hope to save our citizens' lives, our response to Iran's invasion of our sovereign embassy territory has been muted: pleas to third parties, the ruling-out of force, a cosmetic switching of oil trade, a tit-for-tat banking maneuver, a finger-wagging at Iranian students here.

But restraint need not be paralysis. We have a nonviolent weapon that can have an effect in Iran: food. That nation imports 30 percent of its food, and relies on the United States for rice, much of its wheat, corn, and poultry feed-grain (in Persia, chicken feed is not chicken feed).

We should now impose a food embargo on Iran, arranging with alternative grain suppliers like Australia and Canada not to take up the slack. The Soviets could not take up the slack because we make up their grain short-falls. This embargo will not cause starvation in Iran but will push up prices, contribute to the general unrest, and make the point around the world that a superpower is not necessarily muscle-bound.

Just as important as keeping cool is planning ahead: What do we do after the impasse is resolved? Assume that the Shah ultimately returns to Mexico (which has had the foresight to close its embassy in Teheran) and the American hostages are released, do we turn the other cheek, forgive and forget? On the contrary—we should treat this kidnapping with great seriousness and turn this provocation to our advantage.

The Ayatollah's act of aggression offers an opportunity for us to end the collapse of Western influence in the Persian Gulf, and to blunt the Soviet move—through Afghanistan and the Horn of Africa—which threatens the main sources of Western oil.

We should take the position that no legitimate government now exists in Iran, and that we would find intolerable the replacement of mob rule by a Communist regime.

Accordingly, our C.I.A.—already blamed for nonexistent conspiracies—should start conspiring now to aid those ethnic groups in Iran that are resisting the Ayatollah. In the north, the Kurds—once double-crossed by the Shah and the U.S.—should be supplied with weapons, including surface-to-air missiles, to help achieve their autonomy.

In the southwest, where the main oil fields are located, the area is not controlled by Arab oil workers but by two Iranian tribes—the Qashqai and the Bakhtiari—which are not beholden to the anarchists in Teheran. An uprising there would be crucial, especially if the Iranian armed forces are reluctant to crush it.

Mobs are by nature fickle; militant Islam turned out to be an underestimated force in Iran, but it is not the only force. Millions of Iranians are afflicted with an oppression worse than any they have known, and effigy-burning riots for television feed no bellies. Some political or military leader is likely to move into that vacuum, and it is not immoral for us to make sure that the successor to the 80-year-old strongman is not beholden to Moscow.

Elsewhere in the Persian Gulf, the United States should make its military presence felt. The Sultan of Oman is worried about Communist penetration of nearby South Yemen, and has offered to let us make a staging base of the island of Masira. We should take up that offer quickly, and top that with the leasing of the air bases that are being vacated by the Israelis in the Sinai.

The Ayatollah's slap in our face ought to wake us up to the fact that we are not at present capable of the rapid deployment of major military forces. A conventional threat in the Mideast would catch us flat-footed: It would take us more than a month to deliver two Marine divisions and support equipment. (When Mr. Carter announced his training exercise at Guantanamo to amuse the Cubans, our few landing craft had to be pulled out of heavy maintenance.)

Belatedly, Carter budgeteers are weighing the Pentagon secret Persian

Gulf contingency planning study that shows how power could be projected into the area. (Our State Department fussed at not being included in this planning; fortunately for hard-liners, it was not.)

Short-range, we are forced to strip our forces around the globe to create a three-carrier task force in the Indian Ocean. Long-range, we must make up for Mr. Carter's scuttling of the Navy by building Fast Deployment Logistic ships; also, to bolster our meager fleet of heavy-lift aircraft, we must build the "CX"—a new version of the C-5A air transports whose cost overruns in the 1960's still give Defense Secretary Harold Brown nightmares.

With our embassy staff held hostage, it makes sense to bite our tongues for a while. The job of creative diplomacy is neither to admire our own restraint nor to get ready to thump our chests; instead, we should be planning to react to this act of war with a strategy to stop the Soviet reach for the oil lifeline of the West.

PATIENCE IS NOT FORTITUDE

December 17, 1979

WASHINGTON—What is our standard of success in the Iranian crisis? What criterion will determine if the Carter Administration succeeded in meeting the challenge?

In Mr. Carter's own eyes, he will have succeeded by securing the safe return of the hostages through peaceful means, after having refused to deliver the deposed Shah for execution. To the President, success essentially means nobody dead.

Using this criterion, he will be able to contrast his patience and restraint with the action of President Ford following the seizure of the *Mayagüez*, which retrieved our seamen promptly at some cost of life.

If the lives of hostages are our "primary concern"—if success is to be measured in immediate humanitarian terms—then Mr. Carter's approach is likely to be declared a success.

In time, Ruhollah Khomeini's regime will come apart, as a result of the secession of Kurds, Baluchis, and Azerbaizanis, or after a split with other religious leaders, or by a coup from what is left of the military, or after a takeover by Communists. The last of the American hostages—convicted of spying but not executed—would presumably then be freed. Patience would have been rewarded.

But a negotiator who only gets back his P.O.W.'s is not always considered a success. On the contrary, much higher criteria will be put forward:

Did the United States respond to an act of war promptly and effectively? As a result of the Carter response, are terrorists in Iran and elsewhere in the world more or less likely to use kidnapping against Americans as a tool to gain attention and affect policy? Did the United States gain or lose respect among nations who depend on our resolve for protection? Has our extended patience made our nuclear deterrent more or less credible?

Looked at in this light—and with many more than 50 lives at stake—the Carter actions to date will be seen to be not only unsuccessful, but dangerous.

The Administration's initial response to the second invasion of our Teheran Embassy was first to rule out the use of force, then to rule it in, and then out again. Only after Iran moved to withdraw its funds did we freeze its assets. Under pressure to return the Shah, Mr. Carter passed the pressure along to the Shah to get out of our country—in this way, kidnappers were able to punish the Shah by remote control of the U.S. President.

The second U.S. response was to portray itself to the world as the injured party. Before the U.N. and the World Court, we asserted that we were truly deserving of the pity of the world "community." We fairly preened in patience, gloried in impotence, and accepted gratefully the unanimous sympathy of other nations.

By reveling in our victimization, we have heartened terrorists around the world. In Pakistan and Libya, Government officials encourage the sacking of our embassies, which resulted in the murder of Marine guards; in Turkey, four Americans were ambushed and killed. When Pakistan and Libya produce the first of Islam's atom bombs, the magnitude of terrorism's power will take a quantum jump.

With America calling its paralysis "patience," and while the President calls the meaningless ejection of Iranian diplomats "tightening the screws," the world has been doing business as usual with a country at war with the U.S. This is because our patience is viewed with dismay by our friends and with contempt by our enemies.

What should we have done? To prove we could not be coerced by kidnappers, we should have offered the Shah asylum. We should have imposed a food blockade immediately, insisting that no other supplier of grain pick up the slack. We should now be mining the Straits of Hormuz, so that American forces can make the decision about what goes in and out of the Persian Gulf. We would not then have to beg the Japanese to help apply economic pressure on Iran.

The central point is not to succeed in obtaining the release of our hostages by the display of patience. The point is to succeed in the release of our hostages by a demonstration of our impatience. Only in that way can we send the message to every would-be terrorist that the murder or kidnapping of Americans is a losing proposition.

No nukes needed; the choice is not between the present dithering and a rain of bombs, which Carter apologists would have us believe. A range of nonviolent military-economic actions is available, much of which should now be in operation; more important, we should be using this provocation to project U.S. power into new Mideast bases.

Mr. Carter and his men, pleading rather than pressuring, measure their own success in terms of 50 lives to be saved. If these lives are purchased at the cost of thousands of others, and if American inaction invites a Soviet-sponsored grab at the West's oil lifeline, then history—not to mention next year's electorate—will judge where patience ends and fortitude begins.

December 17, 1979

The New York Times

To the Editor:

William Safire's column in today's *Times* ("Patience Is Not Fortitude," December 17, 1979) goes beyond his usual slick and lively Know-Nothingism; it is dangerous and disingenuous. It is also egregiously partisan, which is not surprising; it's just more transparent than usual. In paragraph three, President Ford courageously resolves the *Mayagüez* crisis "at some cost of life." In paragraph eleven, President Carter's pusillanimity results in "the murder of Marine guards." Moral: It's better to die with a Republican in office.

The piece was dangerous in its description of the Government's policy (which has virtually universal support, and it's an unpopular Government) as "dithering." His alternative is blithely to mine the Straits of Hormuz; let America decide who enters the Persian Gulf, as though it were the Hudson River.

Mr. Safire's column was disingenuous in its misrepresentation of world opinion of the Government's handling of the situation. Scant sentences before his suggestion that we make the Persian Gulf an American colony, Mr. Safire lamented that our friends view our policy "with dismay," our enemies "with contempt." This is repulsive demagoguery. Does Mr. Safire believe that, were we to close off the Persian Gulf, the Allies would burst into enthusiastic applause, like so many cheerleaders? Does he believe that Kuwait, Qatar, and Abu Dhabi would view such a move as anything other than an act of hostile arrogance?

If Mr. Safire wants to knock heads, let him go out for touch football in Central Park.

Sincerely,
Jamie James
New York, New York

A TIME FOR DARING

November 26, 1979

WASHINGTON—"Calculated delay" is the phrase chosen by one editorialist to praise the frustrated finger-wagging of the Carter Administration, which refuses to acknowledge that this nation is being warred upon. In the 19th century, the favorite euphemisms were "masterly inactivity" and "disciplined inaction."

The trouble with such praise of folly is that it focuses only on the immediate incident—the taking of hostages—and considers some bloodless retaliation after the hostages are returned, or a more destructive reaction if the captives are killed.

Retaliation now or later is not the issue. Assume the Shah returns to Mexico next week, and the United Nations agrees to hear the Ayatollah's complaints against him for such crimes as the land reform that weakened the mullahs. Then, if the hostages come out, the U.S. will warn other Americans in Iran such as newsmen to get out and avoid being taken hostage as we destroy the Abadan refinery. That would punish Iranians without seriously affecting shipment of crude oil to our nervous allies.

The other scenario: If the current power spasm leads to the trial and murder of United States diplomats, we could destroy Iranian air and naval facilities, seize the island of Kharg, blockade the Persian Gulf, and determine how much food goes in and oil comes out.

Some such tactical retaliation would satisfy our national pride and chastise the wicked, but would do nothing to turn today's diplomatic outrage to our geopolitical advantage.

A power vacuum will soon exist: The Khomeini phenomenon, an amalgam of the new fanaticism and the old rent-a-mob, will go as suddenly as it came. One of the two superpowers will then move strongly into that Persian Gulf vacuum.

The Soviets might try the direct route, with a coup by radicals in Teheran, backed by Kurdish and other tribal revolts elsewhere in Iran. Or they may take an indirect way: Iraq, now the most formidable military force in the region, despises its neighbor. The Arab Moslems in Iraq could seek to liberate their Arab brethren in Iran from the non-Arab Moslem Iranians; with Soviet backing, they would probably succeed, and Moscow would then control the oil lifeline to Western Europe.

The Soviets have not been bashful. With advisers and mercenaries, they have taken strong positions in South Yemen and Ethiopia, although Mr. Brzezinski, ostrichlike, has been pooh-poohing reports of buildups there in recent months. Soviet sponsorship of an Iraqi move into Iran could cripple the West.

The other possibility is for the United States to seize this opportunity to become a welcome military presence at the world's energy jugular.

We have been provoked, our embassy territory invaded, and our nationals captured and harassed. The best part of that is that the aggressor is neither Arab nor Soviet. Rather than merely react, as we are expected to do, we could thoughtfully respond—in a way that projects our forces into the area on a long-term basis. We could recoup the losses of a decade and re-establish our strategic pre-eminence.

First, we should lease the two airfields being returned to the Egyptians by the Israelis in the Sinai. These are among the most sophisticated air bases in the world, built with our equipment, capable of handling our B-52's. If, for example, the occasion came to strike at strategic Mideast targets today, B-52's would have to fly from Guam to Diego Garcia, refuel, and carry out the mission; we and our allies would be better served by a Mideast facility.

Long-term leases of these desert outposts—no population nearby, no security problem—would position us legally as firmly as at Guantanamo. A substantial rental would help ease Egypt's economic woes. To protect the bases, a permanent U.S. ground force would be needed—which could double as an Egypt-Israel peace-keeping force—and could be strengthened by air quickly if Saudi Arabia or the oil emirates were threatened.

At the same time, we should be taking up the quiet offers made to us to sign leases at Bahrain and islands near Oman, stationing permanent naval forces there and ending our bulb-snatching of aircraft carriers.

As part of this strategy to reassure friends of the United States in the Mideast, we should promptly and decisively increase our military aid to the King of Morocco in his fight against Algerian-sponsored radicals.

Mr. Carter would have to set aside his Vietnam-era guilt in order to embrace such a strategy. He would have to confidently urge the rebuilding of our conventional military and naval forces; the 5 percent real increase bruited about at Camp David should be seen as more than a payoff for Senators' votes for SALT.

The Ayatollah's provocation is heaven-sent. The President's job is neither to turn the other cheek nor to retaliate in fury, but to use this incident with audacity to assert American power in the Mideast and to reverse the strategic decline over which he has presided.

A CALL FOR DISUNITY

December 20, 1979

WASHINGTON—A six-week period of appeasement has given Iranian terrorists no incentive to return the hostages. Six weeks of hand-wringing, the ruling-out of force, the dispatching of Ramsey Clark, and the harassing of Iranian students here has given the populace of Iran no reason to pressure the Khomeini regime and its terrorist representatives to return to civilization.

But six weeks of too-little-and-too-late—of protracted crisis and self-congratulation for having the patience of Job—has enabled President Carter to resuscitate his political fortunes by wrapping himself in the mantle of "national unity."

Since the appeasement policy has had no effect in obtaining the release of the hostages but great effect in hypo-ing Presidential popularity, it is fair to ask how the other men who are seeking the President's office are dealing with the telecrisis.

Not one has had the wit or courage to say "I disagree with the President's methods. The best way to free the hostages—and more important, to discourage the taking of many more hostages—would be to stop glorifying our impotence and to start putting real pressure on Iran and all those nations doing business with her."

On the contrary, the political orchestration of "National Unity Day"— of postcard-writing campaigns and the mournful dimming of the national Christmas tree—has caused candidates to shy away from Topic A, as if it would be unpatriotic to criticize the President's failure to respond effectively. Nobody wants to commit the sin of dissent at the time bad policy is being made for fear of being charged with fomenting the appearance of disunity.

Let us handicap the challengers, their tiptoe comments, and their reasons for refusing to say that the emperor is wearing no clothes.

On the left, Senator Kennedy wandered off the unity reservation only long enough to show sympathy for what he thinks is the root cause of the terrorism. When this feint leftward was embraced by the terrorists, who are recognized as villains by most Democrats, Mr. Kennedy hurriedly retreated to "unity."

On the far-left-far-right, Governor Brown—who competes with Kennedy, not Carter, for funds—leaped to the defense of the President and the cause of "unity" when Kennedy broke his three-point position and was called off-side. Brown, anxious to prove how flaky he was not, posed as an establishmentarian. (Now dead in the water, Mr. Brown will return to the land of the political living on January 7, in the Des Moines debate with Kennedy and Carter; as the man with the quickest mind and the least to lose, Brown should win.)

In the center, George Bush—a former C.I.A. chief and U.N. ambassador who took flak this spring when he criticized the Carter policy in Iran—has since been gun-shy on the subject. Of Republicans, he would have the most to gain from an outspoken separation from an appeasement policy, but he is also the most cautious of the bunch; moreover, his natural policy inclination is probably closer to Carter's than, say, to John Connally's.

On the center-right-but-willing-to-listen-to-reason, Senator Howard Baker has been volubly silent. Since he is a man skilled in compromise, and since his central appeal is his ability to attract Democratic votes, he is loath to be the first to poke his spoon into the unity soufflé. His Iowa TV spots call for creation of a 50,000-man mobile strike force, but he does not say what he would do now even if we had one.

On the activist-center-that-poses-as-the-right, John Connally is uncharacteristically restrained. He was burned on his frank but wrongheaded Mideast pitch; anxious to prove he is no bomb thrower, he is passing up his chance to say what he really thinks. Yearning to put some daylight between himself and the current appeasement, he limits himself to fruitless calls for a Presidential "briefing of candidates."

On the right, Ronald Reagan is playing not to lose. He asserted one strong position—that the U.S. should offer asylum to the Shah, which showed his unwillingness to truckle to the truculent—and then adopted the compliant, riskless strategy of not arguing with the man in the White House while he's doing the best a pacifist can. (Of the unannounced candidates, only General Al Haig is zinging the Carter Iran policy, but that is muted by his delay in taking the plunge during the period of enforced consensus.)

This is an election campaign? This is a farce: At least half the candidates strongly disagree with the President's policy on the most important issue of the day, and all walk around stuffing White House "unity" gags in their mouths.

The candidate who says "We have to support the President until the hostages are out" is no improvement over Carter. We have had six weeks of appeasement, six weeks of suppressed debate, and six weeks of failure: Only if candidates start acting like candidates will the President be forced to start acting like a President.

December 23, 1979

The Editor of the New York Times

Dear sirs:

Columnist William Safire's recent calls for some good old-fashioned violence to whip the Iranians in line is truly frigthening to anyone who realizes what is at stake.

The United States needs to do three things in this crisis: *listen* ("You believe the Shah to be a bloody murderer, and that he has robbed your country of billions in national assets"); *stand firm* ("We cannot send the Shah back, or everyone with a real or imagined grievance will seize

American hostages"); and *help* ("We will do everything we can to help you get your case before the world").

It is to President Carter's credit (and the nation's) that he has done much of this. However, he has not done the first well, with the terrible result that the shouts of the Iranians have escalated in an effort to make their point heard (Kennedy listened excellently, but the Administration seized on the public outcry to make political hay against him).

No country in the world has more to gain from the peaceful settlement of issues than the United States. If the lives of the hostages are forfeited and the world becomes an even more dangerous place in which to live, Safire's rabble-rousing (what an accurate phrase!) will bear some of the responsibility.

Thomas J. Johnson, III, Pastor
Central Presbyterian Church
Summit, New Jersey

The News Business

"T O SEE OURSELVES as others see us." That gift from God, as the poet saw it, is available to many of us who put the product of our minds and fingers before the public. It comes in the mail, not only in the form of sharp rejoinders, but in some fairly searching analyses of our work and our motives.

Here are some of my judgments on the business I'm happily in, and some judgments by readers of the business I do.

IF MEDIA WERE KING

May 15, 1978

WASHINGTON—Martin Tolchin, who covers the White House for *The New York Times*, poked his head in my office a little while ago to wonder aloud: "What if the press were really running the country? Could we do it any better?"

Let's dream about that.

No, Walter Cronkite would not be right for President. The obvious choice (Taft, Rockefeller, Reagan, William Seward) never makes it, because he is usually well known enough, and around long enough, to make enemies. Cronkite reminds too many people of Vietnam and Watergate and space shots. Though his voice is of Presidential timbre, Walter would never get the nomination. Put him down for Senate Majority Leader.

Other TV anchormen are similarly marred. John Chancellor has a Stevensonian flavor that could win a nomination but not an election (just thought you'd like to know) so its Chancellor for Ambassador to the United Nations. Harry Reasoner's publicized irritation with his female sidekick would cost his party much-needed support, so Reasoner, talented, independent, with no place to go at the moment, would fit as Governor of California.

The Vice Presidency is a job that requires a willingness to adapt and an ability to listen with great intensity. The slot belongs to Barbara Walters.

The Cabinet could use editors. Ed Kosner of *Newsweek* would be Secretary of Defense, issuing annual posturing statements with a stripe across the corner reading "Crisis of Confidence" or "U.S. Navy: That Sinking Feeling." Clay Felker could profitably shrink the circulation at H.E.W.; at Justice, though, I would turn to a writer, Roger Wilkins, who knows where the bodies are buried.

At Foggy Bottom, Marvin Kalb would make the perfect Secretary of State, with Henry Kissinger trailing along as his biographer. That would mean Bernard Kalb would get Director of Central Intelligence, since the last time we had brothers in those posts the world had a streak of peace and security. (No, not Daniel Schorr for C.I.A., Schorr for Director of the F.B.I.)

In the White House, the Chief of Staff who can knock heads together is publisher Rupert Murdoch; for press secretary, Dan Rather, who knows all about palace guards. For National Security Adviser, *New York Times* reporter Les Gelb—no, he's already director of State's Politico-Military Affairs Bureau; mustn't let reality race ahead of me—so let's give Zbig's office to columnist Joe Kraft (watch out, Marvin Kalb, he'll use the back channel).

Pundits would do best in the advisory area: Anthony Lewis for White House counsel (and ultimately, elevation to the Supreme Court); David Broder to energize the Domestic Council; Mary McGrory to deal with all the pressure groups that demand compassion, and Evans and Novak to watch Kraft and Kalb. *The New Republic*'s Martin Peretz for intellectual-in-residence, handling the Charles River gang, and columnist Pat Buchanan back in as White House speechwriter.

But let me not duck the central question: What kind of media man would do well in the Oval Office? Must be well known, not unliked, reek with trustworthiness. Of the availables, David Brinkley is a touch too acerbic, John Hart a few years too young; that leaves Roger Mudd to be President. A safe choice; that means we can appoint Tom Brokaw to be Ted Kennedy (doing well in the polls, a threat to Mudd if he stumbles). The Mudd Administration would have a choice of Charlotte Curtis, Sally Quinn, or Barbara Howar as activist First Lady.

Of course, if media biggies were kings, most current politicians would gravitate to the real power in the country—the positions vacated by today's press lords. Zbigniew Brzezinski would take over for Kremlinologist Victor Zorza; Walter Mondale would be saying "and that's the way it is" on CBS, Ann Wexler would gather John Moss at *Rolling Stone*.

Hamilton Jordan, bureau chief of *The New York Times* in Washington, would poke his head into the office in which I sit at this moment and ask my replacement, Joseph L. "Jody" Powell: "What if we were really running the country? Could we do it any better?"

Powell would look up from some tendentious diatribe in his typewriter and point down the hall, to the office today occupied by Scotty Reston, which would be occupied then by a man whose Administration's name became the same as Roger's: "Ask Jimmy. He's discovered it's a lot more fun on the outside."

TRACKING DOWN THE COINER OF "THE FOURTH ESTATE"

November 2, 1978

As a card-carrying controversialist—a man convinced that testiness is next to godliness—I usually know when I am about to get into a scrap. But that was not the case on the subject of "The Fourth Estate."

In a piece not long ago about the injustice being perpetrated on my colleague Myron Farber, I wrote in passing that the phrase "Fourth Estate" had been coined in regard to the press by English essayist William Hazlitt, writing about my vituperative hero, pamphleteer William Cobbett.

This incurred the wrath of the quotation mongers. How dare I attribute that hallowed phrase to Hazlitt! "I fear that Safire may have been dazzled by a druid on his recent tour of England," writes a newsman to *The Washington Star*, pointing to a stack of the leading quotation books that attribute this phrase otherwise.

I have read all those quotation books, and they are all wrong.

Bartlett's *Familiar Quotations*, Fourteenth Edition, quotes English historian Thomas Carlyle as writing in 1832 about "the stupendous fourth estate, whose wide world-embracing influences what eye can take in." In 1841, Carlyle used the phrase again and gave everybody a wrong steer to conservative Edmund Burke: "Burke said there were Three Estates in Parliament; but, in the Reporter's Gallery yonder, there sat a Fourth Estate more important far than they all."

In a footnote, Bartlett's seems to gently contradict Carlyle's memory, citing a comment made by Lord Macaulay in 1828: "The gallery in which the reporters sit has become a Fourth Estate of the Realm."

Bergen Evans, in his *Dictionary of Quotations*—the one with the superb index—comes right out and says "Carlyle picked up the term and mis-ascribed it to Burke." The most comprehensive quotation book of all, and the one I cannot do without—Burton Stevenson's *Home Book of Proverbs, Maxims and Famous Phrases*—says of Carlyle's: "The attribution to Burke instead of Macaulay was probably a slip of the pen, as the phrase has not been found in Burke's published works."

Burke buffs have been combing his works for years, looking for the absent phrase that Carlyle, in his sloppiness, promised them. Results: zero. In 18th-century England, the three "estates" were the King, the Clergy, and the Commons; many citations can be found in Henry Fielding and others using Fourth Estate to mean "the mob," but none to mean "the press."

And so the coinage seemed to stand, with the quotation books nervously attributing the phrase to Macaulay, based on a probable mistake by Carlyle. Not a very solid footing, especially since the *Oxford English Dictionary* found a use in 1823 by Lord Brougham, speaking in the House of Commons: That great dictionary noted the phrase "at that time was treated as original."

So there I sat, perusing William Hazlitt as is my wont, on the character of William Cobbett. "One has no notion of him as making use of a fine pen," wrote the great stylist about the angry journalist, "but a great mutton-fist; his style stuns his readers . . . he is too much for any single newspaper antagonist; 'lays waste' a city orator or Member of Parliament, and bears hard upon the government itself. He is a kind of Fourth Estate in the politics of the country."

That was written in 1821, in the publication *Table Talk*—two years before Lord Brougham, seven years before Macaulay, and over a decade before Carlyle began using the phrase. That, to my mind, makes Hazlitt the coiner.

Some people cannot accept this. "To coin terms was not his style," writes David Brussat of Washington, D.C. ". . . by italicizing, he declaimed authorship and responsibility for the term. . . . In his essay 'On Familiar Style,' Hazlitt rejected 'not only all unmeaning pomp, but all low, cant phrases and loose, unconnected, slipshod allusions. . . .'"

Okay. Maybe Hazlitt heard his housemaid mumble "Fourth Estate, the damn press," just as Beethoven might have heard his wife humming the first four notes to the Fifth Symphony while dusting the music room. But the fact remains that Hazlitt wrote it down, and his is the first written record of the use of this phrase in this meaning anywhere. Or at least anywhere that anybody has yet found.

The point here is not to foster quotation-book hatred, or even to undermine our institutions of received wisdom. Rather, the notion is to open up the possibilities that sometimes "everybody" can be wrong. Indeed, I have the queasy feeling that somebody out there is going to send in a citation antedating Hazlitt.

To challenge the conventional wisdom, to upset and offend the orderly minded, to stick it to the stuck-up and to hand back authority's handouts—isn't that what Hazlitt and the others meant by "Fourth Estate"?

SNOOPING AND SNIPING

April 3, 1978

WASHINGTON—"Do you ever get any sleep?" asks a reader in Hamilton, N.Y. "I'm sure you don't, for I expect you lie awake nights thinking up mean things to say about President Carter . . . quite worthy of Westbrook Pegler in his heyday."

In a similar vein, a member of Mr. Carter's Cabinet—knowing I was within earshot—explained his assessment of my motivation to a dinner partner in these words: "He sees things with the perspective of the kind of people who used to be in power. By tearing us down, he is trying to make them look better."

Since this week marks my fifth anniversary in this line of work, a personal word may be in order about what I do and why I do it.

These essays are not intended to be even-handed analyses, sage soul-searchings, or detached observations. On the contrary, I am in the business of writing informed polemics, investigative commentaries that seek to make their points with a satisfying zap, so as to affect people in power and their policy in formation.

In 1973, I was hopelessly defensive; now, I am happily aggressive. One reason is surely that my old colleagues are Out and many who claim to be holier-than-thou are In, but there is more to the change in this space over the past five years than the changing times.

A better reason is in the advice given me at the start by the late Stewart Alsop on how to seduce a reader who disagrees with your point of view: Bait the hook with inside information or surprising slants. Belatedly, I've followed that advice, and the Carter Administration has made my America a land of targets of opportunity.

The trick in having an effect, I've discovered, is not to dazzle 'em with your mouthwork, but to zing in an embarrassing fact and to root for the people and publications who are rooting out corruption. Consider three events of the past week:

1. *The Marston affair.* Agents of the F.B.I. went to the President of the United States and asked him about the phone call he received on November 4, 1977, from Congressman Joshua Eilberg. A serious investigation is now taking place about the use of the President and the Attorney General as tools in a scheme to obstruct justice by a Congressman anxious to oust a pursuing prosecutor.

That embarrassing but purifying investigation would never have taken place but for the tenacity of one United States Senator: Malcolm Wallop of Wyoming, who has used the confirmation hearings of Benjamin Civiletti as the means to force the Justice Department to follow up leads it had no intention of ever following up. Mr. Civiletti is both smooth and artful—the perfect lawyer for a guilty client—and Senator Kennedy has been superciliously scornful of Senator Wallop's questioning, but the Wyoming freshman has proven that one Senator can shame an entire department into doing its job.

2. *Koreagate.* Last week, after 18 months of studied lethargy, the Government finally indicted longtime Congressional satrap Otto Passman, and is expected to indict a handful of others in coming weeks.

Justice would never have moved, nor would the House Ethics Committee have hired a special counsel, but for the needling of Congressman Bruce Caputo, Republican of New York, and the front-page coverage given that story by *The Washington Star.* Both President Carter and Speaker O'Neill will do only what they absolutely must, but there are those who will make it difficult for them to wish that scandal away.

3. *Lance's lawbreaking.* Bert Lance would have achieved his dream of becoming chairman of the Federal Reserve—bailing out the Carter-financing C.&S. Bank, helping Carter fund-raiser Jackson Stephens and his lawyer-director, Arab agent William Fulbright, deliver dozens of key United States banks to Saudi control—were it not for *The New York Times* and, better late than never, Senator Charles Percy, Republican of Illinois.

In these matters, my job is to cheer on the lonely, red-faced whistle blowers, to publicize their progress and to deride their obstructors. Outrage is never out of date.

My motive? If ever I find out what it is, that will be my secret. Nothing so simplistic as vengeance, I hope, or so souring as to make me a nattering nabob of negativism.

Five years into a job that offers more freedom of thought than I ever imagined possible, I find some justification in a cartoon by Brickman. An irate man asks: "You're always knocking the Administration—what are *you* doing for your country?" The not-so-smug reply: "Knocking the Administration."

March 13, 1978

Dear Mr. Safire:

In the past year I believe you've been finding minor discrepancies and inadequacies in Jimmy Carter and his associates, and ballooning them up out of proper proportion. I feel you've become biased and almost manic in what to me seems to be an attempt to discredit Jimmy Carter. To me, you have become more strident than former Vice President Agnew ever was. If I recall correctly some of his more famous (infamous?) utterings were contributions from you?

I wonder if I can induce you to analyze your efforts? Two possibilities occur to me: Are you subconsciously defending Nixon by attacking Carter? Richard Reeves in the January 1977 issue of *Esquire* mentions the same possibility. Reeves also damns you with questionable praise by suggesting that you are best when you're being very mean. The second possibility—are you simply being a good investigative reporter, exposing wrongs that exist?

Undoubtedly, Mr. Carter and his associates have made mistakes. Let us assume that all your accusations are facts—not merely opinions. Even so, I believe that a fair-minded investigator would occasionally come up with some praise for a particular job well done. Rarely do you mention anything that was praiseworthy. The balance toward derogation was overwhelming.

Finally, enclosed is an interesting article by Jack Anderson. He doesn't directly refer to you when he entitles the essay "Witch-Hunters on the Loose." He is referring specifically to prosecutors. It is my contention that the "shoe fits you," Mr. Safire. Please take it off.

Sincerely yours,
Marshall Bergen, M.D.
Jersey City, New Jersey

HERE'S TO MEDIA WARS

November 27, 1978

WASHINGTON—When the *Time-Life* empire (sales: $1.2 billion) declares war on *The Washington Post-Newsweek* empire (sales: $436 million), that's news.

Although unreported by the embarrassed press sections of *Time* or *Newsweek*, the media war broke out recently when *The Washington Star*—purchased this year by *Time*—published, and heavily promoted, a lively five-part series about Katharine Graham, the woman who heads *The Washington Post* and *Newsweek*.

The series about Mrs. Graham was conceived over a year ago by *The Star*'s then-editor James Bellows and written by *Star* staff writer Lynn Rosellini. But publisher Joseph Albritten suppressed it; competing on such a personal basis was not then done. The new publisher, *Time*'s James Shepley, evidently backed up his new editor, Murray Gart, in deciding to launch journalism's *Star Wars*.

Editor Bellows, who is now rebuilding *The Los Angeles Herald Examiner*, says today: "When you see all the stuff that's printed about Jackie Onassis and Joan Crawford, I think it's sad when newspapers turn away from good articles about a powerful, achieving woman like Kay Graham." Not surprisingly, he is running the syndicated series in *The Herald Examiner*.

Surely Mrs. Graham is a newsworthy subject. I first met her in 1970, when we were fellow students—along with columnists Robert Novak, Alan Otten, and David Broder—in a six-week seminar on John Locke's *Second Treatise on Government*. (Novelist Herman Wouk, then getting started on his magnificent *War and Remembrance*, was the star pupil.)

Kay Graham played hooky toward the end. But the seminars were conducted in her executive conference room; she felt her role was not so much to mix it up intellectually as to provide a forum and encouragement for others, which is the way she runs her paper. She relies too much on her Jason Robards-like editor, who has spent four years resting on laurels, but since Mrs. Graham was the first publisher to offer this ex-White House speechwriter a job as newspaper columnist, I have a mixed opinion about her judgment of editorial personnel.

The Star series was no hatchet job: well-researched, sometimes surprisingly revealing, often admiring and sympathetic, and evenhanded in the portrait of what reporter Rosellini saw as the duality of "Katharine the Great" and "Katharine the Terrible."

At *The Post*, ombudsman Charles Seib reacted grumpily: "They relied heavily, as gossip columns do, on unnamed sources." Still he had to concede that "since *The Post* is well known for its gloves-off personality pieces and its readiness to use unidentified sources, there may have been a certain justice in *The Star* series." But he felt the justice had been too rough.

This opening salvo by one journalism conglomerate at another's quarterdeck was aimed at getting *The Star* talked about. *Time* is expected to take its afternoon daily into the morning field soon for direct *Post-Star* confrontation, while *The Post* may lash back with a five-part "Hedley Donovan Story."

Is this news-business rivalry of general news interest? Of course it is: A media power struggle deserves attention, and the people involved ought not to be self-conscious about being participants rather than observers. Tradition is served, too, in the thundering of press titans at each other:

Horace Greeley, Henry Raymond, and James Gordon Bennett knew that news about news is news.

That's why it was good to see *New York Times* executive editor A. M. Rosenthal quoted in the newly vigorous *Esquire* magazine denouncing Rupert Murdoch, new publisher of the *New York* (not *The Washington*) *Post*, for "practising ugly, mean, violent journalism" and prophesying such sensationalism's doom. That shot was well deserved; if Mr. Murdoch has a defense, he is not without a forum.

Media wars—out in the open, with no gentlemen's agreements to reduce the vividness of discourse—are not only of reader interest, they are important to the future of free speech.

To regulate political power, the Constitution sets up checks and balances. Similarly, to regulate the power of media conglomerates, the best way to avoid abridgement of press freedom by government is to simulate more economic and ideological competition: not only between television and the printed word, but among magazines, individual newspapers, and the huge conglomerates of news.

That competition is expressed dryly on balance sheets and with dignity on editorial pages. But even faceless institutions are run by individual men and women blessed with tempers, memories, visions, and vengeances. As editors and publishers and broadcasters begin to zap each other with the zest and spirit hitherto directed at politicians, then their gray institutional competition becomes infused with the color of human personality; the inky juices flow, and the public learns much more about the way the news is made.

Such healthy combat is good for editors and publishers; pundits, of course, are above all that.

December 21, 1978

Dear Mr. Safire,

Well, I never thought that I would write this to you. When you started as a columnist for *The Times*, I was disappointed to say the least. I really couldn't understand what was going on in their minds that made them hire a former Nixon speechwriter. I always read your column, however, and you often made me extremely angry. I remember one night, about a year ago, while I was still going to graduate school in Boston, that I was so angry that I repeatedly called *The New York Times* trying to get hold of you to give you a piece of my mind. Now I can't remember what the issue that had me so mad was, so it must not have been too important.

At any rate, I just wanted to tell you that, over the past couple of years, I have come to look forward to your columns. You can consider this quite a compliment coming from a registered Democrat who was arrested in Washington in 1971 at a peace march. I don't think that my politics have changed a great deal, but I do see better now why conservatives think the way that they do. Some things that you have to say make a great deal of sense to me now, whereas even two years ago I just wrote it all off. My father warned me that this would happen to me, but I never believed him.

Your columns are interesting, informative, and very often display the fact that you must have done a lot of digging to get what you have written. My compliments. I sometimes wish that you would take it a little easier on Mr. Carter. You often show a sort of bitterness in your columns that results, I think, from your feeling that Nixon was run out of office by the liberal press. I don't think that is true, and I certainly don't think that any of Mr. Carter's transgressions even come close to those of Mr. Nixon. I sincerely hope that you are not bitter because bitterness can only hurt—it serves no positive goal.

Thank you for the hours of pleasure that you have given me with your columns, and keep up the good work. I suspect that there are other liberals who feel the same way but they will never admit that to you. Warmest regards for a happy and healthy New Year.

Sincerely,
Kevin Farrell
New York, New York

Index